Puntos de partida

Thalia Dorwick

Ana M. Pérez-Gironés
WESLEYAN UNIVERSITY

Anne Becher
UNIVERSITY OF
COLORADO, BOULDER

SPAN 1441
Beginning Spanish I
Department of Modern Languages
University of Texas at Arlington

Mc
Graw
Hill
Education

7 8 9 0 SCI SCI 20 19

ISBN-13: 978-1-259-95730-7
ISBN-10: 1-259-95730-6

Solutions Program Manager: Joyce Berendes
Project Manager: Gina Schilling

It's more than a text. It's a program.

Success in the language classroom requires so much more than just a text. In any language-learning setting, students require numerous and various opportunities to read, write, hear, and speak. *Puntos de partida* sets the standard for Spanish-language teaching. An innovative program that has been continuously refined for today's classroom, *Puntos* delivers proven pedagogy with clear and effective presentations, comprehensive teaching resources, and powerfully adaptive digital tools.

Now in its anniversary Tenth Edition, *Puntos* builds on the holistic, five-skills approach it pioneered. It's the *Puntos* you know. It's the *Puntos* of today.

Proven Approach

Puntos has been the starting point for over a million students beginning to learn Spanish. The best-selling program combines digital innovations with the program's solid foundation and proven approach.

This is what *Puntos* offers that continues to set the standard for Introductory Spanish programs:

• Comprehensive scope and sequence

Puntos' hallmark approach to vocabulary and grammar focuses on the acquisition of vocabulary during the early stages of language learning (**Capítulo 1: Ante todo**) and then at the start of each chapter throughout the text. Grammar is introduced in thorough explanations, with careful attention given to skill development rather than grammatical knowledge alone.

To this end, the overall organization carefully progresses from formulaic expressions to vocabulary and grammar relevant to daily life and personal interests (studies, family, home, leisure activities), then goes on to prepare students for survival situations (ordering a meal, traveling), and finally branches out to broader themes (current events, social and environment issues). This forward progress is reinforced by a cyclical structure where vocabulary, grammar, and language functions are continuously reviewed and recycled.

• Clear and effective vocabulary and grammar presentations

The thorough, effective grammar explanations in *Puntos* are in keeping with the extensive changes made in the ninth edition. These explanations are now even more accessible to students, featuring conversational language, increased clarity, additional examples, and organization of complex, dense explanations into manageable chunks of concise grammar summary. Students will find the grammar explanations to be clear and comprehensible, and particular care has been taken to bolster those grammar points that traditionally prove difficult.

- Integrated four-skills approach with scaffolded activities that move students from input to open-ended communication

One of the hallmark features of *Puntos* is its careful sequencing of activities, moving students from controlled to free-form tasks. In the tenth edition, this scaffolding is improved and introduced at the individual activity level. Starting with the very first activity following the grammar explanation, additional *Pasos* have been added to give students the opportunity to use the new grammar in a controlled but more personalized way, facilitating practice and communication with their peers as soon as new concepts are introduced. The activities following each vocabulary topic and grammar point also build up to one or more free- expression activities in which students communicate more independently and creatively.

Práctica y comunicación

A. Los gustos y preferencias para las vacaciones

Paso 1. Autoprueba. Complete las siguientes oraciones con -a or -an.

1. Me gust_____ nadar.
2. Por eso me gust_____ las playas caribeñas.
3. A mi familia y a mí nos gust_____ esquiar.
4. Por eso nos gust_____ las vacaciones de invierno.
5. A mi mejor amigo le gust_____ el sol.
6. Por eso siempre le gust_____ la República Dominicana para las vacaciones.
7. ¿A ti te gust_____ las vacaciones activas o relajantes (*relaxing*)?

Paso 2. Use las siguientes frases en oraciones completas para expresar sus gustos.

MODELOS: ¿viajar? → (No) Me gusta viajar.
¿los aviones? → (No) Me gustan los aviones.

1. ¿viajar?   5. ¿el invierno?
2. ¿los viajes con mi familia? 6. ¿las playas caribeñas?
3. ¿los vuelos?   7. ¿los aeropuertos?
4. ¿el calor?   8. ¿viajar en coche?

Paso 3. Ahora, en parejas, túrnense para entrevistarse sobre las ideas del **Paso 2.** Luego díganle al resto de la clase algo que Uds. tienen en común.

MODELO: E1: A mí me gusta viajar. ¿Y a ti?
E2: A mí también. →
A nosotros nos gusta viajar.

- Inclusion of all Spanish-speaking countries

The tenth edition of *Puntos* highlights the proven concept that introducing students to the Spanish-speaking world goes beyond asking them to simply absorb information about each country. Instead, a few key cultural insights, appearing at various moments throughout each chapter, serve to spark students' interest and, by closing with a question that asks students to reflect on cultural comparisons, encourage them to create personal connections with the cultures of the Spanish-speaking world.

EL MUNDO HISPANOHABLANTE*

- El español es la lengua que más se habla* en el mundo* después del* mandarín. Más de* 500 (quinientas) millones de personas hablan español.

- Es la lengua oficial de 20 (veinte) naciones y de Puerto Rico.

*EL...The Spanish-speaking world *la...the language spoken most *world *después... after *Más...More than

Puntos de partida was designed to provide novice and experienced instructors alike with the tools needed to walk into the classroom—be it face-to-face or online—well-prepared to teach an engaging class. As a comprehensive program, *Puntos* offers a wide array of resources and supporting materials, so it functions as a flexible framework that can be tailored to individual teaching situations and goals. Whether you're using the program for your face-to-face, hybrid, or online class, the wealth of resources sets up both instructors and students for success.

• New and enhanced instructor's annotations

The program's user-friendliness and solid teaching support are strengthened in this edition with extensively rewritten annotations in the Instructor's Edition. With improved and added notes, instructors will now find teaching suggestions for each and every grammar presentation and practice activity in the text, with point-by-point suggestions for presenting the material in class, in addition to a wealth of helpful facts and resources, variations on and supplements to the existing material, and suggestions for follow-up and extension. Taking into account that Introductory Spanish classrooms typically contain a mix of true beginners, false beginners, and even heritage speakers, a new streamlined organization and a designated space for expanded suggestions for heritage speakers makes it even easier to meet the needs of students with varying levels of language proficiency.

---

234 ■ doscientos treinta y cuatro   Capítulo 8 De viaje

HERITAGE SPEAKERS

• Hay muchas maneras de decir *autobús* dependiendo del país en que uno se encuentre. Por ejemplo, en México se dice *el camión* o *la ruta* para referirse a un autobús de transporte público. En la Argentina se dice *el colectivo*, mientras que en las Islas Canarias, las Antillas, Cuba y la República Dominicana, se dice *la guagua*. Sin embargo, la palabra *guagua* significa *bebé, niño* o *infante* en el Perú y en otros países andinos. Pregúnteles a los hispanohablantes qué palabra usan ellos para referirse a un autobús.

(*Cont.*)

- Brand-new digital and print testing program

A key part of the instructor resources available with *Puntos* is the comprehensive testing program, now completely rewritten and available in both print and digital formats. Whether you use the testing program as a model to customize your own tests, or you want to quickly and easily assign existing exams or poolable questions to your students, the new testing program offers multiple versions for each chapter from which instructors can draw.

- Updated supplemental activities manual

The tenth edition can be accompanied by the updated *Supplementary Materials to Accompany* Puntos de partida, by Sharon Foerster. The supplementary materials are an updated teacher's guide to *Puntos* and consist of worksheets, short pronunciation practice, listening exercises, grammar worksheets, integrative communication-building activities, comprehensive chapter reviews, and language games.

- In-class grammar and culture presentations on Connect under the Library tab

Connect houses other important resources to support instruction. In addition to the Instructor's Manual and an Instructor's Guide for Connect, you will find a digital Image Bank to support your classroom presentations and activities, as well as updated cultural and grammar content for in-class use. With engaging images and cultural facts about the countries of focus, the updated Cultural PowerPoint Presentations offer students additional contact with culture, and offer the instructor detailed notes and suggestions for how to present these in class. To build on the grammar presentations in the text, Grammar PowerPoint Presentations provide an additional way for students to absorb grammatical knowledge, which is especially useful for hard-to-grasp concepts where students often benefit from multiple and varied modes of presentation.

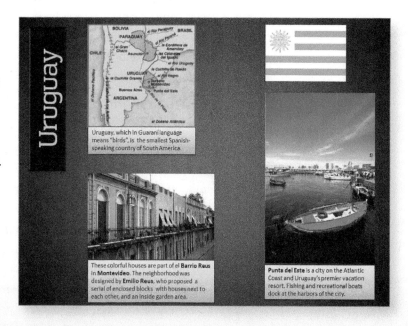

Uruguay, which in Guaraní language means "birds", is the smallest Spanish-speaking country of South America.

These colorful houses are part of el **Barrio Reus** in **Montevideo**. The neighborhood was designed by **Emilio Reus**, who proposed a serial of enclosed blocks with houses next to each other, and an inside garden area.

Punta del Este is a city on the Atlantic Coast and Uruguay's premier vacation resort. Fishing and recreational boats dock at the harbors of the city.

Engaging and Immersive
Digital Tools

Connect is the most powerful and flexible course management system available. Rooted in research on effective student learning practices, the platform integrates adaptive learning tools with dynamic, engaging language practice activities. The result is better student learning of the Spanish language.

• A personalized and adaptive learning and teaching experience

No two students learn a language the same way or at the same rate. Students enter the Introductory Spanish course with a wide range of knowledge and experience, from true beginners to heritage speakers. So how do you know what to teach and to whom?

McGraw-Hill's LearnSmart provides each student with a personalized and adaptive learning experience based on individual needs. As the student works through a series of probes around the vocabulary and grammar presented in each chapter, LearnSmart identifies what the student knows and doesn't know, and continuously adapts the subsequent probes to focus on those areas where the student needs the most help. Each student learns and masters core vocabulary and grammar at his or her own pace and comes to class better prepared to communicate in the target language.

And just as no two students learn a language the same way, no two Spanish courses are taught the same way. Connect provides the instructor with both the ability and flexibility to pull from the robust set of content available in the platform and craft a unique learning path based on the goals of the course. Be it in a face-to-face, hybrid, or fully online course, Connect can adapt to you and to your students to create the ideal learning environment.

• Student-centered

Students learn best when they are involved and interested in the material being taught. *Practice Spanish: Study Abroad*, the market's first 3-D immersive language game designed exclusively by McGraw-Hill Education, brings the language to the students in a fun, engaging, and immersive gaming experience. Students "study abroad" virtually in Colombia where they will create their very own avatar, live with a host family, make new friends, and navigate a variety of real-world scenarios using their quickly developing Spanish language skills. Students earn points and rewards for successfully accomplishing these tasks via their smartphones, tablets, and computers, and instructors have the ability to assign specific tasks, monitor student achievement, and incorporate the game into the classroom experience. *Practice Spanish: Study Abroad* is available upon request. Your Learning Technology Representative can provide more information.

• Robust data

Instructors and students alike want to know how students are performing in the course and where they can improve. The powerful reporting tools in Connect surface actionable data to both instructors and students so steps can be taken by both groups to ensure student success.

The first and only analytics tool of its kind, Connect Insight is a series of visual data displays—each framed by an intuitive question—to provide instructors at-a-glance information regarding how your class is doing. Connect Insight provides analysis on five key insights, available at a moment's notice from your Connect course.

LearnSmart provides powerful reports to view student progress by module and detail with completion breakdown, along with class performance data, frequency of missed questions, and a view into the most challenging learning objectives. Metacognitive reports allow instructors to view statistics on how knowledgeable their students are about their own comprehension and learning. What's more, LearnSmart provides students their own progress reports so they can take full responsibility for their own learning.

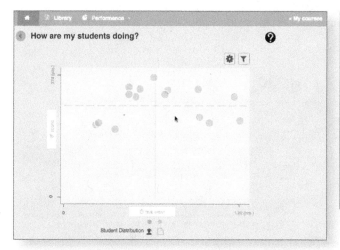

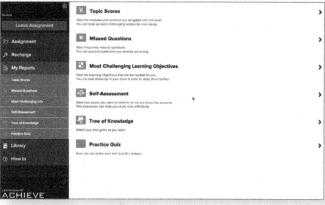

WHAT'S NEW

Functional design and easy reference

- Identifiable goals: Each chapter opener details what students can hope to accomplish.

- Significance of color: Updated color patterns allow for easy navigation and concept identification.

- Visually fresh: Many new photos, realia, and updated drawings.

Solidifying grammar and vocabulary

- Clarity: Grammar explanations are simpler and more straightforward, with particular care given to points that are often challenging for students.

- Grammar summaries: Short summaries now appear at the end of all grammar explanations.

- More input: More models in the target language to guide students through activities.

- Seamless progression: *Práctica* and *Conversación* are now a single section, *Práctica y comunicación*, for seamless transition from controlled to free-form activities, while maintaining careful sequencing. Each initial activity in *Práctica y comunicación* incorporates an *Autoprueba* for students to check their comprehension and builds up to personalized and communicative grammar practice.

- Self-checks: *En resumen* now includes a chapter-ending checklist for students to assess their progress toward attaining the goals stated at the beginning of the chapter.

New opportunities for communicative practice

- Chapter opener: New personal chapter opener questions and answers from native speakers from various parts of the Spanish-speaking world get students listening and talking in the target language from the very first page of each chapter.

- Communicative grammar practice: Grammar activity sections are scaffolded to carefully move students into free-form practice activities after each grammar point.

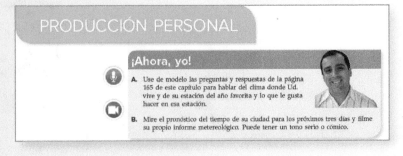

- *Producción personal*: This new chapter-ending section guides students to create a capstone portfolio of writing, speaking, and filming activities.

- Information gap activities: New activities designed for every chapter.

Integrated culture

- Culturally based activities: More grammar and vocabulary exercises center on cultural context.
- *Algo sobre...* : Appearing three to four times per chapter, these new windows into the countries of focus weave culture into the linguistic workflow.
- *A leer*: Readings are simplified and include more interactive activities (*Y ahora, Uds.*).
- *Un poco de todo*: Each section starts with a *Lengua y cultura* activity to practice newly acquired and recycled grammar and vocabulary.

Video integration:

- In each chapter, the *Salu2* (formerly *Telepuntos*) video is divided into two shorter segments, one that is integrated into the vocabulary presentation, providing the opportunity for additional practice, and one that remains at the end of the chapter to reinforce a variety of skills.

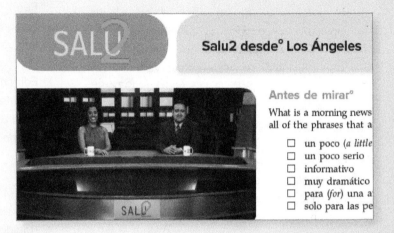

Salu2 desde° Los Ángeles

Antes de mirar°

What is a morning news all of the phrases that a

☐ un poco (*a little*
☐ un poco serio
☐ informativo
☐ muy dramático
☐ para (*for*) una a
☐ solo para las pe

Digital tools

- Embedded audio: Audio recordings throughout the ebook; students hear new vocabulary as it is introduced.
- LearnSmart: Grammar modules for every grammar topic and updated vocabulary modules.
- *Practice Spanish: Study Abroad*: This interactive 3D game, accessible on computers and mobile devices, immerses students in a virtual study abroad experience in Colombia. *Practice Spanish* facilitates real-world application that integrates culture, grammar, and vocabulary.
- English grammar guides: Assignable explanations and practice with basic grammar concepts in English.

Instructor resources

- Even more comprehensive instructor annotations: Strengthened and reorganized annotations have consistent suggestions for expansion, oral practice, and grammar explanations.
- Well-organized: Easy-to-navigate Annotated Instructor's Edition with a dedicated area for heritage speakers.
- Testing program: Completely revised in both digital and print forms.

ABOUT THE AUTHORS

Thalia Dorwick retired as McGraw-Hill's Editor-in-Chief for Humanities, Social Sciences, and Languages. For many years she was also in charge of McGraw-Hill's World Languages college list in Spanish, French, Italian, German, Japanese, and Russian. She has taught at Allegheny College, California State University (Sacramento), and Case Western Reserve University, where she received her Ph.D. in Spanish in 1973. She was recognized as an Outstanding Foreign Language Teacher by the California Foreign Language Teachers Association in 1978. Dr. Dorwick is the coauthor of several textbooks and the author of several articles on language teaching issues. She is a frequent guest speaker on topics related to language learning, and she was also an invited speaker at the II Congreso Internacional de la Lengua Española, in Valladolid, Spain, in October 2001. In retirement, she consults for McGraw-Hill, especially in the area of world languages, which is of personal interest to her. She is a Vice President of the Board of Trustees of Case Western Reserve University and a past President of the Board of Directors of Berkeley Repertory Theatre.

Ana María Pérez-Gironés is an Adjunct Associate Professor of Spanish at Wesleyan University, Middletown, Connecticut, where she teaches and coordinates Spanish language courses. She received a Licenciatura en Filología Anglogermánica from the Universidad de Sevilla in 1985, and her M.A. in General Linguistics from Cornell University in 1988. Professor Pérez-Gironés' professional interests include second language acquisition and the use of technology in language learning. She is a coauthor of *A otro nivel, Puntos en breve,* Second Edition, and *¿Qué tal?,* Seventh Edition. She is also a coauthor of the Student Manuals for Intermediate Grammar Review and Intensive and High Beginner Courses that accompany *Nuevos Destinos.*

Anne Becher received her M.A. in Hispanic Linguistics in 1992 from the University of Colorado—Boulder, and now coordinates the Beginning Spanish One course and teaches pedagogy and methods courses for the Department of Spanish and Portuguese there. She has taught beginning through advanced levels of Spanish since 1996, including several years teaching Modified Spanish classes for students with difficulty learning languages. She has published several reviews in *Hispania,* presents frequently at the Colorado Congress of Foreign Language Teachers (CCFLT) conferences, and has served on the boards of CCFLT and the Colorado chapter of American Association of Teachers of Spanish and Portuguese. She co-edited the bilingual literary journal *La selva subterranea* from 1987–1996.

ACKNOWLEDGMENTS

We would like to thank the overwhelming number of friends and colleagues who served on boards of advisors or as consultants, completed reviews or surveys, and attended symposia or focus groups. Their feedback was indispensible in creating the *Puntos* program. The appearance of their names in the following lists does not necessarily constitute their endorsement of the program or its methodology.

Practice Spanish: Study Abroad Board of Advisors

James Abraham
Glendale Community College

Kalynn Aguirre
Florida Atlantic University

Adam Ballart
Ball State University

Kelly Conroy
Western Kentucky University

Ari Gutman
Auburn University

Patricia Harrigan
Community College of Baltimore County

Felix Kronenberg
Rhodes College

Melissa Logue
Columbus State Community College

Leticia McGrath
Georgia Southern University

David Neville
Elon University

Michelle Ocasio
Valdosta State University

Aaron Salinger
Mount San Antonio College

Jacquelyn Sandone
University of Missouri

Practice Spanish: Study Abroad Colombia Consultants

Lourdes Arevalo
University of California, Los Angeles

Jorge Cubillos
University of Delaware

Fabio Espitia
Grand Valley State University

Martiza Nemoga
University of Pittsburgh

Beatriz Potter
Valdosta State University

Chayree Santiago Thomas
Rowan-Cabarrus Community College

Amy Uribe
Lone Star College

Juan Villa
University of Rhode Island

Practice Spanish: Study Abroad Student Board of Advisors

Kaitlin Anderson
Illinois State University

Jasmine Arias
University of Illinois, Urbana-Champaign

Joyce Bolivar
University of Rhode Island

Mike Churvis
Georgia Perimeter College, Dunwoody

Julian Colonia
University of Rhode Island

Brian de la Cruz
University of Rhode Island

Katherine Foss
University of Rhode Island

Brandi Glenn
Georgia Southern University

Michael R. Herrera
University of Cincinnati

Tricia Hogan
University of Rhode Island

Abigael Mandenberg
University of Illinois, Urbana-Champaign

Jen McGunigal
University of Rhode Island

Johan Molina
University of Rhode Island

Deandra Moorman
University of Cincinnati

Isaac Reeves
Ben Davis University

Gulya Tlegenova
San Diego Mesa College

Kari Uhle
Indiana University

Victoria Vanderaa
Illinois State University

Juan Villa
University of Rhode Island

Kayla Warren
Georgia Southern University

Practice Spanish: Study Abroad Student Ambassadors

Daniel Carroll
Northern Virginia Community College

Marie-Claire Levy
Florida State University

Tuyen Lieu
Central Piedmont Community College

Matt Lozano
Clarke University

Colin McCullough
Ohio University

Emily Ousterhout
Mississippi State University

Paige Tabler
California State University, Chico

Maggie Wilson
George Mason University

Vanessa Wismeier
Loras College

Matt Wolf
Kansas State University

Practice Spanish: Study Abroad Pilots and Beta Testers

James Abraham
Glendale Community College

Julie Alwehieby
Coastline Community College

Melba Amador
Western Kentucky University

Jeanette Banashak
Grand Valley State University

Tulio Cedillo
Lynchburg College

Daren Crasto
Houston Community College

Paul Cristofaro
Minot State University

Luis Delgado
Olive Harvey College

Mark A. Dowell
Randolph Community College

Muriel Gallego
Ohio University

Audrey R. Gertz
Indiana University-Purdue University Indianapolis

Scott Gibby
Austin Community College

Adrienne Gonzalez
University of Denver

Michael Harrison
San Diego Mesa College

Claudia Jaramillo
Purdue University Calumet

Ryan LaBrozzi
Bridgewater State University

Jude Thomas Manzo
Saint Phillip's College

Leticia McGrath
Georgia Southern University

Peggy McNeil
Louisiana State University

Marco Mena
Mass Bay Community College

Wendy Mendez-Hasselman
Palm Beach State College

Jerome Mwinyelle
East Tennessee State University

Danae Orlins
University of Cincinnati

Hector Iglesias Pascual
Ohio University

Erika M Southerland
Muhlenberg College

Amber Workman
California Lutheran University

ACTFL 2014 Workshop Participants

Susana Solera Adoboe
Southern Methodist University

Berta Chópite
Earlham College

Abby Dings
Southwestern University

Jude Thomas Manzo
Saint Phillip's College

Leticia McDoniel
Southern Methodist University

Javier Morin
Del Mar College

Samuel Sommerville
Johnson County Community College

Gloria Yampey-Jorge
Houston Community College

Symposia

Atlanta, GA

Juan Alcarría
Georgia College & State University

Barbara A. Bateman
Georgia Perimeter College

María Elena Bermudez
Georgia State University

María Guadalupe Calatayud
University of North Georgia

Aurora Castillo-Scott
Georgia College & State University

Jose A. Cortés
Georgia Perimeter College

Lisa Davie
Georgia Perimeter College

Janan Fallon
Georgia Perimeter College

Carolina Ganem-Cameron
Georgia Perimeter College

Gael Guzmán Medrano
University of West Georgia

Kristi Hislope
University of North Georgia

Nicolas Hu
University of North Georgia

Melissa Logue
Columbus State Community College

Leda Lozier
The University of Georgia

Raúl Llorente
Georgia State University

Rosaria Meek
University of North Georgia

Oscar H. Morena
Georgia State University

Sharon Nuruddin
Clark Atlanta University

Teresa Pérez-Gamboa
The University of Georgia

Rick Robinson
Georgia Perimeter College

Daniel Sanchez
The University of Georgia

Pamela Simpson
Georgia Perimeter College

Elizabeth Z. Solis
University of West Georgia

Mariana Stone
University of North Georgia

Sherry von Klitzing
Kennesaw State University

Alvaro Torres Calderón
University of North Georgia

Ami L. Travillian-Vonesh
University of North Georgia

Napa, CA

Tanya Chroman
California Polytechnic State University

Laurie de González
University of Oregon

Mari Carmen García
Sacramento City College

Ana Hartig-Ferrer
California Polytechnic State University

Deborah Holmberg
Azusa Pacific University

Keith Johnson
California State University, Fresno

Anne Kelly-Glasoe
South Puget Sound Community College

Milagros Ojermark
Diablo Valley College

Marcelo Paz
California State University, East Bay

Beatriz Robinson
University of Nevada, Reno

Judy Rodríguez
California State University, Sacramento

Julio Torres
University of California, Irvine

Chicago, IL

Maxi Armas
Triton College

An Chung Cheng
University of Toledo

Chyi Chung
Northwestern University

Luis Delgado
Olive-Harvey College

Ronald Gest
Milwaukee Area Technical College

Ileana Hester
Governors State University

Alfonso Illingworth-Rico
Eastern Michigan University

Franklin Inojosa
City Colleges of Chicago

David Migaj
Wilbur Wright College

Octavian Stinga
City Colleges of Chicago

Lucero Tonkinson
City Colleges of Chicago

Los Angeles, CA

Ashlee Balena
University of North Carolina at Wilmington

Tracy Bishop
University of Arkansas

Aymara Boggiano
Rice University

Oscar Cabrera
Community College of Philadelphia

Sara Casler
Sierra College

Christine Cotton
University of Arkansas at Little Rock

Christopher DiCapua
Community College of Philadelphia

Concepción Domenech
University of Wyoming

Mandy Faretta-Stutenberg
Northern Illinois University

Erin Finzer
University of Arkansas at Little Rock

Anna Kalminskaia
University of Nevada, Reno

David Leavell
College of S. Nevada

Maria Manni
University of Maryland, Baltimore County

Anne-Marie Martin
Portland Community College

Juan Carlos Moraga
Folsom Lake College

Christine Núñez
Kutztown University of Pennsylvania

Eva Núñez
Portland State University

Norma Rivera-Hernández
Millersville University of Pennsylvania

Baton Rouge, LA

Gina Breen
Louisiana State University

Brigitte Delzell
Louisiana State University

Dorian Dorado
Louisiana State University

Ann Francois
Louisiana State University

Stephanie Gaillard
Louisiana State University

Amy George-Hirons
Tulane University

Melissa Guerry
Louisiana State University

Sheldon Lotten
Louisiana State University

Cathy Luquette
Louisiana State University

Peggy McNeil
Louisiana State University

Sulagna Mishra
Louisiana State University

John Patin
Louisiana State University

Alfonso Quinones
Louisiana State University

Mariela Sanchez
Southeastern Louisiana University

Jack Yeager
Louisiana State University

Miami, FL

Emmanuel Alvarado
Palm Beach State College

Elisabeth D'Antoni
Broward College Central

Domenica Diraviam
Broward College Central

Mónica Durán
University of Miami, Coral Gables

Trenton Hoy
Broward College Central

Wendy Mendez-Hasselman
Palm Beach State College, Lake Worth

Sandy Oakley
Palm Beach State College, Eissey

Celia Roberts
Broward College Central

Alyse Schoenfeldt
Palm Beach State College, Eissey

Alina Vega-Franco
Broward College Central

Justin White
Florida Atlantic University, Boca Raton

Amelia Island, FL

Flavia Belpoliti
University of Houston

Sarah Bentley
Portland Community College

Sara Casler
Sierra College

Jorge Cubillos
University of Delaware

Paul Larson
Baylor University

María Elizabeth Mahaffey
University of North Carolina, Charlotte

Leticia McGrath
Georgia Southern University

Catherine Ortiz
University of Texas at Arlington

Yanira Paz
University of Kentucky

Carlos Ramírez
University of Pittsburgh

Carmen Sotolongo
El Camino College

Edda Temoche-Weldele
Grossmont College

Amy Uribe
Lone Star College

Karen Zetrouer
Santa Fe Community College

Key West, FL

Michelle Cipriano
Wright State University

Edward Erazo
Broward College–Central

Cindy Espinosa
Central Michigan University

Vanessa Lazo-Wilson
Austin Community College–Round Rock

Kathy Leonard
University of Nevada, Reno

Melissa Logue
Columbus State Community College

Germán Negrón
University of Nevada, Las Vegas

Sylvia Nikopoulos
Central Piedmont Community College

Isabel Parra
University of Cincinnati, Batavia

Carlos Pedroza
Palomar College

Beatriz Potter
Valdosta State University

Latasha Russell
Florida State College, South Campus

Nancy Stucker
Cabrillo College

Lucero Tenorio
Oklahoma State University, Stillwater

Lilia Vidal
Miracosta College

Practice Spanish: Study Abroad - Hollywood, FL

Kelly Conroy
Western Kentucky University

Darren Crasto
Houston Community College, Northwest College

Richard Curry
Texas A & M University

Dorian Dorado
Louisiana State University, Baton Rouge

Leah Fonder-Solano
University of Southern Mississippi

Luz Font
Florida State College, South Campus

Muriel Gallego
Ohio University, Athens

Scott Gibby
Austin Community College, Northridge

Ryan LaBrozzi
Bridgewater State University

Melissa Logue
Columbus State Community College

Alejandro Muñoz
Garces Coastal Carolina University

Aaron Roggia
Oklahoma State University

Aaron Salinger
Mt. San Antonio College

Jacquelyn Sandone
University of Missouri, Columbia

Michael Vrooman
Grand Valley State University

Reviewers

Dean Allbritton
Colby College

Tim Altanero
Austin Community College

Virginia Arreola
Hiram College

Silvia Arroyo
Mississippi State University

Barbara Avila-Shah
University at Buffalo, State University of New York

Wanda Baumgartel
Snead State Community College

Anne Becher
University of Colorado at Boulder

Brian Beeles
Arizona Western College

Clare Bennett
University of Alaska Southeast, Ketchikan

Donna Binkowski
Southern Methodist University

Diane Birginal
Gonzaga University

Joseph Brockway
Mountain View College

Francis Canedo
Northeast State Community College

Beth Cardon
Georgia Perimeter College

Gabriela Carrion
Regis University

Mayra Cortes-Torres
Pima Community College

Laurence Covington
University of the District of Columbia Community College

Darren Crasto
Houston Community College

Betsy Dahms
University of West Georgia

Kit Decker
Piedmont Virginia Community College

Heriberto Del Porto
Westminster College, MO

David Detwiler
MiraCosta College

John Deveny
Oklahoma State University, Stillwater

Dorian Dorado
Louisiana State University

Indira Dortolina
Lone Star College, Univeristy Park

Denise Egidio
Guilford Technical Community College

Hector Fabio Espitia
Grand Valley State University

Abra Figueroa
Oklahoma City Community College

Sarah Finley
University of Kentucky

Timothy Foxsmith
Univeristy of Texas, Arlington

Ellen Lorraine Friedrich
Valdosta State University

Daniel Fulmer
Snead State Community College

Javier A. Galvan
Santa Ana College

Luis Garcia-Torvisco
Gonzaga University

Alejandro Garza
Tarrant County College, Northwest Campus

Scott Gibby
Austin Community College

Debbie Gill
Penn State University, DuBois

Elena Grajeda
Pima Community College

Ileana Gross
University of Colorado Denver

Sergio A. Guzmán
College of Southern Nevada

Karen Hall Zetrouer
Santa Fe College

Patricia Harrigan
Community College of Baltimore County

Haydn
Campbell University

Lynn Healy
Grand Valley State University

Laurie Huffman
Los Medanos College

Elena Iglesias-Villamel
Hiram College

Kelsey Ihinger
University of Wisconsin, Madison

Casilde Isabelli
University of Nevada, Reno

Roberto Jimenez-Arroyo
University of South Florida Sarasota-Manatee

Julie Kleinhans-Urrutia
Austin Community College

Chris Kneifl
University of Oklahoma

Dr Jeremy Larochelle
University of Mary Washington

Luis E Latoja
Columbus State Community College

Rachele Lawton
The Community College of Baltimore County

Vanessa Lazo-Wilson
Austin Community College

Peter Lebron
Moberly Area Community College

Kathleen Leonard
University of Nevada, Reno

Talia Loaiza
Austin Community College

Rosemary LoDato
Houston Community College Southwest

Kathy Lopez
Saginaw Valley State University

Kimberly Louie
Southeast Missouri State University

Monica Malamud
Canada College

Jude Thomas Manzo
Saint Philip's College

Sandra M. Manzon - Omundson
Anoka Ramsey Community College

Ornella Mazzuca
Dutchess Community College

Peggy McNeil
Louisiana State University

Marco Mena
Massbay Community College

Wendy Mendez-Hasselman
Palm Beach State College

Jise L. Mendoza
The University of San Diego

Joseph Menig
Valencia College

Lizette Moon
Houston Community College Northwest

Patricia Moore-Martinez
Temple University

Sandra J. Mulryan
Community College of Baltimore County

Heather Nylen
University of Hawaii at Manoa

Dale Omundson
Anoka-Ramsey Community College

Ann Ortiz
Campbell University

Catherine Ortiz
University of Texas at Arlington

Patricia Orozco Watrel
University of Mary Washington

Philip Pack
Connors State College

Elizabeth Petree
Joliet Junior College

Maria Portal
Hamilton College

Tim Robbins
Drury University

Silvia Roca-Martinez
The Citadel

Angelo J. Rodriguez
Kutztown University of Pennsylvania

Margarita Rodriguez
Lone Star College System

Ulises Rodriguez
Mountain View College

Francisco Salgado
The College of Staten Island

Francisco Salgado-Robles
University of Kentucky

Bethany Sanio
University of Nebraska at Lincoln

Roman Santos
Mohawk Valley Community College

David Schultz
College of Southern Nevada

Dr. Dennis Seager
Oklahoma State University

Georgia Seminet
St. Edward's University

Louis Silvers
Monroe Community College

Natalie Sobalvarro
Merced College

Samuel Sommerville
Johnson County Community College

Stacy Southerland
University of Central Oklahoma

Clay Tanner
The University of Memphis

Joe Terantino
Kennesaw State University

Rosa Tezanos-Pinto
Indiana University-Purdue University Indianapolis

Giovanna Urdangarain
Pacific Lutheran University

Amy Uribe
LoneStar College CyFair

Vangie Vélez-Cobb
Palo Alto College

Hilde Votaw
University of Oklahoma

Michael Vrooman
Grand Valley State University

Natalie S. Wagener
University of Texas, Arlington

Sara Walker
Holy Family University

Tina Ware-Walters
Oklahoma Christian University

Sandra Watts
University of North Carolina, Charlotte

Susan Wehling
Valdosta State University

Christopher Weimer
Oklahoma State University

Joseph Wieczorek
College of Baltimore

Karen Zetrouer
Santa Fe College

The authors wish to thank the following friends and professional colleagues. Their feedback, support, and contributions are greatly appreciated.

- Arni C. Álvarez , Rodrigo Figueroa, Nathan Gordon, Melissa Logue, Christina D. Miller, and Mark Pleiss for their work as user diarists, and Anne Becher and Jeanette Sánchez Naranjo for helping us identify many members of this fine team
- The Teaching Assistants and colleagues of Anne Becher at the University of Colorado, Boulder, whose thought-provoking conversations and annotations truly shaped the revision of the grammar, vocabulary, and activities. "Their work was perhaps the single most important kind of input that I received for this edition."—Thalia Dorwick
- The colleagues of Ana Pérez-Gironés at Wesleyan University
- Dora Y. Marrón Romero and Claudia Sahagún (Broward Community College), for their helpful comments about culture
- Alejandro Lee (Central Washington University), for the many comments and suggestions on the eighth edition
- Laura Chastain, for her meticulous work on the language and linguistic accuracy of the manuscript, over many editions but especially this one

Finally, the authors would like to thank their families and close personal friends for all of their love, support, and patience throughout the creation of this edition. **¡Los queremos mucho!**

Contributors

Kalynn Aguirre, Sarah Alem, Allen Bernier, Denise Nicole Casnettie, Eileen Fancher, Lorena Gómez Mostajo, Danielle Havens, Shelly Hubman, Emilia Illana Mahiques, Constance Kihyet, Christopher LaFond, Lily Martínez, Leticia McGrath, Wendy Mendez-Hasselman, Louise Neary, Ron Nelms, Pennie Nichols, Jodi Parrett, Maritza Salgueiro-Carlisle, John Underwood, Annie Rutter Wendel, Sam Sommerville, Nina Tunac-Basey, Amy Uribe, Alina Vega Franco

Product Team

Editorial and Marketing: Mike Ambrosino, Jorge Arbujas, Allen J. Bernier, Susan Blatty, Chris Brown, Laura Ciporen, Craig Gill, Helen Greenlea, Misha Maclaird, Pennie Nichols, Sadie Ray, Kimberley Sallee, Katie Stevens, Alina Vega Franco

Art, Design, and Production: Matt Backhaus, Amber Bettcher, Francine Cronshaw, Kelly Heinrichs, Patti Isaacs, Lynne Lemley, Erin Melloy DeHeck, Sylvie Pittet, Margaret Potter, Terri Schiesl, Emily Tietz, Beth Thole, Shawntel Schmitt

Media Partners: Aptara, BBC Motion Gallery, Eastern Sky Studios, Hurix, Klic Video Productions, Inc., Laserwords, Latinallure Voiceover, LearningMate

CONTENTS

| Capítulo | VOCABULARY AND PRONUCIATION | GRAMMAR |

VOCABULARY AND PRONUCIATION	GRAMMAR

GET THE MOST FROM YOUR SPANISH STUDIES!

In the 21st century global society we live in now, there is an ever-growing demand for those who have proficiency in more than one language. The Spanish language is at the top of the list in the United States. Regardless of your career path, there is not a single profession that would not benefit from proficiency in Spanish!

In addition to **majoring** or **minoring in Spanish**, the Department of Modern Languages also offers a **B.A. in Translation and Interpreting**. You may also wish to consider other options such as completing one of the **Certificate Programs**. And if you are looking for a way to build your proficiency in the language while expanding your cultural horizons, be sure to check out details of our **Study Abroad Program**. **Accelerated courses for Lower Level Spanish** (1441-1442 and 2313-2314) can help you begin these programs more quickly by taking two levels in one semester. See details for these options below and on the following page.

Full course descriptions for **all undergraduate Spanish courses** are listed at the end of this section of your textbook. For more information, please consult with our **Undergraduate Advisor** in the Department of Modern Languages by sending an email to **modladvisor@uta.edu** or by phoning **817.272.3161**. More information is also available on the Department of Modern Languages website: **http://www.uta.edu/modl**

CERTIFICATE IN SPANISH FOR THE PROFESSIONS

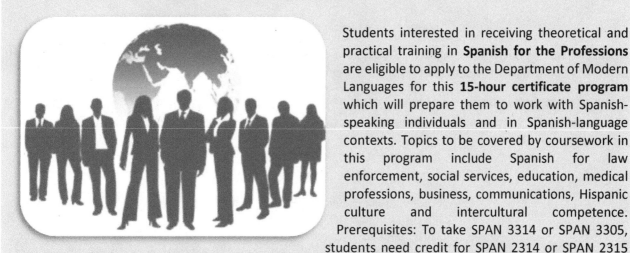

Students interested in receiving theoretical and practical training in **Spanish for the Professions** are eligible to apply to the Department of Modern Languages for this **15-hour certificate program** which will prepare them to work with Spanish-speaking individuals and in Spanish-language contexts. Topics to be covered by coursework in this program include Spanish for law enforcement, social services, education, medical professions, business, communications, Hispanic culture and intercultural competence. Prerequisites: To take SPAN 3314 or SPAN 3305, students need credit for SPAN 2314 or SPAN 2315 with a grade of C or better. Other prerequisites are listed below and also require a grade of C or better.

REQUIRED COURSES:

❖ **SPAN 3314** - Advanced Spanish Grammar OR:
  SPAN 3305 - Advanced Spanish for Heritage Speakers
❖ **SPAN 3315** - Composition through Literature (Prerequisite: SPAN 3314 or SPAN 3305)
❖ **SPAN 3309** - Spanish for the Professions (Prerequisite: SPAN 3315)

❖ **Two (2) 4000-level courses** from the following. (Prerequisites: All <u>required</u> courses above.)
  SPAN 4312 - Intercultural Competence for Global Communication
  SPAN 4334 - Contemporary Hispanic Culture
  SPAN 4335 - Business Spanish
  SPAN 4336 - Topics in Spanish for the Professions

CERTIFICATE IN TRANSLATION

PREREQUISITES:
- ❖ SPAN 3305 - Advanced Spanish for Heritage Speakers OR:
  SPAN 3314 - Advanced Spanish Grammar
- ❖ SPAN 3315 - Composition through Literature

REQUIRED COURSES:
- ❖ SPAN 3340 - Introduction to Translation
- ❖ SPAN 4341 - Business and Legal Translation
- ❖ SPAN 4342 - Medical, Scientific and Technical Translation

translation   traducción

english   inglés

spanish   español

CERTIFICATE IN INTERPRETING

PREREQUISITES:
- ❖ SPAN 2314 - Intermediate Spanish II OR:
  SPAN 2315 - Intermediate Spanish for Heritage Speakers
- ❖ SPAN 3305 - Advanced Spanish for Heritage Speakers OR:
  SPAN 3314 - Advanced Spanish Grammar

REQUIRED COURSES:
- ❖ SPAN 3341 - Introduction to Interpreting
- ❖ SPAN 4343 - Interpreting in Medical Settings
- ❖ SPAN 4344 - Interpreting in Legal Settings

ACCELERATED LOWER LEVEL SPANISH COURSES

ACCELERATED BEGINNING SPANISH: SPAN 1441-032 + SPAN 1442-032. Take Beginning Spanish I and Beginning Spanish II in one semester. This class meets MWF from 10-11:50.

ACCELERATED INTERMEDIATE SPANISH: SPAN 2313-132 + SPAN 2314-132. Take Intermediate Spanish I and Intermediate Spanish II in one semester. This class meets MWF from 10-11:50. Prerequisite: Grade of C or better in SPAN 1442.

SPANISH DEGREE PROGRAMS

B.A. in SPANISH FOR GLOBAL COMPETENCE
B.A. in TRANSLATION AND INTERPRETING
MINOR in SPANISH
Detailed information on the MODL website: **http://www.uta.edu/modl/spanish/Spanish_Programs.php**

SUMMER STUDY ABROAD PROGRAM IN MEXICO

- Study Spanish in Cuernavaca, Mexico — a colonial city in the heart of Mexico known for its eternal spring weather.
- Live with a Mexican family.
- Interact with native speakers.
- Experience Mexican culture first hand: in the classroom, on the cobblestone streets or in the market.
- Attend classes on the beautiful campus of the Spanish Language Institute.
- Students pay in-state tuition to UTA in addition to program fees, room, board, and excursions. Student Financial Aid applies! Scholarships are available at the Department of Modern Languages for eligible students, in addition to UTA.

WEBSITE: **http://utaencuernavaca.wordpress.com**
PROGRAM DIRECTOR: **Dr. Ray Elliott – elliott@uta.edu**

SPANISH COURSE DESCRIPTIONS

SPAN 1441. BEGINNING SPANISH I. 4 Hours. (TCCN = SPAN 1411). Beginning study of Spanish language with emphasis on speaking, listening, reading, and writing. No prerequisites. Native or heritage speakers of Spanish may not take this course.

SPAN 1442. BEGINNING SPANISH II. 4 Hours. (TCCN = SPAN 1412). Continuation of beginning Spanish. Prerequisite: SPAN 1441 with a grade of C or better. Native or heritage speakers of Spanish may not take this course.

SPAN 2301. TOPICS IN SPANISH LITERATURE IN TRANSLATION. 3 Hours. Study of the works of major authors and intellectual trends of a given period or periods. May be repeated for credit as topics or periods vary. SPAN 2301 may be taken to fulfill the foreign language literature requirement. Prerequisite: ENGL 1301 and ENGL 1302.

SPAN 2313. INTERMEDIATE SPANISH I. 3 Hours. (TCCN = SPAN 2311). Intermediate study of Spanish language with emphasis on speaking, listening, reading, and writing. Prerequisite: SPAN 1442 with a grade of C or better. Native or heritage speakers of Spanish may not take this course.

SPAN 2314. INTERMEDIATE SPANISH II. 3 Hours. (TCCN = SPAN 2312). Continuation of intermediate Spanish. Prerequisite: SPAN 2313 with a grade of C or better. Native or heritage speakers of Spanish may not take this course.

SPAN 2315. INTERM SPAN HERITAGE SPEAKERS. 3 Hours. This course focuses on the development of reading, writing, speaking and listening skills in Spanish, as well as an understanding of Hispanic cultures and issues of identity of heritage speakers in the United States. This course is intended for heritage speakers of Spanish and is the equivalent of SPAN 2314. Prerequisite: SPAN 2313 with a Grade of C or better or the equivalent, or consent of the department.

SPAN 2391. CONFERENCE COURSE. 3 Hours. Independent study; consultation with instructor on a regular basis. Prerequisite: Permission of the instructor.

SPAN 3302. HISPANIC LITERATURE IN TRANSLATION. 3 Hours. The works of major authors and intellectual trends of a given period. May be repeated for credit as topics or periods vary. SPAN 3302 cannot be applied toward the B.A. in Spanish or toward a Spanish minor, but may be taken to fulfill the foreign language literature requirement. Prerequisite: 2314 of a Modern or Classical language and 6 hours of English.

SPAN 3303. ADVANCED SPANISH CONVERSATION. 3 Hours. Practice in oral expression with an emphasis on vocabulary building and grammar review. Of special interest to students who wish to improve their skills in pronunciation, comprehension, and oral expression. Credit will not be granted to native or heritage speakers of Spanish. Prerequisite: SPAN 2314 with a grade of C or better.

SPAN 3305. ADVANCED SPANISH FOR HERITAGE SPEAKERS. 3 Hours. A detailed study of Spanish grammar for heritage speakers. Capitalizes upon students' existing language skills, expands their knowledge base, and develops their ability to read, write, and communicate more effectively. Special attention is given to regional and dialectal differences. Prerequisite: SPAN 2315, or the equivalent, with a grade of C or better.

SPAN 3309. SPANISH FOR THE PROFESSIONS. 3 Hours. Practice in Spanish-language skills needed in the professional fields in order to communicate with Spanish-speaking individuals. Emphasis on specialized vocabulary building, role play, and an understanding of Hispanic culture. Topics may include Spanish for law enforcement, social services, education, medicine, business, and communications. Prerequisite: SPAN 3315 with a grade of C or better.

SPAN 3311. SPANISH CULTURE AND CIVILIZATION. 3 Hours. Spanish history with emphasis on cultural, intellectual, and artistic trends and existing social institutions. Prerequisite: SPAN 2314 or SPAN 2315 with a grade of C or better.

SPAN 3312. LATIN AMERICAN CULTURE AND CIVILIZATION. 3 Hours. An interdisciplinary introduction to Latin American society, history and culture. Offered as MAS 3312 and SPAN 3312; credit will be granted for either MAS or SPAN. Prerequisite: SPAN 2314 or SPAN 2315 with a grade of C or better.

SPANISH COURSE DESCRIPTIONS

SPAN 3313. TOPICS IN HISPANIC LANGUAGE, LITERATURE & CULTURE. 3 Hours. Topics may include Peninsular or Latin American film, music, radio, politics, human rights movements, literature, language or Hispanic linguistics. May be repeated as the topic changes. Prerequisite: SPAN 2314 or SPAN 2315 with a grade of C or better.

SPAN 3314. ADVANCED SPANISH GRAMMAR. 3 Hours. A detailed study of Spanish grammar for non-native speakers. Credit will not be granted to native or heritage speakers of Spanish. Prerequisite: SPAN 2314 with a grade of C or better.

SPAN 3315. COMPOSITION THROUGH LITERATURE. 3 Hours. Practice in original composition and critical thinking through the study of selected literary and cultural texts. Of special interest to students who wish to improve their reading comprehension and their writing skills. Prerequisite: SPAN 3305 or SPAN 3314, with grade C or better.

SPAN 3319. INTRODUCTION TO SPANISH LINGUISTICS. 3 Hours. Introductory study of the structure of the Spanish language including phonology, morphology, and syntax, as well as historical, regional, and social variation. Prerequisite: SPAN 3314 or SPAN 3305 with a grade of C or better.

SPAN 3320. INTRODUCTION TO HISPANIC LITERATURE AND CULTURE. 3 Hours. An introduction to the tools of literary and cultural criticism as well as Spanish and Latin American literary history. Study of representative literary texts with the object of developing students' understanding of historical change and cultural crosscurrents. Prerequisite: SPAN 3315 with a grade of C or better.

SPAN 3340. INTRODUCTION TO TRANSLATION. 3 Hours. This course is an introduction to the theory, methods and practice of English to Spanish translation and Spanish to English translation. The student will learn how to address translation problems related to culture and language as well as the fundamentals of translating general material from different fields such as journalism, advertisement, tourism, gastronomy, health, business, etc. The student will also acquire basic knowledge of translation theory. SPAN 3340 cannot be applied toward the B.A. in Spanish. Prerequisite: SPAN 3315 with grade of C or better.

SPAN 3341. INTRODUCTION TO INTERPRETING. 3 Hours. Introduction to the theory, methods and practice of interpreting. The student will become familiar with community interpreting (interpreting in school, medical and legal settings) and interpreting theory. The student will begin to interpret in the simultaneous and consecutive (bilateral) modes. The student will also learn about sight translation. Non-native/heritage speakers are also encouraged to take SPAN 3303 prior to enrolling in SPAN 3341. SPAN 3341 cannot be applied toward the B.A. in Spanish. Prerequisite: SPAN 3305 or SPAN 3314 with a grade of B or better.

SPAN 3345. INTRODUCTION TO COMPUTER-ASSISTED TRANSLATION. 3 Hours. Introduction to computer-assisted translation (CAT), machine translation (MT), translation memory (TM) and terminology management tools in modern translation and localization workflows. Prepares students for real-world careers in the language services industry. For students enrolled in Localization and Translation/Interpreting programs only. SPAN 3345 cannot be applied toward the B.A. in Spanish.

SPAN 3391. CONFERENCE COURSE. 3 Hours. Independent study; consultation with instructor on a regular basis. Offered primarily in summer study abroad programs. May be repeated for credit. Prerequisite: Permission of the instructor.

SPAN 4310. TOPICS IN PENINSULAR SPANISH LITERATURE AND CULTURE TO THE EIGHTEENTH CENTURY. 3 Hours. Topics may include: Medieval Spanish literature and culture, Golden Age Spanish literature and culture, or any particular movement, genre, work or author prior to the eighteenth century. May be repeated for credit when content changes. Prerequisite: SPAN 3315 with a grade of C or better.

SPAN 4311. TOPICS IN PENINSULAR SPANISH LITERATURE AND CULTURE, EIGHTEENTH CENTURY TO THE PRESENT. 3 Hours. Topics may include: Neoclassical peninsular Spanish literature and culture, peninsular Spanish literature and culture of the Romantic period, Realist or Naturalist Spanish literature and culture, peninsular Spanish literature and culture since 1900, as well as any particular movement, genre, work or author from the eighteenth century to the present. May be repeated for credit when content changes. Prerequisite: SPAN 3315 with a grade of C or better.

SPANISH COURSE DESCRIPTIONS

SPAN 4312. INTERCULTURAL COMPETENCE FOR GLOBAL COMMUNICATION. 3 Hours. A study of the cultural differences between the U.S. and the Hispanic world with a focus on the development of intercultural competence: verbal and non-verbal communication, interpersonal skills, effective management strategies, and professional etiquette in multicultural settings. Prerequisite: SPAN 3315 with a grade of C or better.

SPAN 4313. TOPICS IN HISPANIC CULTURE. 3 Hours. Among the topics are Spanish or Latin American music, television, radio, film, and literature as culture. May be repeated for credit as topic changes. Prerequisite: SPAN 3315 with a grade of C or better. Offered as MAS 4313 and SPAN 4313; credit will be given for MAS 4313 or SPAN 4313 but not both in a given semester.

SPAN 4314. TOPICS IN LATIN-AMERICAN LITERATURE AND CULTURE TO MODERNISM. 3 Hours. Topics may include: Colonial Latin-American literature and culture, pre-modern Latin-American literature and culture, Latin-American literature and culture of the Enlightenment, or any particular movement, genre, work or author prior to Modernism. May be repeated for credit when content changes. Prerequisite: SPAN 3315 with a grade of C or better.

SPAN 4315. TOPICS IN CONTEMPORARY LATIN-AMERICAN LITERATURE AND CULTURE, MODERNISM TO THE PRESENT. 3 Hours. Topics may include: Latin-American literature and culture of Modernism, modern Latin-American literature and culture, or any particular movement, genre, work or author from Modernism to the present. May be repeated for credit when content changes. Offered as MAS 4315 and SPAN 4315; credit will be given for MAS 4315 or SPAN 4315 but not both in a given semester. Prerequisite: SPAN 3315 with a grade of C or better.

SPAN 4317. CHICANO LITERATURE. 3 Hours. Mexican-American literature, with special attention to its social, cultural, and linguistic background. Offered as MAS 4317 and SPAN 4317; credit will be given for MAS 4317 or SPAN 4317 but not both in a given semester. Prerequisite: SPAN 3315 with a grade of C or better.

SPAN 4318. MEXICAN LITERATURE. 3 Hours. Studies in Mexican fiction, poetry, drama, and literary essay. Offered as MAS 4318 and SPAN 4318; credit will be given for MAS 4318 or SPAN 4318 but not both in a given semester. Prerequisite: SPAN 3315 with a grade of C or better.

SPAN 4320. TOPICS IN SPANISH LANGUAGE, WRITING AND THEORY. 3 Hours. Review of advanced research methods and topics in Spanish, Latino and Latin American literature, culture and linguistics. Topics may include: literary and cultural theory in relation to Hispanic literature and culture, research trends, and methods in Spanish linguistics. Students conduct original research or writing projects in relation to the course topic. May be repeated for credit as topic changes. Prerequisite: SPAN 3315 with a grade of C or better.

SPAN 4327. WOMEN IN HISPANIC LITERATURE. 3 Hours. Considers women as characters in and writers of Hispanic literature. Includes the analysis of themes, language, and how the writings of women often give voice to lesser known aspects of culture. Offered as SPAN 4327, MAS 4327, and WOMS 4327; credit will be granted only once. Prerequisite: SPAN 3315 with a grade of C or better.

SPAN 4330. TOPICS IN SPANISH LINGUISTICS. 3 Hours. Topics may include: Spanish phonetics and phonology, morphology, syntax, semantics, lexicography, history of the Spanish language, Old Spanish, Spanish sociolinguistics, as well as the application of any theoretical approach to the study of the Spanish language, excluding the study of either peninsular or American Spanish dialectology. May be repeated for credit when content changes. Prerequisite: SPAN 3319 with a grade of C or better.

SPAN 4332. TOPICS IN SPANISH DIALECTOLOGY. 3 Hours. Topics may include: Modern peninsular Spanish dialectology, modern Spanish-American dialectology, Old Spanish dialectology, early American Spanish dialectology, as well as a detailed study of any one dialect or regional dialect of Spanish from either a synchronic or a diachronic perspective. Emphasis may be given to phonetics, phonology, morphology, syntax, semantics, or lexicon, as applied to the study of peninsular or American Spanish dialectology. May be repeated for credit when content changes. Prerequisite: SPAN 3319 with a grade of C or better.

SPANISH COURSE DESCRIPTIONS

SPAN 4334. CULTURE AND ECONOMIC GLOBALIZATION IN THE HISPANIC WORLD. 3 Hours. An introduction to social, political and economic structures in Spain and Latin America, with special emphasis on current events affecting the business world. Prerequisite: SPAN 3315 with a grade of C or better. Exclusively for International Business Spanish students. SPAN 4334 cannot be applied toward the B.A. in Spanish.

SPAN 4335. BUSINESS SPANISH. 3 Hours. An introduction to business terminology, skills needed for writing business letters, conducting telephone conversations, commercial transactions, and international procedures. Operational and strategic issues involved in interaction with Hispanic firms and markets; international trade; competitive, vendor-customer, and collaborative relations. Prerequisite: SPAN 3315 with a grade of C or better. Exclusively for International Business Spanish students. SPAN 4335 cannot be applied toward the B.A. in Spanish.

SPAN 4336. TOPICS IN SPANISH FOR THE PROFESSIONS. 3 HOURS. Development of Spanish-language skills needed to work in a specific profession. Emphasis on reading and formal communication, including technical papers, letters, reports, proposals, and presentations. Topics may include Spanish for legal, medical, educational, or communications fields. May be repeated for credit when content changes. Prerequisite: SPAN 3315 with a grade of C or better.

SPAN 4339. THE ACQUISITION OF SPANISH. 3 Hours. Topics, methods, and techniques specific to the teaching of the Spanish language. Prerequisite: SPAN 3319 with a grade of C or better.

SPAN 4341. BUSINESS AND LEGAL TRANSLATION. 3 Hours. An advanced course in translation with a focus on business and legal texts. Students deepen their knowledge of translation theory and are trained to build and consolidate their skills in specialized translation. May be taken concurrently with SPAN 4342. SPAN 4341 cannot be applied toward the B.A. in Spanish. Prerequisite: SPAN 3340 with a grade of C or better.

SPAN 4342. MEDICAL, SCIENTIFIC & TECH TRANSLATION. 3 Hours. An advanced course in translation with a focus on medical, scientific and technical translation. Students deepen their knowledge of translation theory and are trained to build and consolidate their skills in specialized translation. May be taken concurrently with SPAN 4341. SPAN 4342 cannot be applied toward the B.A. in Spanish. Prerequisite: SPAN 3340 with a grade of C or better.

SPAN 4343. INTERPRETING IN MEDICAL SETTINGS. 3 Hours. A study of different types of interpretation. Medical terminology in English and Spanish will be addressed with a special emphasis on the diverse roles of medical interpreters as well as various locations where they are needed, such as hospital clinics, doctor's offices, and hearings that deal with medical issues. Ethical standards of practice in medical interpreting will be examined. SPAN 4343 cannot be applied toward the B.A. in Spanish. Prerequisite: SPAN 3341 with a grade of B or better.

SPAN 4344. INTERPRETING IN LEGAL SETTINGS. 3 Hours. A study of different types of interpretation. Legal terminology in English and Spanish will be addressed with special emphasis on the diverse roles of legal interpreters as well as various locations where they are needed, such as courtrooms, lawyer's offices, and state, federal, or local law-enforcement facilities. Ethical standards of practice in legal interpreting will be examined. SPAN 4344 cannot be applied toward the B.A. in Spanish. Prerequisite: SPAN 3341 with a grade of B or better.

SPAN 4391. CONFERENCE COURSE. 3 Hours. Independent study in the preparation of a paper on a research topic; consultation with instructor on a regular basis. May be repeated for credit. Prerequisite: two 3000 level courses and permission of the instructor.

SPAN 4393. SPANISH INTERNSHIP. 3 Hours. A combination of field-related experience in the business or service sector with an academic component. Coursework may include journal writing in Spanish, outside readings, and formal presentations. Prerequisite: two 3000 level courses and permission of the instructor.

SPAN 4394. HONORS THESIS / SENIOR PROJECT. 3 Hours. Required of all students in the University Honors College. During the senior year, the student must complete a thesis or a project under the direction of a faculty member in the major department. May not be repeated for credit. Prerequisite: two 3000 level courses and permission of the instructor.

An Invitation to

Puntos de partida

Puntos de partida means *points of departure* in Spanish. This program will be your point of departure for learning Spanish and for learning about Hispanic cultures. With *Puntos de partida*, you will get ready to communicate with Spanish speakers in this country and in other parts of the Spanish-speaking world. To speak a language means much more than just learning its grammar and vocabulary. To know a language is to know the people who speak it. For this reason, *Puntos de partida* will provide you with cultural information to help you understand and appreciate the traditions and values of Spanish-speaking people all over the world. Get ready for the adventure of learning Spanish!

1

Ante todo°

Ante... *First of all*

En este capítulo°

En... *In this chapter*

|SPANISH

www.connectspanish.com

Zócalo (*Main Plaza*),
México, D.F., México

Parque Güell, Barcelona, España

EL MUNDO HISPANOHABLANTE[a]

- El español es la lengua que más se habla[b] en el mundo[c] después del[d] mandarín. Más de[e] 500 (quinientas) millones de personas hablan español.

- Es la lengua oficial de 20 (veinte) naciones y de Puerto Rico.

[a]El...*The Spanish-speaking world* [b]la...*the language spoken most* [c]*world* [d]después... *after* [e]Más...*More than*

- ¡Hola! ¿Cómo está usted?[a]
- ¿Cómo se llama?[b]
- ¿De dónde es?[c]
- ¿Cómo es usted?[d]

[a]¡Hola!... *Hello! How are you?* [b]¿Cómo... *What's your name?* [c]¿De... *Where are you from?* [d]¿Cómo... *What are you like?*

ALEJANDRA HERNÁNDEZ SOTO CONTESTA LAS PREGUNTAS.[a]

- ¡Hola! Estoy[b] muy bien. ¿Y usted?[c]
- Me llamo Alejandra Hernández Soto.
- Soy de[d] Guanajuato, México.
- ¿Cómo soy?[e] Optimista, responsable, sentimental y muy independiente. ¿Y cómo es usted?

[a]contesta... *answers the questions* [b]*I am* [c]¿Y... *And (how are) you?* [d]Soy... *I'm from* [e]¿Cómo... *What am I like?*

PRIMERA° PARTE

First

Saludos° y expresiones de cortesía *Greetings*

Here are some words, phrases, and expressions for meeting and greeting others in Spanish. Can you tell the difference between those that are formal and those that are more informal or familiar (as on a first-name basis)?

Situaciones formales

1.

ELISA VELASCO:	Buenas tardes, señor Gómez.
MARTÍN GÓMEZ:	Muy buenas, señora Velasco. ¿Cómo está?
ELISA VELASCO:	Bien, gracias. ¿Y usted?
MARTÍN GÓMEZ:	Muy bien, gracias. Hasta luego.
ELISA VELASCO:	Adiós.

2.

LUPE:	Buenos días, profesor.
MARTÍN GÓMEZ:	Buenos días. ¿Cómo se llama usted, señorita?
LUPE:	Me llamo Lupe Carrasco.
MARTÍN GÓMEZ:	Mucho gusto, Lupe.
LUPE:	Igualmente.

Situaciones informales

3.

JOSÉ:	¡Hola, Carmen!
CARMEN:	¿Qué tal, José? ¿Cómo estás?
JOSÉ:	Muy bien. ¿Y tú?
CARMEN:	Regular. Nos vemos mañana, ¿eh?
JOSÉ:	Bien. Hasta mañana.

4.

MIGUEL RENÉ:	Hola. Me llamo Miguel René. ¿Y tú? ¿Cómo te llamas?
KARINA:	Me llamo Karina. Mucho gusto.
MIGUEL RENÉ:	Encantado, Karina. Y, ¿de dónde eres?
KARINA:	Soy de Venezuela. ¿Y tú?
MIGUEL RENÉ:	Yo soy de México.

> Translations of short dialogues like the ones on this page will always be at the foot of the page, but you should try to read them without the translations first!

---

1. EV: *Good afternoon, Mr. Gómez.* MG: *Afternoon, Mrs. Velasco. How are you?* EV: *Fine, thank you. And you?* MG: *Very well, thanks. See you later.* EV: *Bye.*
2. L: *Good morning, professor.* MG: *Good morning. What's your name, miss?* L: *My name is Lupe Carrasco.* MG: *Nice to meet you, Lupe.* L: *Likewise.*
3. J: *Hi, Carmen!* C: *How's it going, José? How are you?* J: *Very well. And you?* C: *OK. See you tomorrow, OK?* J: *Fine. Until tomorrow.*
4. MR: *Hello. My name is Miguel René. And you? What's your name?* K: *My name is Karina. Nice to meet you.* MR: *Nice to meet you, Karina. And where are you from?* K: *I'm from Venezuela. And you?* MR: *I'm from Mexico.*

Note the use of red to highlight aspects of Spanish that you should pay special attention to.

	formal		informal	
títulos	**señor (Sr.)**	Mr.		
	señora (Sra.)	Mrs., ma'am		
	señorita (Srta.)	Miss		
	profesor (*for a man*)			
	profesora (*for a woman*)			
saludos	**buenos días**	good morning	**hola**	hi
	buenas tardes	good afternoon/evening		
	buenas noches	good evening/night		
	(muy) buenas	good day (*any time*)		
preguntas (*questions*)	**¿Cómo está?**	How are you?	**¿Cómo estás?** ⎤	How are
			¿Qué tal? ⎬	you?
	¿Y usted?	And you?	**¿Y tú?** ⎦	And you?
	—**¿Cómo se llama (usted)?**		—**¿Cómo te llamas (tú)?**	
	—**Me llamo...**		—**Me llamo...**	
	"What's your name?"		"What's your name?"	
	"My name is . . . "		"My name is . . . "	
	—**¿De dónde es (usted)?**		—**¿De dónde eres (tú)?**	
	—**(Yo) Soy de...**		—**(Yo) Soy de...**	
	"Where are you from?"		"Where are you from?"	
	"I'm from . . . "		"I'm from . . . "	

¡OJO!*

There is no Spanish equivalent for *Ms.;* use **Sra.** or **Srta.**, as appropriate.

¡OJO!

Note the accent marks on Spanish words that ask questions.

Nota **cultural**

Así se dice (*That's how it's said*) introduces optional vocabulary from the Spanish-speaking world.

Los saludos en el mundo° hispano   *world*

Hispanics all over the world hug and kiss when they are greeting each other a lot more frequently than do non-Hispanics in this country. Younger people especially greet in this way, even when they have just met. Two men will typically hug or pat each other on the back, and if they are family, they will sometimes give a kiss on the cheek and embrace, just like women do.

How do you greet your friends? Your relatives?

¿Qué pasa, hombre? (*What's up, man?*)

Así se dice

The following greetings express *What's up?, What's happening?,* or *How's it going?*

¿Qué hay? ¿Qué pasa? ¿Qué hubo? ¿Qué onda? (*Mexico*)

The phrase **por nada** is an alternative to **de nada**.

Nota **comunicativa**

Más° expresiones de cortesía	*More*		
—**Encantado.** (*for a man*) ⎤		**por favor**	please (*also used to get someone's attention*)
—**Encantada.** (*for a woman*) ⎬ "Nice to meet you."			
—**Mucho gusto.** ⎦		**perdón**	pardon me, excuse me (*to ask forgiveness or to get someone's attention*)
—**Igualmente.**	"Likewise."		
Gracias.	Thanks. Thank you.	**(con) permiso**	pardon me, excuse me (*to request permission to pass by or through a group of people*)
Muchas gracias.	Thank you very much.		
De nada. / No hay de qué.	You're welcome.		

You will use these expressions in **Comunicación.**

---

*¡OJO! means Watch out! *or* Pay attention! *in Spanish.*

Comunicación

A. Expresiones de cortesía. How many different ways can you respond to the following greetings and phrases?

1. Buenas tardes.
2. Adiós.
3. ¿Qué tal?
4. Hola, Hola,
5. ¿Cómo está?, Muy buenas, regular, etc
6. Buenas noches.

7. Muchas gracias.
8. Hasta mañana.
9. ¿Cómo se llama usted?
10. Mucho gusto.
11. ¿De dónde eres?
12. Buenos días.

B. Situaciones. If the following people met or passed each other at the times given, what might they say to each other? Role-play the situations with a classmate.

1. Mr. Santana and Miss Pérez, at 5:00 P.M.
2. Mrs. Ortega and Pablo, at 10:00 A.M.
3. Ms. Hernández and Olivia, at 11:00 P.M.
4. you and a classmate, just before your Spanish class

C. Situaciones. What would you say in Spanish in the following situations?

1. Your classmate passes you a handout from the professor.
2. You need to be excused from class to go to the restroom.
3. You just dropped your drink on a friend's book.
4. Your professor thanks you for opening the door for her.
5. You need your professor's attention.

D. Más (More) situaciones. Are the people in this drawing saying **por favor, con permiso,** or **perdón?** ¡OJO! More than one response is possible for some items.

E. Entrevista (Interview)

Paso (Step) 1. Turn to a person sitting next to you and do the following.

- Greet him or her appropriately, that is, with informal forms.
- Ask how he or she is.
- Find out his or her name.
- Ask where he or she is from.
- Conclude the exchange.

Paso 2. Now have a similar conversation with your instructor, using the appropriate formal or familiar forms, according to your instructor's request.

Pronunciación: Las vocales:° *a, e, i, o, u*

vowels

There is a very close relationship between the way Spanish is written and the way it is pronounced. This makes it relatively easy to learn the basics of Spanish spelling and pronunciation.

Many Spanish sounds, however, do not have an exact equivalent in English, so you can't always trust English to be your guide to Spanish pronunciation. Even words that are spelled the same in both languages are usually pronounced quite differently.

English vowels can have many different pronunciations or may be silent. Spanish vowels are always pronounced, and they are almost always pronounced in the same way. They are always short and tense. They are never drawn out with a *u* or *i* glide as in English: **lo** ≠ *low;* **de** ≠ *day.*

> **a:** pronounced like the *a* in *father,* but short and tense
> **e:** pronounced like the *e* in *they,* but without the *i* glide
> **i:** pronounced like the *i* in *machine,* but short and tense*
> **o:** pronounced like the *o* in *home,* but without the *u* glide
> **u:** pronounced like the *u* in *rule,* but short and tense

¡OJO!
The *uh* sound or schwa (which is how most unstressed vowels are pronounced in English: c*a*nal, wait*e*d, at*o*m) does not exist in Spanish.

Práctica

A. Palabras (Words). Repeat the following words after your instructor.

1. hasta	tal	nada	mañana	natural	normal	fascinante
2. me	qué	Pérez	Elena	rebelde	excelente	elegante
3. sí	señorita	permiso	terrible	imposible	tímido	Ibiza
4. yo	con	como	noches	profesor	señor	generoso
5. uno	usted	tú	mucho	Perú	Lupe	Úrsula

B. Nombres. Here is a table of the 10 Spanish names most frequently given to Hispanic babies (male and female) in the U.S. in 2012 (**dos mil doce**).

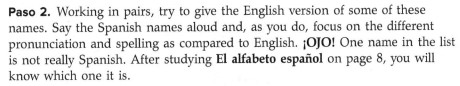

Los 10 nombres de bebé preferidos por los hispanos en el 2012	
Niño	**Niña**
Santiago	Sofía
Matías	Isabella
Sebastián	Valentina
Mateo	Camila
Nicolás	Valeria
Alejandro	Luciana
Samuel	Ximena/Jimena
Diego	Mariana
Daniel	María José
Benjamín	Victoria

From Fox News Latino

Paso 1. Can you find the Spanish word for *boy*? for *girl*? for the phrase *preferred by Hispanics*?

Paso 2. Working in pairs, try to give the English version of some of these names. Say the Spanish names aloud and, as you do, focus on the different pronunciation and spelling as compared to English. **¡OJO!** One name in the list is not really Spanish. After studying **El alfabeto español** on page 8, you will know which one it is.

Paso 3. In pairs, make a list of other Hispanic first names you know and say them out loud, trying to pronounce them in Spanish.

---

*The word **y** (and) is also pronounced like the letter **i**, as is the letter **y** at the end of a word: *¡ay!

El alfabeto español

¡OJO!

The **rr** combination occurs frequently in Spanish, but it is not a separate letter.

The Spanish *alphabet* (**el alfabeto** or **el abecedario**) is slightly different from the English alphabet.

- It has 27 letters (not 26).
- The extra letter is **ñ**.
- The letters **k** and **w** appear only in words borrowed from other languages.

Letters	Names of Letters	Examples			Pronunciation
a	a	Antonio	Ana	la Argentina	
b	be	Benito	Blanca	Bolivia	like Spanish **v**
c	ce	Carlos	Cecilia	Cáceres	**c + a/o/u** = like English *k*; **c + e/i** = like English *s* (in Spain, a *th* sound)
d	de	Domingo	Dolores	Durango	
e	e	Eduardo	Elena	el Ecuador	
f	efe	Felipe	Francisca	Florida	
g	ge	Gerardo	Gloria	Guatemala	**g + e/i** = like hard English *h*; **g + a/o/u** and **gue/gui** = like English *g* in *got*
h	hache	Héctor	Hortensia	Honduras	silent; in **ch** combination = like English *cheese*
i	i	Ignacio	Inés	Ibiza	
j	jota	José	Juana	Jalisco	like hard English *h*; similar to **g + e/i**
k	ca (ka)	(Karl)	(Karina)	(Kansas)	like English *k*
l	ele	Luis	Lola	Lima	like English *l*; when doubled (**ll**), like *y* in English *yes*
m	eme	Manuel	María	México	
n	ene	Nicolás	Nati	Nicaragua	
ñ	eñe	Íñigo	Begoña	España	like *ny* in English *canyon*
o	o	Octavio	Olivia	Oviedo	
p	pe	Pablo	Pilar	Panamá	
q	cu	Enrique	Raquel	Quito	
r	ere	Álvaro	Rosa	Monterrey	like *tt* in English *butter*; trilled at beginning of a word or as **rr**
s	ese	Salvador	Sara	San Juan	
t	te	Tomás	Teresa	Toledo	
u	u	Agustín	Úrsula	el Uruguay	
v	uve	Víctor	Victoria	Venezuela	like Spanish **b**
w	doble uve	(Oswaldo)	(Wilma)	(Washington)	like English *w*
x	equis	Xavier	Ximena	Extremadura	like English *x*; at beginning of a word and in **México, mexicano**, x = Spanish **j**
y	ye	Pelayo	Yolanda	el Paraguay	like *i* in English *machine*
z	ceta (zeta)	Gonzalo	Zoila	Zaragoza	like English *s* (in Spain, a *th* sound); never like English *z*

Práctica

A. Pronunciación. Match the Spanish letters with their equivalent pronunciation and pronounce the example words.

EXAMPLES/SPELLING

1. _C_ mucho: **ch**
2. _e_ Geraldo: **ge** (also: **gi**); Jiménez: **j**
3. _i_ hola: **h**
4. _a_ gusto: **gu** (also: **ga, go**)
5. _f_ me llamo: **ll**
6. _h_ señor: **ñ**
7. ____ profesora: **r**
8. _g_ Ramón: **r** (to start a word); burro: **rr**
9. _d_ nos vemos: **v**

PRONUNCIATION

a. like the *g* in English *garden*
b. similar to *tt* of *butter* when pronounced very quickly
c. like *ch* in English *cheese*
d. like Spanish **b**
e. similar to a "strong" English *h*
f. like *y* in English *yes*
g. a trilled sound, several Spanish **r**'s in a row
h. like the *ny* sound in *canyon*
i. never pronounced

B. ¿Cómo se escribe... ? *(How do you write ... ?)*

Paso 1. Pronounce these U.S. place names in Spanish. Then spell the names aloud in Spanish. All of them are of Hispanic origin: **Toledo, Los Ángeles, Montana, Colorado, El Paso, Florida, Las Vegas, Amarillo, San Francisco.**

Paso 2. Spell your own name aloud in Spanish, and listen as your classmates spell their names. Try to remember as many of their names as you can.

MODELO: Me llamo María: **M** (eme) **a** (a) **r** (ere) **í** (i con acento) **a** (a).

Nota **comunicativa**

Los cognados

As you study Spanish, note that many Spanish and English words are similar or identical in form and meaning. These related words are called *cognates* (**los cognados**). It's useful to begin recognizing and using cognates immediately; they will help you enrich your Spanish vocabulary and develop language proficiency more quickly. Here are some examples.

TO DESCRIBE PEOPLE		TO NAME PLACES AND THINGS	
cruel	optimista	banco	hotel
elegante	paciente	bar	museo
idealista	pesimista	café	oficina
importante	responsable	clase	parque
independiente	sentimental	diccionario	teatro
inteligente	terrible	estudiante	teléfono
interesante	tolerante	examen	televisión

You will practice this vocabulary throughout this chapter.

¿Cómo es usted? (Part 1)

Ángela Suárez del Pino

Ismael Figueroa García

1. —¿Quién **es usted** y cómo **es**?
   — **Soy** Ángela Suárez del Pino. **Soy** optimista y tolerante.

   > Remember to watch for the words in **red**. Check the translation at the bottom of the page only if you need to.

2. —¿Quién **eres tú**?
   — Me llamo Ismael Figueroa García y **soy** estudiante de universidad.
   —Ismael, ¿cómo **eres**?
   — **Soy** inteligente, romántico y responsable.

---

1. *"Who are you and what are you like?" "I'm Ángela Suárez del Pino. I'm optimistic and tolerant."*
2. *"Who are you?" "My name is Ismael Figueroa García, and I'm a university (college) student." "Ismael, what are you like?" "I'm intelligent, romantic, and responsible."*

a verb / **un verbo** = a word that describes an action or a state of being

¡OJO!
In Spanish, subject pronouns are not always used because the verb form indicates the person. See how this works in the dialogues on page 9.

Use the following verb forms to describe yourself or another person.

Subject Pronouns / Pronombres personales*	ser (to be):† Formas singulares	
yo	soy	I am
tú	eres	you (*familiar*) are
usted	es	you (*formal*) are
él	es	he is
ella	es	she is

Comunicación

A. **¿Cómo es usted?** Indique todas las palabras apropiadas (*appropriate words*).

(Yo) Soy...

_____ diligente	_____ pesimista	⨯ independiente
_____ idealista	_____ materialista	⨯ estudiante
⨯ impaciente	_____ normal	_____ diferente
_____ extravagante	_____ profesor	_____ profesora
_____ elegante	⨯ importante	_____ ¿ ?

B. **¿Quién es... ?**

Paso 1. With a classmate, take turns asking and answering questions.

MODELO: arrogante →
ESTUDIANTE 1: ¿Quién es arrogante?
ESTUDIANTE 2: **Enrique Iglesias** es arrogante.

Personas

Enrique Iglesias   Selena Gómez   Penélope Cruz   ¿ ?

1. arrogante   4. materialista   7. elegante
2. independiente   5. impresionante   8. terrible
3. paciente   6. interesante   9. fascinante

Paso 2. Now describe the people in negative terms, using **no** in front of the verb.

MODELO: Enrique Iglesias **no** es arrogante.

C. **Una encuesta (*A poll*)**

Paso 1. Use cognates from **Nota comunicativa** (page 9) and others you have heard or seen to describe the following people and things.

MODELO: Jennifer López → Jennifer López es **independiente.**

1. Jennifer López   3. _____ (programa de televisión)
2. este país (*this country*)   4. _____ (una persona famosa)

Paso 2. Now poll 2 classmates about the same 4 items. Write their answers in the chart.

MODELO: To ask: ESTUDIANTE 1: En tu opinión, ¿cómo es Jennifer López?
        To answer: ESTUDIANTE 2: Es independiente.

Estudiantes (nombre)	Jennifer López	este país	_____ (programa de televisión)	_____ (persona famosa)

*You will learn more about subject pronouns in **Gramática 3** (Capítulo 2) *and* **Gramática 8** (Capítulo 3).
†*You will learn more about **ser** in **Gramática 6** (Capítulo 3).

¡Aquí se habla español!

If you sometimes have the feeling that Spanish is everywhere, that's because it's true, and it may become even more so during your lifetime. Here are some interesting facts.

- Spanish is spoken as a first or second language by about 450 million people. This makes Spanish the second most widely spoken language in the world. (Chinese is the most widely spoken.) Some Spanish speakers also speak an indigenous language, like **náhuatl** in Mexico, **mapuche** in Chile, or **catalán** in Spain.
- Spanish is an official language of 20 countries.
- Over 40 million people in the United States speak Spanish, making it the fourth largest Spanish-speaking country in the world.
- Spanish is the official language (along with English) of Puerto Rico, an **Estado Libre** (*Free State*) associated with the United States.
- Spanish is present in Equatorial Guinea (where it is an official language) and in the Philippines as a heritage from the not so distant past when the islands were colonies of Spain.
- Spanish is second only to English in terms of the number of people studying it worldwide.

La Misión Basílica San Diego de Alcalá, cerca de (*near*) San Diego, California

Knowing a second language has many personal and professional advantages. If you live in a country like the United States, there is no need to explain to you why it's a good thing to study Spanish. The language and its culture are part of the country's historical and cultural past. And, from an economic standpoint, Spanish speakers provide a huge market of consumers of all kinds of goods and services, including the entertainment industry and the world of art.

Spanish is also a great asset for traveling for business or pleasure, within this country or abroad. Like all languages spoken by a large number of people, modern Spanish varies from region to region. The Spanish of Madrid is different from that spoken in Mexico City, Buenos Aires, or Los Angeles. Although these differences are most noticeable in pronunciation ("accent"), they are also found in vocabulary and special expressions used in different areas of the world. But the majority of structures and vocabulary is common to the many varieties of Spanish.

Knowing Spanish also opens the door to a fascinating culture. Actually, *cultures*, plural, would be more accurate. Spanish was the language of one of the most impressive intersections of culture and civilization the world has ever known, when a small group of Spaniards landed on an island in the Caribbean over 500 years ago. No two of the Spanish-speaking American countries that arose from that fusion of European and indigenous cultures (including those of Africans, brought to work as slaves) are alike. They offer a rich and diverse cultural panorama, one that you will learn about in every chapter of *Puntos de partida*.

So . . . welcome to the Spanish-speaking world! Actually, you know, you're already in it.

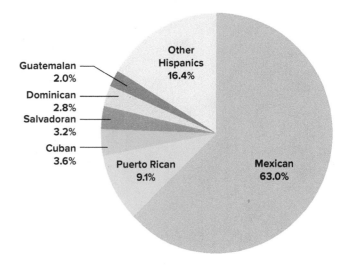

Comparing Origins of U.S. Hispanic Population
Total Hispanic Population
2010 Estimate*
50.5 Million

Guatemalan 2.0%
Dominican 2.8%
Salvadoran 3.2%
Cuban 3.6%
Puerto Rican 9.1%
Other Hispanics 16.4%
Mexican 63.0%

* Source: 2010 U.S. Census

(Alaska)
ESTADOS
UNIDOS

CANADÁ

(Hawaii)
ESTADOS
UNIDOS

ESTADOS
UNIDOS*

MÉXICO

CUBA

REPÚBLICA
DOMINICANA
PUERTO RICO

GUATEMALA
EL SALVADOR
NICARAGUA
COSTA RICA
PANAMÁ

HONDURAS

VENEZUELA

COLOMBIA

ECUADOR

PERÚ

BOLIVIA

PARAGUAY

CHILE

URUGUAY

ARGENTINA

ESPAÑA

GUINEA
ECUATORIAL

ISLAS
FILIPINAS

*The United States is generally expressed as **los Estados Unidos** in Spanish. The phrase is abbreviated in a number of ways:
E.U., EE. UU. (the double vowels indicate plurality), **EEUU** (without the periods), **USA,** and **U.S.A.** (the latter pronounced as
one word). **U.S.A.** is not recommended usage. **Los Estados Unidos de América (E.U.A.)** is also used.

Los números del 0 al 30; *Hay*

En un salón de clase

Hay una profesora. Hay cuatro estudiantes.

Algo... *Something about*

los números

In Spanish-speaking countries, hand-written numbers may look a little different than they do in the U.S.

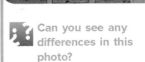
Can you see any differences in this photo?

Los números del 0 al 30

0	cero				
1	uno	11	once	21	veintiuno
2	dos	12	doce	22	veintidós
3	tres	13	trece	23	veintitrés
4	cuatro	14	catorce	24	veinticuatro
5	cinco	15	quince	25	veinticinco
6	seis	16	dieciséis*	26	veintiséis
7	siete	17	diecisiete	27	veintisiete
8	ocho	18	dieciocho	28	veintiocho
9	nueve	19	diecinueve	29	veintinueve
10	diez	20	veinte	30	treinta

¡OJO!

uno, dos,... veinti**uno,** veintidós,...

but

un señor, veinti**ún** señores

una señora, veinti**una** señoras

Nota **comunicativa**

El género (*gender*) y los números

The number *one* has several forms in Spanish. **Uno** is the form used in counting. The forms **un** and **una** are used before *nouns* (**los sustantivos**). How will you know which one to use? It depends on the *gender* (**el género**) of the noun.

All Spanish nouns are either masculine or feminine. For example, the noun **señor** is masculine (*m.*) in gender, and the noun **señora** is feminine (*f.*). (As you will learn, even nouns that are not sex-linked have gender.) Here is how *one* is expressed with these nouns: **un señor, una señora.** The number **veintiuno** has similar forms before nouns: **veintiún señores, veintiuna señoras.** Just get used to using **un** and **una** with nouns now. You'll learn more about gender and number in **Capítulo 2.**

a noun / **un sustantivo** = a word that denotes a person, place, thing, or idea

---

*The numbers 16 to 19 and 21 to 29 can be written as one word (**dieciséis... veintiuno...**) or as three words (**diez y seis... veinte y uno...**).

Hay

The word **hay** expresses both *there is* and *there are* in Spanish. It can be made negative (**no hay**) and can also be used to ask a question: **¿Hay... ?** (*Is there . . . ? Are there . . . ?*)

hay = there is / there are

Hay un teatro en esta universidad, pero **no hay** museo.	There's a theater at this university, but there isn't a museum.
—¿Cuántos estudiantes **hay** en la clase?	"How many students are there in the class?"
—(**Hay**) Treinta.	"(There are) Thirty."

Práctica y comunicación

A. Una canción infantil. (*A children's song.*) This is a popular song for children from all over the Spanish-speaking world. Complete it with the missing numbers. It's basic math!

Dos y dos son <u>cuatro</u>, y ocho _____,

cuatro y dos son <u>seis</u>, y ocho _____,

Seis y dos son <u>ocho</u>, y _____ treinta y dos...

B. Los números. Practique los números, según (*according to*) el modelo.

MODELO: 1 señor → Hay **un** señor.

1. 4 señoras	**6.** 1 idea (*f.*)	**11.** 28 naciones
2. 12 pianos	**7.** 21 ideas (*f.*)	**12.** 5 guitarras
3. 1 café (*m.*)	**8.** 11 personas	**13.** 1 león (*m.*)
4. 21 cafés (*m.*)	**9.** 15 estudiantes	**14.** 30 señores
5. 14 días	**10.** 13 teléfonos	**15.** 20 oficinas

C. Problemas de matemáticas. Express the following simple mathematical equations in Spanish. Note: + (**y**), − (**menos**), = (**son**).

MODELOS: 2 + 2 = 4 → Dos y dos son cuatro.
 4 − 2 = 2 → Cuatro menos dos son dos.

1. 2 + 4 = 6	**8.** 15 − 2 = 13	**15.** 8 − 7 = 1
2. 8 + 17 = 25	**9.** 9 − 9 = 0	**16.** 13 − 9 = 4
3. 11 + 1 = 12	**10.** 13 − 8 = 5	**17.** 2 + 3 + 10 = 15
4. 3 + 18 = 21	**11.** 14 + 12 = 26	**18.** 28 − 6 = 22
5. 9 + 6 = 15	**12.** 23 − 13 = 10	**19.** 30 − 17 = 13
6. 5 + 4 = 9	**13.** 1 + 4 = 5	**20.** 28 − 5 = 23
7. 1 + 13 = 14	**14.** 1 + 3 − 1 = 3	**21.** 19 − 7 = 12

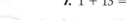

D. Intercambios (*Exchanges*)

1. ¿Cuántos (*How many*) estudiantes hay en la clase de español? ¿Cuántos estudiantes hay en clase hoy (*today*)? ¿Hay tres profesores o un profesor / una profesora?

2. ¿Cuántos días hay en una semana (*week*)? ¿Hay seis? (**No, no hay...)** ¿Cuántos días hay en un fin de semana (*weekend*)? ¿Cuántos días hay en el mes (*month*) de febrero? ¿en el mes de junio? ¿Cuántos meses hay en un año (*year*)?

3. En una universidad, hay muchos edificios (*many buildings*). En esta (*this*) universidad, ¿hay una cafetería? (**Sí, hay... / No, no hay...)** ¿un teatro? ¿un laboratorio de lenguas (*languages*)? ¿un bar? ¿una clínica? ¿un hospital? ¿un museo? ¿muchos estudiantes? ¿muchos profesores?

Los gustos° y preferencias (Part 1)*

Los... Likes

—¿Te gusta el fútbol?
—Sí, ¡me gusta mucho!
— Y a usted, señor, ¿también le gusta el fútbol?
— No, no me gusta el fútbol, pero sí me gusta el fútbol americano.

La selección nacional (*team*) de la Argentina, subcampeona del mundo (*world runner-up*) de fútbol en 2014 (dos mil catorce).

Use these patterns with the verb **gustar** to express likes and dislikes.

Me gusta _libros_.	I like _books_.
No me gusta _pollo_.	I don't like _chicken_.
(No) Te gusta _gatos_. (*familiar*)	You (don't) like _cats_.
(No) Le gusta _gatos_. (*formal*)	
¿Te gusta _limón_? (*familiar*)	Do you like _lemon_?
¿(A usted) Le gusta _limón_? (*formal*)	

In the following activities you will use **el** to mean *the* with masculine nouns and **la** with feminine nouns. Don't try to memorize which words are masculine or feminine.

You will also use Spanish verbs in the infinitive form, which always ends in **-r**. Here are some examples: **estudiar** = *to study*, **comer** = *to eat*. You will be able to guess the meaning of other infinitives from context (the surrounding words).

an infinitive / **un infinitivo** = a verb form that indicates action or state of being without referring to a specific person or time

Práctica y comunicación

A. ¿Yo, tú o usted? Indicate which pronoun you associate with each question or statement.

1. ¿Te gusta la pizza?
2. ¿Le gusta la Coca-Cola?
3. Me gusta mucho el chocolate.

B. Versión bilingüe. Match the ideas.

1. _a_ —¿Te gusta esquiar?
   —No, no me gusta.
2. _c_ —¿Le gusta esquiar?
   —Sí, me gusta.
3. _b_ —Me gusta esquiar.
   —¿Sí? A mí no me gusta.

a. "Do you (*formal*) like to ski?"
   "Yes, I like to."
b. "I like to ski." "Yeah? I don't like to."
c. "Do you (*familiar*) like to ski?"
   "No, I don't like to."

"Do you like soccer?" "Yes, I like it a lot!" "And (what about) you, sir, do you also like soccer?" "No, I don't like soccer, but I do like football."

You will learn more about **gustar** *in* **Gramática 22** (*Capítulo 8*).

C. Los gustos y preferencias

Paso 1. Make a list of six things you like and six things you don't like, following the model. You may choose items from the **Vocabulario útil** box.

MODELO: Me gusta **la clase de español.** No me gusta **la clase de matemáticas.**

> **Vocabulario útil**
>
> Vocabulario útil is not active; that is, you don't need to focus on learning it. But it will help you do this activity.
>
> **el actor** _____, **la actriz** _____
> **el café, el té, la limonada, la Coca-Cola**
> **el/la cantante** (*singer*) _____
> **el cine** (*movies*), **el teatro, la ópera, el arte abstracto, el fútbol**
> **la música moderna, la música clásica, el** *hip hop,* **la música** *country*
> **la pizza, la pasta, la comida** (*food*) **mexicana, la comida de la cafetería**
> _____ **(programa de televisión)**
> _____ **(ciudad** [*city*])

¡OJO!
The word **cantante** is used for both men *and* women.

1. Me gusta _____. No me gusta _____.
2. _____
3. _____
4. _____
5. _____
6. _____

Paso 2. Now ask a classmate if he or she shares your likes and dislikes.

MODELO: **ESTUDIANTE 1:** ¿Te gusta la clase de español?
ESTUDIANTE 2: Sí, me gusta (la clase de español). (No me gusta la clase de español.)
ESTUDIANTE 1: ¿Y la clase de matemáticas?
ESTUDIANTE 2: Sí, también me gusta (la clase de matemáticas). (No me gusta la clase de matemáticas.)

D. Más (*More*) gustos y preferencias

Paso 1. Here are some useful verbs and nouns to talk about what you like. For each item, combine an infinitive (shaded) with a noun to form a sentence that is true for you. The verb **estudiar** is an easily recognizable cognate. Use context to guess the meaning of verbs that are not cognates.

MODELO: Me gusta _____. → Me gusta **estudiar inglés.**

1. beber — café   chocolate   limonada   té
2. comer — enchiladas   ensalada   hamburguesas   pasta   pizza
3. estudiar — computación (*computer science*)   español   historia   inglés   matemáticas
4. hablar — con mis amigos (*with my friends*)   español   por teléfono (*on the phone*)
5. jugar — al basquetbol   al béisbol   al fútbol   al fútbol americano   al tenis
6. tocar — la guitarra   el piano   el violín

Paso 2. Ask a classmate about his or her likes, using your own preferences as a guide.

MODELO: ¿Te gusta **comer enchiladas**?

Paso 3. Now ask your professor if he or she likes certain things. **¡OJO!** Remember to address your professor in a formal manner if that is his or her preference.

MODELO: ¿Le gusta **jugar al tenis**?

¿Qué hora es?

Es la una.   Son las dos.   Son las cinco.

¿Qué hora es? is used to ask *What time is it?* In telling time, one says *Es la una* but *Son las dos (las tres, las cuatro,* and so on).

Es la una y { cuarto. / quince.   Son las dos y { media. / treinta.   Son las cinco y diez.   Son las ocho y veinticinco.

Note that from the hour to the half-hour, Spanish, like English, expresses time by adding minutes or a portion of an hour to the hour.

Son las dos menos { cuarto. / quince.   Son las ocho menos diez.   Son las once menos veinte.

From the half-hour to the hour, Spanish usually expresses time by subtracting minutes or a part of an hour from the *next* hour.

Nota **comunicativa**

Cómo expresar la hora

de la mañana	A.M., in the morning
de la tarde	P.M., in the afternoon (and early evening)
de la noche	P.M., in the evening
en punto	exactly, on the dot, sharp
¿a qué hora... ?	(at) what time . . . ?
a la una (las dos,...)	at 1:00 (2:00, . . .)
Son las cuatro **de la tarde en punto.**	It's exactly 4:00 P.M.
—**¿A qué hora** es la clase de español?	"What time is Spanish class (at)?"
—Es **a las** once **de la mañana.**	"It's at 11:00 A.M."

You will practice these phrases in **Práctica y comunicación.**

> **¡OJO!**
> **Es la... / Son las...** = to tell time
> **A la... / A las...** = to tell *at* what time something happens

Práctica y comunicación

A. ¡Atención! Listen as your instructor says a time of day. Find the clock face that corresponds to the time you heard and say its number in Spanish.

1.   **2.**   **3.**   **4.**

5.   **6.**   **7.**

B. ¿Qué hora es? Express the time in full sentences in Spanish.

1. 1:00	**4.** 1:30 P.M.	**7.** 4:15 A.M.	**10.** 9:50 sharp
2. 6:00	**5.** 3:15 A.M.	**8.** 11:45 exactly	
3. 11:00	**6.** 7:45 P.M.	**9.** 9:10 on the dot	

C. ¡Atención! With a classmate, ask and answer questions about the drawings (**los dibujos**) in **Actividad A.**

MODELO: **ESTUDIANTE 1:** Son las nueve y media de la mañana.

            ESTUDIANTE 2: Es el dibujo 6.

            ESTUDIANTE 1: ¡Correcto! (No es correcto.)

D. Intercambios

Paso 1. Read and practice pronouncing the words in **Vocabulario útil.**

> ### Vocabulario **útil**
>
> | | |
> |---|---|
> | **¿cuándo?** | when? |
> | **los días de la semana*** | the days of the week |
> | **el lunes** | on Monday |
> | **el martes** | on Tuesday |
> | **el miércoles** | on Wednesday |
> | **el jueves** | on Thursday |
> | **el viernes** | on Friday |
> | **el sábado** | on Saturday |
> | **el domingo** | on Sunday |

---

*You will learn more about the days of the week in Spanish in **Capítulo 5.**

Paso 2. With a partner, take turns asking and answering questions about when the following events or activities take place, according to the schedule.

Esta *(This)* **semana**

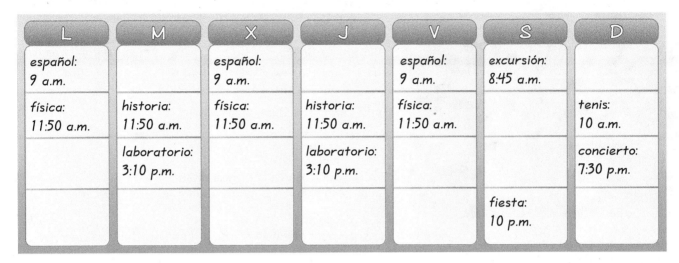

L	M	X	J	V	S	D
español: 9 a.m.		*español:* 9 a.m.		*español:* 9 a.m.	*excursión:* 8:45 a.m.	
física: 11:50 a.m.	*historia:* 11:50 a.m.	*física:* 11:50 a.m.	*historia:* 11:50 a.m.	*física:* 11:50 a.m.		*tenis:* 10 a.m.
	laboratorio: 3:10 p.m.		*laboratorio:* 3:10 p.m.			*concierto:* 7:30 p.m.
					fiesta: 10 p.m.	

MODELO: la clase de español →
  ESTUDIANTE 1: ¿Cuándo es la clase de español?
  ESTUDIANTE 2: El lunes, el miércoles y el viernes a las nueve de la
    mañana.

1. la clase de español
2. la clase de física
3. la clase de historia
4. la sesión de laboratorio
5. la excursión
6. la fiesta
7. el partido *(game)* de tenis
8. el concierto

Paso 3. Now ask when your partner likes to perform the following activities on a given day.

MODELO: cenar *(to have dinner)* →
  ESTUDIANTE 1: ¿Cuándo te gusta cenar **el sábado**?
  ESTUDIANTE 2: El sábado me gusta cenar **a las seis y media**.

1. cenar
2. estudiar español
3. mirar *(to watch)* la televisión
4. ir al *(to go to the)* gimnasio
5. ir al cine
6. ir a una fiesta

E. Situaciones en la calle. Complete los diálogos con un compañero / una compañera.

Diálogo 1: Por la mañana, en la calle *(street)*

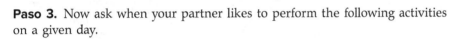

SR. ROLDÁN: Buenos días, Sra. Valdés. ¿Cómo _____?
SRA. VALDÉS: Muy bien. ¿_____ , Sr. Roldán?
SR. ROLDÁN: _____. Perdón, ¿qué hora _____?
SRA. VALDÉS: _____ las _____ (10:30), señor.
SR. ROLDÁN: _____ gracias, señora.

Diálogo 2: Por la tarde

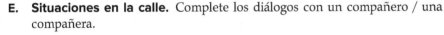

SILVIA: ¡Hola!, muy _____, Julio. ¿Cómo _____?
JULIO: Bien, ¿y _____? ¡Huy!, perdón, ¿qué hora _____?
SILVIA: _____ las _____.
JULIO: ¡Ay!, la clase de historia es a las _____ y diez. Me voy corriendo.[a] ¡Hasta luego!
SILVIA: Oye,[b] ¿nos vemos el sábado en la fiesta?
JULIO: ¡Sí, sí!

[a]Me... I *have to run.* [b]Hey

Salu2 desde° Los Ángeles

from

El presentador (*anchor*) Víctor Gutiérrez y la presentadora Ana García Blanco. *Salu2* es un programa sobre (*about*) la comunidad global de hispanohablantes (*Spanish speakers*).

Antes de mirar°

Antes... *Before watching*

What is a morning news and talk television show usually like? Check all of the phrases that apply.

- ☐ un poco (*a little*) cómico
- ☐ un poco serio
- ☐ informativo
- ☐ muy dramático
- ☐ para (*for*) una audiencia diversa
- ☐ solo para las personas mayores (*only for older people*)

Este° programa

This

This is the introductory program of a new morning show, based in Los Angeles, California.

> Reading part of the script before watching each segment of *Salu2* will help you understand more of the show.

Estrategia

You will not understand every word in *Salu2*. In fact we never catch everything in any program even in our native language. But you will be able to get the gist of the show by catching some key words and phrases that you *do* know and by using context, both in the program as well as in the text and images in this section.

Fragmento del guion°

script

VÍCTOR: Muchas gracias, Laura. La presencia del español en la ciudad de Los Ángeles es impresionante, ¿no crees,[a] Ana?

ANA: Absolutamente. Y personas de todo tipo hablan español, no solo[b] los hispanos. Bueno, es hora de decir[c] adiós por hoy. Espero que les haya gustado nuestro primer programa.[d] Nos vemos muy pronto.[e]

VÍCTOR: Desde el estudio de *Salu2* en la ciudad de Los Ángeles, California, les mandamos[f] saludos a todos los telespectadores y esperamos verlos en nuestro próximo programa.[g] ¡Hasta entonces![h]

[a]¿no... *don't you think* [b]no... *not only* [c]es... *it's time to say* [d]Espero... *I hope you liked our first program.*
[e]muy... *very soon* [f]les... *we send* [g]esperamos... *we hope to see you at our next program* [h]¡Hasta... *Until then!*

> These words and phrases (given in the order in which they appear in the show) will help you understand more when you watch this episode.

Vocabulario del° programa

of the

hoy les presentamos	today we're introducing . . . to all of you
un nombre	a name
antiguo	former
la ciudad	the city
el país	the country, nation
el tema	topic, subject
dentro y fuera de	within and outside of
vamos a hablar/escuchar	we're going to talk/listen to
cuarenta y ocho	forty-eight
les saludo	I'm greeting all of you
la playa	the beach
disculpa	pardon me
¿de dónde vienes?	**¿de dónde eres?**
(yo) vengo de	**(yo) soy de**
¿cuántos años tienes?	how old are you?

If you scan **Después de mirar** *before* watching the show, you will understand more of what is in the program.

Después de mirar°

Después... *After watching*

A. **¿Está claro?** ¿Cierto o falso? Corrija (*Correct*) las oraciones falsas.

	CIERTO	FALSO
1. *Salu2* es un programa matinal (*morning*) de televisión.	☐	☐
2. Es un programa informativo para un público hispanohablante diverso.	☐	☐
3. El estudio está en San Francisco.	☐	☐
4. Hay tres presentadores (*anchors*) y una reportera.	☐	☐
5. Pocas (*Few*) personas hablan español en Los Ángeles.	☐	☐

Laura Sánchez Tejada es reportera. Es de México pero hoy está en California.

B. **¿Quién lo dice?** (**Who says it?**) Indique el presentador: **A** = Ana o **V** = Víctor.

1. «...el Pueblo de Nuestra Señora la Reina de los Ángeles de Porciúncula.» _____

2. «...el nombre de Los Ángeles es un nombre español...» _____

3. «Y vamos a escuchar a personas hispanohablantes de varios países...» _____

4. «...vamos a escuchar a miembros de la comunidad hispana de Los Ángeles.» _____

5. «...es evidente que muchas personas no hispanas sí hablan español.» _____

6. «Y hoy vamos a escuchar los saludos de algunos angelinos...» _____

C. **Un poco más.** (**A little more.**) Match each person with her/his place of origin.

PERSONAS

1. _____ Ricardo

2. _____ Wally

3. _____ Jennifer

4. _____ Michelle y Amy

5. _____ Miriam y Verónica

6. _____ Rubí

ORIGEN

a. Chicago
b. Los Ángeles
c. México
d. Puerto Rico
e. no se sabe (*not known*)

D. **Y ahora, Uds.** (**And now it's your turn.**) Practique su (*your*) pronunciación y su talento como presentador(a). Haga el papel (*Play the role*) de Laura y complete el fragmento con su propia (*your own*) información.

> Buenos días a todos. ¿Cómo están ustedes? Yo estoy muy bien. Me llamo _____ y soy el reportero / la reportera del programa *Salu2*. Les saludo desde[a] _____, en el estado de _____.

[a]Les... *I'm speaking to you (lit. I'm greeting you from)*

Producción personal
Filme los saludos de dos o tres personas en español.

A LEER°

Una lección de geografía

La diversidad del mundo[a] hispano es fabulosa. Lea[b] el texto, mire[c] las fotos ¡y consulte los mapas al final del libro[d]!

1.
El <u>volcán</u> Chimborazo (en el Ecuador), en la <u>cordillera</u> de Los Andes. Los Andes forman la cordillera más larga[e] del mundo (ocho mil quinientos[f] kilómetros), y se extienden por[g] siete naciones de Sudamérica.

3.
Una <u>selva</u>[i] en México. Hay selvas también en otros países[j] en Centroamérica y Sudamérica.

2.
Una <u>playa</u> en la <u>península</u> de Samaná, República Dominicana. En el <u>mar</u> Caribe hay tres <u>islas</u> de habla española. El mundo hispano también tiene[h] <u>costas</u> en el <u>océano</u> Atlántico y en el Pacífico.

4.
El <u>desierto</u> de Atacama, Chile. Es el más árido[k] del mundo. También hay zonas desérticas en otros países hispanos de Norteamérica a Sudamérica: México, el Perú, Bolivia, la Argentina, Colombia. Y también en España.

[a]world [b]Read [c]look at [d]al... *at the back of the book* [e]más... *longest* [f]ocho... *8,500* [g]se... *they pass through* [h]has [i]jungle [j]naciones [k]más... *driest*

5.
El glaciar Perito Moreno, en la Patagonia argentina. Chile y la Argentina tienen[l] territorio en la Patagonia y en el continente de la Antártida.

6.
Madrid, la capital de España, en Europa. Es una ciudad de gran[m] importancia histórica y cultural. En Latinoamérica también hay muchas ciudades grandes,[n] como la Ciudad de México, Buenos Aires, Santiago,...

[l]have [m]great [n]large

Comprensión

A. ¿Qué significa? (*What does it mean?*)

Paso 1. In pairs, decide on the meaning of the Spanish words for geographical features that are underlined in the reading.

Paso 2. With your partner, give examples of these geographical features in the U.S (or other part of the world) and in the Spanish-speaking world.

1. un volcán
2. una cordillera
3. una playa
4. una península
5. un mar
6. un océano
7. un desierto

B. Los nombres de las regiones del mundo. ¿Cómo se dice en español?

1. Latin America
2. Central America
3. North America
4. South America
5. Europe
6. Antarctica

EN RESUMEN En este capítulo

AFTER STUDYING THIS CHAPTER I CAN . . .

☐ meet and greet others appropriately in Spanish (4–5)

☐ pronounce words in Spanish and say the alphabet (7–8)

☐ recognize the meaning of many Spanish cognates (9)

☐ describe myself and others (9–10)

☐ say numbers 0–30 and use **hay** (13–14)

☐ talk about some of my likes and dislikes (15)

☐ tell time (17)

☐ recognize/describe at least 2–3 facts about the Spanish-speaking world

Vocabulario

This is the active vocabulary for *Capítulo 1*. Be sure that you know all the words, including the meaning of the group titles, before beginning **Capítulo 2**.

Saludos y expresiones de cortesía

Buenos días. Buenas tardes. Buenas noches. (Muy) Buenas.
Hola. ¿Qué tal? ¿Cómo estás? ¿Cómo está?
Muy bien. Regular. Bien.
¿Y tú? ¿Y usted?
Adiós. Hasta mañana. Hasta luego. Nos vemos.
¿Cómo te llamas? ¿Cómo se llama usted?
  Me llamo _____.
¿De dónde eres (tú)? ¿De dónde es (usted)?
  (Yo) Soy de _____.
señor (Sr.), señora (Sra.), señorita (Srta.)
profesor, profesora
Gracias. Muchas gracias.
De nada. No hay de qué.
Por favor. Perdón. (Con) Permiso.
Mucho gusto. Igualmente. Encantado/a.

el saludo | greeting

¿Cómo es usted?

All forms of infinitives highlighted in red can be found in Appendix 5.

ser: soy, eres, es

¿Cómo es usted? | What are you like?

Los gustos y preferencias

¿Te gusta _____? ¿(A usted) Le gusta _____?
(Sí,) Me gusta _____. (No,) No me gusta _____.
los gustos | likes

Los números del 0 al 30

cero	diez	veinte
uno	once	treinta
dos	doce	
tres	trece	
cuatro	catorce	
cinco	quince	
seis	dieciséis	
siete	diecisiete	
ocho	dieciocho	
nueve	diecinueve	

¿Qué hora es?

¿qué hora es?	what time is it?
es la... , son las...	
y/menos cuarto (quince)	
y media (treinta)	
en punto	
de la mañana (tarde, noche)	
¿a qué hora... ?, a la(s)...	

Las palabras interrogatives

¿cómo?	how?; what?
¿dónde?	where?
¿qué?	what?
¿quién?	who?

Palabras adicionales

sí/no	yes/no
hay	there is/are
no hay	there is not / are not
¿hay?	is there / are there?
hoy/mañana	today/tomorrow
y/o	and/or
a	to; at (*with time*)
de	of; from
en	in; on; at
muy	very
pero	but
también	also
la palabra	word

Vocabulario personal

Use this space for other words and phrases you learn in this chapter.

| **ESPAÑOL** | **INGLÉS** |

An Introduction to the Rest of

Puntos de partida

Each chapter of the rest of this textbook has a chapter theme and follows a consistent organization. In addition, every chapter focuses on one or more countries of the Spanish-speaking world.

Puntos de partida

- **The opening pages of the chapter:** Here you will begin to learn about each chapter's theme and geographical focus. A Spanish speaker will provide a model of things you will be able to say after studying the vocabulary and grammar in the chapter, which are previewed in **En este capítulo.**
- **Vocabulario: Preparación:** This section presents vocabulary related to each chapter's theme.
- **Pronunciación:** Found in **Capítulos 2–4,** this section presents important aspects of Spanish pronunciation and orthography (spelling).
- **Salu2 ... Segmento 1:** This section will help you to understand a segment of the *Salu2* morning show.
- **Gramática:** This section presents grammar points in context and offers many opportunities for you to practice Spanish, alone and with a partner or group. In a subsection of **Gramática** called **Un poco de todo *(A bit of everything)*,** you will practice all of the grammar points from the chapter

plus review important grammar topics from previous chapters.
- **Salu2 ... Segmento 2:** Here is another segment of the show.
- **A leer** (*Let's read*)**:** In this reading section, you will learn more about the chapter's country of focus (**Lectura cultural**) and also read authentic materials from the Spanish-speaking world (**Del mundo hispano**), including literature.
- **A escuchar *(Let's listen)*:** In this section you will practice authentic listening tasks.
- **Producción personal:** In this section you will create a portfolio that showcases what you can do in Spanish: essays and other real-world writing tasks, oral and video materials, and so on.
- **En resumen: En este capítulo:** This section shows you vocabulary and grammar you need to know from each chapter.

2

En la universidad

En este capítulo°

En... *In this chapter*

www.connectspanish.com

En un salón de clase universitario

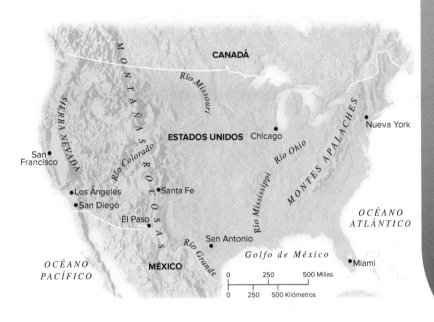

LOS ESTADOS UNIDOS DE AMÉRICA

316 (trescientos dieciséis) millones de habitantes

- En los Estados Unidos hay más de 54 (cincuenta y cuatro) millones de personas de origen hispano.

- Es el quinto[a] país del mundo por[b] número de hispanohablantes.

- En todo el territorio estadounidense, especialmente en el suroeste,[c] hay lugares[d] con nombres[e] en español.

[a]*fifth* [b]*país... country in the world in* [c]*Southwest* [d]*places* [e]*names*

- ¿En qué universidad estudia usted[a]?
- ¿Qué materias[b] estudia este[c] semestre/trimestre?
- ¿Cuál[d] es su[e] clase favorita? (**Mi** clase...)

[a]*estudia... are you studying* [b]*subjects* [c]*this* [d]*Which* [e]*your*

ALEJANDRA HERNÁNDEZ SOTO CONTESTA LAS PREGUNTAS.

- Estudio Relaciones Internacionales en la UNAM, la Universidad Nacional Autónoma de México.

- Este semestre tomo[a] seis clases: estadística, historia, geografía, economía, sistemas políticos, teorías de las relaciones internacionales. ¡Ah! Y también estudio inglés.

- ¿Mi materia favorita este semestre? No sé[b]. ¡Me gusta todo[c]!

[a]*I'm taking* [b]*No... I don't know.* [c]*everything*

En el salón de clase

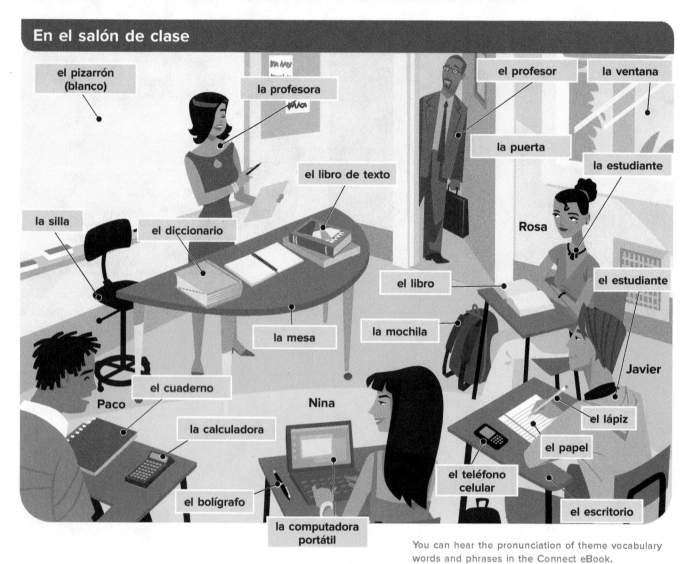

el pizarrón (blanco)

la profesora

el profesor

la ventana

la puerta

el libro de texto

la estudiante

la silla

el diccionario

Rosa

el libro

el estudiante

la mesa

la mochila

el cuaderno

Javier

Paco

Nina

el lápiz

la calculadora

el papel

el teléfono celular

el bolígrafo

el escritorio

la computadora portátil

You can hear the pronunciation of theme vocabulary words and phrases in the Connect eBook.

¿Dónde? Lugares en la universidad

la biblioteca	the library
la cafetería	the cafeteria
el edificio	the building
la librería	the bookstore
la oficina	the office
la residencia	the dormitory
el salón de clase	the classroom

¿Quién? Personas

el bibliotecario	the (male) librarian
la bibliotecaria	the (female) librarian
el compañero (de clase)	the (male) classmate
la compañera (de clase)	the (female) classmate

el compañero de cuarto	the (male) roommate
la compañera de cuarto	the (female) roommate
el consejero	the (male) advisor
la consejera	the (female) advisor
el hombre	the man
la mujer	the woman
el secretario	the (male) secretary
la secretaria	the (female) secretary

¿Qué? Objetos

la computadora (portátil)	(laptop) computer
el dinero	money
el pizarrón (blanco)	(white)board
el teléfono (celular)	(cellular) telephone

Comunicación

A. Identificaciones. ¿Es hombre o mujer?

MODELO: ¿El profesor? → Es hombre.

1. ¿La consejera?
2. ¿La estudiante?
3. ¿El secretario?
4. ¿El estudiante?
5. ¿La bibliotecaria?
6. ¿El compañero de cuarto?

B. ¿Dónde están (*are they*)? Tell where these people are and identify the numbered people and things.

MODELO: El dibujo (*drawing*) 1: **Están** en el salón de clase.
1 → la profesora, 2 → la estudiante,...

Así se dice

el bolígrafo = la pluma, el birome, el esfero
la calculadora = la máquina de calcular
la computadora = el computador (*Latin America*), el ordenador (*Spain*)
la computadora portátil = el portátil (*Latin America, Spain*)
el escritorio = el mesabanco
el pizarrón = el encerado, la pizarra, el tablero
el salón de clase = el aula, la sala (de clase)

In general, use **el profesor / la profesora** to refer to a college teacher, or **el doctor / la doctora**, as appropriate. However, there are many institutional and national differences in usage. Ask your instructor what title to use to address or refer to him or her.

Young people often shorten some words. Can you guess what **el boli** and **la profe** mean?

1.

2.

3.

Algo sobre...°

Algo... *Something about*

la universidad

CAA COLEGIO DE ARQUITECTOS DE LOS ANDES

En el mundo[a] hispanohablante no llaman[b] **colegio** a una institución universitaria. La palabra **colegio** se usa para referirse a[c] a la educación preuniversitaria, aunque[d] con nombres diferentes en diferentes países.[e] También se usa en el nombre de asociaciones de profesionales, como el «Colegio de Arquitectos».

¿Cómo se llama su[f] colegio?

[a]*world* [b]*no... they don't call* [c]*se... is used for talking about* [d]*although* [e]*countries* [f]*your*

Nota **cultural**

más... oldest / del... of the Spanish-speaking world

Las universidades más antiguas° del mundo hispano°

En España
- la Universidad de Salamanca, Salamanca (1218 = mil doscientos veinte)

En Latinoamérica
la Universidad Nacional Mayor de San Marcos, Lima, Perú (1551 = mil quinientos cincuenta y uno)

- la Universidad Nacional Autónoma de México (UNAM), en México, D.F. (Distrito Federal), México (1551 [mil quinientos cincuenta y uno])
- la Universidad Nacional de Córdoba, Argentina (1621 = mil seiscientos veintiuno)
- la Universidad San Francisco Xavier de Chuquisaca, Sucre, Bolivia (1624 = mil seiscientos veinticuatro)
- la Universidad de San Carlos de Guatemala, Antigua, Guatemala (1676 = mil seiscientos setenta y seis)
- la Universidad Nacional de San Antonio Abad del Cusco, Perú (1692 = mil seiscientos noventa y dos)
- la Universidad de San Jerónimo, ahora la Universidad de La Habana, Cuba (1728 = mil setecientos veintiocho)

 ¿Cuál[a] es la universidad más antigua de su país[b]?

[a]*What* [b]*su... your country*

El *campus* de la Universidad de San Marcos, en Lima, Perú

Las materias°

Las... *Subject areas*

The names for most of these subject areas are cognates. See if you can recognize their meaning without looking at the English equivalent. You should learn in particular the names of subject areas that are of interest to you.

la administración de empresas	business administration
las comunicaciones	communications
la economía	economics
el español	Spanish
la filosofía	philosophy
la literatura	literature
las matemáticas	mathematics
la sociología	sociology
las ciencias	sciences
naturales	natural
políticas	political
sociales	social
las humanidades	humanities
las lenguas (extranjeras)	(foreign) languages

Así se dice

la administración de empresas = el comercio, los negocios (*U.S.*)
la computación = la informática (*Spain*)
el español = el castellano (*Spain, Latin America*)

Comunicación

A. Asociaciones. ¿Qué materia(s) asocia usted con (*with*) las siguientes (*following*) personas y cosas (*things*)?

1. la zoología, la botanía, la química
2. Sigmund Freud, B.F. Skinner, Dr. Phil
3. CNN, NBC, ESPN
4. la ética, la moral, la esencia de la realidad
5. Shakespeare, J.K. Rowling, Junot Díaz
6. Frida Kahlo, Pablo Picasso, Salvador Dalí
7. Apple, Microsoft, Google
8. las guerras (*wars*), las elecciones, las civilizaciones antiguas

B. ¿Qué estudia usted? Create sentences about your academic interests by using one word or phrase from each column. Can you guess the meaning of the phrases in the left-hand column? If you need help, they are translated at the bottom of the page*.

MODELOS: Deseo estudiar **español y antropología.**
Necesito estudiar **matemáticas.**

1. (No) Estudio _____.
2. (No) Deseo estudiar _____.
3. (No) Necesito estudiar _____.
4. (No) Me gusta estudiar _____.

+

español, francés, inglés
arte, filosofía, literatura, música
ciencias políticas, historia
antropología, sicología, sociología
biología, física, química
computación, matemáticas, ¿ ?

Vocabulario **útil**

la contabilidad	accounting
la ingeniería	engineering
el mercadeo	marketing
el periodismo	journalism

> These boxes will help you review content you already know on which new material is based.

¿Recuerda usted?°

¿Recuerda... *Do you remember?*

In **Capítulo 1,** you used a number of interrogative words to get information: **¿cómo?, ¿dónde?, ¿qué?,** and **¿quién?** Tell what those words mean in these questions. Then answer the questions.

1. ¿Cómo estás?
2. ¿Cómo es usted?
3. ¿De dónde eres?
4. ¿Qué hora es?
5. ¿Quién es la profesora?

As you listen to your instructor say questions with those words, you will notice that, in Spanish, the voice falls at the end of questions that begin with interrogative words.

¿Qué hora es?   ¿Cómo es usted?

You will learn more about interrogatives in the **Nota comunicativa** on the next page and in **Gramática 4** in this chapter.

an interrogative word / **una palabra interrogativa** =
a word used to ask a question about specific information (*who?, where?,* and so on)

---

*1. *I'm studying (I'm not studying)* **2.** *I want to study (I don't want to study)* **3.** *I need to study (I don't need to study)*
4. *I like to study (I don't like to study)*

Nota comunicativa

Más palabras interrogativas

Use **¿qué?** to mean *what?* when you are asking for a definition or an explanation. Use **¿cuál?** to mean *what?* in all other contexts. You will learn more about using these words in **Gramática 28 (Capítulo 10).**

¿Qué es un hospital?	**¿Qué** es esto (*this*)?
¿Cuál es la capital de Colombia?	**¿Cuál** es tu materia favorita?

Guess the meaning of the following interrogatives from the context in which they appear.

1. —**¿Cuándo** es la clase? —Es mañana, a las nueve.
2. —**¿Cuánto** cuesta (*costs*) el cuaderno? —Dos dólares.

3. —**¿Cuántos** estudiantes hay en la clase? —Hay quince.
4. —**¿Cuántas** naciones hay en Centroamérica? —Hay siete.

Remember to drop your voice at the end of a question that begins with a Spanish interrogative word, the opposite of what happens in English, where the voice usually rises at the end of such questions. This feature of Spanish may cause you to "hear" a Spanish question as a statement at first, but you'll get used to it. Compare these questions.

¿Qué es un tren?	*What's a train?*
¿Cuándo es el programa?	*When is the program?*

You will use many of the preceding interrogative words in **Comunicación C.**

C. Intercambios (*Exchanges*)

¿Dónde le gusta estudiar a usted?

Estrategia

Use **el** or **la** with a title when talking about a person, as in item 3.

el profesor Arana
la señora Castellano
el doctor Brook

Paso 1. Answer the following questions. Pay attention to the words and endings in bold; you have seen most of them before and should be able to guess what they mean.

1. —¿Qué **estudias** este (*this*) semestre/trimestre?
   —**Estudio** _____.

2. —¿Cuál es **tu** (*your*) materia favorita?
   —**Mi** materia favorita es el/la _____.

3. —¿Quién es **tu** profesor(a) en la clase de español?
   —**Es** el profesor / la profesora _____.

4. —¿Cuántas horas **estudias** al día (*per day*)?
   —**Estudio** _____ horas al día.

5. —¿Dónde **estudias**?
   —**Estudio** en _____ (la residencia, la biblioteca, mi cuarto, mi apartamento, la cafetería...).

6. —¿Te **gusta** estudiar por (*in*) la mañana, por la tarde o por la noche (*at night*)?
   —**Me gusta** estudiar por _____.

Paso 2. Now practice the conversation in **Paso 1** with a classmate. Use **¿Y tú?** to ask about your partner.

MODELO: ESTUDIANTE 1: ¿Qué **estudias** este semestre/trimestre?
ESTUDIANTE 2: **Estudio** matemáticas, historia, literatura y español. ¿Y tú?
ESTUDIANTE 1: Yo **estudio** español, biología, física y arte.

«¡Qué bacán!°» Segmento 1

¡Qué... How great!

Antes de mirar°

Antes... *Before watching*

What do you think Víctor and Ana will talk about as they introduce the show? Check all of the phrases that apply.

_____ su (*their*) familia

_____ su concentración/carrera (*major*) en la universidad

_____ el nombre de su universidad

_____ el tráfico en Los Ángeles

_____ el costo de una educación universitaria

Este° segmento

This

Los presentadores introducen el tema (*topic*) del programa: la universidad en el mundo (*world*) hispanohablante.

Víctor y Ana, los presentadores de *Salu2*, que (*who*) hablan de sus (*talk about their*) estudios universitarios

Vocabulario **del segmento**

bienvenidos	welcome	**el país**	country
los telespectadores	TV viewers	**el/la periodista**	journalist
los universitarios	university students	**estudiaste**	did you study
los padres	parents	**pasé**	I spent
con frecuencia pagan	frequently pay for	**en el extranjero**	abroad
bien cara	quite expensive	**marca tu vida**	changes your life
la maestría	master's degree	**vamos a ver**	we're going to see

Estrategia

Before you watch the segment, be sure to read the photo caption and go over the vocabulary list. Don't expect to remember most of the words while watching; they're new and may be difficult for you. But just reading the list will enhance your comprehension, giving you ideas about what to watch for.

Después de mirar°

Después... *After watching*

A. ¿Está claro? Empareje a (*Match*) los presentadores, Ana (**A**) y Víctor (**V**) o a **los dos** (*both*), con las carreras o concentraciones y universidades apropiadas.

LAS CARRERAS O CONCENTRACIONES

_____ sociología

_____ comunicación

_____ inglés

LAS UNIVERSIDADES

_____ UCLA

_____ la Universidad de Panamá

B. Un poco más. (*A little more.*) ¿Cierto o falso? Corrija (*Correct*) las oraciones falsas, según (*according to*) el video.

	CIERTO	FALSO
1. El programa no es interesante para los padres.	☐	☐
2. La universidad es cara.	☐	☐
3. Victor pasó (*spent*) un semestre en España.	☐	☐
4. Ana es de Panamá.	☐	☐

C. Y ahora, Uds. (*And now it's your turn.*) Practique su (*your*) pronunciación y su talento como presentador(a). Complete el fragmento con su propia (*your own*) información y con vocabulario del programa.

Buenos días desde^a _____. Soy _____. Es es un placer^b presentar un nuevo programa de *Salu2*. El tema del programa de hoy es la universidad, un tema muy _____ (adjetivo) para^c los _____ (personas) y los _____ (personas). Estamos en la Universidad de _____, donde yo estudio _____ (materias). ¡Bienvenidos!

^a*from* ^b*pleasure* ^c*for*

Vocabulario: Preparación

treinta y tres ■ **33**

PRONUNCIACIÓN

Diphthongs and Linking

¿Recuerda usted?

Review what you already know about the pronunciation of Spanish vowels by saying the following names and nicknames aloud.

1. Ana   **2.** Pepe   **3.** Pili   **4.** Momo   **5.** Lulú

a diphthong / un **diptongo** = a combination of two vowel sounds in one syllable

Two successive weak vowels (**i, u**) or a combination of a strong vowel (**a, e, o**) and a weak vowel (**i, u**) are pronounced as a single syllable in Spanish, forming a *diphthong* (**un diptongo**): L**ui**s, s**ie**te, c**ua**derno.

When words are combined to form phrases, clauses, and sentences, they are linked together in pronunciation. In spoken Spanish, it is often difficult to hear the word boundaries—that is, where one word ends and another begins.

Práctica

A. Vocales. Más práctica con las vocales.

1. hablar	regular	reservar	compañera
2. trece	clase	papel	general
3. pizarrón	oficina	bolígrafo	libro
4. hombre	profesor	dólares	los
5. universidad	gusto	lugar	mujer

B. Diptongos. Practique las siguientes (*following*) palabras.

1. historia	secretaria	gracias	estudiante	materia
2. bien	Oviedo	siete	ciencias	diez
3. secretario	biblioteca	adiós	diccionario	Antonio
4. cuaderno	Eduardo	el Ecuador	Guatemala	Managua
5. bueno	nueve	luego	pueblo	Venezuela

C. Frases y oraciones (*sentences*). Practice saying each phrase or sentence as if it were one long word, pronounced without a pause.

1. el papel y el lápiz
2. la profesora y la estudiante
3. las ciencias y las matemáticas
4. la historia y la sicología
5. la secretaria y el profesor
6. el inglés y el español
7. la clase en la biblioteca
8. el libro en la librería
9. Es la una y media.
10. Hay siete estudiantes en la oficina.
11. No estoy muy bien.
12. No hay consejero aquí (*here*).

¿Recuerda usted?

As you know, in English and in Spanish, a noun is the name of a person, place, thing, or idea. You have been using nouns since the beginning of *Puntos de partida*. Remember that **el** and **la** mean *the* before nouns. If you can change the Spanish words for *the* to *one* in the following phrases, you already know some of the material in **Gramática 1**.

1. el libro   **2.** la mesa   **3.** el profesor   **4.** la estudiante

1 Naming People, Places, Things, and Ideas (Part 1)

Singular Nouns: Gender and Articles*

Grammar Tutorial **1**
connect |SPANISH
www.connectspanish.com

Gramática en acción: La lista de José María

Note the use of red in **Gramática en acción** to indicate examples of the grammar point of focus.

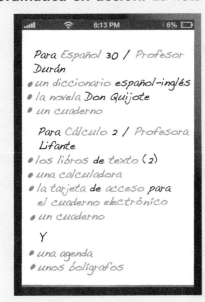

Para Español 30 / Profesor Durán
• un diccionario español-inglés
• la novela Don Quijote
• un cuaderno

Para Cálculo 2 / Profesora Lifante
• los libros de texto (2)
• una calculadora
• la tarjeta de acceso para el cuaderno electrónico
• un cuaderno

Y
• una agenda
• unos bolígrafos

Comprensión

	CIERTO	FALSO
1. La profesora de matemáticas es la profesora Durán.	☐	☐
2. Un cuaderno es para la clase de literatura.	☐	☐
3. La agenda es para la clase de matemáticas.	☐	☐

You use nouns to name people, places, things, and ideas. In Spanish, all *nouns* (**los sustantivos**) have either masculine or feminine *gender* (**el género**). This is a purely grammatical feature; it does not mean that Spanish speakers perceive things or ideas as having male or female attributes.

Since the gender of all nouns must be memorized, it is best to learn the definite article along with the noun; that is, learn **el lápiz** rather than just **lápiz**. The definite article is given with nouns in vocabulary lists in this book.

***José María's list** For Spanish 30 / Professor Durán ■ a Spanish-English dictionary ■ the novel Don Quijote ■ a notebook. for Calculus 2 / Professor Lifante ■ the textbooks (2) ■ a calculator ■ the access card for the electronic workbook ■ a notebook. And ■ a calendar/datebook ■ a few ballpoint pens*

*The grammar sections of Puntos de partida are numbered consecutively throughout the book. If you need to review a particular grammar point, the index will refer you to its page number.

Nouns / **Los sustantivos**				
	Masculine / **Masculino**		Feminine / **Femenino**	
Definite Articles / **Los artículos definidos**	el **hombre** el **libro**	the man the book	la **mujer** la **mesa**	the woman the table
Indefinite Articles / **Los artículos indefinidos**	un **hombre** un **libro**	a man a book	una **mujer** una **mesa**	a woman a table

> *an article* / **un artículo** = a determiner that sets off a noun
> *a definite article* / **un artículo definido** = an article that indicates a specific noun (*the*)
> *an indefinite article* / **un artículo indefinido** = an article that indicates an unspecified noun (*a, an*)

Note the two-column format of grammar explanations. Explanations are on the left, examples are on the right, and red highlighting will help you see what's important.

Gender / El género

1. Masculine Nouns
Nouns that refer to male beings and most other nouns that end in **-o** are *masculine* (**masculino**) in gender.

Sustantivos masculinos

hombre, libro

2. Feminine Nouns
Nouns that refer to female beings and most other nouns that end in **-a, -ción, -sión, -xión, -tad,** and **-dad** are *feminine* (**femenino**) in gender.

Sustantivos femeninos

mujer, mesa, silla
nación, misión, conexión
libertad, universidad

3. Other Endings
Nouns that have other endings and that do not refer to either male or female beings may be masculine or feminine. The gender of these words must be memorized.

el lápiz, el papel, el salón de clase
la clase, la noche, la tarde

4. Spelling Changes
Many nouns that refer to people indicate gender . . .
• by changing the last vowel

OR

• by adding **-a** to the last consonant of the masculine form to make it feminine

el compañero → la compañera
el bibliotecario → la bibliotecaria

un profesor → una profesora

5. Some Nouns that Refer to People
Many other nouns that refer to people have a single form for both masculine and feminine genders. Gender is made clear by context or by an article.

However, a few such nouns that end in **-e** also have a feminine form that ends in **-a.**

Masculino	Femenino
el **estudiante**	la **estudiante**
el **dentista**	la **dentista**
el **presidente**	la **presidenta**
el **cliente**	la **clienta**
el **dependiente** (*clerk*)	la **dependienta**

¡OJO!

A common exception to the normal rules of gender is the word **el día**, which is masculine in gender. Many words ending in **-ma** are also masculine: **el problema, el programa, el sistema,** and so on.

Articles / Los artículos

1. Definite Articles

In English, there is only one *definite article* (**el artículo definido**): *the*.

In Spanish, there are two definite articles for singular nouns, one masculine (**el**) and one feminine (**la**).

Artículo definido: *the*

m. sing. → **el**
f. sing. → **la**

2. Indefinite Articles

In English, the singular *indefinite article* (**el artículo indefinido**) is *a* or *an*.

In Spanish, the indefinite article, like the definite article, must agree with the gender of the noun: **un** for masculine nouns, **una** for feminine nouns.

Un and **una** can mean *one* or *a/an*, depending on context.

Artículo indefinido: *a, an*

m. sing. → **un**
f. sing. → **una**

> **¡OJO!**
> Only the *indefinite* article (never the definite article) is used directly after the word **hay**: Hay **un** libro en la silla. Hay **unos** cuadernos en la mesa.

> One of the first two activities in **Práctica y comunicación** will always include a brief **Autoprueba** (*Self-test*). Take it to see if you understand the basics of the grammar point. The answers are at the bottom of the page.

Práctica y comunicación

A. **Autoprueba.** Escoja (*Choose*) el artículo definido apropiado.

1. el / la libro
2. el / la mujer
3. el / la oficina
4. el / la escritorio
5. el / la libertad
6. el / la acción

Gender Summary

MASCULINO	FEMENINO
el, un	**la, una**
-o	-a
-ma	-ción, -sión, -xión
	-dad, -tad

B. **Los artículos**

Paso 1. Dé (*Give*) el artículo definido apropiado (**el, la**).

1. edificio
2. biblioteca
3. bolígrafo
4. mochila
5. hombre
6. diccionario
7. universidad
8. dinero
9. señora
10. nación
11. bibliotecario
12. calculadora

Paso 2. Ahora (*Now*) dé el artículo indefinido apropiado (**un, una**).

1. día
2. mañana
3. problema
4. lápiz
5. clase
6. papel
7. condición
8. programa

C. **Escenas de la universidad**

Paso 1. Haga una oración (*Form a sentence*) con las palabras indicadas.

MODELO: estudiante / librería → **Hay un** estudiante **en la** librería.

1. consejero / oficina
2. profesora / salón de clase
3. lápiz / mesa
4. cuaderno / escritorio
5. libro / mochila
6. bolígrafo / silla
7. palabra / papel
8. oficina / residencia
9. compañero / biblioteca
10. diccionario / librería

Paso 2. Now create new sentences by changing one of the words in each item in **Paso 1.** Try to come up with as many variations as possible.

MODELOS: Hay un estudiante en **la residencia**. Hay **una profesora** en la librería.

D. Definiciones. En parejas (*pairs*), definan las siguientes (*following*) palabras en español, según (*according to*) el modelo.

MODELO: biblioteca → ESTUDIANTE 1: ¿Qué es una biblioteca?
ESTUDIANTE 2: Es **un edificio**.

CATEGORÍAS: edificio, materia, objeto, persona

1. cliente
2. bolígrafo
3. residencia
4. dependienta
5. hotel (*m.*)
6. computadora
7. computación
8. inglés
9. ¿ ?

E. Nuestra (*Our*) universidad. En parejas, hagan oraciones (*form sentences*) sobre su (*about your*) universidad.

MODELOS: mi consejero/a → El profesor Márquez es mi consejero.
cafetería → Hay una cafetería. Se llama (*It's called*) Foster Hall. (No hay una cafetería.).

Estrategia
Remember to use the article **el** or **la** to refer to someone who has a title: **el profesor Márquez.**

1. mi consejero/a
2. mi profesor(a) de _____ (materia)
3. residencia
4. biblioteca principal
5. cafetería
6. edificio de clases

Grammar Tutorial 2
connect
|SPANISH
www.connectspanish.com

2 Naming People, Places, Things, and Ideas (Part 2)

Nouns and Articles: Plural Forms

Gramática en acción: Un anuncio

You don't have to understand all of the words in this ad (**anuncio**) to get its general meaning.

What is it an ad for?

ᵃen... *abroad*

Comprensión

1. How many nouns (including proper nouns) can you find in the ad? Can you guess the meaning of most of them?
2. Some of the nouns in the ad are plural. Can you tell how to make nouns plural in Spanish?
3. Look for the Spanish equivalent of these words: *adults, preparation, program, courses.*
4. The word **idioma** is a false cognate; it never means *idiom*. What do you think it means?

	Singular	Plural	
Nouns Ending in a Vowel	el **libro**	los **libros**	the books
	la **mesa**	las **mesas**	the tables
	un **libro**	unos **libros**	some books
	una **mesa**	unas **mesas**	some tables
Nouns Ending in a Consonant	la universidad	las **universidades**	the universities
	un papel	unos **papeles**	some papers

1. **Plural Endings**
   Spanish nouns that end in a vowel form plurals by adding **-s.** Nouns that end in a consonant add **-es.** Nouns that end in the consonant **-z** change the **-z** to **-c** before adding **-es: lápiz → lápices.**

<table>
<tr><td colspan="2">Sustantivos plurales</td></tr>
<tr><td colspan="2" align="center">vowel + -s</td></tr>
<tr><td colspan="2" align="center">consonant + -es</td></tr>
<tr><td colspan="2" align="center">-z → -ces</td></tr>
</table>

2. **Plural of Articles**
   The definite and indefinite articles also have plural forms: **el → los, la → las, un → unos, una → unas. Unos** and **unas** mean *some, several,* or *a few.*

<table>
<tr><td colspan="2">Artículos plurales</td></tr>
<tr><td>el → los</td><td>un → unos</td></tr>
<tr><td>la → las</td><td>una → unas</td></tr>
</table>

3. **Groups of People**
   In Spanish, the masculine plural form of a noun is used to refer to a group that includes both males and females.

   los amigos = *the friends* (all male or both male and female)
   las amigas = *the friends* (only female)
   unos extranjeros = *some foreigners* (all male or both male and female)
   unas extranjeras = *some foreign women*

Práctica y comunicación

<table>
<tr><td colspan="2">Plural Forms Summary</td></tr>
<tr><td>el → los</td><td>un → unos</td></tr>
<tr><td>la → las</td><td>una → unas</td></tr>
<tr><td colspan="2" align="center">vowel + -s</td></tr>
<tr><td colspan="2" align="center">consonant + -es</td></tr>
<tr><td colspan="2" align="center">-z → -ces</td></tr>
</table>

A. **Autoprueba.** Empareje (*Match*) los sustantivos con los artículos apropiados.

1. libros		**a.** el
2. hombre		**b.** las
3. librería		**c.** unos
4. profesoras		**d.** una

B. **Cambios (*Changes*)**

Paso 1. Singular → plural.

1. la mesa	**4.** la oficina	**7.** una universidad
2. el papel	**5.** un cuaderno	**8.** un bolígrafo
3. el amigo	**6.** un lápiz	**9.** un teléfono

Paso 2. Plural → singular.

1. los profesores	**4.** los estudiantes	**7.** unas residencias
2. las computadoras	**5.** unos hombres	**8.** unas sillas
3. las bibliotecarias	**6.** unas tardes	**9.** unos escritorios

Prác. A: Answers, Paso 1. 1. c 2. a 3. d 4. b

C. **Identificaciones.** Nombre (*Name*) las personas, los objetos y los lugares.

MODELOS: Hay _____ en _____. → Hay **unos estudiantes** en **el salón de clase.**
Hay **un profesor** en **el laboratorio.**

1.

2.

D. **¡Ojo alerta!***

Paso 1. ¿Cuáles son las semejanzas (*similarities*) y las diferencias entre (*between*) los dos salones de clase? Hay por lo menos (*at least*) seis diferencias.

En el dibujo A, hay _____.
En el dibujo B, hay solo (*only*) _____.
En el escritorio del dibujo A, hay _____.
En el escritorio del dibujo B, (no) hay _____.

Paso 2. Ahora indique qué hay en su propio (*your own*) salón de clase.

MODELO: En mi salón de clase hay _____. En mi escritorio hay _____.

---

*In Spanish, activities like this one are often called **¡Ojo alerta!** = *Eagle Eye!*

These sentences contain Spanish verbs that you have already used. Pick them out.

1. Soy estudiante en la Universidad de _____.
2. Este (*This*) semestre/trimestre, estudio español.
3. En el futuro, deseo estudiar francés.

If you selected **estudiar** in addition to three other words, you did very well! You will learn more about Spanish verbs and how they are used in **Gramática 3**.

3 Expressing Actions
Subject Pronouns (Part 1): Present Tense of **-ar** Verbs; Negation

Grammar Tutorial 3
connect |SPANISH
www.connectspanish.com

Gramática en acción: ¿Una escena típica?

Manu habla enfrente de la clase porque hoy es su presentación. Pero... ¡varias personas no escuchan!

- Laila manda un mensaje por teléfono.
- Kevin y Lisa trabajan en otras materias.
- Teresa mira por la ventana.
- ¿Y Ud.? ¿También desea estar en otro lugar?

Comprensión

En la escena...

1. ¿Cuántos estudiantes hablan?
2. ¿Cuántas personas escuchan la presentación?
3. ¿Quién manda un mensaje por teléfono?
4. ¿Quién estudia chino?

Subject Pronouns / Los pronombres personales

Singular		Plural	
yo	I	**nosotros / nosotras**	we
tú	you (*familiar*)	**vosotros / vosotras**	you (*familiar, Spain*)
usted (Ud.)*	you (*formal*)	**ustedes (Uds.)***	you (*formal*)
él	he	**ellos**	they (*m., m. + f.*)
ella	she	**ellas**	they (*f.*)

a subject / **un sujeto** = the person or thing that performs the action in a sentence

a pronoun / **un pronombre** = a word that takes the place of a noun or represents a person

---

A typical scene? *Manu is talking in front of the class because today is his presentation. But . . . several people are not listening! • Laila is sending a text message on her phone. • Kevin and Lisa are working on other subjects. • Teresa is looking out the window. • And you? Do you want to be somewhere else too?*

*****Usted** *and* **ustedes** *are frequently abbreviated in writing as* **Ud.** *or* **Vd.,** *and* **Uds.** *or* **Vds.,** *respectively.*

1. Subject Pronouns

The person that performs the action in a sentence is expressed by *subject pronouns* (**los pronombres personales**).

In Spanish, many subject pronouns have masculine and feminine forms. The masculine plural form is used to refer to a group of males as well as to a group of males and females.

Manuel	→	**él**	*he*
Sara	→	**ella**	*she*
Manuel + Juan	→	**ellos**	*they*
Manuel + Sara	→	**ellos**	*they*
María + Sara	→	**ellas**	*they*

2. Pronouns for *you*

Spanish has different words for *you*.

- In general, **tú** is used with a friend or a family member.
- **Usted** is used with people with whom the speaker has a more formal or distant relationship.

tú → friend, family member
usted (Ud.) → formal or distant relationship

The situations in which **tú** and **usted** are used also vary among different countries and regions.

3. Plural of *you*

In Latin American Spanish, the plural for both **usted** and **tú** is **ustedes**.

In Spain, however, **vosotros/vosotras** is the plural of **tú**, while **ustedes** is used as the plural of **usted** exclusively.

Latinoamérica

tú
usted (Ud.) } → **ustedes (Uds.)**

España

tú → **vosotros/vosotras**
usted (Ud.) → **ustedes (Uds.)**

4. Omitting Subject Pronouns

Subject pronouns are not used as frequently in Spanish as they are in English, and they may usually be omitted. You will learn more about the uses of Spanish subject pronouns in **Gramática 8** (**Cap. 3**).

Present Tense of -ar Verbs / El tiempo presente de los verbos *-ar*

1. Infinitives

As you know, the *infinitive* (**el infinitivo**) of a verb indicates the action or state of being, with no reference to who or what performs the action or when it is done (present, past, or future).

Infinitives in English are indicated by *to: to* speak, *to* eat, *to* live.

In Spanish, all infinitives end in **-ar, -er,** or **-ir.**

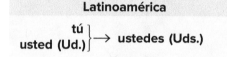

-ar:	**hablar**	to speak
-er:	**comer**	to eat
-ir:	**vivir**	to live

an infinitive / **un infinitivo** = a verb form that indicates action or state of being without reference to person, tense, or number	*a tense* / **un tiempo** = the quality of a verb form that indicates time: present, past, or future

2. Conjugating Verbs

To *conjugate* (**conjugar**) a verb means to give the various forms of the verb with their corresponding subjects: *I speak, you speak, she speaks,* and so on.

All regular Spanish verbs are conjugated by adding *personal endings* (**las terminaciones personales**) that reflect the subject doing the action. These are added to the *stem* (**la raíz**), which is the infinitive minus the infinitive ending.

Infinitive / **Infinitivo**		Stem / **Raíz**
habl**ar**	→	habl-
com**er**	→	com-
viv**ir**	→	viv-

3. Present Tense Endings

The personal endings that are added to the stem of all regular **-ar** verbs to form the *present tense* (**el presente**) are listed at the right. The chart below shows those same endings attached to the stem of the infinitive **hablar** (**habl-**).

Las terminaciones -ar del tiempo presente

-o, -as, -a, -amos, -áis, -an

		hablar (to speak; to talk): habl-			
	Singular			**Plural**	
(yo)	habl**o**	I speak	(nosotros) (nosotras)	habl**amos**	we speak
(tú)	habl**as**	you speak	(vosotros) (vosotros)	habl**áis**	you speak
(Ud.) (él) (ella)	habl**a**	you speak he speaks she speaks	(Uds.) (ellos) (ellas)	habl**an**	you speak they (*m., m. + f.*) speak they (*f.*) speak

4. Important -ar Verbs

Here are some **-ar** verbs used in this chapter.

Los verbos -ar

bailar	to dance
buscar	to look for
cantar	to sing
comprar	to buy
desear	to want
enseñar	to teach
escuchar	to listen (to)
estudiar	to study
hablar	to speak; to talk
mandar un mensaje	to (send a) text
necesitar	to need
pagar	to pay (for)
practicar	to practice
regresar	to return (*to a place*)
tocar	to play (*a musical instrument*)
tomar	to take; to drink
trabajar	to work

¡OJO!

Note that in Spanish the meaning of the English word *for* is included in the verbs **buscar** (*to look for*) and **pagar** (*to pay for*); *to* is included in **escuchar** (*to listen to*).

5. **Conjugated Verb +** *Infinitive*

As in English, when two Spanish verbs are used in a row and there is no change of subject, the second verb is usually in the infinitive form.

Necesito mandar un mensaje.
I need to send a text (message).

Me gusta bailar.
I like to dance.

6. **Tense**

In both English and Spanish, conjugated verb forms also indicate the *time* or *tense* (**el tiempo**) of the action: *I speak* (present), *I spoke* (past).

Some English equivalents of the present tense forms of Spanish verbs are shown at the right.

	I speak	Simple present tense
hablo	I am speaking	Present progressive (indicates an action in progress)
	I will speak	Near future action

¡OJO!

The exact English equivalent of a Spanish verb form depends on the context in which the verb appears. In the following sentence, the word **mañana** indicates a future action, so **hablo** means *I will:* **Hablo con Juan mañana.**

Negation / La negación

In Spanish the word **no** is placed before the conjugated verb to make a negative sentence.

subject + **no** *+ verb*

El estudiante **no habla** español.
The student doesn't speak Spanish.

No, **no necesito** dinero.
No, I don't need money.

Práctica y comunicación

A. Asociaciones. ¿Qué verbos asocia Ud. con las siguientes ideas? Dé (*Give*) infinitivos.

MODELO: la música → escuchar, tocar, bailar, ...

1. español
2. mucho (*a lot of*) dinero
3. en la librería
4. en el salón de clase
5. un coche (*car*)
6. a la residencia
7. Coca-Cola o café (*coffee*)
8. la música

Summary of -ar Verb Endings		
(yo) -o	(nosotros/as) -amos	
(tú) -as	(vosotros/as) -áis	
(Uds., el/ella) -a	(Uds., ellos/as) -an	

B. Mi compañero/a y yo

Paso 1. Autoprueba. Complete los verbos con las terminaciones apropiadas.

1. (yo) pag_____
2. (tú) toc_____
3. (ella) habl_____
4. (nosotras) compr_____
5. (Ud.) escuch_____
6. (ellos) trabaj_____

Paso 2. ¿Sí o no? Complete las oraciones de forma personal. Use **no** delante del (*in front of the*) verbo si es necesario.

MODELO: **1.** Necesit _____ un coche. → Necesito un coche. (**No** necesito un coche.)

1. Necesit___ un coche.
2. Trabaj___ en la biblioteca de la universidad
3. Cant___ en un coro (*choir*).
4. Tom___ una clase de ciencias sociales este (*this*) semestre.
5. Bail___ salsa en las fiestas.
6. Habl___ inglés como (*as a*) lengua nativa.
7. Mand___ muchos mensajes todos los días (*every day*).
8. Toc___ un instrumento musical.

Paso 3. En parejas (*pairs*), hagan y contesten preguntas (*ask and answer questions*) basadas en el **Paso 2.**

MODELO: Necesito un coche. → ESTUDIANTE 1: ¿**Necesitas** un coche?

ESTUDIANTE 2: Sí, **necesito** un coche. (No, **no necesito** un coche.)

Prác. A: Answers. Paso 1. 1. pago 2. tocas 3. habla 4. compramos 5. escucha 6. trabajan

44 ■ cuarenta y cuatro

Capítulo 2 En la universidad

C. Una o más personas

Paso 1. Cambie por (*Change to*) un sujeto plural.

MODELOS: Él no desea tomar café. →
         Ellos no **desean** tomar café.
         Yo no deseo tomar café. →
         Nosotros no **deseamos** tomar café.

1. Ella no desea estudiar francés (*French*).
2. Ud. baila muy bien el tango.
3. ¿Mandas muchos (*a lot of*) mensajes?
4. Escucho la radio con frecuencia.

Paso 2. Ahora cambie por un sujeto singular. En los números 2 y 4 hay más de una opción.

1. Ellas no buscan el dinero.
2. Los estudiantes no necesitan seis clases.
3. Pagamos mucho dinero de matrícula (*tuition*).
4. ¿Compran Uds. muchos libros?

D. La fiesta de Marcos

Paso 1. Complete el párrafo con las formas apropiadas de los verbos entre paréntesis.

Esta noche[a] hay una fiesta en casa de Marcos.[b] Marcos es de Guatemala y su compañero de apartamento, Julio, es de Honduras. Hay quince amigos en la fiesta. Una persona (tocar[1]) la guitarra y las otras personas (cantar[2]) o (escuchar[3]). ¡Yo solo (desear[4]) bailar!

Marta (hablar[5]) con Nati mucho tiempo.[c] Pero Nati (desear[6]) bailar con Miguel, el estudiante mexicano, porque[d] él (bailar[7]) muy bien. Eduardo, Marcos y yo (bailar[8]) en grupo.

A las once de la noche Julio (buscar[9]) pizza para todos.[e] Pero todos (pagar[10]).

¡La fiesta es fantástica! (*Yo:* Practicar[11]) español toda la noche[f] porque todos los amigos de Marcos (hablar[12]) español. ¡Eduardo y yo (regresar[12]) a casa[g] a las dos de la mañana!

¿A Ud. le gustan las fiestas?

[a]Esta... *Tonight* [b]en... *at Marco's place (lit., house)* [c]mucho... *for a long time* [d]*because*
[e]para... *for everyone* [f]toda... *all night* [g]a... *home*

Paso 2. Comprensión. Indique si las siguientes (*following*) oraciones son **ciertas, falsas** o **no se sabe** (*not known*). Luego (*Then*) indique dónde está la información correcta en el texto.

	CIERTO	FALSO	NO SE SABE
1. La persona que (*who*) habla es hispanohablante.	☐	☐	☐
2. Nati baila muy bien.	☐	☐	☐
3. Marcos y Julio compran la pizza.	☐	☐	☐
4. Todos tocan la guitarra y bailan.	☐	☐	☐
5. Marta habla mucho (*a lot*) en la fiesta.	☐	☐	☐

E. **Oraciones lógicas.** Form eight complete logical sentences by using one word or phrase from each column. Many combinations are possible. Use the correct form of the verbs and make any sentences negative.

MODELO: Yo no estudio francés.

yo tú (un[a] estudiante) nosotros (los miembros de esta clase) los estudiantes de aquí el extranjero un secretario una profesora de español una dependienta	+ (no)	buscar comprar enseñar estudiar hablar mandar pagar regresar tocar tomar trabajar	+	la guitarra, el piano, el violín el edificio de ciencias en la cafetería, en la universidad, en casa (*at home*) en una oficina, en una librería a casa muy tarde (*very late*)/temprano (*early*) a la biblioteca a las dos muchos/pocos mensajes francés, alemán (*German*), italiano, inglés bien el español los libros de texto, la matrícula libros y cuadernos en la librería

> **¡OJO!**
> Remember that the verb form that follows **desear** or **necesitar** is the infinitive, just as in English.

+ (no) { desear / necesitar } +
- tomar una clase de computación
- hablar bien el español
- estudiar más
- comprar una calculadora, una mochila
- pagar la matrícula en septiembre

> **¡OJO!**
> Remember that **de la mañana (tarde, noche)** are used when a specific hour of the day is mentioned. Also, remember to use **a la una / a las dos (tres...)** to express a specific time of day.
>
> Generalmente estudio en casa **por** la mañana.
>
> Hoy estudio con Javier en la biblioteca **a las** diez **de** la mañana.

Nota **comunicativa**

Cómo expresar las partes del día

You can use the preposition **por** to mean *in* or *during* when expressing the part of the day in which something happens.

Estudio **por** la mañana y trabajo **por** la tarde. **Por** la noche, estoy en casa.
I study in the morning and I work in the afternoon. At night I'm at home.

You will practice these phrases in **Práctica F.**

F. **Intercambios** *(Exchanges)*

Paso 1. Use los siguientes verbos y frases para crear (*create*) cinco preguntas (*questions*) interesantes.

MODELO: ¿**Cantas** bien?

1. cantar o bailar 2. estudiar o trabajar 3. necesitar 4. tomar 5. tomar	+	bien/mal (*poorly*), mucho/poco (*a little*) muchas/pocas (*few*) horas, todos los días dinero, libros, una computadora, pagar la matrícula _____ (número de clases) / café o té por la mañana clases por la mañana / por la tarde / por la noche

 Paso 2. En parejas, túrnense (*take turns*) para hacer y contestar (*answer*) sus (*your*) preguntas del **Paso 1.**

MODELO: **ESTUDIANTE 1:** ¿Cantas bien?
ESTUDIANTE 2: Sí, **canto** bien. (No, **canto** mal.)

Nota **comunicativa**

El verbo *estar*

Estar is a Spanish **-ar** verb that means *to be*. You have already used forms of it to ask how others are feeling or to tell where things are located. Here is the complete present tense conjugation of **estar.** Note that the **yo** form is irregular. The other forms take regular **-ar** endings, and some have an accent to maintain the stress pattern.

(yo)	est**oy**	I am	**(nosotros/as)**	est**amos**	we are
(tú)	est**ás**	you are	**(vosotros/as)**	est**áis**	you are
(Ud.)	est**á**	you are	**(Uds.)**	est**án**	you are
(él/ella)	est**á**	he/she is	**(ellos/ellas)**	est**án**	they are

You will learn the uses of the verb **estar,** along with those of **ser** (a second Spanish verb that means *to be*) gradually, over the next several chapters. Review what you already know by answering these questions.

1. ¿Cómo está Ud. en este momento (*right now*)?
2. ¿Cómo están sus (*your*) compañeros? (**Mis** compañeros...)
3. ¿Dónde está Ud. en este momento?

You will use **estar** in **Práctica G**.

G. ¿Dónde están? Tell where these people are and what they are doing.

MODELO: **FOTO 1**: La Sra. Martínez _____. →
La Sra. Martínez **está en una oficina. Trabaja por la tarde. Necesita...**

Vocabulario **útil**

buscar información	**tomar apuntes**
hablar por teléfono	to take notes
mandar un mensaje	**usar una computadora**
preparar la lección	
pronunciar las palabras	

¡OJO!

Remember to use the definite article with titles when you are talking *about* a person: **el señor Santana, la profesora Aguilar,** and so on.

1. La Srta. Martínez _____.

Trabaja por _____.

Necesita _____.

2. Estas (*These*) personas _____.

El profesor _____.

Una estudiante _____.

Muchos (*Many*) estudiantes _____.

4 Getting Information (Part 1)
Asking Yes/No Questions

connect |SPANISH
www.connectspanish.com

Gramática en acción: La matriculación

PENÉLOPE: ... y ahora necesito una clase más por la mañana. ¿Hay sitio en la clase de Sociología 2?

JAVIER: A ver... No, no hay.

PENÉLOPE: ¿Hay una clase de historia o de matemáticas?

JAVIER: Solo por la noche. ¿Deseas tomar una clase por la noche?

PENÉLOPE: ¡Ay, chico, es imposible! Trabajo por la noche.

JAVIER: Pues... ¿qué tal la clase de Literatura Hispana en los Estados Unidos?

PENÉLOPE: ¡Perfecto! ¡Me gusta mucho Sandra Cisneros! ¿Cuándo es la clase?

Comprensión

1. ¿Necesita Penélope dos clases más?
2. ¿Hay sitio en Sociología 2?
3. ¿Cuál es el problema con los cursos de historia y matemáticas?
4. ¿Qué curso recomienda Javier por fin?

You have been asking questions since the beginning of *Puntos de partida*, and you learned more about asking questions in **Nota comunicativa (page 32).** This section will help you review all that you know about this topic as well as learn another way to ask questions in Spanish.

1. Types of Questions
There are two kinds of questions (**las preguntas**) in English and in Spanish.

- *Information questions* ask for information, for facts. They typically begin with *interrogative words* (**las palabras interrogativas**). You have already learned a number of them.

Preguntas informativas
—¿Qué lengua habla Ud.?
—Hablo español.

¡OJO!
Remember that intonation drops at the end of an information question in Spanish, whereas it rises in English.

- *Yes/No questions* can be answered by a simple **sí** or **no**.

Preguntas sí/no
—¿Habla Ud. francés?
—No.

Registration PENÉLOPE: . . . and now I need one more class in the morning. Is there room in Sociology 2? JAVIER: Let's see . . . No, there isn't (room). PENÉLOPE: Is there a history or a math class? JAVIER: Only at night. Do you want to take a night class? PENÉLOPE: Come on, that's impossible! I work at night. JAVIER: Well . . . what about the class about Hispanic Literature in the U.S.? PENÉLOPE: Perfect! I love Sandra Cisneros!

2. Forming Yes/No Questions

There are two ways to form this kind of question.

- *Rising intonation:* The simplest way is to make your voice rise at the end of a statement. Doing so makes the statement into a question.

- *Inversion:* Another way to form yes/no questions is to invert (transpose) the order of the subject and verb, in addition to making your voice rise at the end of the question. You can also put the subject all the way at the end of the question.

STATEMENT:	Ud. trabaja aquí todos los días. *You work here every day.*
QUESTION:	¿Ud. trabaja aquí todos los días? *Do you work here every day?*
STATEMENT:	Ud. trabaja aquí todos los días.
QUESTION:	¿Trabaja Ud. aquí todos los días?
STATEMENT:	María manda muchos mensajes.
QUESTION:	¿Manda muchos mensajes María?

Práctica y comunicación

A. Preguntas

Summary of Questions

- with interrogatives
- with intonation
- by inverting the subject and verb

Paso 1. Autoprueba. ¿Cómo se dice (*How do you say it*) en inglés?

1. ¿Habla Ud. inglés?
2. ¿Necesitan Uds. otra clase?
3. ¿Tomas biología?
4. ¿Trabajo mañana?

Paso 2. Ahora exprese las siguientes oraciones como preguntas. **¡OJO!** Hay dos formas.

MODELO: Alicia toca el violín. → ¿**Toca Alicia** el violín? ¿**Alicia toca** el violín?

1. Susana toca la guitarra.
2. Los estudiantes compran muchos libros.
3. Uds. miran el teléfono en clase.
4. Diego manda mensajes en clase.
5. Uds. toman cinco clases este semestre/trimestre.

Paso 3. Ahora, en parejas, usen las oraciones del **Paso 2** para hacer y contestar preguntas. **¡OJO!** No es necesario usar los pronombres **tú** y **yo** en la pregunta o en la respuesta (*answer*).

MODELO: tocar la guitarra →

ESTUDIANTE 1: ¿**Tocas** la guitarra?
ESTUDIANTE 2: SÍ, **toco** la guitarra. (No, no **toco** la guitarra.)

B. Una conversación inventada.
Imagine that you have just met Diego, a new person on campus. You asked him some questions and he gave you the following answers. What were the questions that you asked?

MODELO: Sí, estudio antropología. → ¿**Estudias** antropología?

1. Sí, soy estadounidense (*from the United States*).
2. Sí, estudio con frecuencia.
3. No, no toco el piano. Toco la guitarra clásica.
4. No, no deseo trabajar más horas.
5. No, no hablo francés, pero hablo italiano un poco.
6. No, no soy reservado. ¡Soy muy extrovertido!

Prác. A: Answers, Paso 1. 1. Do you speak English? 2. Do you (pl.) need another class? 3. Are you taking (a) biology (class)? 4. Do (Will) I work tomorrow?

C. Intercambios: Sus (*Your*) actividades

Paso 1. Use the following cues as a guide to form questions that you will ask a classmate. You may ask other questions as well. Write the questions on a sheet of paper. **¡OJO!** Use the **tú** form of the verbs.

MODELO: escuchar música por la mañana →
           ¿**Escuchas** música por la mañana?

1. estudiar en la biblioteca todos los días
2. practicar español con un amigo o amiga
3. tomar mucho / un poco de (*a little bit of*) café por la mañana
4. bailar mucho en las fiestas
5. cantar en la ducha (*shower*)
6. regresar a casa muy tarde los fines de semana
7. comprar los libros en la librería de la universidad
8. mandar muchos mensajes
9. trabajar los fines de semana
10. usar (*to use*) un diccionario bilingüe online

Paso 2. Now use the questions to get information from your partner. Jot down his or her answers for use in **Paso 3**.

MODELO: **ESTUDIANTE 1:** ¿Escuchas música por la mañana?
          ESTUDIANTE 2: Sí, (No, no) **escucho** música por la mañana.

Paso 3. With the information you gathered in **Paso 2**, report your partner's answers to the class. (You will use the **él/ella** form of the verbs when reporting.)

MODELO: Jenny no **escucha** música por la mañana.

D. Una encuesta (*poll*): ¿Qué clases tomas?

Paso 1. Make a list in Spanish of the classes you are taking. Ask your instructor or use a dictionary to find the names of classes you don't know how to say in Spanish. If you ask your instructor, remember to ask in Spanish: **¿Cómo se dice _____ en español?**

Paso 2. Circulate, asking yes/no questions to find classmates who are taking the same classes as you. Write down their answers.

MODELO: **ESTUDIANTE 1:** Carlos, ¿tomas una clase de matemáticas?
          ESTUDIANTE 2: Sí, tomo matemáticas. Tomo Cálculo 2.

Paso 3. Report back the information you have learned to the whole class.

MODELO: Carlos y yo tomamos matemáticas. Jennie y yo... Solo yo tomo geología.

Algo... *Something about*

Algo sobre°...

los Departamentos de Estudios Latinos en las universidades de los Estados Unidos

La importancia de la población hispana en los Estados Unidos se refleja[a] en el mundo[b] académico. Muchas universidades tienen[c] departamentos o concentraciones[d] que investigan[e] y enseñan temas[f] relacionados con los latinos en los Estados Unidos. En los estados del suroeste,[g] se ofrecen[h] regularmente Estudios Chicanos, especializados en la población norteamericana de origen mexicano.

¿Hay un programa o un área de concentración de estudios especializados en los latinos en su[i] universidad?

[a]se... *is reflected* [b]*world* [c]*have* [d]*majors* [e]*que... that research* [f]*topics* [g]*Southwest* [h]se... *are offered* [i]*your*

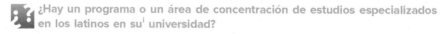

Un poco de todo

A. Lengua y cultura: Dos universidades fabulosas... y diferentes

Paso 1. Complete the following description of two well-known universities. Give the correct form of the verbs in parentheses, as suggested by context. When the subject pronoun is in *italics,* don't use it in the sentence. When two possibilities are given in parentheses, select the correct word.

¿Cómo es la universidad perfecta? Hay muchas opciones. Por ejemplo, (hay / es[1]) dos (universidad / universidades[2]) muy famosas en los Estados Unidos. La primera[a] es (el / la[3]) Universidad de Texas, en Austin. ¡Es (un / una[4]) universidad muy grande[b]! Hay veinticuatro grupos sociales para estudiantes hispanos y una (librería / biblioteca[5]) con una colección latinoamericana fantástica, la Colección Latinoamericana Benson. (Los / Las[6]) materias más populares en la UT son: administración de empresas, ingeniería, humanidades y comunicaciones. Muchos estudiantes (tomar[7]) cursos en (el / la[8]) Instituto de Estudios Latinoamericanos y en (el / la[9]) Centro para Estudios Mexicoamericanos.

Stanford, en (el / la[10]) estado de California, es una universidad menos grande.[c] Tiene[d] una residencia para estudiantes de español, la Casa Zapata. Allí,[e] (los / las[11]) estudiantes (practicar[12]) español y (participar[13]) en celebraciones hispanas. Las materias más populares en Stanford son:[f] biología, economía, inglés y ciencias políticas. (El / La[14]) problema en Stanford es que los estudiantes (pagar[15]) mucho por[g] la matrícula.

¿Prefiere Ud. la UT o Stanford? ¿(*Ud.:* Desear[16]) (estudia / estudiar[17]) en California o en Texas?

La Colección Latinoamericana Benson, una colección comprensiva de libros, documentos, revistas (*magazines*) y periódicos (*newspapers*) relacionados con (*related to*) Latinoamérica

[a]La... *The first one* [b]*big* [c]*menos... smaller* [d]*It has* [e]*There* [f]*are* [g]*for*

Paso 2. Comprensión. Las siguientes oraciones son falsas. Corríjalas. (*Correct them.*)

1. En la Universidad de Texas hay dos grupos sociales para estudiantes hispanos.
2. En el Instituto de Estudios Latinoamericanos hay pocos (*few*) estudiantes.
3. La Universidad de Stanford está en Texas.
4. La Casa Zapata es una biblioteca importante.

Paso 3. Ahora complete la siguiente información sobre su (*about your*) universidad.

Mi universidad est_____ en el estado de _____.

En mi universidad...
1. muchos / pocos (*many/few*) estudiantes tom_____ clases de español.
2. hay / no hay un centro o un / una programa de estudios latinoamericanos.
3. hay / no hay organizaciones de estudiantes latinos
4. las materias más populares son: _____.
5. los estudiantes pag_____ mucho / poco dinero.

B. ¿Qué pasa (*What's happening*) en la fiesta?

Paso 1. En parejas, describan la escena.

MODELO: En la fiesta, Pilar y Ana bailan. Nora...

> **Vocabulario útil**
>
> **descansar** to rest
> **escuchar**
> **fumar** to smoke
> **hablar**
> **mirar** to watch
>   **una película** a movie
>   **la tele** TV
> **tocar**
>   **la batería** drum set
>   **la guitarra**
>   **el piano**
> **tomar refrescos** soft drinks

Paso 2. Ahora comparen la escena con las fiestas en su (*your*) universidad. Usen **nosotros.**

MODELO: En las fiestas, mis amigos y yo **bailamos.**

En **su**° comunidad
your

As you know, all Spanish-speaking countries use the word **universidad** to refer to colleges or universities, big or small, public or private. But there is a lot of variation in the words that Spanish speakers use for *elementary school*, *middle school*, and *high school*. There is also variation in how the following words and phrases are expressed: (*academic*) *grade* (and the symbols used to give grades), *to pass, to fail*.

PREGUNTAS POSIBLES

- Ask someone who was raised in a Hispanic country what language is used in his or her country to express different levels of schooling and the grading system.
- Ask the person to describe his or her educational experience in the country of origin.
- If relevant, ask for a comparison with the educational system in this country.

SALU2

Antes de mirar°

Antes... *Before watching*

Conteste (*Answer*) las siguientes preguntas.

1. ¿Desea Ud. estudiar en un país (*country*) hispanohablante? ¿En qué país(es)?

2. En ese (*that*) país, ¿desea vivir (*to live*) con una familia o en una residencia de estudiantes?

Muchos (*Many*) estudiantes extranjeros viven (*live*) con familias peruanas hospitalarias (*welcoming*). Así (*So*), practican el español todo el tiempo (*all the time*) y aprenden (*they learn*) por experiencia la cultura de manera directa y personal.

Este° segmento

This

Desde (*From*) Lima, Perú, Laura presenta un reportaje sobre la Universidad del Pacífico, un lugar muy interesante para estudiar español.

Vocabulario del segmento

la ciudad	city	**los negocios**	business
el sitio	place, site	**la mercadotecnia**	marketing
el barrio	neighborhood	**la contabilidad**	accounting
lindo/a	pretty, cute	**pequeño/a**	small
se especializa	it specializes	**se sienten como**	feel like
la carrera	concentration, major	**miembros**	members

Fragmento del guion°

script

Esta universidad limeña^a atrae^b a numerosos estudiantes internacionales por varias razones.^c Primero,^d la universidad cuenta con^e modernas instalaciones,^f como la biblioteca. Segundo,^g está muy cerca del^h centro histórico de Lima. Pero lo más importante es que la universidad tiene^i un estupendo Centro de Idiomas.

^a*in Lima* ^b*attracts* ^c*por... for various reasons* ^d*First* ^e*cuenta... has* ^f*facilities* ^g*Second* ^h*está... it is very close to the* ^i*has*

Después de° mirar

Después... *After*

A.   ¿Está claro? ¿Cierto o falso? Corrija (*Correct*) las oraciones falsas según (*according to*) el video.

		CIERTO	FALSO
1. La ciudad de Lima...			
	a. es pequeña.	☐	☐
	b. tiene (*has*) barrios modernos.	☐	☐
	c. tiene sitios arquelógicos de los incas.	☐	☐
2. La Universidad del Pacífico...			
	a. es rural.	☐	☐
	b. es pública.	☐	☐
	c. tiene un centro para estudiar lenguas.	☐	☐
	d. se especializa en Humanidades.	☐	☐

B.   Un poco más. Conteste las siguientes preguntas.

1. ¿En qué materias se especializa la Universidad del Pacífico?

2. ¿Cuándo hay clases para los estudiantes extranjeros, por la mañana o por la tarde? ¿Qué hay por la tarde?

C.   Y ahora, Uds. En parejas, usen algunas (*some*) ideas del programa y del capítulo para hablar de su universidad.

MODELO: Esta (*This*) universidad es pública/privada. Se especializa en...

A LEER°

A... *Let's read*

Antes de leer°

Antes... *Before reading*

¿Hay muchos estudiantes de origen hispano en su universidad? ¿Hay organizaciones para ellos? ¿Es Ud. miembro de una organización estudiantil?

Lectura cultural: Los Estados Unidos

La presencia latina en las universidades norteamericanas

En la actualidad[a] hay muchos estudiantes latinos en las universidades de los Estados Unidos.

Las organizaciones de estudiantes latinos
La experiencia universitaria típica en los Estados Unidos incluye[b] la participación en organizaciones de estudiantes con diversos intereses. Por eso,[c] las universidades estadounidenses tienen[d] una variada representación de organizaciones latinas.

- Algunas[e] son para todos los hispanos de la universidad, como **Latinos Unidos.**
- Otras son para un grupo específico, como **Fuerza Quisqueyana** (estudiantes dominicanos) o **(La) Raza** (estudiantes mexicanoamericanos o chicanos).

Las organizaciones latinas coordinan eventos sociales y académicos: bailes de gala[f] con música hispana, conferencias de escritores[g] hispanohablantes, servicios sociales, etcétera. Con frecuencia, también hay una Casa Latina, donde miembros de la organización viven juntos.[h]

[a]En... *Currently* [b]*includes* [c]Por... *For this reason* [d]*have* [e]*Some (organizations)* [f]bailes... *formal dances* [g]*writers* [h]viven... *live together*

El mural *Resurrection of the Green Planet*, del artista chicano Ernesto de la Loza, en *East Los Angeles*

Un símbolo latino en los Estados Unidos: Los murales y el arte urbano

La tradición muralista mexicana está muy presente en las comunidades latinas de los Estados Unidos, especialmente en California y los estados del Suroeste.[a] Presenta motivos indigenistas,[b] históricos y sociales. Ahora hay ejemplos del arte urbano en los grandes[c] museos, desde[d] grafitis hasta[e] murales.

[a]*Southwest* [b]motivos... *indigenous (native) themes or elements* [c]*great* [d]*from* [e]*to*

En **otros** países° hispanos

countries

- **En todo el mundo[a] hispanohablante** Hay universidades nacionales que son gratuitas[b] o muy económicas en comparación con las universidades privadas. Las universidades nacionales son con frecuencia las más prestigiosas y antiguas[c] del país.

- **En el Ecuador** Hay dos ciclos escolares: uno para la región de la sierra, de octubre a junio, y el otro para la costa, de abril a enero.[d] Es para evitar que haya escuela en los meses de lluvia,[e] porque[f] hay peligro de inundaciones.[g]

[a]*world* [b]que... *that are free* [c]las... *the most prestigious and oldest* [d]*January* [e]para... *to avoid having school in the months of the rainy season* [f]*because* [g]peligro... *danger of flooding*

COMPRENSIÓN

Empareje (*Match*) la información de las dos columnas.

A	B
1. el Ecuador	a. ejemplos del arte latino
2. los murales	b. asociación de estudiantes dominicanos
3. bailes de gala	c. un país (*country*) con dos ciclos académicos
4. Fuerza Quisqueyana	d. ejemplo de un evento social

 Y ahora, Uds.

- ¿Son Uds. miembros de organizaciones estudiantiles? ¿De cuál(es)?
- ¿Hay ejemplos del arte mural en su (*your*) ciudad?

Del mundo hispano°

Del... *From the Hispanic world*

Antes de leer°

Antes... *Before reading*

What is a good way for an adult to learn another language? On the job (**el trabajo**), with friends who speak the language, in school (**una escuela**)? Can you think of other ways? Explain your answer. In a school, how many other learners would there ideally be in each class? How many days per week would the class meet? How many hours per day?

Lectura: Un anuncio° de Inglés USA

Lectura... *Reading: An ad*

Comprensión

A. Traducciones. (*Translations.*) Empareje (*Match*) las frases en español del anuncio con sus equivalentes en inglés.

1. _____ una hora de descanso
2. _____ el almuerzo
3. _____ semanas
4. _____ mayor

   a. *more*
   b. *an hour-long break*
   c. *weeks*
   d. *lunch*

B. En el anuncio. Busque (*Look for*) la siguiente información en el anuncio.

1. ¿Cómo se llama la escuela?
2. ¿Dónde está la escuela?
3. ¿Cuántos estudiantes hay en una clase?
4. ¿Qué tipo de estudiantes hay en la escuela?
5. ¿Cuántas horas de clase hay al (*per*) día?

INGLES USA ★

CURSOS INTENSIVOS INDIVIDUALES en CINCINNATI, OHIO, USA.

especial para empresas y altos ejecutivos[a]

Hotel y almuerzo de lunes a sábado incluídos[b] en el precio paquete

PROGRAMA:
7 horas diarias de clases, lunes a sábado con una hora de descanso para el almuerzo con el profesor.

Duración de 2 a 4 semanas

Para mayor información:

FUNDADA EN 1972[c]

CINCILINGUA INC.°

322 East Fourth Street
Cincinnati, Ohio 45202 U.S.A.
(513) 721-8782
FAX: (513) 721-8819
www.cincilingua.com

[a]para... *for business and corporate executives* [b]*included* [c]*mil novecientos setenta y dos*

Un anuncio° para los cursos de verano° de la Universidad Internacional
A... *Let's listen / ad / summer*

Antes de escuchar°
Antes... *Before listening*

What kind of information do you expect to hear in an ad for a summer course?

Vocabulario **para escuchar**			
el anuncio	ad	**la semana**	week
el verano	summer	**julio**	July
mayo	May	**agosto**	August

Después de escuchar°
Después... *After listening*

A. **Información básica.** Indique las respuestas (*answers*) apropiadas.

1. El período de matrícula es en...

_____ mayo   _____ junio   _____ julio   _____ agosto

2. Hay cursos de...

_____ 2 semanas _____ 4 semanas _____ 8 semanas _____ 10 semanas

3. Con seguridad (*For sure*) hay cursos de... según (*according to*) el anuncio.

_____ sociología _____ arte   _____ matemáticas _____ literatura

4. Por internet se ofrecen (*are offered*) cursos de...

_____ alemán   _____ filosofía   _____ italiano   _____ portugués

B. **Más información.** Según (*According to*) el anuncio, ¿cuál es el nombre de la residencia? ¿la dirección (*address*) de la página web? ¿el teléfono de contacto?

PRODUCCIÓN PERSONAL

¡Ahora, yo!

A. Use de (*as a*) modelo las preguntas y respuestas (*answers*) de la página 27 de este capítulo para hablar de sus propios estudios universitarios (*own university studies*).

B. Con las preguntas de la página 27 como modelo, filme una o dos entrevistas con compañeros de clase sobre (*about*) las materias que estudian y su especialización universitaria.

A ESCRIBIR°
Un ensayo sobre este° semestre/trimestre

A... *Let's write*

ensayo... *essay*
about this

¿Qué estudia Ud.? ¿Trabaja? ¿Es su horario (*schedule*) este semestre/trimestre muy diferente del (*from the*) horario de sus (*your*) compañeros de clase? ¿O es similar?

Preparar

Paso 1. Primero (*First*), complete la columna de la izquierda (*left-hand column*) con información personal. Luego entreviste a (*Then interview*) un compañero / una compañera y complete la columna de la derecha.

Yo	Mi compañero/a
Mi especialización[a] es / puede ser[b]:	Su[c] especialización es / puede ser:
Clases que[d] tomo este semestre/ trimestre:	Clases que toma este semestre/ trimestre:
Mi clase favorita es:	Su clase favorita es:
No trabajo. / Trabajo en...	No trabaja. / Trabaja en...
(No) Me gusta este semestre/ trimestre.	(No) Le gusta[e] este semestre/trimestre.

[a]*major* [b]*puede... might be* [c]*His/ Her* [d]*that* [e]*Le... He/She likes*

Paso 2. Ahora combine la información para escribir un ensayo. Hay más ayuda (*help*) en Connect.

Más ideas para su portafolio

- Make a list of reasons why you are studying Spanish. No reason is too silly or too small!
- Make a list of things you'd like to be able to do eventually with your Spanish. Let your imagination run wild!
- If you have been playing *Practice Spanish: Study Abroad,* in Quest 1 you saw the importance of the *plaza*. Where can *plazas* generally be found? How do people use them within their communities?

Sugerencia: You are now ready to play Quest 1 in **Practice Spanish: Study Abroad** (www.mhpractice.com).

Visit **www.connectspanish.com** to practice the vocabulary and grammar points covered in this chapter.

AFTER STUDYING THIS CHAPTER I CAN . . .

☐ name people, places, and things in the classroom and the university (28)

☐ name academic subject areas (30)

☐ recognize nouns and articles as masculine or feminine, singular or plural (35–36, 37–39)

☐ talk about actions with **-ar** verbs and subject pronouns (41–44)

☐ ask questions with interrogatives and yes/no questions with proper intonation (32, 48–49)

☐ recognize/describe at least two to three aspects of the Hispanic population of the U.S.

Gramática en breve

1. **Singular nouns: Gender and Articles**
    Noun Endings
    Masculine: **-o**
    Feminine: **-a, -ión, -dad, -tad**
    Masculine or feminine: **-e**

2. **Nouns and Articles: Plural Forms**
    Plural Endings

    -o ⟶   -os
    -a ⟶   -as
    -e ⟶   -es
    z   ⟶   -ces
    consonant   +-es

Definite Articles		**Indefinite Articles**	
Masculine	el ⟶ los	un ⟶ unos
Feminine	la ⟶ las	una ⟶ unas

3. **Subject Pronouns; Present Tense of -ar Verbs; Negation**
    Subject Pronouns
    yo, tú, Ud., él, ella, nosotros/as, vosotros/as, Uds., ellos/as

    Regular -ar Verb Endings
    -o, -as, -a, -amos, -áis, -an

4. **Asking Yes/No Questions**
    • Rising intonation
    • Inversion of word order:
    subject + *verb* ⟶ *verb* + *subject*

Vocabulario

¡OJO!

• Infinitives listed in colored text in **Vocabulario** lists are conjugated in all tenses and moods in Appendix 5.
• Be sure that you know the meaning of the group headings in addition to the meaning of the words in each group.
• If you are not sure of the meaning of a word, you can look it up in the end-of-book Spanish-English Vocabulary.)

Los verbos

bailar	to dance
buscar	to look for
cantar	to sing
comprar	to buy
desear	to want
enseñar	to teach
escuchar	to listen (to)
estar **(estoy, estás,...)**	to be
estudiar	to study
hablar	to speak; to talk
hablar por teléfono	to talk on the phone
mandar un mensaje	to (send a) text
necesitar	to need
pagar	to pay (for)
practicar	to practice
regresar	to return (*to a place*)
regresar a casa	to go home
tocar	to play (*a musical instrument*)
tomar	to take; to drink
trabajar	to work

Las personas

el/la amigo/a	friend
el/la bibliotecario/a	librarian
el/la cliente/a	client
el/la compañero/a (de clase)	classmate
el/la compañero/a de cuarto	roommate
el/la consejero/a	advisor
el/la dependiente/a	clerk
el/la estudiante	student
el/la extranjero/a	foreigner
el hombre	man
la mujer	woman
el/la secretario/a	secretary

Repaso: el/la profesor(a)

> **Repaso** (*Review*) indicates vocabulary listed as active in this chapter that you learned in previous chapters.

Los lugares

el apartamento	apartment
la biblioteca	library
la cafetería	cafeteria
el cuarto	room
el edificio	building
la fiesta	party
la librería	bookstore
el lugar	place
la oficina	office
la residencia	dormitory
el salón de clase	classroom
la universidad	university

Los objetos

el bolígrafo	pen
la calculadora	calculator
la computadora	computer
la computadora portátil	laptop (computer)
el cuaderno	notebook
el diccionario	dictionary
el dinero	money
el escritorio	desk
el lápiz (*pl.* lápices)	pencil
el libro (de texto)	(text)book
la mesa	table
la mochila	backpack
el papel	paper
el pizarrón (blanco)	(white)board
la puerta	door
la silla	chair
el teléfono (celular)	(cell) phone
la ventana	window

Las materias

la administración de empresas	business administration
la ciencia	science
la computación	computer science
la física	physics
la materia	subject area
la química	chemistry
la sicología	psychology

Cognados: el arte, las ciencias naturales/políticas/sociales, las comunicaciones, la economía, la filosofía, la historia, las humanidades, la literatura, las matemáticas, la sociología

Cognado(s) lists vocabulary you should be able to recognize because the words are close cognates of English.

Las lenguas (extranjeras)

el alemán	German
el español	Spanish
el francés	French
el inglés	English
el italiano	Italian
la lengua (extranjera)	(foreign) language

Otros sustantivos

el café	coffee
la clase	class (*of students*); class, course (*academic*)
el día	day
la matrícula	tuition

Las palabras interrogativas

¿cuál?	what?; which?
¿cuándo?	when?
¿cuánto?	how much?
¿cuántos/as?	how many?

Repaso: ¿cómo?, ¿(de) dónde?, ¿qué?, ¿quién?

¿Cuándo?

ahora	now
con frecuencia	frequently
el fin de semana	weekend
por la mañana/tarde	in the morning/afternoon
por la noche	at night, in the evening
tarde/temprano	late/early
todos los días	every day

Los pronombres personales

yo	I
tú	you (*fam. sing.*)
Ud.	you (*form, sing.*)
él	he
ella	she
nosotros/as	we
vosotros/as	you (*fam., plural*)
Uds.	you (*form., plural*)
ellos/as	they

Palabras adicionales

aquí	here
con	with
en casa	at home
mal	poorly
más	more
mucho (*adverb*)	much; a lot
poco (*adverb*)	(a) little
un poco (de)	a little bit (of)
solo	only

Repaso: no

Vocabulario personal

Use this space for other words and phrases you learn in this chapter.

ESPAÑOL	INGLÉS

3

La familia

En este° capítulo

this

www.connectspanish.com

Una familia mexicana, en una celebración especial

MÉXICO

120 (ciento veinte) millones de habitantes

- El nombre oficial de México es Estados Unidos Mexicanos. Hay 31 estados mexicanos.

- Es el primer país del mundo por[a] número de hispanohablantes.

- Un 64% (sesenta y cuatro por ciento) de los hispanos de los Estados Unidos de América son de origen mexicano.

[a]*el… the number one country in the world by*

- ¿Cómo es su[a] familia, grande[b] o pequeña[c]? (**Mi** familia…)
- ¿Cuántas personas hay en su familia más cercana[d]?
- ¿Cómo se llama su padre[e]/madre? (**Mi** padre/madre…)
- ¿Le gusta celebrar su cumpleaños[f] con sus amigos? (…con **mis** amigos) ¿con su familia? (…con **mi** familia)

[a]*your* [b]*big* [c]*small* [d]*más… closest* [e]*father* [f]*birthday*

ALEJANDRA HERNÁNDEZ SOTO CONTESTA LAS PREGUNTAS.

- Mi familia más cercana es pequeña porque[a] soy hija única.[b]

- Pero mi familia extendida es muy grande: tengo seis tías[c] y tíos y doce primos.[d]

- Mi padre se llama Juan y mi madre se llama Susana. Yo me llamo como mi abuela[e] materna.

- Me gusta celebrar mi cumpleaños con mis padres y también con mis amigos pero ¡por separado!

[a]*because* [b]*hija… an only child* [c]*aunts* [d]*cousins* [e]*grandmother*

VOCABULARIO: PREPARACIÓN

You can hear the pronunciation of theme vocabulary words and phrases in the Connect eBook.

La familia y los parientes°

relatives

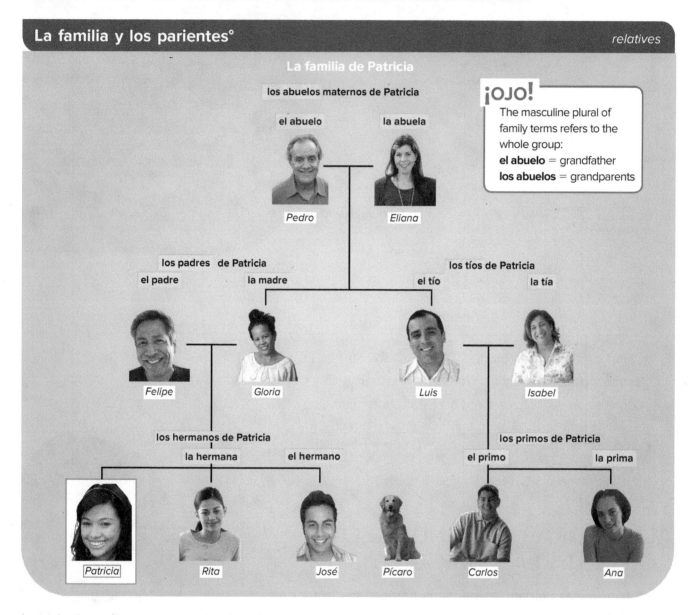

La familia de Patricia

los abuelos maternos de Patricia

el abuelo — la abuela

Pedro — Eliana

¡OJO!
The masculine plural of family terms refers to the whole group:
el abuelo = grandfather
los abuelos = grandparents

los padres de Patricia
el padre — la madre

los tíos de Patricia
el tío — la tía

Felipe — Gloria

Luis — Isabel

los hermanos de Patricia
la hermana — el hermano

los primos de Patricia
el primo — la prima

Patricia — Rita — José — Pícaro — Carlos — Ana

la madre (mamá)	mother (mom)
el padre (papá)	father (dad)
los padres	parents
la hija	daughter
el hijo	son
los hijos	children
la esposa / la mujer	wife
el esposo / el marido	husband
la nieta	granddaughter
el nieto	grandson
la sobrina	niece
el sobrino	nephew

Las mascotas°

Las... *Pets*

el gato	cat
el pájaro	bird
el perro	dog

Remember that the complete conjugation of infinitives in red is given in Appendix 5.

Formas del verbo tener°

to have

tengo	I have
tienes	you (*fam.*) have
tiene	you (*form.*) have, he/she has

Learn as many of the following terms for additional family relationships as you need to describe your own family as completely as possible. Write the terms you learn in **Vocabulario personal** (page 97).

el padrastro / la madrastra	stepfather / stepmother
el hijastro / la hijastra	stepson / stepdaughter
el hermanastro / la hermanastra	stepbrother / stepsister
el medio hermano / la media hermana	half-brother / half-sister
el suegro / la suegra	father-in-law / mother-in-law
el yerno / la nuera	son-in-law / daughter-in-law
el cuñado / la cuñada	brother-in-law / sister-in-law
...(ya) murió	...has (already) died

Comunicación

A. La familia de Patricia. Mire (*Look at*) el árbol (*tree*) genealógico de Patricia en la página 62 (sesenta y dos). Indique si las siguientes oraciones son ciertas o falsas. Corrija (*Correct*) las oraciones falsas.

	CIERTO	FALSO
1. José es el hermano de Ana.	☐	☐
2. Eliana es la abuela de Patricia.	☐	☐
3. Ana es la sobrina de Felipe y Gloria.	☐	☐
4. Patricia y José son (*are*) primos.	☐	☐
5. Gloria es la tía de José.	☐	☐
6. Carlos es el sobrino de Isabel.	☐	☐
7. Pedro es el padre de Luis y Gloria.	☐	☐
8. Isabel y Gloria son las esposas de Luis y Felipe, respectivamente.	☐	☐

B. ¿Quién es?

Paso 1. Complete las siguientes oraciones lógicamente.

1. La madre de mi (*my*) padre es mi _____.
2. El hijo de mi tío es mi _____.
3. La hermana de mi padre es mi _____.
4. El esposo (marido) de mi abuela es mi _____.

Paso 2. Ahora defina la relación de estas (*these*) personas, según (*according to*) el modelo de las oraciones del **Paso 1.**

MODELOS: El _____ de mi _____ es mi _____.
La _____ de mi _____ es mi _____.

1. prima   **2.** sobrino   **3.** tío   **4.** abuelo

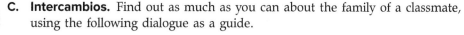

C. Intercambios. Find out as much as you can about the family of a classmate, using the following dialogue as a guide.

MODELO: E1:* ¿Cuántos hermanos tienes?
E2: Bueno,[a] tengo dos hermanos.
E1: ¿Cómo se llaman tus hermanos?
E2: Se llaman Dixon y Lisa.
E1: ¿Y cuántos primos tienes?
E2: ¡Uf! Tengo un montón.[b] Más de[c] veinte.
E1: ¿Tienes una mascota?
E2: Sí, tengo un perro. Se llama Bear.

[a]Well [b]bunch [c]Más... More than

_____

*From this point on in the text, ESTUDIANTE 1 and ESTUDIANTE 2 will be abbreviated as **E1** and **E2,** respectively.*

The terms **mamá/mami** and **papá/papi** are used to speak *to* one's parents.

Many Spanish speakers use the terms **abuelito/tata** and **abuelita/nana** to speak *to* their grandparents.

Here is vocabulary for referring to non-traditional types of families:

- **una familia reconstituida** (family whose parents were previously married and have other children with previous spouses)
- **una unión civil**
- **una pareja de hecho** (non-married couple with formalized status)
- **un matrimonio entre personas del mismo sexo**

¡OJO!
¿cuántos? (*with male relatives*)
¿cuántas? (*with female relatives*)

INSTITUTO FEDERAL ELECTORAL
MEXICO REGISTRO FEDERAL DE ELECTORES
CREDENCIAL PARA VOTAR

NOMBRE
GOMEZ
VELAZQUEZ
MARGARITA

EDAD 26
SEXO M

DOMICILIO
C.PITAGORAS 1253 INT. 4
COL. MORELOS 06100
CUAJIMALPA DE MORELOS, D.F.
CLAVE DE REGISTRO GMVLMR80070501M000
CURP GOVM800705MCLMLR01 AÑO DE REGISTRO 2008 02
ESTADO 09 MUNICIPIO 004 SECCION 0747
LOCALIDAD 005 EMISION 2008 VIGENCIA 2018

FIRMA

En esta credencial para votar, de México, están el nombre y los dos apellidos de la persona: primero, los apellidos y después (*next*), el nombre.

Nota **cultural**

El sistema hispano de apellidos° *last names*

En los países hispanos las personas llevan sistemáticamente dos apellidos oficiales. Típicamente, el primer[a] apellido es el del[b] padre y el segundo,[c] el de la madre.

PADRE	MADRE
Antonio **Lázaro** Ochoa	Marina **Aguirre** Salmero

HIJOS
Marta **Lázaro Aguirre**
Jacobo **Lázaro Aguirre**

 Según el sistema hispano, ¿cómo se llamaría Ud.?[d]

[a]*first* [b]*el... that of the* [c]*second* [d]*¿cómo... what would your name be?*

Los números del 31 al 100

Continúe las secuencias:

- treinta y uno, treinta y dos...
- ochenta y cuatro, ochenta y cinco...

31	treinta y uno	**40**	cuarenta
32	treinta y dos	**50**	cincuenta
33	treinta y tres	**60**	sesenta
34	treinta y cuatro	**70**	setenta
35	treinta y cinco	**80**	ochenta
36	treinta y seis	**90**	noventa
37	treinta y siete	**100**	cien
38	treinta y ocho		
39	treinta y nueve		

setenta y ocho años
cincuenta y cinco años
treinta y nueve años
cuarenta y cinco años
cuarenta y siete años
ochenta y cinco años
«El abuelito Pedro tiene 85 años.»
«La abuelita Eliana tiene 78 años.»

Beginning with 31, Spanish numbers are *not* written in a combined form. **Treinta y uno,**[*] **cuarenta y dos, sesenta y tres,** and so on, must be three separate words.

Cien is used before nouns and in counting.

cien casas	a (one) hundred houses
noventa y ocho, noventa y nueve, cien	ninety-eight, ninety-nine, one hundred

Comunicación

A. Más problemas de matemáticas. Recuerde (*Remember*): + **y,** − **menos,** = **son.**

1. 30 + 50 = 80
2. 45 + 45 = 90
3. 68 − 28 = 40
4. 77 + 23 = 100
5. 100 − 40 = 60
6. 55 + 15 = 70

---

[*]*Remember that when* **uno** *is part of a compound number (***treinta y uno,** *and so on), it becomes* **un** *before a masculine noun and* **una** *before a feminine noun:* **setenta y un hombres; cincuenta y una mesas.**

B. Un directorio de teléfonos de la clase. Interview five classmates to find out their full names, Spanish-style, and phone numbers. Follow the model of this directory from **México**: last name, last name, first name. **¡OJO!** In many Hispanic countries phone numbers are said with an initial single digit, then in groups of two, as in the model.

MODELO: E1: ¿Cómo te llamas y cuál es tu número de teléfono?

E2: Me llamo **Smith Wiliams, John** y mi número (de teléfono) es **el 215-8194** (dos-quince-ochenta y uno-noventa y cuatro).

LAZARO AGUIRRE, A. –Schez Pacheco, 12	413 0146
LAZCANO DEL MORAL, A. –Ibiza, 2	472 6868
LEAL ANTON, J. –Pozo, 6	222 3944
LOPEZ BARTOLÓME, J. –Palma, 61	323 2027
LOPEZ CABRA,J. –E. Solana, 113	407 5807
LOPEZ GONZALEZ, J. A. –Ibiza, 21	409 5225
LOPEZ GUTIERREZ, G. –5. Cameros, 1	486 8494
LOPEZ MARIN, V. –Illescas, 31	218 6630
LOPEZ MARIN, V. –Valmojado, 321	722 2823
LOPEZ NUÑEZ. J. –Pl. Pinazo, s/n	796 0051
LOPEZ NUÑEZ, M. –Rocafort, Bl. 289	768 5387
LOPEZ RODRIGUEZ, C. –Pl. Jesus, 9	429 3250
LOPEZ TRAPERO, A. –Cam. Ingenieros, 5	462 9253
LOPEZ VEGA, J. – M. Santa Ana, 7	231 3121
LORENZO MARTINEZ, A. –P. Laborde, 53	771 2800
LOSADA MIRON, M. –Padilla, 31	276 3973

Nota **comunicativa**

Cómo expresar la edad:° *tener... años*   *age*

In Spanish, age is expressed with the phrase **tener... años** (literally, *to have . . . years*).

NORA: ¿Cuántos **años** tienes, abuela?

ABUELA: Setenta y ocho. ¿Y cuántos **años tienes** tú?

NORA: Yo **tengo** ocho.

You will practice telling how old people are in **Comunicación C.**

C. Hablemos (*Let's talk*) de la edad (*age*)

Paso 1. Complete las siguientes oraciones.

1. Yo tengo _____ años.
2. La persona mayor (*oldest*) de mi familia es **mi** _____. Tiene _____ años.
3. La persona más joven (*youngest*) de mi familia es **mi** _____. Tiene _____ años.
4. En mi opinión, una persona es vieja (*old*) cuando tiene _____ años.
5. La edad ideal para casarse (*for getting married*) es a los _____ años.
6. La edad ideal para tener hijos es a los _____ años.

Paso 2. Ahora haga (*form*) preguntas basadas en las oraciones del **Paso 1** y haga (*conduct*) una encuesta (*poll*) entre (*with*) un mínimo de seis compañeros de clase.

Estrategia

En el **Paso 2**, cambie (*change*) la palabra **mi (en negrilla)** para formar las preguntas, según el modelo:

mi → tu

MODELO: 2. E1: ¿Quién es la persona mayor de **tu** familia? ¿Cuántos años tiene?

E2: Es **mi** abuela. Tiene noventa y siete años.

Paso 3. Finalmente, presente sus (*your*) resultados a la clase.

Algo sobre...

los estados[a] mexicanos

El escudo (símbolo) de los Estados Unidos Mexicanos es un águila sobre un nopal.

México tiene 32 entidades federativas: 31 estados y 1 distrito federal, que[b] es la capital, la Ciudad de México. Los mexicanos la llaman[c] el D.F.

 ¿Cuántos estados hay en los Estados Unidos? La capital, Washington D.C., ¿es un estado?

[a]*states* [b]*which* [c]*la... call it (i.e., the capital)*

Vocabulario: Preparación

sesenta y cinco ■ **65**

Los adjetivos

guapo	handsome, good-looking
bonito	pretty
feo	ugly
grande	large, big
pequeño	small
simpático	nice, likeable
antipático	unpleasant, unlikeable
corto	short (*in length*)
largo	long
bueno	good
malo	bad
listo	smart, clever
tonto	silly, foolish
trabajador	hardworking
perezoso	lazy
rico	rich
pobre	poor
delgado	thin, slender
gordo	fat

To describe a masculine singular noun, use **alt**o, **baj**o, and so on; use **alt**a, **baj**a, and so on for feminine singular nouns.

Comunicación

A. Descripciones

Paso 1. En parejas, describan estas (*these*) imágenes opuestas (*opposite*).

MODELO: Un _____ es y _____ el otro es _____.

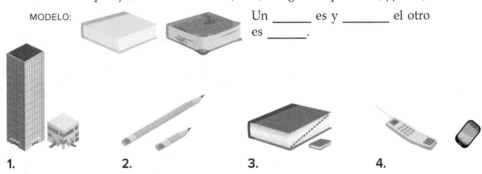

1. 2. 3. 4.

Paso 2. Ahora describan a estas personas e* ideas.

MODELO: fumar (*to smoke*) → Fumar es malo. No es bueno.

1. bailar
2. Stephen Hawkins
3. Bill Gates
4. estudiar toda la noche

5. el edificio Empire State
6. Frankenstein
7. un átomo

B. ¿Cómo es?

Describe a famous male personality, using as many adjectives as possible so that your classmates can guess who the person is. Use cognate adjectives that you have seen in **Capítulos 1** and **2**.

MODELO: Es un hombre importante; controla una compañía de *software* muy importante. Es muy trabajador y muy rico. → Bill Gates

---

*Notice that the word **y** becomes **e** before a word that starts with the sound **i: español e inglés, matemáticas e historia**.*

«Padres modernos» Segmento 1

Antes de mirar°

Antes... *Before watching*

¿Tiene Ud.... ?

_____ abuelos que viven cerca (*who live nearby*)
_____ muchos parientes
_____ hijos
_____ padrinos (*godparents*) (un padrino / una madrina)
_____ ahijados (*godchildren*) (un ahijado / una ahijada)

Este° segmento

This

Ana García Blanco y Víctor Gutiérrez presentan un programa sobre (*about*) la familia. También hablan de personas importantes en su vida familiar (*their family life*).

Hoy Víctor toma una taza grande (*big cup*) de café. ¿Por qué?

Vocabulario del segmento

disfrutar	to enjoy	**cuidar a**	to take care of
enfermo/a	sick	**¡Vivan las abuelas!**	Hooray for grandmothers!
cansado/a	tired	**los amigos íntimos**	very close friends

Estrategia

Before you watch, scan **Actividades A** and **B** in **Después de mirar.** Knowing what tasks you need to do after watching will help you focus on information to pay attention to as you watch the segment.

Después de mirar°

Después... *After watching*

A. ¿Está claro? Empareje (*Match*) las personas con las relaciones familiares del segmento.

LAS PERSONAS

____ **1.** Víctor
____ **2.** la abuela
____ **3.** Sarita
____ **4.** Marina
____ **5.** Ana
____ **6.** Leticia

LAS RELACIONES FAMILIARES

a. la esposa de Víctor
b. la mamá de Víctor
c. la hija de Víctor
d. la tía y madrina de Leticia
e. la sobrina de Ana
f. el papá de Sarita

B. Un poco más. ¿Cierto o falso? Corrija las oraciones falsas, según el video.

	CIERTO	FALSO
1. Víctor toma aspirinas porque (*because*) está cansado.	☐	☐
2. Víctor está enfermo.	☐	☐
3. La esposa de Víctor cuida a Sarita hoy.	☐	☐
4. Los padrinos y los amigos íntimos son (*are*) personas importantes y fundamentales en muchas familias.	☐	☐

C. Y ahora, Uds. Practique su (*your*) pronunciación y su talento como presentador(a). Complete el fragmento con su propia (*your own*) información y con vocabulario del programa.

Muy buenos días desde nuestro estudio en _____. ¿Cómo están Uds.? Yo estoy _____ hoy. El tema del programa de hoy es la familia. ¿Qué personas son[a] muy importantes en su[b] familia, además de[c] los padres? ¿Son importantes también los _____ (personas)? En mi caso, mi _____ y mi _____ son personas fundamentales. ¡Viva mi _____ ! ¡Vivan mis _____ !

[a]*are* [b]*your* [c]además... *besides*

PRONUNCIACIÓN

Stress and Written Accent Marks (Part 1)

Some Spanish words have *written accent marks* over one of the vowels. That mark is called **el acento (ortográfico).** It means that the syllable containing the accented vowel is stressed when the word is pronounced, as in the word **bolígrafo (bo-LÍ-gra-fo),** for example.

Although all Spanish words of more than one syllable have a stressed vowel, most words do not have a written accent mark. Most words have the spoken stress exactly where native speakers of Spanish would predict it. These two simple rules tell you which syllable is stressed when there is no written accent on the word.

¡OJO!

You will learn about words that have a written accent mark in **Capítulo 4.**

1. Las palabras llanas, words ending in a vowel, **-n,** or **-s**

Las palabras llanas have the word stress on the *second-to-last syllable* (**la penúltima sílaba**). When they end in a vowel, **-n,** or **-s,** they don't need a written accent mark. This is the largest group of Spanish words; it includes most nouns and adjectives as well as their plurals, most verb forms, and so on. Here are some examples.

　　　me-sa　　　me-xi-ca-no　　　e-xa-men　　　gra-cias　　　e-res

2. Las palabras agudas, words ending in a consonant other than **-n** or **-s**

Las palabras agudas have the word stress on the *last syllable* (**la última sílaba**). When they end in consonants other than **-n** or **-s** (typically **-d, -l,** and **-r**), they don't need a written accent mark. This group includes all infinitives and many common words that end in **-dad, -or,** and **-al.** Here are some examples.

　　　us-ted　　　es-pa-ñol　　　pro-fe-sor　　　es-tar　　　doc-tor

Práctica

Estrategia

llana (ends in a vowel, **-n,** or **-s**) = stress on the second-to-last syllable

aguda (ends in a consonant other than **-n** or **-s**) = stress on the last syllable

A.　Tipos de palabras: ¿Llanas o agudas? None of these words needs a written accent mark. Categorize each one as **llana** or **aguda,** then pronounce the word.

1. can-tan	**5.** me-sa	**9.** se-ñor
2. ar-te	**6.** es-pa-ñol	**10.** na-tu-ral
3. cla-se	**7.** a-mi-gos	**11.** com-pu-ta-do-ra
4. mu-jer	**8.** us-ted	**12.** bai-las

B.　Vocales. Indicate the stressed vowel in the following words.

1. mo-chi-la	**4.** i-gual-men-te	**7.** li-be-ral
2. me-nos	**5.** E-cua-dor	**8.** hu-ma-ni-dad
3. re-gu-lar	**6.** e-le-gan-te	

Grammar Tutorial 5
connect
|SPANISH
www.connectspanish.com

5 **Describing**
Adjectives: Gender, Number, and Position

Gramática en acción: Un poema sencillo

Amigo
Fiel
Amable
Simpático
¡Lo admiro!

Amiga
Fiel
Amable
Simpática
¡La admiro!

¿Y Ud.?

According to their form, which of the following adjectives can be used to describe each person? Which can refer to you?

Marta:
Mario: { fiel   amable   simpática   simpático }

Adjectives (**Los adjetivos**) are words used to talk about nouns or pronouns. Adjectives may describe or tell how many of something there are.

large desk   **few** desks

tall woman   **several** women

an adjective / **un adjetivo** = a word used to describe a noun or a pronoun

You have been using adjectives to describe people since **Capítulo 1.** In this section, you will learn more about describing the people and things around you.

Adjectives with *ser* / Los adjetivos con *ser*

In Spanish, forms of **ser** are used with adjectives that describe basic, inherent qualities or characteristics of the nouns or pronouns they modify. **Ser** establishes the "norm," that is, what is considered basic reality: *snow is cold, water is wet.*

Tú **eres amable.**
You're kind. (You're a kind person.)

El diccionario **es grande.**
The dictionary is big.

Mi hermana **es trabajadora.**
My sister is hardworking.

A simple poem *Friend Loyal Kind Nice I admire him/her!*

Forms of Adjectives / Las formas de los adjetivos

Spanish adjectives "agree" with the noun or pronoun they modify. This agreement is shown in two ways:

- gender agreement (masculine or feminine): **una amiga alta**
- number agreement (singular or plural): **los amigos ricos**

For this reason, Spanish adjectives have more than one form.

> *agreement* / **la concordancia** = when one word "agrees," or must be coordinated, with an aspect of another (for example, *he + speaks* but *you + speak*)

1. Adjectives Ending in -o

Adjectives that end in **-o (alto)** have four forms, showing gender and number.

Adjetivos con 4 formas		
	Masculino	**Femenino**
Singular	amigo alto	amiga alta
Plural	amigos altos	amigas altas

2. Adjectives Ending in -e or a Consonant

Adjectives that end in **-e (amable)** or in most consonants (**fiel**) have only two forms, a singular and a plural form. The plural of adjectives is formed in the same way as that of nouns, by adding **-s** or **-es.**

Adjetivos con 2 formas		
	Masculino	**Femenino**
Singular	amigo amable amigo fiel	amiga amable amiga fiel
Plural	amigos amables amigos fieles	amigas amables amigas fieles

> **¡OJO!**
> When the adjective **joven** is made plural, an accent mark is added to retain the original stress:
> **joven ⟶ jóvenes.**

3. Adjectives Ending in -dor

Like adjectives that end in **-o,** these adjectives also have four forms.

Adjetivos con 4 formas		
	Masculino	**Femenino**
Singular	amigo trabajador	amiga trabajadora
Plural	amigos trabajadores	amigas trabajadoras

4. Nationality Adjectives

Many adjectives of nationality have four forms.

> **¡OJO!**
> Nationality adjectives ending in **-e** generally have only two forms: **estadounidense(s)** (from the United States), **canadiense(s).**

	Masculino	**Femenino**
Singular	el doctor mexicano español	la doctora mexicana española
Plural	los doctores mexicanos españoles	las doctoras mexicanas españolas

5. Names of Languages

The names of many languages—which are masculine in gender—are the same as the masculine singular form of the corresponding adjective of nationality.

Lengua	Adjetivo
el inglés	inglés, inglesa, ingleses, inglesas
el francés	francés, francesa, franceses, francesas
el italiano	italiano, italiana, italianos, italianas
el alemán	alemán, alemana, alemanes, alemanas

> **¡OJO!**
> Note that in Spanish the names of languages and adjectives of nationality are not capitalized, but the names of countries are: **el español, española,** but **España.**

> **¡OJO!**
> When the last syllable of an adjective has a written accent mark (**inglés, alemán**), the accent is dropped in the feminine and plural forms, as shown in the box above.

Position of Adjectives / La posición de los adjetivos

As you have probably noticed, adjectives do not always precede the noun in Spanish as they do in English. Note the following rules for adjective placement.

1. Adjectives of Quantity

Like numbers, adjectives of quantity *precede* the noun, as do the interrogatives **¿cuánto/a?** and **¿cuántos/as?**

> **¡OJO!**
>
> **Otro/a** is an adjective of quantity. By itself it means *another* or *other*. The indefinite article is never used with **otro/a.**

Hay **muchas sillas** y **dos escritorios.**
There are many chairs and two desks.

¿Cuánto **dinero** necesitas?
How much money do you need?

Busco otro **coche.**
I'm looking for another car.

2. Adjectives of Quality

Adjectives that describe the qualities of a noun and distinguish it from others generally *follow* the noun. Adjectives of nationality are included in this category.

un **perro** listo
un **dependiente** trabajador
una **mujer** delgada y morena
un **profesor** español

3. *Bueno* and *malo*

The adjectives **bueno** and **malo** may *precede or follow* the noun they modify. When they precede a masculine singular noun, they shorten to **buen** and **mal,** respectively.

un buen **perro** / un **perro** bueno
una buena **perra** / una **perra** buena

un mal **día** / un **día** malo
una mala **noche** / una **noche** mala

4. *Grande*

The adjective **grande** may also *precede or follow* the noun.

• When it precedes a singular noun—masculine or feminine—it shortens to **gran** and means *great* or *impressive.*
• When it follows the noun, it means *large* or *big.*

Nueva York es una gran **ciudad.**
New York is a great (impressive) city.

Nueva York es una **ciudad** grande.
New York is a large city.

Forms of *this/these* / Formas de *este/estos*

1. *This/These*

The adjective *this/these* has four forms in Spanish.* Learn to recognize them when you see them.

este hijo	this son
esta hija	this daughter
estos hijos	these sons
estas hijas	these daughters

2. *Esto*

You have already seen the neuter demonstrative **esto.** It refers to something that is as yet unidentified.

¿Qué es esto?
What is this?

---

*You will learn all forms of this type of adjective (this, that, these, those) in **Gramática 9 (Cap. 4).**

Adjective Agreement Summary

SINGULAR ENDINGS	PLURAL ENDINGS
-o, -a	-os, -as
-e	-es
-[consonant]	-[consonant] + -es
-dor, -dora	-dores, -doras

A. La familia

Paso 1. Autoprueba. Complete los adjetivos con la forma apropiada.

1. El padre es alt_____ y trabajador_____.
2. La madre es baj_____ y amabl_____.
3. Los abuelos son viej_____ y simpátic_____.
4. Las hijas son pequeñ_____ y adorabl_____.
5. Hay much_____ parientes en la familia.
6. La familia tiene buen_____ amigos.

Paso 2. Ahora complete las siguientes oraciones según la familia de Ud.

1. Mi padre/hermano/tío es _____ y _____.
2. Mi madre/hermana/tía es _____ y _____.
3. Mis abuelos son (*are*) _____ y _____. (Mi abuelo/a es _____ y _____.)
4. _____ (nombre) y _____ (nombre) son buen_____ amigos/amigas de mi familia

 Paso 3. Ahora, en parejas, túrnense para hacer y contestar (*take turns asking and answering*) preguntas sobre su (*about your*) familia. Usen las oraciones del **Paso 2** como modelo.

MODELO: **E1:** Mis abuelos son mexicanos y simpáticos.
¿Y tus abuelos?
E2: Mis abuelos son estadounidenses y viejos.

B. Descripciones

Paso 1. Haga oraciones con los siguientes adjetivos para describirse (*to describe yourself*). ¡**OJO!** Use la forma apropiada del adjetivo.

Soy...
No soy...

1. alto
2. trabajadora
3. estadounidense
4. rico
5. rubia
6. fiel
7. simpático
8. europeo
9. gordo
10. hispana (latina)*
11. dedicado
12. social
13. estudiosa
14. listo

Paso 2. Ahora haga oraciones para describir a su (*your*) padre/madre, a su esposo/a o a su mejor amigo/a (*best friend*).

MODELOS: Mi mejor amiga es moren**a**, simpátic**a** y pobre.
Mi esposo es alt**o**, trabaja**dor** y muy dedica**do**.

Algo sobre...

una pintora mexicana

Frida Kahlo es una pintora mexicana muy famosa. Fue[a] la esposa del famoso muralista mexicano Diego Rivera. Los dos vivieron[b] por un tiempo en los Estados Unidos, en Nueva York y San Francisco.

En sus obras,[c] Frida se enfoca en sí misma.[d] Sus obras son autorretratos[e] que incluyen elementos de la cultura mexicana.

Frida Kahlo con su esposo, Diego Rivera

 ¿Hay pintoras famosas en los Estados Unidos?

[a]*She was* [b]*lived* [c]*sus... her works* [d]*se... looks inward at herself* [e]*self-portraits*

---

*Hispano/a *is a general term used by most Hispanics to refer to themselves. The term* **latino/a** *is often used by Hispanics born in this country.*

Prác. A, Paso 1: Answers: **1.** alto, trabajador (no change) **2.** baja, amable **3.** viejos, simpáticos **4.** pequeñas, adorables **5.** muchos **6.** buenos

C. La familia de Carlos. Estos son los parientes de Carlos (página 62). Complete las oraciones con los adjetivos apropiados según su forma.

1. **El tío Felipe** es _____. (trabajador / alto / nueva / gran / amable)
2. **Los abuelos** son _____. (rubio / antipático / inteligentes / viejos / religiosos / sinceras)
3. **Mi tía Gloria,** la madre de Patricia, es _____. (rubio / elegante / sentimental / buenas / gordas / simpática)
4. **Mis primos** son _____. (trabajadores / morenos / lógica / bajas / mala)

D. ¡Dolores es igual! Cambie (*Exchange*) **Diego** por **Dolores.**

Diego es un buen estudiante. Es listo y trabajador y estudia mucho. Es estadounidense de origen mexicano, y por eso^a habla español. Desea ser profesor de antropología. Diego es moreno, guapo y atlético. Le gustan las fiestas grandes y tiene buenos amigos en la universidad. Tiene parientes estadounidenses y mexicanos. Diego tiene 20 años.

^apor... *for that reason*

Nota **comunicativa**

Otras nacionalidades

You learned some nationality adjectives on page 70. Here are some more. If you don't find the adjective(s) you need to describe yourself and your family, ask your instructor. Write the adjectives you need in **Vocabulario personal** (page 97).

Norteamérica	Centroamérica y el Caribe	Sudamérica		Europa y Asia	
canadiense	costarricense	argentino/a	ecuatoriano/a	chino/a	japonés, japonesa
mexicano/a	cubano/a	boliviano/a	paraguayo/a	coreano/a	pakistaní (*pl.* pakistaníes)
	dominicano/a	brasileño/a	peruano/a	indio/a	palestino/a
	guatemalteco/a	chileno/a	uruguayo/a	israelí (*pl.* israelíes)	ruso/a
	hondureño/a	colombiano/a	venezolano/a	iraní (*pl.* iraníes)	tailandés, tailandesa
	nicaragüense			iraquí (*pl.* iraquíes)	vietnamita
	panameño/a				
	salvadoreño/a				

You will use many of these adjectives in **Práctica E.**

E. Países (*Countries*) y nacionalidades del mundo (*world*)

Paso 1. Diga (*Tell*) la nacionalidad de las siguientes personas.

1. Monique es de Francia; es _____.
2. Piero y Andri son del Uruguay; son _____.
3. Indira y su (*her*) hermana son de la India; son _____.
4. Ronaldo y Ronaldinho son del Brasil; son _____.
5. Saji es un hombre del Japón; es _____.
6. La familia Musharraf es de Pakistán; son (*they are*) _____.
7. Paul es de Inglaterra; es _____.
8. Samuel y su (*his*) hermana son de Guatemala; son _____.
9. Sonia es de la Argentina; es _____.
10. Ramón y José son de Colombia; son _____.
11. Jimena es de Costa Rica; es _____.
12. Bill y Susan son de California; son _____.

¡OJO!

Recuerde (*Remember*): Los adjetivos de nacionalidad y los nombres de las lenguas no comienzan con letra mayúscula (*capital letter*).

Paso 2. En parejas, hagan oraciones con las nacionalidades hispanas, según el modelo. Busquen (*Look for*) los nombres de las naciones hispanas en el mapa de la página 12.

MODELO: E1: ¿Una mujer de Costa Rica?
E2: Es **costarricense.** ¿Y un hombre?
E1: Es **costarricense.** ¿Una mujer de El Salvador?
E2: Es...

F. Una mujer sorprendente (*surprising*)

Paso 1. Complete con las terminaciones apropiadas la siguiente descripción de una mujer muy especial.

Sor (*Sister*) Juana Inés de la Cruz, 1651 – 1695 (mil seiscientos cincuenta y uno hasta mil seiscientos noventa y cinco)

Sor[a] Juana Inés de la Cruz es una mujer religios___[1] mexican___[2] del siglo[b] XVII. Es una gran__[3] poeta y una mujer muy inteligent___[4] y muy ilustrad___[c5] para su[d] época. Es muy famos___[6] internacionalmente. Escribió[e] much___[7] poemas important___[8] de la literatura hispan___[9].

[a]*Sister* [b]*century* [c]*ilustrado/a = educated* [d]*para... for her* [e]*She wrote*

Paso 2. Comprensión. ¿Cierto o falso? Corrija las oraciones falsas.

	CIERTO	FALSO
1. Sor Juana es de Nicaragua.	☐	☐
2. Escribió poemas en español.	☐	☐
3. Es famosa solamente en México.	☐	☐

G. Asociaciones. En grupos, hablen (*talk*) de las personas o cosas (*things*) que (*that*) asocian con las siguientes frases. Expresen acuerdo (*agreement*) o desacuerdo (*disagreement*) con **(No) Estoy de acuerdo.**

MODELO: un gran hombre →
E1: Creo que (*I believe that*) **mi padre** es un gran hombre.
E2: No estoy de acuerdo.

1. un mal restaurante
2. un buen programa de televisión
3. una gran mujer, un gran hombre
4. un buen libro (¿una novela?), un libro horrible
5. un buen coche
6. una buena computadora

H. Descripciones. En parejas, describan a su (*your*) familia, haciendo (*forming*) oraciones completas con estas palabras, con cualquier (*any*) otro adjetivo que conozcan (*that you may know*) y con los adjetivos de nacionalidad. **¡OJO!** Cuidado (*Be careful*) con la forma de los adjetivos.

MODELO: Mi familia no es grande. Es pequeña. Mi padre tiene 50 años.
Es pakistaní de nacimiento (*by birth*).

mi familia mi padre/madre mi esposo/esposa mi ¿ ? (otro pariente) mi perro/gato	**+** (no) es **+** **+** tiene... años	agresivo amable animado (*lively*) antipático bueno cariñoso (*affectionate*) comprensivo (*understanding*) difícil (*difficult*)	famoso grande (im)paciente importante inteligente interesante malo nuevo	pequeño sensible (*sensitive*) sentimental serio simpático tolerante travieso (*mischievous*) viejo

¿Recuerda Ud.?

Before beginning **Gramática 6,** review the forms and uses of **ser** that you know already by answering these questions.

1. ¿Es Ud. estudiante o profesor(a)?
2. ¿Cómo es Ud.? ¿Es una persona sentimental? ¿inteligente? ¿paciente? ¿elegante?
3. ¿Qué hora es? ¿A qué hora es la clase de español?
4. ¿Qué es un hospital? ¿Es una persona? ¿un objeto? ¿un edificio?

Grammar Tutorial 6
connect SPANISH
www.connectspanish.com

6 Expressing *to be*

Present Tense of *ser;* Summary of Uses (Part 2)

Gramática en acción: Presentaciones

Lea lo que dice Francisco y luego complete su descripción de su esposa.

— Hola. Me llamo Francisco Durán Ferrer, pero todos me llaman Pancho.

- **Soy** profesor de la universidad.
- **Soy** alto y moreno.
- **Soy** de Guanajuato, México.

—¿Y Lola Benítez Velasco, mi esposa?

- **Es** _____ (profesión).
- **Es** _____ y _____ (descripción).
- **Es** de _____ (origen).

Vocabulario útil

guapa, pesimista, muy inteligente
Jalisco (un estado de México)
médica en el Hospital Central, profesora también

ser (*to be*)			
(yo)	soy	(nosotros/as)	somos
(tú)	eres	(vosotros/as)	sois
(Ud.)		(Uds.)	
(él)	es	(ellos)	son
(ella)		(ellas)	

As you know, two Spanish verbs mean *to be:* **ser** and **estar.** They are not interchangeable; the meaning the speaker wants to convey determines their use. Here, you will review the uses of **ser** that you already know and learn some new ones. Remember to use **estar** to express location and to ask how someone is feeling. You will learn more about **estar** in **Gramática 15–16 (Cap. 6).**

Some basic uses of **ser** are presented on the following pages. You have used or seen all of them already in this and previous chapters.

_____

Introductions *Read what Francisco says and then complete his description of his wife. Hello! My name is Francisco Durán Ferrer, but everyone calls me Pancho. ▪ I'm a university professor. ▪ I'm tall and brunet. ▪ I'm from Guanajuato, Mexico. And Lola Benítez, Velasco, my wife? ▪ She's _____. ▪ She's _____ and _____. ▪ She's from _____.*

Identification / La identificación

To *identify* people (including their profession) and things

> ### ¡OJO!
> Note that the indefinite article is not used after **ser** before unmodified (undescribed) nouns of profession: **Carmen es profesora.** *but* **Carmen es una buena profesora.**

Yo **soy estudiante.**
Alicia y yo **somos hermanas.**
La doctora Ramos **es profesora.**
Esto **es un libro.**

Description / La descripción

To *describe* people and things*

Soy sentimental.
I'm sentimental (a sentimental person).

El coche **es muy viejo.**
The car is very old.

Origin / El origen

With **de,** to express *origin*

Somos de Chile, pero nuestros padres **son de la Argentina. ¿De dónde es** Ud.?
We're from Chile, but our parents are from Argentina. Where are you from?

Generalizations / Las generalizaciones

To express *generalizations* (with **es** + *adjective*)

> ### ¡OJO!
> Note that **es** + *adjective* is followed by an infinitive in this context, just like in English.

Es necesario estudiar. Por eso no **es posible** mirar la televisión todos los días.
It's necessary to study. For that reason (That's why) it's not possible to watch television every day.

Here are two basic functions of **ser** that you have not yet practiced.

Possession / Las posesiones

With **de,** to express *possession,* to whom something belongs.

> ### ¡OJO!
> Note that there is no **'s** in Spanish.

—Este **es** el perro **de Carla.** ¿De quién son las gatas?
—**Son** las gatas **de Jorge.**
"This is Carla's dog. Whose are those (fem.) cats?"
"They're Jorge's cats."

The masculine singular article **el** contracts with **de** to form **del.** (No other article contracts with **de.**)

Esta **es** la casa **del** abuelo.
Esta **es** la casa **de la** abuela.

Use **¿de quién es... ?** to ask to whom something belongs.

—¿De quién es esta casa?
—Es del abuelo.
"Whose house is this?"
"It's grandfather's."

> ### ¡OJO!
> The subject pronoun **él** never contracts with **de: Es la casa** de él.

Destination / El destino

With **para,** to tell for whom or what something *is intended*

¿Romeo y Julieta? **Es para** la clase de inglés.
Romeo and Juliet? It's for English class.

—¿**Para** quién **son** los regalos?
¿Para mi nieto?
"Who are the presents for?" For my grandson?"

---

*You practiced this use of **ser** in **Gramática 5** in this chapter.

Práctica y comunicación

Summary of Uses of *ser*

- to identify
- to describe
- to express origin
- to express generalizations
- to express possession
- to express whom or what something is intended for

A. Así es mi familia (*That's what my family is like*)

Paso 1. Autoprueba. Complete las frases con las formas apropiadas del verbo **ser.**

1. yo _____
2. tú _____
3. Ud. _____
4. Pedro _____
5. tú y yo _____
6. Pedro y Alicia _____
7. Ud. y sus (*your*) amigos _____
8. tú y tus amigos _____

Paso 2. Complete las siguientes oraciones con formas del verbo **ser** y el adjetivo o frase apropiados.

1. Yo _____ miembro de una familia grande / pequeña.
2. Mi familia _____ de origen (*f.*) _____ (adjetivo de nacionaliad).
3. Mi familia más cercana (*closest*) y yo _____ del estado / país de(l) _____.
4. Otros parientes de mi familia _____ de _____ (estado o país).
5. Mi abuelo paterno / materno / abuela paterno / materna _____ de_____ (estado o país).
6. En mi familia, (no) _____ normal celebrar fiestas familiares / bailar en las fiestas familiares / estar en contacto con frecuencia...

Paso 3. Ahora use formas del verbo **ser** y las ideas del **Paso 2** para entrevistar (*interview*) a un compañero o una compañera.

1. ¿_____ miembro de una familia grande o pequeña?
2. ¿De qué nacionalidad _____ tu familia?
3. ¿De qué estado o país _____ tu familia y tú?
4. ¿De dónde _____ otros de tus parientes?
5. ¿De dónde _____ tu abuelo paterno/materno / tu abuela paterna/materna?
6. En tu familia, ¿_____ normal _____?

B. Nacionalidades

Paso 1. ¿De dónde son, según los nombres, apellidos y ciudades?

MODELO: João Gonçalves, Lisboa → João Gonçalves **es de** Portugal.

1. John Doe, Nueva York
2. Karl Lotze, Berlín
3. Graziana Lazzarino, Roma
4. Mongkut, Bangkok
5. María Gómez, San Salvador
6. Claudette Moreau, París
7. Timothy Windsor, Londres
8. Hai Chow, Beijing

Naciones

Alemania
China
El Salvador
los Estados Unidos
Francia
Inglaterra
Italia
Portugal
Tailandia

Paso 2. Ahora, dé su (*your*) información personal. ¿De dónde es Ud.? ¿De este estado / una metrópoli / un área rural? ¿Es de otro país?

C. Personas extranjeras

Paso 1. ¿Quiénes son, de dónde son y dónde trabajan ahora?

MODELO: **Teresa:** actriz / de Madrid / en Cleveland →
Teresa **es** actriz. **Es** de Madrid. **Ahora trabaja** en Cleveland.

1. **Carlos Miguel:** médico / de Cuba / en Milwaukee
2. **Pilar:** profesora / de Barcelona / en Miami
3. **Mariela:** dependienta / de Buenos Aires / en Nueva York
4. **Juan:** dentista* / de Lima / en Los Ángeles

Estrategia

Form complete sentences by supplying the missing verbs (indicated by /), as in the model.

Paso 2. Ahora hable sobre (*talk about*) un amigo o pariente, según el modelo del **Paso 1.**

---

*A number of professions end in **-ista** in both masculine and feminine forms. The article indicates gender: **el/la dentista, el/la artista,** and so on.

*Prác. A, Paso 1: Answers: **1.** soy **2.** eres **3.** es **4.** es **5.** somos **6.** son **7.** son **9.** sois/son*

D. ¿De quién es? Las siguientes cosas (*things*), ¿son de la rica actriz Jennifer Sánchez o de Martín Osborne, el estudiante (pobre, naturalmente)? En parejas, hagan y contesten preguntas. Las respuestas pueden (*can*) variar.

MODELO: la mochila →
  E1: ¿De quién es la mochila?
  E2: Es la mochila **del** estudiante. (La mochila es **del** estudiante.)

Estrategia

Use **son** with plural items:
¿De quién son los... ? Son...

1. la casa grande
2. la computadora
3. la limosina
4. los libros de texto
5. el Óscar
6. los exámenes
7. los ex esposos
8. el teléfono celular
9. los mensajes

E. ¡Somos como una familia!

Paso 1. Complete el párrafo con las formas correctas de **ser** o con **hay**.

Me llamo Antonia y _____[1] de Chicago. (Yo) _____[2] estudiante de ingeniería en la Universidad de Illinois. En mis clases _____[3] estudiantes de todas partes[a] y muchos de ellos _____[4] hispanos. Mi familia _____[5] de origen mexicano y aunque nunca he vivido[b] en México, hablo bastante bien[c] el español. Me gusta hablar español con mi amigo Javier. Javier _____[6] de Costa Rica y estudia ingeniería también. Javier y yo _____[7] los asistentes del profesor Thomas; por eso pasamos mucho tiempo juntos.[d] Javier _____[8] muy guapo y simpático, pero nosotros solo _____[9] buenos amigos. Javier _____[10] el novio[e] de mi mejor[f] amiga.

[a]*places* [b]aunque... *although I have never lived* [c]bastante... *rather well* [d]pasamos... *we spend a lot of time together* [e]*boyfriend* [f]*best*

Paso 2. Comprensión. ¿Cierto o falso? Corrija las oraciones falsas.

	CIERTO	FALSO
1. Antonia es una persona muy sociable.	☐	☐
2. Es de México.	☐	☐
3. Antonia y Javier son novios.	☐	☐

Nota **comunicativa**

Cómo dar° explicaciones: Porque y para + *infinitive* — *to give*

porque because

—¿Por qué trabajas tanto?
—¡**Porque** necesitamos dinero!

"Why do you work so much?"
"Because we need money!"

para + *inf.* in order to (*do something*)

—¿Por qué necesitamos una televisión nueva?
—Pues... **para** mirar el partido de fútbol...
  ¡Es la Copa Mundial!

"Why do we need a new TV set?"
"Well ... (in order) to watch the soccer game ... It's the World Cup!"

¡OJO!

Note: **porque** (one word, no accent) versus the interrogative **¿por qué?** (two words, accent on **qué**), meaning *why?*

You will practice using these words in **Práctica F.**

F. El regalo ideal

Paso 1. Look at Diego's list of gifts and what his family members like. With a partner, decide who receives each gift and why. A sample item is done for you.

MODELO: la camiseta (*t-shirt*) de la selección (*team*) nacional de México →
E1: **¿Para quién** es la camiseta de la selección nacional de México?
E2: **Es para** la prima.
E1: **¿Por qué?**
E2: **Porque** le gusta (*she likes*) el fútbol.

LOS REGALOS DE DIEGO

1. _____ una calculadora grande
2. _____ unas entradas (*tickets*) para un concierto
3. _____ un teléfono celular
4. _____ la última (*latest*) novela de Isabel Allende
5. _____ una suscripción para un canal de fútbol
6. _____ dinero

LOS MIEMBROS DE LA FAMILIA DE DIEGO

a. el primo: Desea estudiar en el extranjero (*abroad*).
b. el padre: Le gusta mucho mirar el fútbol.
c. los abuelos: Les gusta mucho la música clásica.
d. el hermano: Estudia ingeniería y toma clases de matemáticas
e. la hermana pequeña: Tiene 11 años y no tiene teléfono propio (*of her own*).
f. la madre: Le gusta mucho leer (*to read*).

Paso 2. With a partner, exchange ideas about good gifts for members of your family and also about good gifts for you.

MODELO: Para mi mamá, deseo comprar ropa, porque ella necesita ropa nueva. Yo necesito ropa nueva también.

G. ¿Qué opina Ud.? Exprese opiniones originales, afirmativas o negativas, con estas palabras como base.

MODELO: En mi opinión, **es importante hablar español en la clase de español.**

(no) es importante
(no) es muy práctico
(no) es necesario
(no) es absurdo
(no) es fascinante
(no) es una lata (*pain, drag*)
(no) es posible

+

mirar la televisión todos los días
hablar español en la clase
tener muchas mascotas
llegar (*to arrive*) a clase puntualmente
tomar café en el salón de clase
hablar con los animales / las plantas
tomar mucho café y fumar cigarrillos
trabajar dieciocho horas al día
tener muchos hermanos
ser amable con todos los miembros de la familia
estar mucho tiempo (*a lot of time*) con la familia

¿Recuerda Ud.?

You have already learned one way to express possession in Spanish: **de** + *noun*. Express these ideas in Spanish.

1. Juan's house
2. Jorge and Estela's grandfather
3. the man's niece
4. the student's book

You will learn another way to express possession in **Gramática 7.**

Grammar Tutorial 7

7 Expressing Possession

Unstressed Possessive Adjectives (Part 1)*

Gramática en acción: Invitación y posesión

los señores Ortega

los señores Gil

A. «¡Pasen, por favor! Nuestra casa es su casa.»

Juanita

Joaquín

B. «¡No son tus juguetes! ¡Son mis juguetes!»

Comprensión

En el dibujo A:
1. ¿De quién es la casa?
2. ¿Quiénes visitan la casa?

En el dibujo B:
3. ¿De quién son los juguetes?
4. ¿Quién desea jugar (*to play*) con los juguetes?

Possessive adjectives (**Los adjetivos posesivos**) are words that tell *to whom* or *to what* something belongs: *my* (book), *his* (sweater). You have already seen and used several possessive adjectives in Spanish. Here is the complete set.

Possessive Adjectives / Los adjetivos posesivos

my	mi hijo/hija	our	nuestro hijo	nuestra hija
	mis hijos/hijas		nuestros hijos	nuestras hijas
your (*fam.*)	tu hijo/hija	your (*fam.*)	vuestro hijo	vuestra hija
	tus hijos/hijas		vuestros hijos	vuestras hijas
your (*form.*), his, her, its	su hijo/hija	your (*form.*), their	su hijo / hija	
	sus hijos/hijas		sus hijos / hijas	

> *a possessive adjective /* **un adjetivo posesivo** = an adjective that expresses who owns or has something

1. Agreement with Person or Thing Possessed

In Spanish, the ending of a possessive adjective agrees in form with the person or thing owned, not with the owner or possessor. Note that these possessive adjectives are placed before the noun.

The possessive adjectives **mi(s)**, **tu(s)**, and **su(s)** show agreement in number only (as seen in the chart above). **Nuestro/a/os/as** and **vuestro/a/os/as**, like all adjectives that end in **-o**, show agreement in both number and gender.

Es { mi / tu / su } hermano.   Son { mis / tus / sus } hermanos.

Es { nuestra / vuestra / su } familia.   Son { nuestras / vuestras / sus } familias.

Invitation and Ownership A. "Come in, please! Our house is your house." *B.* "They're not your toys! They're my toys!"

*Another kind of possessive is called the stressed possessive adjective. It can be used as a noun. You will learn more about using stressed possessive adjectives in **Capítulo 17**.

2. Su(s)

As you have seen, the word **su(s)** has several equivalents in English: *your* (sing.), *his, her, its, your* (pl.), and *their*. Usually its meaning is clear in context. When the meaning is not clear, the construction *de + pronoun* is used to indicate possession.

su **hijo** = **el** hijo **de** } Ud., Uds.
él/ella
ellos/ellas

sus **hijos** = **los** hijos **de** } Ud., Uds.
él/ella
ellos/ellas

3. Su(s) *versus vuestro/a/os/as*

The forms **vuestro/a/os/as** are the possessives that correspond to the subject pronoun **vosotros.** They are only used in Spain.

Latin America

Uds. ⟶ su, sus

Spain

vosotros ⟶ vuestro/a/os/as

Uds. ⟶ su, sus

Práctica y comunicación

A. Las posesiones

> **Summary of possessive Adjectives**
>
> mi(s) nuestro/a(s)
> tu(s) vuestro/a(s)
> su(s)

Paso 1. Autoprueba. Complete la tabla con los posesivos apropiados. ¡OJO! Preste atención a (*Pay attention to*) las personas y los sustantivos. ¿Son masculinos o femeninos? ¿singulares o plurales? Siga (*Follow*) el modelo del número 1.

Personas	Adjetivos posesivos	Sustantivos
1. yo	**mi**	compañero de clase
2. nosotros = mi compañero/a y yo		computadoras
3. Ud.		mesa
4. los otros compañeros de clase		escritorios
5. tú		teléfono celular
6. Luisa		profesoras

Paso 2. Ahora indique los sustantivos posibles para cada (*each*) adjetivo posesivo según su forma.

1. su: problema primos dinero tías escritorios familia
2. tus: perro idea hijos profesoras abuelo examen
3. mi: ventana médicos cuarto coche abuela gatos
4. sus: animales oficina nietas padre hermana abuelo
5. nuestras: guitarra libros materias lápiz sobrinas tía
6. nuestros: gustos consejero parientes puertas clases residencia

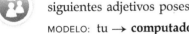

Paso 3. Ahora, en parejas, indiquen tres sustantivos para cada uno de los siguientes adjetivos posesivos.

MODELO: tu ⟶ **computadora, tía, perro**

Adjetivos posesivos (personas)	Tres sustantivos
1. mis	
2. su (de los compañeros de clase)	
3. sus (del profesor / de la profesora)	
4. nuestras (de nosotros dos)	

Prác. A, Paso 1: Answers: 2. nuestras **3.** su **4.** sus **5.** tu **6.** sus

B. ¿Cuáles son sus hijos? Empareje (*Match*) las fotos de padres e hijos.

LOS PADRES

LOS HIJOS

1. Su hija es _____.

a. David

2. Sus hijos son _____.

b. Sara

3. Sus hijas son _____.

c. Maribel y Julia

4. Su hijo es _____.

d. Joaquín y Rosa

C. David y su familia

David

Paso 1. Describa a la familia de David.

MODELO: familia / pequeño →
    Su familia **es** pequeñ**a.**

1. hijo / guapo
2. perro / feo
3. hija / rubio
4. padre / viejito
5. esposa / bonito

Paso 2. Ahora imagine que Ud. es David y modifique (*change*) las respuestas (*answers*).

MODELO: familia / pequeño →
    Mi familia es pequeñ**a.**

Paso 3. Ahora imagine que Ud. es la esposa de David. Hable por (*Speak for*) Ud. y por su esposo. Modifique solo las respuestas del 1 al 3.

MODELO: familia / pequeño →
    Nuestra familia es pequeñ**a.**

D. ¿Sí o no? Are the following things or people in your classroom right now? In these items, **su(s)** = *your* (**de Ud.**).

MODELOS: ¿su libro? → Sí, **mi** libro está en mi mochila. (No, **mi** libro está en casa.)
    ¿los amigos de Uds.? → No, **nuestros** amigos no están en el salón de clase. Están en la cafetería.

1. ¿su computadora portátil?
2. ¿los libros de Uds.?
3. ¿el profesor / la profesora de Uds.?
4. ¿la computadora del profesor / de la profesora de Uds.?
5. ¿los teléfonos celulares de Uds.?
6. ¿su silla?
7. ¿sus padres? / ¿su esposo/a?
8. ¿la mochila de otro estudiante?
9. ¿su dinero? (la cartera = *wallet*)

E. Intercambios

Paso 1. With a partner, take turns asking and answering questions about your families. Talk about what family members are like, their ages, some things they do, and so on. Use the model as a guide. Take notes on what your partner says.

MODELO: tu abuela →
> E1: Mi abuela es alta. ¿Y tu abuela? ¿Es alta?
> E2: Bueno, no. Mi abuela es baja.
> E1: ¿Cuántos años tiene?...

1. tu familia en general
2. tus padres
3. tus abuelos
4. tus hermanos/hijos
5. tu esposo/a / compañero/a de cuarto/casa

Paso 2. Tell the class one thing that you and your partner have in common.

MODELO: Nuestras abuelas tienen 75 años.

¿Recuerda Ud.?

The personal endings used with **-ar** verbs share some characteristics with **-er** and **-ir** verbs, which you will learn in **Gramática 8**. Review the present tense endings of **-ar** verbs by telling which subject pronoun(s) you associate with each of these endings.

1. -amos **2.** -as **3.** -áis **4.** -an **5.** -o **6.** -a

8 Expressing Actions
Present Tense of -er and -ir Verbs; Subject Pronouns (Part 2)

Gramática en acción: Un estudiante típico

- Se llama Samuel Flores Toledo.
- Estudia en la UNAM (Universidad Nacional Autónoma de México).
- Vive con su familia en la Ciudad de México, el D.F. (Distrito Federal).
- Come pizza y tacos con frecuencia.
- Bebe café por la mañana.
- Recibe muchos e-mails de sus primos del Canadá.
- Lee y escribe mucho para su especialización.
- Aprende inglés porque desea visitar a su familia en Ontario.

¿Y Ud.? Complete las oraciones con formas verbales que terminan en **-o** (= **yo**) y con información personal.

1. Yo (no) vivo con mi familia.
2. (No) Com_____ muchos tacos.
3. Recib_____ muchos e-mails de _____.
4. Le_____ y escrib_____ mucho para mi clase de _____.
5. Aprend_____ español en esta clase.

Samuel Flores Toledo

A typical student ■ *His name is Samuel Flores Toledo.* ■ *He studies at UNAM (the National Autonomous University of Mexico).* ■ *He lives with his family in Mexico City,* **el D.F.** *(Federal District).* ■ *He frequently eats pizza and tacos.* ■ *He drinks coffee in the morning.* ■ *He gets a lot of e-mails from his cousins in Canada.* ■ *He reads and writes a lot for his major.* ■ *He's learning English because he wants to visit his family in Ontario.*

1. Present Tense Endings

The present tense of **-er** and **-ir** verbs is formed by adding personal endings to the stem of the verb (the infinitive minus its **-er/-ir** ending). The personal endings for **-er** and **-ir** verbs are the same except for the first and second person plural.

¡OJO!

Only the endings for **nosotros** and **vosotros** are different for -**er** and -**ir** verbs.

Las terminaciones -er/-ir del tiempo presente			
-er		**-ir**	
-o	-emos	-o	-imos
-es	-éis	-es	-ís
-e	-en	-e	-en

comer (to eat)				vivir (to live)			
(yo)	**como**	(nosotros/as)	**comemos**	(yo)	**vivo**	(nosotros/as)	**vivimos**
(tú)	**comes**	(vosotros/as)	**coméis**	(tú)	**vives**	(vosotros/as)	**vivís**
(Ud.) (él) (ella)	**come**	(Uds.) (ellos) (ellas)	**comen**	(Ud.) (él) (ella)	**vive**	(Uds.) (ellos) (ellas)	**viven**

2. Important -er/-ir Verbs

These are the frequently used **-er** and **-ir** verbs you will find in this chapter.

comer
beber
leer
escribir

-er verbs		-ir verbs	
aprender	to learn	**abrir**	to open
aprender +a + inf.	to learn how to (do something)	**asistir (a)**	to attend, go to (a class, a function)
beber	to drink		
comer	to eat	**escribir**	to write
comprender	to understand	**recibir**	to receive
creer (en)	to think; to believe (in)	**vivir**	to live
deber + inf.	should, must, ought to (do something)		
leer	to read		
vender	to sell		

- **Deber,** like **desear** and **necesitar,** is followed by an infinitive.

- **Aprender + a +**infinitive means to learn how to (do something).

Debes leer tus e-mails todos los días.
You should read your e-mails on a daily basis.

Muchos niños **aprenden a hablar** español con sus abuelos.
Many children learn to speak Spanish with their grandparents.

3. English Equivalents of the Present Tense

Remember that the Spanish present tense has a number of present tense equivalents in English. It can also be used to express future meaning.

como = *I eat, I am eating, I will eat*

Uses of Subject Pronouns / Los usos de los pronombres personales

In English, a verb must have an expressed subject (a noun or pronoun): *the train arrives*, *she says*. In Spanish, however, as you have probably noticed, an expressed subject is not required. Verbs are accompanied by a subject pronoun only for clarification, emphasis, or contrast.

- *Clarification:* When the context does not make the subject clear, the subject pronoun is expressed. This happens most frequently with third person singular and plural verb forms.

Unclear: Escribe cartas. Nunca **escribe** cartas. →
Ella escribe cartas. **Él** nunca escribe cartas.
She writes letters. He never writes letters.

- *Emphasis:* Subject pronouns are used in Spanish to emphasize the subject when in English you would stress it with your voice.

—¿Quién debe pagar?   *"Who should pay?"*
—¡**Tú** debes pagar!   *"**You** should pay!"*

- *Contrast:* Contrast is a special case of emphasis. Subject pronouns are used to contrast the actions of two individuals or groups.

Ellos leen mucho; **nosotros** leemos poco.
***They** read a lot; **we** read little.*

¡OJO!

Avoid using subject pronouns in Spanish when they are not necessary. The overuse of subject pronouns sounds overbearing to native speakers of Spanish.

Unnecessary: Yo soy de Tampa. **Yo** soy estudiante universitario. **Yo** vivo con mi familia.

Natural: (Yo) Soy de Tampa. Soy estudiante universitario. Vivo con mi familia.

Práctica y comunicación

A. Asociaciones. Empareje las ideas y cosas (*things*) con el verbo más lógico. Luego (*Then*) dé otras ideas para cada (*each*) verbo.

MODELO: 1. abrir → e: abrir **una puerta** También: abrir **una ventana**...

Summary of -er/-ir Verb Endings			
(yo)	-o	(nosotros/as)	–emos / -imos
(tú)	-es	(vosotros/as)	-éis / -ís
(Uds., el/ella)	-e	(Uds., ellos/as)	-en

VERBOS
1. abrir
2. aprender
3. asistir a
4. beber
5. comer
6. deber
7. escribir
8. leer
9. vivir

IDEAS Y COSAS
a. una revista (*magazine*)
b. una composición
c. un té
d. las materias
e. una puerta
f. un concierto
g. tacos
h. estudiar más
i. en un apartamento

Algo sobre...

la comida[a] de México

El maíz[b] es el producto esencial en la comida de los mexicanos y otros pueblos[c] americanos desde[d] 1500 a. C. (mil quinientos antes de Cristo). Es la base para las tortillas y los tamales. El tamal consiste en masa[e] de maíz con otros ingredientes, envuelta[f] y cocida[g] en hojas[h] de maíz (u* hojas de otras plantas, como el plátano[i]).

 En su opinión, ¿qué ingrediente(s) son esenciales en la comida de su país de origen?

[a]*food* [b]*corn* [c]*peoples* [d]*since* [e]*dough* [f]*wrapped* [g]*steamed* [h]*leaves* [i]*plantain*

Un delicioso tamal mexicano

---

*Notice that the word **o** becomes **u** before a word that starts with the sound **o**: inglés **u** otra materia, pesimista **u** optimista. In* **Algo sobre...** *above, the word* **hoja** *starts with the sound* **o**, *since the letter* **h** *is silent in Spanish.*

B. En la clase de español

Paso 1. Autoprueba. Complete los verbos con las terminaciones apropiadas.

1. yo: com_____, viv_____
2. tú: aprend_____, escrib_____
3. él: cre_____, abr_____
4. nosotros: le_____, asist_____
5. Uds.: comprend_____, recib_____

Paso 2. Ahora use las siguientes ideas para expresar acciones que Ud. hace (*do*) o no hace en la clase de español.

MODELO: comer en clase → **Como** en clase. (No **como** en clase.)

1. escribir respuestas en el libro de texto
2. aprender palabras nuevas
3. asistir a clase todos los días
4. beber café en clase
5. comprender las instrucciones para las actividades
6. abrir regalos

Paso 3. Ahora, en parejas, túrnense para hacer y contestar preguntas basadas en el **Paso 2**. Luego (*Then*) digan (*tell*) a la clase algo (*something*) que Uds. tienen en común.

MODELO: escribir respuestas en el libro texto →
    E1: ¿Escribes respuestas en el libro de texto?
    E2: No, no escribo respuestas en el libro de texto.
    E2: Yo tampoco. (*Me neither.*) (Yo sí.)
EN COMÚN: Nosotros/as dos (no) escribimos respuestas en el libro de texto.

C. Diego habla de su padre.
Complete el siguiente párrafo con la forma correcta de los verbos entre paréntesis.

Mi padre (vender[1]) coches y trabaja mucho. Mis hermanos y yo (aprender[2]) mucho de papá. Según mi padre, los jóvenes (deber[3]) (asistir[4]) a clase todos los días, porque es su obligación. Papá también (creer[5]) que no es necesario mirar la televisión por la noche. Es más interesante (leer[6]) el periódico,[a] una revista o un buen libro. Por eso (*nosotros:* leer[7]) o (escribir[8]) por la noche y no miramos la televisión. Yo admiro a mi papá y (creer[9]) que él (comprender[10]) la importancia de la educación.

[a]*newspaper*

Comprensión. ¿Cierto o falso? Corrija las oraciones falsas.

	CIERTO	FALSO
1. Diego y sus hermanos venden coches.	☐	☐
2. Diego mira mucho la televisión.	☐	☐
3. El padre de Diego lee mucho.	☐	☐

Prác. B, Paso 1: Answers: 1. como, vivo **2.** aprendes, escribes **3.** cree, abre **4.** leemos, asistimos **5.** comprenden, reciben

Una escena típica de una tamalada

D. Este domingo, tamalada

Paso 1. Una tamalada consiste en hacer (*making*) y comer tamales. Hay familias que hacen una tamalada en ocasiones especiales.

Complete las siguientes oraciones con la forma apropiada de un verbo de **Vocabulario útil**. El número 2 entre paréntesis indica que Ud. debe usar el verbo dos veces (*twice*) en las oraciones.

> **¡OJO!**
>
> Hay verbos de todos tipos en la lista: **-ar, -er, -ir,** irregular.

> **Vocabulario útil**
>
> aprender, asistir, beber, celebrar, comprender, creer, deber, leer (2), mirar, preparar, ser (2), vivir

1. Hoy todos nosotros _____¹ el cumpleaños (*birthday*) de mi abuela y, como es domingo, hay una tamalada.
2. Toda la familia _____² a la tamalada en nuestra casa.
3. Mis padres y mis tíos _____³ los tamales, con la ayuda (*help*) de las mujeres de la familia.
4. Después de comer (*After eating*), los adultos _____⁴ café.
5. Muchos _____⁵ la tele y mi padre _____⁶ el periódico.
6. Yo _____⁷ un libro a los niños pequeños. Mi prima Lucy _____⁸ descansar (*rest*) porque solo tiene 2 años.
7. Mi primo Rudy, que (*who*) _____⁹ en Oklahoma, no _____¹⁰ todo porque su español no _____¹¹ perfecto. Pero _____¹² rápido.
8. Yo _____¹³ que todos en mi familia _____¹⁴ cocineros (*cooks*) excelentes.

Paso 2. Comprensión. Complete las oraciones con información del **Paso 1.**

1. _____ es un ejemplo de una fiesta familiar.
2. Esta familia celebra _____ de la abuela.
3. _____ preparan los tamales; _____ ayudan (*help*).
4. Después de comer, unos _____ y _____.
5. La persona que narra la historia (*story*) _____.
6. Rudy no _____ bien el español.

Nota **comunicativa**

Cómo expresar la frecuencia de las acciones

AT THE BEGINNING OR END OF A SENTENCE

a veces	sometimes, at times
con frecuencia	frequently
siempre	always
todos los días	every day
una vez a la semana	once a week

AT THE BEGINNING OF A SENTENCE

casi nunca	almost never
nunca	never

Hablo con mis amigos **todos los días.** Hablo con mis padres **una vez a la semana. Casi nunca** hablo con mis abuelos. Y **nunca** hablo con mis tíos que viven en Italia.

You will use these expressions in **Práctica E.**

Algo sobre...

una gran ciudad mexicana

Más de[a] 21 millones de personas viven en el área metropolitana de la Ciudad de México, o el Distrito Federal. Los mexicanos lo llaman[b] simplemente el D.F.

México, D.F.

 ¿Cuántos habitantes hay en su ciudad?

[a]Más... *More than* [b]lo... *call it*

E. ¿Con qué frecuencia?

Paso 1. Indique con oraciones completas la frecuencia con que Ud. hace (*do*) las siguientes actividades.

EXPRESIONES DE FRECUENCIA:

todos los días   con frecuencia   a veces   casi nunca   nunca

MODELO: 1. recibir un e-mail de **sus** padres/abuelos →
Todos los días recibo e-mails de **mis** abuelos. / **Nunca recibo** un e-mail de **mis** abuelos.

1. recibir un e-mail de sus padres/abuelos
2. escribir en su Facebook
3. usar la computadora en una clase
4. comer pizza
5. leer revistas
6. beber café
7. comprar cosas por (*on the*) internet
8. vender sus libros al final del semestre/trimestre

 Paso 2. Ahora compare sus oraciones con las (*those*) de dos compañeros/as. Luego (*Then*) digan (*tell*) a la clase algo (*something*) que Uds. tienen en común.

MODELO: 1. recibir un e-mail de **sus** padres/abuelos →
EN COMÚN: Todos los días los/las tres recibimos un e-mail de **nuestros** abuelos. (Nunca recibimos un e-mail de **nuestros** abuelos.)

 **F. Intercambios.** Use las siguientes frases para entrevistar a un compañero o una compañera. Use expresiones de frecuencia cuando sea (*it is*) apropiado. Luego (*Then*) digan (*tell*) a la clase algo (*something*) que Uds. tienen en común.

MODELO: leer + novelas de horror
→ Carmen, ¿lees novelas de horror a veces?
EN COMÚN: Los/Las dos leemos novelas de horror a veces. (Nunca leemos novelas de horror.)

(nombre de estudiante),
    tú
tus padres/hijos
tus abuelos
tu mejor (*best*) amigo/a

+

abrir
beber
comprender
escribir
leer
recibir
vender
vivir
¿ ?

+

mucho / poco

la situación / los problemas de los estudiantes
Coca-Cola/café antes de (*before*) la clase
tu ropa (*clothing*), un estéreo viejo
la puerta a (*for*) las mujeres / los hombres

novelas de ciencia ficción / de horror
el periódico / una revista todos los días
muchas/pocas cartas, novelas, revistas
muchos/pocos ejercicios, libros, regalos

en una casa / un apartamento / una residencia
en otra ciudad / en otro estado/país
en un cuaderno / con un bolígrafo/lápiz

+ deber **+** mirar mucho la televisión
llegar a casa temprano

Un poco de todo

¿América?

En la cultura hispana se enseña que[a] América es un continente que incluye Norteamérica, Centroamérica y Sudamérica. Por eso[b] el término **americano/a** se usa[c] para referirse[d] a las personas o cosas de todo el continente, no solo de los Estados Unidos. La palabra **estadounidense** se aplica a los Estados Unidos en particular.

México es un país norteamericano. Por eso los mexicanos son americanos, ¿no?

 ¿Cuántos continentes hay en este hemisferio según se enseña[e] en los Estados Unidos?

¡América!

[a]se... *people are taught that* [b]Por... *That's why* [c]se... *is used* [d]para... *to refer* [e]según... *as is taught*

A. Lengua y cultura: Las familias

Paso 1. Complete the following paragraphs about families. Give the correct form of the words in parentheses, as suggested by context.

¿Existe la familia hispana típica? La idea de que las familias hispanas son muy (grande[1]) es un estereotipo del pasado,[a] especialmente en las (grande[2]) ciudades. Ahora, la norma (ser[3]) una familia con dos o tres hijos. Es difícil tener (mucho[4]) hijos cuando el padre y la madre (trabajar[5]) fuera de la casa,[b] y cuando los abuelos o tías no (vivir[6]) en casa para cuidar[c] a los niños.

A pesar de[d] la reducción en el número de hijos, los hispanos (creer[7]) que la familia es su institución (principal[8]). Muchos hispanos mantienen[e] relaciones con parientes que (estar[9]) en otro país y muchos les mandan[f] dinero y regalos para ayudarlos.[g] En las reuniones (familiar[10]) también es frecuente incluir a parientes de (vario[11]) generaciones.

En su opinión, ¿hay (mucho[12]) diferencias entre su familia y las familias hispanas que conoce[h]?

Una familia mexicana que celebra un día especial

[a]*past* [b]fuera... *outside the home* [c]cuidar... *care for* [d]A... *In spite of* [e]*keep up, maintain* [f]les... *send to them* [g]*help them* [h]*you know*

Paso 2. Comprensión. ¿Cierto o falso? Corrija (*Correct*) las oraciones falsas.

	CIERTO	FALSO
1. Todas las familias hispanas son grandes.	☐	☐
2. Por lo general (*Generally*), las familias urbanas son pequeñas.	☐	☐
3. Para los hispanos, la familia es una institución social fundamental.	☐	☐

Paso 3. Ahora, en parejas, contesten la pregunta del final de **Lengua y cultura:** «¿Hay muchas diferencias entre su familia y las familias hispanas que conoce?» Deben escribir 3–4 oraciones para expresar su opinión. Usen las oraciones de **Lengua y cultura** como modelo y hagan los cambios (*changes*) necesarios. **¡OJO!** No es necesario usar todo el texto original.

MODELOS: En **nuestra** opinión (no) hay muchas diferencias entre **nuestras** familias y las familias hispanas.
No estamos de acuerdo. Yo creo que... pero mi compañera cree...
En la familia típica estadounidense/mexicana, hay...

B. Una fiesta. There is a Spanish saying, **«Una fiesta se hace** (*is made*) **con tres personas: una canta, otra baila y la otra toca.»** Working in groups of four, use this saying as a model to tell what the following things are "made of."

MODELO: una clase → Una clase se hace con un profesor o una profesora. Esta persona enseña la clase. También hay unos estudiantes. Desean aprender la materia y estudian mucho. Leen su libro de texto y escriben informes (*papers*). También hay un salón de clase, un pizarrón...

¿Cómo se hace... ?

1. una clase de español
2. una fiesta en esta universidad
3. una universidad
4. una familia

En **su** comunidad

Entreviste a (*Interview*) una persona hispana de su universidad o ciudad sobre (*about*) su familia.

PREGUNTAS POSIBLES

- ¿Tiene esta persona una familia grande o pequeña? ¿Cuáles son los miembros de la familia?
- ¿Cuál es el país de origen de los abuelos de la persona? ¿Viven solos (*alone*) o con un pariente?
- ¿Los parientes se reúnen (*get together*) con frecuencia? ¿En qué ocasiones?

SALU2

«Padres modernos» Segmento 2

Antes de mirar°

Antes... *Before watching*

Conteste las siguientes preguntas.

1. ¿De dónde es su familia?
2. ¿Tiene parientes en ese (*that*) país?
3. ¿Cree que su familia es muy unida (*close*)?

Este segmento

Laura entrevista (*interviews*) a los miembros de una familia mexicana que vive en Los Ángeles.

Las hermanas Minerva (de blanco [*in white*]) y Araceli Rubio, con sus hijos. Todos extrañan (*miss*) a los parientes que están en México.

Vocabulario del segmento

único/a	unique; only
una vida mejor	a better life
mil novecientos noventa y nueve	1999
mayor	oldest
estar solo/a	to be alone
han crecido juntos	they've grown up together
dejar atrás	to leave behind

Fragmento del guion°

script

El año pasado hubo[a] una celebración especial en México. Una sobrina de Minerva y Araceli cumplió 15 años.[b] Mine fue[c] a México para estar en la celebración de la quinceañera[d] de su prima. Fue[e] una buena oportunidad de estar cerca del[f] resto de su familia y ver[g] a todos los parientes: abuelos, tíos, primos. ¡Fue una fiesta fantástica!

[a]*El... Last year there was* [b]*cumplió... turned 15* [c]*went* [d]*fifteenth birthday* [e]*It was* [f]*cerca... close to the* [g]*to see*

Después de mirar°

Después... *After watching*

A. ¿Está claro? ¿Cierto o falso? Corrija las oraciones falsas según el video.

	CIERTO	FALSO
1. Minerva tiene dos hijas.	☐	☐
2. Las hijas de Minerva viven en California.	☐	☐
3. Araceli tiene 3 hijos.	☐	☐
4. Los hijos de Araceli y de Minerva no son unidos.	☐	☐

B. Un poco más. Conteste las siguientes preguntas.

1. ¿Qué miembros de esta familia viven en los Estados Unidos?
2. ¿Qué celebración importante para la familia de Minerva y Araceli hubo en México?

C. Y ahora, Uds. En grupos, hablen de (*talk about*) la familia. ¿Es importante la familia extendida en su caso? ¿Qué parientes incluye? ¿Incluye a parientes que viven en otro país? ¿Cómo es su familia? ¿Es tradicional? ¿patriarcal? ¿matriarcal?

A LEER°

A... *Let's read*

Antes de leer

¿Es normal para los jóvenes estadounidenses vivir con su familia cuando tienen 20 años o más? Si Ud. vive con su familia, ¿le gusta? ¿Le gusta vivir cerca de (*close to*) su familia?

Lectura cultural: México
La institución de la familia en México

or tradición,[a] las familias en México son muy unidas. Esto tiene ventajas[b] para los niños y adolescentes: tienen el apoyo[c] de sus padres, hermanos y parientes cercanos.[d] Pero hay personas que creen que esta unión familiar presenta problemas. Cuando los jóvenes viven con sus padres hasta que[e] son adultos, pueden perder[f] parte de su identidad individual. Muchos jóvenes viven con su familia hasta que contraen matrimonio.[g] Y si no contraen matrimonio, siempre viven en casa de sus padres.

Aquí hay unas cifras para pensar.[h]

- El 90,5% (noventa coma cinco por ciento) de los hogares[i] mexicanos es de tipo familiar, es decir,[j] entre[k] las personas que los forman[l] existe una relación familiar.
- El 18,5% de los hogares familiares es monoparental. Las mujeres son responsables de su familia[m] en el 84% de los hogares monoparentales.
- México, D.F. tiene la mayor[n] proporción de hogares monoparentales en el país: el 24,3%.

[a]Por... *Traditionally* [b]*advantages* [c]*support* [d]*close* [e]*hasta... until* [f]*pueden... they can lose* [g]*hasta... until they marry* [h]*cifras... numbers to think about* [i]*homes* [j]*es... that is* [k]*among* [l]*los... make them up* [m]*responsables... the heads of the household* [n]*greatest*

La Pirámide del Sol (*Sun*) en la antigua ciudad de Teotihuacán, cerca de (*close to*) la Ciudad de México. Tiene 63,5 metros de altura (*height*).

Un símbolo mexicano: Los centros arqueológicos

Hay muchos por todo el país, pero los más importantes son las ruinas mayas de Chichén Itzá (cerca de[a] Cancún), el complejo[b] de Teotihuacán (cerca del D.F.) y las ruinas zapotecas (cerca de Oaxaca).

[a]cerca... *close to* [b]*building complex*

COMPRENSIÓN

¿Cierto o falso? Identifique la parte de los textos donde aparece la información.

	CIERTO	FALSO
1. La unidad de la familia mexicana tiene aspectos positivos para los hijos.	☐	☐
2. Para los jóvenes, vivir con la familia es siempre ideal.	☐	☐
3. La estructura familiar mexicana es única en el mundo hispanohablante.	☐	☐
4. En México hay ruinas de solo una cultura indígena.	☐	☐

En otros países hispanos

En todo el mundo hispanohablante Es impresionante cómo los hispanos de todos los países coinciden en cuanto a[a] la importancia de la familia. También es típico en todo el mundo hispano que los hijos se independicen tarde.

[a]en... *with regards to*

 Y ahora, Uds.

- ¿Creen Uds. que la unión familiar es una ventaja o una desventaja?
- ¿Hay ejemplos de ruinas arqueológicas en su estado?

Del mundo hispano

Antes de leer°

Antes... *Before reading*

Match the sentences with the numbers given in **Números útiles**. If you don't know, guess! **¡OJO!** In Spanish, decimals are marked with a comma: 3.4 = **3,4 (tres coma cuatro)**.

Números útiles: 1,32; 1,65; 2; 2,06; 2,2; 3; 4; 5; 6; 8; 40

1. _____: número de semanas de un embarazo (*pregnancy*) normal
2. _____: número de bebés, si son mellizos o gemelos (*twins*)
3. _____: número de bebés, si son octillizos
4. _____: número de bebés, si son quintillizos
5. _____: número de bebés, si son trillizos
6. _____: número de libras (*pounds*) en 1 kilogramo
7. _____: promedio (*average number*) de hijos por mujer en Puerto Rico
8. _____: promedio de hijos por mujer en España
9. _____: promedio de hijos por mujer en los Estados Unidos

Lectura: Un parto° excepcional en la República Dominicana

birth

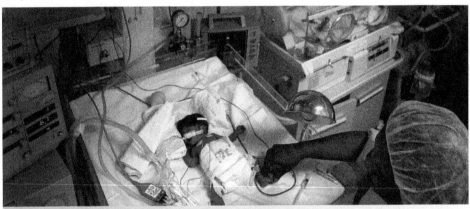

Uno de los sextillizos dominicanos

27 de diciembre, Hospital Plaza de la Salud, Santo Domingo, República Dominicana: Máxima Pérez y su esposo Emilio Figueroa son ahora los padres de sextillizos. Pérez se sometió a[a] un tratamiento de fertilidad y dio a luz[b] mediante una cesárea. Los bebés nacieron tras[c] 29 semanas de embarazo y pesaron[d] entre 800 y 1.000 gramos. Es la primera vez[e] que en el país se produce un parto de seis criaturas.

[a]*se... went through* [b]*dio... gave birth* [c]*nacieron... were born after* [d]*they weighed* [e]*la... the first time*

Comprensión

A. Resumen de la noticia (*Summary of the news item*).

Para resumir la información de la noticia, complete las oraciones con las palabras apropiadas.

esposo   fertilidad   padres   República   seis   sextillizos

Noticias de la _____[1] Dominicana:

La Sra. Máxima Pérez y su _____,[2] el Sr. Emilio Figueroa, son ahora los _____[3] de _____[4] hijos, gracias a un tratamiento de _____.[5] No hay otro caso de _____[6] en la historia del país.

B. En el texto. Encuentre (*Find*) las siguientes ideas y palabras en la noticia.

1. *birth*
2. *babies* (2 *words*)
3. *through a C-section*
4. *fertility treatment*

A ESCUCHAR°

La familia de Lucía Jiménez Flores

A... *Let's listen*

Vocabulario para escuchar

la escuela	school
la cuñada	sister-in-law
travieso/a	troublemaker
las mellizas	twins
juntas	together

Antes de escuchar

¿Tiene Ud. hermanos casados (*married*)? ¿Tiene buenas relaciones con sus cuñados (*in-laws*)? ¿Tiene padrinos (*godparents*) o es padrino o madrina de un niño?

Después de escuchar°

Después... *After listening*

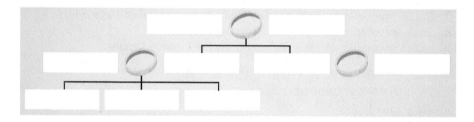

A. **El árbol genealógico de la familia.** Complete el árbol genealógico con los nombres de los miembros de la familia.

B. **¿Quién es quién?** Complete las oraciones.

1. La cuñada de Lucía se llama _____.
2. El cuñado de José se llama _____.
3. Lucía tiene tres _____.
4. La abuela de Camila tiene _____ años.
5. El nombre del padre de Lucía es _____.
6. La familia de Lucía es de _____ (ciudad).
7. En México, Lucía tiene muchos _____.

PRODUCCIÓN PERSONAL

¡Ahora, yo!

A. Use de (*as a*) modelo las preguntas y respuestas de la página 61 de este capítulo para hablar de su propia (*own*) familia.

B. Con las preguntas de la página 61 como modelo, filme una o dos entrevistas con personas que hablan de sus familias.

A ESCRIBIR

Un ensayo sobre° la familia

ensayo... *essay about*

¿Cómo es la familia «moderna» estadounidense? ¿Es diversa? ¿complicada? ¿Hay una familia estereotípica? ¿Qué une (*unites*) a los miembros de una familia?

Preparar

Paso 1. Use las siguientes preguntas para entrevistar a varios compañeros de clase. Sus respuestas le darán (*will give you*) información específica para defender sus ideas en su ensayo. Repase (*Review*) el vocabulario de **Más parientes** (pág. 63) antes de empezar.

- ¿Viven tus padres en el mismo domicilio (*same residence*)?
- ¿Cuántos hermanos tienes?
- ¿Tienes padrastro / madrastra / hermanastro/a(s) / hijastro/a(s) / medio/a(s) hermano/a(s) / ?
- ¿Viven tus abuelos en el mismo estado?
- ¿Cuál es el país de origen de tu familia?
- _____ (una pregunta propia [*of your own*])

Paso 2. Ahora use sus opiniones y las respuestas de sus compañeros para escribir un ensayo sobre la familia moderna. Hay más ayuda (*help*) en Connect.

Más ideas para su portafolio

- Busque (*Look for*) una fotografía de su familia y seleccione un adjetivo especial para cada persona de la foto.

- Escriba un breve poema sobre (*about*) una persona de su familia que es muy especial para Ud. Aquí está el modelo de la página 69.

Amigo	Amiga
Fiel	Fiel
Amable	Amable
Simpático	Simpática
¡Lo admiro!	¡La admiro!

Sugerencia: You are now ready to play Quest 2 in **Practice Spanish: Study Abroad** (www.mhpractice.com).

- Dé tres palabras favoritas de este capítulo para Ud. ¿Por qué son interesantes para Ud.? ¿Con qué las asocia Ud. (*do you associate them*)?

- Si ha estado jugando (*have been playing*) Practice Spanish: Study Abroad, en Quest 2 Ud. conoció (*met*) a un fantasma (*ghost*) que se llama la Mancarita. Dibuje (*Draw*) a la Mancarita y luego escriba 4 oraciones describiéndola (*describing her*).

EN RESUMEN En este capítulo

LEARNSMART
Visit **www.connectspanish.com** to practice the vocabulary and grammar points covered in this chapter.

AFTER STUDYING THIS CHAPTER I CAN . . .

☐ name family members (62–63)

☐ count from 31 to 100 (64)

☐ describe people, places, things, and ideas using adjectives and the verb **ser** (66, 69–71)

☐ also use **ser** to identify and to expres origin, generalizations, possession, and destination (75–77)

☐ use possessive adjectives to distinguish what's mine and what belongs to others (80–81)

☐ talk about more actions with **-er** and **-ir** verbs (83–85)

☐ avoid subject pronouns but use them to clarify or emphasize the subject (85)

☐ recognize/describe at least 2–3 aspects of Mexican cultures

Gramática en breve

5. Adjectives: Gender, Number, and Position

Adjective Endings

Singular	Plural
-o	-os
-a	-as
-e	-es
-[consonant]	-[consonant] + -es

6. Present Tense of *ser;* Summary of Uses

ser: soy, eres, es, somos, sois, son

Uses of **ser**: identification, description, origin, generalizations, possession, destination

de + el → del

7. Unstressed Possessive Adjectives

yo → mi(s) nosotros → nuestro/a(s)
tú → tu(s) vosotros → vuestro/a(s)
Ud., él, → su(s) Uds., ellos, → su(s)
ella ellas

8. Present Tense of *-er* and *-ir* Verbs; Subject Pronouns

Regular -er Verb Endings

-o, -es, -e, -emos, -éis, -en

Regular -ir Verb Endings

-o, -es, -e, -imos, -ís, -en

When to use subject pronouns: for clarification, emphasis, and contrast.

Vocabulario

Los verbos

abrir	to open
aprender	to learn
aprender a + *inf.*	to learn how to (*do something*)
asistir (a)	to attend, go to (a *class, a function*)
beber	to drink
comer	to eat
comprender	to understand
creer (en)	to think; to believe (in)
deber + *inf.*	should; must; ought to (*do something*)
escribir	to write
leer	to read
llegar	to arrive
mirar	to look at; to watch
mirar la tele(visión)	to watch television
recibir	to receive
ser (soy, eres,...)	to be (I am, you are . . .)
vender	to sell
vivir	to live

La familia y los parientes

el/la abuelo/a	grandfather/grandmother
los abuelos	grandparents
el/la esposo/a	husband/wife
el/la hermano/a	brother/sister
los hermanos	siblings
el/la hijo/a	son/daughter
los hijos	children
la madre (mamá)	mother (mom)
el marido	husband
la mujer	wife
el/la nieto/a	grandson/granddaughter
el/la niño/a	small child; boy/girl
el padre (papá)	father (dad)
los padres	parents
el pariente	relative
el/la primo/a	cousin
los primos	cousins
el/la sobrino/a	nephew/niece
el/la tío/a	uncle/aunt
los tíos	aunts and uncles

Las mascotas

el gato	cat
la mascota	pet
el pájaro	bird
el perro	dog

Otros sustantivos

la carta	letter
la casa	house, home
la ciudad	city
el coche	car
el estado	state
el/la médico/a	(medical) doctor
el mundo	world
el país	country
el periódico	newspaper
el regalo	present, gift
la revista	magazine

Los adjetivos

alto/a	tall
amable	kind; nice
antipático/a	unpleasant, unlikeable
bajo/a	short (*in height*)
bonito/a	pretty
buen, bueno/a	good
corto/a	short (*in length*)
delgado/a	thin, slender
este/a	this
estos/as	these
feo/a	ugly
fiel	faithful
gordo/a	fat
gran, grande	large, big; great
guapo/a	handsome, good-looking
joven	young
largo/a	long
listo/a	smart; clever
mal, malo/a	bad
moreno/a	brunet(te)
mucho/a	a lot (of)
muchos/as	many
nuevo/a	new
otro/a	other, another
pequeño/a	small
perezoso/a	lazy
pobre	poor
rico/a	rich
rubio/a	blond(e)
simpático/a	nice, likeable
todo/a	all; every
tonto/a	silly, foolish
trabajador(a)	hardworking
viejo/a	old

Cognados: hispano/a, inteligente, necesario/a, posible

Los adjetivos de nacionalidad

alemán/alemana	German
español(a)	Spanish
estadounidense	U.S.
inglés/inglesa	English
mexicano/a	Mexican

Los adjetivos posesivos

mi(s)	my
tu(s)	your (*fam. sing.*)
nuestro/a(s)	our
vuestro/a(s)	your (*fam. pl., Sp.*)
su(s)	his, hers, its; your (*form. sing.*); their; your (*form. pl.*)

Los números del 31 al 100

treinta, cuarenta, cincuenta, sesenta, setenta, ochenta, noventa, cien

¿Con qué frecuencia... ?

a veces	sometimes, at times
casi	almost
casi nunca	almost never
nunca	never
siempre	always
una vez a la semana	once a week

Repaso: con frecuencia, todos los días

Palabras adicionales

¿de quién?	whose?
del (de + el)	of the, from the
estar de acuerdo / no estar de acuerdo	to agree / to disagree
esto	this (*neuter*)
para	(intended) *for*
para + *inf.*	in order to (*do something*)
por eso	for that reason
¿por qué?	why?
porque	because
que	that, which; who
según	according to
tener... años (tengo, tienes, tiene)	to be . . . years old

Repaso: ¿de dónde es Ud.?

Vocabulario personal

Remember to use this space for other words and phrases you learn in this chapter.

ESPAÑOL	INGLÉS

4

De compras°

De... *Shopping*

|SPANISH

www.connectspanish.com

En este capítulo

En un mercado (*market*), en Tecpán, Guatemala

Mar Caribe

MÉXICO

BELICE

GUATEMALA
Chichicastenango
•San Pedro Sula
HONDURAS
Ciudad de Guatemala
Antigua
⊕Tegucigalpa

EL SALVADOR
NICARAGUA

OCÉANO
PACÍFICO

COSTA RICA
PANAMÁ

0   100   200 Millas
0   100   200 Kilómetros

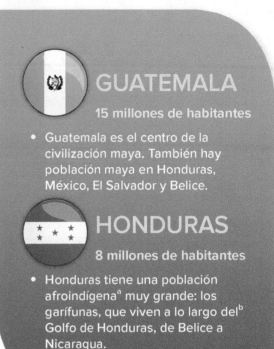

GUATEMALA
15 millones de habitantes

- Guatemala es el centro de la civilización maya. También hay población maya en Honduras, México, El Salvador y Belice.

HONDURAS
8 millones de habitantes

- Honduras tiene una población afroindígena[a] muy grande: los garífunas, que viven a lo largo del[b] Golfo de Honduras, de Belice a Nicaragua.

[a]*native African* [b]*a... along the*

- ¿Qué tipo de ropa[a] le gusta llevar[b] con más frecuencia, ropa formal o informal?
- ¿Prefiere usar ropa de muchos colores o prefiere la ropa de colores muy básicos, como el blanco y el negro[c]? (**Prefiero...**)
- ¿Le gusta ir de compras[d] o prefiere comprar por[e] internet? Cuando va[f] de compras, ¿va a centros comerciales o a pequeñas tiendas[g] locales? (**Voy...**)

[a]*clothing* [b]*to wear* [c]*el... white and black* [d]*ir... to go shopping* [e]*on the* [f]*you go* [g]*shops*

ALEJANDRA HERNÁNDEZ SOTO CONTESTA LAS PREGUNTAS.

- Me gusta todo tipo de ropa. Para ir[a] a la universidad todos los días, llevo ropa cómoda:[b] *jeans*, camisetas[c] y suéteres grandes, zapatos bajos o deportivos.[d] Pero me gusta la ropa elegante para ocasiones especiales.
- Me gusta mucho combinar el negro con el blanco y colores vivos,[e] como el rojo[f] y el turquesa.
- Prefiero ir de compras. Con frecuencia voy a un centro comercial. Pero a veces, voy a tiendas pequeñas en el centro que tienen cosas un poco diferentes. ¡Nunca compro por internet!

[a]*go* [b]*comfortable* [c]*T-shirts* [d]*zapatos... low or sporty shoes* [e]*strong, vibrant* [f]*red*

VOCABULARIO: PREPARACIÓN

De compras: La ropa°

De... *Shopping: Clothing*

- la chaqueta
- la camiseta
- los pantalones cortos
- las chanclas
- la blusa
- el cinturón
- la falda
- el bolso
- los zapatos
- la camisa
- los pantalones
- los tenis

1.   2.   3.

You can hear the pronunciation of theme vocabulary words and phrases in the Connect eBook.

Los verbos

comprar	to buy
llevar	to wear; to carry; to take
regatear	to haggle; to bargain
usar	to wear; to use
vender	to sell
venden de todo	they sell (have) everything

Los lugares

el almacén	department store
el centro	downtown
el centro comercial	shopping mall

el mercado	market (place)
la plaza	plaza
la tienda	shop, store

¿Cuánto cuesta(n)?

la ganga	bargain
el precio	price
el precio fijo	fixed (set) price
las rebajas	sales, reductions
barato/a	inexpensive
caro/a	expensive
cómodo/a	comfortable

Otras palabras y expresiones útiles

el abrigo	coat	**las sandalias**	sandals
los aretes	earrings	**el sombrero**	hat
las botas	boots	**la sudadera**	sweatshirt
los calcetines	socks	**el suéter**	sweater
la cartera	wallet; handbag	**el traje**	suit
la chaqueta	jacket (*for a woman or a man*)	**el traje de baño**	bathing suit
la corbata	tie	**el vestido**	dress
las gafas de sol	sun glasses	**de cuadros (lunares, rayas)**	plaid (polka-dot, striped)
la gorra	baseball cap	**Es de (algodón, cuero, lana, oro, plata, seda)**	it is made of (cotton, leather, wool, gold, silver, silk)
el impermeable	raincoat		
los *jeans*	blue jeans, jeans		
las medias	stockings	**Es de última moda.**	It's trendy (hot).
el reloj	watch	**Está de moda.**	
la ropa interior	underwear		

Así se dice

el almacén = los grandes almacenes (*Spain*)
el bolso = la bolsa (*Mexico*)
la camiseta = la polera (*Argentina*), la playera (*Mexico*), el polo (*Peru*)
la cartera = la billetera (*Argentina, El Salvador*); *coin purse* = el monedero

la falda = la pollera (*Argentina, Uruguay*)
los *jeans* = los mahones (*Puerto Rico, Dominican Republic*), los vaqueros (*Spain*)
el suéter = el jersey (*Spain*), el pulóver (*Argentina*)

To talk about sales, you can say **hay rebajas** or say that something **está de/en rebaja** or **está en liquidación/venta**.

Comunicación

A. La ropa

Paso 1. ¿Qué ropa llevan estas personas?

Vocabulario **útil**

el chico	guy
la chica	girl
el hombre	
la mujer	

vestido

botas

pantalones

1.   **2.**   **3.**

Paso 2. De estas personas, ¿quién trabaja hoy? ¿Quién probablemente no trabaja en este momento? ¿Quién va a (*is going to*) una fiesta?

---

*Note another use of **ser** + **de**: to tell what material something is made of.

B. Asociaciones. Complete las siguientes oraciones lógicamente con palabras de **De compras: La ropa.**

1. Un _____ es una tienda grande, con muchos departamentos.
2. No es posible _____ cuando hay precios fijos.
3. En la librería, _____ de todo: textos y otros libros, cuadernos, lápices,...
4. Hay grandes _____ en las tiendas al final de la temporada (*season*), en las cuales (*in which*) todo es muy barato.
5. Siempre hay *boutiques* en los _____.
6. El _____ de una ciudad es con frecuencia la parte histórica.
7. Esta ropa es para fiestas formales: _____.
8. La ropa de _____ (materia) es muy elegante.

C. El estilo personal. Complete las siguientes oraciones lógicamente para hablar de sus preferencias con relación a la ropa.

1. Para ir a la universidad, llevo _____.
2. Para ir a las fiestas con los amigos, llevo _____.
3. Para pasar un día en la playa (*beach*), me gusta llevar _____.
4. Para estar en casa todo el día, me gusta llevar _____.
5. Nunca uso _____.
6. No puedo vivir sin (*I can't live without*) ____ y ____.

Estrategia

Remember that the preposition **para** followed by an infinitive can be used to express *in order to*.

Para ir al centro, me gusta llevar pantalones, una camiseta y sandalias. (*In order*) *To go downtown, I like to wear pants, a T-shirt, and sandals.*

¡OJO!

The inverted question mark comes immediately before the tag question, not at the beginning of the statement.

Nota comunicativa

Preguntas coletilla (*tag*)

Tag phrases can change statements into questions.

Aquí venden de todo,	¿no?	They sell everything here, right?
	¿verdad?	(don't they?)
No necesito impermeable hoy, ¿verdad?		I don't need a raincoat today, do I?

¿Verdad? is found after affirmative or negative statements; **¿no?** is usually found after affirmative statements only.

You will practice using tag phrases in **Comunicación D.**

D. Intercambios. En parejas, usen las coletillas **¿no?** y **¿verdad?** para intercambiar (*exchange*) información de sus hábitos y preferencias sobre (*about*) las compras.

MODELO: Hay un buen centro comercial cerca de (*close to*) tu casa. →
    E1: Hay un buen centro comercial cerca de tu casa, ¿no? (¿verdad?)
    E2: Sí, hay un centro comercial muy grande a cinco millas (*five miles away*) de mi casa. (No, no hay un buen centro comercial cerca de mi casa.)

1. Hay un buen centro comercial cerca de tu casa.
2. Te gusta la ropa deportiva (*sports*) más que la ropa elegante.
3. Tienes muchos zapatos.
4. Te gusta llevar ropa de moda.
5. No compras en las tiendas de ropa usada (*used*).
6. Compras muchas cosas (*things*) por internet.
7. No hay muchos mercados en esta ciudad.

Los colores: ¿De qué color es?

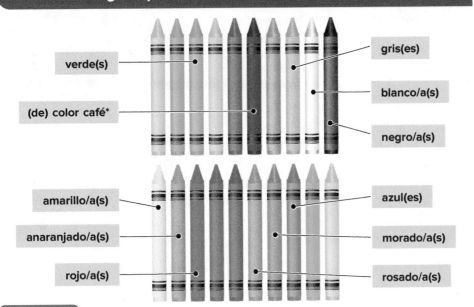

verde(s)

(de) color café*

gris(es)

blanco/a(s)

negro/a(s)

amarillo/a(s)

anaranjado/a(s)

rojo/a(s)

azul(es)

morado/a(s)

rosado/a(s)

¡OJO!

The names of colors are masculine, like the word **color: el rojo, el azul,** and so on. Note that three colors (**azul, gris, verde**) have only one singular form for masculine and feminine: **el traje azul, la camisa azul.**

Así se dice

anaranjado = naranja
(de) color café = marrón, pardo
morado = (de) color violeta, púrpura, purpúreo
rosado = (de) color rosa, rosa

Note that some Spanish speakers use **marrón** for objects and **pardo** for animals. Brown hair and eye color are often expressed with **castaño.**

Comunicación

A. **Un cuadro colorido (*colorful painting*).** Hay muchos colores en este cuadro de Edwin Guillermo. ¿Cuáles son?

El cortejo (Courting), de Erwin Guillermo

Algo sobre...

un artista guatemalteco

Erwin Guillermo (1951– [mil novecientos cincuenta y uno]) vive y trabaja en la Ciudad de Guatemala. Su estilo es representativo del arte contemporáneo guatemalteco: es muy expresivo y simbólico. Con frecuencia, como se ve[a] en este cuadro,[b] las figuras de Guillermo tienen una forma estilizada y sensual, con muchos colores.

 ¿Le gusta el estilo del cuadro de Guillermo? ¿Qué pintor(a) le gusta mucho a Ud.?

[a]*se... is seen* [b]*painting*

---

*The expression (**de) color café** is *invariable*; that is, it does not show gender or number agreement with the noun it modifes: **el sombrero (de) color café, la falda (de) color café, los pantalones (de) color café.**

Nota cultural

La ropa tradicional en el mundo hispano

La ropa tradicional en el mundo hispano es muy diversa, porque hay muchos países y regiones diferentes. Algunas prendas[a] son ahora conocidas[b] en todo el mundo:

- la guayabera[c] (Caribe)
- el poncho (los Andes)
- el traje de flamenco (España)

En los países de cultura maya

En estos países hay tejidos muy bellos y coloridos.[d] Varían según la región y forman parte de la ropa habitual de las mujeres indígenas. Una prenda distintiva es el huipil, una especie de blusa, que varía de región a región.

 ¿Hay ropa tradicional en este país?

[a]articles of clothing [b]known [c]elegant short-sleeved shirt worn outside the pants [d]tejidos... beautiful and colorful textiles

Una mujer guatemalteca que hace tejidos (is weaving)

B. Asociaciones. ¿Qué asocia Ud. con los siguientes colores?

1. gris
2. verde
3. blanco y negro
4. amarillo
5. rojo
6. azul

C. ¡Ojo alerta! ¿Escaparates (Window displays) idénticos? These window displays are almost alike . . . but not quite! Can you find at least nine differences between them?

MODELO: En el dibujo A hay _____, pero en el dibujo B hay _____.

A.

B.

D. ¿De qué color es?

Paso 1. Describa el color de la ropa y de las cosas (*things*) de sus compañeros.

MODELO: El bolígrafo de Anita es amarillo. Un libro de Anita es azul...

Paso 2. Ahora describa la ropa que lleva una persona de la clase sin decir (*without saying*) su nombre. Sus compañeros tienen que (*have to*) identificar a la persona de la descripción.

MODELO: **E1:** Lleva botas negras, una camiseta blanca y *jeans*.
E2: Es Anne.

Los números a partir del 100°

a... *from 100 on*

Continúe las secuencias:

- noventa y nueve, cien, ciento uno...
- mil, dos mil...
- un millón, dos millones...

100	cien, ciento	**700**	setecientos/as
101	ciento uno/una	**800**	ochocientos/as
200	doscientos/as	**900**	novecientos/as
300	trescientos/as	**1.000**	mil
400	cuatrocientos/as	**2.000**	dos mil
500	quinientos/as	**1.000.000**	un millón
600	seiscientos/as	**2.000.000**	dos millones

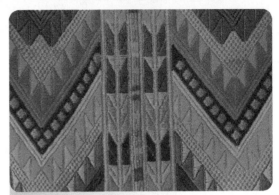

Este huipil guatemalteco hecho a mano (*hand-made*) cuesta 750 (setecientos cincuenta) quetzales.

- **Cien** is used in counting and when referring to exactly one hundred of something: **cien** dólares.
- **Ciento** is used in combination with numbers from 1 to 99 to express the numbers 101 to 199: ...noventa y nueve, cien, **ciento** uno, **ciento** dos...
- **Cien** is used before numbers greater than 100: **cien mil, cien millones.**
- When counting, the masculine form of words containing **cientos** is used: **...doscientos uno, doscientos dos...**
- When the numbers 200 to 900 modify a noun, they must agree in gender: **doscientos veintiún dólares, quinientas ocho sillas.**
- **Mil** means *one thousand* or *a thousand*. It does not have a plural form in counting, but **millón** does. When followed directly by a noun, **millón (dos millones,** and so on) must be followed by **de.**

mil gracias	
3.000 habitantes	**tres mil habitantes**
14.000.000 *de* habitantes	**catorce millones *de* habitantes**

- Years are expressed like regular numbers in Spanish.

1899	**mil ochocientos noventa y nueve**
2008	**dos mil ocho**

¡OJO!

In many parts of the Spanish-speaking world, a period **(punto)** is used where a comma **(coma)** is used in English and viceversa.
$1.500 $1.000.000 $10,45   65,9%

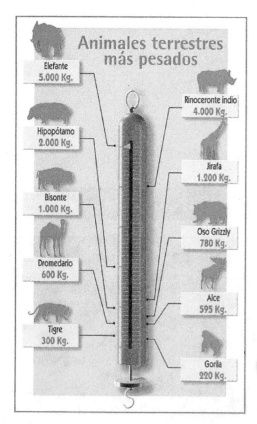

Animales terrestres más pesados

Elefante
5.000 Kg.

Rinoceronte indio
4.000 Kg.

Hipopótamo
2.000 Kg.

Jirafa
1.200 Kg.

Bisonte
1.000 Kg.

Oso Grizzly
780 Kg.

Dromedario
600 Kg.

Alce
595 Kg.

Tigre
300 Kg.

Gorila
220 Kg.

Estrategia

un kilo = 2.2. libras
(aproximadamente)

Comunicación

A. ¿Cuánto cuestan? Exprese los siguientes precios en dólares en español.

1. unos *jeans* de moda: $100
2. unos tenis tipo NBA: $150
3. un anillo (*ring*) de diamantes: $1.200
4. unos aretes (*earrings*) de oro: $225
5. una tela (*fabric*) de artesanía local de excelente calidad: $400
6. un cinturón de cuero de un diseñador (*designer*) famoso: $330
7. un coche europeo: $75.000
8. una casa grande en una zona residencial muy exclusiva: $2.000.000
9. un edificio de apartamentos: $15.800.000

B. ¿Cuánto pesan? (*How much do they weigh?*)

Paso 1. Estos son los animales terrestres más grandes. ¿Cuánto pesan en kilos? **¡OJO!** Use el artículo masculino para todos los nombres, menos para (*except for*) **jirafa.**

MODELO: El elefante pesa cinco mil kilos.

Paso 2. Ahora, en parejas, calculen cuánto pesan aproximadamente en kilos o en libras (*pounds*) los siguientes animales y objetos.

MODELO: E1: ¿Cuánto crees que pesa un perro grande?
E2: Creo que pesa más de (*more than*) 25 kilos.
E1: Estoy de acuerdo. (No estoy de acuerdo. Creo que pesa más de 30 kilos.)

1. un perro/gato
2. su mochila con los libros
3. un coche
4. su libro de español
5. el animal más grande del mundo

C. Más o menos

Paso 1. With a classmate, determine how much the following items probably cost, using **¿Cuánto cuesta(n)... ?** Keep track of the prices that you decide on. Follow the model.

MODELO: una chaqueta de cuero →
E1: ¿Cuánto cuesta una chaqueta de cuero?
E2: Cuesta doscientos dólares.

1. un iPhone de último (*latest*) modelo
2. un coche nuevo/usado
3. una computadora portátil de último modelo
4. la matrícula de esta universidad
5. un reloj de oro muy elegante
6. unos tenis (**¡OJO! cuestan**)
7. una casa en esta ciudad

Paso 2. Now compare the prices you selected with those of others in the class. What is the most expensive thing on the list? (**¿Cuál es la cosa más cara** [*most expensive*]**?**) What is the least expensive? (**¿Cuál es la más barata?**)

D. Fechas (*Dates*) importantes. Exprese las siguientes fechas en español.

1. este año, el año pasado y el próximo (*next*) año
2. el año de su nacimiento (*birth*)
3. 1821, el año de la independencia de Guatemala y Honduras (de España)
4. 1776, el año de la independencia de los Estados Unidos (de Inglaterra)

«¡Moda,° moda, moda!» Segmento 1 — *Fashion*

Antes de mirar

¿Qué estilo de ropa prefiere Ud.? Indique sus preferencias después de leer (*after reading*) la descripción del estudio de Vilma (foto).

_____ siempre ropa cómoda e informal
_____ ropa elegante de alta costura y de tiendas exclusivas
_____ ropa variada, a veces informal, a veces elegante
_____ ropa muy juvenil y deportiva (*youthful and sporty*)

Este segmento

El tema de este programa es la moda. El segmento incluye una entrevista (*inverview*) con una diseñadora (*designer*) puertorriqueña.

«En el estudio de Vilma, vemos (*we see*) vestidos (*costumes*) de épocas históricas para obras de teatro (*plays*), vestidos de alta costura (*designer*) y su nueva línea de prendas (*garments*) reversibles de cuero.»

Vocabulario del segmento

te ves	you look	**acá/allá**	here/there
no creas	don't get the idea	**mismo/a**	same
el significado	meaning	**la marca**	brand, label
Cuéntanos.	Tell us (about it).	**hablé**	I spoke
primero vamos	first let's go	**Ropajes**	Apparel
el clima	climate	**desarrollamos**	we develop
la playa	beach	**la enseñanza**	teaching
Colón llegó	Columbus arrived	**todo el mundo**	everybody
el segundo viaje	second voyage		

Estrategia

You can pick up vocabulary that will be in the segment by reading the photo caption, **Este segmento,** and **Vocabulario del segmento,** doing **Antes de mirar,** and scanning **Después de mirar** before you watch the segment!

Después de mirar

A. ¿Está claro? Las siguientes oraciones son falsas. Corríjalas (*Correct them*), según el video.

1. Ana y Víctor están hoy en Puerto Rico.
2. Víctor lleva una camiseta hoy porque va (*he's going*) a la playa.
3. Solo hay influencia de España en Puerto Rico.
4. El estilo de Ropajes Inc. es juvenil e informal.

B. Un poco más. Empareje (*Match*) las ideas de la **Columna A** con la forma correcta de una palabra de la **Columna B.**

COLUMNA A
1. _____ el clima de Puerto Rico
2. _____ las playas de Puerto Rico
3. _____ la apariencia de Víctor hoy, en camiseta
4. _____ la diseñadora Vilma Martínez
5. _____ las prendas de cuero de la nueva línea

COLUMNA B
a. bonito
b. relajado (*relaxed*)
c. reversible
d. fundador (*founder*)
e. suave (*mild*)

C. Y ahora, Uds. En parejas, imaginen que son los presentadores del programa de hoy sobre la ropa y la moda. Sigan el modelo de este segmento y hagan una breve introducción al programa, incluyendo (*including*):

- un saludo + una presentación personal + el lugar donde Uds. están
- un comentario informal sobre la ropa de uno de Uds. o su estilo (o sobre la ropa que Uds. llevan hoy o su propio [*own*] estilo). (Usen vocabulario de **Antes de mirar** y de **Vocabulario: Preparación.**)
- una breve introducción al próximo (*upcoming*) reportaje sobre la moda o sobre una tienda en particular

PRONUNCIACIÓN

Stress and Written Accent Marks (Part 2)

 ¿Recuerda Ud.?

In the **Pronunciación** section of **Capítulo 3**, you learned that most Spanish words do not need a written accent mark because their pronunciation is completely predictable. Review the two basic rules of Spanish word stress in words that do not have a written accent mark by looking at the examples and completing the rules. The stressed syllable is underlined.

- Examples: **li**bro, **me**sa, e**xa**men, i**ma**gen, **e**res, **gra**cias

  A word that ends in a _____, _____, or _____ is stressed on the next-to-last syllable.

- Examples: bai**lar**, us**ted**, pa**pel**, es**toy**

  A word that ends in _____ is stressed on the last syllable.

In Spanish, the written accent mark is used in the following situations.

1. A written accent mark is needed when a word does not follow the two basic rules reviewed in **¿Recuerda Ud.?**

Look at the words in this group.

ta-bú	a-le-mán	in-glés
ca-fé	na-ción	es-tás

The preceding words end in a vowel, **-n,** or **-s,** so one would predict that they would be stressed on the *second-to-last syllable* (**la penúltima sílaba**). But the written accent mark shows that they are in fact accented on the *last syllable* (**la última sílaba**).

Now look at the words in this group.

lá-piz   dó-lar   ál-bum   á-gil   dó-cil

The preceding words end in a consonant (other than **-n** or **-s**), so one would predict that they would be stressed on the last syllable. But the written accent mark shows that they are in fact accented on the next-to-last syllable.

2. All words that are stressed on the *third-to-last syllable* (**la antepenúltima sílaba**) must have a written accent mark, regardless of which letter they end in. These are called **palabras esdrújulas.**

bo-lí-gra-fo   ma-trí-cu-la   ma-te-má-ti-cas

3. When two consecutive vowels do not form a diphthong (see **Pronunciación, Cap. 2**), the weak vowel (**i, u**) that receives the spoken stress will have a written accent mark. This pattern is very frequent in words that end in **-ía.**

Ma-rí-a	po-li-cí-a	as-tro-no-mí-a
dí-a	bio-lo-gí-a	

> **¡OJO!**
> Contrast the pronunciation of those words with the following words in which the vowels **i** and **a** *do* form a diphthong: **Pa**tricia, **Fran**cia, in**fan**cia, dis**tan**cia.

4. Some one-syllable words have accents to distinguish them from other words that are pronounced the same but have different meanings. This type of accent does not follow the general rules of accentuation; it is called the *diacritic accent* (**el acento diacrítico**). Here are some of the most common examples.

él (*he*)/el (*the*)
sí (*yes*)/si (*if*)
tú (*you*)/tu (*your*)
mí (*me*)/mi (*my*)

5. Interrogative and exclamatory words have a written accent on the stressed vowel. For example:

¿quién?
¿dónde?
¡Qué ganga! (*What a bargain!*)

6. Accent marks are also added to preserve the original stress of a word when the word is changed in some way, for example, when it becomes plural. Here are some examples:

joven → jóvenes   examen → exámenes

You will learn about other situations in which accents are added for this reason in upcoming chapters.

> **¡OJO!**
> As you know, the accent mark is sometimes dropped when a word is made plural.
> pantalón   pantalones
> francés   franceses
> nación   naciones

Práctica

A. **Sílabas.** The following words have been separated into syllables for you. Read them aloud, paying careful attention to where the spoken stress should fall. Don't worry about the meaning of words you haven't heard before. The rules you have learned will help you pronounce them correctly.

1. a-quí | pa-pá | a-diós | bus-qué
2. prác-ti-co | mur-cié-la-go | te-lé-fo-no | ar-chi-pié-la-go
3. Ji-mé-nez | Ro-drí-guez | Pé-rez | Gó-mez
4. si-co-lo-gí-a | so-cio-lo-gí-a | sa-bi-du-rí-a | e-ner-gí-a
5. his-to-ria | te-ra-pia | Pre-to-ria | me-mo-ria

B. **Reglas. (Rules.)** Indicate the stressed vowel of each word in the following list. Give one of the three reasons from the list to explain the stressed vowel of each word.

1. exámenes
2. lápiz
3. necesitar
4. perezoso
5. actitud
6. acciones
7. dólares
8. francés
9. Están
10. hombre
11. peso
12. mujer
13. plástico
14. María
15. Rodríguez
16. Patricia

GRAMÁTICA

 ¿Recuerda Ud.?

You learned the four forms of the demonstrative adjective **este** in **Gramática 5 (Cap. 3).** Review them now by completing these phrases.

1. est_____ pantalones   **2.** est_____ falda   **3.** est_____ blusas   **4.** est_____ abrigo

9 Pointing Out People and Things
Demonstrative Adjectives (Part 2) and Pronouns

Grammar Tutorial 9
connect
|SPANISH
www.connectspanish.com

Gramática en acción: Suéteres a buenos precios

el vendedor

Jorge   Susana

Susana busca un suéter con su amigo Jorge.

SUSANA: ¿Cuánto cuesta este suéter?

VENDEDOR: Bueno, ese que Ud. tiene en la mano cuesta 800 quetzales. Este aquí cuesta 700 quetzales.

SUSANA: ¡Qué caros!

VENDEDOR: Es que todos son de pura lana. Mire aquellos suéteres de rayas sobre aquella mesa. Solo cuestan 300 quetzales. Son acrílicos.

SUSANA: Muchas gracias.

Comprensión

¿Quién habla, Susana, su amigo Jorge o el vendedor?

1. «Estos suéteres de rayas son bonitos. Y solo cuestan 300 quetzales.»
2. «Los suéteres en aquella mesa no son de pura lana.»
3. «Compro este suéter. Me gusta la ropa de lana.»
4. «Estos suéteres acrílicos son más baratos que aquellos de lana.»

Demonstrative Adjectives / Los adjetivos demostrativos

Singular			Plural			Adverbs / Los adverbios
this	este abrigo	esta gorra	these	estos abrigos	estas gorras	aquí = here
that	ese abrigo	esa gorra	those	esos abrigos	esas gorras	allí = there
	aquel abrigo	aquella gorra		aquellos abrigos	aquellas gorras	allá = way over there

an adverb / **un adverbio** = a word (such as *very* and *quickly*) that modifies a verb, adjective, or another adverb

¡OJO!
Note that the final -e in the singular forms **este** and **ese** changes to an -o- in the plural: **estos, esos.**

Sweaters at good prices *Susana is looking for a sweater with her friend Jorge. SUSANA: How much is this sweater? SALESMAN: Well, that one that you have in your hand costs 800 quetzales. This one here costs 700 quetzales. SUSANA: (They're) So expensive! SALESMAN: It's because they're all made of pure wool. Take a look at those striped sweaters on that table (over there). They only cost 300 quetzales. They're acrylic. SUSANA: Thanks a lot.*

1. Agreement

Demonstrative adjectives are used to indicate a specific noun or nouns. In Spanish, **los adjetivos demostrativos** precede the nouns they modify. They also agree in number and gender with the nouns.

> *a demonstrative adjective /* **un adjetivo demostrativo** = an adjective used to indicate a particular person, place, thing, or idea

2. Using *este* and *ese*

Forms of **este** (*this, these*) and **ese** (*that, those*) are used just like *this/these* and *that/those* in English.

- When two people are speaking, forms of **este** are used to refer to nouns that are close to the speaker in space or time.
- Forms of **ese** refer to nouns that are close to the person spoken *to*.
- When the noun is distant from both speakers, forms of **ese** are used.

¿Esos pantalones?

No, aquellos allá.

3. Using *ese* and *aquel*

There are two ways to say *that/those* in Spanish.

- Forms of **ese** refer to nouns that are not close to the speaker(s) (point 2).
- Forms of **aquel** refer to nouns that are even farther away from the speaker(s).

In the chart on page 110, the *adverbs* (**los adverbios**) **aquí, allí,** and **allá** are associated with the forms of **este, ese,** and **aquel,** respectively. However, it is not obligatory to use these words with the demonstrative adjectives.

Este niño es mi hijo. **Ese** joven allí es mi hijo también. Y **aquel** señor allá es mi esposo.
This boy is my son. That young man there is also my son. And that man way over there is my husband.

Demonstrative Pronouns / Los pronombres demostrativos

1. Demonstrative Pronouns

In English, the *demonstrative pronouns* are the demonstrative adjective + the word *one(s),* as in the examples to the right. In Spanish, **los pronombres demostrativos** are the same as demonstrative adjectives, except that the noun is not used and there is no direct equivalent for English *one(s).**

2. Agreement

In Spanish, demonstrative pronouns agree in gender and number with the noun they are replacing: **ese libro, en la mesa** ⟶ **ese, en la mesa.**

—¿Te gusta **aquella** casa allá?
—¿Cuál?
—**Aquella,** la de las ventanas grandes.
—¡Ah, **aquella!** Sí, me gusta mucho. Mucho más que **esta...**

*"Do you like **that** house way over there?"*
"Which one?"
***"That one,** the one with the big windows."*
*"Oh, **that one!** Yes, I like it a lot. A lot more than **this one . . ."***

3. Neuter Demonstrative Pronouns

Use the neuter demonstrative pronouns **esto, eso,** and **aquello** to refer to as yet unidentified objects or to a whole idea, concept, or situation.

¿Qué es **esto?**
What is this?

Eso es todo.
That's it. / That's all.
¡**Aquello** es terrible!
That's terrible!

¡OJO!

Esto es una mochila. (to identify in general)
This is a backpack.

Esta es mi mochila. (to identify one out of a group)
This (one) is my backpack.

---

*Some Spanish speakers to use accents on demonstrative pronouns: **este coche y ése, aquella casa y ésta.** However, it is correct in modern Spanish, according to the **Real Academia Española** in Spain, to omit the accent on these forms when context makes the meaning clear (see Appendix 2).*

Summary of Demonstratives

near	**este/a, estos/as, esto**
far	**ese/a, esos/as, eso**
farther	**aquel(la), aquellos/as, aquello**

Práctica y comunicación

A. Una cuestión de perspectiva

Paso 1. Autoprueba. Empareje las palabras con su significado apropiado en inglés.

1. estas
2. aquellos
3. ese
4. esas
5. este

a. *that*
b. *those* (*over there*)
c. *these*
d. *this*
e. *those*

Paso 2. Autoprueba. Ahora empareje los siguientes demostrativos con los objetos apropiados.

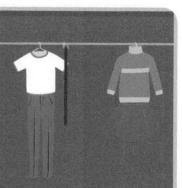

1. esta _____
2. estas _____
3. este _____
4. aquel _____
5. aquellos _____
6. esos _____

Paso 3. Ahora, en parejas, desde el lugar donde Uds. están, usen los siguientes demostrativos para identificar los objetos de la clase.

1. estos _____ y esta _____
2. ese _____ y esas _____
3. aquel _____ y aquellos _____

B. Cambios (*Changes*)

Paso 1. Cambie (*Change*) las formas de **este** por **ese** y añada (*add*) **también,** según el modelo.

MODELO: Este abrigo es muy grande. →
    Ese abrigo **también** es muy grande.

1. Esta falda es muy pequeña.
2. Este diccionario es muy largo.
3. Este libro es muy bueno.
4. Esta corbata es muy fea.

Paso 2. Ahora cambie **este** por **aquel** y añada **allá** también.

MODELO: Este abrigo es muy grande. →
    Aquel abrigo **allá también** es muy grande.

Paso 3. Finalmente, cambie las oraciones del singular al plural.

MODELO: Este abrigo es muy grande. →
    Est**os** abrigo**s** **son** muy grandes.

Prác. A: Answers, Paso 1. 1. c 2. b 3. a 4. e 5. d
Answers, Paso 2. 1. gorra 2. chanclas 3. traje de baño 4. suéter 5. zapatos/tenis 6. pantalones

112 ■ ciento doce

Capítulo 4 De compras

C. Situaciones. Empareje (*Match*) cada (*each*) situación de la columna A con un comentario de la columna B.

                    A   B

1. _____ Aquí hay un regalo para Ud.   **a.** ¡Eso es un desastre!
2. _____ Ocurre un accidente de coche.   **b.** ¡Eso es magnífico!
3. _____ No hay clases mañana.   **c.** ¿Qué es esto?
4. _____ La matrícula cuesta más este semestre/   **d.** ¡Eso es terrible!
            trimestre.
5. _____ Ud. tiene A en su examen de español.

D. En una tienda

Paso 1. Complete el siguiente diálogo con los demostrativos apropiados. Asuma (*Take*) el punto de vista (*point of view*) del vendedor y el cliente.

VENDEDOR: ¿Qué suéter le gusta?

¿_____¹ rojo que está aquí?

CLIENTE: No, el rojo no.

VENDEDOR: ¿_____² suéter amarillo?

CLIENTE: No, tampocoª el amarillo.

¡Me gusta _____³

anaranjado de allá!

ªNo... *No, not* [*the yellow one*] *either*

Paso 2. Ahora indique el demostrativo apropiado para los pantalones de cada maniquí, según la perspectiva de los dos hombres.

1. _____ pantalones negros
2. _____ pantalones azules
3. _____ pantalones color kaki

E. En la alcoba (*bedroom*) de Ernesto. Working with a partner, imagine that you are the person depicted in the drawing, who is looking into Ernesto's bedroom. Some objects and items of clothing are close to you, some are a bit farther away, and some are at the other end of the room. Describe them as accurately as you can, using the appropriate demonstrative adjectives and all of the vocabulary you have learned so far.

MODELOS: _____ gato es blanco y
         _____ gato es negro.
         _____ libro es verde.

> **Vocabulario útil**
>
> **la cama**   bed
> **el estante**   book shelf
> **la mesita**   nightstand

F. En el salón de clase

Paso 1. En parejas, usen demostrativos para identificar cinco pares (*pairs*) de personas o cosas en el salón de clase.

MODELO: Esta chica es rubia. Aquella chica cerca de la puerta es morena.

Paso 2. Ahora compartan (*share*) sus oraciones con el resto de la clase. Sus compañeros deben adivinar (*guess*) a qué personas u objetos Uds. se refieren.

> **Vocabulario útil**
>
> **cerca de**   near
> **lejos de** far from

¿Recuerda Ud.?

You began using the singular forms of the verb **tener** in **Capítulo 3.** Review them by completing the following verb forms.

1. tú t___nes
2. yo te____o
3. Julio t___ne

You will learn about similar patterns in **Gramática 10.**

Grammar Tutorial **10**

connect

|SPANISH

www.connectspanish.com

 10 **Expressing Actions and States**

Tener, venir, poder, preferir, querer;
Some Idioms with **tener**

Gramática en acción: Un mensaje telefónico

Hola, Jorge. Soy Jaqui. Esta tarde tengo que comprar un regalo para Miguel y no quiero ir sola. ¿Vienes conmigo? Podemos encontrarnos en ese centro comercial que está cerca de tu casa. O si prefieres, puedo pasar por ti antes. ¡Llámame!

Comprensión

Ahora vuelva a contar (*retell*) el mensaje de Jaqui. Estas formas verbales son como **tiene**.

1. Jaqui tien_____que comprar un regalo.
2. Quier_____ir de compras con Jorge.
3. Pued_____encontrarse con Jorge en el centro comercial.
4. O si Jorge prefier_____, Jaqui pued_____pasar por la casa de él.

Tener, venir, poder, preferir, querer

> Remember that infinitives in red are conjugated in their entirety in Appendix 5.

tener (to have)		venir (to come)		poder (to be able, can)		preferir (to prefer)		querer (to want)	
tengo	tenemos	vengo	venimos	puedo	podemos	prefiero	preferimos	quiero	queremos
tienes	tenéis	vienes	venís	puedes	podéis	prefieres	preferís	quieres	queréis
tiene	tienen	viene	vienen	puede	pueden	prefiere	prefieren	quiere	quieren

---

A phone message *Hello, Jorge. It's Jaqui. This afternoon I have to buy a gift for Miguel, and I don't want to go alone. Will you come with me? We can meet at that shopping center that's near your house. Or if you prefer, I can come by for you ahead of time. Call me!*

The five verbs shown on the preceding page share a number of characteristics.

- The **yo** forms of **tener** and **venir** are irregular.

- In other forms of **tener** and **venir**, and in **preferir** and **querer**, when the stem vowel **e** is stressed, it becomes **ie**.

- Similarly, the stem vowel **o** in **poder** becomes **ue** when stressed.

- Like **deber**, **desear**, and **necesitar**, the verbs **poder**, **preferir**, and **querer** can be followed by an infinitive.

Verbs like these are called *stem-changing verbs*. You will learn more verbs of this type in **Gramática 13 (Cap. 5).**

tener: yo **tengo**, tú **tienes** (e → ie)...
venir: yo **vengo**, tú **vienes** (e → ie)...
preferir, querer: (e → ie)
poder: (o → ue)

In vocabulary lists, these changes are shown in parenthesis after the infinitive: **poder (puedo).**

¿Puedes correr muy rápido?
Can you run very fast?

¿Qué **quieres/prefieres** hacer hoy?
What do you want/prefer to do today?

Prefiero **no ir** a la biblioteca el sábado por la noche.
I prefer not to go to the library Saturday night.

¡OJO!
The **nosotros** and **vosotros** forms of these verbs do not have changes in the stem vowel because it is not stressed.

¡OJO!
You will learn to use the verb **hacer** (*to do or to make*) in **Gramática 12 (Cap. 5).** Learn to recognize it in questions and direction lines.

Some Idioms with tener / Algunos modismos con *tener*

1. Conditions or States

Many ideas expressed in English with the verb *to be* are expressed in Spanish with *idioms* (**los modismos**) that use **tener.**

Idioms are often different from one language to another. For example, in English, *to pull Mary's leg* usually means *to tease her*, not *to grab her leg and pull it*. In Spanish, *to pull Mary's leg* is **tomarle el pelo a Mary** (lit., *to take hold of Mary's hair*).

You already know one **tener** idiom: **tener... años.** Here are some more **tener** idioms. They all describe a condition or state. Based on the drawings, can you guess what these idioms mean?

an idiom / **un modismo** = an expression whose meaning cannot be inferred from the literal meaning of the words that form it

tener **sueño**

tener **prisa**

tener **razón**

no tener **razón**

tener **miedo (de)**

Note that **de** (in **tener miedo de**) can be followed by an infinitive or a noun.

Tengo miedo **de estar** solo aquí. ¡Tengo miedo **de la oscuridad**!
I'm afraid of being alone here. I'm afraid of the dark!

2. *Tener* Idioms + *Infinitive*

Other **tener** idioms include the following:

tener ganas de + *infinitive* = to feel like (*doing something*)

tener que + *infinitive* = to have to (*do something*)

¡OJO!

Note that the English equivalent of the infinitive in expressions with **tener ganas** is expressed with *-ing*, not with the infinitive as in Spanish.

Tengo ganas de comer.
I feel like eating.

¿No tiene Ud. que leer este capítulo?
Don't you have to read this chapter?

Summary of Verbs

tener: tengo, tienes...
venir: vengo, vienes...
poder: puedo...
preferir: prefiero...
querer: quiero...

Práctica y comunicación

A. Esta semana

Paso 1. Autoprueba. Complete los siguientes verbos.

1. p_____do, p_____des, p_____demos
2. pref_____ro, pref_____mos, pref_____ren
3. qu_____ro, qu_____re, qu_____remos
4. t_____o, t_____nes, t_____nemos
5. v _____o, v_____ne, v_____nimos

Paso 2. Ahora complete las siguientes oraciones con uno de los verbos o frases. Debe añadir (*add*) información de sus actividades esta semana y el nombre de un día de la semana. Solo debe repetir el verbo **tener**.

Verbos: poder   preferir   querer   tener   tener ganas   venir

Esta semana yo...

1. _____ clase de _____ (materia) el _____.
2. (no) _____ que estudiar mucho el _____.
3. (no) _____ estudiar en la biblioteca el _____.
4. _____ (no) estudiar en la biblioteca el _____ por la noche.
5. (no) _____ de mirar _____ (programa de televisión) el _____.
6. (no) _____ a la universidad el _____ / todos los días.

Paso 3. Finalmente, en parejas, usen sus oraciones del **Paso 2** como base para hacer y contestar preguntas. Luego (*Then*) digan (*tell*) a la clase algo (*something*) que Uds. tienen en común.

MODELO: 1. Tengo clase de chino el martes. →
    E1: ¿**Tienes** clase de chino el martes?
    E2: No, no estudio chino. Pero **tengo** clase de química el martes.

B. Situaciones. Empareje las situaciones con las respuestas apropiadas.

SITUACIONES

1. _____ El niño es muy pequeño.
2. _____ En esa casa, hay un perro furioso.
3. _____ Son las tres de la mañana.
4. _____ Pablito: «Dos y dos son... seis».
5. _____ Pablito: «Buenos Aires es la capital de la Argentina».
6. _____ Tenemos que estar en el centro a las tres y ya son (*it's already*) las tres menos cuarto.
7. _____ Mañana tengo un examen.

RESPUESTAS

a. Tengo mucho sueño.
b. Yo tengo miedo de ese perro.
c. Solo tiene dos años.
d. Tiene razón.
e. Por eso tengo que estudiar mucho.
f. No tiene razón.
g. Por eso tenemos mucha prisa.

Prác. A, Paso 1: Answers: 1. puedo, puedes, podemos 2. prefiero, preferimos, prefieren 3. quiero, quiere, queremos 4. tengo, tienes, tenemos 5. vengo, viene, venimos

Nota **comunicativa**

Mucho y poco

In this chapter, you learned that words like **aquí, allí,** and **allá** are *adverbs* (**los adverbios**), words that modify a verb (*run **quickly***), an adjective (***very** smart*), or another adverb (***very** quickly*). One very common Spanish adverb that you have used frequently is **muy** (*very*).

In the first chapters of *Puntos de partida*, you have used the words **mucho** and **poco** as both adjectives and adverbs. In English and in Spanish, adverbs are invariable in form. Spanish adjectives, however, agree in gender and number with the words they modify, as you know.

ADVERBIOS:	**mucho**	Rosa estudia **mucho.**	*Rosa studies a lot.*
	poco	Julio come **poco.**	*Julio doesn't eat much.*
ADJETIVOS:	**mucho/a(s)**	Rosa tiene **mucha** ropa.	*Rosa has a lot of clothes.*
		Tiene **muchos** zapatos.	*She has a lot of shoes.*
	poco/a(s)	Julio come **poca** pasta.	*Julio doesn't eat much pasta.*
		Come **pocos** postres.	*He eats few desserts.*

You will use these words in **Práctica C, D,** and **E.**

C. En mi armario (*closet*)

Paso 1. Haga rápidamente una lista aproximada de su ropa y complementos (*accessories*). Escriba (*Write*) **muchos, muchas, pocos, pocas** o **no tengo,** según sea (*is*) apropiado.

	MUCHOS/AS	POCOS/AS	NO TENGO
camisas/blusas			
camisetas			
pantalones largos			
pantalones cortos			
faldas			
vestidos			
chaquetas			
zapatos (de todo tipo)			
botas			
complementos			

Paso 2. Ahora, en parejas, túrnense para hacer y contestar preguntas sobre cuánta ropa tienen y de qué tipo.

MODELO: E1: ¿Tienes muchas camisas?
E2: No, no tengo muchas camisas. Solo tengo dos o tres. ¿Y tú?
E1: Yo tengo más de 6.

Paso 3. Para terminar, hagan una evaluación mutua de su vestuario (*wardrobe*). ¿Qué es obvio que prefieren llevar o no llevar? ¿Tienen su propio (*own*) estilo? ¿Qué tienen en exceso? ¿Qué tienen que comprar?

Vocabulario **útil**

demasiados/as	too many
deportivo/a	sporty
más/menos	more/less
de + *number*	than

D. Circunstancias personales

Paso 1. Choose a partner, but before working with him or her, try to predict the choices he or she will make in each of the following cases.

MODELO: tener muchos / pocos libros en su cuarto →
            Mi compañero tiene pocos libros en su cuarto.

1. estudiar mucho / poco este semestre/trimestre
2. querer tomar muchas / pocas clases de ciencias en la universidad
3. venir en coche / en autobús / a pie (*on foot*) a la universidad todos los días
4. preferir estudiar en la biblioteca / casa / la residencia
5. tener muchas / pocas cosas con el logotipo (*logo*) de la universidad
6. poder correr (*run*) una milla en menos / más de (*than*) cinco minutos
7. tener muchas ganas de estudiar / bailar esta noche
8. tener mucha / poca ropa
9. preferir el verde / rojo / amarillo
10. preferir usar botas / zapatos / sandalias / tenis / chanclas

Paso 2. Now, using tag questions (*preguntas coletilla*), ask your partner questions to find out if you guessed correctly in **Paso 1.**

MODELO: E1: Tienes muchos libros en tu cuarto, ¿verdad?
      E2: Sí, tengo muchos libros en mi cuarto. (No, tengo pocos libros.)

E. Intercambios. En parejas, túrnense para entrevistarse sobre los siguientes temas. Deben añadir (*add*) una pregunta original para cada (*each*) verbo.

VERBO INICIAL	OPCIONES
preferir	¿los gatos o los perros? ¿mirar una película (*movie*) en casa o en el cine (*movie theater*)? ¿la ropa elegante o la ropa cómoda? ¿ ?
tener	¿mucho dinero o muchas deudas (*debts*)? ¿una familia grande o pequeña? ¿sueño en clase con frecuencia? ¿ ?
venir	¿a clase tarde o temprano? ¿de una familia anglosajona, hispana o de otro origen? ¿a clase todos los días? ¿ ?
(¿qué?) querer	¿comprar esta semana? ¿comprar en el futuro? ¿mirar en la tele esta noche? ¿ ?
poder	¿hablar una lengua extranjera? ¿vivir sin (*without*) dinero? ¿escribir poemas? ¿ ?

Gramática en acción: ¿Adónde vas?

El Mercado Central, Ciudad de Guatemala

Rosa y Casandra son compañeras de casa.

CASANDRA: ¿Adónde vas?

ROSA: Voy al Mercado Central.

CASANDRA: ¿Qué vas a comprar allá?

ROSA: Voy a comprar unos regalos para mi familia en Nueva Jersey.

CASANDRA: ¿Vas a viajar a los Estados Unidos pronto?

ROSA: Sí, en quince días. ¿Por qué no vienes conmigo al Mercado?

CASANDRA: ¡Sí! Vamos.

Comprensión

¿Cierto o falso? Corrija las oraciones falsas.

	CIERTO	FALSO
1. Rosa va a estudiar.	☐	☐
2. Rosa va a comprar regalos.	☐	☐
3. Casandra va a los Estados Unidos.	☐	☐

The Verb ir / El verbo ir

ir (to go)			
(yo)	voy	(nosotros/as)	vamos
(tú)	vas	(vosotros/as)	vais
(Ud., él, ella)	va	(Uds., ellos/as)	van

Ir is the irregular Spanish verb used to express *to go*.

Rosa va al centro.
Rosa is going downtown.
¿Adónde vas tú?
Where are you going?

The first person plural of **ir, vamos** (*we go, are going, do go*), is also used to express *let's go.*

Vamos a clase ahora mismo.
Let's go to class right now.

The Contraction al / La contracción al

As you can see in the preceding examples, the verb **ir** is often used with the preposition **a** to indicate where someone is going (to).

When **a** is followed by **el**, it contracts to **al**, just as **de + el → del (Capítulo 3). Al** and **del** are the only *contractions* (**las contracciones**) in Spanish.

a + el → al

Voy al centro comercial.
I'm going to the mall.

Vamos a la tienda.
We're going to the store.

Where are you going? Rosa and Casandra are housemates. ***CASSANDRA:*** *Where are you going?* ***ROSA:*** *I'm going to the Central Market.* ***CASSANDRA:*** *What are you going to buy there?* ***ROSA:*** *I'm going to buy some presents for my family in New Jersey.* ***CASSANDRA:*** *Are you going to travel to the United States soon?* ***ROSA:*** *Yes, in two weeks. Why don't you come to the Market with me?* ***CASSANDRA:*** *Yes! Let's go.*

Using ir to Talk About the Future / El uso de *ir* para hablar del futuro

You can use the verb **ir** + **a** + *infinitive* to talk about the future in Spanish.

¡OJO!

This structure is like **aprender** + **a** + *infinitive*, which you learned in **Gramática 8 (Cap. 3)**.

¡OJO!

This use of **a** is different from the use of **a** to indicate where someone is going.

Voy al centro para comer.
I'm going downtown *to eat.*

Van a venir a la fiesta esta noche.
They're coming to the party tonight.
Voy a comer en un restaurante en el centro.
I'm going to eat at a downtown restaurant.

Práctica y comunicación

Summary of *ir*

voy, vas...

ir + a + infinitivo

A. Mañana

Paso 1. Autoprueba. Complete las siguientes frases con formas del verbo **ir.**

1. tú _____
2. nosotros _____
3. yo _____
4. Uds. _____
5. Ud. _____

Paso 2. Ahora use las siguientes frases para expresar lo que (*what*) Ud. va a hacer o no hacer mañana.

MODELO: estudiar → Mañana **no voy a** estudiar.

1. ir a un centro comercial
2. comer en la cafetería de la universidad
3. estudiar en la biblioteca
4. escribir e-mails
5. venir a la clase de español
6. poder hacer toda mi tarea (*homework*)
7. bailar en una discoteca

Paso 3. Ahora use las frases del **Paso 2** para entrevistar a un compañero o una compañera.

MODELO: estudiar → ¿**Vas a** estudiar mañana?

B. ¿Adónde van de compras? Haga oraciones completas, usando (*using*) **ir.**
¡OJO! a + el → al.

MODELO: Marta / el centro → Marta **va al** centro.

1. tú y yo / la *boutique* Regalitos
2. Francisco / el almacén Goya
3. Juan y Raúl / el centro comercial
4. (tú) / el Mercado Central
5. Ud. / la tienda Gómez
6. yo / ¿ ?

C. ¿Adónde va Ud. si... ? ¿Cuántas oraciones puede hacer?

Vocabulario útil

el cine movie theater
el mercadillo flea market

Me gusta **+** leer.
ir de compras.
buscar gangas y regatear.
hablar con mis amigos.
comer en restaurantes.
mirar programas de detectives.
ver películas (*movies*).
+ Por eso voy a _____.

Prác. A, Paso 1: Answers: 1. vas 2. vamos 3. voy 4. van 5. va

120 ■ ciento veinte

Capítulo 4 De compras

D. Intercambios

Paso 1. En parejas, túrnense para hacer y contestar preguntas sobre sus planes para el fin de semana. Aquí hay unas actividades posibles. Traten de obtener (*Try to get*) mucha información. **¡OJO! ¿adónde?** = *where to?*

MODELO: ir de compras → **¿Vas a ir** de compras **este fin de semana**? ¿**Adónde** vas a ir? ¿**Por qué** vas a ese centro comercial? ¿**Qué** vas a comprar?

1. ir de compras
2. leer una novela
3. asistir a un concierto
4. estudiar para un examen
5. ir a una fiesta
6. escribir una carta
7. ir a bailar
8. escribir un enayo (*essay*)
9. practicar un deporte (*sport*)
10. mirar mucho la televisión

Paso 2. Ahora digan (*tell*) al resto de la clase un plan que Uds. tienen en común y otra actividad para la que (*which*) tienen distintos planes.

Un poco de todo

Algo sobre...

las compras en Guatemala y Honduras

Igual que^a en los Estados Unidos, en el mundo hispano abundan^b los centros comerciales. De hecho,^c en algunos^d países, como en Guatemala y Honduras, se llaman «malls». Algunos centros comerciales están en el centro de la ciudad y otros en las afueras.^e En las tiendas de los centros comerciales los precios son siempre fijos.

 ¿Hay grandes centros comerciales en el centro de su ciudad? ¿O están en las afueras?

^aIgual... *Similar to* ^b*there are many* ^cDe... *In fact* ^d*some* ^een... *in the outskirts*

City Mall, San Pedro Sula, Honduras. Es probablemente el centro comercial más grande y moderno de todo el país.

A. Lengua y cultura: Pero, ¿no se puede[*] *(can't one)* regatear?

Paso 1. Complete the following paragraphs about shopping. Give the correct form of the words in parentheses, as suggested by context. When two possibilities are given in parentheses, select the correct word.

¿**A** Ud. le gusta ir de compras? En (los / las¹) ciudades hispanas, hay una (grande²) variedad de tiendas para (ir³) de compras. Hay almacenes, centros comerciales y *boutiques* (elegante⁴), como en (este⁵) país, en donde los precios son siempre (fijo⁶).

También hay tiendas que (vender⁷) un solo^a producto. Por ejemplo,^b en una zapatería solo hay zapatos. En español el sufijo **-ería** se usa^c para (formar⁸) el nombre de la tienda. ¿Dónde (creer⁹) Ud. que venden papel y (otro¹⁰) artículos de escritorio^d? ¿A qué tienda (ir¹¹) a ir Ud. a comprar fruta?

Finalmente, vamos (a / de¹²) mencionar los mercados porque hay muchos en el mundo hispano. En (este¹³) mercados hay (pequeño¹⁴) tiendas permanentes o temporales^e donde Ud. (poder¹⁵) encontrar^f desde comida^g típica hasta artesanías^h locales o ropa interior. Allí los compradoresⁱ (regatear¹⁶) los precios, porque el primer^j precio casi siempre (ir¹⁷) a ser muy alto.

^a*single* ^bPor... *For example* ^cse... *is used* ^dartículos... *writing implements* ^e*temporary* ^f*find* ^g*food* ^h*arts and crafts* ⁱ*shoppers, buyers* ^j*first*

---

*Note that sometimes placing the word **se** before a verb changes its meaning slightly: **puede** = he/she/you can; **se puede** = one can. You will learn how to use this structure in **Capítulo 8**.*

Una zapatería, en Quetzaltenango, Guatemala

Paso 2. Comprensión. Complete las oraciones.

1. En las ciudades hispanas hay *boutiques,*

tiendas, _____, _____ y

_____.

2. El nombre de muchas tiendas especializadas en un

tipo de producto termina en _____.

3. Una tienda de zapatos se llama una _____.

4. Si a Ud. le gusta practicar español y regatear, debe ir a

_____.

Paso 3. En parejas, hagan una lista de los lugares para ir de compras que hay en la ciudad donde Uds. estudian. No olviden (*Don't forget*) su propio *campus.* ¿Hay muchas opciones o pocas? ¿Son fijos los precios en todos los lugares? ¿Tienen una tienda favorita entre todas? Luego (*Then*) comparen sus respuestas con las (*those*) de otras parejas. ¿Hay una tienda favorita de toda la clase?

B. Encuesta *(Poll)*

Paso 1. Entreviste a (*Interview*) un mínimo de seis compañeros de clase para saber (*to find out*) la siguiente información. Apunte (*Write down*) sus respuestas.

• un aspecto de la moda actual (*current*) que tiene ganas de tener o llevar
• algo (*something*) dictado por la moda que cree que es absurda

> ### Vocabulario útil
>
> **un agujero** (hole) **en la nariz** (nose) / **la lengua** (tongue)
> **unos aretes de oro**
> **unos** *jeans* **de Ralph Lauren o Narciso Rodríguez**
> **llevar faldas muy cortas/largas**
> **llevar la gorra de atrás para adelante** (backwards)
> **llevar los pantalones muy bajos** (low) / **estrechos** (tight)
> **los tatuajes**

Paso 2. Organice los resultados de su encuesta para presentarlos al resto de la clase. **¡OJO! nadie** = *no one.*

MODELO: Seis estudiantes quieren tener tatuajes. Nadie quiere comprar aretes de oro. Tres estudiantes creen que es bueno llevar faldas muy, muy cortas. Uno/a cree...

En su comunidad

Entreviste a (*Interview*) una persona hispana de su universidad o ciudad para informarse de (*find out about*) sus preferencias con respecto a las compras y la moda.

> ### PREGUNTAS POSIBLES
>
> • ¿Cuáles son las tiendas favoritas de esta persona para comprar comida (*food*)? ¿para comprar ropa?
> • ¿Hay mercados en su país de origen? ¿Qué venden en los mercados? ¿Se puede regatear allí?
> • En su opinión, ¿dónde hay más preocupación por la ropa, en este país o en su país de origen?

SALU2

«¡Moda, moda, moda!» Segmento 2

Antes de mirar

Conteste las siguientes preguntas.

1. ¿Prefiere Ud. las camisetas o con diseños o mensajes (*messages*) o sin nada? ¿Tiene una camiseta muy especial?
2. En general, ¿hay algunas marcas (*brands*) que Ud. prefiere? ¿Qué le gusta especialmente de esas marcas? ¿los diseños? ¿los colores? ¿el precio?

Este segmento

En este segmento del programa, Laura entrevista a otro diseñador puertorriqueño y los presentadores hablan del tipo de ropa de su preferencia.

Javier Claudio es dueño (*owner*) de la tienda Icónica, que se especializa en diseños (*designs*) de camisetas.

Fragmento del guion

Yo creo que en Puerto Rico por la condición del Caribe, que es un clima tropical y es caluroso,[a] pues los jóvenes universitarios mayormente andan[b] siempre en *T-shirts* y mahones,[c] quizás[d] andan también en pantalones cortos, ¿no? y tenis. De hecho, eso fue lo que me llevó a mí a hacer[e] la marca Icónica.

[a]*hot* [b]*mayormente... mostly wear* [c]*jeans (only in Puerto Rico)* [d]*maybe* [e]*De... In fact, that's what motivated me to create*

Vocabulario del segmento

se hace	becomes	nos recuerda	it reminds us
como dice el nombre	as the name suggests	importantísimos	very important
nos representan	respresents us	¡Ay, mi'jo!	Oh, boy!
la venta	sale	en todas partes	everywhere
¡Bien padres!	Very cool!	vestida impecablemente	impeccably dressed

Después de mirar

A. ¿Está claro? ¿Quién dice (*says*) las siguientes oraciones? Conteste con la inicial del nombre de la persona: Ana (**A**), Javier (**J**), Laura (**L**) o Víctor (**V**).

1. «...donde el viejo San Juan se hace global con los diseños de camisetas.»
2. «...como dice el nombre, son íconos de la cultura popular, ... »
3. «Icónica es otro ejemplo (*example*) de globalización, en este caso de productos hispanos.»
4. «Nos recuerda que en el mundo de la alta costura (*high fashion*) hay nombres hispanos importantísimos, ... »
5. «El próximo segmento nos lleva a una tienda aquí en Los Ángeles.»

B. Un poco más. Conteste las siguientes preguntas.

1. ¿Cómo se llama la tienda de Javier? ¿Por qué se llama así (*like that*)?
2. ¿Qué diseñadores importantes nombra Ana?
3. ¿Dónde compra ropa Ana?

C. Y ahora, Uds. En parejas, hablen de los estilos o marcas de ropa que se mencionan en el programa y de los estilos o marcas que Uds. prefieren. Expliquen por qué. Luego digan (*tell*) a la clase una cosa que Uds. tienen en común o una en que son muy diferentes.

A LEER

¿Hay mercados de artesanías (*arts and crafts*) en la zona donde Ud. vive? ¿Son fijos los precios en esos mercados?

Lectura cultural: Guatemala y Honduras

Los mercados

En Guatemala y Honduras hay mercados donde se puede comprar artículos de artesanía a buen precio. Son famosos los mercados guatemaltecos de las ciudades de Guatemala, Antigua, Chichicastenango y Quezaltenango. En estos mercados existe la costumbre[a] del «regateo»: el comprador[b] de un artículo debe negociar el precio con el vendedor.[c] Los vendedores invitan a los compradores a regatear y con frecuencia se escucha decir:[d] « ...pero tiene rebaja, ofrezca un precio[e]».

En Guatemala, los tejidos[f] de tradición maya son especialmente populares entre los turistas por su colorido y belleza.[g] En Honduras, además de[h] artesanías, los turistas también compran café, ron,[i] vainilla, cerámica y puros.[j]

[a]*custom* [b]*buyer, customer* [c]*seller* [d]*se... one hears people say* [e]*pero... but a discount is possible, make an offer* [f]*weavings* [g]*por... for their colors and beauty* [h]*además... besides* [i]*rum* [j]*cigars*

Los gemelos (*twins*) Hunahpú y Xbalanqué, que juegan a la pelota (*play a ball game*) en Xibalba, el otro mundo (*underworld*) de los mayas, según el *Popol Vuh*

En **otros** países hispanos

- **En todo el mundo hispanohablante** En los países hispanohablantes es común encontrar[a] ropa con tallas[b] similares a las[c] de los Estados Unidos (XS, S, M, L y XL). Pero si la ropa es hecha[d] en un país hispano, se usan con frecuencia las iniciales de los adjetivos en español:

  CH = chico (México y Latinoamérica)
  P = pequeño (España)
  M = mediano
  G = grande
  EG = extra grande
  EEG = extra extra grande

- A la talla de los zapatos se le llama[e] «número». En España y en muchos países latinoamericanos, los números de zapatos para los adultos van del 35 al 46. Los números 37, 38 y 39 son muy comunes para las mujeres y, para los hombres, los números 41, 42 y 43 son muy populares.

- **En los países andinos** En estos países hay una lana[f] excelente que viene de los camélidos[g] de la región: la llama, la vicuña, la alpaca y el guanaco. La lana de estos animales es de excelente calidad y se utiliza para hacer[h] suéteres, gorras,[i] guantes,[j] ponchos, mantas,[k] etcétera.

[a]*to find* [b]*sizes* [c]*those* [d]*made* [e]*A... Shoe size is called a* [f]*wool* [g]*camel-like animals* [h]*making* [i]*knitted caps* [j]*gloves* [k]*blankets*

Un símbolo guatemalteco y hondureño: El *Popol Vuh*

La cultura maya es el sustrato fundamental de Guatemala y Honduras. El *Popol Vuh* es el libro sagrado[a] de los mayas, escrito en el siglo XVI.[b] Es la historia de la creación del mundo, según las creencias[c] mayas.

[a]*sacred* [b]*escrito... written in the 16th century* [c]*beliefs*

COMPRENSIÓN

Conteste las siguientes preguntas.

1. ¿En qué ciudades de Guatemala hay mercados de artesanías?
2. ¿Qué es el regateo?
3. ¿Cómo se indica la talla de la ropa y de los zapatos en el mundo hispanohablante?
4. ¿Dónde hay muchos productos de lana?
5. ¿En dónde se describe la creación del mundo, según los mayas?

 Y ahora, Uds.

- ¿Qué productos compran los turistas en la zona donde Uds. viven?
- ¿Cuál es el libro sagrado de su religión o la religión de su familia? ¿En qué lengua se escribió (*was it written*) originalmente?

Del mundo hispano

Antes de leer

Conteste las siguientes preguntas.

1. ¿Qué significa para Ud. la frase «ropa activa»?

2. ¿Cuándo y dónde es buena idea usar «ropa activa»? ¿Tiene Ud. ropa de este tipo?

3. Para Ud., ¿es importante que la ropa tenga (*have*) las siguientes cualidades? Explique por qué sí o por qué no.

- Repeler los mosquitos.
- Servir para proveer (*provide*) protección solar.
- Ser impermeable.
- Neutralizar malos olores (*odors*).

Lectura: Un artículo sobre la ropa

Algo[a] más que ropa
por Gregori Dolz

➡ Desde[b] las calles[c] de Manhattan a las colinas nevadas[d] de Aspen, Exofficio proporciona[e] a sus clientes algo más que ropa activa. Parte de sus beneficios ayudan a[f] causas medioambientales[g] como la Conservation Alliance o World Concern, que auxilian[h] a comunidades necesitadas[i] de todo el mundo. Además,[j] sus prendas[k] proporcionan protección contra los insectos, contra el sol[l] y el agua, contra los olores corporales[m] y muchas otras inconveniencias.

» www.exofficio.com

[a]*Something* [b]*From* [c]*streets* [d]*colinas... snowy hills* [e]*offers* [f]*ayudan... help* [g]*environmental* [h]*help*
[i]*needy* [j]*In addition* [k]*ropa* [l]*sun* [m]*bodily*

Comprensión

A. Un resumen del artículo. Las tres oraciones del artículo «Algo más que ropa» describen tres de las características de la compañía Exofficio y de la ropa que vende. Empareje (*Match*) las tres oraciones del artículo con los siguientes resúmenes.

_____ **a.** La compañía dona (*donates*) parte de sus ganancias (*earnings*) a organizaciones conservacionistas y humanitarias.

_____ **b.** La ropa de Exofficio protege (*protects*) contra diversos inconvenientes.

_____ **c.** Uno puede usar la ropa de Exofficio en muchos lugares diferentes.

B. Ud. y Exofficio

Indique la importancia que tienen para Ud. las siguientes características de Exofficio y la ropa que produce. Luego explique sus respuestas.

	MUY IMPORTANTE	IMPORTANTE	POCO IMPORTANTE	NADA IMPORTANTE
1. La compañía dona parte de sus ganancias a varias causas.	☐	☐	☐	☐
2. Es ropa protectora.	☐	☐	☐	☐
3. Es «ropa activa» que uno puede usar en muchas situaciones.	☐	☐	☐	☐

A ESCUCHAR

Los planes de Lidia y Cristina para ir de compras

Antes de escuchar

¿Espera Ud. (*Do you wait for*) las rebajas para ir de compras? ¿Para comprar qué tipo de cosas (*things*) busca Ud. rebajas? ¿para comprar ropa? ¿objetos electrónicos?

Vocabulario **para escuchar**	
la llamada (telephone) call	**empiezan** they start
¿Qué onda? What's up? (*Mexico*)	**¡Qué padre!** Great! (*Mexico*)
conmigo with me	

Después de escuchar

A. ¿Cierto o falso? Las siguientes oraciones son falsas. Corríjalas (*Correct them*).

1. Las rebajas empiezan hoy.
2. Cristina tiene clases mañana por la mañana.
3. Lidia no tiene clases mañana.
4. Cristina y Lidia van a encontrarse (*meet up*) en la universidad.
5. Lidia no tiene hermanos.

B. Intercambios. Invente la parte que falta (*is missing*) de los intercambios, usando expresiones del diálogo.

1. —_____
   —Hola, soy yo.
2. —_____
   —Muy bien. ¿Y tú?
3. —_____
   —Perfecto. En Zara, a las 7.

PRODUCCIÓN PERSONAL

¡Ahora, yo!

 A. Use de (*as a*) modelo las preguntas y respuestas de la página 99 de este capítulo para hablar de su ropa favorita y su propio (*own*) estilo de vestir.

 B. Con las preguntas de la página 99 como modelo, filme una o dos entrevistas con personas que hablan de su estilo de vestir y de sus tiendas de ropa favoritas.

A ESCRIBIR

Un ensayo sobre los estilos en el *campus*

¿Cree Ud. que hay un estilo de ropa que llevan los estudiantes universitarios en general o hay más de un estilo? En su opinión, ¿se ven (*are seen*) en este *campus* las tendencias de la moda (*fashion*) que predominan en el resto del país?

Preparar

Paso 1. En parejas, hagan una lista del estilo o los estilos de moda típicos en su universidad. Para cada estilo, hagan una lista de la ropa más característica del estilo, con una descripción básica (por ejemplo: pantalones negros muy estrechos...). La siguiente tabla va a ayudarles (*help you*) a organizar sus ideas. ¡Deben incluir a los profesores también! Pónganle (*Give*) un nombre a cada (*each*) estilo si no lo tiene todavía (*yet*). ¡Sean (*Be*) originales!

	Primer (*1st*) lugar en popularidad en el *campus*	Segundo (*2nd*) lugar en popularidad	Tercer (*3rd*) lugar en popularidad
¿Nombre del estilo?			
Personas (estudiantes, profesores, personal administrativo...)			
Descripción de la ropa			

Paso 2. Ahora use sus ideas para escribir un ensayo sobre la moda en su universidad. Incluya unas oraciones sobre su propio (*own*) estilo. Hay más ayuda (*help*) en Connect.

Sugerencia: You are now ready to play Quest 2 in **Practice Spanish: Study Abroad** (www.mhpractice.com).

Más ideas para su portafolio

- Busque (*Find*) una fotografía reciente de Ud. llevando (*wearing*) ropa bonita o interesante en una ocasión especial y descríbala (*describe it*).

- Busque la página web de su tienda o marca favorita y determine si tiene una página en español. Si la tiene (*If it has one*), incluya (*include*) unos detalles de la página.

- Si ha estado jugando (*have been playing*) Practice Spanish: Study Abroad, en Quest 2 Ud. pasó su primer día (*spent your first day*) en el Instituto de Lenguas y tuvo que aprender sobre (*had to learn about*) sus clases y el campus. Ahora cree un folleto (*brochure*) para estudiantes nuevos sobre la universidad a la que asiste Ud. Incluya (*Include*) detalles (*details*) sobre las clases y las actividades que ofrece (*that it offers*).

EN RESUMEN En este capítulo

Visit **www.connectspanish.com** to practice the vocabulary and grammar points covered in this chapter.

AFTER STUDYING THIS CHAPTER I CAN . . .

☐ name items of clothing and use color adjectives (100–101, 103)

☐ talk about shopping (100)

☐ count beyond 100 and express years (105)

☐ use demonstratives to describe people and things at different distances (110–112)

☐ talk about more actions with a different kind of **-er** and **-ir** verbs (114–115)

☐ use very frequent expressions with **tener** (115–116)

☐ talk about where I'm going and what I'm going to do in the near future, using the verb **ir** (119–120)

☐ recognize/describe at least 2–3 aspects of Guatemalan and Honduran cultures

Gramática en breve

9. Demonstrative Adjectives and Pronouns

this → *these*	*that/those*	*that/those* (*over there*)
este → **estos**	**ese** → **esos**	**aquel** → **aquellos**
esta → **estas**	**esa** → **esas**	**aquella** → **aquellas**
neuter: **esto**	neuter: **eso**	neuter: **aquello**

10. *Tener, venir, poder, preferir, querer;* Some Idioms with *tener*

tener: **tengo, tienes, tiene, tenemos, tenéis, tienen**

venir: **vengo, vienes, viene, venimos, venís, vienen**

poder: **puedo, puedes, puede, podemos, podéis, pueden**

preferir: **prefiero, prefieres, prefiere, preferimos, preferís, prefieren**

querer: **quiero, quieres, quiere, queremos, queréis, quieren**

Idioms with **tener:**

tener miedo de / prisa / razón / sueño
  no tener razón
tener ganas de + *inf.* **/ que** + *inf.*

11. *Ir;* The Contraction *al; Ir* + *a* + *inf.*

ir: **voy, vas, va, vamos, vais, van**

a + el → al

Vocabulario

Remember that changes like **e → ie** and **o → ue** will be shown like this in vocabulary lists.

Los verbos

ir (voy, vas,...)	to go
ir a + *inf.*	to be going to (*do something*)
poder (puedo)	to be able, can
preferir (prefiero)	to prefer
querer (quiero)	to want
tener (tengo, tienes,...)	to have
venir (vengo, vienes,...)	to come

La ropa

llevar	to wear; to carry; to take
usar	to wear; to use
el abrigo	coat
los aretes	earrings
la blusa	blouse
el bolso	purse
las botas	boots
los calcetines	socks
la camisa	shirt
la camiseta	T-shirt
la cartera	wallet; handbag
las chanclas	flip-flops
la chaqueta	jacket
el cinturón	belt
la corbata	tie
la falda	skirt
las gafas de sol	sun glasses
la gorra	baseball cap
el impermeable	raincoat
las medias	stockings
los pantalones	pants
los pantalones cortos	shorts
el reloj	watch
la ropa	clothing
la ropa interior	underwear
las sandalias	sandals
el sombrero	hat
la sudadera	sweatshirt
el traje	suit
el traje de baño	swimsuit
el vestido	dress
los zapatos	shoes

Cognados: los *jeans*, el suéter, los tenis

De compras

ir (voy, vas...) de compras	to go shopping
regatear	to haggle; to bargain

Repaso: comprar, vender

la ganga	bargain
el precio (fijo)	(fixed, set) price
las rebajas	sales, reductions
¿cuánto cuesta(n)?	how much does it (do they) cost?
de todo	everything
Es de última moda. } Está de moda. }	It's trendy (hot).

Las materias

de...	
cuadros	plaid
lunares	polka-dot
rayas	striped
es de...	it is made of . . .
algodón (m.)	cotton
cuero	leather
lana	wool
oro	gold
plata	silver
seda	silk
la materia	material

Los lugares

el almacén	department store
el centro	downtown
el centro comercial	shopping mall
el mercado	market(place)
la tienda	shop, store

Cognado: la plaza

Los colores

amarillo/a	yellow
anaranjado/a	orange
azul	blue
blanco/a	white
(de) color café	brown
gris	gray
morado/a	purple
negro/a	black
rojo/a	red
rosado/a	pink
verde	green

Otros sustantivos

el/la chico/a	guy/girl
el examen	exam, test

Los adjetivos

barato/a	inexpensive
caro/a	expensive
cómodo/a	comfortable
poco/a	little, few

Repaso: mucho/a

Los números a partir del 100

ciento, ciento uno, ciento dos... ciento noventa y nueve, doscientos/as, trescientos/as, cuatrocientos/as, quinientos/as, seiscientos/as, setecientos/as, ochocientos/as, novecientos/as, mil, un millón (de)

Repaso: cien

Las formas demostrativas

aquel, aquella, aquellos/as	that, those ([way] over there)
aquello (neuter)	that ([way] over there)
ese/a, esos/as	that, those
eso (neuter)	that

Repaso: este/a, esto (neuter), estos/as

Palabras adicionales

¿adónde?	where (to)?
al (a + el)	to the
allá	(way) over there
allí	there
si	if
sobre	about
tener...	
ganas de + inf.	to feel like (doing something)
miedo (de)	to be afraid (of)
prisa	to be in a hurry
que + inf.	to have to (do something)
razón	to be right
sueño	to be sleepy
no tener razón	to be wrong
vamos	let's go
¿no?, ¿verdad?	right, don't they (you, and so on)?

Repaso: aquí, mucho (adv.), poco (adv.), tener... años

Vocabulario personal

5

En casa

En este capítulo

www.connectspanish.com

Casas de muchos colores en una calle (*street*) del centro de Granada, Nicaragua

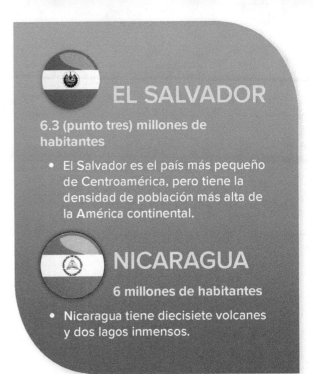

EL SALVADOR

6.3 (punto tres) millones de habitantes

- El Salvador es el país más pequeño de Centroamérica, pero tiene la densidad de población más alta de la América continental.

NICARAGUA

6 millones de habitantes

- Nicaragua tiene diecisiete volcanes y dos lagos inmensos.

- ¿Dónde vive Ud.? ¿En qué parte de la ciudad? ¿en el centro, en la zona universitaria o en una zona residencial? ¿Vive en una residencia, en una casa o en un apartamento?

- ¿Cómo es su alcoba,[a] grande o pequeña? ¿Tiene un cuarto de baño propio[b]?

- ¿Cómo se siente Ud.[c] cuando está en casa? (**Me siento...**)

[a]*bedroom* [b]*un... your own bathroom* [c]*se... do you feel*

MANUEL GIL DEL VALLE CONTESTA LAS PREGUNTAS.

- Vivo en Managua, en un apartamento en una zona residencial que está a 5 kilómetros del centro de la ciudad.

- Es un apartamento muy cómodo, con tres alcobas y dos baños. Mi mujer y yo tenemos la alcoba de matrimonio,[a] que es muy amplia y luminosa y tiene su propio[b] baño. La alcoba de mis hijas también está muy bien, pero no tiene cuarto de baño propio. La otra alcoba es más pequeña y funciona como un estudio.

- Me gusta mucho estar en casa. Allí me siento bien porque puedo descansar y relajarme.[c] Pero sobre todo[d] porque en mi casa estoy con mi mujer y mis hijas, que son lo más importante en mi vida.[e]

[a]*alcoba... master bedroom (lit., of the marriage)* [b]*own* [c]*descansar... rest and relax* [d]*sobre... especially* [e]*lo... the most important thing in my life*

Los muebles,° los cuartos y otras partes de la casa
Los... *Furniture*

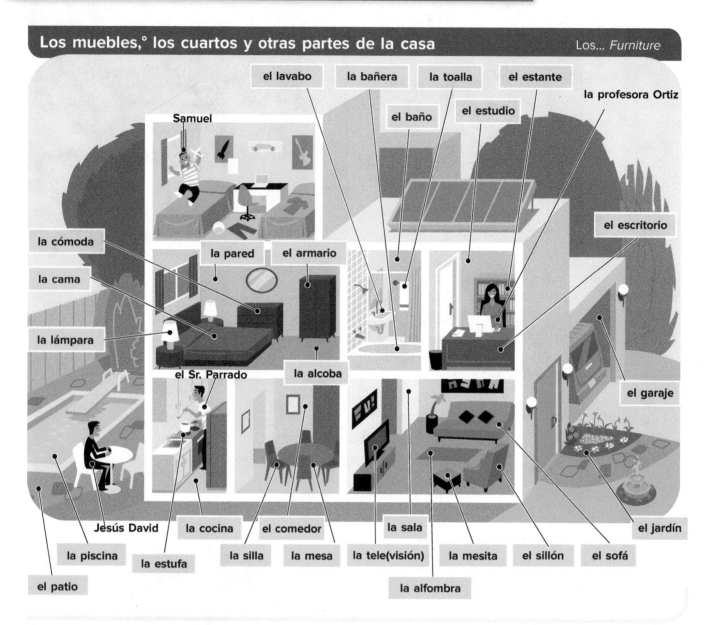

el lavabo · la bañera · la toalla · el estante · la profesora Ortiz · el baño · el estudio · Samuel · la cómoda · la cama · la lámpara · la pared · el armario · el escritorio · el Sr. Parrado · la alcoba · el garaje · Jesús David · la piscina · la estufa · la cocina · el comedor · la sala · la mesita · el sillón · el sofá · el jardín · el patio · la silla · la mesa · la tele(visión) · la alfombra

You can hear the pronunciation of theme vocabulary words and phrases in the Connect eBook.

Así se dice

el armario = el ropero
la bañera = la tina
el estudio = el despacho (*Sp.*)
el lavabo = la pileta (*L.A.*)

la piscina = la alberca (*Mex.*), la pileta (*Arg.*)
la sala = el living
la televisión = el televisor

There is great variation in the ways in which Spanish-speakers refer to the bedroom. It is called **la habitación** (also a synonym for any room of a house) by many native speakers, **el dormitorio** by Argentines, and **la recámara** by Mexicans.

---

*This is the first group of words you will learn for talking about where you live and the things found in your room, house, or apartment. You will learn additional vocabulary for those topics in **Capítulos 10** and **12**.*

Comunicación

A. Asociaciones. ¿Qué cuarto(s) o lugar de la casa asocia Ud. con estas actividades? **¡OJO! se** + *verb* = *"one (does something)"*.

1. Es donde se trabaja en la computadora.
2. Es donde se come con toda la familia.
3. La parte de la casa para el coche.
4. Allí se nada (*one swims*).
5. Allí se duerme (*one sleeps*).
6. Es donde se prepara la comida (*food*).

B. Asociaciones

Paso 1. En parejas, hagan y contesten preguntas para hacer una lista de los muebles o partes de la casa que Uds. asocian con las siguientes actividades.

1. estudiar para un examen
2. dormir la siesta (*to take a nap*) por la tarde
3. pasar (*to spend*) una noche en casa con la familia
4. celebrar con una comida (*meal*) especial
5. lavar (*to wash*) el perro
6. hablar de temas (*topics*) serios con los amigos (padres, esposo/a, hijos)

Paso 2. Ahora comparen sus respuestas con las (*those*) del resto de la clase. ¿Tienen todos las mismas costumbres (*same customs*)?

C. Esta casa

Paso 1. En parejas, identifiquen las partes de esta casa y lo que (*what*) hay en cada (*each*) una. Usen colores también.

MODELO: **E1:** El número 1 corresponde al **garaje.**
       E2: ¿Qué hay en el garaje?
       E1: Hay **un coche verde** y...

> **Vocabulario útil**
>
> **la bicicleta**
> **las cortinas**
> **la planta**

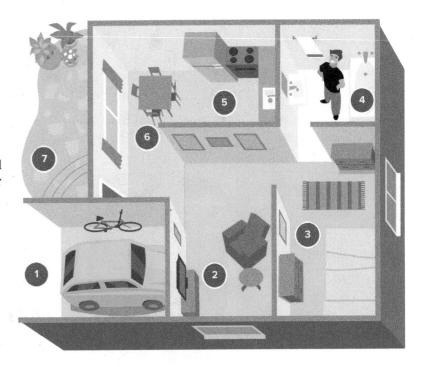

Paso 2. Ahora expandan el plano de esta casa para incorporar dos partes más. Deben pensar (*think*) en la utilidad (*purpose*) que tienen esas partes y poner (*put in*) los muebles apropiados. Luego (*Then*) prepárense para describir sus cambios.

Paso 3. Describan al resto de la clase las nuevas partes de la casa sin (*without*) leer.

MODELO: Las nuevas partes de nuestra casa son... En el/la _____ hay...

Nota **cultural**

Las casas en el mundo hispano

La palabra **casa** se usa de manera genérica en español para significar hogar,[a] como en estos ejemplos.

ir/regresar a casa	to go/return home
estar en casa	to be at home
Estás en tu casa.	Welcome. (*Lit.* You're in your home.)

Hay una gran variedad de tipos de casas en el mundo hispano y no se puede decir que haya[b] «una casa típica». Las construcciones dependen del[c] uso, de la zona (rural o urbana), del clima y de las tradiciones históricas y culturales. Y, por supuesto,[d] del factor económico.

En las ciudades, la mayoría de las personas no vive en casas sino[e] en apartamentos. Otras palabras para apartamento son **piso** (España) y **departamento** (México, Argentina).

[a]*home* [b]*decir... say that there is* [c]*on the* [d]*por... of course* [e]*but rather*

El Museo Casa Natal de Rubén Darío, en Ciudad Darío, Nicaragua

En su ciudad, ¿es más común vivir en un apartamento o en una casa? En su estado o país, ¿hay un estilo de casas predominante o tradicional?

¿Qué día es hoy?

¡OJO!

To express *on* with days of the week, use **el** (for singular) or **los** (to generalize), as appropriate. The word **en** is not used with days of the week in Spanish. See *Nota comunicativa,* page 135.

lunes

1. Javier asiste a clase el lunes a las ocho.

martes

2. Javier mira la televisión el martes.

miércoles

3. Javier va al gimnasio el miércoles.

jueves

4. Javier trabaja cuatro horas el jueves.

viernes

5. El viernes va al mercado con unos amigos.

el fin de semana (sábado y domingo)

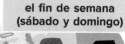

6. El fin de semana juega al basquetbol con sus amigos.

Hoy es viernes (domingo,...).	Today is Friday (Sunday, . . .).
Mañana es sábado (lunes,...).	Tomorrow is Saturday (Monday, . . .).
Ayer fue martes (miércoles,...).	Yesterday was Tuesday (Wednesday, . . .).
el fin de semana	the weekend
pasado mañana	the day after tomorrow
anteayer	the day before yesterday
el próximo jueves (viernes,...)	next Thursday (Friday, . . .)
el jueves (viernes,...) que viene	
la próxima semana	next week
la semana que viene	

- In Spanish-speaking countries, the week usually starts with **lunes.**
- The days of the week are not capitalized in Spanish.
- The words **sábado** and **domingo** have plural forms: **sábados, domingos.** All other days of the week end in **-s**; they use the same form for the plural as they do for the singular. See examples in **Nota comunicativa.**

Nota comunicativa

Cómo expresar *on* con los días de la semana

The definite article (singular or plural) is used to express **on** with the days of the week in Spanish.

    el + *day* = on (Monday, Tuesday . . .)

        Esta semana, tengo que ir al mercado **el** lunes.

        This week, I have to go to the market on Monday.

    los + *day* (plural form, if any) = on (Mondays, Tuesdays . . .)

        Por lo general voy al mercado **los** viernes o **los** sábados.

        I generally go to the market on Fridays or on Saturdays.

You will use **el** and **los** with days of the week in **Comunicación A** and **B**.

Comunicación

A. La semana

  Paso 1. Complete las oraciones.

    1. Hoy es _____. Mañana es _____.

    2. Ayer fue _____ y anteayer fue _____.

    3. Si hoy es sábado, mañana es _____. Ayer fue _____.

    4. Si ayer fue domingo, hoy es _____ y mañana es _____.

    5. Hay clase de español los _____, _____ y _____.

    6. No tengo clases los _____ ni (*nor*) los _____.

    7. Mi próximo examen de _____ es este _____.

    8. Trabajo los _____ por la mañana/tarde/noche.

    9. Los _____ por la tarde nunca estudio en la biblioteca.

    10. Casi todos los _____ salgo (*I go out*) con mis amigos.

  Paso 2. En parejas, intercambien (*exchange*) la información de los números 6–10. Luego digan (*tell*) a la clase las actividades que tienen en común.

B. Mi semana. Primero (*First*), indique lo que Ud. va a hacer **el** (lunes...) que viene. Luego indique una actividad típica de todos **los** (lunes...). Siga los modelos.

MODELOS: **El lunes** tengo que ir al gimnasio. (Voy a ir al gimnasio **el lunes**.)
Por lo general (Generalmente) voy al gimnasio **los lunes**.

Estrategia

Remember to use an infinitive after **ir a** if you want to use a verb. To express a place after **ir a,** remember to form the contraction **al** if necessary. The infinitive is used after all of the other verbs in the middle column.

lunes martes miércoles jueves viernes sábado domingo	**+**	ir a + *place* ir a + *inf.* deber desear necesitar poder preferir tener ganas de tener que	**+**	el bar la biblioteca el centro el cine (*movies*) el gimnasio el museo el parque ¿ ? descansar (*to rest*) en cama hasta muy tarde jugar (*to play*) al (tenis, golf, voleibol, basquetbol) ¿ ?

¿Cuándo? • Las preposiciones (Part 1)*

1. Antes de la fiesta, Rosa prepara la ensalada.

2. Durante la fiesta, Rosa baila y baila hasta el final.

3. Después de la fiesta, Rosa limpia la sala.

a preposition / **una preposición** = a word or phrase that specifies the relationship of one word to another

Prepositions link words or phrases to other words or phrases. The prepositions are indicated in the following sentences. Can you tell what words or phrases are linked by them?

1. The book is **on** the table.
2. The homework is **for** tomorrow.
3. Los sábados siempre descanso **hasta** muy tarde.
4. Voy a mirar la tele **después de** comer.

---

*You will learn prepositions that express spatial relationships in the **Vocabulario: Preparación** section of **Capítulo 6.**

136 ■ ciento treinta y seis

Capítulo 5 En casa

You have already used many common Spanish prepositions, including: **a, con, de, en, hasta** (as in **hasta mañana**), **para,** and **por** (*in*, *during*, as in **por la mañana**).

In English, prepositions are often followed by the *-ing* form of a verb. However, in Spanish, the infinitive is the only verb form that can follow a preposition. You learned this with the expressions **para** + *inf.* and **ir a** + *inf.*

¿Adónde vas **después de** estudiar?	*Where are you going after studying (after you study)?*
Tengo ganas de comer **antes de** mirar la tele esta noche.	*I feel like eating before watching TV (before I watch TV) tonight.*

Comunicación

A.   ¿Cuándo?

Paso 1. Complete las siguientes oraciones lógicamente. Puede usar sustantivos, infinitivos, días de la semana, etcétera.

1. Por lo general, prefiero estudiar antes de / después de las nueve de la noche.
2. Siempre tengo mucho sueño durante la clase de _____.
3. Voy a la clase de español antes de / después de la clase de _____.
4. Los _____ (día o días), estoy en la universidad hasta _____ (hora).
5. No puedo ir a fiestas durante la semana. Voy los _____ (día o días).
6. Tengo que estudiar en esta universidad hasta el año _____.

Paso 2. Ahora entreviste (*interview*) a un compañero o una compañera, usando (*using*) las oraciones del **Paso 1.**

MODELOS:: ¿Prefieres estudiar antes de las nueve de la noche?
¿Prefieres estudiar antes o después de las nueve de la noche?
¿Cuándo prefieres estudiar, antes o después de las nueve de la noche?

B.   Intercambios. En parejas, túrnense para entrevistarse. Hagan sus preguntas, usando una palabra o frases de cada columna.

estudiar
hablar por teléfono
leer
trabajar
¿ ?
	+ antes de
	después de
	durante
	hasta
		+ tu programa favorito de
		  televisión
		las clases
		las conferencias (*lectures*)
		  de _____
		los viernes por la noche, los
		  domingos por la mañana...
		estudiar, mirar la tele,...
		las tres de la mañana,
		  medianoche (*midnight*),
		  muy tarde,...
		¿ ?

«Vivir con la familia» Segmento 1

«Bueno, mientras (*while*) asisto a la universidad vivo con mis padres. Lo mejor (*The best part*) de vivir con mis padres es la convivencia (*living together*) con ellos y lo peor (*the worst thing*) es que tengo que acatar sus reglas (*follow their rules*).»

Antes de mirar

Conteste las siguientes preguntas.

1. ¿Dónde vive Ud. ahora mientras (*while*) asiste a la universidad? ¿En una residencia universitaria? ¿en un apartamento compartido (*shared*) con otros estudiantes? ¿con su familia?

2. ¿Dónde vive la mayoría (*majority*) de los estudiantes de su universidad?

Este segmento

El tema del reportaje (*report*) de este segmento es dónde viven los estudiantes universitarios estadounidenses y mexicanos.

Vocabulario **del segmento**

les vuelven a dar la bienvenida	welcome you again
¡En efecto!	You're so right!
lejos de	far from
en cambio	in contrast
no deja su hogar	don't leave home
la colonia	neighborhood (*Mex.*)
lo más céntrico	very centrally located
el apoyo que me dan	the support they give me
la novia	girlfriend
los familiares	relatives
las facilidades	facilities, conveniences

Después de mirar

A. ¿Está claro? Complete las siguientes oraciones según el video.

1. Según Víctor, muchos/pocos estudiantes estadounidenses asisten a una universidad que está lejos de su casa.
2. La mayoría de los estudiantes entrevistados (*interviewed*) vive/no vive con su familia.
3. Según unos estudiantes, uno tiene que/no tiene que acatar las reglas de la familia.
4. Para estos estudiantes, la compañía o convivencia es/no es importante.
5. Según un estudiante, cuando uno vive con la familia, no es necesario pagar las facilidades/la matrícula.

B. Un poco más. Conteste las siguientes preguntas.

1. Según los estudiantes mexicanos entrevistados, ¿qué es lo mejor de vivir con la familia? ¿Y lo peor?
2. Según Víctor, ¿por qué es caro asistir a la universidad en los Estados Unidos?

 C. Y ahora, Uds. En grupos, expresen sus opiniones sobre la idea de vivir con la familia mientras uno asiste a la universidad. ¿Qué es lo mejor y lo peor?

¿Recuerda Ud.?

Most of the verbs presented in **Gramática 12** share a first person singular irregularity with two verbs that you learned in **Capítulo 4.** Review what you know about those two verbs by completing their first person forms.

(yo) ven_____o   (yo) ten_____o

12 Expressing Actions

Hacer, oír, poner, salir, traer, ver

Grammar Tutorial 12
connect
|SPANISH
www.connectspanish.com

Gramática en acción: Aspectos de la vida de Rigoberto

1. Traigo muchos libros al salón de clase.

2. No oigo bien. Por eso hago muchas preguntas en clase.

3. Pongo la tele y veo mi programa favorito.

4. Salgo con Elena los fines de semana.

Comprensión

1. ¿Qué trae Rigoberto al salón de clase?
2. ¿Por qué hace muchas preguntas en clase? ¿Ve bien? ¿Oye bien?
3. ¿A qué hora pone la tele? ¿Por qué prefiere mirar la tele a esa hora?
4. ¿Con quién sale?

hacer (to do; to make)		oír (to hear)		poner (to put; to place)		salir (to leave; to go out)		traer (to bring)		ver (to see)	
hago	hacemos	oigo	oímos	pongo	ponemos	salgo	salimos	traigo	traemos	veo	vemos
haces	hacéis	oyes	oís	pones	ponéis	sales	salís	traes	traéis	ves	veis
hace	hacen	oye	oyen	pone	ponen	sale	salen	trae	traen	ve	ven

Aspects of Rigoberto's life **1.** I bring a lot of books to class. **2.** I don't hear well. That's why I ask a lot of questions in class. **3.** I turn on the TV and watch my favorite program. **4.** I go out with Elena on weekends.

1. hacer

Hacer expresses English *to do* or *to make* in many contexts.

Pero, Julio, ¿qué **haces**?
But, Julio, what are you doing?

Siempre **hago** la tarea en la cafetería.
I always do my homework in the cafeteria.

Hacer is also used in a number of common idioms.

hacer un viaje
hacer una pregunta

Quieren **hacer** un viaje al Perú.
They want to take a trip to Peru.

Los niños siempre **hacen** muchas preguntas.
Children always ask a lot of questions.

Hacer is also used to express *to do* with physical and academic exercises. Note that the singular **ejercicio** is used to express *to exercise* in a gym, but the plural **ejercicios** is used for aerobics.

Hace ejercicio en el gimnasio, pero **hace** ejercicios aeróbicos en casa.
She exercises in the gym but does aerobics at home.

Alicia **hace** los ejercicios en el cuaderno.
Alicia does the exercises in the notebook.

2. oír

Oír means *to hear*.
The command forms of **oír** are used to attract someone's attention in the same way that English uses *Listen!* or *Hey!*

oye (tú)   **oiga** (Ud.)   **oigan** (Uds.)

¡OJO!

oír = to hear
escuchar = to listen to
Some native speakers of Spanish use **oír** to mean *to listen to* things like music or the news. But **escuchar** can never mean *to hear*.

No **oigo** bien a la profesora.
I can't hear the professor well.

Oye, Juan, ¿vas a la fiesta?
Hey, Juan, are you going to the party?

¡**Oigan**! ¡Silencio, por favor!
Listen! Silence, please!

Oímos/Escuchamos música en clase.
We listen to music in class.

No **oigo** bien por el ruido.
I can't hear well because of the noise.

3. poner

Poner means *to put* or *to place*. Many Spanish speakers use **poner** with appliances to express *to turn on*.

Voy a **poner** la televisión.
I'm going to turn on the TV.

Siempre **pongo** leche y mucho azúcar en el café.
I always put milk and a lot of sugar in my coffee.

4. salir

Salir means *to leave* or *to go out*. Note in the examples at the right how different prepositions are used with it to express different meanings.

salir de + *place*
salir con + *person*
salir para + *destination*

Here's another useful expression: **salir bien/mal**, which means *to turn/come out well/poorly, to do well/poorly.*

Salgo con el hermano de Cecilia.
I'm going out with / dating Cecilia's brother.

Salimos para la sierra pasado mañana.
We're leaving for the mountains the day after tomorrow.

Todo va a **salir** bien.
Everything is going to turn out OK (well).

No quiero **salir** mal en esta clase.
I don't want to do poorly in this class.

Salen de la clase ahora.
They're leaving class now.

5. *traer*

Traer means *to bring.*

¡OJO!

Traer and **llevar** are somewhat related in meaning, but they are actually antonyms, like *bring* and *take* in English. **Traer** expresses *to bring* as in *to have* something *with* or *on* one. It also expresses *to bring* something *to* the person who is speaking. **Llevar** means *to take* someone or something *to* a place.

¿Por qué no **traes** ese radio a la cocina?
Why don't you bring that radio to the kitchen?

¿Cuánto dinero **traes** hoy?
How much money do you have (on you, did you bring) today?

¿Por qué no me **traes** una de las sillas del comedor?
Why don't you bring me one of the chairs from the dining room?

Este año voy a **llevar** a mi familia a Nicaragua.
This year I'm going to take my family to Nicaragua.

6. *ver*

Ver means *to see.* It can also mean *to watch* as in watching television or a movie, which is also expressed with the verb **mirar.**

¡OJO!

Mirar never expresses *to see* (except with movies). It only means *to watch, look at.*

No **veo** bien sin mis lentes.
I don't see well without my glasses.

Los niños **ven/miran** una película.
The kids are watching a movie.

Práctica y comunicación

A. Mi rutina

Paso 1. Autoprueba. Dé la forma indicada para cada verbo.

1. hacer: yo
2. oír: ellos
3. poner: yo
4. salir: yo
5. traer: yo
6. ver: yo

Verb Summary

hacer, oír, poner, salir, traer	= -g-
oír	= -y-
ver	veo

Paso 2. Ahora complete las siguientes oraciones lógicamente usando los verbos del **Paso 1** solo una vez. Añada (*Add*) una expresión de tiempo a cada oración y la palabra **no,** si es necesario.

Expresiones de tiempo

Before or after the verb: **los lunes/martes/…, los fines de semana, (casi) todos los días, a veces…**

Before the verb: **(casi) siempre, (casi) nunca**

1. _____ ejercicio en el gimnasio_____.
2. _____ a mis amigos los _____ por la _____.
3. _____ de casa antes de las _____ de la mañana.
4. _____ mi libro de texto a la clase de español _____.
5. _____ las noticias (*news*) por la tele _____.
6. _____ la ropa en la cómoda y el armario _____ .

Paso 3. Ahora, en parejas, túrnense para hacer y contestar preguntas basadas en las oraciones del **Paso 2.** Luego digan (*tell*) a la clase algo (*something*) que Uds. tienen en común o que hacen de manera muy diferente o peculiar.

MODELO: Hago ejercicio en el gimnasio casi todos días. →
¿Con qué frecuencia haces ejercicio en el gimnasio? (¿Haces ejercicio en el gimnasio todos los días?) →
Hannah y yo casi nunca hacemos ejercicio en el gimnasio.

Prác. A, Paso 1: Answers: hago 2. oyen 3. pongo 4. salgo 5. traigo 6. veo

B. Lógicamente

Paso 1. Complete las siguientes oraciones con la forma apropiada de **hacer, oír, poner, salir, traer** o **ver.** Use **no** cuando es necesario para que (*so that*) las oraciones sean (*will be*) apropiadas para Ud.

MODELO: Los estudiantes de esta clase _____ mucha tarea. →
Los estudiantes de esta clase **hacemos/hacen** mucha tarea.

1. (Yo) _____ la tele por la noche.
2. Siempre (tú) _____ los sábados por la noche con tus amigos.
3. (Nosotros) _____ el libro de texto de español a clase.
4. Muchas personas no _____ ejercicio.
5. Los hispanos _____ mucho la radio.
6. Yo _____ azúcar (*sugar*) en mi café.
7. Mi amigo va a _____ un viaje a Nicaragua en diciembre.
8. En general, (yo) _____ bien en los exámenes.
9. Me gusta _____ películas extranjeras.

Paso 2. Use las respuestas del **Paso 1** para hacerle preguntas a un compañero o una compañera. ¿Está siempre de acuerdo con Ud. su compañero/a?

MODELO: Los estudiantes de esta clase **hacemos** mucha tarea. →
¿**Crees que** los estudiantes de esta clase hacemos mucha tarea?

C. Los nuevos verbos

Paso 1. Lea (*Read*) el siguiente afiche (*poster*), que ilustra una expresión idiomática.

LOS TRES MONOS^a SABIOS

NO OÍR, NO VER, NO HABLAR

^amonos... *smart monkeys*

1. ¿Qué dicen los monos sabios en inglés?
2. ¿Qué diría (*would say*) cada mono en español hablando (*speaking*) en primera persona?
3. ¿Dónde sería (*would it be*) apropiado colgar (*to hang*) un afiche como este?

Paso 2. Los nuevos verbos se usan en más expresiones idiomáticas. Pero el significado (*meaning*) de los modismos no es siempre transparente. ¿Puede Ud. emparejar cada expresión con su significado?

EXPRESIONES

1. _____ poner un granito de arena (*sand*)
2. _____ poner en duda
3. _____ poner un límite a
4. _____ traer algo (*something*) entre manos (*hands*)
5. _____ salir en las noticias
6. _____ hacer un papel (*role*)
7. _____ ver para creer

SIGNIFICADOS

a. ¡tener sus 15 minutos de fama!
b. decir (*to say*) que algo (*something*) es cuestionable
c. necesitar la observación personal para aceptar que una cosa es verdad
d. hacer una pequeña contribución
e. decidir hasta dónde queremos llegar
f. tener un plan
g. actuar en una película o una obra de teatro (*play*)

Algo sobre...

los lagos de Nicaragua

En Nicaragua hay dos lagos inmensos: el lago de Nicaragua (o Cocibolca) y el lago de Managua (o Xolotlán). Los dos están unidos por el río[a] Tipitapa. El Cocibolca es el lago más grande[b] de Centroamérica y, después del lago Titicaca en Bolivia, es el lago más grande de Latinoamérica. En el Cocibolca hay volcanes e islas.

 ¿Cómo se llama el lago más grande de este país? ¿y el río más grande?

[a]*river* [b]*más... biggest*

El lago de Nicaragua, con el volcán Maderas al fondo (*in the background*)

D. Consecuencias lógicas. En parejas, indiquen acciones lógicas o consecuencias relacionadas con cada situación. No se limiten a usar los verbos de esta sección del libro. ¡Sean (*Be*) creativos y audaces (*daring*)!

1. Me gusta nadar (*to swim*) en los lagos. Por eso...
2. Todos los días usamos este libro en la clase de español. Por eso...
3. Mis hijos / compañeros de cuarto hacen mucho ruido en la sala. Por eso...
4. La televisión no funciona. Por eso...
5. Hay mucho ruido en el salón de clase. Por eso...
6. Estoy en la biblioteca y ¡no puedo estudiar más! Por eso...
7. Queremos bailar y necesitamos música. Por eso...
8. No comprendo la lección. Por eso...
9. Me gusta hacer ecoturismo y hablar español. Por eso...

Vocabulario útil	
gritar «¡silencio!»	to shout "silence!"
hacer una cita	to make an appointment
los vecinos	neighbors

E. Intercambios

Paso 1. En parejas, hagan y contesten las siguientes preguntas.

EN CASA

1. ¿Qué pones en el armario? ¿y en la cómoda? ¿en el cajón (*drawer*) del escritorio?
2. ¿Pones la televisión con frecuencia cuando estás en casa? ¿Qué programa(s) ves todos los días? ¿Qué programa muy popular no ves nunca? (**Nunca veo...**) ¿Cuál es el canal de televisión que más miras? ¿Por qué te gusta tanto (*so much*)?
3. ¿Pones el radio con frecuencia? ¿Prefieres oír las noticias por radio o verlas (*to see them*) en la televisión? ¿Cuál es la estación de radio que más escuchas? ¿Por qué te gusta tanto?

(Continúa.)

MIS ACTIVIDADES

4. ¿Qué haces los _____ (día) por la noche? ¿Cuándo sales con los amigos? ¿Adónde van cuando salen juntos (*together*)?

5. ¿Te gusta hacer ejercicio? ¿Haces ejercicios aeróbicos? ¿Dónde haces ejercicio?

PARA LAS CLASES

6. Generalmente, ¿qué traes a clase todos los días? ¿Crees que traes más cosas (*things*) que tus compañeros o menos? ¿Sales a veces para la clase sin tu libro de texto? ¿sin dinero? ¿Qué trae tu profesor(a) de español a clase?

7. ¿A qué hora sales para las clases los lunes? ¿A qué hora sales de clase los viernes?

8. ¿Cuándo haces la tarea? ¿Por la mañana? ¿Dónde haces la tarea? ¿En casa? ¿Haces la tarea mientras (*while*) ves la televisión? ¿mientras oyes música?

9. ¿Siempre sales bien en los exámenes? ¿En qué clase no sales bien? ¿Qué haces si sales mal en un examen?

Paso 2. Ahora digan (*tell*) a la clase dos o tres cosas que Uds. tienen en común.

MODELO: Jim y yo nunca ponemos la ropa en el armario. Hacemos ejercicio todos los días: Jim hace ejercicios aeróbicos y yo voy al gimnasio. Los dos vemos el programa _____ los lunes por la noche; es nuestro programa favorito.

Algo sobre...

las casas tradicionales centroamericanas

En Centroamérica y en otros países latinoamericanos hay casas de bajareque, un tipo de construcción tradicional de origen precolombino.[a] Se usan materiales locales y económicos: paredes sostenidas por palos[b] y rellenas de barro y cañas.[c] Las casas de bajareque son generalmente humildes,[d] pero también son construcciones ecológicas y sismorresistentes,[e] una característica importante para una región de alta actividad sísmica como es Centroamérica.

 En los Estados Unidos, ¿es la construcción de las casas típicas del norte diferente de la (*that*) de las casas del sur?

[a]*pre-Columbian* [b]*sostenidas... held up by sticks or logs* [c]*rellenas... filled with mud and reeds* [d]*humble* [e]*resistant to earthquakes*

Una casa de bajareque, en Nicaragua

¿Recuerda Ud.?

The change in the stem vowels of **preferir**, **querer**, and **poder** was presented in **Gramática 10**. Review the forms of **preferir**, **querer**, and **poder** now.

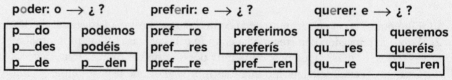

poder: o → ¿?

p__do	podemos
p__des	podéis
p__de	p__den

preferir: e → ¿?

pref__ro	preferimos
pref__res	preferís
pref__re	pref__ren

querer: e → ¿?

qu__ro	queremos
qu__res	queréis
qu__re	qu__ren

If you could complete those verb forms correctly, you already know most of the important information in **Gramática 13**.

13 Expressing Actions

Present Tense of Stem-changing Verbs (Part 2)

Grammar Tutorial 13

connect

|SPANISH

www.connectspanish.com

Gramática en acción: ¿Una fiesta exitosa?

Es la noche del sábado y todos están en una fiesta en casa de Ernesto.

- Aurora duerme en el sofá.
- Samuel juega a las cartas... a solas.
- Ernesto sirve las bebidas. Kevin pide una Coca-Cola.
- Noemí sale y vuelve con más amigas.
- ¿Es una fiesta exitosa? ¿Qué piensa Ud.? ¿Por qué?

¿Y Ud.? ¿Qué hace en las fiestas?

1. ¿Duerme Ud. en el sofá?
2. ¿Juega a las cartas?
3. ¿Sirve las bebidas?
4. ¿Pide Coca-Cola?
5. ¿Sale y vuelve con más amigos?

e → ie: p**e**nsar (to think)		o → ue: v**o**lver (to return)		e → i: p**e**dir (to ask for; to order)	
p**ie**nso	pensamos	v**ue**lvo	volvemos	p**i**do	pedimos
p**ie**nsas	pensáis	v**ue**lves	volvéis	p**i**des	pedís
p**ie**nsa	p**ie**nsan	v**ue**lve	v**ue**lven	p**i**de	p**i**den

1. **Stem-changing Verbs**

   You have already used three *stem-changing verbs* (**los verbos que cambian el radical**): **poder, preferir,** and **querer.** And you also know two other verbs that are similar (**tener** and **venir**), but whose first person singular forms are irregular.

A successful party? It's Saturday night and everybody is at a party at Ernesto's house. • Aurora is sleeping on the couch. • Samuel is playing cards … alone. • Ernesto is serving beverages. Kevin asks for a Coke. • Noemí leaves and comes back with more friends. • Is it a successful party? What do you think? Why?

Gramática

2. Stem Vowel Changes

There are three groups of stem-changing verbs. You already know about the first two.

- verbs like **preferir** and **querer,** in which the stem vowel **e** becomes **ie** in stressed syllables
- verbs like **poder,** in which the stem vowel **o** becomes **ue** in stressed syllables

Here is the third group.

- verbs in which the stem vowel **e** becomes **i**

The stem-changing pattern of all three groups is shown at the right. The stem vowels are stressed (and so they change) in all present tense forms except **nosotros** and **vosotros.** All three groups follow this regular pattern, which looks like a boot.

¡OJO!

Nosotros and **vosotros** forms *do not* have a stem vowel change.

Las vocales que cambian el radical

e → ie

-ie-	-e-
-ie-	-e-
-ie-	-ie-

o → ue

-ue-	-o-
-ue-	-o-
-ue-	-ue-

e → i

-i-	-e-
-i-	-e-
-i-	-i-

---

3. Important Stem-changing Verbs

Some stem-changing verbs practiced in this chapter include the following.

e → ie

cerrar (cierro)

cerrar (cierro)	to close
empezar (empiezo)	to begin, start
entender (entiendo)	to understand
pensar (pienso)	to think
perder (pierdo)	to lose; to miss *(an event)*

o (u) → ue

dormir (duermo)

almorzar (almuerzo)	to have lunch
dormir (duermo)	to sleep
jugar (juego)	to play *(a game, sport)*
volver (vuelvo)	to return *(to a place)*

¡OJO!

Jugar *is the only* **u → ue** *stem-changing verb in Spanish.* **Jugar** *is usually followed by* **al** *when used with the name of a sport:* **Juego al tenis.** *Some Spanish speakers, however, omit the* **al.** *Just* **a** *is used before the names of other games:* **Juego a las cartas.**

e → i

servir (sirvo) (para)

| pedir (pido) | to ask for; to order |
| servir (sirvo) | to serve; to be used *(for)* |

As you learned with **poder, preferir,** and **querer,** stem-changing verbs will be indicated in vocabulary lists with the **yo** form in parentheses, as shown here.

4. *Verb + a + Infinitive*
Like **aprender** and **ir,** the stem-changing verbs **empezar** and **volver** are followed by **a** before an infinitive.

The meaning of **empezar** does not change in this structure, but **volver a** + *infinitive* expresses *to do* (something) *again.*

Uds. **empiezan a hablar** muy bien el español.
You're starting to speak Spanish very well.

¿Cuándo **vuelves a jugar** al tenis?
When are you going to play tennis again?

5. *Conjugated Verb + Infinitive*
Like other verbs you already know (**desear, necesitar, deber,...**), **pensar** can be followed directly by an infinitive. In that case, it expresses *to intend, plan.*

The phrase **pensar en** can be used to express *to think about.*

¿Cuándo **piensas** almorzar?
When do you plan to eat lunch?

—¿En qué **piensas**?
—**Pienso** en las cosas que tengo que hacer el domingo.
"What are you thinking about?"
"I'm thinking about the things I have to do on Sunday."

Pensar de indicates one's opinion about someone or something. The answer to a question with **pensar de** usually starts with **Pienso que...**

—¿Qué **piensas** de esa situación?
—¡**Pienso** que es un desastre!
"What do you think about that situation?"
"I think (that) it's a real mess!"

—¿Qué **piensas** del nuevo apartamento de Cristina?
—**Pienso** que es elegante. . . pero ¡muy caro!
"What do you think of/about Cristina's new apartment?"
"I think (that) it's fancy. . . but very expensive!"

6. Present Tense Equivalents
Remember that the Spanish present tense has a number of present tense equivalents in English. It can also be used to express future meaning.

cierro = *I close, I am closing, I will close*

Práctica y comunicación

Stem-Change Summary

empezar (empiezo)
volver (vuelvo)
jugar (juego)
pedir (pido)

A. Asociaciones

Paso 1. Dé por lo menos un infinitivo que asocia con las siguientes ideas y cosas.

1. una bebida
2. una lección
3. a casa
4. una cama
5. una hamburguesa
6. el tenis
7. una opinión
8. una puerta
9. las llaves (*keys*)
10. la cocina
11. una siesta
12. un favor
13. las cartas
14. una palabra o frase
15. la música

Paso 2. Explique para qué sirven las siguientes cosas.

MODELO: las cartas → **Sirven para** jugar.

1. las llaves
2. una cama
3. una bandeja (*tray*)
4. un menú
5. un diccionario
6. el cerebro (*brain*)

B. La vida (*Life*) en la universidad

Paso 1. Autoprueba. Dé la forma de cada verbo para **yo** y para **nosotros.**

1. almorzar
2. entender
3. pedir
4. perder

5. dormir
6. jugar
7. pensar
8. volver

Paso 2. Ahora complete las siguientes oraciones lógicamente usando los verbos del **Paso 1** solo una vez. Añada (*Add*) una expresión de tiempo y/o la palabra **no,** si es necesario.

Expresiones de tiempo

Before or after the verb: **los lunes/martes/... , los fines de semana, (casi) todos los días, a veces...**

Before the verb: **(casi) siempre, (casi) nunca**

1. _____ la siesta _____.
2. _____ en la cafetería _____.
3. _____ pizza para almorzar _____.
4. _____ a las cartas con mi familia _____.
5. _____ en mis notas (*grades*) _____.
6. _____ mi carnet de identificación de la universidad _____.
7. _____ a casa de mis padres / de mi familia _____.
8. _____ muchas cosas en mi clase de _____ (materia).

 Paso 3. Ahora, en parejas, túrnense para hacer y contestar preguntas basadas en las oraciones del **Paso 2.** Luego digan (*tell*) a la clase algo (*something*) que Uds. tienen en común o que hacen de manera muy diferente o peculiar.

MODELOS: Duermo la siesta casi todos días. →
¿Con qué frecuencia duermes la siesta? (¿Duermes la siesta todos los días?) →
Jacob y yo dormimos la siesta casi todos los días.

C. Una tarde típica en casa.
¿Cuáles son las actividades de todos? Haga oraciones completas, usando una palabra o frase de cada columna.

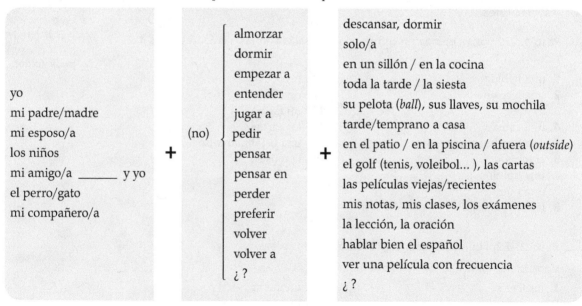

yo		descansar, dormir
mi padre/madre	almorzar	solo/a
mi esposo/a	dormir	en un sillón / en la cocina
los niños	empezar a	toda la tarde / la siesta
mi amigo/a _____ y yo	entender	su pelota (*ball*), sus llaves, su mochila
el perro/gato	jugar a	tarde/temprano a casa
mi compañero/a	**+** (no) pedir **+**	en el patio / en la piscina / afuera (*outside*)
	pensar	el golf (tenis, voleibol...), las cartas
	pensar en	las películas viejas/recientes
	perder	mis notas, mis clases, los exámenes
	preferir	la lección, la oración
	volver	hablar bien el español
	volver a	ver una película con frecuencia
	¿ ?	¿ ?

D. Una semana ideal... ¡y posible!

Paso 1. ¿Qué va a hacer Ud. la semana que viene? Organice la próxima semana en la siguiente agenda. Escriba frases con el infinitivo, por ejemplo: **ver la televisión.** Incluya actividades que tiene que hacer, pero también algunas (*some*) que tiene ganas de hacer.

	por la mañana	por la tarde	por la noche
lunes			
martes			
miércoles			
jueves			
viernes			
sábado			
domingo			

Paso 2. En parejas, hablen de su horario (*schedule*) para esta semana, basándose (*based on*) en la agenda del **Paso 1.** Luego digan (*tell*) algunas (*some*) respuestas interesantes a la clase.

MODELO: ver la televisión →
    E1: ¿Qué **piensas** hacer el domingo por la tarde?
    E2: **Pienso** ver la televisión. Y tú, ¿qué haces el domingo?
    E1: El domingo **juego** al tenis con mi amigo Alex.

Estrategia

e → ie
o → ue
e → i

E. Intercambios.
En parejas, túrnense para hacer y contestar preguntas sobre los temas siguientes con las frases sugeridas (*suggested*).

MODELOS: almorzar (¿dónde? ¿con quién? ¿a qué hora?) →
    Por lo general, ¿dónde **almuerzas** de lunes a viernes?
    ¿Con quién **vas a almorzar** hoy?
    ¿A qué hora **piensas almorzar** el domingo?

1. almorzar (¿dónde? ¿con quién? ¿a qué hora?)
2. perder (¿qué? ¿dónde? ¿con frecuencia? ¿siempre?)
3. dormir (¿cuántas horas? ¿mucho o poco? ¿siestas frecuentes o infrecuentes? ¿largas o cortas?)
4. jugar (¿juegos de mesa [*board games*]? ¿cuáles? ¿con quién? ¿dónde?)

Estrategia

generalizations: present tense
future: **ir + a** + *inf.*
definite plans: **pensar** + *inf.*

¿Recuerda Ud.?

In **Capítulo 1,** you learned how to ask what someone's name is and express your own name by using phrases with the verb **llamar.** Show what you remember by completing the following phrases.

1. (yo) _____ llamo   **2.** (tú) _____ llamas   **3.** Ud. _____ llama

The words with which you completed those phrases are part of a pronoun system that you will learn about in **Gramática 14.**

14 Expressing -self/-selves
Reflexive Pronouns (Part 1)*

Gramática en acción: La rutina diaria de Andrés

La rutina de Andrés empieza a las siete y media.

1.

2.

3.

4.

5.

6.

7.

(1) Me despierto a las siete y media y me levanto en seguida. Primero, (2) me ducho y luego (3) me cepillo los dientes. (4) Me peino, (5) me pongo la bata y (6) voy al cuarto a vestirme. Por fin, (7) salgo para la universidad. No tomo nada antes de salir porque, por lo general, ¡tengo prisa!

¿Y Ud.? ¿Cómo es su rutina diaria?

1. Yo me levanto a las _____ .
2. Me ducho por la mañana / noche.
3. Me visto en el baño / mi cuarto.
4. Me peino antes de / después de vestirme.
5. Antes de salir para las clases, tomo / no tomo el desayuno (*breakfast*).

Verbs Used Reflexively / Los verbos que se usan con pronombres reflexivos

bañarse (*to take a bath, bathe*)					
(yo)	**me baño**	I take a bath	(nosotros)	**nos bañamos**	we take a bath
(tú)	**te bañas**	you take a bath	(vosotros)	**os bañáis**	you take a bath
(Ud.)		⌈ you take a bath	(Uds.)		⌈ you take a bath
(él)	**se baña**	⟨ he takes a bath	(ellos)	**se bañan**	⟨ they take a bath
(ella)		⌊ she takes a bath	(ellas)		⌊ they take a bath

_____

Andrés's daily routine *Andrés's routine begins at seven-thirty. (1) I wake up at seven-thirty and I get up right away. First, (2) I take a shower and then (3) I brush my teeth. (4) I comb my hair, (5) I put on my robe, and (6) I go to my room to get dressed. Finally, (7) I leave for the university. I don't eat or drink anything before leaving because I'm generally in a hurry!*
You will learn how to use reflexive pronouns to express each other in **Gramática 32 (Cap. 11).**

1. Reflexive Pronouns

In Spanish, some verbs are used reflexively, that is, with reflexive pronouns that indicate that the subject is doing something *to* or *for himself, herself, itself,* and so on. The reflexive pronouns that correspond to the subject must accompany the verb, coming before it: **yo → me; tú → te; él, ella, Ud. → se; nosotros → nos; vosotros → os; ellos, ellas, Uds. → se.**

The pronoun **-se** at the end of an infinitive indicates that the verb is used reflexively: **bañarse** (to take a bath; to bathe oneself).

¡OJO!
Verbs used reflexively often do not have an exact parallel in English, and there is not always a reflexive pronoun in the translation.

Los pronombres reflexivos

yo	me	myself
tú	te	yourself (*fam., sing.*)
Ud./él/ella	se	himself, herself, itself; yourself (*form. sing.*)
nosotros/as	nos	ourselves
vosotros/as	os	yourselves (*fam. pl. Sp.*)
Uds./ellos/as.	se	themselves; yourselves (*form. pl.*)

me baño = I take a bath (bathe myself)
me ducho = I shower (take a shower)

2. Important Verbs Used Reflexively

Many English verbs that describe parts of one's daily routine—to get up, to take a bath, and so on—are expressed in Spanish with a reflexive construction. Here are some that are frequently used.

¡OJO!
Notice that some of these reflexive verbs also have stem changes: **e → ie, o → ue, e → i.**

despertarse (me despierto)

ducharse

afeitarse

vestirse (me visto)

sentarse (me siento)

> Note the **-se** on the end of these infinitives. This is how reflexive verbs will be shown in vocabulary lists.

acostarse (me acuesto)	to go to bed
afeitarse	to shave
bañarse	to take a bath, bathe
cepillarse los dientes	to brush one's teeth
despertarse (me despierto)	to wake up
divertirse (me divierto)	to have a good time, enjoy oneself
dormirse (me duermo)	to fall asleep

ducharse	to take a shower
levantarse	to get up (out of bed); to stand up
llamarse	to be called
peinarse	to brush/comb one's hair
ponerse (me pongo)	to put on (*an article of clothing*)
quitarse	to take off (*an article of clothing*)
sentarse (me siento)	to sit down
vestirse (me visto)	to get dressed

¡OJO!
After **ponerse** and **quitarse**, the definite article, not the possessive as in English, is used with articles of clothing.

Me siento y **me quito** los zapatos. Luego **me quito** los pantalones y la camisa y **me pongo** la bata.
I sit down and take off my shoes. Then I take off my pants and shirt and put on my bathrobe.

3. Placement of Reflexive Pronouns

Reflexive pronouns are placed before a conjugated verb. In a negative sentence, they are placed between the word **no** and the conjugated verb: **No se bañan.**

When a conjugated verb is followed by an infinitive that is used reflexively, the reflexive pronouns may either precede the conjugated verb or be attached to the infinitive.

Me levanto temprano todos los días.
I get up early every day.
No me levanto temprano todos los días.
I do not get up early every day.

Me tengo que levantar temprano.
Tengo que **levantarme** temprano.
I have to get up early.

Debo **acostarme** más temprano.
Me debo acostar más temprano.
I should go to bed earlier.

Me levanto a las siete, **me ducho** y **me visto** antes de **peinarme.**
Mi esposo **se baña,** yo **me ducho** y los dos **nos peinamos** antes de las seis.

> **¡OJO!**
> The reflexive pronoun must be repeated with each verb in a series of verbs.

4. Nonreflexive Use of Verbs

All of these verbs can also be used nonreflexively, often with a different meaning. Some examples of this appear at right.

dormir = to sleep   **dormirse** = to fall asleep

poner = to put, place   **ponerse** = to put on

Algo sobre...

la costa centroamericana

Los países centroamericanos tienen costa en los océanos Pacífico y Atlántico (el mar Caribe), excepto El Salvador, que solo tiene costa en el Pacífico. El Salvador es un poco más pequeño que el estado de Massachusetts. Así que aunque[a] solo tiene costa en el Pacífico, ¡el mar nunca está muy lejos[b] para ir a bañarse!

 ¿Tiene su estado (o país) costa marítima? ¿En qué océano o mar?

[a]Así... *So although* [b]*far*

Playa la Paz, El Salvador, un lugar ideal para bañarse y hacer *surfing*

Práctica y comunicación

A. Asociaciones. Dé todas las palabras que pueda (*you can*) asociar con los siguientes infinitivos. Piense (*Think*) en grupos de palabras que Ud. ya conoce (*you already know*): los cuartos de una casa, los muebles, la ropa, otros verbos, los adverbios, etcétera.

Reflexive Pronoun Summary	
yo	→ me
tú	→ te
Ud., él, ella	→ se
nosotros/as	→ nos
vosotros/as	→ os
Uds., ellos, ellas	→ se

1. llamarse
2. levantarse
3. bañarse
4. sentarse
5. ponerse
6. despertarse
7. divertirse
8. acostarse

B. Su rutina diaria

Paso 1. Autoprueba. Empareje los pronombres reflexivos con los verbos apropiados.

PRONOMBRES

1. me _____
2. te _____
3. se _____
4. nos _____

VERBOS

a. acuesta
b. baño
c. ponemos

d. duermen
e. despierta
f. vistes

Paso 2. Complete las siguientes oraciones lógicamente con verbos en la primera persona singular (**yo**) y **no** si es necesario. Luego indique si Ud. hace las acciones **los lunes, los sábados** o los dos días. No repita los verbos.

VERBOS: acostarse, despertarse, divertirse, ducharse, levantarse, ponerse

1. _____ con el reloj despertador (*alarm clock*).
2. _____ antes de salir de casa.
3. _____ muy tarde después de una fiesta con mis amigos.
4. _____ mucho durante toda la tarde con amigos.
5. _____ ropa deportiva (*sports*) y tenis.
6. No _____ inmediatamente después de despertarme.

Paso 3. Ahora, en parejas, túrnense para hacer y contestar preguntas basadas en las oraciones del **Paso 2.** Luego digan (*tell*) a la clase algo (*something*) que Uds. tienen en común o que hacen de manera muy diferente o peculiar.

MODELOS: 1. Me despierto con el reloj despertador los lunes. →
¿Te despiertas con el despertador los lunes? →
Sam y yo nos despertamos con el reloj despertador los lunes.

Nota comunicativa

Cómo expresar una secuencia de acciones

The following adverbs and expressions will help you indicate the sequence of actions or events.

primero	first	**finalmente**	finally
luego, después	then, later, next	**por fin**	finally
en seguida	immediately		

Primero, me ducho y me visto. **Luego,** tomo un café y leo el periódico.
Después, me cepillo los dientes. **Finalmente,** salgo para el trabajo.

You will use these words and phrases in **Práctica C.**

C. Un día típico

Paso 1. Complete las siguientes oraciones lógicamente para describir su rutina diaria. Use el pronombre reflexivo cuando sea necesario. **¡OJO!** Use el infinitivo después de las preposiciones.

1. Me levanto después de _____.
2. Primero, (yo) _____ y luego _____.
3. Me visto antes de / después de _____.
4. Luego me siento a la mesa para _____.
5. Me gusta estudiar antes de _____ o después de _____.
6. Por la noche me divierto y luego _____.
7. Me acuesto antes de / después de _____ y finalmente _____.

Paso 2. Con las oraciones del **Paso 1,** describa los hábitos de su esposo/a, su compañero/a de cuarto/casa, sus hijos...

Prác. B, Paso 1: Answers: 1. b 2. f 3. a, d, e 4. c

D. El día de Ángela. Ángela es dependienta en una tienda de ropa para jóvenes en El Paso. ¿Cómo es un día normal de trabajo para ella? Complete la narración con los verbos apropiados, según los dibujos. **¡OJO!** Algunos (*Some*) verbos se usan más de una vez (*more than once*).

1.

2.

3.

4.

5.

6.

1. Me despierto a las nueve de la mañana y _____ en seguida. (Yo) _____ rápidamente y salgo de casa sin _____. Llego a la tienda a las diez menos diez de la mañana con mis compañeras de trabajo. Primero (yo) _____ mi trabajo, ordenando (*putting in order*) la ropa. La ropa de la tienda _____ muy bonita.
2. A las diez abren la tienda y los clientes _____ a llegar.
3. Mis compañeras no _____ español. Por eso yo siempre atiendo a los clientes hispanos.
4. (Yo) _____ a las doce y media con mi amiga Susie, que trabaja en una zapatería. Generalmente podemos _____ en la pizzería San Marcos y casi siempre _____ pizza.
5. Luego, (yo) _____ a la tienda y _____ a trabajar. Nunca _____ la siesta.
6. Por fin, la supervisora _____ la tienda a las seis en punto. Luego yo _____ a casa. _____ la ropa de trabajo (*work clothes*) y _____ un vestido y zapatos elegantes. _____ salir a bailar con unos amigos... ¡y no pienso ir a _____ hasta muy, muy tarde!.

E. Intercambios: Su rutina

Paso 1. En parejas, túrnense para entrevistarse. Hagan preguntas, usando las ideas de las tres columnas y otras de su imaginación. Usen una palabra o frase de cada columna y traten de (*try to*) explicar sus acciones.

(Continúa.)

MODELO: **E1:** ¿A qué hora te acuestas?

E2: Siempre me acuesto muy tarde porque trabajo hasta las once de la noche en un restaurante. Luego tengo que estudiar un poco.

| ¿a qué hora? ¿con quién? ¿cuándo? ¿dónde? ¿durante _____? ¿hasta qué hora? | **+** | acostarse afeitarse cepillarse los dientes despertarse dormirse ducharse/bañarse levantarse peinarse sentarse vestirse/ponerse _____ volver | **+** | los días de la semana los fines de semana los lunes (martes...) todos los días tarde/temprano solo/a |

Paso 2. Ahora digan (*tell*) a la clase un detalle (*detail*) interesante, raro o indiscreto de la vida (*life*) de su compañero/a.

MODELO: Sebastián se duerme a la una todas las noches con su perro y con sus dos gatos. ¡Debe tener una cama muy grande!

Un poco de todo

A. Lengua y cultura: Una tradición extendida: El Día de la Cruz (Cross)

Paso 1. Complete the following paragraphs about a special holiday. Give the correct form of the words in parentheses, as suggested by context. When two possibilities are given in parentheses, select the correct word.

Nicaragua y El Salvador tienen tradiciones que reflejan su mezcla[a] étnica y cultural. Una de estas tradiciones es la fiesta (del / de la[1]) Día de la Cruz, una fiesta religiosa que se celebra el 3 de mayo en El Salvador, en Nicaragua y en (otro[2]) países hispanohablantes, incluyendo España. ¿(Por qué / Porque[3]) es una tradición tan[b] extendida la celebración del Día de la Cruz? Porque todos son países en donde muchas personas (pero no todas) observan las (tradición[4]) católicas.

En algunos[c] pueblos y (ciudad[5]) hay procesiones[d] que (salir[6]) por los barrios.[e] Muchas familias salvadoreñas (poner[7]) una cruz en su patio. Las (cruz[8]) están adornadas con mucha fruta y con fruta y flores[f] (con / de[9]) papel. Las personas (vestirse[10]) con ropa especial y (celebrar[11]) el día con comidas y bebidas típicas, con (su[12]) familia y con sus amigos.

En El Salvador la celebración del 3 de mayo (unir[g][13]) el culto a la cruz de los cristianos con el culto a la tierra[h] de los indígenas. En el mes de mayo se cosecha[i] la fruta y también (empezar[14]) las lluvias.[j] (Por / Para[15]) eso es un (bueno[16]) momento para dar gracias[k] a la tierra. Además,[l] los campesinos (pedir[17]) una buena cosecha para el año entrante,[m] según la tradición indígena. Esto es solo *un* ejemplo de cómo la influencia indígena y la española se unen en las tradiciones latinoamericanas.

[a]reflejan... *show their mixture* [b]*so* [c]*some* [d]*religious parades, processions* [e]por... *out from (individual) neighborhoods* [f]*flowers* [g]*to join, unite* [h]*earth* [i]*se... is harvested* [j]*rains* [k]dar... *thank* [l]*Besides* [m]*coming*

El Día de la Cruz en Panchimalco, El Salvador

Paso 2. Comprensión. ¿Cierto o falso? Corrija las oraciones falsas.

	CIERTO	FALSO
1. Nicaragua y El Salvador tienen mucho en común.	☐	☐
2. El Día de la Cruz es una celebración política.	☐	☐
3. No hay comidas y bebidas especiales para el Día de la Cruz.	☐	☐
4. En la celebración del Día de la Cruz, se unen las tradiciones cristianas con las indígenas.	☐	☐

Paso 3. Conteste las siguientes preguntas con un compañero o una compañera.

1. ¿Hay fiestas religiosas en esta ciudad o en este estado? ¿Cuáles son?

2. En este país, ¿celebramos la cosecha (*harvest*)? ¿Cómo se llama en inglés la fiesta con que se celebra?

B. Hábitos

Paso 1. Todos tenemos nuestros hábitos. Indique en qué cuarto o parte de la casa Ud. hace las siguientes actividades. También debe especificar qué muebles y objetos usa.

MODELO: Por lo general, estudio en la alcoba, en mi escritorio. Pero a veces también leo y hago la tarea en la cama. Uso...

1. estudiar

2. dormir la siesta o acostarse por la noche

3. quitarse los zapatos

4. bañarse o ducharse

5. desayunar

6. vestirse

7. divertirse

8. ser desorganizado/a o ser muy organizado/a

Paso 2. Ahora, en parejas, túrnense para hacer y contestar preguntas basadas en las acciones del **Paso 1.**

MODELO: E1: ¿Dónde estudias, por lo general?
E2: Por lo general, estudio en la alcoba, en mi escritorio y a veces también en la cama. ¿Y tú?

Paso 3. Finalmente, digan (*tell*) a la clase algo (*something*) que tienen en común o que hacen de manera muy diferente.

MODELO: Maribel y yo estudiamos en la alcoba, por lo general. Pero preferimos hacer la tarea en la cama, no en el escritorio porque...

En **su** comunidad

Entreviste a (*Interview*) una persona hispana de su universidad o ciudad sobre las viviendas (*housing*) de su país de origen.

PREGUNTAS POSIBLES

- ¿En qué tipo de vivienda vive la mayoría de las personas en su país de origen?
- ¿Hay un tipo o estilo de casa «típico»? ¿Cómo es?
- ¿Dónde vive su familia?

SALU2

«Vivir con la familia» Segmento 2

Antes de mirar

Conteste las siguientes preguntas.

1. ¿Piensa Ud. pasar un tiempo en otro país mientras (*while*) completa sus estudios universitarios? ¿A qué país piensa ir? ¿Por qué quiere ir a ese país?
2. ¿Cuáles son las ventajas (*advantages*) y desventajas de vivir con una familia en otro país?

Este segmento

Desde México, D.F., Laura ofrece un reportaje sobre una mujer que espera recibir (*hopes to house*) a estudiantes extranjeros en su casa.

Lorena Campus Verduzco quiere rentar un cuarto en su casa a un estudiante extranjero, porque su hija se va a casar (*get married*) y no quiere quedarse sola (*to be left alone*).

Vocabulario del segmento

bienvenidos	welcome	por lo regular	generally
mostrarnos	showing us	la carrera	university studies
el próximo curso	next academic year	hasta que no se casan	until they get married
disfrutar	to enjoy	la costumbre	custom
la actual habitante	the current inhabitant	grandes	adults
debido a que	due to (the fact) that	la gente	people
la luz	light	el hogar	home
cuentas con	you have	hasta cierto punto	up to a point
se la va a pasar	he/she is going to be	nos despedimos	we'll say good-bye

Fragmento del guion

Bueno,[a] aquí en casa va a tener todas las comodidades[b] como si estuviera[c] en su propia[d] casa. Porque a mí me gusta tener ordenado el cuarto,[e] entonces no va a haber necesidad de que él vaya a pagar lavandería,[f] aquí mismo lo podemos hacer. Va a comer comida casera[g] muy rica.[h] Y aparte[i] va a tener compañía...

[a]*Well* [b]*comforts* [c]*como... as if he were* [d]*own* [e]*tener... to have the room tidy* [f]*entonces... so there is no need for him to pay for laundry* [g]*homemade* [h]*muy... very tasty* [i]*besides*

Después de mirar

A. ¿Está claro? ¿Cierto o falso? Corrija las oraciones falsas.

	CIERTO	FALSO
1. Lorena y su familia viven en Guadalajara, México.	☐	☐
2. Lorena tiene tres hijos.	☐	☐
3. La hija de Lorena que se va a casar se llama Luisa.	☐	☐
4. Por lo general, los jóvenes mexicanos viven con sus padres durante y después de sus estudios universitarios.	☐	☐

B. Un poco más. Describa el cuarto para un estudiante extranjero. ¿De quién es ahora el cuarto? ¿Cómo es? ¿Qué tiene?

C. Y ahora, Uds. En parejas, imaginen que son los presentadores de *Salu2*. Preparen un cierre (*closing*) diferente para este segmento, incluyendo:

- una idea general como resumen del segmento
- una despedida (*sign-off*) con el nombre del programa y la ciudad de origen
- un anticipo (*preview*) del próximo programa (¡tienen libertad de imaginar!)

A LEER

¿Vienen sus amigos a su apartamento o casa con frecuencia? ¿Es formal o familiar (*relaxed*) su actitud?

Lectura cultural: El Salvador y Nicaragua
La vivienda[a]

Como en todo el mundo, la vivienda en El Salvador y Nicaragua puede variar mucho. Hay lujosas[b] mansiones para las personas ricas y casas muy pobres y humildes[c] con un solo cuarto para toda una familia. En las ciudades principales hay edificios de apartamentos, como en cualquier[d] otro país.

En las ciudades de León y Granada, en Nicaragua, hay hermosas[e] casas de la época colonial. Estas casas cuentan con[f] muchos cuartos y tienen techos de tejas,[g] un jardín en medio de la casa y un patio trasero.[h]

[a]La... *Housing* [b]*luxurious* [c]*humble, simple* [d]*any* [e]*beautiful* [f]*cuentan... tienen* [g]*techos... tiled roofs* [h]*out back*

El volcán Izalco, también llamado «el Faro (*Lighthouse*) del Pacífico», todo un símbolo salvadoreño

En otros países hispanos

En todo el mundo hispanohablante Los hispanos en general tienen un concepto muy generoso de la hospitalidad en su hogar[a] y les gusta ofrecer algo[b] de comer y beber a sus invitados.[c] Otra característica es que la hospitalidad en los hogares hispanos es más formal que en los Estados Unidos, una formalidad que los hispanos comprenden bien. Por ejemplo, es una falta[d] de respeto abrir el refrigerador en la casa de un amigo sin su permiso, aun si[e] se trate de[f] la casa de un amigo íntimo.

[a]*home* [b]*ofrecer... to offer something* [c]*guests (in their home)* [d]*lack* [e]*aun... even if* [f]*se... it involves*

Un símbolo de El Salvador y Nicaragua: Los volcanes·

Los volcanes son una imagen representativa en estos dos países, que están dentro del llamado[a] Arco[b] Volcánico Centroamericano. En Nicaragua solamente,[c] hay diecisiete volcanes. Por eso, los escudos de las banderas[d] nicaragüense y salvadoreña muestran[e] una cordillera[f] con cinco volcanes.

[a]*dentro... inside the so-called* [b]*Rim, Arch* [c]*En... In Nicaragua alone* [d]*flags* [e]*show* [f]*mountain range*

COMPRENSIÓN
Conteste las siguientes preguntas.

1. ¿En qué son similares las viviendas en El Salvador y Nicaragua a las (*those*) del resto del mundo?
2. En general, ¿cómo es la hospitalidad de los hispanos?
3. ¿Por qué se consideran los volcanes un símbolo del país en Nicaragua y El Salvador?

Y ahora, Uds.

- En la zona donde Uds. viven, ¿qué tipo de vivienda es más común?
- En su región o estado, ¿qué se destaca (*stands out*) en la geografía? ¿Volcanes o montañas? ¿ríos (*rivers*)? ¿la costa?

Del mundo hispano

Antes de leer

¿Cómo es su casa? Piense en la casa de su familia o en el lugar donde vive ahora y dé la siguiente información.

1. Número de alcobas y de baños
2. Área en pies cuadrados (*square feet*), aproximadamente
3. ¿Tiene cocina? ¿patio? ¿jardín? ¿garaje? (¿Para cuántos coches?)
4. ¿Qué otras comodidades (*facilities*) tiene? (piscina, gimnasio, etcétera)

Lectura: Anuncios de bienes raíces°

Anuncios... *Real estate ads*

ᵃCocina... *kitchen with built-in cabinets and kitchen appliances* ᵇcuarto... *servant quarters* ᶜacabados... *first-class finishing touches*

Comprensión

A. Características de las viviendas mexicanas. Para cada vivienda, busque (*look for*) la siguiente información:

1. número de recámaras
2. número de baños
3. tamaño (*size*) de la construcción (**C**) y del terreno (**T**)
4. capacidad para coches
5. precio
6. otros atractivos

B. Estas viviendas. Conteste las siguientes preguntas.

1. ¿Cuál es la vivienda más grande (*biggest*)? ¿más pequeña? ¿más cara?
2. ¿Cuántos dígitos tienen los números de teléfono en esta ciudad?
3. ¿Cuál es la vivienda más apropiada para las siguientes personas: una familia con 3 hijos, una pareja sin hijos, una persona que vive sola? Explique su respuesta.
4. ¿Cuál es la vivienda más apropiada para Ud.? Explique su respuesta.

Ernesto y Víctor necesitan muchos muebles

Vocabulario para escuchar

amueblar	to furnish
ya	already
la plasma	flat-screen TV

Antes de escuchar

¿Qué es más usual entre los estudiantes universitarios: alquilar (*to rent*) un apartamento amueblado o uno sin amueblar (*furnished or unfurnished*)? ¿Tiene Ud. muchos muebles propios (*of your own*) donde Ud. vive? En su cuarto, casa o apartamento, ¿qué cosas son de Ud.?

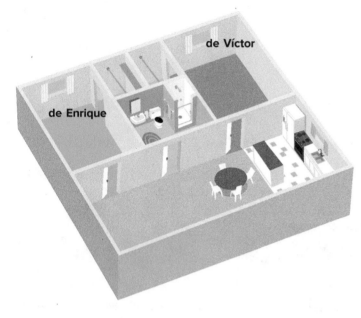

de Víctor

de Enrique

Después de escuchar

A. ¿Qué necesitan? Enrique y Víctor acaban de alquilar (*have just rented*) un apartamento que tiene muy pocos muebles, pero no importa porque ellos tienen varias cosas. Dibuje (*Draw*) o escriba en el plano del apartamento el nombre de los muebles y cosas que ellos ya tienen para cada cuarto.

B. Más detalles. Conteste las siguientes preguntas.

1. ¿Qué cosas tienen que comprar Víctor y Enrique para sus alcobas?
2. ¿Qué parte de la casa no mencionan en la conversación?
3. ¿Qué muebles no necesitan comprar para la sala comedor?
4. ¿Cuántos televisores tienen entre los dos?

PRODUCCIÓN PERSONAL

¡Ahora, yo!

A. Use de (*as a*) modelo las preguntas y respuestas de la página 131 de este capítulo para hablar de su casa y su alcoba.

B. Con las preguntas de la página 131 como modelo, filme una o dos entrevistas con estudiantes de su universidad que hablan del lugar donde viven mientras (*while*) asisten a la universidad.

A ESCRIBIR

Un ensayo sobre una semana típica de los estudiantes universitarios

¿Cree Ud. que los estudiantes universitarios en general tienen una manera típica de vivir? Y, en particular, ¿los estudiantes de su universidad? ¿Por qué?

Preparar

Paso 1. En una hoja de papel aparte, complete una tabla como la siguiente con información sobre 5 o 6 actividades que Ud. hace de lunes a viernes y durante el fin de semana en una semana típica. Luego entreviste (*interview*) a dos compañeros de clase sobre sus actividades y complete la tabla con su respectiva información.

	de lunes a viernes	fines de semana
Ud.		
compañero/a A		
compañero/a B		

Paso 2. Ahora use la información para escribir un ensayo sobre la semana típica de los estudiantes de su universidad, si cree que es posible hablar de una semana típica. Hay más ayuda (*help*) en Connect.

Más ideas para su portafolio

- Incluya (*Include*) una foto de su cuarto o alcoba y descríbalo (*describe it*).
- Describa con muchos detalles la casa de sus sueños (*dreams*).
- Describa un día ideal para Ud. ¿Qué día de la semana es, dónde está Ud. y qué hace durante todo el día?
- Si ha estado jugando (*have been playing*) Practice Spanish: Study Abroad, en Quest 3 Ud. almorzó (*had lunch*) en la casa de su familia colombiana. ¿Cómo es la casa? Dibuje el plano (*Draw the floorplan*) de la casa de su familia colombiana, incluyendo (*including*) todos los cuartos que Ud. recuerde (*that you remember*). Luego, nombre (*name*) dos actividades que se hacen (*are done*) en cada cuarto.

Sugerencia: You are now ready to play Quest 3 in **Practice Spanish: Study Abroad** (www.mhpractice.com).

LEARNSMART

Visit **www.connectspanish.com** to practice the vocabulary and grammar points covered in this chapter.

AFTER STUDYING THIS CHAPTER I CAN. . .

☐ name the parts of a house or apartment and furniture (132)

☐ use the names of the days of the week as well as other time expressions (134–135)

☐ use some words and expressions that put actions in sequence (136–137, 153)

☐ use important irregular and stem-changing verbs (139–141, 145–147)

☐ talk about my daily routine and other actions that require reflexive pronouns (150–152)

☐ recognize/describe at least 2–3 aspects of Salvadoran and Nicaraguan cultures

Gramática en breve

12. Present Tense of *hacer, oír, poner, salir, traer, ver*

hacer: **ha**go, **ha**ces, **ha**ce, **ha**cemos, **ha**céis, **ha**cen

oír: **oi**go, **o**yes, **o**ye, **oí**mos, **oís**, **o**yen

poner: **pon**go, **po**nes, **po**ne, **po**nemos, **po**néis, **po**nen

salir: **sal**go, **sa**les, **sa**le, **sa**limos, **sa**lís, **sa**len

traer: **trai**go, **tra**es, **tra**e, **tra**emos, **tra**éis, **tra**en

ver: **v**eo, **v**es, **v**e, **v**emos, **v**eis, **v**en

13. Present Tense of Stem-changing Verbs

Stem-changing Patterns

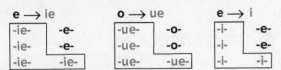

e → ie   o → ue   e → i

-ie-	-e-		-ue-	-o-		-i-	-e-
-ie-	-e-		-ue-	-o-		-i-	-e-
-ie-	-ie-		-ue-	-ue-		-i-	-i-

14. Reflexive Pronouns

yo → me	nosotros/as → nos
tú → te	vosotros/as → os
Ud./él/ella → se	Uds./ellos/ellas → se

Vocabulario

Los verbos

almorzar (almuerzo)	to have lunch
cerrar (cierro)	to close
descansar	to rest
dormir (duermo)	to sleep
dormir la siesta	to take a nap

empezar (empiezo)	to begin, start
empezar a + *inf.*	to begin to (*do something*)
entender (entiendo)	to understand
hacer	to do; to make
hacer ejercicio	to exercise
hacer un viaje	to take a trip
hacer una pregunta	to ask a question
jugar (juego) (a; al)	to play (*a game; a sport*)
oír (oigo, oyes,...)	to hear; to listen to (*music, the radio*)
pedir (pido)	to ask for; to order
pensar (pienso) (en)	to think (about)
pensar de/que	to think of, have an opinion about/that
pensar + *inf.*	to intend, plan to (*do something*)
perder (pierdo)	to lose; to miss (*an event*)
poner (pongo)	to put; to place; to turn on (*an appliance*)
salir (salgo) (de)	to leave (*a place*)
salir bien/mal	to turn/come out well/badly; to do well/poorly
salir con	to go out with, date
salir para	to leave for (*a place*)
servir (sirvo)	to serve
servir para	to be used for
traer (traigo)	to bring
ver (veo)	to see; to watch (*a program, movie*)
volver (vuelvo)	to return (*to a place*)
volver a + *inf.*	to (*do something*) again

Los verbos que se usan con pronombres reflexivos

acostarse (me acuesto)	to go to bed
afeitarse	to shave
bañarse	to take a bath, bathe
cepillarse los dientes	to brush one's teeth
despertarse (me despierto)	to wake up
divertirse (me divierto)	to have a good time, enjoy oneself
dormirse (me duermo)	to fall asleep
ducharse	to take a shower
levantarse	to get up (out of bed); to stand up
llamarse	to be called
peinarse	to brush/comb one's hair
ponerse (me pongo)	to put on (*an article of clothing*)
quitarse	to take off (*an article of clothing*)
sentarse (me siento)	to sit down
vestirse (me visto)	to get dressed

Los cuartos y otras partes de una casa

la alcoba	bedroom
el baño	bathroom
la cocina	kitchen
el comedor	dining room
el estudio	office (in a home)
el jardín	garden
la pared	wall
el patio	patio; yard
la piscina	swimming pool
la sala	living room

Cognado: el garaje

Repaso: la casa, el cuarto

Los muebles y otras cosas de una casa

la alfombra	rug
el armario	armoire, free-standing closet
la bañera	bathtub
la cama	bed
la cómoda	bureau; dresser
el estante	bookshelf
la estufa	stove
la lámpara	lamp
el lavabo	(bathroom) sink
la mesita	end table
el mueble	piece of furniture
el sillón	armchair
la toalla	towel

Cognado: el sofá

Repaso: el escritorio, la mesa, la silla, la tele(visión)

Otros sustantivos

la bebida	drink
el cine	movies; movie theater
la cosa	thing
el diente	tooth
el ejercicio	exercise
la llave	key
la nota	grade
las noticias	news
la película	movie
la pregunta	question
el ruido	noise
la rutina	routine
la tarea	homework
el viaje	trip

Los adjetivos

cada inv.*	each, every
diario/a	daily
siguiente	following
solo/a	alone

Las preposiciones

antes de	before
después de	after
durante	during
sin	without

Repaso: a, con, de, en, hasta, para, por (in, during)

¿Qué día es hoy?

los días de la semana:
    lunes, martes, miércoles, jueves, viernes, sábado, domingo

anteayer	the day before yesterday
ayer fue (miércoles...)	yesterday was (Wednesday. . .)
el lunes (martes...)	on Monday (Tuesday. . .)
los lunes (los martes...)	on Mondays (Tuesdays. . .)
pasado mañana	the day after tomorrow
el próximo (martes...)	next (Tuesday. . .)
la próxima semana	next week
la semana (el lunes...) que viene	next week (Monday. . .)

Repaso: el día, el fin de semana, hoy, mañana

Palabras adicionales

después adv.	then, later, next
en seguida	immediately
finalmente	finally
lo que	what, that which
luego	then, later, next
por fin	finally
por lo general	generally
primero	first

Vocabulario personal

---

*The abbreviation inv. means invariable, unchanging (in form). The adjective **cada** is used with masculine and feminine nouns (**cada libro, cada mesa**), and since its meaning (each) is singular, it is never used with plural nouns.

6

Las estaciones y el tiempo°

Las... *Seasons and the weather*

|SPANISH

www.connectspanish.com

En este capítulo

Una catarata (*waterfall*) del río Celeste, en el Parque National Volcán Tenorio, Costa Rica

COSTA RICA

4.8 (punto ocho) millones de habitantes

- La Constitución de Costa Rica prohíbe la organización de fuerzas armadas.[a]

- El ecoturismo es fundamental para la economía de Costa Rica y para **preservar** sus **bosques**[b] y **selvas,**[c] **que cubren**[d] un 30% (por ciento) de su territorio.

[a]fuerzas... *armed forces* [b]*forests* [c]*jungles* [d]*cover*

Mar Caribe

MÉXICO   BELICE

GUATEMALA   HONDURAS

EL SALVADOR   NICARAGUA

Lago de Nicaragua

Parque Nacional la Amistad

COSTA RICA   PANAMÁ

OCÉANO PACÍFICO

⊛ San José

0   100   200 Millas

0   100   200 Kilómetros

- ¿Cómo es el clima de su país?

- ¿Qué le gusta hacer cuando el tiempo[a] es bueno?

- ¿Cuál es su estación[b] favorita?

[a]*weather* [b]*season*

MANUEL GIL DEL VALLE CONTESTA LAS PREGUNTAS.

- El clima de Managua es poco variado. Solo hay dos estaciones, una lluviosa[a] y otra seca.[b] La temperatura diaria varía poco: alrededor de[c] 30 grados de máxima y 21 de mínima. Es decir,[d] hace calor[e] todo el año.

- Bueno,[f] no hago nada[g] en especial, porque no hay una estación de calor y otra de frío.[h]

- Prefiero la estación seca. Es que[i] puede llover[j] mucho durante la estación lluviosa y no me gusta estar mojado.[k]

[a]una... *a rainy one* [b]otra... *a dry one* [c]alrededor... *around* [d]Es... *That is* [e]hace... *it's hot* [f]*Well* [g]no... *I don't do anything* [h]*cold* [i]Es... *That's because* [j]*rain* [k]*wet*

¿Qué tiempo hace hoy?°

¿Qué... *What's the weather like today?*

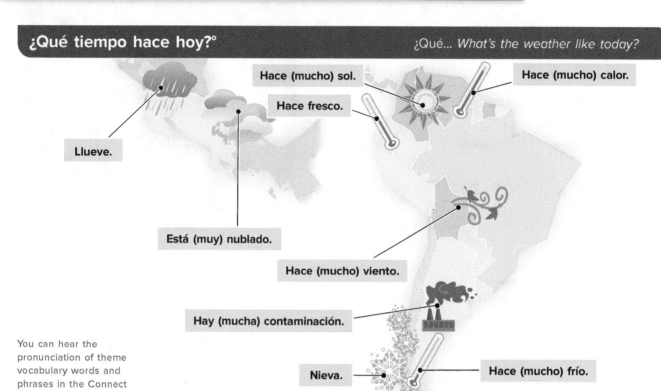

Hace (mucho) sol.

Hace fresco.

Hace (mucho) calor.

Llueve.

Está (muy) nublado.

Hace (mucho) viento.

Hay (mucha) contaminación.

Nieva.

Hace (mucho) frío.

You can hear the pronunciation of theme vocabulary words and phrases in the Connect eBook.

¡OJO!

el tiempo = *weather* and *time* in general, but: *What time is it?* = **¿Qué hora es?**

¡OJO!

There is no Spanish equivalent for the English subject *it* in these weather expressions. The verb alone (**hace, está, hay**) is sufficient.

- Many weather conditions are expressed with **hace** (**hacer**).

Hace (muy) buen/mal tiempo	It's very good/bad weather. It's (very) nice/bad out.
Hace (mucho) calor/fresco/frío/ sol/viento.	It's (very) hot/cool/cold/sunny/ windy.

- The words **calor** (*heat*), **fresco** (*coolness*), **frío** (*cold*), **sol** (*sun*), and **viento** (*wind*) are all nouns, which is why the adjective **mucho** is used with them, not an adverb (as in English, which uses *very*).
- *To rain* and *to snow* are expressed with stem-changing verbs. Only the third person singular is used.

  llover: llueve   it rains, it's raining   **nevar: nieva**   it snows, it's snowing

- There are also weather expressions with the verbs **está** and **hay**.

Está (muy) nublado.	It's (very) cloudy.
Hay (mucha) contaminación.	There's (a lot of) pollution.

Así se dice

Here are some other weather expressions that you might hear.

Está nublado. = Está nubloso.
Nieva. = Está nevoso.
Llueve. = Está lluvioso.
Hace sol. = Está soleado.

Comunicación

A. El tiempo y la ropa. Diga qué tiempo hace, según la ropa de cada persona.

MODELO: Todos llevan traje de baño y chanclas. →
  Hace calor. (Hace buen tiempo.)

1. María lleva pantalones cortos y camiseta.
2. Juan lleva suéter, pero no lleva chaqueta.
3. Roberto lleva sudadera y chaqueta.
4. Ramón lleva impermeable y botas y también tiene paraguas (*umbrella*).
5. Todos llevan abrigo, botas y sombrero.

B. El clima en el mundo

Paso 1. ¿Qué clima o condición asocia Ud. con las siguientes ciudades?

1. Seattle, Washington
2. Los Ángeles, California
3. San José, Costa Rica
4. Buffalo, Nueva York
5. Waikikí, Hawái
6. Chicago, Illinois

Paso 2. ¿Qué clima o condición asocia Ud. con los siguientes lugares?

1. un desierto
2. una playa (*beach*)
3. una montaña muy, muy alta
4. una ciudad grande
5. la Antártida
6. una zona tropical
7. una zona templada
8. Londres

C. El tiempo y las actividades. Haga oraciones completas, indicando una actividad apropiada para cada situación. Es necesario conjugar los verbos a la derecha (*right*).

cuando hace buen/mal tiempo cuando hace calor cuando hace frío cuando hay mucha contaminación cuando llueve cuando nieva	**+** (no) **+**	jugar al basquetbol/voleibol con mis amigos almorzar afuera (*outside*) / en el parque divertirse en el parque / en la playa con mis amigos salir de casa volver a casa trabajar o estudiar quedarse (*to stay*) en casa

Nota **comunicativa**

Otras expresiones con *tener*

Other conditions are expressed in Spanish with **tener** idioms—not with *to be,* as in English.

tener (mucho) calor	to be/feel (very) warm, hot
tener (mucho) frío	to be/feel (very) cold

These expressions are used to describe people or animals only. *To be comfortable*—neither hot nor cold—is expressed with **estar bien.**

You will use these expressions in **Comunicación D.**

D. ¿Tienen frío o calor? ¿Están bien? En parejas, describan el tiempo que hace en cada dibujo. También deben indicar cómo están las personas. Si Uds. creen que no tienen ni (*neither*) frío ni (*or*) calor, pueden decir (*say*): «Está(n) bien».

1.   2.   3.   4.   5.   6.

Los meses y las estaciones° del año

seasons

**Las cuatro estaciones
en el hemisferio norte**

el invierno

diciembre

enero

febrero

la primavera

marzo

abril

mayo

el otoño

septiembre

octubre

noviembre

el verano

junio

julio

agosto

<table>
<tr><td>

Así se dice

Other ways to ask what day it is include:

¿Qué día es hoy?
¿A cuántos estamos?

In the last sentence, **cuántos** is masculine because it refers to **días** (*m.*).

</td></tr>
</table>

¿Cuál es la fecha de hoy?
¿Qué fecha es hoy? }   What's today's date?

(Hoy) Es el primero de abril.   (Today is) It's the first of April.
(Hoy) Es el cinco de febrero.   (Today is) It's the fifth of February.

- The ordinal number **primero (1°)** is used to express the first day of the month. Cardinal numbers (**dos, tres,** and so on) are used for other days.
- The definite article **el** is used before the date. However, when the day of the week is expressed, **el** is omitted: **Hoy es jueves, 3 de octubre.**
- As you know, **mil** is used to express the year (**el año**) after 999.

  1950 mil novecientos cincuenta   2011 dos mil once

Comunicación

A. **¿Cuántos días hay en cada mes?** Piense en el poema que se usa en inglés para recordar (*remember*) el número de días en cada mes: *Thirty days . . .* Aquí está el poema en español. Para completarlo (*complete it*), Ud. tiene que hacer rimar los dos primeros versos (*lines*).

Treinta días tiene _____,
Con abril, _____ y _____.
De veintiocho solo hay uno,
Y los demás,ᵃ treinta y uno.

ᵃlos... *the rest*

B. Las fechas

Paso 1. Exprese estas fechas en español. ¿En qué estación caen (*do they fall*)?

MODELO: February 15 ⟶ Es el quince de febrero. Cae (*It falls*) en invierno.

1. March 7
2. August 24
3. December 1
4. June 5
5. September 19, 1997
6. May 30, 1842
7. January 31, 1660
8. July 4, 1776

Paso 2. ¿Cuándo se celebran (día y mes)?*

1. el Día del Año Nuevo
2. el Día de los Enamorados (de San Valentín)
3. la Navidad (*Christmas*)
4. el Día de los Inocentes (*Fools*), en los Estados Unidos
5. su cumpleaños (*birthday*)
6. el cumpleaños de su novio/a (*boyfriend/girlfriend*), esposo/a, mejor (*best*) amigo/a,...

Nota cultural

El clima en el mundo hispano

El mundo hispanohablante es inmenso. Se extiende en las Américas desde los Estados Unidos hasta la Argentina. Por eso, el clima de los países hispanohablantes es muy variado.

- No todos los países tienen cuatro estaciones. Costa Rica y otros países centroamericanos y sudamericanos solo tienen dos: una estación seca[a] y otra húmeda, con mucha lluvia. Esto es normal en los países de la zona tropical.
- El Niño, un fenómeno meteorológico, afecta directamente a varios países hispanos. Está caracterizado por temperaturas más calientes de lo normal[b] en la zona ecuatorial del océano Pacífico. El fenómeno se llama El Niño porque se presenta típicamente alrededor de[c] Navidad, época en que nace el Niño Jesús.[d]

[a]*dry* [b]*más... warmer than normal* [c]*alrededor... around* [d]*nace... the Baby Jesus is born (Christian faiths)*

La costa del Perú, donde se descubrió (*was discovered*) el fenómeno de El Niño en el siglo (*century*) XIX

 ¿Cómo es el clima de su estado o país? ¿Están las estaciones bien diferenciadas?

C. Intercambios

Paso 1. En parejas, túrnense para entrevistarse sobre los siguientes temas. Deben obtener detalles interesantes y personales de su compañero/a.

MODELO: la fecha de su cumpleaños ⟶
¿Cuál es la fecha de tu cumpleaños? ¿Qué tiempo hace, generalmente, ese día? ¿Cómo celebras tu cumpleaños?

1. la fecha de su cumpleaños
2. su signo del horóscopo
3. su estación favorita
4. una estación que no le gusta

Paso 2. Digan a la clase lo que Uds. tienen en común.

MODELO: Nosotras tenemos el cumpleaños en abril. La fecha de María es el 16 y mi fecha es el 18. Nuestro signo es Aries. Las dos (*Both of us*) preferimos la primavera. ¿Por qué? Porque nuestro cumpleaños es en primavera y es una estación muy bonita.

Los signos del horóscopo

Aries	Libra
Tauro	Escorpión
Géminis	Sagitario
Cáncer	Capricornio
Leo	Acuario
Virgo	Piscis

---

*Remember that the word **se** before a verb changes the verb's meaning slightly. **¿Cuándo se celebran?** = When are they celebrated? You will see this construction throughout **Puntos de partida**. You will learn about this usage in **Capítulo 8**.

¿Dónde está? Las preposiciones (Part 2)

Pablito está a la derecha de Teresa.

Teresa está entre Carmen y Pablito.

El libro está encima de la mesa.

La mochila está debajo de la mesa.

La maestra habla: «Todos los estudiantes están delante de mí».

Nueva York está al norte de Miami. México está al sur de los Estados Unidos.

cerca de	close to	**al lado de**	alongside of	**a la derecha de**	to the right of
lejos de	far from	**entre**	between, among	**a la izquierda de**	to the left of
debajo de	below	**delante de**	in front of	**al norte/sur/**	to the north/south/
encima de	on top of	**detrás de**	behind	**este/oeste de**	east/west of

¡OJO!

Note that **mí** has a written accent, but **ti** does not. This diacritical accent (**Capítulo 4**) distinguishes the object of a preposition (**mí**) from the possessive adjective (**mi**).

- In Spanish, the *pronoun objects of prepositions* (**los pronombres preposicionales**) are identical in form to the subject pronouns, except for **mí** and **ti**.

  Julio está *delante de mí*.   Julio is in front of me.
  María está *detrás de ti*.   María is behind you.
  Me siento *a la izquierda de ella*.   I sit on her left.

- The pronouns **mí** and **ti** combine with the preposition **con** to form **conmigo** (*with me*) and **contigo** (*with you*), respectively.

  —¿Vienes *conmigo*?   "Are you coming with me?"
  —Sí, voy *contigo*.   "Yes, I'll go with you."

Comunicación

A. En el salón de clase

Paso 1. Describa a las personas o cosas de su clase en relación con Ud. Siga el modelo. Use **nadie** (*no one*) cuando sea (*it's*) necesario.

MODELO: está cerca de la puerta. → **Jaime** está cerca de la puerta.

Una persona o una cosa que...
1. está cerca/lejos de la puerta.
2. está detrás de la mesa del profesor / de la profesora.
3. está delante del pizarrón.
4. está a su izquierda/derecha.
5. habla con Ud. en la clase.
6. hoy trabaja con Ud.

(Continúa.)

Paso 2. Con un compañero / una compañera, escoja (*choose*) a una persona o un objeto en el salón de clase. Luego, sin nombrarlo/la (*without naming him/her/it*), use las preposiciones de lugar para explicar dónde está. Su compañero/a va a adivinar (*guess*) qué persona, objeto o mueble es.

MODELO: Está a la derecha de Paul ahora, pero generalmente se sienta detrás de mí. Siempre llega a clase conmigo. ¿Quién es?

B. **¿De qué país se habla?**

Paso 1. Escuche la descripción de un país de Sudamérica que da (*gives*) su profesor(a). ¿Cuál es ese país?

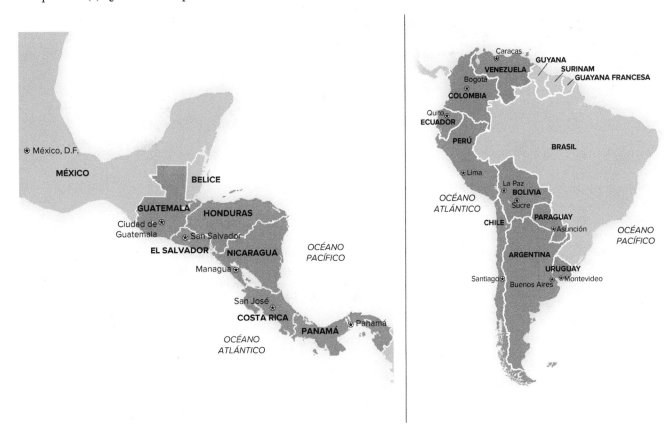

Paso 2. Ahora describa un país de Sudamérica. Sus compañeros de clase van a decir cuál es. Siga (*Follow*) el modelo, usando todas las frases que sean (*are*) apropiadas.

MODELO: Este país está al norte/sur/este/oeste de _____. También está cerca de _____. Pero está lejos de _____ . Está entre _____ y _____. Su capital es _____. ¿Cómo se llama?

C. **Intercambios.** Find out as much information as you can about the location of each others' hometown or state, or country of origin. You should also tell what the weather is like.

MODELO: E1: ¿De dónde eres?
E2: Soy de Tylertown.
E1: ¿Dónde está Tylertown?
E2: Está en el estado de _____, al oeste de _____.
E1: ¿Cómo es el clima?

SALU2

«En la Mitad del Mundo°» Segmento 1

Mitad... *Middle of the World*

El monumento a la Mitad del Mundo: «Aquí turistas ecuatorianos y de todos los países vienen a poner un pie (*foot*) en cada hemisferio.»

Antes de mirar

Indique todas las opciones que son ciertas para Ud.

- ☐ Donde yo vivo hay cuatro estaciones.
- ☐ Me gusta el clima cálido (*warm*) y seco (*dry*). ¡Me gusta el sol!
- ☐ Prefiero el invierno porque me gusta el frío y la nieve (*snow*).
- ☐ Llueve mucho aquí. Afortunadamente me gusta mucho la lluvia (*rain*).

Este segmento

Este segmento incluye un reportaje sobre aspectos del clima y la geografía del Ecuador. Para empezar, los presentadores intercambian comentarios sobre el clima del país de Ana, Panamá.

Estrategia

This segment includes a lot of vocabulary that you learned in **Vocabulario: Preparación.** You will understand the segment more easily if you review that vocabulary before watching. Consider adding some additional weather-related vocabulary to **Vocabulario personal** (at the end of the chapter).

Vocabulario del segmento

rico/a	beautiful	**reflejar**	to reflect
disfrutando	enjoying	**olvidar**	to forget
la temporada	season	**montañoso/a**	mountainous
mejor te quedas	you better stay	**atravesar (atravieso)**	to cross
me gustaría	I would like	**el corazón**	heart
la infatigable viajera	tireless traveler	**segundo/a**	second
lluvioso/a	rainy	**rodear**	to surround
a nivel del mar	at sea level	**contrarrestar**	to react (with), counteract
el grado centígrado	Celsius degree		
la humedad	humidity		

Después de mirar

A. ¿Está claro? Las siguientes oraciones son falsas. Corríjalas. (*Correct them.*)

1. A Ana no le gusta la nieve.
2. El clima de Panamá es muy diferente del clima del Ecuador.
3. La Mitad del Mundo es una ciudad del Ecuador.
4. En los países tropicales hay dos temporadas, una cálida y otra fría.
5. En Quito no llueve mucho.

B. Un poco más. Conteste las siguientes preguntas.

1. ¿Es muy cálido el clima en todas las zonas tropicales del mundo? Dé un ejemplo.
2. ¿Qué factor geográfico afecta el clima del Ecuador?

C. Y ahora, Uds. En parejas, hablen sobre si les gustaría (*you would like*) vivir en un lugar con un clima como el (*like that*) de Quito o como el de la costa ecuatoriana, que es mucho más cálido. Expliquen por qué.

MODELO:: Me gustaría vivir en un lugar con un clima similar al (*to that*) de Quito porque me gusta la lluvia...

GRAMÁTICA

15 *¿Qué están haciendo?*

Present Progressive: **Estar + -ndo**

GRAMÁTICA

GRAMÁTICA

Grammar Tutorial 15
connect
|SPANISH
www.connectspanish.com

15 *¿Qué están haciendo?*

Present Progressive: **Estar + -ndo**

Gramática en acción: ¿Qué está haciendo Elisa esta tarde?

Elisa es periodista. Por eso escribe y habla mucho por teléfono en su trabajo. Pero ahora mismo no está trabajando. Está descansando en casa. Está oyendo música, leyendo una novela y tomando un café.

¿Y Ud.?

En el salón de clase, ¿quién está haciendo las siguientes cosas en este momento? **¡OJO!** **nadie** = *nobody*.

1. _____ está hablando en su teléfono celular.
2. _____ está leyendo un periódico.
3. _____ está tomando un café.
4. _____ está mandando mensajes.
5. _____ está escuchando su iPod.

The Progressive / El progresivo

estoy		I am	
estás		you (*fam.*) are	
está	**tom**ando	he, she, it, you (*form.*) are	drinking
estamos	**com**iendo	we are	eating
estáis	**abr**iendo	you (*pl. fam.*) are	opening
están		they, you (*pl. form.*) are	

Uses of the Progressive / Los usos del progresivo

1. The Progressive
Spanish and English form the *progressive* (**el progresivo**) in similar ways, as you can see in the preceding chart, but the use of the progressive is not the same in both languages.

> *the progressive* / **el progresivo** = a verb form that expresses continuing or developing action

---

What's Elisa doing this afternoon? *Elisa is a journalist. That's why she writes and talks a lot on the phone in her job. But she's not working right now. She's resting at home. She's listening to music, reading a novel, and having a cup of coffee.*

Gramática

ciento setenta y tres ■ **173**

2. Uses of the Progressive

As shown in the example sentences, English uses the present progressive to tell:

- what is happening *right now* (1)
- what is happening *over a period of time* (2)
- what is *going to* happen (3)

   However, in Spanish, the present progressive is used primarily to express an action that *is happening right now* (1).

   To express actions that are happening over a period of time, Spanish generally uses uses the simple present tense (2).

   To express actions that are going to happen, Spanish uses the simple present tense or **ir + a + infinitive** (3), but never the progressive.

1. *Ramón is eating right* now.
   Ramón **está comiendo** ahora mismo.

2. *Adelaida is studying* chemistry *this semester.*
   Adelaida **estudia** química este semestre.

3. *We're buying the house tomorrow.*
   Compramos (Vamos a comprar) la casa mañana.

Forming the Present Progressive / La formación del presente progresivo

1. Spanish Present Progressive

The Spanish *present progressive* (**el presente progresivo**) is formed with **estar** plus the *present participle* (**el gerundio**).

The present participle is formed by adding **-ando** to the stem of **-ar** verbs and **-iendo** to the stem of **-er** and **-ir** verbs.

The present participle never varies; it always ends in **-o**.

> *a present participle / un* **gerundio** = the verb form that ends in *-ing* in English

estar + *present participle*

tomar → **tom**ando	taking; drinking
comprender → **comprend**iendo	understanding
abrir → **abr**iendo	opening

¡OJO!

Unaccented **i** represents the sound [y] in the participle ending **-iendo: comiendo, viviendo.** Unaccented **i** between two vowels becomes the letter **y**.

leer: le + iendo → leyendo
oír: o + iendo → oyendo

---

2. Present Participle of -*ir* Stem-changing Verbs

-Ir stem-changing verbs also have a stem change in the present participle.

- The stem vowel **e** changes to **i**.
- The stem vowel **o** changes to **u**.

   As you can see, sometimes that change is the same as in the present tense (as in **pedir**) and sometimes it is different (as in **preferir** and **dormir**).

   The verbs you have learned so far that show this second change are: **divertirse, dormir(se), pedir, preferir, servir,** and **vestirse.**

preferir (**prefie**ro) (**i**) → **prefi**riendo
pedir (**pi**do) (**i**) → **pi**diendo
dormir (**duer**mo) (**u**) → **dur**miendo

Note that (**duer**mo) shows you the present tense stem change for **dor**mir: o → ue. The (**u**) shows you the change in the present participle of **dor**mir: o → u (**dur**miendo).

In vocabulary lists from this point on in *Puntos de partida*, this second stem change will be shown in parentheses after the first person singular form of the verb.

---

3. Position of Reflexive Pronouns

Reflexive pronouns can be attached to a present participle or precede the conjugated form of **estar**. Note the accent that is added to the present participle when pronouns are attached.

Pablo **se está** bañando.
Pablo está **bañándose.** } *Pablo is taking a bath.*

¡OJO!

When a verb used reflexively follows expressions like **empezar a,** the pronoun is usually placed at the end of the infinitive: **Estoy empezando a vestirme.**

Práctica y comunicación

A. Un sábado típico

Paso 1. Autoprueba. Complete el gerundio de los siguientes verbos con una de las siguientes terminaciones.

a. -ando **b. -iendo** **c. -yendo**

1. acost______
2. bañ______
3. durm______
4. hac______
5. le______
6. pid______
7. prefir______
8. divirt______
9. cre______
10. empez______

Paso 2. Ahora piense en su rutina de un sábado típico. Indique dos acciones que es posible que Ud. esté (*might be*) haciendo a las siguientes horas. Hay una lista de **Frases útiles,** pero Ud. puede modificarlas (*change them*) o añadir otras.

MODELO: a las ocho de la mañana ⟶
A las ocho de la mañana estoy durmiendo o duchándome.

1. a las 8 de la mañana
2. a las 10:30 de la mañana
3. al mediodía (*noon*)
4. a las 4 de la tarde
5. a las 9 de la noche
6. a la medianoche (*midnight*)

Frases útiles

almorzar	levantarse
despertarse	oír música
dormir (la siesta)	pedir una pizza
ducharse	ver una película
estudiar	volver a casa
hacer ejercicio	

Paso 3. Ahora, en parejas, túrnense para determinar si hacen las mismas (*same*) cosas a la misma hora.

MODELO: **E1:** A las ocho de la mañana los sábados, ¿estás durmiendo?
E2: No, a esa hora estoy trabajando.

B. Hoy, en casa de Lola.

Hoy no es un día como todos los días para la familia de Lola, porque su tío de Costa Rica está de visita. Complete las siguientes oraciones para expresar lo que está pasando (*happening*).

MODELO: Casi siempre, Lola almuerza con su hija. Hoy Lola... (almorzar con su tío en un restaurante) ⟶
Hoy Lola **está almorzando** con su tío en un restaurante.

1. Generalmente, Lola pasa la mañana en la universidad. Hoy Lola... (pasar el día con su tío Ricardo)
2. Casi siempre, Lola toma un café en la cafetería después de sus clases. Hoy Lola y su tío... (tomar un café en casa)
3. De lunes a viernes, Marta, la hija de Lola, va a la escuela (*school*) por la tarde. Pero esta tarde ella... (jugar con Ricardo)
4. Generalmente, la familia cena (*has dinner*) a las nueve. Esta noche todos... (cenar a las diez)

Prác. A, Paso 1: Answers: **1.** a **2.** a **3.** b **4.** b **5.** c **6.** b **7.** b **8.** b **9.** c **10.** a

Summary of Present Progressive

estar + -ando
-iendo
-yendo

Algo sobre...

los valores[a] de los costarricenses

El Parque Nacional Rincón de la Vieja, parte de la importante industria ecoturística de Costa Rica

Dos cualidades caracterizan el país de Costa Rica. Una es la paz.[b] Esta nación no tiene fuerzas armadas[c] desde 1948. Hay una expresión que ilustra este sentimiento nacional: «Donde haya[d] un costarricense, habrá[e] paz.» La segunda[f] característica es la importancia que la ecología tiene para el país. Costa Rica no solo preserva su biodiversidad; también la explota.[g]

¿Qué cualidades caracterizan este país? ¿Es la paz un valor estadounidense?

[a]*values* [b]*peace* [c]fuerzas... *armed forces* [d]Donde... *Wherever there is* [e]*there will be* [f]*second* [g]la... *she uses it*

C. En casa con la familia Duarte

Paso 1. Describa lo que pasa en cada dibujo, explicando quién está haciendo la acción —el padre, la madre, la hija, los gemelos (*twins*), el perro— y a qué hora. Use los verbos de la lista u otros verbos, si desea. Puede hacer más de (*than*) una oración para cada dibujo, si quiere. **¡OJO!** Hay verbos reflexivos en las listas.

MODELO: salir de la ducha (*shower*) ⟶ El padre **está saliendo** de la ducha a las seis de la mañana.

Por la mañana: A las seis de la mañana

Verbos

dormir todavía (*still*)
leer el periódico
levantarse
salir de la ducha
tomar un café

1.   2.   3.   4.

Más tarde: A las ocho de la mañana

Verbos

desayunar
leer sus e-mails
pensar en el examen que tiene hoy
salir para la universidad
trabajar en la oficina
vestirse

5.   6.   7.   8.

Por la tarde: A las seis y media de la tarde

Verbos

hacer la tarea
jugar
leer un libro de texto
preparar la cena (*dinner*)
quitarse la ropa

9.   10.   11.   12.

Paso 2. Ahora explique qué hacen Ud. y otros miembros de su familia o sus compañeros de cuarto/casa a la misma hora que ve en los dibujos.

Nota comunicativa

El gerundio con otros verbos

As in English, the Spanish present participle **(el gerundio)** can be used with verbs other than **estar**. The following verbs are commonly used with the present participle.

- **pasar tiempo** + *present participle*

  ¿Pasas mucho tiempo **haciendo** la tarea?

  to spend time (doing something)

  Do you spend a lot of time doing homework?

- **seguir (sigo) (i) / continuar (continúo)*** + *present participle*

  Sigue lloviendo mucho.

  to continue (doing something)

  It continues to rain / raininig a lot.

- **divertirse (me divierto) (i)** + *present participle*

  ¿Te diviertes mucho **bailando** salsa?

  to enjoy (doing something)

  Do you have a good time dancing salsa?

> Remember that the letter in parentheses indicates the change in the present participle of the verb, which in this case would be **siguiendo**.

You will use these verbs in **Comunicación D** and **E**.

¡OJO!
Note the present tense forms of **continuar**, which have an accent on the **u** when it is stressed (like the boot pattern of stem-changing verbs):

continúo	**continuamos**
continúas	**continuáis**
continúa	**continúan**

¡OJO!
If the second verb in these constructions is reflexive, its reflexive pronoun must agree with the subject.

Me divierto **bañándome** en el mar.
I enjoy bathing in the sea.

D. Intercambios

Paso 1. Use las siguientes ideas para hacer cinco oraciones sobre sus hábitos.

infinitivo → gerundio

continuar/seguir
divertirse
estar
pasar más tiempo
pasar mucho/poco tiempo

+

bailar hasta la medianoche
estudiar / leer / ¿ ?
hablar español después de la clase
mandar mensajes
mirar la tele / **oír** música
ser amigo/a de mi mejor (*best*) amigo/a de la escuela primaria
trabajar (en ¿ ?)
¿ ?

Paso 2. Ahora, en parejas, túrnense para entrevistarse sobre los mismos temas. Luego compartan (*share*) con la clase algo (*something*) que tienen en común.

MODELOS: ¿Pasas mucho tiempo mirando la tele? ¿Cuántas horas al (*per*) día? ¿Cuál es tu programa favorito?

E. ¿Qué están haciendo?
Imagine lo que están haciendo las siguientes personas ahora mismo. Use una palabra o frase de cada columna y la forma progresiva.

yo
mi mejor amigo/a
mis padres
mi equipo (*team*) deportivo favorito
el/la líder (*leader*) de este país
el profesor / la profesora de español
_____ (un compañero / una compañera que está ausente hoy)

+

descansar, dormir(se), escribir, hacer, jugar (al), leer, practicar, trabajar, ¿ ?

divertirse + *inf.*, seguir + *inf.*,

+

fútbol/basquetbol
un libro / una novela
a los estudiantes / a sus consejeros
la tarea / un informe
ejercicio físico
¿ ?

You have been using forms of **ser** and **estar** since **Capítulo 1.** The following section will help you consolidate everything you know so far about these two verbs, both of which express *to be* in Spanish. You will learn a bit more about them as well.

Before you begin **Gramática 16,** think in particular about the following questions: **¿Cómo está Ud.? ¿Cómo es Ud.?** What do these questions tell you about the difference between **ser** and **estar?**

Grammar Tutorial 16
connect
|SPANISH
www.connectspanish.com

16 ¿Ser o estar?

Summary of the Uses of **ser** and **estar**

Gramática en acción: Una conversación a larga distancia

Aquí hay un lado de la conversación entre una esposa que **está** en un viaje de negocios y su esposo, que **está** en casa. Habla el esposo.

Aló. [...] ¿Cómo **estás**, querida? [...] ¿Dónde **estás** ahora? [...] ¿Qué hora **es** allí? [...] ¡Huy!, **es** muy tarde. Y el hotel, ¿cómo **es**? [...] Oye, ¿qué **estás** haciendo ahora? [...] Ay, lo siento. **Estás** muy ocupada. ¿Con quién tienes cita mañana? [...] ¿Quién **es** el dueño de la compañía? [...] Ah, él **es** de Costa Rica, ¿verdad? [...] Bueno, ¿qué tiempo hace allí? [...] Muy bien. Hasta luego, ¿eh? [...] Adiós.

Comprensión

Complete las oraciones con **es** o **está.**

1. El esposo _____ en casa.
2. La esposa _____ una mujer de negocios.
3. La esposa _____ en un viaje de negocios.
4. No sabemos (*We don't know*) cómo _____ el hotel.
5. _____ muy tarde donde _____ la esposa.
6. La esposa _____ trabajando ahora.
7. El dueño de la compañía _____ de Costa Rica.

A long-distance conversation *Here is one side of a conversation between a wife who is on a business trip and her husband, who is at home. The husband is speaking. Hello . . . How are you, dear? . . . Where are you now? . . . What time is it there? . . . Wow, it's very late. And how's the hotel? . . . Hey, what are you doing now? . . . Gosh, I'm sorry. You're very busy. Who do you have an appointment with tomorrow? . . . Who's the owner of the company? . . . Ah, he's from Costa Rica, isn't he? . . . Well, what's the weather like there? . . . Great. See you later, OK? . . . Good-bye.*

Summary of the Uses of ser / Resumen de los usos de ser

- To *identify* people (including their profession) and things

  Ella **es doctora.**
  Tikal **es una ciudad maya.**

- To express *nationality;* with **de** to express *origin*

  Son cubanos.
  Son de La Habana.

- With **de** to tell of what *material* something is made

  Este bolígrafo **es de plástico.**

- With **de** to express *possession*

  Es de Carlota.

- With **para** to tell *for whom something is intended*

  El regalo **es para** Sara.

- To tell *time* and give the *date*

  Son las once.
  Es la una y media.
  Hoy **es martes,** tres de octubre.

- With *adjectives* that describe *basic, inherent characteristics*

  Ramona **es inteligente.**

- To form many *generalizations* or *impersonal expressions* (only **es**)

  Es necesario llegar temprano.
  Es importante estudiar.

Summary of the Uses of estar / Resumen de los usos de estar

- To tell *location*

  El libro **está en la mesa.**

- To describe *health*

  Estoy muy **bien,** gracias.

- With *adjectives* that describe *conditions*

  Estoy muy **ocupada.**

- In a number of *fixed expressions*

  (No) Estoy de acuerdo.
  Está bien. (*It's fine, OK.*)

- With *present participles* to form the *progressive tense*

  Estoy estudiando ahora mismo.

Ser *and* estar with Adjectives / Ser y estar con adjetivos

1. **Ser = Fundamental Characteristics**
   Ser is used with adjectives that describe the *fundamental qualities* (**las características fundamentales**) of a person, place, or thing.

   Esa mesa **es** muy **baja.**
   That table is very short.

   Sus calcetines **son morados.**
   His socks are purple.

   Este sillón **es cómodo.**
   This armchair is comfortable.

   Sus padres **son cariñosos.**
   Their parents are affectionate people.

2. **Estar = Conditions**
   Estar is used with adjectives to express *conditions* (**las condiciones**) or observations that are true at a given moment but that do not describe inherent qualities of the noun. The adjectives on the next page are generally used with **estar.**

abierto/a	open	**desordenado/a**	messy	**ocupado/a**	busy
aburrido/a	bored	**enfermo/a**	sick	**ordenado/a**	neat
alegre	happy	**furioso/a**	furious, angry	**preocupado/a**	worried
cansado/a	tired	**limpio/a**	clean	**seguro/a**	sure, certain
cerrado/a	closed	**loco/a**	crazy	**sucio/a**	dirty
congelado/a	frozen; very cold	**molesto/a**	annoyed	**triste**	sad
contento/a	content, happy	**nervioso/a**	nervous		

3. *Ser* or *estar*?

Many adjectives can be used with either **ser** or **estar**, depending on what the speaker intends to communicate. In general, when *to be* implies *looks, feels,* or *appears,* **estar** is used. Compare the use of **ser** and **estar** in the sample sentences.

Daniel **es guapo.**
Daniel is handsome. (He is a handsome person.)
Daniel **está muy guapo** esta noche.
Daniel looks very nice (handsome) tonight.

Amalia **es muy simpática**, pero hoy **está muy seria**.
Amalia is very nice, but she's very serious today.

Algo sobre...

la democracia en Costa Rica

Costa Rica se considera un país modelo en el mundo hispano. Lleva disfrutando de paz[a] y democracia desde 1948, un período muy largo en comparación con otros países hispanohablantes. Ese año, hubo[b] una rebelión después de unas elecciones problemáticas. Entonces[c] se creó[d] una nueva constitución con una asamblea[e] democráticamente elegida.[f] José Figueres Ferrer, el líder de la rebelión, fue el primer presidente elegido bajo[g] la nueva constitución. Es considerado un héroe nacional.

 ¿Cuánto tiempo lleva su país disfrutando de la democracia? ¿Quién es considerado un héroe / una heroína nacional en su país?

[a]Lleva... *It has been enjoying peace* [b]*there was* [c]*Then* [d]*se... was created* [e]*assembly* [f]*elected* [g]*under*

Luis Guillermo Solís Rivera, presidente de Costa Rica desde 2014

Summary of *ser* and *estar*

ser = inherent qualities
identification
nationality, origin
material
possession
for whom
time, date
generalizations

estar = conditions
location
present progressive
fixed expressions

Práctica y comunicación

A. ¿Soy o estoy?

Paso 1. Autoprueba. ¿**Ser** o **estar**? ¿Cuál es el verbo apropiado para cada caso?

___ **1.** to describe a health condition
___ **2.** to tell time
___ **3.** to describe inherent characteristics
___ **4.** to tell where a thing or person is located
___ **5.** to tell someone's profession

___ **6.** to say who something belongs to
___ **7.** to tell where someone is from
___ **8.** to describe a temporary condition
___ **9.** to make a generalization
___ **10.** to tell what something is intended for

Prác. A Paso 1: Answers: 1. estar **2.** ser **3.** ser **4.** estar **5.** ser **6.** ser **7.** ser **8.** estar **9.** ser (es) **10.** ser

Paso 2. Ahora complete las siguientes oraciones con **estoy** o **soy.** También identifique la razón para usar cada verbo, usando los números de las explicaciones del **Paso 1.**

RAZÓN DEL **PASO 1**

a. _____ bien. _____
b. _____ simpático/a. _____
c. _____ contento/a de tomar español este semestre. _____
d. _____ estudiante universitario/a. _____
e. _____ de (ciudad, estado o país). _____

Paso 3. Ahora, en parejas, túrnense para hacer y contestar preguntas basadas en el **Paso 2.** Luego digan a la clase algo (*something*) que Uds. tienen en común.

MODELO: a. Estoy bien. →
E1: ¿Cómo estás?
E2: Estoy muy bien. ¿Y tú?
EN COMÚN: Los dos estamos bien hoy.

B. Un regalo estupendo. Use **es** o **está** para describir el siguiente regalo que los padres de su compañero/a de cuarto acaban de comprarle (*just bought for him/her*).

La computadora...

1. _____ en la mesa del comedor.
2. _____ un regalo de cumpleaños.
3. _____ para mi compañero de cuarto.
4. _____ de la tienda Computec.
5. _____ en una caja (*box*) verde.
6. _____ de los padres de mi compañero.
7. _____ un regalo muy caro, pero estupendo.
8. _____ de metal y plástico gris.
9. _____ una IBM último modelo.
10. _____ muy fácil (*easy*) de usar.

Nota **comunicativa**

El uso de adjetivos + *por*

Por often expresses *because of* or *about (*as in *due to)*, especially with adjectives such as **contento/a, furioso/a, nervioso/a,** and **preocupado/a.**

Amalia está preocupada **por** los exámenes finales.
Amalia is worried about her final exams.

You will use **por** in this way in **Práctica C** and **D.**

C. ¿Quiénes son? En parejas, hagan oraciones con **ser** o **estar,** inventando detalles para describir a las personas y cosas que se ven en la foto.

1. ¿quiénes?
2. ¿de qué país?
3. simpáticos/antipáticos / ¿ ?
4. en este momento, contentos/tristes / ¿ ?
5. molestos/cansados por el viaje / ¿ ?
6. aquí por un mes / una semana / ¿ ?
7. ¿ ?

Gabriela nuestros primos de San José Julio

D. Publicidad

Paso 1. Complete el siguiente anuncio (*ad*) con la forma apropiada de **ser**, **estar** o **hay**, según el contexto.

Costa Rica... belleza[a] natural

¿(*T*ú: _____[1]) de una gran ciudad? ¿(*Tú:* _____[2]) una persona aventurera? ¿(_____[3]) la naturaleza una gran atracción en tu vida[b]? ¿(_____[4]) preocupado/a por los cambios[c] en el clima global? Entonces,[d] Costa Rica (_____[5]) el país para ti. Imagina: (_____[6]) en un lugar cerca del mar[e] en donde (_____[7]) increíbles especies de animales y plantas: iguanas, caimanes, orquídeas, heliconias...

(*Nosotros:* _____[8]) los expertos en turismo natural en Costa Rica. Todos nuestros guías[f] (_____[9]) costarricenses de nacimiento,[g] pero (*ellos:* _____[10]) contentos de conocer[h] a personas de todo el mundo y hacer nuevos amigos. Con sus conocimientos,[i] con su gran paciencia, con su español, (*ellos:* _____[11]) como profesores... pero sus clases (_____[12]) mucho más interesantes que las clases académicas... ¡y menos difíciles!

No (_____[13]) necesario viajar[j] a Costa Rica en una estación específica. (_____[14]) bueno viajar a Costa Rica en cualquier[k] mes del año. ¡Ven![l] ¡Costa Rica (_____[15]) esperándote[m]!

[a]*beauty* [b]*life* [c]*changes* [d]*Then* [e]*sea, ocean* [f]*guides* [g]*de...by birth* [h]*de... to meet* [i]*knowledge* [j]*to travel* [k]*any* [l]*Come (to visit)!* [m]*waiting for you*

Paso 2. Comprensión. ¿Cierto o falso? Corrija las oraciones falsas.

	CIERTO	FALSO
1. En Costa Rica, la naturaleza tiene mucha importancia para el turismo.	☐	☐
2. El turista no va a ver animales exóticos allí.	☐	☐
3. El turista puede aprender español allí.	☐	☐
4. No todas las estaciones son apropiadas para el turismo.	☐	☐

E. Una conversación entre esposos

Paso 1. En parejas, organicen el diálogo entre el marido de la página 178 (**Columna A**) y su esposa (**Columna B**), que está en un viaje de negocios. Primero, emparejen los elementos de las dos columnas. El esposo empieza el diálogo, contestando el teléfono.

A

1. _____ Aló.
2. _____ Bien. ¿Cómo estás tú, querida?
3. _____ ¿Dónde estás ahora?
4. _____ ¿Qué hora es allí?
5. _____ ¡Huy!, es muy tarde. Y el hotel, ¿cómo es?
6. _____ Oye, ¿qué estás haciendo ahora?
7. _____ Ay, lo siento. Estás muy ocupada. ¿Con quién tienes cita mañana?
8. _____ ¿Quién es el dueño de la compañía?
9. _____ Ah, él es de Costa Rica, ¿verdad?
10. _____ Bueno, ¿qué tiempo hace allí?
11. _____ Bueno. Mañana hablamos más. Buenas noches.

B

a. _____ muy moderno y _____ muy limpio.
b. Sí, pero ahora _____ trabajando en Nueva York.
c. _____ las once de la noche.
d. Hola, querido. ¿Qué tal?
e. El señor Cortina.
f. _____ leyendo unos informes para la reunión de mañana. _____ que leer uno más todavía.
g. Sí. Hasta mañana.
h. _____ en el hotel, en Nueva York.
i. _____ un poco cansada por el viaje y _____ sueño.
j. _____ fresco y _____ nublado.
k. Con un señor de Computec.

Paso 2. Ahora completen las oraciones de la señora con la forma correcta de **estar, hacer, ser** o **tener**. Luego practiquen la conversación completa.

Una heliconia

F. Una tarde terrible

Paso 1. Hoy es un día desastroso para la familia Castañeda. Ud. va a describir su casa en el **Paso 2.** Para prepararse, repase (*review*) primero unos adjetivos, cambiando (*exchanging*) las palabras rosadas por antónimos en las siguientes oraciones.

1. No hace buen tiempo; hace _____.
2. El bebé no está bien; está _____.
3. El gato no está limpio; está _____.
4. El esposo no está tranquilo; está _____ por el bebé.
5. El garaje no está cerrado; está _____.
6. Los niños no están tranquilos; están _____, porque tienen miedo.
7. La esposa no está contenta; está _____ por el tiempo.
8. El baño no está ordenado; está _____.

Paso 2. Ahora use los adjetivos del **Paso 1** y otros que Ud. conozca (*you know*) para expresar lo que *están haciendo* todos los miembros de la familia *en este momento*. Póngales (*Give*) nombres a todos y exprese su *estado de ánimo* (*their feelings*) o sus deseos. ¡Use su imaginación! Si puede, diga también lo que *usualmente hacen* estas personas a esta hora.

Estrategia

lo que están haciendo =
el presente progresivo

el estado de ánimo =
el presente simple

lo que usualmente hacen =
el presente simple

Vocabulario útil

la cena	dinner	**ladrar**	to bark
cenar	to have dinner	**llorar**	to cry
cocinar	to cook	**los truenos y**	thunder and
conducir (conduzco)*	to drive	**relámpagos**	lightning

---

*Only the first person singular of the verb **conducir** is irregular, as noted. The other forms of the present tense are regular: conduces, conduce...

G. Ana y Estela. Conteste las preguntas para describir el siguiente dibujo de un cuarto de dos estudiantes. ¡OJO! Invente otros detalles necesarios.

1. ¿Quiénes son las dos compañeras de cuarto?
2. ¿Dónde estudian? ¿Qué estudian?
3. ¿De dónde son?
4. ¿Cómo son?
5. ¿Dónde están en este momento?
6. ¿Qué hay en el cuarto?
7. ¿Cómo está el cuarto?
8. ¿Son ordenadas las dos o desordenadas?

H. Intercambios. ¿Cómo están Uds. en estas situaciones? En parejas, túrnense para hacer y contestar preguntas, según el modelo.

MODELO: cuando / tener mucha tarea ⟶
    E1: ¿Cómo estás cuando **tienes** mucha tarea?
    E2: Estoy cansado y estresado, como ahora. ¿Y tú?
    E3: Yo también.

1. cuando / tener mucha tarea / una tarea fácil/difícil
2. cuando / no tener trabajo académico
3. cuando / sacar (to get) A/D en un examen
4. en verano/invierno
5. cuando llueve/nieva
6. los lunes por la mañana / los domingos por la tarde / los...
7. después de una fiesta / un examen
8. durante la clase de _____
9. ¿ ?

Grammar Tutorial 17
connect
|SPANISH
www.connectspanish.com

Gramática en acción: Buenos Aires y San José

El centro de Buenos Aires, Argentina

El centro de San José, Costa Rica

- Buenos Aires es más grande que San José.
- Tiene más edificios altos que San José.
- Generalmente, en Buenos Aires no hace tanto calor como en San José.

Pero...
- San José es menos antigua que Buenos Aires.
- No tiene tantos habitantes como Buenos Aires.
- Sin embargo, los costarricenses son tan simpáticos como los argentinos.

¿Y Ud.?

1. Mi ciudad/pueblo...
   - (no) es tan grande como Chicago.
   - es más/menos cosmopolita que San Francisco.

2. Me gusta _____ (nombre de mi ciudad/pueblo)...
   - más que _____ (nombre de otra ciudad).
   - menos que _____ (nombre de otra ciudad).
   - tanto como _____ (nombre de otra ciudad).

Algo sobre...

San José y Buenos Aires

San José
- Fundada en 1738 y capital de Costa Rica desde 1823
- Población: 288.000 habitantes
- Clima: 2 estaciones; 23° C promedio todo el año

Buenos Aires
- Fundada en 1580 y capital de la Argentina desde 1853
- Población: 2.891.000 habitantes
- Clima: 4 estaciones; 26° C de máximas temperaturas (diciembre–febrero) y 14° C de mínimas (junio–agosto).

La ciudad donde Ud. vive, ¿es una ciudad capital? ¿Cuántos habitantes tiene, aproximadamente? ¿Cuántas estaciones hay?

ªaverage

In English *comparisons* (**las comparaciones**) are formed in a variety of ways. Equal comparisons are expressed with the word *as*. Unequal comparisons are expressed with the adverbs *more* or *less*, or by adding *-er* to the end of the adjective.

as cold *as*
as many *as*

more intelligent,
less important
tall**er**, smart**er**

a comparative / **un comparativo** = a form of or structure with nouns, adjectives, and adverbs used to compare nouns, qualities, or actions

---

Buenos Aires and San José *Buenos Aires is bigger than San José. • It has more tall buildings than San José. • It is not as hot in Buenos Aires as it is in San José, generally. But . . . San José is newer (lit., less ancient) than Buenos Aires. • It doesn't have as many inhabitants as Buenos Aires. • Nevertheless, Costa Ricans are as nice as Argentines.*

Comparatives / **Los comparativos**

Inequality / **La desigualdad**				Equality / **La igualdad**	
más... que	more . . . than	**menos... que**	less . . . than	**tan... como**	as . . . as
más que	more than	**menos que**	less than	**tant**o/a/os/as**... como**	as much/many . . . as
				tanto como	as much as

Inequality / La desigualdad: más/menos... que, más/menos que

1. Comparing Adjectives, Adverbs, and Verbs

Elena habla: «Juan es más alto que yo. Y corre más rápido que yo.»

Para describir

> más/menos + *adjective* + que
> more/less + *adjective* } + *than*
> *adjective* + -er

Juan es **más alto** que Elena.
Juan is taller than Elena (is).

Elena es **menos alta** que Juan.
Elena is shorter than Juan (is).

Para describir cómo se hace una acción

> más/menos + *adverb* + que
> more/less + *adverb* } + *than*
> *adverb* + -er

Juan corre **más rápido** que Elena.
Juan runs faster (more quickly) than Elena (does).

Elena corre **menos rápido** que Juan.
Elena runs slower (less quickly) than Juan (does).

¡OJO!
While the repetition of a verb is optional in English, as shown in the examples with (*is*) and (*does*), the second verb is *never* repeated in Spanish.

Para expresar la frecuencia o intensidad de una acción

> *verb* + más/menos que
> *verb* + more/less than

Juan **corre** más que Elena.
Juan runs more than Elena (does).

Elena **corre** menos que Juan.
Elena runs less than Juan (does).

2. Comparing Nouns

Carmen habla: «Rigoberto tiene más coches que yo.»

Para comparar la cantidad

> más/menos + *noun* + que
> more/less (fewer) + *noun* + than

Rigoberto tiene **más coches** que Carmen.
Rigoberto has more cars than Carmen (does).

Carmen tiene **menos coches** que Rigoberto.
Carmen has fewer cars than Rigoberto (does).

3. *More/Fewer than* + *number*

Juan habla: «Elena tiene menos lápices que yo.»

¡OJO!
The preposition **de** is used instead of **que** when the comparison is followed by a number.

Para expresar una cantidad

> más/menos de + *number* + *noun*
> more/fewer than + *number* + *noun*

Juan tiene **más de dos** lápices.
Juan has more than two pencils.

Elena tiene **menos de dos** lápices.
Elena has fewer than two pencils.

1. Comparing Adjectives, Adverbs, and Verbs

Ernesto

Patricia

¡OJO!
Remember that the second verb, indicated in parentheses, optional in English, is *never* repeated in Spanish.

Patricia habla: «Ernesto es tan alto y tan delgado como yo»

Ernesto

MARTES

JUEVES

SÁBADO

Ernesto habla: «Patrica juega tan agresivamente como yo. También juega tanto como yo.»

Para describir

tan + *adjective* + como

as + adjective + as

Patricia es tan **alta** como Ernesto. También es tan **delgada** como él.
Patricia is as tall as Ernesto (is). She's also as thin as he (is).

Para describir cómo se hace una acción

tan + *adverb* + como

as + adverb + as

Patricia juega al tenis tan **bien** como Ernesto. También juega tan **agresivamente** como él.
Patricia plays tennis as well as Ernesto (does). She also plays as aggressively as he (does).

Para expresar la frecuencia o intensidad de una acción

verb + tanto como

verb + as much as

Patricia **juega** al tenis tanto como Ernesto. También **gana** tanto como él.
Patricia plays tennis as much as Ernesto (does). She also wins as much (often) as he (does).

---

2. Comparing Nouns

Ernesto   Patricia

¡OJO!
Like all adjectives, **tanto** must agree in gender and number with the noun it modifies: **tanto dinero, tanta prisa, tantos abrigos, tantas hermanas.**

Ernesto

Patricia habla: «Ernesto tiene tantos hermanos como yo.»

Para comparar la cantidad

tanto/a/os/as + *noun* + como

as much/many + noun + as

Ernesto tiene tantos **trofeos** como Patricia. También tiene tantas **raquetas de tenis** como ella.
Ernesto has as many trophies as Patricia (does). He also has as many tennis rackets as she (does).

Patricia y Ernesto tienen tantas **hermanas** como hermanos.
Patricia and Ernesto each have as many sisters as (they have) brothers.

Gramática   Patricia

Irregular Forms / Las formas irregulares

- **bueno/a/os/as** *adj.* → mejor, mejores (que)

  Estos coches son **buenos,** pero esos son **mejores** (que estos).
  These cars are good, but those are better (than these).

- **bien** *adv.* → mejor (que)

  Yo hablo español **bien,** pero mi amigo Dennis lo habla **mejor** (que yo).
  I speak Spanish well, but my friend Dennis speaks it better (than I [do]).

- **malo/a/os/as** *adj.* → peor, peores (que)

  La nueva película de este director es **mala,** pero su primera es **peor.**
  This director's new movie is bad, but his first one is worse.

- **mal** *adv.* → peor (que)

  La profesora canta **mal,** pero yo canto **peor** (que ella).
  The professor sings badly, but I sing worse (than she [does]).

- **viejo/a/os/as** → mayor, mayores (que)

  La abuela es **viejita,** pero el abuelo es **mayor** *que* ella.
  Grandmother is old, but grandfather is older than she (is).

- **joven, jóvenes** → menor, menores (que)

  Delia es **joven,** pero su esposo es todavía **menor** que ella.
  Delia is young, but her husband is even younger than she (is).

Comparison Summary

| más... que / más que/de | menos... que / menos que/de | tan... como / tanto/a/os/as... / como tanto como |

Práctica y comunicación

A. Comparaciones

Paso 1. Autoprueba. Complete las frases con la palabra comparativa apropiada.

a. como   **b.** que

1. más + _____   **3.** peor + _____   **5.** menos + _____
2. tantos + _____   **4.** tan + _____   **6.** tanta + _____

Paso 2. Ahora compárese *(compare yourself)* con su mejor amigo/a, haciendo oraciones con los siguientes verbos y las formas comparativas del **Paso 1** u otras.

MODELO: tener años → Tengo **tantos años como** mi mejor amiga. (Soy [un año] **mayor/menor que** mi mejor amiga.)

1. tener años   **3.** bailar   **5.** ser inteligente
2. tomar cursos   **4.** tener dinero   **6.** tener pasión por el/la

Paso 3. Ahora, en parejas, usen las oraciones del **Paso 2** para entrevistarse. Luego digan a la clase algo *(something)* que tienen en común.

MODELO: E1: Tengo tantos años como mi mejor amiga. ¿Y tú?
        E2: Sí, tengo tantos años como mi mejor amiga. (No, soy [un año] mayor que mi mejor amiga.)
        EN COMÚN: Las dos tenemos tantos años como nuestras mejores amigas.
                  (Las dos no tenemos tantos años como nuestras mejores amigas.)

Prác. A, Paso 1: Answers: 1. b 2. a 3. b 4. a 5. b 6. a

188 ■ ciento ochenta y ocho

Capítulo 6 Las estaciones y el tiempo

B. Alfredo y Gloria

Alfredo
San José, Costa Rica
Profesor universitario
Casado. (*Married*) Vive en una casa
    cerca del *campus*.
Dos hijos

Gloria
Punta Arenas, Chile
Estudiante universitaria
Vive en una casa en el centro
    con ocho compañeros.
No tiene hijos.

Paso 1. ¿Quién probablemente tiene más de las siguientes cosas y cualidades y quién tiene menos? **¡OJO!** Los dos son similares en los números 4, 5 y 6.

1. botas de invierno
2. camisas de manga (*sleeves*) corta
3. chanclas

4. inteligencia
5. parientes
6. camisetas

Paso 2. ¿Quién probablemente hace más o hace menos? **¡OJO!** Los dos son similares en los números 4, 5 y 6.

1. ganar (*to earn*) dinero
2. salir con sus amigos
3. dormir

4. levantarse temprano
5. hacer ejercicio
6. trabajar

Paso 3. Use los comparativos irregulares para hablar de Alfredo y Gloria.

1. Es obvio que Alfredo tiene más años: es _____ _____ Gloria.
2. Los padres de Alfredo tienen más de 65 años. Sin duda, los padres de Gloria son _____ _____ los padres de Alfredo.
3. Gloria toma clases de danza. Así que (*So*), Gloria baila _____ _____ Alfredo.

C. Opiniones

Paso 1. Complete las siguientes declaraciones para expresar su opinión.

MODELO: el cine / la televisión : ser / interesante →
El cine **es más** interesante **que** la televisión. (**tan... como**)

1. el fútbol / el fútbol americano: ser / divertido
2. la clase de historia / la clase de español: ser / interesante
3. en esta universidad, las artes / los deportes (*sports*): ser / importante
4. el español / el inglés: ser / difícil
5. mis amigos / mis padres: divertirse con
6. los niños / los adultos: dormir
7. los profesores / los estudiantes: trabajar
8. en primavera / en otoño: llover

Paso 2. Ahora en parejas, comparen sus respuestas y expliquen sus opiniones. Luego digan a la clase una idea que los dos comparten (*share*).

D. Más opiniones

Paso 1. Compare las siguientes personas y cosas para expresar su opinión sobre ellas. Puede añadir (*add*) más palabras si quiere.

MODELO: el basquetbol y el golf: interesante, rápido, fácil de aprender →
El basquetbol es **menos** interesante **que** el golf.

1. Meryl Streep y Cameron Díaz: joven, bonito, tener premios Óscar, actriz
2. Ud. y sus padres (hijos): joven, conservador, tener experiencia, desordenado
3. un Prius y un Cadillac: grande, barato, gastar (*to use*) gasolina, elegante
4. los perros y los gatos: independiente, inteligente, cariñoso, activo
5. Texas y Delaware: grande, tener habitantes, petróleo, estar lejos de California

(Continúa.)

Paso 2. En parejas, comparen sus opiniones. Traten de (*Try to*) explicar sus razones. Luego digan a la clase algo (*something*) que tienen en común.

MODELO: el basquetbol y el golf: interesante, rápido →
    E1: El basquetbol es **menos** interesante **que** el golf.
    E2: No estoy de acuerdo. El basquetbol es **más** interesante **que** el golf porque es **más** rápido.

E. Comparaciones. Complete las siguientes oraciones según su experiencia personal.

1. En mi familia, yo soy mayor que _____ y menor que _____.
2. En esta clase, _____ estudia tanto como yo.
3. En esta universidad, los estudiantes _____ más que _____.
4. _____ es más guapo que Juanes.
5. _____ es más guapa que Shakira.
6. _____ tiene tanto talento como Carlos Santana.

F. La familia de Lucía y Miguel

Paso 1. En parejas, miren la foto e identifiquen a los miembros de la familia de Lucía. Piensen en la edad (*age*) de cada persona.

el abuelo Jaime

Lucía   Miguel   la abuela Lucía

Amalia

Lucía, con su esposo, sus padres y sus hijos

Sami

Sancho

MODELO: Sancho es mayor que sus hermanos.

Paso 2. Comparen a cada miembro de la familia con otra persona.

MODELO: Amalia es menor que Sancho pero es más alta que él.

Paso 3. Ahora comparen a los miembros de su propia (*own*) familia. Haga por lo menos cinco declaraciones.

MODELOS: E1: Mi hermana Mary es mayor que yo, pero yo soy más alto que ella.
    E2: Mi abuela es mayor que mi abuelo, pero ella es más activa que él.

G. La rutina diaria... en invierno y en verano

Paso 1. ¿Es diferente nuestra rutina diaria en cada estación? Complete las siguientes oraciones sobre su rutina.

	EN INVIERNO	EN VERANO
1. me levanto a _____ (hora)	_____	_____
2. almuerzo en _____	_____	_____
3. me divierto con mis amigos / mi familia en _____	_____	_____
4. estudio _____ horas todos los días	_____	_____
5. estoy / me quedo en _____ (lugar) por la noche	_____	_____
6. me acuesto a _____ (hora)	_____	_____

Vocabulario útil

afuera outside

el gimnasio
el parque

Paso 2. En parejas, comparen sus actividades de invierno con las de verano.

MODELO: E1: En invierno, ¿te levantas más temprano que en verano?
    E2: No, en invierno, me levanto tan temprano como en verano.
        (No, en invierno, me levanto a la misma hora que en verano.)

Paso 3. Ahora digan a la clase una o dos cosas que Uds. tienen en común.

MODELO: Nosotros nos levantamos más tarde en verano que en invierno. En verano no hay clases y, por lo general, nos acostamos más tarde.

Un poco de todo

A. Lengua y cultura: Dos hemisferios

Paso 1. Complete the following paragraphs with the correct forms of the words in parentheses, as suggested by context. When two possibilities are given in parentheses, select the correct word.

¿Sabe Ud.ª algo de las diferencias entre los hemisferios del norte y del sur? Hay (mucho¹) diferencias entre el clima del hemisferio norte y el del hemisferio sur.

Cuando (ser / estar²) invierno en este país, por ejemplo, (ser / estar³) verano en la Argentina, en Bolivia, en Chile... Cuando yo (salir⁴) para la universidad en enero, con frecuencia tengo que (llevar⁵) abrigo y botas. En (los / las⁶) países del hemisferio sur, un estudiante (poder⁷) asistir (a / de⁸) un concierto en febrero llevando solo pantalones (corto⁹), camiseta y sandalias.

En muchas partes de este país, (antes de / durante¹⁰) las vacaciones de diciembre, casi siempre (hacer¹¹) frío y a veces (nevar¹²). En (grande¹³) parte de Sudamérica, al otro lado del ecuador, hace calor y (muy / mucho¹⁴) sol durante (ese¹⁵) mes. A veces en los periódicos, hay fotos de personas que (tomar¹⁶) el sol y nadanᵇ en las playas sudamericanas en enero.

Es diciembre en Buenos Aires. ¿Qué tiempo hace?

Tengo un amigo que (ir¹⁷) a (hacer / tomar¹⁸) un viaje a Buenos Aires. Él me diceᶜ que allí la Navidadᵈ (ser / estar¹⁹) una fiesta de verano y que todos (llevar²⁰) ropa como la queᵉ llevamos nosotros en julio. Pareceᶠ increíble, ¿verdad?

ª¿Sabe... *Do you know* ᵇ*are swimming* ᶜÉl... *He tells me* ᵈ*Christmas* ᵉla... *that which* ᶠ*It seems*

Paso 2. Comprensión. ¿Probable o improbable?

	PROBABLE	IMPROBABLE
1. Los estudiantes argentinos van a la playa en julio.	☐	☐
2. Muchas personas sudamericanas hacen viajes de vacaciones en enero.	☐	☐
3. En Santiago (Chile) hace frío en diciembre.	☐	☐

Paso 3. En parejas, lean el anuncio (*ad*) del inicio del año escolar (*school*) en el Perú (página 192). Luego conteste las siguientes preguntas.

1. ¿En qué mes cae (*occurs*) el inicio del año escolar en los Estados Unidos? ¿En qué estación cae?

2. ¿En qué mes empieza en el Perú? ¿En qué estación cae?

3. ¿Por qué la escuela empieza en meses diferentes en los dos países?

4. ¿Cuándo son las vacaciones de verano en los Estados Unidos?

5. ¿Cuándo creen Uds. que empiezan las vacaciones de verano en el Perú?

Buen inicio del año escolar

10 de marzo

B. Expresiones

Paso 1. Las comparaciones se usan mucho en refranes y expresiones populares e idiomáticas. En parejas, lean las siguientes expresiones. ¿Tienen equivalentes en inglés?

1. pesar (*to weigh*) menos que un mosquito
2. ser más pesado (*overbearing, boring*) que el matrimonio
3. ser más bueno que el pan (*bread*)
4. ser más largo que un día sin pan
5. estar más claro que el agua (*water*)
6. ser más alto que un pino (*pine tree*)
7. ser tan rápido como un chisme (*rumor*)

Paso 2. Ahora, en parejas, inventen por lo menos cuatro expresiones que se parecen a las (*resemble those*) del **Paso 1.** Pueden cambiar la terminación de las expresiones del **Paso 1** (**pesar menos que...** ¿ ?) o crear expresiones originales (**ser tan divertido como...** , **ser más larga que una semana sin...**).

Al crear (*When you are creating*) las expresiones, piensen en cosas y cualidades que, en la cultura de este país, son generalmente positivas o negativas. En las expresiones del **Paso 1,** por ejemplo, se usa la palabra **pan** dos veces. ¿Cómo se presenta el pan en la cultura hispana en estas expresiones, como una cosa muy positiva o negativa?

En **su** comunidad

Entreviste (*Interview*) a una persona hispana de su universidad o ciudad sobre el clima de su país de origen y los horarios (*schedules*) de clases durante el año.

PREGUNTAS POSIBLES

- ¿Hay en su país cuatro estaciones o solo dos?
- ¿Coinciden con las estaciones del lugar donde Ud. vive ahora?
- ¿Cómo es el clima en cada estación?
- ¿En qué mes empiezan las clases en las escuelas? ¿Y en qué mes terminan?
- ¿Es igual para los ciclos de la universidad?

«En la Mitad del Mundo» Segmento 2

Antes de mirar

Indique todas las palabras que Ud. asocia con las artesanías (*crafts*). ¿Tiene otras asociaciones?

_____	la tradición	_____	su país
_____	mercados al aire libre (*open air*)	_____	la modernidad
		_____	centros comerciales
_____	la gente (*people*) mayor	_____	la gente joven
		_____	otros países

Este segmento

Laura presenta un reportaje sobre la tradición artesanal textil en la ciudad ecuatoriana de Otavalo y habla con un maestro tejedor.

El Sr. José Cotocachi, maestro tejedor (*master weaver*) de tercera (*third*) generación que mantiene (*maintains*) la tradición textil de su familia

Fragmento del guion

LAURA: La lengua materna de José es el quechua, la lengua que hablaban[a] los incas y que hoy siguen hablando muchas personas desde Ecuador hasta Chile. José nos enseñó[b] cómo él mismo[c] hace los tintes[d] para la lana que usa en los tejidos de su taller.[e] Estos tintes son completamente naturales y los colores son increíbles. Vemos cómo un insecto tan pequeño, la cochinilla, produce un intenso color rojo.

JOSÉ: Si es que le guardo[f] un año o dos años mejor todavía más fuerte[g]... y bueno un poco de ácido natural... llegó [a ser] un poquito claro.[h]

[a]*used to speak* [b]*nos... showed us* [c]*él... he himself* [d]*dyes* [e]*tejidos... fabrics of his shop* [f]*Si... If I keep it* [g]*todavía... even stronger* [h]*llegó... it got lighter*

Vocabulario del segmento

rodeado/a de	surrounded by
sobre todo	especially
la bufanda	scarf
tuve	I had
la transmite	he teaches it
era	it was
duro/a	hard, difficult
no ha cambiado	has not changed
la venta masiva	mass distribution
nos explicó	explained to us
los negocios	businesses
la feria	fair
trabajábamos	used to work
ya salíamos	we were already leaving
ya no es así	it's not that way any more

Después de mirar

A. **¿Está claro?** Las siguientes oraciones son falsas. Corríjalas (*Correct them*) según el video.

1. Otavalo está en la costa del Ecuador.
2. Allí hace mucho calor.
3. Otavalo es famosa por su gran centro comercial.
4. La ciudad no tiene población indígena.
5. José es el único (*only*) tejedor en su familia.

B. **Un poco más.** Conteste las siguientes preguntas.

1. Además del (*Besides*) español, ¿qué otra lengua se habla en el Ecuador?
2. ¿Qué prendas (*articles of clothing*) textiles producen los artesanos otavaleños?
3. ¿Qué pasa en una feria?

C. **Y ahora, Uds.** En parejas, preparen un resumen informativo de este segmento de *Salu2*. Deben crear (*create*) un texto que pudiera (*could*) ser útil a turistas.

A LEER

¿Es muy variado el clima en el país donde Ud. vive?

Lectura cultural: Costa Rica
El clima de Costa Rica

Se puede decir[a] que el clima de Costa Rica es tropical. Esto significa que propiamente[b] no tiene una estación de invierno. Lo que sí tiene son dos temporadas:[c] una seca[d] y otra lluviosa.[e] En la mayor parte del país, esta última[f] ocurre entre mayo y noviembre. En las zonas más lluviosas del país, las lluvias son muy copiosas[g] y llegan a ocasionar muchas inundaciones.[h]

Sin embargo, el clima de Costa Rica es muy diverso. Esto llama mucho la atención de los turistas, ya que[i] en pocas horas se puede pasar de un clima lluvioso en las montañas a uno caluroso[j] en la playa.

[a]say [b]really [c]seasons [d]dry [e]rainy [f]last one (i.e., last season) [g]heavy
[h]llegan... they cause a lot of floods [i]ya... since [j]uno... a warm one (i.e., warm climate)

Una carreta de Sarchí, Costa Rica

En otros países hispanos

- **En Chile** En este país se encuentra[a] el desierto de Atacama, el más seco del mundo.

- **En España** La diversidad climática y geográfica de este país europeo es espectacular para su tamaño.[b] La zona más caliente de Europa (el área de Córdoba y Sevilla) coexiste con una de las cordilleras[c] más altas del continente (la Sierra Nevada). Hasta hay[d] una zona desértica (en Almería).

[a]se... is found [b]size [c]mountain ranges [d]Hasta... There's even

COMPRENSIÓN

Conteste las siguientes preguntas.

1. ¿Por qué no tiene el clima costarricense cuatro estaciones?
2. ¿Cuáles son los meses secos en Costa Rica?
3. ¿Dónde está el desierto de Atacama?
4. ¿Qué aspecto del clima y la geografía de España es interesante?
5. ¿Para qué sirve una carreta?

Un símbolo costarricense: La carreta

Como método de transporte tradicional, las carretas no son exclusivas de Costa Rica. Allí su uso se asocia con las plantaciones de café. Sin embargo, sí es puramente costarricense decorar las carretas con bellos diseños[a] y colores. Por eso, las carretas son un símbolo nacional del trabajo y la cultura costarricense. La ciudad de Sarchí, al norte de la capital, es el centro artesanal de estas carretas.

[a]bellos... beautiful designs

 Y ahora, Uds.

Uds. ya saben (know by now) muchos detalles sobre la geografía y el clima del mundo hispanohablante. En grupos, seleccionen un país de ese mundo donde les gustaría (you would like) vivir. También deben escribir una lista de razones que justifiquen su decisión, para presentar a la clase.

Del mundo hispano

Antes de leer

Conteste las siguientes preguntas.

1. ¿Qué tipo de calendario(s) usa Ud.?
2. Mire el calendario que aparece en esta lectura. ¿Qué día de la semana se representa con la X? ¿Por qué cree que se usa la X?
3. ¿Cuál es el primer día de la semana en los calendarios de los países hispanos?

Lectura: Un calendario especial

CURIOSIDADES ¿Se pueden usar calendarios de otros años?

ENERO							
L	M	X	J	V	S	D	
			1	2	3	4	
5	6	7	8	9	10	11	
12	13	14	15	16	17	18	
19	20	21	22	23	24	25	
26	27	28	29	30	31		

FEBRERO						
L	M	X	J	V	S	D
						1
2	3	4	5	6	7	8
9	10	11	12	13	14	15
16	17	18	19	20	21	22
23	24	25	26	27	28	

MARZO						
L	M	X	J	V	S	D
						1
2	3	4	5	6	7	8
9	10	11	12	13	14	15
16	17	18	19	20	21	22
23/30	24/31	25	26	27	28	29

ABRIL						
L	M	X	J	V	S	D
	1	2	3	4	5	
6	7	8	9	10	11	12
13	14	15	16	17	19	20
21	22	23	24	25	26	27
28	29	30				

MAYO						
L	M	X	J	V	S	D
			1	2	3	
4	5	6	7	8	9	10
11	12	13	14	15	16	17
18	19	20	21	22	23	24
25	26	27	28	29	30	31

JUNIO						
L	M	X	J	V	S	D
1	2	3	4	5	6	7
8	9	10	11	12	13	14
15	16	17	18	19	20	21
22	23	24	25	26	27	28
29	30					

JULIO						
L	M	X	J	V	S	D
	1	2	3	4	5	
6	7	8	9	10	11	12
13	14	15	16	17	18	19
20	21	22	23	24	25	26
27	28	29	30	31		

AGOSTO						
L	M	X	J	V	S	D
					1	2
3	4	5	6	7	8	9
10	11	12	13	14	15	16
17	18	19	20	21	22	23
24/31	25	26	27	28	29	30

SEPTIEMBRE						
L	M	X	J	V	S	D
1	2	3	4	5	6	
7	8	9	10	11	12	13
14	15	16	17	18	19	20
21	22	23	24	25	26	27
28	29	30				

REPETIMOS CADA 28 AÑOS

¿Alguien[a] guarda el calendario de hace 28 años? Si la respuesta es afirmativa, es el momento de sacarlo,[b] ya que[c] coincide día por día con el de este año 2010. Esa ha sido[d] la curiosa iniciativa que la asociación ecologista más importante de Italia, Legambiente, ha puesto en marcha[e] para promover el reciclaje. Resulta que, cada 28 años, los calendarios se repiten, siendo iguales en todas sus fechas. La explicación es que cada año solo puede comenzar en un día de la semana, por lo que existirían[f] 7 calendarios posibles... si no existieran años bisiestos.[g] Según los cálculos, al repetirse los años bisiestos cada 4 años, y los normales cada 7, el ciclo dura 28 años.

Y la próxima...
¿Cuándo nació la corbata?

[a]*Anyone* [b]*take it out* [c]*ya... since* [d]*ha... has been* [e]*ha... has put in motion* [f]*por... in which case, there would be* [g]*años... leap years*

Comprensión

A. Según el texto. Conteste las siguientes preguntas.

1. ¿Cómo se llaman los años de 366 días?
2. ¿Con qué frecuencia se repiten los calendarios?
3. ¿Qué es Legambiente?
4. ¿Qué acción recomienda Legambiente?
5. Además de (*Besides*) servir para el año 2010, ¿para qué otros años del pasado y del futuro puede servir el calendario de la Lectura?

B. Comentario. ¿Cree Ud. que es buena idea seguir la recomendación de Legambiente? ¿Es algo práctico y fácil de hacer? Explique sus razones.

El pronóstico° del tiempo en la Argentina   *report*

Vocabulario **para escuchar**

despejado	clear, no clouds	el granizo	hail
los grados	degrees	la borrasca	storm
soleado	sunny	la bajada	dip, lowering
la franja	coastal area	bajo	below

Antes de escuchar

¿Mira Ud. el pronóstico del tiempo todos los días? ¿Le gustan los pronósticos con muchos detalles o solo quiere saber (*know*) la información básica, como la temperatura máxima y mínima y si va a hacer sol o va a llover?

Después de escuchar

A. Temperaturas y condiciones atmosféricas. Complete los espacios en blanco (*blanks*) en el mapa con las temperaturas máximas y mínimas. También dibuje (*draw*) el símbolo correspondiente a las condiciones atmosféricas que se mencionan.

Se espera nieve.   Se espera lluvia.

Se espera granizo.   Se espera sol.

B. El pronóstico en general. Conteste las siguientes preguntas.

1. ¿Qué tiempo va a hacer el domingo en la mayoría de las regiones argentinas?
2. ¿Qué estación es hoy en la Argentina?

(mapa de la Argentina con las ciudades:) BOLIVIA, PARAGUAY, JUJUY, Salta, BRASIL, CHILE, ARGENTINA, Córdoba, Mendoza, URUGUAY, PAMPA, Buenos Aires, San Carlos de Bariloche, Río Gallegos

PRODUCCIÓN PERSONAL

¡Ahora, yo!

A. Use de modelo las preguntas y respuestas de la página 165 de este capítulo para hablar del clima donde Ud. vive y de su estación del año favorita y lo que le gusta hacer en esa estación.

B. Mire el pronóstico del tiempo de su ciudad para los próximos tres días y filme su propio informe metereológico. Puede tener un tono serio o cómico.

A ESCRIBIR
Un ensayo sobre sus preferencias climáticas

Preparar

Paso 1. Piense en la estación del año que Ud. prefiere. ¿Por qué prefiere esa estación? ¿Con qué la asocia (*do you associate it*)? ¿Cuál es la estación del año que menos le gusta? ¿Por qué?

Paso 2. Entreviste a dos compañeros de clase sobre la estación del año que más les gusta y la que (*that which*) menos les gusta. También debe preguntarles por qué. Complete el cuadro con su respectivo información y también con sus propias (*your own*) respuestas a las preguntas.

nombre	estación preferida	estación que menos le gusta	¿por qué?
yo			
compañero/a 1			
compañero/a 2			

Paso 3. Ahora use sus opiniones y las respuestas de sus compañeros para escribir su ensayo. Hay más ayuda (*help*) en Connect.

Más ideas para su portafolio

- Incluya una imagen del mapa del tiempo de una ciudad donde Ud. desea vivir. Explique por qué le gusta (o no le gusta) el tiempo de esta ciudad.

- Dé tres palabras que Ud. asocia con el clima del estado donde vive y tres palabras que asocia con el clima del estado o país donde le gustaría (*you would like*) vivir en el futuro. Incluya una foto que represente el clima de su estado o el clima del país de su futuro.

- Si ha estado jugando (*have been playing*) Practice Spanish: Study Abroad, en Quest 4 Ud. participó (*participated*) en una telenovela (*soap opera*) sobre una compañía que se especializa en (*specializes in*) la moda. Hay muchos diseñadores (*designers*) de ropa y modelos hispanos famosos, por ejemplo Carolina Herrera, Paloma Picasso, Narciso Rodríguez, Oscar de la Renta, Cristóbal Balenciaga y Manolo Blahnik. Busque información en el internet sobre dos hispanos famosos en la industria de la moda y escriba por lo menos 6 oraciones comparándolos (*comparing them*). Incluya (*Include*) una foto de cada uno y escriba 2-3 oraciones sobre la ropa que llevan en la foto.

Sugerencia: You are now ready to play Quest 4 in **Practice Spanish: Study Abroad** (www.mhpractice.com).

EN RESUMEN En este capítulo

LEARNSMART
Visit **www.connectspanish.com** to practice the vocabulary and grammar points covered in this chapter.

AFTER STUDYING THIS CHAPTER I CAN . . .

- ☐ talk about the weather (166)
- ☐ talk about months and seasons of the year and express dates (168)
- ☐ use prepositions and cardinal points to locate people, places, and things (170)
- ☐ use the present progressive to express what I'm doing right now (174–174)
- ☐ use the verbs **ser** and **estar** correctly, especially with adjectives (178–180)
- ☐ compare people, places, things, and actions (185–188)
- ☐ recognize/describe at least 2–3 aspects of Costa Rican cultures

Gramática en breve

15. Present Progressive   estar + -ndo
-ar ⟶ -ando
-er/-ir ⟶ -iendo

Unaccented **-i-** ⟶ **-y-** (le**y**endo)

-ir Stem-changing Verbs: e ⟶ i (p**i**diendo)
o ⟶ u (d**u**rmiendo)

16. Summary of the Uses of *ser* and *estar*

ser	estar
inherent qualities, characteristics	mental, physical, health conditions
identification (including profession)	location present progressive
nationality, origin	fixed expressions
material	
possession	
for whom intended	
time and date	
generalizations	

Idioms with tener (expressing *to be*)

tener (mucho) calor, (mucho) frío

17. Comparisons

Comparisons of Inequality	Comparisons of Equality
más/menos... que	**tan... como**
más/menos que	**tanto/a/os/as... como**
más/menos de + *número*	
mayor/menor que	
mejor/peor que	

VOCABULARIO

Los verbos

celebrar	to celebrate
continuar (continúo)	to continue
pasar	to spend (*time*); to happen
quedarse	to stay, remain (*in a place*)
seguir (sigo) (i)	to continue, to follow
Repaso: divertirse (me divierto) (i)	

Remember that the parenthetical letter gives you the stem change for the present participle.

¿Qué tiempo hace?

el clima	climate
el tiempo	weather; time
está (muy) nublado	it's (very) cloudy, overcast
hace...	it's ...
(muy) buen/mal tiempo	(very) good/bad weather (very) nice out
(mucho) calor	(very) hot
(mucho) fresco	(very) cool
(mucho) frío	(very) cold
(mucho) sol	(very) sunny
(mucho) viento	(very) windy
hay (mucha) contaminación	there's (lots of) pollution
llover: llueve	to rain: it rains, it's raining
nevar: nieva	to snow: it snows, it's snowing
¿qué tiempo hace?	what's the weather like?

Los meses del año

el año	year
la fecha	date (*calendar*)
el mes	month
¿Cual es la fecha de hoy? ¿Qué fecha es hoy?	What's today's date?
el primero de	the first of (*month*)

enero	abril	julio	octubre
febrero	mayo	agosto	noviembre
marzo	junio	septiembre	diciembre

Las estaciones del año

la estación	season
la primavera	spring
el verano	summer
el otoño	fall, autumn
el invierno	winter

Los lugares

la capital	capital city
la playa	beach

Otros sustantivos

el cumpleaños	birthday
la medianoche	midnight
el mediodía	noon
el/la novio/a	boyfriend/girlfriend
la respuesta	answer

Los adjetivos

abierto/a	open
aburrido/a	bored
alegre	happy
cansado/a	tired
cariñoso/a	affectionate
cerrado/a	closed
congelado/a	frozen; very cold
contento/a	content, happy
desordenado/a	messy
difícil	hard, difficult
enfermo/a	sick
fácil	easy
furioso/a	furious, angry
limpio/a	clean
loco/a	crazy
mismo/a	same
molesto/a	annoyed
nervioso/a	nervous
ocupado/a	busy
ordenado/a	neat
preocupado/a	worried
querido/a	dear
seguro/a	sure, certain
sucio/a	dirty
triste	sad

Las comparaciones

más/menos de + number	more/fewer than + *number*
más/menos que	more/less than
más/menos... que	more/less (-er) . . . than

tan... como	as . . . as
tanto como	as much as
tanto/a(s)... como	as much/many . . . as
mayor (que)	older (than)
mejor (que)	better (than); best
menor (que)	younger (than)
peor (que)	worse (than)

Las preposiciones

a la derecha de	to the right of
a la izquierda de	to the left of
al lado de	alongside of
cerca de	close to
debajo de	below
delante de	in front of
detrás de	behind
encima de	on top of
entre	between; among
lejos de	far from

Los puntos cardinales

el norte, el sur, el este, el oeste

Palabras adicionales

afuera	outdoors
ahora mismo	right now
conmigo	with me
contigo	with you (*fam.*)
esta noche	tonight
está bien	it's fine, OK
estar bien	to be comfortable (*temperature*)
mí (*obj. of prep.*)	me
por	about; because of
sin embargo	nevertheless
tener (mucho) calor	to be (very) warm, hot
tener (mucho) frío	to be (very) cold
ti (*obj. of prep.*)	you (*fam.*)
todavía	still

Vocabulario personal

ÍNDICE

CAPÍTULO
1

Communicative Goals for Capítulo 1

By the end of this chapter, you should be able to:

- meet and greet others ❑
- describe yourself and others ❑
- count to 30 and do simple math ❑
- talk about likes and dislikes ❑
- tell time ❑
- get information by asking questions ❑

Grammatical Structures

You should know:

- **ser** ❑
- some interrogative words ❑
- **gustar** ❑
- **hay** ❑

PRONUNCIACIÓN

There are only five vowel sounds in Spanish. Listen carefully as your instructor pronounces each word group, then repeat.

A: Panamá–ciudad--Caracas–capital--Caracas es la capital.--Caracas es la capital de Venezuela.--España--Madrid–Madrid es la capital de España.--Islas--Islas Canarias--Nicaragua--Managua–Managua es la capital de Nicaragua.

E: México--Monterrey--Monterrey está--Monterrey está en México.--Venezuela--Cartagena--Belice--Ecuador--Palenque--América--Barcelona--Sevilla--Sevilla está--Sevilla está en España.

I: Islas--Lima--Lima es la capital.--Lima es la capital del Perú.--Quito--Quito es la capital del Ecuador.--Bolivia--Bolivia está--Bolivia está en América Latina.--país--Brasil--Brasil es un país.--Chile--Potosí--Potosí está en Bolivia.

O: Colombia--Bogotá--Bogotá es la capital de Colombia.--Orinoco--Costa--Costa Rica--San José es la capital de Costa Rica.--Ecuador--Andorra--Andorra está al norte de España.--Honduras--Copán--Copán está en Honduras.

U: Acapulco--Cancún--península--Yucatán--Cancún está--Cancún está en la península de Yucatán.--Cuba--República--Perú--Cuzco--Cuzco está en el Perú.--Machu Picchu--Uruguay--Cataluña--Honduras

COGNATES PRACTICE: LOS GUSTOS

A. Choose two things you like and two things you don't like in each category.

LUGARES

el restaurante vegetariano   el museo de arte moderno

la universidad prestigiosa   el club exclusivo

el parque zoológico   la cafetería universitaria

Me gusta _____ pero no me gusta _____.

Me gusta _____ pero no me gusta _____.

PERSONAS

la profesora excéntrica   el piloto incompetente

el director flexible   el detective paciente

el actor arrogante   la artista prolífica

Me gusta _____ pero no me gusta _____.

Me gusta _____ pero no me gusta _____.

COSAS

el perfume exótico   la novela romántica

el refrigerador enorme   el café expreso

el volcán gigantesco   la biología marina

Me gusta _____ pero no me gusta _____.

Me gusta _____ pero no me gusta _____.

B. With a partner, ask each other questions to find out what they like and don't like in each category.

¿Te gusta _____?

PRÁCTICA: LA HORA Y LOS SALUDOS

Use the clocks shown and the greetings below to answer the questions.

<u>Los saludos</u>: Buenos días   Buenas tardes   Buenas noches

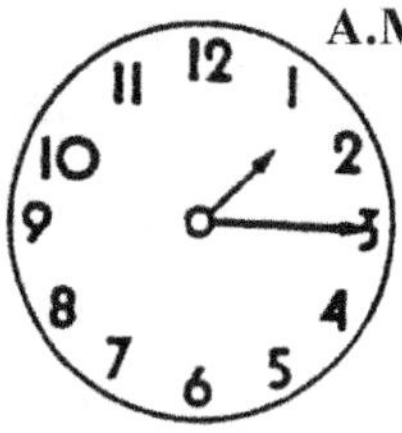

¿Qué hora es en Madrid? _____

¿Qué saludo usas? _____

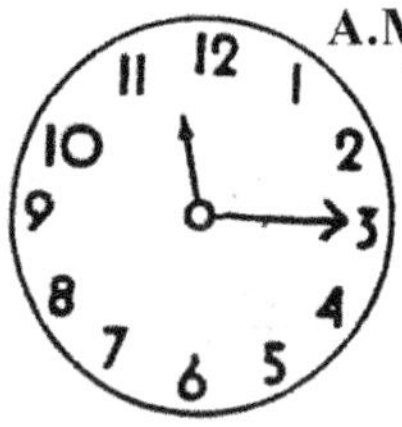

¿Qué hora es en Buenos Aires? _____

¿Qué saludo usas? _____

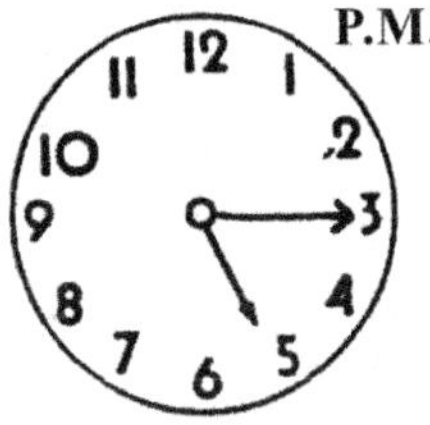

¿Qué hora es en San Francisco? _____

¿Qué saludo usas? _____

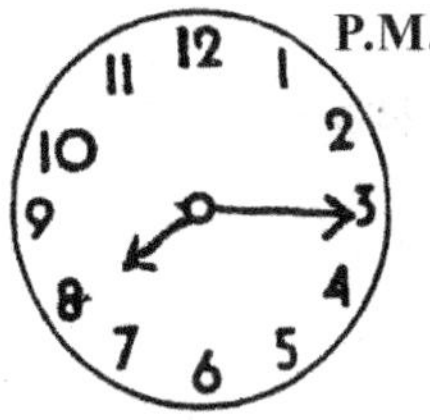

¿Qué hora es en Nueva York? _____

¿Qué saludo usas? _____

En este momento (*Right now*), ¿qué hora es? _____

¿Qué hora es en Madrid? _____

¿Qué saludo usas en Madrid en este momento? _____

PRÁCTICA: PREGUNTAS Y RESPUESTAS

Some students are talking about classes and the new semester. Complete each conversation with the correct question word: **¿cómo?, ¿dónde?, ¿quién?,** or **¿qué?**

Laura: ¿ _____ es tu clase de español?
David: ¡Es fabulosa! Es mi clase favorita.

Anita: ¿ _____ es la orientación para (*for*) estudiantes internacionales?
Tomás: Es en el auditorio Rubén Darío.

Sonia: ¿A _____ hora es la fiesta?
Pablo: Es a las ocho de la noche.

Laura: ¿ _____ es el profesor de ciencias?
David: Es muy inteligente, pero un poco tímido.

Rubén: ¿ _____ se llama tu libro de texto (*textbook*)?
Elisa: El libro se llama *Puntos de partida.*

Diego: ¿De _____ eres?
Anita: Soy de Venezuela. ¿Y tú?

Laura: ¿ _____ hay en el centro estudiantil (*student union*)?
Sonia: Hay de todo... unas oficinas, una cafetería, un banco...

Pablo: ¿ _____ está el profesor ahora?
Marta: Está en la oficina.

Marta: ¿ _____ te llamas?
David: Me llamo David Ramos. ¿Y tú?

Juana: ¿ _____ hora es?
Julio: Son las diez y cinco.

Rubén: ¿ _____ te gusta comer pizza?
Tomás: Me gusta comer pizza en Pizza Hut.

Anita: Hola, Elisa. ¿ _____ estás hoy?
Elisa: Muy bien, gracias. ¿Y tú?

Sonia: ¿ _____ es el profesor de español?
Marta: Es el profesor Gómez.

REPASO: CAPÍTULO 1

I. Vocabulario

A. La hora. Create a question for the following answers:

1. ¿ _____?

   Son las once y veinte de la mañana.

2. ¿ _____?

   La clase de sociología es a las dos de la tarde.

3. ¿ _____?

   Regreso a casa a las cinco y media.

B. Expresa en español.

1. Excuse me, miss. What time is it?

   _____

2. It is 7 p.m. on the dot.

   _____

3. Spanish class is at 11 a.m., but History class is at 4.

   _____

C. Los números. Complete the sentences with the written form of the numbers given.

1. En mi clase de biología, hay (17) _____ muchachos y (21) _____ muchachas.

2. Hoy necesito comprar (*buy*) mis libros. El libro de inglés cuesta (30) _____ dólares. También necesito comprar (6) _____ cuadernos (*notebooks*) y (12) _____ bolígrafos (*pens*). Ahora hay (7) _____ clientes en la librería (*bookstore*), pero solo (1) _____ dependienta (*clerk*).

3. En el departamento de idiomas (*languages*) hay (29) _____ profesores. (21) _____ profesores son de Europa o América Latina.

II. Gramática

A. Gustar. Answer in complete sentences.

1. ¿Te gusta la clase de matemáticas? _____

2. ¿Te gusta estudiar la gramática? _____

3. ¿Te gusta la universidad? _____

4. ¿Te gusta tomar café? _____

B. Preguntas. Answer in complete sentences.

1. ¿Cómo te llamas? _____

2. ¿De dónde eres? _____

3. ¿A qué hora es la clase de español? _____

4. ¿Cuántos estudiantes hay en la clase de español? (aproximadamente) _____

5. ¿Dónde te gusta estudiar? _____

III. Diálogo

Write a short dialogue in which:

- Luis introduces himself to Marta
- Marta asks him where he's from
- Luis answers and asks if she likes Spanish class
- Marta answers and says she'll see him tomorrow

_____

_____

_____

_____

_____

_____

_____

_____

BINGO: GUSTAR

_____ la clase de español	_____ estudiar español	_____ el arte moderno	_____ la fruta	_____ el chocolate
_____ visitar los parques nacionales	_____ la salsa	_____ el programa _Big Bang Theory_	_____ la universidad	_____ Shakira
_____ Taco Bell	_____ el basquetbol	_____ la pizza	_____ la limonada	_____ la música clásica
_____ la televisión	_____ practicar yoga	_____ el profesor / la profesora	_____ el café	_____ conversar por teléfono
_____ practicar la pronunciación	_____ la música latina	_____ la ópera	_____ Enrique Iglesias	_____ Jennifer López

CAPÍTULO
2

Communicative Goals for Chapter 2

By the end of the chapter, you should be able to:

- talk about your college or university ❏
- discuss your schedule, courses, professors ❏
- talk about activities you do on campus ❏
- get information by asking questions ❏

Grammatical Structures

You should know:

- articles ❏
- **-ar** verbs ❏
- **estar** ❏
- negation ❏
- interrogative words ❏

PRONUNCIACIÓN

A: las matemáticas--Marta--A Marta no le gustan las matemáticas.-- cifras--Hay cifras.--Hay cifras sin parar.--la calculadora--salva--La calculadora me salva.--sumar--sumar y restar--sumar, restar y multiplicar--El alemán--A Ana--A Ana le encanta el alemán.

E: Eliseo--Mérida--Eliseo es de Mérida, México.--estudia--ciencias--Estudia ciencias en los Estados Unidos.--le encantan--las ciencias geológicas--A Eliseo le encantan las ciencias geológicas.--el estudiante--egoísta--Es el estudiante menos egoísta de la clase.

I: la química--la química y la física--La química y la física son ciencias.--Inés--le interesa--A Inés le interesa la ingeniería.--Iñigo Irizarry--Íñigo Irizarry es ingeniero.--Es un ingeniero inteligente e impresionante.

O: Begoña--español--Begoña enseña español.--a las once--Begoña enseña español a las once todos los días.--obligatorio--Es una clase obligatoria.--sus horas de oficina--Sus horas de oficina son a las once y a las dos los miércoles.

U: la universidad--la universidad pública--A Lupe le gusta la universidad pública.--La universidad pública es muy popular.--Hugo--Hugo estudia humanidades.--A Hugo le gustan sus cursos universitarios.--Umberto--Umberto y Hugo son los únicos alumnos uruguayos.

LISTENING COMPREHENSION

#1 · You will hear a passage about Roberto and Luis. The first time, listen for the answers to the **Cierto/Falso** statements below. The second time, listen for the answers to the short-answer questions.

¿Cierto o falso?

1. ☐ C ☐ F   Los dos amigos son estudiantes.

2. ☐ C ☐ F   Uno de los amigos habla muchas lenguas.

3. ☐ C ☐ F   Luis no trabaja porque es estudiante.

4. ☐ C ☐ F   Están contentos en la universidad porque las librerías son buenas.

Preguntas. Answer with short Spanish sentences.

1. ¿Cómo se llaman los dos amigos?

_____

2. ¿Estudian los dos?

_____

3. ¿Dónde trabaja Luis?

_____

4. ¿Qué enseña Roberto?

_____

5. ¿Por qué trabaja Luis?

_____

#2   You will hear a short passage about Ramón and María. Listen for the answers to the **Cierto/Falso** statements below.

¿Cierto o falso?

1. ☐ C ☐ F   Ramón y María son estudiantes italianos.

2. ☐ C ☐ F   Estudian en Buenos Aires.

3. ☐ C ☐ F   Son de Madrid.

4. ☐ C ☐ F   Estudian por la mañana.

5. ☐ C ☐ F   Escuchan muchas lenguas extranjeras en el café.

6. ☐ C ☐ F   Ramón y María tocan música en el café.

PRÁCTICA: LOS ARTÍCULOS DEFINIDOS E INDEFINIDOS

Complete each sentence with the correct definite or indefinite article, according to the context.

los artículos definidos	
el	la
los	las

los artículos indefinidos	
un	una
unos	unas

1. Hay _____ diccionarios españoles en _____ Biblioteca Internacional.

2. _____ exámenes de _____ estudiantes están en _____ mesa de _____ profesora Bonilla.

3. _____ programa de música clásica es en _____ teatro de _____ universidad, mañana por _____ tarde.

4. En _____ librería, hay _____ lápices especiales y _____ cuadernos perfectos para _____ clase de arte.

5. _____ oficina de _____ profesora Méndez está en _____ Departamento de Lenguas. _____ número de teléfono es 555-0047.

6. Hay _____ problemas graves con _____ programas de computadoras en _____ laboratorio de lenguas.

7. _____ director del Centro Internacional está aquí todos _____ días a _____ dos de _____ tarde.

8. Hay _____ clase de computación por _____ noche.

9. _____ estudiantes de _____ clase de inglés desean hablar con _____ consejera ahora.

10. _____ problema con _____ universidad es que es muy grande (big).

11. Todos _____ estudiantes necesitan pagar _____ matrícula hoy, antes de (before) _____ seis de _____ tarde.

12. En _____ mochila del estudiante nuevo, hay _____ papeles, _____ lápices, _____ calculadora y _____ mapa (masc.) de _____ universidad.

PRESENT TENSE OF -AR VERBS

bailar	enseñar	practicar
buscar	estudiar	regresar (a casa)
cantar	hablar	tocar
comprar	necesitar	tomar
desear	pagar	trabajar

Complete the sentences with the correct form of a logical verb from the list. Remember the endings: **-o, -as, -a, -amos, -áis, -an.**

En la universidad:

1. ¿ _____ (nosotros) español por la noche?
2. La profesora Ybarra no _____ inglés.
3. ¿Cuántas clases _____ (tú) este (*this*) semestre?
4. Elena _____ en la biblioteca.
5. ¿Cuándo _____ (nosotros) la matrícula?

En el café:

6. Jorge y Pedro _____ más café.
7. Patricia no _____ la guitarra.
8. Nosotros _____ una canción (*song*) de Carlos Santana.
9. Clara _____ una Coca-Cola.
10. Paco no _____ bailar con la estudiante italiana.

En la librería:

11. Sara no _____ un diccionario.
12. Raúl _____ un cuaderno y una calculadora también.
13. ¿ _____ (tú) los libros con cheque?
14. Los clientes _____ con una dependienta.
15. Los dependientes no _____ muchas horas hoy.

En la residencia:

16. Nuria _____ una compañera de cuarto.
17. Tomás _____ alemán con el estudiante de Berlín.
18. Este fin de semana, nosotros _____ visitar a mi familia.
19. Yolanda _____ con su (*her*) mamá en México.
20. ¿ _____ Uds. tomar un café por la tarde?

PRÁCTICA: FORMAS PLURALES Y *ESTAR*

Change the sentences to the plural following the model.

Modelo: Ella busca la oficina de la consejera. →
Ellas buscan las oficinas de las consejeras.

1. Hay una palabra en el pizarrón.

2. Yo deseo comprar una mochila y un cuaderno.

3. La profesora busca un lápiz y un diccionario.

4. Mi amigo canta una canción (*song*).

5. El secretario trabaja en una oficina.

Answer the questions about where people are, using the cues in parentheses. Then write another sentence explaining where everyone is not.

Modelo: ¿Dónde estás ahora? (biblioteca) →
Estoy en la biblioteca ahora. No estoy en casa.

6. ¿Dónde está tu amigo ahora? (cafetería)

7. ¿Dónde está tu compañero/a de cuarto ahora? (residencia)

8. ¿Dónde está la profesora de español ahora? (oficina)

9. ¿Dónde están los estudiantes de la clase de español ahora? (salón de clase)

10. ¿Dónde estamos todos los sábados (*Saturdays*)? (fiesta)

PRÁCTICA: PREGUNTAS Y RESPUESTAS

Create a logical question for each answer.

Modelo: ¿Dónde está la profesora Guzmán ahora?
La profesora Guzman está en la oficina ahora.

1. _____
Este (*This*) semestre, estudio química, literatura, español y filosofía.

2. _____
El profesor Dávila enseña tres clases.

3. _____
Necesitamos comprar más bolígrafos y cuadernos.

4. _____
El estudiante extranjero se llama Fernando.

5. _____
Tomás regresa a la residencia por la tarde.

6. _____
Porque deseo hablar español con mis amigos de México.

7. _____
Roberto paga $392 por los libros de texto.

8. _____
Pago la matrícula con un cheque.

9. _____
Mercedes trabaja en la biblioteca.

10. _____
Beatriz y Lourdes hablan español.

11. _____
Yo compro una mochila; mi amigo compra una calculadora.

12. _____
Practicamos en el laboratorio de lenguas.

REPASO: CAPÍTULO 2

I. Vocabulario

Complete each row with the actions, people, places, things, and times you associate with the word listed. Use the **Capítulo 2** vocabulary list on pp. 58–59 of *Puntos*.

	Acciones	Personas	Lugares	Objetos	¿Cuándo?
Modelo:	bailar	los amigos	el apartamento	la guitarra	por la noche
	estudiar				
		el cliente			
			la biblioteca		
				el teléfono celular	
					con frecuencia

II. Gramática

A. <u>Los artículos</u>

(definido)

_____ profesor

_____ mujer

_____ libro

_____ problema

_____ clases

_____ noches

_____ drama

(indefinido)

_____ hombre

_____ oficina

_____ tarde

_____ profesores

_____ días

_____ secretario

_____ biblioteca

B. <u>Formas plurales</u>. Change to the plural.

el actor _____

la universidad _____

una calculadora _____

un problema _____

la señorita _____

un dólar _____

la nación _____

el papel _____

una mujer _____

un lápiz _____

C. Pronombres.

1. What pronoun would you use to talk **about** the following people?

   el profesor de historia _____

   los estudiantes de la clase de español _____

   Beyoncé y Shakira _____

   tus (*your*) amigos y tú _____

2. What pronoun would you use to talk **to** the following people?

   el presidente de la universidad _____

   un niño (*child*) _____

   tu amigo/a _____

   tus amigas _____

D. Verbos. Choose the most logical verb and then conjugate it correctly.

1. Los estudiantes de español _____ (trabajar / tocar) mucho.

2. Nosotros _____ (practicar / desear) hablar español.

3. La profesora Gómez _____ (bailar / enseñar) a las once.

4. Los estudiantes _____ (necesitar / mirar) estudiar todas las noches.

5. ¿Tú _____ (estudiar / buscar) español también?

6. ¿Qué otros (*other*) cursos _____ (pagar / tomar) tú este semestre?

7. Yo _____ (practicar / desear) español con unos amigos.

8. ¿Tú _____ (desear / enseñar) tomar un café con nosotros?

E. ¿Dónde están? Write a sentence saying where everyone is. Use the correct form of **estar.**

1. Marcos / la biblioteca _____

2. Antonia y yo / la residencia _____

3. tú / la fiesta _____

4. los profesores / la oficina _____

5. yo / el apartamento _____

6. Natalia / la cafetería _____

F. Palabras interrogativas. Use the following question words and verbs to create eight questions about people and actions in the drawings, then add your own answers.

¿A qué hora?	¿Cuándo?	¿Por qué?
¿Cómo?	¿Cuánto?	¿Qué?
¿Cuál?	¿Dónde?	¿Quién?

buscar	enseñar	pagar	tomar
comprar	hablar	regresar	trabajar
desear	necesitar		

la profesora Gil

el Sr. Miranda

Marcos

1. Pregunta _____
   Respuesta _____

2. Pregunta _____
   Respuesta _____

3. Pregunta _____
   Respuesta _____

4. Pregunta _____
   Respuesta _____

5. Pregunta _____
   Respuesta _____

6. Pregunta _____
   Respuesta _____

7. Pregunta _____
   Respuesta _____

8. Pregunta _____
   Respuesta _____

G. La negación. Answer the questions negatively.

1. ¿Toman Uds. siestas en la clase de español?

   _____

2. ¿Necesita Bill Gates más dinero?

   _____

3. ¿Te gusta el brócoli?

   _____

4. ¿Compran los estudiantes los libros de texto en una biblioteca?

   _____

5. ¿Hablan Uds. español perfectamente?

   _____

III. Diálogo

Write a short dialogue in which Mario and Anita talk about

- their classes
- what they need to do this afternoon (**esta tarde**)
- what they want to do this weekend (**este fin de semana**)

_____

_____

_____

_____

_____

_____

_____

INFORMATION GAP ACTIVITY: ¿QUÉ CLASES TOMAS?

Fill out the first chart below in Spanish with your class schedule. Include the name and time of the class, referring to your book if you need to check how to say a class subject in Spanish.

lunes	martes	miércoles	jueves	viernes

Now find a partner and, using the model questions below, fill out the second chart with information about his or her schedule. After you and your partner have exchanged information, check to make sure you have each other's schedules written correctly.

Modelo: ¿Tomas una clase el lunes (el martes, el miércoles, etc.)?
Sí, tomo el álgebra.
¿A qué hora?
A las once de la mañana.

lunes	martes	miércoles	Jueves	Viernes

¿Es posible tomar un café juntos (*together*) un día? ¿Cuándo?

Speaking Activities

BINGO: EN LA UNIVERSIDAD

baila salsa.	manda mensajes en clase.	no estudia los fines de semana (weekend).	trabaja en un café.	necesita comprar unos libros.
habla por teléfono todos los días.	desea comprar una computadora.	busca un apartamento.	estudia computación.	no está en clase hoy.
escucha música con frecuencia.	busca un(a) compañero/a de cuarto.	trabaja en la universidad.	toca la guitarra.	practica el español todos los días.
toca mucho café.	toca la flauta.	canta en las fiestas.	necesita pagar la matrícula.	es dependiente/a.
necesita estudiar más.	toma cinco clases este semestre.	toma una siesta todos los días.	trabaja en una oficina.	estudia sicología.

COMMUNICATIVE GOALS PRACTICE #1

Talk about the scene in the bookstore for 45 seconds. "Show off" all you have learned up to this point in the semester. Check the **Communicative Goals** boxes at the beginning of each chapter of your Supplement to see all that you should be able to do. You may use your imagination to add more details in your descriptions, but do not try to go beyond what we have been covering in class. For this first oral proficiency practice, the following seven topics are suggested.

1. Time	4. Courses they take	6. Actions taking place
2. Where they are	5. Likes and dislikes	7. Phone numbers
3. Languages they speak		

Use these topics to perform at least ten communicative goals. Do not repeat topics more than once. You can include two questions you would ask characters from the image as part of your ten communicative goals.

Susana   Pedro   Lupita

CAPÍTULO
3

Communicative Goals for Chapter 3

By the end of the chapter, you should be able to:

- describe friends and family ☐
- tell your age ☐
- identify a person's nationality ☐
- indicate purpose and reason for doing something ☐
- tell what belongs to you and others ☐

Grammatical Structures

You should know:

- **ser** ☐
- possessive adjectives ☐
- **-er** and **-ir** verbs ☐
- placement of adjectives ☐

PRONUNCIACIÓN

Listen and repeat after your instructor. Then practice in pairs.

1. Tu tía Tula tiene treinta tortillas tostadas.
2. Mi padre y mi primo, Paquito, practican con su profesor Pablo Pérez.
3. Imelda es impaciente, incompetente e indiscreta.
4. Patricia Pineda es práctica, patriótica y poética.
5. Lola López Ludwig, la alemana, está en Lima hasta el lunes.
6. El general Geraldo Germán es religioso y generoso.

LISTENING COMPREHENSION

#1. You will hear a passage about a student named Carlos Padilla. Listen for the answers to the **Cierto/Falso** statements below.

¿Cierto o falso?

1. ☐ C ☐ F Carlos estudia en la Universidad de los Andes.
2. ☐ C ☐ F Vive con su familia.
3. ☐ C ☐ F Es alto y moreno.
4. ☐ C ☐ F Tiene dos hermanos y una hermana.
5. ☐ C ☐ F Tiene un perro.

#2. You will hear a conversation that takes place in a local supermarket. Listen for the answers to the questions below.

1. ¿Dónde trabaja Catalina? ¿Por qué?
2. ¿Está el Sr. Hernández en el supermercado por la mañana o por la tarde?
3. ¿Cómo se llama la esposa del Sr. Hernández?
4. ¿Cuántas hijas hay en la familia Hernández?
5. ¿Cómo se llama el perro?
6. ¿Dónde trabaja el Sr. Hernández? ¿Y su mujer?

FAMILY TREE DIAGRAM

Listen as your instructor reads a description of a family. Fill in the names of the family members and their ages as you hear them.

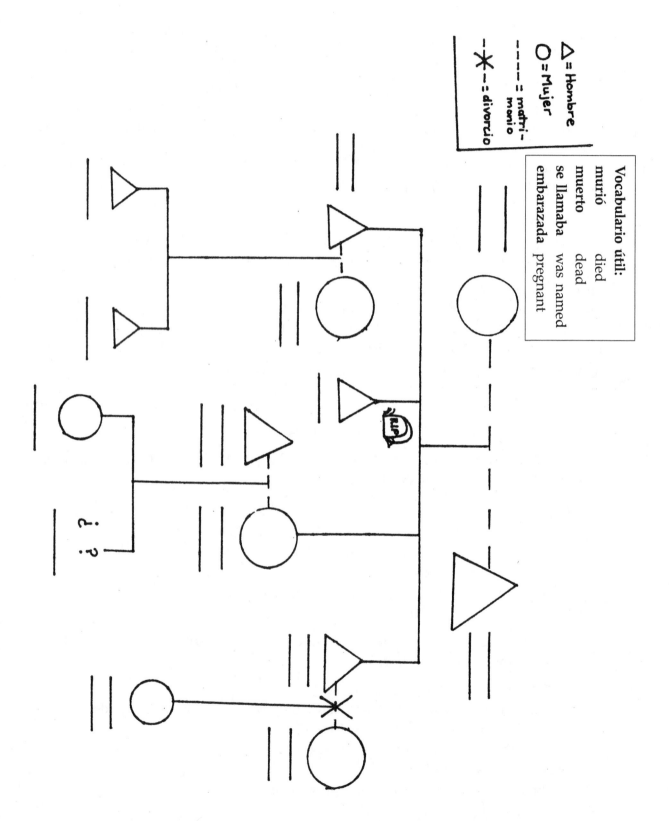

¿CÓMO ES ESTA FAMILIA?

Look at the drawing of the family tree, then use the adjectives presented in the vocabulary section of this chapter of your textbook to describe each person or group of people listed. Use your imagination, and try to use at least two adjectives for each person or group.

Modelo: Juanito   _____

                    Juanito es   joven,   listo   y   guapo

1. Joaquín _____

2. Manolito _____

3. Mercedes y Elena _____

4. Luis _____

5. Josefina _____

6. Sultán _____

7. Carmencita y Manolito _____

8. Joaquín y Josefina _____

9. Michín _____

10. Juan _____

PRÁCTICA: DESCRIPCIONES Y PREGUNTAS

Describe each person, give his/her nationality and age, and then write three questions you might ask that person. Try to include one question starting with **¿Con qué frecuencia...?**

Palabras interrogativas:
¿Qué? ¿Cómo? ¿Cuándo? ¿Dónde? ¿Quién? ¿Cuánto? ¿A qué hora? ¿Por qué?

Modelo: Nina es alta, morena y delgada.
Es peruana y tiene 21 años.

1. Nina, ¿qué lees?
2. ¿Con qué frecuencia estudias en la biblioteca?
3. ¿A qué universidad asistes?

PRÁCTICA: LAS NACIONALIDADES

Complete the table with the answers to the three questions below.

	¿De dónde es?	¿Qué nacionalidad es?	¿Qué lengua habla?
1	Greta es de Alemania.		
2		Chiyo es japonesa.	
3			Sofía habla italiano.
4		Ramón es español.	
5	Helen es de Corea.		
6		Juan Pablo es mexicano.	
7	Juanita es de Bolivia.		
8		Diana es inglesa.	

¿Cierto o falso? Correct the false statements, using the map below.

1. Mercedes es de Asunción.
   □ C   □ F   Es uruguaya. _____

2. José Carlos es de Buenos Aires.
   □ C   □ F   Es argentino. _____

3. Maricarmen es de Quito.
   □ C   □ F   Es peruana. _____

4. Paco y Pepe son de Bogotá.
   □ C   □ F   Son venezolanos. _____

5. Las hermanas Ramos son de Santiago.
   □ C   □ F   Son chilenas. _____

6. Lola es de Caracas.
   □ C   □ F   Es venezolana. _____

7. Enrique y Adriana son de Montevideo.
   □ C   □ F   Son argentinos. _____

8. Gilberto es de Lima.
   □ C   □ F   Es peruano. _____

PRÁCTICA: EXPLAINING YOUR REASONS

Answer the questions using **porque** (because) or **para** + *infinitive* (in order to . . .).

Modelo: ¿Por qué vendes tu bicicleta?
Vendo mi bicicleta **para comprar** otra bicicleta nueva.
Vendo mi bicicleta **porque** necesito el dinero.

1. ¿Por qué deseas aprender español?

   _____

2. ¿Por qué estudias en esta universidad?

   _____

3. ¿Por qué practican los estudiantes en el laboratorio?

   _____

4. ¿Por qué tomas café por la mañana?

   _____

5. ¿Por qué debes asistir a la clase de español todos los días?

   _____

6. ¿Por qué vives en una casa (un apartamento / una residencia)?

   _____

7. ¿Por qué tomas una siesta a veces?

   _____

8. ¿Por qué miras la televisión?

   _____

9. ¿Por qué toman siestas los estudiantes?

   _____

10. ¿Por qué necesitan estudiar Uds. antes del (*before the*) examen?

    _____

11. ¿Por qué a veces regresas a casa tarde los fines de semana?

    _____

12. ¿Por qué es necesario pagar la matrícula pronto?

    _____

13. ¿Por qué es importante hablar otra lengua?

    _____

PRÁCTICA: LOS POSESIVOS

Complete the passages with the correct form of the possessive adjectives indicated.

mi, mis	nuestro/a(s)
tu, tus	vuestro/a(s)
su, sus	su, sus

Un regalo apropiado para su cumpleaños (*birthday*)

Los Sres. Osorio buscan un regalo para (1. *their*) _____ hijo Héctor, porque es (2. *his*) _____ cumpleaños el sábado. La Sra. Osorio cree que Héctor necesita una mascota. (3. *His*) _____ animales favoritos son los perros, por eso ella desea comprarle un pastor alemán (*German shepherd*). El Sr. Osorio explica: «(4. *My*) _____ amor (*love*), Héctor no es muy responsable. Además (*Besides*), (5. *your*) _____ mamá y (6. *his*) _____ tíos tienen mascotas y vivimos cerca de (*near*) ellos. Es mejor (*better*) buscar un regalo más útil (*useful*) para (7. *our*) _____ hijo». Por eso, los Osorio visitan la tienda (*store*) de (8. *their*) _____ amigo, Alfredo, y compran una computadora.

Una familia grande

¿Cómo es (1. *your*) _____ familia? En (2. *my*) _____ familia, hay muchas personas. (3. *My*) _____ abuelos paternos tienen seis hijos. (4. *Their*) _____ hijos se llaman José María, Laura, Victoria, Mateo, Blanca y Arturo. (5. *My*) _____ padre es Arturo, el hijo menor. Nosotros vivimos en Chicago, pero todos (6. *our*) _____ tíos y primos viven en Oklahoma.

La familia de mamá es grande también. (7. *My*) _____ mamá es de Guadalajara, México, y (8. *her*) _____ tres hermanas viven allí. También viven allí (9. *her*) _____ padres, (10. *my*) _____ abuelos maternos. La abuela piensa (*thinks*) que (11. *her*) _____ hija debe regresar a México para vivir, pero a mamá le gusta (12. *her*) _____ vida (*life*) aquí. Pero vamos a Guadalajara todos los años para visitar a todos (13. *our*) _____ parientes. En Guadalajara, nos quedamos (*we stay*) con (14. *my*) _____ tíos Enrique y Teresita o con (15. *my*) _____ abuelos. (16. *Their*) _____ casas son relativamente grandes, y hay lugar para todos.

PRÁCTICA: ENSALADA DE PALABRAS

Complete the following passage by writing the correct form of the words in parentheses, according to context. When given a choice between two verbs, choose the most logical one; change adjectives to agree with the nouns they modify.

(1. Estudiar - yo) _____ el español porque (2. ser) _____ importante hablar un idioma (3. extranjero / extranjera) _____. Mi amigo Brian tiene una novia (*girlfriend*) (4. colombiano / colombiana) _____ y por eso él (5. tomar) _____ la clase; él desea (6. hablar) _____ con ella.

Mi primera (*first*) clase (7. ser/estar) _____ a (8. los/las) _____ nueve de la mañana; en mi clase (9. hay/están) _____ veintitrés estudiantes. Generalmente, Brian y yo (10. llegar/trabajar) _____ a las nueve menos tres pero la profesora no (11. llegar) _____ hasta (*until*) las nueve. Ella (12. te llama/ se llama) _____ Beatriz y (13. ser/tener) _____ 28 años. (14. Los/Las) _____ estudiantes de la clase (15. ser) _____ muy diferentes y por eso es (16. un/una) _____ grupo interesante. (17. Muchos / Muchas) _____ estudiantes (18. practicar/tocar) _____ un deporte (*sport*); otros (19. trabajar) _____, pero todos nosotros (20. estudiar) _____ mucho.

En general, me (21. gustar) _____ la clase. A veces escribimos composiciones (22. cortos / cortas) _____; también (23. practicar) _____ en el laboratorio y (24. escuchar) _____ canciones (*songs*) en español. Después de (*after*) clase, no (25. desear - yo) _____ estudiar más y (26. necesitar) _____ descansar (*rest*). Por eso, voy (*I go*) con Brian y nosotros (27. tomar) _____ un café o una Coca-Cola Después (*Afterwards*), (28. regresar - yo) _____ a la residencia para estudiar y tal vez (*maybe*) para tomar (29. un/una) _____ siesta (30. corto) _____.

PRÁCTICA: SOPA DE VERBOS

Complete the passages. Choose the most logical verb for the context and write the correct form for the subject given.

Mi vida en la universidad

Este semestre, yo (tomar / vivir) _____ en un apartamento. Mi compañero de casa (me llamo / se llama) _____ Ernesto. No me gusta vivir con él, porque (ser / tener) _____ egoísta y perezoso. Por ejemplo, (tocar / tomar) _____ la guitarra a las dos de la mañana y siempre (llegar / hablar) _____ por teléfono. ¡Yo (asistir / creer) _____ que (deber / comprender) _____ buscar un nuevo compañero de casa pronto!

Muchos de mis amigos (vivir / mirar) _____ en residencias universitarias. Los sábados, nosotros (asistir a / llegar) _____ conciertos o fiestas. A veces, nosotros (comer / beber) _____ en un restaurante italiano que nos gusta mucho. Los domingos, yo siempre (creer / tomar) _____ un café en mi café favorito y (leer / escribir) _____ el periódico. Después (*After*), cuando (abrir / recibir) _____ la biblioteca a las doce, yo (estudiar / hablar) _____ allí (*there*) para mis clases el lunes.

Una visita a casa

Yo (vender / vivir) _____ en la universidad, pero mi familia (vivir / asistir a) _____ en Tampa. Con frecuencia, yo (regresar / llegar) _____ a casa los fines de semana para visitar a mi familia. Cuando yo (mirar / llegar) _____ a casa, siempre hay una comida (*meal*) especial. Nosotros (creer / comer) _____ y (hablar / leer) _____ de mi vida en la universidad. Después, nosotros (mirar/tomar) _____ la televisión y a veces yo (tomar / tocar) _____ una siesta. Por la noche, yo (escribir / hablar) _____ por teléfono con mis amigos de Tampa, y vamos (*we go*) a un club para (estudiar / escuchar) _____ música y (bailar / practicar) _____. Mi mamá (comprar / creer) _____ que yo (deber / desear) _____ visitar más. También dice (*she says*) que yo (necesitar / aprender) _____ regresar a casa más. Mis padres no (escuchar / comprender) _____ que yo (trabajar / necesitar) _____ estudiar. Por eso, (llegar / ser) _____ imposible visitar a mis padres todos los fines de semana.

REPASO: CAPÍTULO 3

I. Vocabulario

A. Los adjetivos y la concordancia. Complete the following sentences, paying attention to agreement. Try to list at least three adjectives for each person.

1. Yo soy _____.

2. Mi mejor (*best*) amigo/a es _____.

3. Mi pariente favorito/a es _____.

B. Definiciones

1. La hermana de mi padre es mi _____.

2. El padre de mi madre es mi _____.

3. El hijo de mi hermana es mi _____.

4. La madre de mi sobrino es mi _____.

5. Las hijas de mis tíos son mis _____.

II. Gramática

A. **Ser** and Possession. Look at the image below, then answer the questions.

el primo

el tío

las hijas   la tía   la madre   el padre

1. ¿De quién es la computadora? _____

2. ¿De quién son las dos camisas? _____

3. ¿De quién son los dos perros? _____

4. ¿De quién es el coche? _____

5. ¿De quiénes son los helados (*ice cream*)? _____

B. <u>Los usos del verbo **ser**</u>. Complete the passage with the correct form of the verb **ser**.

¡Hola! Me llamo Carlos Domínguez. _____ estudiante de ingeniería.

_____ alto, delgado y un poco perezoso. Mi familia y yo _____ de

Madrid. Mi padre José _____ periodista y mi madre Sara _____ maestra.

Tengo dos hermanas menores, Elena y Sarita. Ellas _____ estudiantes también.

C. <u>La nacionalidad</u>.

1. Johnny Depp es un actor _____.

2. Acapulco y Veracruz son ciudades _____.

3. El tequila es una bebida (*drink*) _____.

4. El Ferrari es un coche _____.

5. Berlín es una ciudad _____.

D. <u>Los posesivos</u>. Aunt Hortensia is helping everybody find things and get organized for the first day of school. Complete her sentences with the correct form of the possessive.

1. José, (*your*) _____ cuadernos están en (*your*) _____ coche.

2. Liliana, Rafael, aquí tengo (*your*) _____ libros.

3. Aquí están dos lápices de Beatriz. Hay más en (*her*) _____ escritorio.

4. ¿Dónde está (*my*) _____ calculadora?

5. Creo que (*our*) _____ mochilas están en (*their*) _____ cuarto.

E. <u>Un domingo en casa</u>. Complete the sentences with the correct form of the most logical verb in parentheses.

1. Después de misa (*After mass*), nosotros (llegar / hablar) _____ a casa a la una.

2. Por la tarde, papá y yo (leer / abrir) _____ el periódico.

3. Mi hermanita menor (*younger*), Patricia, (vender / aprender) _____ un nuevo juego (*game*) en la computadora.

4. Mamá (estar / escribir) _____ una carta a los abuelos.

5. A veces, la tía Raquel y mis primos (comer / vivir) _____ con nosotros.

6. Todos nosotros (escuchar / mirar) _____ un programa a las seis en la tele.

7. Yo (ser / regresar) _____ a mi residencia en la universidad por la noche.

III. ¿Qué dices (*do you say*)? What do you say in Spanish in each of these situations?

1. You want to find out whose backpack is in your car.

   _____

2. Explain to your roommate your reasons for not studying tonight.

   _____

3. Find out how often your friends study in the library.

   _____

4. You need to find out the capital of Venezuela.

   _____

IV. Diálogo

Your exchange-student roommate is coming home for the weekend with you. Write a short dialogue in which

- your roommate asks about your family
- you describe your family and say what you do together when you come home
- you ask your roommate about his/her family and what they do when they're together

_____

_____

_____

_____

_____

_____

_____

_____

BINGO FAMILIAR

una abuela viuda (widowed)	un perro y un gato	4 abuelos vivos (living)	una sobrina muy joven	un padre guapo
un pariente divorciado	2 hermanos mayores	más de 8 primos	un tío soltero	un pariente de otro país
un/una hermano/a menor	gemelos/as (twins) en la familia	un/una primo/a que vive en California	un/una sobrino/a travieso/a (mischievous)	una tía gorda y simpática
una madre que trabaja	una familia rica	una pariente embarazada (pregnant)	una familia loca	un esposo / una esposa
un/una hermano/a que busca esposo/a	un/una primo/a antipático/a	un/una hermano/a tonto/a	un hermano que vende cosas en e-bay	muchas reunions familiares

COMMUNICATIVE GOALS PRACTICE #2

Try to talk about the party scene below for about 45 seconds. "Show off" all you have learned up to this point in the semester. Check the **Communicative Goals** boxes at the beginning of each chapter of your Supplement to see all that you should be able to do. You may use your imagination to add more details, but do not try to go beyond what we have been covering in class. For this second oral proficiency practice, the following eight topics are suggested:

1. Time	4. Age and nationality	7. Family relationships
2. Appearance	5. Telephone numbers	8. Actions taking place
3. Personality	6. Likes and dislikes	

After you've finished your description, work with a partner taking turns to ask questions of at least two of the characters in the scene. Your partner, using his/her imagination, will answer the questions.

¿Cómo? ¿Qué? ¿Cuál? ¿Cuándo? ¿Cuánto/a(s)? ¿Cuándo? ¿Dónde? ¿De dónde? ¿Quién? ¿Por qué? ¿De quién?

ROUND ROBIN: GRAMMAR MONITOR ACTIVITY

In this activity you will work in groups of three. Each partner will alternate roles until all three of you have (1) described one of the women; (2) asked questions; and (3) served as the grammar monitor.

Partner A: Describe one of the women at the party. Include her physical characteristics, her personality and what she likes to do.

Partner B: Listen carefully as Partner A describes one of the women. Then ask two questions to get more information about her.

Partner C: As the grammar monitor, your job is to listen for agreement errors that Partners A and B may make. Jot down any errors you may hear. Example: **Nati es alta y delgado**. Note that **delgado** should be **delgada**. When Partners A and B are finished, give them feedback on whether or not they are doing well on noun/adjective agreement.

Now switch roles. Partner A takes the role of Partner B (the person asking questions), Partner B takes the role of Partner C (the grammar monitor), and Partner C takes the role of Partner A (the describer).

GUIDED WRITING AND SPEAKING:
LA FAMILIA ANFITRIONA (*HOST*) DE ROSA

A. Study the image and then work with a partner to form six questions about Rosa's host family in Mexico. Use different interrogative words for each question.

¿Cómo? ¿Qué? ¿Cuál? ¿Cuándo? ¿Cuánto/a/os/as? ¿Cuándo? ¿Dónde? ¿Quién? ¿Por qué?

Use your imagination and the vocabulary from this chapter and previous chapters.

1. _____

2. _____

3. _____

4. _____

5. _____

6. _____

B. Imagine you are Rosa. Write an email to your best friend telling her about your host family. Include a description of the family members (ages, physical and personality characteristics), their likes and dislikes, and what the family members do on the weekends.

_____

_____

_____

_____

_____

C. With a partner, role-play a dialogue between Rosa and one of the characters in the drawing.

Speaking Activities

Communicative Goals for Chapter 4

By the end of the chapter, you should be able to:

- discuss clothing and shopping ❑
- ask for and give prices ❑
- point out people and things ❑
- discuss preferences and wishes ❑
- talk about the future ❑

Grammatical Structures

You should know:

- demonstrative adjectives ❑
- stem-changing verbs ❑
- **tener** idioms ❑
- **ir** + **a** + infinitive ❑
- the contractions **al** and **del** ❑

PRONUNCIACIÓN

A. **Stress and Written Accents:** Listen as your instructor pronounces each of the following words. Underline the stressed syllable. Then take turns with a partner and pronounce the words in the list.

1. tra-ba-ja-dor

2. nues-tro

3. so-bri-no

4. dic-cio-na-rio

5. cal-cu-la-do-ra

6. a-le-mán

7. so-cio-lo-gí-a

8. plás-ti-co

9. a-crí-li-co

10. dó-la-res

11. a-bri-go

12. se-te-cien-tos

13. a-na-ran-ja-do

14. u-ni-ver-si-dad

15. pá-ja-ro

16. ro-mán-ti-ca

17. al-ma-cén

18. de-par-ta-men-to

19. mi-llón

20. mo-chi-la

21. te-lé-fo-no

22. pan-ta-lo-nes

23. a-que-llas

24. re-ba-jas

A. El inventario del Almacén Matilde. Your instructor will read the list of clothing items, the number of each item left in the store at the end of the year, and the price in Mexican pesos of each unit. Write the articles, the number, and price in the chart below.

Artículos	Número (cantidad)	Precio cada uno (*each unit*)

B. Grandes rebajas en ZARA. You will hear prices for various clothing items on sale at ZARA in Santiago, Chile. Write the prices in pesos as your instructor reads them.

Vocabulario útil

los guantes   gloves

la bufanda   scarf

LISTENING COMPREHENSION: LOS HORARIOS (*SCHEDULES*)

Listen as your instructor reads a paragraph describing the schedules of four students. As you listen, fill in the chart with information about each person's schedule. After you complete the chart, use the information you've written to answer the question below.

Vocabulario útil

antes de before   **después de** after

	María	Juan	José	Sara
8-9 a.m.				
9-10 a.m.				
10-11 a.m.				
11-12 a.m.				
12-1 p.m.				
1-2 p.m.				
2-3 p.m.				
3-4 p.m.				
4-5 p.m.				
5-6 p.m.				

¿Cuándo pueden reunirse (*get together*) los cuatro estudiantes por dos horas para estudiar para su examen de español? _____

PRÁCTICA: DEMONSTRATIVE ADJECTIVES

A. Paula and her friend, Regina, are trying to make some decisions about what clothing to buy for their big party. Fill in the dialogue with the appropriate demonstrative adjective.

Paula: ¿Te gustan _____ vestidos o prefieres _____ vestidos
                               these   *those*
          largos allá?

Regina: La verdad es que no me gustan los vestidos en _____ tienda.
                                                              this

          Prefiero los vestidos de _____ tienda de ropa elegante en el centro.
                                        that

Paula: De acuerdo, pero quieres comprar _____ chaqueta rosada, ¿verdad?
                                                 that

Regina: Claro (*Sure*), y también _____ cinturón es bonito y no muy caro. Vamos
                                         this
          a comprar _____ dos cosas (*things*) aquí y podemos comprar los vestidos
                         these
          en la otra tienda.

Paula: _____ es una buena idea.
          That

B. Ana and Yoli are looking at a family photo album. Complete their conversation with the correct demonstrative adjective.

Ana: Yoli, ¿qué es _____?
                             this

Yoli: Es un álbum de fotos de mi familia. ¿Quieres ver las fotos?

Ana: Sí, por supuesto. ¿Quiénes son _____ dos chicos aquí?
                                              these

Yoli: Son mis primos Fede y Manuel. Y _____ dos muchachos allá son
                                               those
          mis hermanos mayores (*older*), Sergio y Daniel.

Ana: ¿Y _____ señora tan elegante?
              that

Yoli: Es mi tía abuela, Carmencita. Y _____ señora en la chaqueta de
                                              that, over there
          rayas es una vecina (*neighbor*), doña Victoria.

Ana: Y _____ personas aquí son tus padres, ¿verdad?
              these

Yoli: No, son mi tío Guillermo y mi tía Lupe.

PRÁCTICA: PLANES Y PREFERENCIAS

Explain what the following people are going to do, have to do, and feel like doing this weekend. Combine the subjects with the activities listed below.

yo mi mejor (*best*) amigo/a el profesor / la profesora los compañeros de clase nosotros / as	+	ver una una exhibición en el museo visitar a unos amigos estudiar para el examen bailar en una discoteca trabajar leer una novela descansar hablar por teléfono aprender los verbos irregulares

¿Qué **van a hacer** (*going to do*) estas personas este fin de semana?

1. _____

2. _____

3. _____

4. _____

5. _____

¿Qué **tienen que hacer** este fin de semana?

1. _____

2. _____

3. _____

4. _____

5. _____

Pero en realidad, ¿qué **tienen ganas de hacer** este fin de semana?

1. _____

2. _____

3. _____

4. _____

5. _____

VERB WORKSHEET

I have to read. _____

I want to read. _____

I'm going to read. _____

I can read. _____

I feel like reading. _____

I prefer to read. _____

We don't have to go. _____

We don't need to go. _____

We're not going to go. _____

We can't go. _____

Marta has to return. _____

Marta wants to return. _____

Marta feels like returning. _____

Marta is going to return. _____

Marta can return. _____

They prefer to pay. _____

They don't feel like paying. _____

They need to pay. _____

They are going to pay. _____

They want to pay. _____

They have to pay. _____

PRÁCTICA: PREPOSITIONS AND CONTRACTIONS

Complete the sentences with the missing prepositions, contractions, and articles.

de	del	a	al	la	los	las

La familia

1. Humberto es el sobrino _____ _____ Sra. López.

2. La novia _____ mi hermano es guapa.

3. Mis abuelos son _____ Bolivia.

4. El hermano _____ doctor Sánchez está en Australia ahora.

5. La foto es _____ hermano de Ana.

6. Vamos _____ _____ casa _____ _____ primos _____ Ana el sábado.

7. Elena recibe mucho dinero _____ sus abuelos.

8. Mi padre va _____ laboratorio _____ _____ ocho de la mañana.

9. El color _____ coche _____ mi padre es rojo.

De compras

1. Vamos _____ almacén _____ _____ Hermanos Ramos.

2. La chaqueta _____ algodón es muy bonita.

3. La ropa _____ profesor Jaenes es muy cara.

4. Mis hijas van _____ supermercado para comprar café.

5. Llegan _____ _____ tienda _____ _____ dos de la tarde.

6. El impermeable _____ niño es _____ plástico.

7. El nombre _____ almacén donde compramos nuestra ropa es Galerías.

PRÁCTICA: ENSALADA GRAMATICAL: ESTE FIN DE SEMANA

Me gusta asistir a (1. este / esta) _____ universidad, porque es

muy (2. gran / grande) _____ y siempre hay mucho que hacer (3. las / los)

_____ fines de semana. Este fin de semana, por ejemplo, (4. está / hay)

_____ un partido (*game*) de fútbol norteamericano entre (5. mi/su) _____

universidad y (6. nuestro) _____ rivales. Muchos estudiantes de la otra universidad

(7. venir / llevar) _____ a ver (*see*) el partido, y muchísimos estudiantes de

nuestra universidad (8. asistir / ser) _____ también. El partido (9. es / está)

_____ el sábado (10. en / a) _____ las cuatro de la tarde. Todo (11. el /

la) _____ día antes (12. de / del) _____ partido, hay muchas fiestas.

Pero, ¡qué terrible! La clase de español (13. tener que / tener ganas de) _____

tomar (14. un / el) _____ examen el viernes antes del partido. Los estudiantes

(15. desear / necesitar) _____ tomar el examen (16. el / la) _____ jueves,

pero los profesores dicen (*say*) que eso es imposible. Ahora los estudiantes no están muy

(17. contento) _____, y (18. creer / comer) _____ que los profesores

son antipáticos. Es (19. un / una) _____ problema, pero la clase simplemente no

(20. poder / tener) _____ tomar la prueba antes. Por eso, todos los estudiantes

(21. ir / desear) _____ a salir inmediatamente después de clase. Tienen mucha

(22. razón / prisa) _____ y (23. querer / ir) _____ terminar de tomar el

examen pronto.

¿(24. Cuándo / Qué) _____ otros eventos hay este fin de semana? Bueno, mis

compañeros de cuarto, Ramón y Esteban, (25. venir / desear) _____ ir al cine (*movies*)

(26. este / esta) _____ noche. A Ramón le (27. gusta / gustan) _____

las películas (*films*) de ciencia-ficción, pero Esteban (28. preferir / querer) _____

las películas extranjeras. Y el sábado (29. por / a) _____ la noche, mi amiga Leticia

quiere ir a un concierto de música (30. latinoamericano) _____. Mis (31. hijos /

primos) _____ Juanjo y Rebeca tienen (32. ganas / sueño) _____ de ir

(33. al / a la) _____ museo de la universidad el domingo por la mañana. Yo (34. ir /

querer) _____ a ir con ellos, y después, por (35. el / la) _____ tarde, voy

al centro comercial. Ahora hay unas (36. tiendas / rebajas) _____ fabulosas en mi

almacén (37. favorito) _____. Quiero (38. comprar / regatear) _____ una

blusa (39. de / a) _____ seda, (40. unos / as) _____ pantalones (41. corto)

_____, unas camisetas y tal vez (42. un / una) _____ traje de baño.

Después, por la noche yo (43. necesitar / tener) _____ (44. a / que) _____

estudiar para mis exámenes (45. el / la) _____ lunes.

REPASO: CAPÍTULO 4

I. Vocabulario

A. 1. ¿Qué ropa llevamos en julio? ¿en diciembre? ¿en abril?

_____

2. ¿Qué ropa generalmente llevas a clase?

_____

B. ¡Qué desastre! You picked up someone else's suitcase at the airport. For the lost baggage form, describe some of the unique items in the suitcase you picked up, then describe the unique items in your own suitcase. Be careful with agreement.

Someone else's suitcase	Your suitcase
an old suit	an orange shirt
a grey bathing suit	some new sandals
a red raincoat	yellow shorts
purple socks	a blue and red scarf

1. En la otra maleta (_suitcase_), hay:

_____

_____

2. Pero en <u>mi</u> maleta hay:

_____

_____

II. Gramática

A. <u>Demostrativos</u>. Complete the sentences with the correct demonstrative adjective.

1. Quiero ir a (_this_) _____ tienda, no a (_that, over there_) _____ mercado.

2. ¿Es para mí? ¡(_This_) _____ es una sorpresa!

3. (_That_) _____ niño es su hijo.

4. (_This_)· _____ semana voy a estudiar más.

5. (_Those_) _____ señoras vienen a hablar con mi mamá.

6. ¿Qué quieres hacer (_this_) _____ tarde? ¿Solo comer? ¿(_That_) _____ es todo?

7. —¿Qué es (_that_) _____?

   —¿(_This_) _____? Es un sombrero.

B. Los verbos nuevos. Complete with the correct form of the most logical verb.

Estudiantes irresponsables. (Verbos posibles: **tener, venir, querer, poder**)

1. ¿Por qué _____ Uds. a clase sin los libros de texto?

2. Si Uds. _____ aprender, _____ que llegar a clase con los libros.

3. Nosotros no _____ estudiar los verbos nuevos hoy porque

   Uds. no _____ los libros.

De compras. (Verbos posibles: **preferir, tener, querer, poder**)

Dependienta: ¿Qué camiseta 4. _____, la roja o la verde?

   Lupita: (Yo) 5. _____ la roja, pero 6. _____ que comprar la

   verde porque mi madre 7. _____ el color verde.

Dependienta: 8. _____ comprar la roja para Ud. y la verde para su madre.

C. Expresiones con **tener**. Summarize the situations using an expression with **tener**.

1. Son las tres de la mañana, y estamos en la biblioteca porque hay un examen mañana.

   _____

2. Marco cree que la capital del estado de California es Los Ángeles.

   _____

3. Trabajo en el laboratorio de computadoras a las tres. Ya (*Already*) son las tres y cinco.

   _____

4. Estoy solo en casa, mirando (*watching*) una película (*film*) de horror en la televisión.

   _____

D. **Ir + a +** *infinitive*. Answer the questions in a complete sentence.

1. ¿Cuándo vas a regresar a casa hoy?

   _____

2. ¿Cuándo vas a estudiar para el examen de español?

_____

3. ¿Qué van a hacer (*to do*) tú y tus amigos este fin de semana?

_____

4. ¿Qué vas a hacer esta noche?

_____

E. <u>Preguntas personales</u>. Contesta las preguntas con una oración completa.

<u>Tú</u>:

1. ¿Qué quieres hacer (*to do*) mañana?

_____

2. ¿Qué ropa prefieres llevar a las fiestas?

_____

3. ¿Con quién hablas cuando tienes miedo? ¿Por qué?

_____

4. ¿Con qué frecuencia vienes a la clase de español?

_____

<u>Tú y tus amigos</u>:

5. ¿Prefieren Uds. las clases por la mañana o por la tarde? ¿Por qué?

_____

6. ¿Cuántos libros tienen que comprar para la clase de español? ¿Y para tus otras clases?

_____

7. ¿Dónde prefieren estudiar Uds., en casa o en la biblioteca? ¿Por qué?

_____

8. ¿Por qué quieren Uds. aprender español?

_____

F. Preguntas y respuestas. Form eight questions about the lives of the rich and famous by combining the question words from Column A with the verbs in Column B, and the celebrities. Then answer your own questions, based on what you think these celebrities are doing.

Modelo: ¿Qué tiene que hacer Tiger Woods mañana?
Tiene que comprar una gorra nueva.

¿Qué?	ir + a + *infinitive*	Barack Obama
¿Cómo?	necesitar	Bill Gates
¿Cuándo?	tener que + *infinitive*	Johnny Depp
¿Adónde?	preferir	Lady Gaga
¿Cuánto/a/os/as?	querer	LeBron James
¿A qué hora?	poder	Jennifer López
¿Por qué?	tener ganas de + *infinitive*	Brad Pitt
¿Quién?	deber	Anderson Cooper

_____

_____

_____

_____

_____

_____

_____

ENTREVISTA: LOS PLANES DE LA CLASE DE ESPAÑOL

Take a stroll around the room and ask your classmates about their plans for the future, and in turn answer their questions about your plans. Use the **ir + a +** *infinitive* structure to form your questions and replies, and <u>write down</u> the responses you get on this sheet. Ask a different question of each classmate.

Modelo:

> You: Pete, ¿qué vas a hacer después de (*after*) clase?
>
> Pete: Voy a regresar a la residencia y voy a tomar una siesta.
>
> (You write):   Pete va a regresar a la residencia y va a tomar una siesta.

¿Qué vas a hacer... (*What are you going to do . . .*)

después de clase?

_____

esta noche?

_____

mañana antes de (*before*) la clase de español?

_____

este fin de semana?

_____

para las vacaciones de primavera (*spring break*)?

_____

antes de tus exámenes finales?

_____

después de tus exámenes finales?

_____

después de graduarte (*after graduating*)?

_____

INFORMATION GAP ACTIVITY: EL REGALO PERFECTO

You and your partner need gifts for your imaginary family members, listed under *Pariente* in the chart below, but first you need to find out more about these relatives. Ask your partner questions and fill in the missing pieces of information on your chart, and answer your partner's questions using the information in your chart. Then discuss gift ideas together and write your suggestions below.

<u>Preguntas útiles:</u>

¿Cuántos años tiene _____?   ¿Qué tipo de ropa prefiere llevar?

¿Cuál es el color favorito de _____?   ¿Qué le gusta hacer?

Compañero/a #1

Pariente	*Tiene _____ años*	*Su color favorito es...*	*Prefiere llevar...*	*Le gusta...*	*Un buen regalo es...*
el tío Javier		el rojo		jugar al golf y tenis	
la abuela	67		moda de Gucci y Chanel		
el primo Carlos		el negro		ir a clubes, escuchar música	
Mamá	46		ropa informal		

Compañero/a #2

Pariente	*Tiene _____ años*	*Su color favorito es...*	*Prefiere llevar...*	*Le gusta...*	*Un buen Regalo es...*
el tío Javier	34		ropa deportiva (*sporty*)		
la abuela		el rosado		asistir a conciertos, ir a museos	
el primo Carlos	21		ropa de los años 60 y 70		
Mamá		el verde		trabajar en el jardín, tocar el piano	

Speaking Activities

GUIDED WRITING AND SPEAKING: UNA CAFETERÍA

A. Study the image and then work with a partner to form six questions about the scene in the cafeteria. Find a new partner to answer your questions. Use your imagination and the vocabulary from Chapters 1-4.

¿Por qué?	¿Quién?	¿Dónde?	¿Cómo?	¿A qué hora?	¿Qué?

1. _____

2. _____

3. _____

4. _____

5. _____

6. _____

B. Next, imagine you are one of the characters in the drawing. Write a 100-word e-mail home about your classes, roommate, dorm and new friends.

C. Now, with a partner, role-play a dialogue between any two characters in the drawing. One person tries to make plans and the other person turns him/her down. Use the following expressions to extend and decline an invitation: **¿Te gustaría...?** (*Would you like. . .?*) **¿Por qué no vamos a...? Cuánto me gustaría, pero..., Lo siento, es que..., Es que no puedo..., Gracias, pero tengo que...**

DIÁLOGOS

With a classmate, write a short dialogue based on one of these situations. Use the cues as a guide. Be prepared to role-play your dialogue with your partner for the class.

1. **Ropa para la boda** (*wedding*) You and your friend are invited to a wedding, and you both need something to wear. Have a conversation in which you and your friend

   - decide where you are going to go clothes shopping, and what you have to buy;
   - describe your ideal outfit (type of clothing, color, material);
   - talk about what you feel like doing after shopping.

   _____

   _____

   _____

   _____

   _____

2. **De vacaciones en Puerto Rico** You and your roommate are packing for a Spring Break trip to Puerto Rico. With your roommate discuss

   - what clothing you have and what you need to buy;
   - what you want to do in Puerto Rico and where you're going to go;
   - why you prefer going to Puerto Rico instead of going to your parents' house.

   _____

   _____

   _____

   _____

   _____

Expresiones útiles

¿Por qué no vamos a...?	Está bien./Vale. (*Okay.*)
¿Qué te parece...? (*What do you think of . . .?*)	Me parece...
No me gusta para nada.	Bárbaro./Estupendo./Regio. (*Great.*)
Es divertido/aburrido. (*It's fun/boring.*)	Para mí... (*In my opinion . . .*)
¡Suena bien! (*Sounds good!*)	Es ideal/una pesadilla. (*It's perfect/a nightmare.*)

Speaking Activities

KEY LANGUAGE FUNCTIONS: DESCRIPTION

One of the major goals of this course is to help you learn enough vocabulary and grammar to be able to describe yourself and other people accurately. In order to do this well, you need vocabulary to describe physical characteristics and personality traits, and you need to know how to conjugate the verb **ser.** You also need to be very aware of noun-adjective agreement **(la mujer rubia, mis primos locos).**

To construct a description →   Vocabulary →   Linguistic Tools Needed:
- correct conjugation of **ser**
- noun-adjective agreement

Take turns with a partner describing the following people. Include what the person looks like and something about his/her personality. Try to give three sentences for each person. Don't forget your vocabulary from previous chapters and the linguistic tools shown above.

1. A famous person

2. Your roommate

3. Your instructor

4. Your craziest relative

5. The oldest person you know

6. A child in your family

7. Yourself

8. One of your classmates

CAPÍTULO
5

Communicative Goals for Chapter 5
By the end of the chapter, you should be able to:

- discuss weekly and daily routines ☐
- describe where you live ☐

Grammatical Structures
You should know:

- more stem-changing verbs ☐
- reflexive pronouns ☐

PRONUNCIACIÓN

A.   Listen as your instructor reads these sentences, then practice them with a partner.

1.   Esta semana salgo con Víctor Vásquez el viernes, César Serrat el sábado y Diana Dolores del Duero el domingo.

2.   Las sicólogas suecas, Sara y Susana, venden sillones, sofás y sillas super-sofisticadas.

3.   Conchita Correa quiere comprar una casa en Cáceres con comedor cómodo y cama de agua.

4.   Pablo y Pilar piensan poner unos pocos preciosos platos portugueses en las paredes y unas plantas pequeñas en el patio.

LISTENING COMPREHENSION: UNA CASA NUEVA

You will hear a friend describing her plans for furnishing her new house. On the left, list what she and her housemate already have for the house; on the right, list what they still need. You will hear the passage twice.

Vocabulario útil

ya   already

<u>Ellas tienen:</u>

_____

_____

_____

_____

_____

<u>Ellas necesitan:</u>

_____

_____

_____

_____

_____

LISTENING COMPREHENSION: LA RUTINA DE CHELA

Listen as your instructor reads a passage describing Chela's weekday and weekend routines. The first time you listen, fill in the chart below with the times Chela does the activities during the week and on Sundays. The second time, listen for the answers to the true-false statements.

	los días de entresemana (*during the week*)	los domingos
Se acuesta a las...		
Se despierta a las...		
Se levanta a las...		
Se ducha y se viste a las...		
Se sienta para comer o tomar algo a las...		

¿Cierto o falso? Corrige las oraciones falsas.

1. ☐ C ☐ F   Chela tiene la misma (*same*) rutina todos los días.

2. ☐ C ☐ F   Se acuesta más temprano el domingo que durante la semana.

3. ☐ C ☐ F   Insiste en comer algo (*something*) por la mañana todos los días.

4. ☐ C ☐ F   Por lo general, tiene prisa por la mañana durante la semana.

5. ☐ C ☐ F   Trabaja a las nueve y cuarto en la universidad.

6. ☐ C ☐ F   Chela prefiere levantarse inmediatamente después de despertarse.

7. ☐ C ☐ F   Los domingos, antes de leer el periódico, se ducha y se viste.

LOS VERBOS NUEVOS: IRREGULAR AND STEM-CHANGING

irreg. → yo	e → ie	o (u) → ue	e → i
hacer	cerrar	almorzar	pedir
poner	empezar	dormir	servir
salir	pensar	jugar	
	perder	volver	
	preferir		

1. Marta y José _____ al tenis todos los días. Después, _____ en el Café Continental, _____ a su apartamento y _____ una siesta corta.

2. En ese restaurante (ellos) _____ comida italiana muy buena. Siempre (yo) _____ ir allí cuando _____ con mis amigos. (Nosotros) _____ una pizza grande casi siempre.

3. (Yo) _____ a Boston mañana, donde _____ un trabajo (*job*) nuevo. (Yo) _____ que mi nuevo trabajo va a ser interesante.

4. No me gusta _____ al basquetbol con mi amiga Luisa, porque cuando ella _____, está furiosa y _____ a su casa en seguida. (Yo) _____ jugar con Rafael y Gabriela.

5. ¡Mi compañero de cuarto es un desastre! Siempre me _____ cosas: dinero, comida (*food*), mi camisa favorita... ¡Y después, (él) _____ todas mis cosas! (Él) _____ todo el día, no _____ la puerta del baño nunca, y _____ a casa muy tarde todas las noches. _____ que voy a buscar otro compañero el próximo semestre.

6. Quiero estar en buena forma (*good shape*). Por eso, (yo) _____ ocho horas de noche, _____ siempre una ensalada, _____ deportes y _____ ejercicio.

PRÁCTICA DE VERBOS

Complete las siguientes oraciones con la forma correcta del verbo más lógico entre parénthesis.

En la universidad

1. ¿(Entender / Pensar - tú) _____ todas las palabras nuevas?

2. En clase mañana, (tener / ir - nosotros) _____ que tomar un examen.

3. Si tú (tener / traer) _____ un examen, entonces (*then*) debes (ver / leer) _____ tu libro de texto.

4. La profesora (vender / venir) _____ a clase tarde a veces.

En la residencia

5. (Salir / Servir - ellos) _____ tacos, hamburguesas y pizza en la cafetería.

6. Patricio no (poner / poder) _____ descansar ahora, porque su compañero de cuarto quiere (oír / ver) _____ el partido (*game*) de béisbol en la tele.

7. Yolanda (volver / vivir) _____ tarde a la residencia porque hoy (entender / empezar) _____ su nuevo trabajo en la librería.

8. Yo no (deber / dormir) _____ bien en la residencia, porque mis compañeros de cuarto (tener / hacer) _____ mucho ruido.

En el centro

9. Yo (almorzar / beber) _____ en el centro todos los días.

10. En ese almacén, Uds. pueden (comprar / regatear) _____ de todo.

11. Cuando yo (ser / salir) _____ con mis amigos, nosotros (ver / ir) _____ al Café «La Mallorquina» para tomar café y hablar.

12. ¿Qué (hacer / ir) _____ tú esta tarde? ¿(Venir / Querer) _____ ir de compras conmigo?

La familia

13. Mis tíos siempre nos (traer / venir) _____ regalos cómicos para nuestros cumpleaños (*birthdays*).

14. Este fin de semana, nosotros (pedir / pensar) _____ visitar a los tíos.

15. En casa de mis tíos, yo (ver / jugar) _____ con mis primitos y Ana (ser / salir) _____ con la tía Isa.

16. Después de (ver/oír) _____ a los tíos, Ana y yo (pensar / pedir) _____ ir a la casa de nuestros amigos también.

ENSALADA GRAMATICAL I: STEM-CHANGING VERBS

Complete los siguientes pasajes con la forma correcta de las palabras entre paréntesis.

1. Mis amigas Sara y Anita _____ (almorzar) en casa, pero yo (preferir) _____ almorzar en un café. Hay un café en mi barrio donde (servir-ellos) _____ comida (*food*) italiana muy (bueno) _____. Siempre (pedir-yo) _____ el mismo plato: lasagna. Después de almorzar, (volver-yo) _____ a (el / la) _____ universidad y (empezar) _____ a estudiar.

2. (Dormir-yo) _____ ocho horas de noche, pero mi amigo José (dormir) _____ solo cinco o seis. (Mucho) _____ veces, él (estar) _____ cansado porque (este) _____ días (trabajar) _____ en un almacén veinticinco horas (de / a) _____ la semana. (Creer - yo) _____ que José (deber) _____ descansar más. Pero (ir - él) _____ a la biblioteca todas las noches y no (volver) _____ a la residencia hasta (los / las) _____ doce, cuando la biblioteca se (cerrar) _____. José (pensar) _____ ser profesor de español en el futuro; por eso, (tener) _____ que trabajar mucho ahora.

3. (Este) _____ fin de semana, no (querer - yo) _____ estudiar. (Pensar - yo) _____ salir con unos amigos. Nosotros (ir) _____ a ir al cine o tal vez a un partido de béisbol. (Mi) _____ amigos y yo (pensar) _____ que el béisbol es un deporte (*sport*) muy (divertido) _____, pero (este) _____ año nuestro equipo (*team*) favorito (perder) _____ mucho. A veces, después (de/del) _____ partido, nosotros (jugar) _____ en el parque. Yo no (jugar) _____ muy bien, pero mi amiga Beatriz (ser) _____ excelente.

ENSALADA GRAMATICAL II:
UN LUNES DIFÍCIL PARA PEPE

Complete the following passage, conjugating the verbs in parentheses. Remember that in Spanish the subject is not always directly stated, so read carefully. Answer the questions at the end of the passage.

No me (1. gustar) _____ levantarme los lunes porque siempre (2. tener - yo) _____ muchos problemas ese día. Por ejemplo, (3. tener) _____ clase a las ocho de la mañana. Es la clase de español. Normalmente no está mal la clase pero hoy (4. ser) _____ una excepción. (5. Estar -yo) _____ muy cansado y no (6. poder) _____ escuchar a la profesora. ¡Casi me (7. dormir) _____ en clase! Además (*Besides*), (8. tener - yo) _____ hambre y mi estómago (9. hacer) _____ mucho ruido. En clase (10. Practicar - nosotros) _____ la gramática un poco; también (11. hacer) _____ unos diálogos. Unos estudiantes no (12. entender) _____ los verbos irregulares porque estos verbos (13. ser) _____ muy difíciles. Esta noche (14. ir - yo) _____ a estudiar con una amiga de mi clase, pero ahora (15. preferir) _____ ir a la cafetería para tomar un café colombiano.

<u>Preguntas</u>

1. ¿Qué problemas tiene Pepe esta mañana?

   _____

2. ¿Qué hacen en clase hoy?

   _____

3. ¿Qué no entienden unos estudiantes? ¿Por qué?

   _____

4. ¿Qué va a hacer Pepe esta noche?

   _____

5. ¿Qué prefiere hacer ahora?

   _____

6. ¿Por qué necesita un café colombiano?

   _____

PRÁCTICA: REFLEXIVE ACTIONS

Complete the passages below. Remember to use the correct reflexive pronoun to match the subject.

me acuesto	**nos** acostamos
te acuestas	**os** acostáis
se acuesta	**se** acuestan

I. Tengo una familia muy grande. Todos los días, mis hermanos y yo (1. *get dressed*)

_____ antes de salir para la escuela. Los hermanos pequeños (2. *bathe*)

_____ por la noche, pero yo (3. *shower*) _____ y (4. *wash*)

_____ el pelo (*hair*) por la mañana. Mi hermana Cristina está cansada

porque no (5. *goes to bed*) _____ hasta muy tarde. Mi hermano Joaquín

trabaja en un banco. Es muy elegante y todos los días (6. *he puts on*) _____

una corbata de seda. Papá (7. *shaves*) _____ todos los días justo en el

momento en que Mamá necesita (8. *comb her hair*) _____, y los dos tienen

que compartir el espejo (*share the mirror*). Nosotros siempre (9. *enjoy ourselves*)

_____ mucho con seis personas, dos perros y un gato en la familia.

II. ¡BZZZZZZZ! Yo (1. acostarse / despertarse) _____ a las siete y media de

la mañana, pero no (2. levantarse / sentarse) _____ hasta las ocho. Tomo

un café y luego voy al baño para (3. ponerse la ropa / ducharse) _____.

Después de planchar (*iron*) una blusa muy rápido, (4. vestirse / afeitarse)

_____. Desayuno y miro el programa «¡Buenos días!» en la tele. Después,

(5. ponerse / comprarse) _____ los zapatos y un suéter porque hace frío y

salgo para la universidad.

Cuando regreso a casa por la tarde, estoy cansada. (6. Peinarse / Acostarse)

_____ en el sofá para mirar el noticiero de las cinco. Empiezo a

estudiar a las siete y media, y estudio hasta las diez y media. Después, (7. lavarse /

quitarse) _____ la ropa, (8. ponerse / vestirse) _____ el

pijama, (9. cepillarse / peinarse) _____ los dientes y (10. lavarse / afeitarse)

_____ la cara. Por fin, (11. acostarse / dormirse) _____ a las

once, y, después de leer un rato (*awhile*), (12. dormirse / despertarse) _____.

¡Hasta mañana!

REFLEXIVE ACTIONS: LA RUTINA DE MARISOL Y CARLOS

Use reflexive verbs to write six questions about Marisol and Carlos' morning routine. Then with a partner, answer each other's questions.

Verbos útiles:

afeitarse
bañarse
despertarse
levantarse
peinarse
ponerse
quitarse
vestirse

_____

_____

_____

_____

_____

_____

REPASO: CAPÍTULO 5

I. Vocabulario

A. Correspondencias. Match the word on the left with an associated action or actions on the right.

la cama	afeitarse
el baño	levantarse
la alcoba	ducharse
la sala	almorzar
la cocina	hacer la tarea
el comedor	poner / quitar la mesa
el escritorio	vestirse
la cómoda	acostarse
	peinarse

B. La rutina de Diego. Using the drawings as a guide, write a short paragraph describing a typical morning for Diego.

_____

_____

_____

_____

_____

_____

C. <u>La rutina diaria</u>. Now use six reflexive verbs to describe your daily routine.

_____

_____

_____

_____

_____

_____

D. <u>Los días de la semana</u>. What do you do or like to do on different days of the week? Complete the sentences.

1. Los lunes, generalmente...

_____.

2. Los miércoles, prefiero...

_____.

3. Los jueves, voy a...

_____.

4. Los viernes, salgo con...

_____.

5. Los sábados, no me gusta...

_____.

6. Los domingos, me gusta...

_____.

II. <u>Gramática</u>

A. <u>Verbos nuevos</u>. Complete the sentences with the correct form of one of the verbs according to the context. In each section, each verb will only be used once.

<u>En casa los domingos</u>: **despertarse / almorzar / salir / afeitarse / jugar / sentarse / dormir / volver / ponerse / ducharse**

1. Papá _____ en el sofá y Javier _____ en el baño.

2. Mamá _____ un poco tarde, a las nueve, y después _____ con la tía Mercedes.

3. (Yo) _____ en el sillón grande para leer el periódico.

4. Mi hermano Daniel _____ al fútbol en el parque y después

   _____ a casa, _____ y

   _____ mejor (*better*) ropa para visitar a su novia.

5. Todos _____ juntos (*together*) a las dos en la cocina. ¡Tenemos

   hambre!

<u>En la residencia</u>: **hacer / salir / bañarse / servir / acostarse / ducharse / dormir / volver / afeitarse / perder**

1. En la cafetería, (ellos) _____ comida (*food*) buena y barata.

2. Mi compañero, Martín, tiene una vida (*life*) complicada: _____

   con tres chicas a la vez (*at the same time*), siempre _____ a la

   residencia muy tarde y con frecuencia _____ su tarea.

3. Todos usamos un baño común. Allí (nosotros) _____,

   _____, _____, etcétera.

4. No _____ muy bien de noche porque los muchachos en el otro

   cuarto _____ mucho ruido y _____ a las tres

   de la mañana.

III. <u>Diálogo</u>

Ana and Lola are trying to decide if they would make good roommates.
Write a dialogue in which they discuss:

Ana   Lola

- their daily routines
- their study habits
- the kind of music they like
- what they do to have fun on the weekends

_____

_____

_____

_____

_____

_____

_____

¡A CONVERSAR!: EN UNA FIESTA

Pretend you are at a party. Use these questions to get to know the other guests.

Una presentación:
- Hola, ¿qué tal? Eres _____, ¿verdad?
- Soy _____, mucho gusto.
- Encantado / Encantada (Igualmente).

En la universidad

¿De dónde eres?	¿Te gusta la universidad? ¿Por qué?
¿Dónde vives este semestre?	¿Cuál es tu especialización?
¿Te gusta tu residencia / casa?	¿Qué quieres hacer en el futuro?

La familia

¿Tienes una familia grande?	¿Qué hacen tus hermanos?
¿Cómo son tus padres?	¿Cuántos años tienes tú?
¿Dónde viven ellos?	¿Qué te gusta hacer con tu familia?
¿Tienes hermanos? ¿Cuántos años tienen?	¿Cuándo viene tu familia de visita?

La comida

¿Tienes un restaurante favorito?	¿Dónde comes normalmente?
¿Cuáles?	¿Comes con tu familia frecuentemente?
¿Cómo es? ¿Qué sirven?	¿Qué te gusta comer cuando vuelves a casa?

El tiempo libre

¿Qué te gusta hacer en tu tiempo libre?	¿Qué programas te gustan?
¿Qué haces los viernes por la noche?	¿Te gusta bailar?
¿Miras mucho la televisión?	¿Adónde te gusta ir los fines de semana?

Una despedida:
Con permiso, tengo que hablar con _____.
Hasta luego. Ha sido un placer (*It's been a pleasure*).

Posibles reacciones
Vale. (*Okay.*)   Claro. (*Of course.*)
¡Qué va! (*No way!*)   ¿De verdad? (*Really?*)
¡No me digas! (*You're kidding!*)   ¡Qué interesante! (*How interesting!*)
¡Qué casualidad! (*What a coincidence!*)   ¡Qué bien! (*How nice!*)

GUIDED WRITING AND SPEAKING: EN CASA

A. Using the drawing and your imagination, answer the following questions in complete sentences in Spanish. Pay careful attention to the way the questions are phrased in order to use the correct structures in your answers.

1. What day of the week is it? How do you know?
2. With whom is Rosalía talking?
3. Who is Isabel and what is she doing with her daughter?
4. What is Carlitos doing?
5. What does doña Lupe want to do this afternoon?
6. What time does Sergio usually wake up from his nap?

B. Next, imagine you're an exchange student living with this family. Write a 100–word e-mail home about how you spend a typical Sunday with them.

C. With a partner, role-play a dialogue between any two characters in the drawing.

ROUND ROBIN: GRAMMAR MONITOR ACTIVITY

In this activity you will work in groups of three. Each partner will alternate roles until all three of you have (1) described the routine of one of the characters; (2) asked questions to get more information; and (3) served as the grammar monitor.

Matilde y Jorge

Rocío y Pepe

Guille y Sara

Partner A: Describe one of the characters. Include personality characteristics and how he/she is feeling today. Then use your imagination to describe a typical day for this person.

Partner B: Listen carefully as Partner A describes one of the characters and his/her routine. Then ask two questions to get more information about him/her.

Partner C: As the grammar monitor, your job is to listen for agreement errors that Partners A and B may make. Write down any errors you may hear. Also listen for the proper use of the reflexive verbs. Example: *Rocío es alta y delgado. Levanta a las seis.* Note that *delgado* should be *delgada* and that the verb should be *se levanta*. When Partners A and B are finished, give them feedback on whether or not they are doing well on noun/adjective agreement and reflexive verbs.

Now switch roles. Partner A takes the role of Partner B (the person asking questions), Partner B takes the role of Partner C (the grammar monitor), and Partner C takes the role of Partner A (the describer).

BINGO: MI CASA Y MI RUTINA

se levanta a las siete.	tiene una cama de agua (*water bed*).	sale todos los viernes.	hace su tarea en la cama.	se afeita antes de la clase de español.
no tiene televisión.	tiene una alfombra en su alcoba.	va a salir de casa este fin de semana.	la alcoba de es un desastre.	se duerme en clase a veces.
canta mientras (*while*) se ducha.	almuerza en McDonald's mucho.	juega al tenis muy bien.	vuelve a casa muy tarde los viernes por la noche.	se levanta temprano los sábados.
va a la iglesia (*church*) los domingos.	tiene que despertarse temprano los domingos.	estudia en la cocina.	sale con alguien esta noche.	va a ir a una fiesta este sábado.
tiene tres clases los martes.	siempre hace su tarea para la clase de español.	tiene un sofá feo.	siempre se divierte los sábados.	hace deportes los fines de semana.

COMMUNICATIVE GOALS PRACTICE #3

Try to talk about the Muñoz family for 60 seconds. "Show off" all you have learned up to this point in the semester. Check the **Communicative Goals** boxes at the beginning of each chapter of your Supplement to see all that you should be able to do. For this second oral proficiency practice, the following topics are suggested. Try to use connectors (**porque, pero, y, también, por eso**) to make your description sound more fluent and natural.

1. Time	4. Description of their house
2. Description (age, personality, physical appearance, clothing)	5. Actions taking place
	6. Future plans
3. Family relationships	7. Routines of family members

Laura   Ben   Memo

Lourdes   Nando

After you've finished your description, work with a partner, taking turns to ask questions of at least two of the characters in the scene. Your partner, using his/her imagination, will answer the questions.

¿Cómo? ¿Qué? ¿Cuál? ¿Cuándo? ¿Cuánto/a/os/as? ¿Cuándo? ¿Dónde? ¿De donde? ¿Quién? ¿Por qué? ¿De quién?

Communicative Goals for Chapter 6

By the end of the chapter, you should be able to:

- talk about the weather ❏
- describe what you do seasonally ❏
- point out where things are located ❏
- talk about what you are doing right now ❏
- describe personality traits and conditions ❏
- make simple comparisons ❏

Grammatical Structures

You should know:

- prepositions of place ❏ ❏
- present progressive ❏ ❏
- **ser** vs. **estar** ❏ ❏
- **más/menos... que** ❏ ❏
- **tan... como** ❏ ❏
- **tanto/a/os/as... como** ❏ ❏

PRONUNCIACIÓN: LOS SONIDOS *RR* Y *R*

Remember that Spanish has two **r** sounds. The single **r** is pronounced like the double *d* in *ladder*; the trilled **r** is written **rr** between vowels (**carro**), and **r** at the beginning of a word (**rosa**). Listen as your instructor pronounces these pairs of words, then repeat.

ahora / ahorra	coro / corro	caro / carro
cero / cerro	pero / perro	coral / corral

Now listen as your instructor reads these sentences, then practice them with a partner.

1. El perro pardo es para Laura Rosario Romano.
2. Los ricos requieren ropa cara y carros rápidos.
3. Ahora es la hora de revisar los horribles errores de Ricardo.
4. Las rosas amarillas son para la prima de Ramiro.
5. Los ratones ruidosos corren rápidamente por los corredores.

Listen as your instructor reads some Spanish proverbs, then repeat. Can you match each proverb to its English equivalent?

_____ 1. Al perro viejo, no hay tus tus.

_____ 2. Cuando a Roma fueres, haz como vieres.

_____ 3. La ropa sucia se debe lavar en casa.

_____ 4. Perro ladrador, poco mordedor.

_____ 5. Donde más hondo el río, hace menos ruido.

_____ 6. Cuando una puerta se cierra, ciento se abren.

a. Still waters run deep.
b. A dog's bark is worse than its bite.
c. When one door shuts, another one opens.
d. You can't teach an old dog new tricks.
e. When in Rome, do as the Romans do.
f. Don't air your dirty laundry in public.

LISTENING COMPREHENSION: EL BOLETÍN METEOROLÓGICO

You will hear brief weather reports for five U.S. cities. As you listen, write the name of the city next to the drawing that best matches its weather description. Then complete the chart by listening for the high and low temperatures for that city and the weather forecast for the next day. One drawing will not be used. You will hear the reports twice.

	Ciudad	Temperaturas máximas y mínimas	Tiempo para mañana

LISTENING COMPREHENSION: ¿QUIÉN ES?

Your instructor will describe the people in the following drawings. Listen and fill in the names of the people being described.

PRÁCTICA: PRESENT PROGRESSIVE

¡Qué noche más divertida! Write a short paragraph about what everyone is doing at the Bar Paladino tonight. Use the present progressive.

Vocabulario útil

el mesero / el camarero   waiter

_____

_____

_____

_____

_____

Now answer the questions about the scene above.

1. ¿De dónde **es** Carlos?

_____

2. ¿Dónde **están** todos en este momento?

_____

3. ¿Cómo **es** Ana?

_____

4. ¿Cómo **está** el camarero después de trabajar ocho horas?

_____

5. ¿De qué **es** la falda de Ana?

_____

6. ¿Por qué **está** contento Jaime?

_____

7. Tomás piensa que el Bar Paladino **es** aburrido. ¿Por qué no **está** de acuerdo Ana?

_____

8. ¿A qué hora **es** el concierto de Madonna en la tele?

_____

¿SER O ESTAR?

With a partner, read the sentences and decide if you would need to use **ser** or **estar** for each. Explain your reasons.

1. Who <u>is</u> that gorgeous guy?

_____

2. The bride <u>is</u> beautiful.

_____

3. Yes, and the groom <u>looks</u> handsome in his tux.

_____

4. Where <u>is</u> the father of the bride?

_____

5. <u>He's</u> in the bar across the street.

_____

6. <u>He's</u> furious because weddings <u>are</u> expensive.

_____

7. When <u>is</u> the ceremony?

_____

8. <u>It's</u> at 4.

_____

9. <u>It's</u> hard to see the bride from here.

_____

10. Which one <u>is</u> the bride's mother?

_____

11. <u>She's</u> the tall lady up front.

_____

12. She <u>is</u> very emotional!

_____

13. For whom <u>are</u> all those presents?

_____

14. They <u>are</u> for the newlyweds, of course!

_____

15. Where <u>is</u> the groom from?

_____

16. <u>He's</u> from Seattle.

_____

17. <u>I'm</u> so happy I could cry.

_____

¿SER O ESTAR?: PÁRRAFO

Complete the following paragraphs with the correct form of either **ser** or **estar**.

Hoy 1. _____ martes, y los estudiantes 2. _____ en el salón

de clase. 3. _____ las once y media, más o menos. ¿Qué pasa ahora en la clase

de español? Bueno, en este momento hacemos un ejercicio de gramática. En general, a los

estudiantes no les gusta mucho la gramática; unos 4. _____ aburridos ahora. Otros

5. _____ preocupados porque no comprenden las diferencias entre los dos verbos

ser y **estar**. Unos estudiantes miran a la profesora, y otros piensan en otras cosas: una siesta,

el fin de semana, etcétera.

¿Cómo 6. _____ los estudiantes de nuestra clase? Unos 7. _____

altos, otros 8. _____ rubios y otros 9. _____ de otros países. A veces,

cuando los estudiantes llegan a clase, 10. _____ cansados porque trabajan mucho y

11. _____ preocupados por sus problemas académicos. Hoy, sin embargo, nadie

(*nobody*) 12. _____ nervioso o de mal humor; la verdad es que todos parecen (*seem*)

13. _____ relativamente contentos. ¿Todos los estudiantes 14. _____ en

clase hoy o no? ¿Quiénes no 15. _____ aquí? ¿Qué 16. _____ haciendo

las personas ausentes.?

A la profesora le gusta la clase porque los estudiantes 17. _____

inteligentes, trabajadores y simpáticos. ¿Cómo 18. _____ la profesora hoy? Pues,

desgraciadamente (*unfortunately*) no 19. _____ muy bien; 20. _____

cansada. Pero normalmente ella 21. _____ una persona alegre.

En este momento los estudiantes 22. _____ ocupados con la gramática.

Hablamos de los verbos **ser** y **estar.** A veces 23. _____ difícil entender los usos

de los dos verbos. Pero 24. _____ muy importante saber (*to know*) cuándo se dice

(*one says*) **ser** y cuándo se dice **estar**. Uds. 25. _____ de acuerdo, ¿verdad?

VERBOS: ¿SER O ESTAR?

Select the correct words or phrases from those given to complete the following sentences.

Ejemplo: Ernesto Pérez es _____. (ocupado / cansado / aquí / profesor)
Ernesto Pérez es <u>profesor</u>.

1. Estoy en el hospital porque soy _____.
(enfermo / doctor / aquí / cerca)

2. Mi amigo está _____ hoy.
(cantante / de España / contento / argentino)

3. Sofía no es _____, pero vive ahora en Colombia.
(nerviosa / en el centro / colombiana / cerca)

4. Después de clase, estás _____.
(inteligente / viejo / cansado / de Alemania)

5. Nuestros perros son muy _____.
(frustrados / perezosos / enfermos / preocupados)

6. Hoy la profesora está _____.
(de Chile / actriz / preocupada / alta)

7. —¿Cómo estás?
—Estoy _____, gracias.
(de Uruguay / difícil / bien / inteligente)

8. Necesito un libro pero ahora la biblioteca está _____.
(grande / cerrada / alta / vieja)

9. Creo que mis padres están _____ ahora.
(simpáticos / inteligentes / en casa / morenos)

10. Vamos a estudiar más tarde; ahora estamos _____.
(presidentes / trabajadores / cansados / aquí)

11. La familia de Miguel es _____.
(cerca de la biblioteca / en la oficina / de acuerdo / de Panamá)

12. La mesa es _____.
(de plástico / en mi nombre / cerca de la puerta / detrás del profesor)

13. Estos platos están _____.
(de porcelana / de mi madre / sucios / viejos)

14. La playa está muy _____.
(bonita / cerca de aquí / grande / fea)

15. El libro es _____.
(cerrado / caro / encima del escritorio / debajo de la mesa)

¿SER O ESTAR?: PICTURE DESCRIPTIONS

Look at the four pairs of drawings below. For each pair of drawings, write:

- one sentence with **ser**, describing a person or a place in the drawing;
- one sentence with **estar**, explaining how one of the people feels, where she is, or what she is doing right now;
- one additional sentence about the drawing, using **ser** or **estar**

1. _____

2. _____

3. _____

1. _____

2. _____

3. _____

1. _____

2. _____

3. _____

1. _____

2. _____

3. _____

PRÁCTICA: LAS COMPARACIONES

I. Compare the pairs of items listed, using the adjective and the symbol to guide you.

1. Oprah Winfrey/Bill Gates/rico (+)

2. Rafael Nadal/Roger Federer/talentoso (=)

3. Chris Rock/Jon Stewart/cómico (+)

4. la vida (*life*) privada de Britney Spears/la vida privada de Lindsey Lohan/escandaloso (=)

5. Marc Anthony/los Beatles/popular (−)

6. los perros/los gatos/cariñoso (+)

7. Brad Pitt/Orlando Bloom/guapo (+)

8. Cameron Díaz/Meryl Streep/viejo (−) (¡OJO!)

II. Make five comparative statements about the people pictured, using the verbs below.

Alicia / Pedro (estudiar)

Delia / Pedro (comer)

Alicia / Delia (levantarse temprano)

Delia / Alicia (tener tiempo libre)

Alicia / Pedro (dormir)

Alicia   Delia   Pedro

1. _____

2. _____

3. _____

4. _____

5. _____

REPASO: CAPÍTULO 6

I. Vocabulario

A. ¿Qué tiempo hace? Based on the short descriptions of what people are doing or wearing, write a sentence saying what the weather is like:

1. Los turistas van a las montañas para esquiar: _____

2. Tomamos el sol y jugamos al voleibol en la playa: _____

3. E1 cielo (*sky*) está gris y estoy triste: _____

4. ¿Dónde están mis botas y mi impermeable? _____

5. ¡Uff! ¡Necesito tomar agua! _____

6. En Los Ángeles, no puedo ver ni respirar (*nor breathe*): _____

7. ¿Qué tal si vamos al parque para estudiar? _____

B. Asociaciones. ¿Qué asocias con los meses y las estaciones? Think of three associations for each month or season.

el otoño: _____

junio: _____

diciembre: _____

el verano: _____

septiembre: _____

diciembre: _____

la primavera: _____

C. ¿Dónde está? Un poco de geografía. Read the following statements and mark them as **cierto** or **falso**. Then check your answers using the maps in your book.

1. ☐ C ☐ F   Nicaragua está al sur de México.

2. ☐ C ☐ F   Portugal está al oeste de España.

3. ☐ C ☐ F   Venezuela está cerca de Chile.

4. ☐ C ☐ F   E1 Salvador está entre Guatemala y Honduras.

5. ☐ C ☐ F   Panamá está lejos de Colombia.

6. ☐ C ☐ F   La Argentina está al lado de Chile.

7. ☐ C ☐ F   Tegucigalpa está al oeste de San Salvador.

8. ☐ C ☐ F   La Ciudad de México está al este de la Ciudad de Guatemala.

II. Gramática

A. ¿Ser o estar? Would you use **ser** or **estar** to talk about the following things? Indicate "S" or "E" next to each one, then check your work on **pp. 178–180** of *Puntos*. Write a sentence in Spanish for each item.

1. ☐ S ☐ E possession

   _____

2. ☐ S ☐ E someone's current condition or emotional state

   _____

3. ☐ S ☐ E what something is made of

   _____

4. ☐ S ☐ E time

   _____

5. ☐ S ☐ E inherent personality traits

   _____

6. ☐ S ☐ E where something is

   _____

7. ☐ S ☐ E agreeing with someone

   _____

8. ☐ S ☐ E identifying someone or something

   _____

9. ☐ S ☐ E nationality/origin

   _____

B. Ser vs. estar. Complete the passage.

Hoy _____ jueves. _____ un día horrible. Llueve y hace mucho

frío. Tengo que _____ en casa todo el día. No puedo ir al parque. Pero

_____ posible ir al cine. La película que dan (*they are showing*) en el Cine Rex

_____ muy interesante. _____ a las dos y veinte de la tarde. Voy a

llamar a mis amigos. Si ellos _____ de acuerdo, todos vamos al cine esta tarde.

¡Va a _____ fenomenal!

C. Comparativos. Make comparative statements about the people depicted below. Use the cues in parentheses to determine if the comparisons are equal or unequal.

1. clases / Gloria / Inés (=)

_____

2. refrescos (*cold drinks*) / José / Ramón (=)

_____

3. amigos / Carlos / José (−)

_____

4. tarea / Gloria / Roberto (+)

_____

5. comer / Luis / José (+)

_____

6. ver televisión / Roberto / Inés (+)

_____

7. leer / Carlos / Gloria (=)

_____

8. estudiar / Luis / Gloria (−)

_____

D. ¿Qué están haciendo en este momento? Use the present progressive to tell what each member of the Hernández family is doing right now. Be careful with the reflexive pronouns.

1. _____
2. _____
3. _____
4. _____
5. _____
6. _____

E. Un sábado típico. Suppose that today is a typical Saturday. Using five different verbs in the present progressive, tell what you are doing at the following times.

1. Son las siete y cuarto de la mañana. _____

2. Son las diez de la mañana. _____

3. Es la una y media de la tarde. _____

4. Son las seis y media de la tarde. _____

5. Son las doce menos cuarto de la noche. _____

F. ¿Cuál fue (*was*) la pregunta? Write an appropriate question for the answers given.

1. ¿_____?

   Bogotá está en Colombia.

2. ¿_____?

   Los países centroamericanos son Guatemala, Honduras, El Salvador, Nicaragua, Costa Rica y Panamá.

3. ¿_____?

   Para mis próximas vacaciones, voy a Chile para esquiar.

4. ¿_____?

   Hay más de 122 millones de habitantes en México.

5. ¿_____?

   Carlos Fuentes, el escritor (*writer*), es de México.

III. Diálogo

You are sitting next to a good-looking stranger on a flight to Central America. Write a short dialogue in which you:

- introduce yourselves, say where you are from and what you do;
- discuss where you are going and make two comparisons between your destination and your seatmate's destination;
- make plans to meet again.

_____

_____

_____

_____

_____

_____

_____

ENTREVISTA: ¿CÓMO ESTÁS?

In class we've practiced using the verb **estar** to describe conditions (**Estoy alegre, aburrido/a, furioso/a**). Now find out how one of your classmates feels in the following situations. Take turns asking and answering the following questions with a classmate, following the cues below. Use the adjectives on **p. 180** of *Puntos* in your answers.

1. Cuando tienes mucho trabajo, ¿cómo estás?

   Cuando tengo mucho trabajo, estoy _____.

2. Los lunes por la mañana, ¿cómo estás?

3. Antes de los exámenes, ¿cómo estás?

4. Cuando llueve, ¿cómo estás?

5. Los viernes por la noche, ¿cómo estás?

6. Después de la clase de español, ¿cómo estás?

7. Cuando estás con tu familia, ¿cómo estás?

8. Antes de una cita (*date*), ¿cómo estás?

9. Cuando no comprendes el español, ¿cómo estás?

10. Cuando sacas (*you get*) una «A» en tu examen de español, ¿cómo estás?

11. Cuando te acuestas tarde, ¿cómo estás al día siguiente?

Speaking Activities

KEY LANGUAGE FUNCTIONS: DESCRIPTION AND COMPARISON

At this point in the course, you should be able to describe and compare people and places. To do this accurately, you should know how to use **ser** and **estar**, know the rules for noun-adjective agreement, and know how to make comparisons of equality and inequality.

 To construct a description → Vocabulary → Linguistic Tools Needed:
- **ser** vs. **estar**
- noun-adjective agreement

Take turns with a partner describing the following places. Include what you usually do in those places and how you feel when you are there. Don't forget your vocabulary from previous chapters and the linguistic tools listed above.

1. Your living room
2. Your favorite place to go on Saturday nights
3. Your favorite place to hang out on campus
4. Your favorite place to go in the summer

 To construct a comparison → Vocabulary → Linguistic Tools Needed:
- **ser** vs. **estar**
- noun-adjective agreement
- **más/menos... que** ($\neq$)
- **tan... como** ($=$)
- **tanto/as/os/as... como** ($=$)

Take turns with a partner making comparisons between the following people, places, and sentiments. Don't forget your vocabulary from previous chapters and the linguistic tools listed above.

1. Compare yourself and a relative.
2. Compare your apartment or dorm and your parents' house.
3. Compare your wardrobe and your roommate's wardrobe.
4. Compare how you feel during finals and how you feel during spring break.

GUIDED WRITING AND SPEAKING: EN LA RESIDENCIA

A. Using the drawing and your imagination, answer the following questions in complete Spanish sentences. Pay careful attention to the way the questions are phrased in order to use the correct structures in your answers.

1. What's the weather like in Mérida today?
2. Who is sitting to the left of Germán?
3. Why is Germán worried?
4. Why does Profesor Campos think that Dina is smarter than Riqui and Nicolás?
5. What does Nicolás feel like doing?
6. Which of the students has to leave for class in five minutes?
7. Why is Nicolás tired and when does he typically get up?
8. Who likes to get up early?
9. Who studies as much as Ana María?
10. Where is Professor Alonso from?

B. Now imagine you are one of the characters in the drawing. Write an entry in your journal, comparing life in the dorm to life at home, and your college friends to your high-school friends.

C. With a partner, role-play a dialogue between any two characters in the drawing.

Speaking Activities

ADJECTIVE A word that describes a noun or pronoun.

una casa **grande**
a **big** house

Ana es **inteligente.**
*Ana is **smart.***

Demonstrative adjective An adjective that points out a particular noun.

este chico, **esos** libros, **aquellas** personas
***this** boy, **those** books, **those** people (over there)*

Interrogative adjective An adjective used to form questions.

¿Qué cuaderno?
***Which** notebook?*

¿Cuáles son los carteles que buscas?
Which ones are the posters (that) you're looking for?

Possessive adjective (unstressed) An adjective that indicates possession or a special relationship.

sus coches
***their** cars*

mi hermana
***my** sister*

Possessive adjective (stressed) An adjective that more emphatically describes possession.*

Es **una** amiga **mía.**
*She's **my** friend. / She's a friend **of mine.***

Es **un** coche **suyo.**
*It's **her** car. / It's a car **of hers.***

ADVERB A word that describes an adjective, a verb, or another adverb.

Roberto es **muy** alto.
*Roberto is **very** tall.*

María escribe **bien.**
*María writes **well.***

Van **demasiado** rápido.
*They are going **too** quickly.*

ARTICLE A determiner that sets off a noun.

el país
***the** country*

Definite article An article that indicates a specific noun.

la silla
***the** chair*

las mujeres
***the** women*

Indefinite article An article that indicates an unspecified noun.

un chico
***a** boy*

una ciudad
***a** city*

unas zanahorias
*(**some**) carrots*

---

*See Appendix 3 on page A–7 for more information.

CLAUSE A construction that contains a subject and a verb.

Main (Independent) clause A clause that can stand on its own because it expresses a complete thought. **Busco una muchacha.**

I'm looking for a girl.

Si yo fuera rica, **me compraría una casa.**
*If I were rich, **I would buy a house.***

Subordinate (Dependent) clause A clause that cannot stand on its own because it does not express a complete thought.

Busco a la muchacha **que juega al tenis.**
*I'm looking for the girl **who plays tennis.***

Si yo fuera rica, me compraría una casa.
***If I were rich,** I would buy a house.*

COMPARATIVE The form of adjectives and adverbs used to compare two nouns or actions.

Luis es menos **hablador** que Julián.
*Luis is **less talkative than** Julián.*

Luis corre más **rápido** que Julián.
*Luis runs **faster than** Julián.*

CONJUGATION The different forms of a verb for a particular tense or mood. A present indicative conjugation:

(yo) **habl**o	(nosotros/as) **habl**amos
(tú) **habl**as	(vosotros/as) **habl**áis
(Ud.) **habl**a	(Uds.) **habl**an
(él/ella) **habl**a	(ellos/as) **habl**an

I speak	*we speak*
you (fam. sing.) speak	*you (fam. pl.) speak*
you (form. sing.) speak	*you (pl.) speak*
he/she speaks	*they speak*

CONJUNCTION An expression that connects words, phrases, or clauses.

Cristóbal **y** Diana
*Cristóbal **and** Diana*

Hace frío, **pero** hace buen tiempo.
*It's cold, **but** it's nice out.*

DIRECT OBJECT The noun or pronoun that receives the action of a verb.

Veo **la caja.**
*I see **the box.***

La veo.
*I see **it.***

GENDER A grammatical category of words. In Spanish, there are two genders: masculine and feminine.

	MASCULINE	FEMININE
ARTICLES AND NOUNS:	**el** disco compacto	**la** cinta
PRONOUNS:	**él**	**ella**
ADJECTIVES:	bonito, listo	bonita, lista
PAST PARTICIPLES:	El informe está **escrito.**	La composición está **escrita.**

IMPERATIVE *See Mood.*

IMPERFECT (*IMPERFECTO*) In Spanish, a verb tense that expresses a past action with no specific beginning or ending.

Nadábamos con frecuencia.
*We **used to swim** often.*

IMPERSONAL CONSTRUCTION One that contains a third person singular verb but no specific subject in Spanish. The subject of English impersonal constructions is generally *it*.

Es importante que...
It is important that . . .

Es necesario que...
It is necessary that . . .

INDICATIVE *See* Mood.

INDIRECT OBJECT The noun or pronoun that indicates *for who(m)* or *to who(m)* an action is performed. In Spanish, the indirect object pronoun is usually included, even when the indirect object is explicitly stated as a noun.

Marcos **le** da el suéter **a Raquel**. / Marcos **le** da el suéter.
*Marcos gives the sweater **to Raquel**. / Marcos gives **her** the sweater.*

INFINITIVE The form of a verb introduced in English by *to: to play, to sell, to come.* In Spanish dictionaries, the infinitive form of the verb appears as the main entry.

Luisa va a **comprar** un periódico.
*Luisa is going **to buy** a newspaper.*

MOOD A set of categories for verbs indicating the attitude of the speaker toward what he or she is saying.

Imperative mood A verb form expressing a command.

¡**Ten** cuidado!
***Be** careful!*

Indicative mood A verb form denoting actions or states considered facts.

Voy a la biblioteca.
***I'm going** to the library.*

Subjunctive mood A verb form, uncommon in English, used in Spanish primarily in subordinate clauses after expressions of desire, doubt, or emotion. Spanish constructions with the subjunctive have many possible English equivalents.

Quiero que **vayas** inmediatamente.
*I want you **to go** immediately.*

NOUN A word that denotes a person, place, thing, or idea. Proper nouns are capitalized names.

abogado, ciudad, periódico, libertad, Luisa
lawyer, city, newspaper, freedom, Luisa

NUMBER

Cardinal number A number that expresses an amount.

una silla, **tres** estudiantes
one *chair,* **three** *students*

Ordinal number A number that indicates position in a series.

la **primera** silla, el **tercer** estudiante
*the **first** chair, the **third** student*

PAST PARTICIPLE The form of a verb used in compound tenses (*see* Perfect Tenses). Used with forms of *to have* or *to be* in English and with **ser, estar,** or **haber** in Spanish.

comido, terminado, perdido
eaten, finished, lost

PERFECT TENSES Compound tenses that combine the auxiliary verb **haber** with a past participle.

Present perfect indicative This form uses a present indicative form of **haber**. The use of the Spanish present perfect generally parallels that of the English present perfect.

No **he viajado** nunca a México.
*I've never **traveled** to Mexico.*

Past perfect indicative This form uses **haber** in the imperfect tense to talk about something that had or had not been done before a given time in the past.

Antes de 2008, **no había estudiado** español.
*Before 2008, **I hadn't studied** Spanish.*

Present perfect subjunctive This form uses the present subjunctive of **haber** to express a present perfect action when the subjunctive is required.

¡Ojalá que Marisa **haya llegado** a su destino!
*I hope (that) Marisa **has arrived** at her destination!*

PERSON The form of a pronoun or verb that indicates the person involved in an action.

	SINGULAR	PLURAL
FIRST PERSON:	*I* / **yo**	*we* / **nosotros/as**
SECOND PERSON:	*you* / **tú, Ud.**	*you* / **vosotros/as, Uds.**
THIRD PERSON:	*he, she* / **él, ella**	*they* / **ellos, ellas**

PREPOSITION A word or phrase that specifies the relationship of one word (usually a noun or pronoun) to another. The relationship is usually spatial or temporal.

a la escuela
to *school*

cerca de la biblioteca
near *the library*

con él
with *him*

antes de la medianoche
before *midnight*

PRESENT PARTICIPLE The verb form that ends in -*ing* in English. Used with forms of *to be* in English and with **estar** in Spanish to form the progressive.

hablando, comiendo, pidiendo
speaking, eating, asking

PRETERITE (*PRETÉRITO*) In Spanish, a verb tense that expresses a past action with a specific beginning and ending.

Salí para Roma el jueves.
I left *for Rome on Thursday.*

PROGRESSIVE The verb that expresses continuing or developing action.

Julio **está durmiendo** ahora.
*Julio **is sleeping** now.*

Anita **estaba comiendo** cuando sonó el teléfono.
*Anita **was eating** when the phone rang.*

PRONOUN A word that refers to a person (I, you) or that is used in place of one or more nouns.

Demonstrative pronoun A pronoun that singles out a particular person, place, thing, or idea.

Aquí están dos libros. **Este** es interesante, pero **ese** es aburrido.
*Here are two books. **This one** is interesting, but **that one** is boring.*

Interrogative pronoun A pronoun used to ask a question.

¿**Quién** es él?
Who *is he?*

¿**Qué** prefieres?
What *do you prefer?*

Object pronoun A pronoun that replaces a direct object noun or an indirect object noun. Both direct and indirect object pronouns can be used together in the same sentence.

Si **me** llamas más tarde, **te** doy el número de teléfono de David.
*If you call **me** later, I'll give **you** David's phone number.*

Veo a **Alejandro. Lo** veo.
*I see **Alejandro.** I see **him.***

However, when the pronouns **le** or **les** appear before **lo, la, los,** or **las, le** or **les** changes to **se.**

Le doy **el libro** a Juana.
*I give the book **to Juana.***

Se lo doy (a ella).
*I give **it** to **her.***

Reflexive pronoun A pronoun that represents the same person as the subject of the verb.

Me miro en el espejo.
*I look at **myself** in the mirror.*

Relative pronoun A pronoun that introduces a dependent clause and denotes a noun already mentioned.

El hombre con **quien** hablaba era mi vecino.
*The man with **whom** I was talking was my neighbor.*

Aquí está el bolígrafo **que** buscas.
*Here is the pen (**that**) you're looking for.*

Subject pronoun A pronoun representing the person, place, thing, or idea performing the action of a verb.

Lucas y Julia juegan al tenis.
***Lucas and Julia** are playing tennis.*

Ellos juegan al tenis.
***They** are playing tennis.*

SUBJECT The word(s) denoting the person, place, thing, or idea performing an action or existing in a state.

Sara trabaja aquí.
***Sara** works here.*

¡**Buenos Aires** es una ciudad magnífica!
***Buenos Aires** is a great city!*

Mis **libros** y mi **computadora** están allí.
*My **books** and my **computer** are over there.*

SUBJUNCTIVE *See Mood.*

SUPERLATIVE The form of adjectives or adverbs used to compare three or more nouns or actions. In English, the superlative is marked by *most, least,* or *-est.*

Escogí el **vestido** más **caro.**
*I chose **the most expensive** dress.*

Ana es la **persona** menos **habladora** que conozco.
*Ana is **the least talkative person** I know.*

TENSE The form of a verb indicating time: present, past, or future.

Raúl **era, es** y siempre **será** mi mejor amigo.
*Raúl **was, is,** and always **will be** my best friend.*

VERB A word that reports an action or state.

Maribel **llegó.**
*Maribel **arrived.***

La niña **estaba** cansada.
*The child **was** tired.*

Auxiliary verb A verb in conjuction with a participle to convey distinctions of tense and mood. In Spanish, one auxiliary verb is **haber.**

Han viajado por todas partes del mundo.
*They **have** traveled everywhere in the world.*

Reflexive verb A verb whose subject and object are the same.

Juan **se corta** la cara cuando **se afeita.**
*Juan **cuts himself** when he **shaves** (**himself**).*

APPENDIX 2 — Using Adjectives as Nouns

Nominalization means using an adjective as a noun. In Spanish, adjectives can be nominalized in a number of ways, all of which involve dropping the noun that accompanies the adjective, then using the adjective in combination with an article or other word. One kind of adjective, the demonstrative, can simply be used alone. In most cases, these usages parallel those of English, although the English equivalent may be phrased differently from the Spanish.

Article + Adjective

Simply omit the noun from an *article + noun + adjective* phrase.

    el **libro** azul ⟶ **el azul** (*the blue one*)
    la **hermana** casada ⟶ **la casada** (*the married one*)
    el **señor** mexicano ⟶ **el mexicano** (*the Mexican one*)
    los **pantalones** baratos ⟶ **los baratos**
       (*the inexpensive ones*)

You can also drop the first noun in an *article + noun + **de** + noun* phrase.

    la **casa** de Julio ⟶ **la de Julio** (*Julio's*)
    los **coches** del Sr. Martínez ⟶ **los del Sr. Martínez**
       (*Mr. Martínez's*)

In both cases, the construction is used to refer to a noun that has already been mentioned. The English equivalent uses *one* or *ones,* or a possessive without the noun.

    — ¿Necesitas el **libro** grande?
    — No. Necesito **el pequeño.**
    "Do you need the big book?"
    "No. I need the small one."

    — ¿Usamos el **coche** de Ernesto?
    — No. Usemos **el de Ana.**
    "Shall we use Ernesto's car?"
    "No. Let's use Ana's."

Note that in the preceding examples the noun is mentioned in the first part of the exchange (**libro, coche**) but not in the response or rejoinder.

Note also that a demonstrative can be used to nominalize an adjective: **este rojo** (*this red one*), **esos azules** (*those blue ones*).

Lo + Adjective

As seen in **Capítulo 11, lo** combines with the masculine singular form of an adjective to describe general qualities or characteristics. The English equivalent is expressed with words like *part* or *thing.*

lo mejor   *the best thing (part), what's best*
lo mismo   *the same thing*
lo cómico   *the funny thing (part), what's funny*

Article + Stressed Possessive Adjective

The stressed possessive adjectives—but not the unstressed possessives—can be used as possessive pronouns: **la maleta suya** ⟶ **la suya.** The article and the possessive form agree in gender and number with the noun to which they refer.

    Este es mi **banco.** ¿Dónde está el **suyo**?
    This is my bank. Where is yours?

    Sus **bebidas** están preparadas; las **nuestras,** no.
    Their drinks are ready; ours aren't.

    No es la **maleta** de Juan; es la **mía.**
    It isn't Juan's suitcase; it's mine.

Note that the definite article is frequently omitted after forms of **ser: ¿Esa maleta? Es suya.**

Demonstrative Pronouns

The demonstrative adjective can be used alone, without a noun. An accent mark can be added to the demonstrative pronoun (**éste, ése, aquél**) to distinguish it from the demonstrative adjectives if context does not make meaning clear.

    Necesito este diccionario y **ese (ése).**
    I need this dictionary and that one.

    Estas señoras y **aquellas (aquéllas)** son las
      hermanas de Sara, ¿no?
    These women and those (over there) are Sara's
      sisters, aren't they?

It is acceptable in modern Spanish, according to the **Real Academia Española,** to omit the accent on demonstrative pronouns when context makes the meaning clear and no ambiguity is possible.

APPENDIX 3 More About Stressed Possessives

When in English you would emphasize the possessive with your voice or with *of mine* (*of yours, of his*, and so on), you will use the *stressed possessives* (**las formas tónicas de los posesivos**) in Spanish. As the term implies, they are more emphatic than the *unstressed forms* (**las formas átonas de los posesivos**).

The stressed forms follow the noun, and the noun *must* be preceded by a definite or indefinite article or by a demonstrative adjective. The stressed forms agree with the noun modified in number and gender. In the following examples, boldface italic type in the English translations indicates voice stress.

Es **su** perro.	*It's her dog.*

But:

Es **un** perro **suyo**.	*It's **her** dog (i.e., not ours).* *It's a dog of hers.*
El perro **suyo** se llama King.	***Her** dog is named King.*
Ese perro **suyo** es bravo.	*That dog of hers is fierce.*

Es **su** maleta.	*It's **his** suitcase.*

But:

Es **una** maleta **suya**.	*It's **his** suitcase.*
La maleta **suya** está perdida.	***His** suitcase (i.e., not ours) is lost.*
Esa maleta **suya** está perdida.	*That suitcase of his is lost.*

The stressed possessives are often used as nouns. See **Appendix 2: Using Adjectives as Nouns.**

APPENDIX 4

Additional Perfect Forms (Indicative and Subjunctive)

As you know, some indicative verb tenses have corresponding perfect forms in the indicative and subjunctive moods. Here is the present tense system.

el presente:	yo hablo, como, pongo
el presente perfecto:	yo he hablado, comido, puesto
el presente perfecto de subjuntivo:	(que) yo haya hablado, comido, puesto

Other indicative forms that you have learned also have corresponding perfect indicative and subjunctive forms. Here are the most important ones, along with examples of their use. In each case, the tense or mood is formed with the appropriate form of **haber.**

El pluscuamperfecto de subjuntivo

yo:	hubiera hablado, comido, vivido, *and so on.*
tú:	hubieras hablado, comido, vivido, *and so on.*
Ud./él/ella:	hubiera hablado, comido, vivido, *and so on.*
nosotros:	hubiéramos hablado, comido, vivido, *and so on.*
vosotros:	hubierais hablado, comido, vivido, *and so on.*
Uds./ellos/ellas:	hubieran hablado, comido, vivido, *and so on.*

These forms correspond to **el pluscuamperfecto de indicativo (past perfect indicative) (Capítulo 15)**. The **pluscuamperfecto de subjuntivo** is most frequently used in **si** clause sentences, along with the conditional perfect. See examples in the second column.

El futuro perfecto

yo:	habré hablado, comido, vivido, *and so on.*
tú:	habrás hablado, comido, vivido, *and so on.*
Ud./él/ella:	habrá hablado, comido, vivido, *and so on.*
nosotros:	habremos hablado, comido, vivido, *and so on.*
vosotros:	habréis hablado, comido, vivido, *and so on.*
Uds./ellos/ellas:	habrán hablado, comido, vivido, *and so on.*

These forms correspond to **el futuro (Capítulo 17)** and are most frequently used to tell what *will have already happened* at some point in the future. (In contrast, the future is used to tell what *will happen*.)

Mañana **hablaré** con Miguel.
I'll speak with Miguel tomorrow.

Para las tres, ya **habré hablado** con Miguel.
By 3:00, I'll already have spoken with Miguel.

El año que viene **visitaremos** a los nietos.
We'll visit our grandchildren next year.

Para las Navidades, ya **habremos visitado** a los nietos.
We'll already have visited our grandchildren by Christmas.

El condicional perfecto

yo:	habría hablado, comido, vivido, *and so on.*
tú:	habrías hablado, comido, vivido, *and so on.*
Ud./él/ella:	habría hablado, comido, vivido, *and so on.*
nosotros:	habríamos hablado, comido, vivido, *and so on.*
vosotros:	habríais hablado, comido, vivido, *and so on.*
Uds./ellos/ellas:	habrían hablado, comido, vivido, *and so on.*

These forms correspond to **el condicional (Capítulo 18)**. These forms are frequently used to tell what *would have happened* at some point in the past. (In contrast, the conditional tells what one *would do*.)

Yo **hablaría** con Miguel.
I would speak with Miguel (if I were you, at some point in the future).

Yo **habría hablado** con Miguel.
I would have spoken with Miguel (if I had been you, at some point in the past).

Si Clause: Sentences About the Past

You have learned (**Capítulo 18**) to use the past subjunctive and conditional to speculate about the present in **si** clause sentences: what *would happen* if a particular event *were* (or *were not*) to occur.

Si **tuviera** el tiempo, **aprendería** francés.
If I had the time, I would learn French.

The perfect forms of the past subjunctive and the conditional are used to speculate about the past: what *would have happened* if a particular event *had* (or *had not*) occurred.

En la escuela superior, si **hubiera tenido** el tiempo, **habría aprendido** francés.
In high school, if I had had the time, I would have learned French.

A. Regular Verbs: Simple Tenses

Infinitive Present Participle Past Participle	INDICATIVE					SUBJUNCTIVE		IMPERATIVE
	Present	Imperfect	Preterite	Future	Conditional	Present	Imperfect	
hablar hablando hablado	hablo	hablaba	hablé	hablaré	hablaría	hable	hablara	
	hablas	hablabas	hablaste	hablarás	hablarías	hables	hablaras	habla tú, no hables
	habla	hablaba	habló	hablará	hablaría	hable	hablara	hable Ud.
	hablamos	hablábamos	hablamos	hablaremos	hablaríamos	hablemos	habláramos	hablemos
	habláis	hablabais	hablasteis	hablaréis	hablaríais	habléis	hablarais	hablad, no habléis
	hablan	hablaban	hablaron	hablarán	hablarían	hablen	hablaran	hablen
comer comiendo comido	como	comía	comí	comeré	comería	coma	comiera	
	comes	comías	comiste	comerás	comerías	comas	comieras	come tú, no comas
	come	comía	comió	comerá	comería	coma	comiera	coma Ud.
	comemos	comíamos	comimos	comeremos	comeríamos	comamos	comiéramos	comamos
	coméis	comíais	comisteis	comeréis	comeríais	comáis	comierais	comed, no comáis
	comen	comían	comieron	comerán	comerían	coman	comieran	coman
vivir viviendo vivido	vivo	vivía	viví	viviré	viviría	viva	viviera	
	vives	vivías	viviste	vivirás	vivirías	vivas	vivieras	vive tú, no vivas
	vive	vivía	vivió	vivirá	viviría	viva	viviera	viva Ud.
	vivimos	vivíamos	vivimos	viviremos	viviríamos	vivamos	viviéramos	vivamos
	vivís	vivíais	vivisteis	viviréis	viviríais	viváis	vivierais	vivid, no viváis
	viven	vivían	vivieron	vivirán	vivirían	vivan	vivieran	vivan

B. Regular Verbs: Perfect Tenses

INDICATIVE					SUBJUNCTIVE	
Present Perfect	Past Perfect	Preterite Perfect	Future Perfect	Conditional Perfect	Present Perfect	Past Perfect
he	había	hube	habré	habría	haya	hubiera
has	habías	hubiste	habrás	habrías	hayas	hubieras
ha hablado	había hablado	hubo hablado	habrá hablado	habría hablado	haya hablado	hubiera hablado
hemos comido	habíamos comido	hubimos comido	habremos comido	habríamos comido	hayamos comido	hubiéramos comido
habéis vivido	habíais vivido	hubisteis vivido	habréis vivido	habríais vivido	hayáis vivido	hubierais vivido
han	habían	hubieron	habrán	habrían	hayan	hubieran

C. Irregular Verbs

Infinitive / Present Participle / Past Participle	INDICATIVE					SUBJUNCTIVE		IMPERATIVE
	Present	Imperfect	Preterite	Future	Conditional	Present	Imperfect	
andar	ando	andaba	anduve	andaré	andaría	ande	anduviera	
andando	andas	andabas	anduviste	andarás	andarías	andes	anduvieras	anda tú, no andes
andado	anda	andaba	anduvo	andará	andaría	ande	anduviera	ande Ud.
	andamos	andábamos	anduvimos	andaremos	andaríamos	andemos	anduviéramos	andemos
	andáis	andabais	anduvisteis	andaréis	andaríais	andéis	anduvierais	andad, no andéis
	andan	andaban	anduvieron	andarán	andarían	anden	anduvieran	anden
caber	quepo	cabía	cupe	cabré	cabría	quepa	cupiera	cabe tú,
cabiendo	cabes	cabías	cupiste	cabrás	cabrías	quepas	cupieras	no quepas
cabido	cabe	cabía	cupo	cabrá	cabría	quepa	cupiera	quepa Ud.
	cabemos	cabíamos	cupimos	cabremos	cabríamos	quepamos	cupiéramos	quepamos
	cabéis	cabíais	cupisteis	cabréis	cabríais	quepáis	cupierais	cabed, no quepáis
	caben	cabían	cupieron	cabrán	cabrían	quepan	cupieran	quepan

Infinitive Present Participle Past Participle	INDICATIVE					SUBJUNCTIVE		IMPERATIVE
	Present	Imperfect	Preterite	Future	Conditional	Present	Imperfect	
caer cayendo caído	caigo caes cae caemos caéis caen	caía caías caía caíamos caíais caían	caí caíste cayó caímos caísteis cayeron	caeré caerás caerá caeremos caeréis caerán	caería caerías caería caeríamos caeríais caerían	caiga caigas caiga caigamos caigáis caigan	cayera cayeras cayera cayéramos cayerais cayeran	cae tú, no caigas caiga Ud. caigamos caed, no caigáis caigan
creer creyendo creído	creo crees cree creemos creéis creen	creía creías creía creíamos creíais creían	creí creíste creyó creímos creísteis creyeron	creeré creerás creerá creeremos creeréis creerán	creería creerías creería creeríamos creeríais creerían	crea creas crea creamos creáis crean	creyera creyeras creyera creyéramos creyerais creyeran	cree tú, no creas crea Ud. creamos creed, no creáis crean
dar dando dado	doy das da damos dais dan	daba dabas daba dábamos dabais daban	di diste dio dimos disteis dieron	daré darás dará daremos daréis darán	daría darías daría daríamos daríais darían	dé des dé demos deis den	diera dieras diera diéramos dierais dieran	da tú, no des dé Ud. demos dad, no deis den
decir diciendo dicho	digo dices dice decimos decís dicen	decía decías decía decíamos decíais decían	dije dijiste dijo dijimos dijisteis dijeron	diré dirás dirá diremos diréis dirán	diría dirías diría diríamos diríais dirían	diga digas diga digamos digáis digan	dijera dijeras dijera dijéramos dijerais dijeran	di tú, no digas diga Ud. digamos decid, no digáis digan

Infinitive Present Participle Past Participle	INDICATIVE					SUBJUNCTIVE		IMPERATIVE
	Present	Imperfect	Preterite	Future	Conditional	Present	Imperfect	
estar estando estado	estoy estás está estamos estáis están	estaba estabas estaba estábamos estabais estaban	estuve estuviste estuvo estuvimos estuvisteis estuvieron	estaré estarás estará estaremos estaréis estarán	estaría estarías estaría estaríamos estaríais estarían	esté estés esté estemos estéis estén	estuviera estuvieras estuviera estuviéramos estuvierais estuviera	está tú, no estés esté Ud. estemos estad, no estéis estén
haber habiendo habido	he has ha hemos habéis han	había habías había habíamos habíais habían	hube hubiste hubo hubimos hubisteis hubieron	habré habrás habrá habremos habréis habrán	habría habrías habría habríamos habríais habrían	haya hayas haya hayamos hayáis hayan	hubiera hubieras hubiera hubiéramos hubierais hubieran	
hacer haciendo hecho	hago haces hace hacemos hacéis hacen	hacía hacías hacía hacíamos hacíais hacían	hice hiciste hizo hicimos hicisteis hicieron	haré harás hará haremos haréis harán	haría harías haría haríamos haríais harían	haga hagas haga hagamos hagáis hagan	hiciera hicieras hiciera hiciéramos hicierais hicieran	haz tú, no hagas haga Ud. hagamos haced, no hagáis hagan
ir yendo ido	voy vas va vamos vais van	iba ibas iba íbamos ibais iban	fui fuiste fue fuimos fuisteis fueron	iré irás irá iremos iréis irán	iría irías iría iríamos iríais irían	vaya vayas vaya vayamos vayáis vayan	fuera fueras fuera fuéramos fuerais fueran	ve tú, no vayas vaya Ud. vayamos id, no vayáis vayan

C. Irregular Verbs (continued)

Infinitive Present Participle Past Participle	INDICATIVE Present	Imperfect	Preterite	Future	Conditional	SUBJUNCTIVE Present	Imperfect	IMPERATIVE
oír oyendo oído	oigo oyes oye oímos oís oyen	oía oías oía oíamos oíais oían	oí oíste oyó oímos oísteis oyeron	oiré oirás oirá oiremos oiréis oirán	oiría oirías oiría oiríamos oiríais oirían	oiga oigas oiga oigamos oigáis oigan	oyera oyeras oyera oyéramos oyerais oyeran	oye tú, no oigas oiga Ud. oigamos oíd, no oigáis oigan
poder pudiendo podido	puedo puedes puede podemos podéis pueden	podía podías podía podíamos podíais podían	pude pudiste pudo pudimos pudisteis pudieron	podré podrás podrá podremos podréis podrán	podría podrías podría podríamos podríais podrían	pueda puedas pueda podamos podáis puedan	pudiera pudieras pudiera pudiéramos pudierais pudieran	
poner poniendo puesto	pongo pones pone ponemos ponéis ponen	ponía ponías ponía poníamos poníais ponían	puse pusiste puso pusimos pusisteis pusieron	pondré pondrás pondrá pondremos pondréis pondrán	pondría pondrías pondría pondríamos pondríais pondrían	ponga pongas ponga pongamos pongáis pongan	pusiera pusieras pusiera pusiéramos pusierais pusieran	pon tú, no pongas ponga Ud. pongamos poned, no pongáis pongan
querer queriendo querido	quiero quieres quiere queremos queréis quieren	quería querías quería queríamos queríais querían	quise quisiste quiso quisimos quisisteis quisieron	querré querrás querrá querremos querréis querrán	querría querrías querría querríamos querríais querrían	quiera quieras quiera queramos queráis quieran	quisiera quisieras quisiera quisiéramos quisierais quisieran	quiere tú, no quieras quiera Ud. queramos quered, no queráis quieran

Infinitive Present Participle Past Participle	INDICATIVE					SUBJUNCTIVE		IMPERATIVE
	Present	Imperfect	Preterite	Future	Conditional	Present	Imperfect	
saber sabiendo sabido	sé sabes sabe sabemos sabéis saben	sabía sabías sabía sabíamos sabíais sabían	supe supiste supo supimos supisteis supieron	sabré sabrás sabrá sabremos sabréis sabrán	sabría sabrías sabría sabríamos sabríais sabrían	sepa sepas sepa sepamos sepáis sepan	supiera supieras supiera supiéramos supierais supieran	sabe tú, no sepas sepa Ud. sepamos sabed, no sepáis sepan
salir saliendo salido	salgo sales sale salimos salís salen	salía salías salía salíamos salíais salían	salí saliste salió salimos salisteis salieron	saldré saldrás saldrá saldremos saldréis saldrán	saldría saldrías saldría saldríamos saldríais saldrían	salga salgas salga salgamos salgáis salgan	saliera salieras saliera saliéramos salierais salieran	sal tú, no salgas salga Ud. salgamos salid, no salgáis salgan
ser siendo sido	soy eres es somos sois son	era eras era éramos erais eran	fui fuiste fue fuimos fuisteis fueron	seré serás será seremos seréis serán	sería serías sería seríamos seríais serían	sea seas sea seamos seáis sean	fuera fueras fuera fuéramos fuerais fueran	sé tú, no seas sea Ud. seamos sed, no seáis sean
tener teniendo tenido	tengo tienes tiene tenemos tenéis tienen	tenía tenías tenía teníamos teníais tenían	tuve tuviste tuvo tuvimos tuvisteis tuvieron	tendré tendrás tendrá tendremos tendréis tendrán	tendría tendrías tendría tendríamos tendríais tendrían	tenga tengas tenga tengamos tengáis tengan	tuviera tuvieras tuviera tuviéramos tuvierais tuvieran	ten tú, no tengas tenga Ud. tengamos tened, no tengáis tengan

C. Irregular Verbs (continued)

Infinitive Present Participle Past Participle	INDICATIVE						SUBJUNCTIVE		IMPERATIVE
	Present	Imperfect	Preterite	Future	Conditional		Present	Imperfect	
traer trayendo traído	traigo traes trae traemos traéis traen	traía traías traía traíamos traíais traían	traje trajiste trajo trajimos trajisteis trajeron	traeré traerás traerá traeremos traeréis traerán	traería traerías traería traeríamos traeríais traerían		traiga traigas traiga traigamos traigáis traigan	trajera trajeras trajera trajéramos trajerais trajeran	trae tú, no traigas traiga Ud. traigamos traed, no traigáis traigan
venir viniendo venido	vengo vienes viene venimos venís vienen	venía venías venía veníamos veníais venían	vine viniste vino vinimos vinisteis vinieron	vendré vendrás vendrá vendremos vendréis vendrán	vendría vendrías vendría vendríamos vendríais vendrían		venga vengas venga vengamos vengáis vengan	viniera vinieras viniera viniéramos vinierais vinieran	ven tú, no vengas venga Ud. vengamos venid, no vengáis vengan
ver viendo visto	veo ves ve vemos veis ven	veía veías veía veíamos veíais veían	vi viste vio vimos visteis vieron	veré verás verá veremos veréis verán	vería verías vería veríamos veríais verían		vea veas vea veamos veáis vean	viera vieras viera viéramos vierais vieran	ve tú, no veas vea Ud. veamos ved, no veáis vean

D. Stem-Changing and Spelling Change Verbs

Infinitive Present Participle Past Participle	INDICATIVE					SUBJUNCTIVE		IMPERATIVE
	Present	Imperfect	Preterite	Future	Conditional	Present	Imperfect	
pensar (pienso) pensando pensado	pienso piensas piensa pensamos pensáis piensan	pensaba pensabas pensaba pensábamos pensabais pensaban	pensé pensaste pensó pensamos pensasteis pensaron	pensaré pensarás pensará pensaremos pensaréis pensarán	pensaría pensarías pensaría pensaríamos pensaríais pensarían	piense pienses piense pensemos penséis piensen	pensara pensaras pensara pensáramos pensarais pensaran	piensa tú, no pienses piense Ud. pensemos pensad, no penséis piensen
volver (vuelvo) volviendo vuelto	vuelvo vuelves vuelve volvemos volvéis vuelven	volvía volvías volvía volvíamos volvíais volvían	volví volviste volvió volvimos volvisteis volvieron	volveré volverás volverá volveremos volveréis volverán	volvería volverías volvería volveríamos volveríais volverían	vuelva vuelvas vuelva volvamos volváis vuelvan	volviera volvieras volviera volviéramos volvierais volvieran	vuelve tú, no vuelvas vuelva Ud. volvamos volved, no volváis vuelvan
dormir (duermo) (u) durmiendo dormido	duermo duermes duerme dormimos dormís duermen	dormía dormías dormía dormíamos dormíais dormían	dormí dormiste durmió dormimos dormisteis durmieron	dormiré dormirás dormirá dormiremos dormiréis dormirán	dormiría dormirías dormiría dormiríamos dormiríais dormirían	duerma duermas duerma durmamos durmáis duerman	durmiera durmieras durmiera durmiéramos durmierais durmieran	duerme tú, no duermas duerma Ud. durmamos dormid, no durmáis duerman
sentir (siento) (i) sintiendo sentido	siento sientes siente sentimos sentís sienten	sentía sentías sentía sentíamos sentíais sentían	sentí sentiste sintió sentimos sentisteis sintieron	sentiré sentirás sentirá sentiremos sentiréis sentirán	sentiría sentirías sentiría sentiríamos sentiríais sentirían	sienta sientas sienta sintamos sintáis sientan	sintiera sintieras sintiera sintiéramos sintierais sintieran	siente tú, no sientas sienta Ud. sintamos sentid, no sintáis sientan
pedir (pido) (i) pidiendo pedido	pido pides pide pedimos pedís piden	pedía pedías pedía pedíamos pedíais pedían	pedí pediste pidió pedimos pedisteis pidieron	pediré pedirás pedirá pediremos pediréis pedirán	pediría pedirías pediría pediríamos pediríais pedirían	pida pidas pida pidamos pidáis pidan	pidiera pidieras pidiera pidiéramos pidierais pidieran	pide tú, no pidas pida Ud. pidamos pedid, no pidáis pidan

D. Stem-Changing and Spelling Change Verbs (continued)

Infinitive / Present Participle / Past Participle	INDICATIVE					SUBJUNCTIVE		IMPERATIVE
	Present	Imperfect	Preterite	Future	Conditional	Present	Imperfect	
reír (río) (i) riendo reído	río	reía	reí	reiré	reiría	ría	riera	ríe tú, no rías
	ríes	reías	reíste	reirás	reirías	rías	rieras	ría Ud.
	ríe	reía	rio	reirá	reiría	ría	riera	riamos
	reímos	reíamos	reímos	reiremos	reiríamos	riamos	riéramos	reíd, no riáis
	reís	reíais	reísteis	reiréis	reiríais	riáis	rierais	rían
	ríen	reían	rieron	reirán	reirían	rían	rieran	
seguir (sigo) (i) siguiendo seguido	sigo	seguía	seguí	seguiré	seguiría	siga	siguiera	sigue tú, no sigas
	sigues	seguías	seguiste	seguirás	seguirías	sigas	siguieras	siga Ud.
	sigue	seguía	siguió	seguirá	seguiría	siga	siguiera	sigamos
	seguimos	seguíamos	seguimos	seguiremos	seguiríamos	sigamos	siguiéramos	seguid, no sigáis
	seguís	seguíais	seguisteis	seguiréis	seguiríais	sigáis	siguierais	sigan
	siguen	seguían	siguieron	seguirán	seguirían	sigan	siguieran	
construir (construyo) construyendo construido	construyo	construía	construí	construiré	construiría	construya	construyera	construye tú, no construyas
	construyes	construías	construiste	construirás	construirías	construyas	construyeras	construya Ud.
	construye	construía	construyó	construirá	construiría	construya	construyera	construyamos
	construimos	construíamos	construimos	construiremos	construiríamos	construyamos	construyéramos	construid, no construyáis
	construís	construíais	construisteis	construiréis	construiríais	construyáis	construyerais	construyan
	construyen	construían	construyeron	construirán	construirían	construyan	construyeran	
conducir (conduzco) conduciendo conducido	conduzco	conducía	conduje	conduciré	conduciría	conduzca	condujera	conduce tú, no conduzcas
	conduces	conducías	condujiste	conducirás	conducirías	conduzcas	condujeras	conduzca Ud.
	conduce	conducía	condujo	conducirá	conduciría	conduzca	condujera	conduzcamos
	conducimos	conducíamos	condujimos	conduciremos	conduciríamos	conduzcamos	condujéramos	conducid, no conduzcáis
	conducís	conducíais	condujisteis	conduciréis	conduciríais	conduzcáis	condujerais	conduzcan
	conducen	conducían	condujeron	conducirán	conducirían	conduzcan	condujeran	

VOCABULARIES

This **Spanish-English Vocabulary** contains all the words that appear in the text, with the following exceptions: (1) most close or identical cognates that do not appear in the chapter vocabulary lists; (2) most conjugated verb forms; (3) diminutives ending in **-ito/a;** (4) absolute superlatives in **-ísimo/a;** (5) most adverbs ending in **-mente,** and (6) words listed or glossed in the **Vocabulario del segmento** and **Fragmento del guion** features of the **Salu2** sections. Active vocabulary is indicated by the number of the chapter in which a word or given meaning is first listed (**1** = **Capítulo 1**); vocabulary that is glossed in the text is not considered to be active vocabulary and is not numbered. Only meanings that are used in the text are given. The **English-Spanish Vocabulary** is based on the chapter lists of active vocabulary.

The gender of nouns is indicated, except for masculine nouns ending in **-o** and feminine nouns ending in **-a.** Because **ch** and **ll** are no longer considered separate letters, words beginning with **ch** and **ll** are found as they would be found in English. The letter **ñ** follows the letter **n: añadir** follows **anuncio,** for example.

Irregular verbs found in the verb charts of Appendix 5 are set all in color: andar. No changes are indicated for them in these vocabularies. Verbs with stem changes or spelling changes in the *present tense* show the **yo** form of the present tense in parentheses with the stem-vowel or spelling changes indicated in color: **sentarse (me siento); conocer (conozco); escoger (escojo); actuar (actúo).** Verbs with stem changes in the third person *preterite* and the *present participle* show the stem vowel (**i** or **u**) in parentheses after the present tense **yo** form: **preferir (prefiero) (i); morirse (me muero) (u).** Verbs with any other spelling changes in the first person *preterite* or *present subjunctive* show the change in parentheses: **buscar (qu); pagar (gu); empezar (empiezo) (c); averiguar (ü).**

The following abbreviations are used:

adj.	adjective	*inv.*	invariable form
adv.	adverb	*L.A.*	Latin America
Arg.	Argentina	*m.*	masculine
C.A.	Central America	*Mex.*	Mexico
Carib.	Caribbean	*n.*	noun
Col.	Colombia	*obj. (of prep.)*	object (of a preposition)
conj.	conjunction	*pl.*	plural
def. art.	definite article	*poss.*	possessive
d.o.	direct object	*p.p.*	past participle
f.	feminine	*prep.*	preposition
fam.	familiar	*pron.*	pronoun
form.	formal	*refl. pron.*	reflexive pronoun
gram.	grammatical term	*s.*	singular
Guat.	Guatemala	*sl.*	slang
ind. art.	indefinite article	*Sp.*	Spain
inf.	infinitive	*sub. pron.*	subject pronoun
i.o.	indirect object		
interj.	interjection		

Spanish-English Vocabulary

A

a to; at (*with time*) (1); **a base de** based on; **a causa de** because of; **a continuación** following; **a este respecto** in this regard; **a la derecha de** to the right of (6); **a la izquierda de** to the left of (6); **a la moda** in fashion, in a stylish way; **a la(s)...** at . . . (*time of day*) (1); **a menos que** unless (16); **a partir de** beyond (4); **a pesar de** in spite of; **a plazos** in installments (17); **¿a qué hora... ?** at what time . . . ? (1); **a solas** alone; **a tiempo** on time (8); **a través de** across, through; throughout; **¿a usted le gusta... ?** do you (*form. s.*) like . . . ? (1); **a veces** sometimes, at times (3); **a ver** let's see
abacería grocery store
abajo below; underneath
abandonar to abandon
abarcar (qu) to cover (*a topic*)
abarrotes *m. pl.* groceries
abecedario alphabet
abierto/a (*p.p. of* **abrir**) open (6)
abogado/a lawyer (17)
abogar (gu) to advocate
abolengo lineage
abolicionista *m., f.* abolitionist
aborto abortion
abrazar(se) (c) to embrace (11)
abrazo hug, embrace
abreviatura abbreviation
abrigo coat (4)
abril *m.* April (6)
abrir (*pp.* **abierto**) to open (3)
abrumador(a) overwhelming
absoluto/a absolute
abstenerse (*like* **tener**) to refrain
absurdo/a absurd; **es absurdo que** it's absurd that (13)
abuelo/a grandfather/grandmother (3); *m. pl.* grandparents (3)
abundante abundant
aburrido/a bored (6); **ser aburrido/a** to be boring (10)
aburrimiento boredom
aburrir (*like* **gustar**) to bore (13); **aburrirse** to get bored (10)
abuso abuse
abyecto/a wretched
acá here
acabar to finish (14); to run out of (14); **acabar de** + *inf.* to have just (*done something*) (7)
academia academy
académico/a *adj.* academic (14); **año académico** school year; **vida académica** academic life (14)

acampar to camp; **tienda de acampar** tent
acaso: por si acaso just in case (14)
acatar to obey
acceso access
accesorio accessory
accidente *m.* accident (14)
acción *f.* action; **Día** (*m.*) **de Acción de Gracias** Thanksgiving
aceite (*m.*) **(de oliva)** (olive) oil (7)
acelerado/a fast, accelerated (15)
acelerar to accelerate; to speed up
acento accent; **acento diacrítico** diacritical mark; **acento ortográfico** accent mark
acentuación *f.* accent mark
acentuado/a accentuated
aceptable acceptable
aceptar to accept
acera sidewalk (15)
acerca de *prep.* about, concerning, regarding
acercarse (qu) (a) to come near to
acertar (acierto) to guess correctly
ácido acid
acompañar to accompany
acondicionado/a: aire (*m.*) **acondicionado** air conditioning
aconsejable advisable
aconsejar to advise
acontecer to occur
acontecimiento event, happening (18)
acordarse (me acuerdo) (de) to remember (13)
acordeón *m.* accordion
acoso harassment, bullying
acostarse (me acuesto) to go to bed (5)
acostumbrarse (a) to become accustomed (to); to get used (to)
acribillar to bombard
acrílico/a acrylic
actitud *f.* attitude
actividad *f.* activity
activo/a active
acto act
actor *m.* actor (13)
actriz *f.* (*pl.* **actrices**) actress (13)
actuación *f.* performance
actual *adj.* current, present-day (12)
actualidad: de/en la actualidad currently, right now (10)
actualizar(c) to update
actuar (actúo) to act (13)
acuario aquarium; **Acuario** Aquarius
acuático/a aquatic
acudir (a) to go (to)
acueducto aqueduct

acuerdo agreement; **(no) estar de acuerdo** to (dis)agree (3)
acumular to accumulate
acusón, acusona tattler
adaptación *f.* adaptation
adaptarse (a) to adapt (to)
adecuado/a appropriate
adelante forward
adelgazar (c) to lose weight
además *adv.* moreover; **además de** *prep.* besides
adentro inside
adicción *f.* addiction
adicional additional (1)
adiós good-bye (1)
adivinar to guess (9)
adjetivo *gram.* adjective (3); **adjetivo de nacionalidad** adjective of nationality (3); **adjetivo posesivo** possessive adjective (3)
administración *f.* administration; **administración de empresas** business administration (2)
administrar to administer; to manage; to run
admiración *f.* admiration
admirar to admire
admitir to admit
adolescencia adolescence (16)
adolescente *m., f.* adolescent, teenager; **de adolescente** as an adolescent (10)
¿adónde? where (to)? (4)
adoptar to adopt
adoquinado/a cobblestoned
adorar to adore
adquirir to acquire
adquisitivo/a: poder (*m.*) **adquisitivo** purchasing power
aduana customs (*at a border*) (8); **pasar por la aduana** to go/pass through customs (8)
adulto/a adult
adverbio *gram.* adverb
adverso/a adverse
advertencia warning
adyacente adjacent
aéreo/a aerial
aeróbico/a: hacer ejercicios aeróbicos to do aerobics (11)
aerolínea airline
aeropuerto airport (8)
afán *m.* effort
afanoso/a laborious, hard
afectación *f.* affectation
afectar to affect
afectivo/a: estado afectivo emotional state (9)
afecto affection

afeitarse to shave (5)
afición f. hobby (10)
aficionado/a fan; **ser aficionado/a (a)** to be a fan (of) (10)
afiliación f. affiliation
afiliado/a (a) affiliated (with)
afín related
afinidad f. compatibility
afirmación f. statement
afirmar to affirm
afirmativo/a affirmative
afluente affluent
afortunado/a fortunate, lucky
africano/a n., adj. African
afroamerindo/a n., adj. Afro-Amerindian
afroantillano/a Afro-Antillian
afroperuano/a Afro-Peruvian
afuera adv. outdoors (6)
afueras f. pl. outskirts (12); suburbs (12)
agencia agency; **agencia de compra-venta (de coches)** used car dealership; **agencia de viajes** travel agency
agenda agenda; date book
agente m., f. agent (8); **agente de viajes** travel agent
ágil agile
agitar to agitate
agnóstico/a agnostic
agobiado/a overwhelmed
agosto August (6)
agotar to empty; to drain
agradable agreeable, pleasant
agradar (like **gustar**) to please
agradecimiento n. thanks
agregar (gu) to add
agresivo/a aggressive
agrícola adj. m., f. agricultural
agricultor(a) farmer (15)
agricultura farming, agriculture (15)
agrio/a bitter
agroturismo agritourism
agroturista m., f. agritourist
agroturístico/a adj. of rural tourism
agrupar to group
agua f. (but **el agua**) **(mineral)** (mineral) water (7)
aguacate m. avocado (7)
aguar (ü) to dilute; water down
agudo/a sharp
águila f. (but **el águila**) eagle
agujero hole
ahí there
ahijado/a godson/goddaughter
ahora now (2); **ahora mismo** right now (6)
ahorrar to save (money) (17)
ahorro savings
ahorros: cuenta de ahorros savings account

aimara n. Aymara
airado/a angry; annoyed
aire m. air (15); **aire acondicionado** air conditioning; **al aire libre** outdoors (10)
ajedrez m. chess; **jugar (juego) (gu) al ajedrez** to play chess (10)
ajo garlic
al (contraction of **a** + **el**) to the (4); **al** + inf. while (doing something); **al aire** (m.) **libre** outdoors (10); **al alcance** within reach; **al instante** right away; **al lado de** alongside of (6); **al menos** at least; **al principio de** at the beginning of (17)
alameda tree-lined avenue
alberca swimming pool (Mex.)
álbum m. album
alcance: al alcance within reach
alcanzar (c) to reach; to achieve
alce m. elk; moose
alcoba bedroom (5)
alcohol m. alcohol
alcohólico/a alcoholic; **bebida alcohólica** alcoholic beverage
alegrarse (de) to be happy (about) (12)
alegre happy (6)
alemán m. German (language) (2)
alemán, alemana n., adj. German (3)
Alemania Germany
alergia allergy
alérgico/a allergic
alerta: ojo alerta eagle eye
alfabeto alphabet
alfombra rug (5)
algo something; anything (7)
algodón m. cotton (4); **de algodón** adj. (made of) cotton (4)
alguien someone, anyone (7)
algún (alguna/os/as) some, any (7); **alguna vez** once; ever
alimentación f. diet
alimenticio/a of eating
alimento food
aliviar to alleviate
allá (way) over there (4)
allí there (4)
alma m. soul
almacén m. department store (4)
almacenamiento: espacio de almacenamiento storage space (12)
almacenar to store; to save (12)
almohada pillow
almorzar (almuerzo) (c) to have lunch (5)
almuerzo lunch (7)
¿aló? hello? (telephone greeting)
alojarse to lodge
alpinismo mountain climbing; **practicar (qu) el alpinismo** to mountain climb

alquilar v. to rent (12)
alquiler m. rent (12)
alrededor (de) around
alternar to take turns
alternativa n. alternative
alternativo/a adj. alternative
altiplanicie f. high plateau
altiplano high plateau
altitud f. height; altitude
alto/a tall (3); **de alta costura** high fashion; **de alto riesgo** high risk
altura altitude
alucinante incredible
alumno/a student
aluvial alluvial
amabilidad f. kindness
amable kind; nice (3)
amanecer m. dawn
amar to love (16)
amarillo/a yellow (4)
amasijo dough; mixture
Amazonas m. s. Amazon (River)
amazónico/a adj. Amazonian; **Selva Amazónica** Amazon Jungle
ambiental environmental
ambiente m. atmosphere; environment; **medio ambiente** environment (15)
ambigüedad f. ambiguity
ámbito area
ambos/as both
ambulante adj. traveling
América: América Latina Latin America; **Estados** (m. pl.) **Unidos de América** United States of America
americano/a American; **fútbol** (m.) **americano** football
amerindo/a n., adj. Amerindian
amigo/a friend (2)
amistad f. friendship (16)
amistoso/a friendly (16)
amo/a (but **el ama**) **de casa** housekeeper (17)
amoníaco ammonia
amor m. love (16)
amoroso/a loving
ampliar (amplío) to widen
amplio/a wide; large; spacious
amueblado/a furnished
amueblar to furnish
amuleto charm; amulet
amurallado/a walled
analfabetismo n. illiteracy
analfabeto/a illiterate
análisis m. inv. analysis
analista m., f. analyst; **analista de sistemas** systems analyst (17)
analizar (c) to analyze
ananá m. pineapple
anaranjado/a orange (4)
ancho/a wide

anciano/a *n.* old person; *adj.* old; ancient; **residencia de ancianos** nursing home (12)

Andalucía Andalusia

andaluz(a) *n., adj.* Andalusian

andante: caballero andante knight-errant

andar to walk; **andar en bicicleta** to ride a bicycle; **cinta de andar** treadmill

andino/a Andean

anécdota anecdote

anémico/a anemic

anfibio amphibian

anfitrión, anfitriona host (*of an event*) (9)

ángel *m.* angel

angelino/a *adj.* from Los Angeles; *n.* person from Los Angeles

angloparlante *adj.* English-speaking

anglosajón, anglosajona Anglo Saxon

angosto/a narrow

ángulo angle

angustia anguish

anillo ring

ánima *f.* (*but* **el ánima**) soul

animado/a lively; animated; **dibujos** (*m. pl.*) **animados** cartoons

animal *m.* animal (15); **animal de peluche** (*m.*) stuffed animal; **animal doméstico** pet

animar(se) to cheer up; **animarse a** to get up the courage to (*do something*)

ánimo: estado de ánimo state of mind

aniversario anniversary

anoche *adv.* last night (11)

anónimo/a anonymous

ansiedad *f.* anxiety (14)

ansioso/a anxious

antártico/a *adj.* Antarctic

Antártida Antarctica

ante *prep.* before; in front of

anteayer *adv.* the day before yesterday (5)

antecedente *m. gram.* antecedent

anteojos *m. pl.* glasses (11)

antepenúltimo/a third from the end

anterior previous, preceding

antes *adv.* before; **antes de** *prep.* before (5); **antes de Cristo (a.C.)** before Christ (B.C.); **antes (de) que** *conj.* before (16)

antibiótico antibiotic (11)

anticipar to anticipate

anticipo advance

anticuado/a antiquated

antídoto antidote

antiguo/a old; ancient; former

antillano/a *adj.* of/from the Antilles

Antillas (*f. pl.*) **Mayores** Greater Antilles

antipático/a unpleasant (3)

antónimo antonym

antropología anthropology

antropólogo/a anthropologist

anual annual

anualmente annually

anunciar to announce (8)

anuncio announcement; advertisement

añadir to add

año year (6); **año académico** school year; **año bisiesto** leap year; **el año entrante** next year; **Año Nuevo** New Year; **año pasado** last year; **el año que viene** next year; **cumplir años** to have a birthday (9); **este año** this year; **fin** (*m.*) **de año** end of the year (9); tener... **años** to be . . . years old (3)

apagar (gu) to turn off (12)

apagón *m.* blackout

aparato appliance; **aparato doméstico** home appliance (10)

aparcamiento parking place; parking lot

aparcar (qu) to park

aparecer (aparezco) to appear

apariencia appearance

apartamento apartment (2)

aparte also

apellido surname

apenas barely

aperitivo appetizer

apetecer (apetezco) (*like* **gustar**) to appeal to

apetito appetite

apio celery

aplicación *f.* application

aplicar (qu) to apply

aportar to contribute

apóstol *m., f.* apostle

apoyar to support

apoyo support; help

app *f.* app(lication) (12)

apreciar to appreciate

aprender to learn (3); **aprender a + *inf.*** to learn how to (*do something*) (3)

aprendizaje *m.* learning

apropiado/a appropriate

aproximadamente approximately

aproximado/a approximate

aptitud *f.* aptitude

apuntar to write down; **apuntarse** to enroll; to add one's name to the list

apuntes *m. pl.* notes (*academic*) (14)

aquel, aquella *adj.* that ([way] over there) (4); *pron.* that one ([way] over there)

aquello (*neuter pron.*) that ([way] over there) (4)

aquellos/as *adj.* those [way] over there) (4) *pron.* those ones ([way] over there)

aquí here (2)

árabe *m.* Arabic (*language*); *n., adj. m., f.* Arab

Arabia Saudita Saudi Arabia

arábico/a *adj.* Arabic

arado *n.* plow

araña spider

árbol *m.* tree (9); **árbol genealógico** family tree

arcángel *m.* archangel

archipiélago archipelago

archivo (computer) file (12)

arco arch

ardilla squirrel

área *f.* (*but* **el área**) area, region

arena sand

arepa *patty made of cornmeal and flour and stuffed with different foods*

aretes *m. pl.* earrings (4)

argentino/a *n., adj.* Argentine

argumento argument; plot

árido/a arid, dry

aristocrático/a aristocratic

arma weapon

armado/a: fuerzas armadas armed forces

armar un bochinche to throw a (loud) party

armario armoire, free-standing closet (5)

armonía harmony

arpa *f.* (*but* **el arpa**) harp

arqueológico/a archaeological

arquitecto/a architect (13)

arquitectónico/a architectural

arquitectura architecture (13)

arraigado/a deeply rooted

arrancar (qu) to start up (*a car*) (15)

arreglar to fix; to repair (15)

arrepentido/a sorry; repentant

arriba (de) *prep.* above

arroba @ (12)

arrodillarse to kneel

arrogancia arrogance

arrogante arrogant

arroz *m.* (*pl.* **arroces**) rice (7)

arruinar to ruin

arte *m.* art (2); **artes** *f. pl.* the arts (13); **bellas artes** fine arts; **obra de arte** work of art (13)

arteria artery

arterial: presión (*f.*) **arterial** blood pressure

artesanía arts and crafts (13)

artesano/a artisan

Ártico *adj.* Arctic

artículo article; **artículo (in)definido** *gram.* (in)definite article

artista *m., f.* artist (13)

artístico/a artistic (13); **expresión** (*f.*) **artística** artistic expression (13)

arvejas *f. pl.* green peas (7)

asado/a roast(ed) (7); **lechón** (*m.*) **asado** roast suckling pig; **pollo asado** roast chicken (7)

asaltar to rob

asamblea assembly

ascendencia ancestry, descent

ascensor *m.* elevator (12)

asco: ¡qué asco! yuck!

asegurar to assure; **asegurarse (de que)** to make certain (that)

asentamiento settlement

asentarse (me asiento) to settle

asesinar to assassinate (18)

asesinato assassination; murder (18)

asesino *m., f.* murderer

así thus; so; **así como** as well as; **así que** therefore, consequently, so

asiático/a *adj.* Asian

asiento seat (8)

asignar to assign

asimismo additionally

asistencia sanitaria health care

asistente (*m., f.*) **de vuelo** flight attendant (8)

asistir (a) to attend; to go to (*a class, function*) (3)

asma *m.* asthma

asociación *f.* association

asociado/a associated; **estado libre asociado** commonwealth

asociar to associate

aspecto aspect

aspiradora vacuum cleaner (10); **pasar la aspiradora** to vacuum (10)

aspirante *m., f.* candidate; applicant (17)

aspirar to vacuum

aspirina aspirin

astronauta *m., f.* astronaut (17)

asumir to assume

asunto matter

asustar to scare

atacar (qu) to attack

ataque (*m.*) **(terrorista)** (terrorist) attack (18)

atar to tie

Atenas Athens

atención *f.* attention; **poner atención** to pay attention

atender (atiendo) to look after

atenerse (like tener) to accept

ateo/a atheist

ático attic

Atlántico Atlantic

atleta *m., f.* athlete

atmosférico/a atmospheric

átomo atom

atracción *f.* attraction

atractivo/a attractive

atraer (*like* **traer**) (*like* **gustar**) to draw; to attract (13)

atrás *adv.* back, backward; behind; **de atrás** backwards

atrasado/a (*with* **estar**) late (8)

atravesar (atravieso) to go through

atributo attribute

atún *m.* tuna (7)

audaz (*pl.* **audaces**) bold, daring

audiencia audience

auditivo/a aural

aula *f.* (*but* **el aula**) classroom

aumentar to increase

aumento raise

aun *adv.* even

aún *adv.* still, yet

aunque although

auriculares *m. pl.* headphones

auscultar to listen (*with a stethoscope*)

ausencia absence

ausente absent

austeridad *f.* austerity

australiano/a *n., adj.* Australian

auténtico/a authentic

auto auto (15)

autobiográfico/a autobiographical

autobús *m.* bus (8); **estación** (*f.*) **de autobuses** bus station (8); **ir en autobús** to go/travel by bus (8); **parada del autobús** bus stop (12)

autóctono/a indigenous

autoestima self-esteem

automático/a automatic; **cajero automático** automatic teller machine (ATM) (17)

automóvil *m.* automobile

automovilístico/a *adj.* automobile (15)

automutilación *f.* self-mutilation

autonomía autonomy; region

autónomo/a autonomous

autopista freeway; interstate (15)

autoprueba self-test

autor(a) author (13)

autoridad *f.* authority

autorizado/a authorized

autorretrato self-portrait

autostop: hacer autostop to hitchhike

autosuficiencia self-sufficiency

autosuficiente self-sufficient

auxiliar to help; to assist

avance *m.* preview

avanzado/a advanced

ave *f.* (*but* **el ave**) bird

avenida avenue (12)

aventura adventure

aventurero/a adventurous

aventurismo adventure tourism

aventurista *m., f.* adventure tourist

avergonzado/a embarrassed (9)

avión *m.* airplane (8); **ir en avión** to go/travel by plane (8); **volar (vuelo) en avión** to fly; to go by plane (8)

avisar to warn

aviso warning

¡ay! *interj.* ah!; ouch!

ayer yesterday; **ayer fue (miércoles...)** yesterday was (Wednesday . . .) (5)

ayuda help (7)

ayudante *m., f.* assistant

ayudar to help (7); **ayudar a** + *inf.* to help to (*do something*) (7)

ayuntamiento local government

azteca *n., adj. m., f.* Aztec

azúcar *m.* sugar (7)

azul blue (4)

azulejo tile

B

baba saliva; **se le cae la baba por** he/she is drooling over

bacán: ¡qué bacán! fantastic!

bahía bay

bailable danceable

bailaor(a) flamenco dancer

bailar to dance (2)

bailarín, bailarina dancer (13)

baile *m.* dance (13)

bajada ebb; dip

bajar to lower; to download (12); **bajarse (de)** to get down (from) (8); to get off (of) (*a vehicle*) (8)

bajareque *n.* mud wall

bajo *prep.* under; **estar bajo muchas presiones** to be under a lot of pressure (14)

bajo/a short (*in height*) (3); low

balcón *m.* balcony

ballena whale (15)

ballet *m.* ballet (13)

baloncesto basketball

banana banana (7)

banano banana tree

bancario/a: tarjeta bancaria debit card (17)

banco bank (17)

banda band

bandeja tray

bandera flag

bandoneón *m.* large concertina

bañarse to take a bath (5)

bañera bathtub (5)

baño bathroom (5); **traje** (*m.*) **de baño** swimsuit (4)

bar *m.* bar; **ir a un bar** to go to a bar (10)

barato/a inexpensive (4)

barba beard

barbacoa barbecue (7)

barcelonés, barcelonesa of Barcelona (*Sp.*)

barco boat, ship (8); **ir en barco** to go/ travel by boat, ship (8)

barra bar

barrer (el piso) to sweep (the floor) (10)

barriga belly

barrio neighborhood (12)

barro mud

basarse en to base one's ideas/ opinions on

base *f.* base; **a base de** based on; **base de datos** data base; **con base en** based on

básico/a basic

basquetbol *m.* basketball (10)

bastante rather, sufficiently; enough (16)

bastar to be enough

basura trash (10); **sacar (qu) la basura** to take out the trash (10)

bata robe

batalla battle

batería drum set (15)

bautizo baptism

bebé *m., f.* baby

beber to drink (3)

bebida drink (5); **bebida alcohólica** alcoholic beverage

beca scholarship

béisbol *m.* baseball (10)

beisbolista *m., f.* baseball player

Bélgica Belgium

belleza beauty

bello/a beautiful (15); **bellas artes** (*f. pl.*) fine arts

bendecir (*like* **decir**) to bless; **que Dios te bendiga** God bless you

bendito/a blessed

beneficio benefit

besar to kiss; **besarse** to kiss each other (11)

beso kiss

bestia beast

Biblia Bible

biblioteca library (2)

bibliotecario/a librarian (2)

bicentenario bicentennial

bicho insect

bici *f.* bike

bicicleta bicycle; **andar en bicicleta** to ride a bicycle; **pasear en bicicleta** to ride a bicycle (10)

bien *adv.* well (1); **caerle bien a alguien** to make a good impression on someone; **empleo bien pagado** well-paid job/position (17); **está bien** it's fine, OK (6); **estar bien** to be well; to be comfortable (*temperature*) (6); **llevarse bien (con)** to get along well (with) (16); **muy bien** fine, very well (1);

pasarlo bien to have a good time (9); **portarse bien** to behave (9); **salir bien** to come/turn out well (5); to do well (5)

bienes raíces *m. pl.* real estate

bienestar *m.* well-being (11)

bienvenida *n.* welcome

bienvenido/a *adj.* welcome

bife *m.* beef

bilingüe bilingual

billete *m.* bill (*money*) (17); ticket (*Sp.*) (8); **billete de ida** one-way ticket (8); **billete de ida y vuelta** round-trip ticket (8); **billete electrónico** e-ticket (8)

binacional binational

biodiversidad *f.* biodiversity

biografía biography

biología biology

bioluminiscencia bioluminescence

bioquímica biochemistry

bisabuelo/a great-grandfather/ great-grandmother

bisiesto/a: año bisiesto leap year

bisonte *m.* bison

bistec *m.* steak (7)

blanco/a white (4); **pizarrón** (*m.*) **blanco** whiteboard (2); **vino blanco** white wine (7)

blando/a soft

blog *m.* blog (12)

bloqueador (*m.*) **solar** sunscreen (8)

bloqueo de llamadas call blocker

bluejeans *m. pl.* jeans

blusa blouse (4)

boca mouth (11)

bocadillo sandwich (*Sp.*)

bochinche: armar un bochinche to throw a (loud) party

bocina horn (*car*) (15)

boda wedding (*ceremony*) (16)

bodega grocery store (*Carib.*)

bogotano/a *adj.* from Bogotá, Colombia

bola ball

bolero love song

boleto ticket (*L.A.*) (8); **boleto de ida** one-way ticket (8); **boleto de ida y vuelta** round-trip ticket; **boleto electrónico** e-ticket (8)

bolígrafo pen (2)

bolívar *m. Venezuelan currency unit*

boliviano/a *n., adj.* Bolivian

bolso purse (4)

bomba bomb (18)

bombardeo bombing

bombero/a firefighter

bombilla light bulb

bombo legüero Argentine drum

bonanza boom (*economic*)

bongó bongo

bonito/a pretty (3)

boricua *n., adj.* Puerto Rican

Borinquen *indigenous name of Puerto Rico*

borinqueño/a *adj.* Puerto Rican

borrador *m.* draft

borrasca storm

bosque *m.* forest (15); **bosque tropical lluvioso** tropical rain forest

bostezo yawn

botanas *f. pl.* (*Mex.*) appetizers (9)

botanía botany

botánico/a botanical

botar to throw out

botas *f. pl.* boots (4)

botella bottle

botón *m.* button

boxeador(a) boxer

brasileño/a *n., adj.* Brazilian

brazo arm (11)

brecha gap; **brecha digital** digital gap; **brecha salarial** wage gap

Bretaña: Gran Bretaña Great Britain

breve brief

británico/a British

bronce *m.* bronze

broncear to tan

bruja witch

brujo wizard; warlock

bruto/a: producto nacional bruto gross national product

bucear to scuba dive; to snorkel

budismo Buddhism

budista *n., adj. m., f.* Buddhist

buen, bueno/a good (3); **¡buen provecho!** enjoy your meal! **buenas noches** good night (1); **buenas tardes** good afternoon (1); **buenos días** good morning (1); **lo bueno** the good news/thing (11); **muy buenas** good afternoon/evening (1); **tener buena suerte** to have good luck; to be lucky (14)

buey *sl.* dude (*Mex.*)

bufanda scarf

burlarse de to make fun of

buscar (qu) to look for (2); **buscar en internet** to look for on the internet (12)

búsqueda search

buzón (*m.*) **de voz** voice mailbox (12)

C

caballero knight; **caballero andante** knight-errant

caballo horse (10); **montar a caballo** to ride a horse (10)

caber to fit (*into an area*)

cabeza head (11); **dolor** (*m.*) **de cabeza** headache

cabina cabin (*on a ship*) (8)

cacerola casserole dish

cacique, cacica chief

cada *inv.* each, every (5); **cada vez más** increasingly; **cada vez mayor** greater and greater

cadena chain

caer to fall; to drop (14); **caer en** to fall on (*day of the week*); **caerle bien/ mal a alguien** to make a good/bad impression on someone; **caerse** to fall down (14); **se le cae la baba por** he/she is drooling over

café *m.* coffee (2)

cafeína caffeine

cafetal *m.* coffee plantation

cafetera coffeemaker (10)

cafetería cafeteria (2)

cafetero coffee plantation worker

caída fall (*from a height*)

caimán *m.* alligator

caja box

cajero/a cashier; teller (17); **cajero automático** automatic teller machine (ATM) (17)

cajón *m.* drawer

calabaza pumpkin; squash

calabozo prison cell

calamar *m.* squid

calcetines *m. pl.* socks (4)

calculadora calculator (2)

calcular to calculate

cálculo calculus

calefacción *f.* heating (12)

calendario calendar (14)

calentador(a) *adj.* warming

calentar (caliento) to warm

calidad *f.* quality (*excellence*)

cálido/a hot

caliente hot (*temperature*) (7)

calificación *f.* grade

caligrafía calligraphy; handwriting

callar to silence

calle *f.* street (12)

callejero/a *adj.* (of the) street

calma calm

calmarse to calm down

calor *m.* heat; **hacer (mucho) calor** to be very hot (6); **tener (mucho) calor** to be (very) warm, hot (6)

caloría calorie

caluroso/a hot

cama bed (5); **guardar cama** to stay in bed (11); **hacer la cama** to make the bed (10); **tender (tiendo) la cama** to make the bed

cámara camera (12)

camarero/a waiter/waitress (7)

camarones *m. pl.* shrimp (7)

cambiar (de) to change (12)

cambio change; **cambio climático** climate change

camélidos *m. pl.* (*zool.*) Camelidae

camello camel

caminadora treadmill (11)

caminar to walk (10)

caminata: dar una caminata to hike; to go for a hike (10)

caminero/a: furia caminera road rage

camino road; path

camión *m.* truck

camioneta station wagon (8); van (8)

camisa shirt (4)

camiseta T-shirt (4)

campamento campsite

campaña campaign; **tienda de campaña** tent (8)

campeón, campeona champion

campeonato championship

campesino/a peasant (15)

camping *m.* campground (8); **hacer** *camping* to go camping (8)

campo field; countryside (15)

Canadá Canada; **Día** (*m.*) **del Canadá** Canada Day

canadiense *n., adj. m., f.* Canadian

canal *m.* channel (12); canal (7)

canario canary

cancelar to cancel

cáncer *m.* cancer

cancha field; court (*tennis*)

canción *f.* song (7)

candidato/a candidate (18); **postularse (para un cargo) como candidato/a** to run (for a position) as a candidate (18)

cansado/a tired (6)

cansancio fatigue

cansarse to get tired (11)

cantante *m., f.* singer (13)

cantaor(a) flamenco singer

cantar to sing (2)

cantautor(a) singer, songwriter

cantidad *f.* quantity

cantinero/a bartender

caña sugar cane

cañonazo cannon shot

capa layer (15); **capa de ozono** ozone layer (15)

capacidad *f.* capacity

capaz (*pl.* **capaces**) able

Caperucita Roja Little Red Ridinghood

capilla chapel

capital *f.* capital city (6)

capitán, capitana captain

capítulo chapter

Capricornio Capricorn

cara face

caracola large shell

característica *n.* characteristic

característico/a *adj.* characteristic

caracterizar (c) to characterize

caramañola *torpedo-shaped meat pie of Colombia and Panama*

cárcel *f.* jail

cardinal: punto cardinal cardinal point (6)

cardiólogo cardiologist

carga load; **carga de trabajo** workload

cargar (gu) a una cuenta to charge to an account (17)

cargo (political) office (18); **postularse para un cargo (como candidato/a)** to run for a position (as a candidate) (18)

Caribe *m.* Caribbean; **mar** (*m.*) **Caribe** Caribbean Sea

caribeño/a Caribbean

caricatura caricature

cariño affection (16)

cariñoso/a affectionate (6)

carnaval *m.* carnival

carne *f.* meat (7)

carnet (*m.*) **de identificación / de identidad** identification card

carnicería butcher's shop

caro/a expensive (4)

carpa tent

carpeta folder (12)

carpintero/a carpenter

carrera career

carreta cart, wagon

carretera highway (15)

carretilla wheelbarrow

carril *m.* lane

carro (descapotable) (convertible) car (15)

carta letter (3); card; **jugar (juego) (gu) a las cartas** to play cards (10)

cartera wallet; handbag (4)

cartón *m.* cardboard

casa house, home (3); **amo/a** (*but el ama*) **de casa** housekeeper (17) **casa natal** house where someone was born; **en casa** at home (2); **limpiar la casa** to clean (the) house (10); **regresar a casa** to go home (2)

casabe *m.* tortilla-type bread made of cassava

casado/a married; **estar casado/a (con)** to be married (to) (16); **recién casado/a (con)** newlywed (to) (16); **ser casado/a** to be a married person (16)

casarse (con) to marry (16)

cascanueces *m. inv.* nutcracker

caserío hamlet; farmhouse

casero/a home-made

casi *adv.* almost (3); **casi nunca** almost never (3)

caso case; **en caso de (que)** in case (16)

castaño/a brown (chestnut-colored)

castañuelas *f. pl.* castinets

castellano Spanish (language)

castigar (gu) to punish

cata (de vino) (wine) tasting

catalán *m.* Catalan (*language*); **catalán, catalana** *adj.* Catalan

catálogo catalogue

Cataluña Catalonia

catarata waterfall

catarro cold (*health condition*)

catedral *f.* cathedral

categoría category

catolicismo Catholicism

católico/a *n., adj.* Catholic

catorce fourteen (1)

caucásico/a Caucasian

causa cause; **a causa de** because of

causar to cause

cava cellar

cazador(a) hunter

cazar (c) to hunt

CD *m.* CD (compact disc) (12)

CD-ROM *m.* CD-ROM (12)

cebolla onion (7)

cédula identity card

celda cell (*prison*)

celebración *f.* celebration

celebrar to celebrate (6)

celíaco/a gluten intolerant

celos *m. pl.* jealousy

celta *n., adj. m., f.* Celtic

celular: (teléfono) celular *m.* cell phone (2)

cementerio cemetery

cena dinner, supper (7)

cenar to have (eat) dinner, supper (7)

Cenicienta Cinderella

centavo cent

centígrado Celsius

céntrico/a central

centro center (*political*) (18); downtown (4); **centro comercial** shopping mall (4)

Centroamérica Central America

centroamericano/a Central American

cepillarse los dientes to brush one's teeth (5)

cerámica pottery; ceramics (13)

cerca *adv.* near, nearby, close; **cerca de** close to (6)

cercano/a *adj.* close, near

cerdo pork; **chuleta de cerdo** pork chop (7)

cereal *m.* cereal (7)

cerebro brain (11)

ceremonia ceremony

cero zero (1)

cerrado/a closed (6)

cerrar (cierro) to close (5); **cerrarse** to close; to finish

cerro hill

certeza certainty

cerveza beer (7)

cesárea C-section

césped *m.* lawn; grass

cesto basket

ceviche *m. raw fish dish*

champán *m.* champagne (9)

champiñones *m. pl.* mushrooms (7)

chanclas *f. pl.* flip-flops (4)

chaqueta jacket (4)

charango *stringed instrument*

charco puddle

charlar to chat

chatear to chat

chateo *n.* chat (12)

chauchas *f. pl.* green beans (*Arg.*)

cheque *m.* check (17); **con cheque** by check (17)

chequeo check-up (11)

chévere *sl.* cool

chibcha *n., adj. m., f. indigenous people of the Colombian Andes*

chicha *natural fruit soft drink*

chicle *m.* gum

chico/a guy/girl (4)

chileno/a *n., adj.* Chilean

chino Chinese (*language*)

chino/a *n., adj.* Chinese

chisme *m.* gossip

chiste *m.* joke (8)

chocante shocking

chocar (qu) con/contra to run into, bump against (14)

chocolate *m.* chocolate

chofer *m., f.* driver

choque *m.* collision, crash (18)

chuleta (de cerdo) (pork) chop (7)

churro *strip of fried dough*

cibernauto/a of the internet

ciclismo bicycling (10)

ciclo cycle

ciclón *m.* cyclone

ciego/a blind

cien one hundred (3)

ciencia science (2); **ciencia ficción** science fiction; **ciencias** (*f. pl.*) **naturales** natural sciences (2); **ciencias** (*f. pl.*) **políticas** political science (2); **ciencias** (*f. pl.*) **sociales** social sciences (2)

científico/a scientist

ciento one hundred (4); **ciento dos** one hundred two (4); **ciento noventa y nueve** one hundred ninety-nine (4); **ciento uno** one hundred one (4)

cierto/a true **es cierto que** it's certain that (13)

ciervo deer; stag

cifra figure, number

cigarrillo cigarette

cinco five (1)

cincuenta fifty (3)

cine *m. s.* movies (5); movie theater (5)

cineasta *m., f.* filmmaker

cinematográfico/a *adj.* movie, film

cinta: cinta de andar/correr treadmill; **cinta rodante** treadmill

cinturón *m.* belt (4)

circulación *f.* traffic (15)

circular to circulate

círculo circle

circunstancia circumstance

cirugía surgery

cisne *m.* swan

cita date; appointment (11)

citar to cite, quote

ciudad *f.* city (3)

ciudadano/a citizen (18)

cívico/a civic; **responsabilidad** (*f.*) **cívica** civic duty (18)

civil civil; **guerra civil** civil war

civilización *f.* civilization

clarificar (qu) to clarify

claro/a clear

clase *f.* class (*of students*) (2); class, course (*academic*) (2); **compañero/a (de clase)** classmate (2); **dar clases** to teach class; **salón** (*m.*) **de clase** classroom (2)

clásico/a classic(al) (13)

clasificar (qu) to classify

cláusula *gram.* clause

clave *f. n., adj.* key

clic: hacer clic to click (12)

clicar (qu) to click

cliente/a client (2)

clima *m.* climate (6)

climático/a *adj.* climate; **cambio climático** climate change

clínica clinic

cliquear to click

clóset *m.* closet

coalición *f.* coalition

cobrar to cash (*a check*) (17); to charge (*someone for an item or service*) (17)

cobre *m.* copper

coche *m.* car (3); **agencia de compra-venta (de coches)** used car dealership

cochera garage; carport

cochinilla cochineal

cocido/a *adj.* cooked

cocina kitchen (5); cuisine (7)

cocinar to cook (7)

cocinero/a cook; chef (17)
coco coconut
cocodrilo crocodile
cóctel *m.* cocktail party
codiciado/a coveted
código code
codirector(a) codirector
codo elbow
coexistir to coexist
coger (cojo) to take (*things*) (*Sp.*)
cognado *gram.* cognate
coherente coherent
cohesión *f.* cohesion
coincidencia coincidence
coincidir to coincide
cola line (*of people*) (8); **hacer cola** to
   stand in line (8)
colaborar to collaborate
colección *f.* collection
coleccionar to collect
colectivo bus
colega *m., f.* colleague
colegio school
colérico/a furious
colesterol *m.* cholesterol
coletilla tag (*as in* tag question)
colgar (cuelgo) (gu) to post (*on the
   internet*)
colina hill
collar *m.* necklace
colmado small grocery store
   (*Carib.*)
colocar (qu) to place
colombiano/a Colombian
colonia colony
colonización *f.* colonization
colonizador(a) colonist
colonizar (c) to colonize
colono/a settler
coloquial colloquial
color *m.* color (4)
colorado/a red-colored
colorido/a colorful
columna column
comadre *f.* godmother
combatir to combat
combinación *f.* combination
combinar to combine
comedia comedy (13)
comediante *m., f.* comedian
comedor *m.* dining room (5)
comentar to talk about
comentario comment
comentarista *m., f.* commentator
comenzar (comienzo) (c) to begin;
   comenzar a + *inf.* to begin
   to + *inf.*
comer to eat (3); **comerse** to eat up
comercial: centro comercial shopping
   mall (4)
comercio business, commerce; **libre
   comercio** free trade

comestibles *m. pl.* groceries,
   foodstuff (7)
cometa *m.* comet
cometer to commit
cómico/a funny; **tira cómica** comic strip
comida food (7); meal (7); **comida
   rápida** fast food
comienzo beginning
comillas *f. pl.* quotation marks
como like; as; **así como** as well as; **tan...
   como** as . . . as (6); **tanto como** as
   much as (6)
¿cómo? how?; what? (1); **¿cómo es
   usted?** what are you (*form. s.*) like?
   (1); **¿cómo está?** how are you (*form.
   s.*)? (1); **¿cómo estás?** how are you
   (*fam. s.*)? (1); **¿cómo se llama
   usted?** what is your (*form. s.*)
   name? (1); **¿cómo se llega a... ?**
   how do you get to . . . ? (15); **¿cómo
   te llamas?** what is your (*fam. s.*)
   name? (1)
cómoda bureau; dresser (5)
comodidad *f.* convenience
cómodo/a comfortable (4)
compacto/a: disco compacto (**CD** *m.*)
   compact disc (CD) (12)
compadre *m.* godfather
compañero/a companion; friend;
   compañero/a (de clase) classmate
   (2); **compañero/a de cuarto**
   roommate (2)
compañía company
comparación *f.* comparison (6)
comparar to compare
comparativo/a comparative
compartir to share
compasión *f.* compassion
compensar to make up for
competencia competition
competente competent
competición *f.* competition
competitivo/a competitive
complejo/a complex
complemento (in)directo *gram.* (in)
   direct object
completar to complete
completo/a complete; **trabajo de
   tiempo completo** full-time job (14)
complicación *f.* complication
componer (*like* **poner**) to compose (13)
comportamiento behavior
composición *f.* composition
compositor(a) composer (13)
compostero composter
comprador(a) buyer
comprar to buy (2)
compras: de compras shopping (4); **ir
   de compras** to go shopping (4)
**compra-venta: agencia de compra-
   venta (de coches)** used car
   dealership

comprender to understand (3)
comprensible understandable
comprensión *f.* understanding;
   comprehension
comprensivo/a *adj.* understanding
comprobar (compruebo) to prove
comprometido/a committed
compuesto/a composed; compound
   (*gram.*)
compulsivo/a compulsive
computación *f.* computer
   science (2)
computadora computer (2);
   computadora portátil laptop
   (computer) (2)
común common
comunicación *f.* communication; *pl.*
   communication (*subject*) (2); **medio
   de comunicación** medium of
   communication (18)
comunicarse (qu) to communicate
comunicativo/a communicative
comunidad *f.* community
comunión *f.* communion
comunitario/a *adj.* community
con with (2); **chocar (qu) con** to
   run into, bump against (14);
   comunicarse (qu) (con) to
   communicate (with) (18); **con base
   en** based on; **con cheque** by check
   (17); **con cuidado** carefully; **con
   frecuencia** frequently (2); **con
   permiso** excuse me (1); **¿con qué
   frecuencia... ?** how often . . . ? (3);
   con respecto a regarding; **con tal
   de** *prep.* provided (16); **con tal (de)
   que** *conj.* provided (that) (16); **darse
   con** to run into; **pegarse (gu) con** to
   run/bump into (14)
conceder to concede
concentración *f.* concentration
concentrar to concentrate
concepto concept
conciencia conscience
concienciación *f. n.* conscious-raising
concierto concert (10); **ir a un concierto**
   to go to a concert (10)
conciso/a concise
conclusión *f.* conclusion
concordancia *gram.* agreement
concreto: en concreto in particular
concursante *m., f.* contestant
concurso contest
condenado/a condemned
condición *f.* condition
condicional *gram.* conditional
cóndor *m.* condor
conducción *f.* driving
conducir (conduzco) to drive (15);
   licencia de conducir driver's
   license (15)
conductor(a) driver (15)

conectar to connect; **conectarse** to connect (12)

conector *m.* connector

conejo/a rabbit

conexión *f.* connection

conferencia lecture

confesional confessional

confianza confidence

confiar (confío) to trust

configurar to configure

confirmar to confirm

conflicto conflict

confluencia *n.* coming-together

confundido/a confused

congelado/a frozen; very cold (6)

congelador *m.* freezer (10)

congestión *f.* congestion

congresista *m., f.* member of congress

congreso congress; **representante** (*m., f.*) **al congreso** Congressional representative (18)

conjugación *f. gram.* conjugation

conjugar (gu) *gram.* to conjugate

conjunción *f. gram.* conjunction (16); **conjunción de tiempo** conjunction of time (17)

conjunto group

conllevar to involve

conmemorar to commemorate

conmigo with me (6)

Cono Sur Southern Cone

conocer (conozco) to know, be acquainted, familiar with (7); to meet (7); **conocerse** to meet (16)

conocimiento knowledge

conquista conquest

conquistador(a) conqueror

consciente conscious, aware

consecuencia consequence

consecutivo/a consecutive

conseguir (*like* **seguir**) to get; to obtain (9); **conseguir + *inf.*** to succeed in (*doing something*) (9)

consejero/a advisor (2)

consejo (piece of) advice (7)

conservación *f.* conservation

conservacionista conservationist

conservador(a) conservative

conservar to save; to conserve (15)

consideración *f.* consideration

considerar to consider

consigo with himself, herself, themselves

consiguiente: por consiguiente as a result

consistencia consistency

consistir (en) to consist (of)

constante constant

constar (de) to consist of

constatar to confirm

constipado/a: estar constipado/a to have a cold

constitución *f.* constitution

constituir (*like* **construir**) to constitute

construcción *f.* construction

construir (construyo) to build (15)

consuelo consolation

consulta consultation

consultar to consult

consultorio (medical) office (11); consultation

consumidor(a) consumer

consumir to consume

consumo consumption

contabilidad *f.* accounting

contable *m., f.* accountant (*Sp.*)

contacto contact; **lentes** (*m. pl.*) **de contacto** contact lenses (11); **mantenerse** (*like* **tener**) **en contacto** to stay in touch

contador(a) accountant (17)

contaminación *f.* pollution (6)

contaminado/a contaminated, polluted (15)

contaminar to pollute (15)

contar (cuento) to tell; to narrate (8)

contemplación *f.* contemplation

contemplar to contemplate

contemporáneo/a contemporary

contenedor *m.* container

contener (*like* **tener**) to contain

contenido contents

contento/a content, happy (6)

contestar to answer (7)

contexto context

contigo with you (*fam.*) (6)

continente *m.* continent

contingencia contingency

continuación: a continuación following

continuar (continúo) to continue (6)

contra against; **chocar (qu)/pegarse (gu) contra** to run into; to bump against (14); **darse contra** to run into

contrabajo double bass (*musical instrument*)

contradecir (*like* **decir**) to contradict

contraer (*like* **traer**) to contract

contrario contrary

contrarrestar to resist

contraseña password (12)

contrastar to contrast

contraste *m.* contrast

contrastivo/a contrasting

contribución *f.* contribution

contribuir (*like* **construir**) to contribute

control *m.* control; **control de seguridad** security (check) (8); **control remoto** remote control (12); **pasar por el control de seguridad** to go/pass through security (check) (8)

controlador(a) controller

controlar to control

convencer (convenzo) to convince

convención *f.* convention; system

conversación *f.* conversation

conversar to converse

convertir (convierto) (i) to convert

convivencia cohabitation; living together

convivir to live together

coordinar to coordinate

copa (wine) glass; **Copa del Mundo** World Cup (*soccer*); **Copa Mundial** World Cup (*soccer*)

copia copy; **hacer copia** to copy

copiar to copy (12)

copioso/a copious

coquí *m. small frog of Puerto Rico*

corazón *m.* heart (11)

corbata tie (4)

cordillera mountain range

coreano/a *n., adj.* Korean

cormorán cormorant (*aquatic bird*)

coro chorus

corona crown

corporación *f.* corporation

correcto/a correct

corregir (corrijo) (i) to correct

correo mail

correo electrónico e-mail (12)

correr to run (10); **cinta de correr** treadmill

correspondencia correspondence

corresponder (a) to correspond (to)

correspondiente *m., f.* correspondent; *adj.* corresponding

corrido *Mexican folk song*

corriente: cuenta corriente checking account; **estar al corriente** to be up to date

cortar to cut

cortejo courting

cortés *m., f.* polite

cortesía courtesy; **expresión** (*f.*) **de cortesía** courteous expression (1)

cortijo country house

cortina curtain

corto *n.* short segment

corto/a short (*in length*) (3); **pantalones** (*m. pl.*) **cortos** shorts (4)

cosa thing (5)

cosecha harvest; crop

cosechar to harvest

cosmético/a cosmetic

cosmopolita *m., f.* cosmopolitan

cosmovisión *f.* world view

costa coast

costar (cuesto) to cost

costarricense *n., adj. m., f.* Costa Rican

costero/a coastal

costo cost

costoso/a expensive

costumbre *f.* custom

costura: de alta costura high fashion

cotidiano/a daily

country *m.* country music

creación *f.* creation

crear to create (13)
creatividad *f.* creativity
creativo/a creative
crecer (crezco) to grow (16)
crecimiento *n.* rise, growth
credencial *f.* identity card
crédito credit; **tarjeta de crédito** credit card (7)
creencia belief
creer (en) to think; to believe (in) (3); **no creer** to not think/believe (13)
creíble believable
crema cream
cremoso/a creamy
creyente *m., f.* believer
criado/a servant
criatura child
crimen *m. (pl. crímenes)* crime
criollo/a *n., adj.* creole
cristal *m.* glass
cristianismo Christianity
cristiano/a *n., adj.* Christian
Cristo Christ; **antes de Cristo (a.C.)** before Christ (B.C.); **después de Cristo (a.D.)** Anno Domini (A.D.)
crítica criticism
criticar (qu) to criticize
crítico/a critic
crónica chronicle
crónico/a chronic
cronológico/a chronological
croqueta croquette
crucero cruise (ship) (8)
crudo/a raw
cruz *f. (pl. cruces)* cross; **Día** *(m.)* **de la Cruz** Day of the Cross
cruzar (c) to cross; **cruzarse con** to cross paths with
cuaderno notebook (2)
cuadrado *n.* square
cuadrado/a *adj.* square
cuadro painting (*specific piece*) (13); **de cuadros** plaid (4)
cuajar to fit in
cual: el/la cual, lo cual, los/las cuales which
¿cuál(es)? what? (2); which? (2); **¿cuál es la fecha de hoy?** what's today's date? (6); **¿cuál es tu onda?** what's your style?
cualidad *f.* quality (*characteristic*)
cualquier *adj.* any
cuando when
¿cuándo? when? (2)
cuanto: en cuanto as soon as (17); **en cuanto a** regarding
¿cuánto? how much? (2); **¿cuánto cuesta(n)?** how much does it (do they) cost? (4); **¿cuánto tiempo hace que... ?** how long ago (*did something happen*)? / for how long (*has something been happening*)?

¿cuántos/as? how many? (2)
cuáquero/a *n.* Quaker
cuarenta forty (3)
Cuaresma Lent
cuartel *m.* barracks
cuarto room (2); one-fourth; quarter (of an hour); **compañero/a de cuarto** roommate (2); **menos cuarto** a quarter to (*hour*) (1); **y cuarto** a quarter (fifteen minutes) after (*the hour*) (1)
cuarto/a *adj.* fourth (13)
cuate *sl. m., f.* buddy, pal
cuatro four (1)
cuatrocientos/as four hundred (4)
cubano/a *n., adj.* Cuban
cubanoamericano/a *n., adj.* Cuban American
cubierto/a (*p.p. of* **cubrir**) covered
cubiertos *m. pl.* cutlery
cubrir (*p.p.* **cubierto**) to cover (15)
cucaracha cockroach
cuchara spoon
cucharada spoonful
cuchillo knife
cuello neck
cuenta check, bill (7); **cargar (gu) a una cuenta** to charge to an account (17); **cuenta corriente** checking account
cuento story
cuerda string
cuero leather (4); **de cuero** leather (4)
cuerpo (humano) (human) body (11)
cuervo crow
cuestión *f.* question (*issue*); matter (17)
cuestionable questionable
cuestionario questionnaire
cuidado care; *interj.* careful!; **con cuidado** carefully; **tener cuidado** to be careful
cuidar a to care for; **cuidarse** to take care of oneself (11)
culebra snake
culinario/a culinary
culminar to culminate
culpa fault; **tener la culpa** to be at fault
cultivar to cultivate
cultivo cultivation
culto cult; **rendir (rindo) (i) culto** to worship
cultrún *m.* ceremonial Mapuche drum
cultura culture
cultural cultural; **tradición** *(f.)* **cultural** cultural tradition (13)
cumbia *Colombian folk dance now popular throughout Latin America*
cumbre *f.* summit
cumpleaños *m. inv.* birthday (6); **pastel** *(m.)* **de cumpleaños** birthday cake (9)
cumplir to fulfill; **cumplir años** to have a birthday (9)

cuñado/a brother-in-law, sister-in-law
cupo quota; capacity (*space*)
cupón *m.* coupon
cura cure
curación *f.* cure
curar to cure
curativo/a curing, curative
curioso/a curious
currículum *m.* résumé (17)
cursi in poor taste; trite
curso course; **programa** *(m.)* **del curso** course syllabus (14)
cuyo/a whose

D

dama lady
danza dance (13)
daño: hacerse daño to hurt oneself (14); **hacerse daño en** to hurt one's (*body part*) (14)
dar to give (8); **dar clases** to teach class; **dar un paseo** to take a walk (10); **dar una caminata** to hike; to go for a hike (10); **dar una fiesta** to throw a party (9); **darse con/contra** to run into; **darse la mano** to shake hands (11)
darwinista *m., f.* Darwinian
datar to date back to
datos *m. pl.* data; **base** *(f.)* **de datos** data base
de of (1); from (1); **de adolescente** *adj.* adolescent (10) **de algodón** *m.* (*made of*) cotton (4); **de alta costura** high fashion; **de alto riesgo** high risk; **de atrás** backwards; **de compras** shopping (4); **de cuadros** plaid (4); **de cuero** leather (4); **¿de dónde eres (tú)?** where are you (*fam. s.*) from? (1); **¿de dónde es usted?** where are you (*form. s.*) from? (1); **de estatura mediana** of medium height; **de exposición** expository; **de forma presencial** in person; **de la actualidad** currently, right now (10); **de la mañana** in the morning, A.M. (1); **de la noche** in the evening, P.M. (1); **de la tarde** in the afternon, P.M. (1); **de lana** wool (4); **de lunares** polka-dot (4); **de manera que** so that, in such a way that; **de modo que** in such a way that; **de nada** you're welcome (1); **de niño/a** as a child (10); **de oro** gold (4); **de plata** silver (4); **¿de quién?** whose? (3); **de rayas** striped (4); **de remate** hopeless(ly); **de repente** suddenly (11); **de seda** silk (4); **de todo** everything (4); **de todo tipo** of all kinds; **de vacaciones** on vacation (8); **¿de veras?** really?; **de viaje** on a trip, traveling (8); **es de...** it is made of . . . (4)

debajo de below (6)

debate *m.* debate

debatir to debate

deber *n. m.* responsibility (18); obligation (18)

deber *v. + inf.* should, must, ought to (*do something*) (3)

debido/a a due to; because of

débito debit

década decade

decadencia decadence

decente decent

decidir to decide

décimo/a tenth (13)

decimotercer(o/a) thirteenth

decir to say; to tell (8); **eso quiere decir...** that means . . . (11)

decisión *f.* decision

declaración *f.* statement

declarar to state

decoración *f.* decoration

decorar to decorate

decorativo/a decorative

dedicarse (qu) (a) to dedicate oneself (to)

dedo (de la mano) finger (11); **dedo del pie** toe (11)

deducir (deduzco) (*like* **conducir**) to deduce

defender (defiendo) to defend

defensa defense

defensor(a) defender

deficiencia deficiency

deficiente deficient

definición *f.* definition

definido: artículo definido *gram.* definite article

definir to define

degustar to taste

dejar to leave; to let, allow; to quit (17); **dejar de** + *inf.* to stop (*doing something*) (11)

del (*contraction of* **de** + **el**) of the; from the (3)

delante de in front of (6)

delegación *f.* delegation

delfín *m.* dolphin

delgado/a thin, slender (3)

deliberado/a deliberate

delicia delicacy

delicioso/a delicious

delito crime (15)

demanda demand

demás: los/las demás the rest, others (12)

demasiado *adv.* too (9)

demasiado/a *adj.* too much (9); too many (9)

democracia democracy

demócrata *m., f.* democrat

democrático/a democratic

demonio demon, devil

demora delay (8)

demostración *f.* demonstration

demostrar (demuestro) to demonstrate

demostrativo/a *gram.* demonstrative (4)

denominación *f.* denomination

densidad *f.* density

denso/a dense (15)

dentista *m., f.* dentist (11)

dentro inside; **dentro de** inside; within; in (*time*)

departamento department

dependencia dependence

depender (de) to depend (on)

dependiente/a clerk (2)

deporte *m.* sport (10); **practicar (qu)** to play (*a sport*)

deportista *m., f.* athlete

deportivo/a *adj.* sporting, sports; sports-loving (10)

depositar to deposit (17)

depósito deposit

depresión *f.* depression

deprimido/a depressed

derecha *n.* right side; **a la derecha de** to the right of (6)

derecho right (18); **(todo) derecho** straight ahead (15)

derivación *f.* branch, offshoot

derivarse (de) to derive (from)

derramar to spill

desacuerdo disagreement

desafío challenge

desagradable disagreeable

desahogarse (gu) to let off steam; to vent

desamor *m.* lack of affection

desaparecer (desaparezco) to disappear

desarrollar to develop (15)

desarrollo development (15)

desastre *m.* disaster (14)

desastroso/a disastrous

desayunar to have (eat) breakfast (7)

desayuno breakfast (7)

descansar to rest (5)

descanso rest

descapotable: carro descapotable convertible (car) (15)

descargar (gu) to download (12)

descendiente *m., f.* descendent

descentralizado/a decentralized

descifrar to decipher; to figure out

desconectar to unplug; to disconnect

desconocido/a unknown

descontento/a unhappy

descortés *m., f.* rude, impolite

describir (*p.p.* **descrito**) to describe

descripción *f.* description

descriptivo/a descriptive

descrito/a (*p.p. of* **describir**) described

descubierto/a (*p.p. of* **descubrir**) discovered

descubrimiento discovery

descubrir (*p.p.* **descubierto**) to discover (15)

desde *prep.* from; since

desear to want (2)

desempleo unemployment

deseo wish

desequilibrio imbalance

desértico/a *adj.* desert

desesperanza desperation

desfile *m.* parade

desgracia misfortune; disgrace

desgraciadamente unfortunately (11)

deshumanización *f.* dehumanization

desierto desert

designación *f.* designation

designar to appoint; to designate

desigualdad *f.* inequality (18)

desilusión *f.* disillusion

desinflado/a: llanta desinflada flat tire (15)

desocupado/a empty; available

desordenado/a messy (6)

desorganizado/a unorganized

despacio *adv.* slowly

despedida farewell

despedir (*like* **pedir**) to let (*someone*) go (17); to fire (*someone*) (*from a job*) (17); **despedirse (de)** to say good-bye (to) (9)

despejado/a clear (*sky*)

desperdiciar to waste

desperdicio waste

despertador *m.* alarm clock (14)

despertarse (me despierto) to wake up (5)

despierto/a (*p.p. of* **despertar**) awake

despistado/a absent-minded; forgetful

después *adv.* afterwards (5); **después de** *prep.* after (5); **después de Cristo (a.D.)** Anno Domini (A.D.); **después (de) que** *conj.* after (17)

destacar (qu) to emphasize; **destacarse** to stand out

destino destination (8); destiny

destrucción *f.* destruction

destruir (*like* **construir**) to destroy (15)

desventaja disadvantage

detalle *m.* detail (9)

detective *m., f.* detective

detenerse (*like* **tener**) to stop

determinación *f.* determination

determinado/a specific

determinante decisive

determinar to determine

detestar to detest

detrás de behind (6)

deuda debt

devolver (*like* **volver**) to return (*something to someone*) (14)

devoto/a devout

día *m.* day (2); **buenos días** good morning (1); **Día de Acción de**

Gracias Thanksgiving; **Día de la Cruz** Day of the Cross; **Día de la Madre** Mother's Day; **Día de los Difuntos** Day of the Dead; **Día de los Muertos** Day of the Dead; **Día de San Patricio** St. Patrick's Day; **Día de San Valentín** St. Valentine's Day; **Día del Padre** Father's Day; **día festivo** holiday (9); **Día Internacional de la No Violencia Contra la Mujer** International No Violence Against Women Day; **días de la semana** days of the week (5); **estar al día** to be up to date (18); **¿qué día es hoy?** what day is today? (5); **todos los días** every day (2)

diabetes *f. inv.* **(juvenil)** (childhood) diabetes

diabético/a diabetic

diablo devil

diacrítico/a: acento diacrítico diacritical mark

diagnosticar (qu) to diagnose

diágrafo group of letters that represent a single sound

dialecto dialect

diálogo dialogue

diamante *m.* diamond

diariamente daily

diario/a daily (5)

dibujante *m., f.* comic strip artist (13)

dibujar to draw (13)

dibujo drawing (13); **dibujos** (*m. pl.*) **animados** cartoons

diccionario dictionary (2)

dicho saying

diciembre *m.* December (6)

dictador(a) dictator (18)

dictadura dictatorship (18)

dictar to dictate

diecinueve nineteen (1)

dieciocho eighteen (1)

dieciséis sixteen (1)

diecisiete seventeen (1)

diente *m.* tooth (5); **cepillarse los dientes** to brush one's teeth (5)

dieta dieta (7); **estar a dieta** to be on a diet (7)

dietético/a *adj.* diet

diez ten (1)

diferencia difference; **a diferencia de** unlike

diferenciado/a differentiated

diferente different

difícil hard, difficult (6)

dificultad *f.* difficulty

difundir to disseminate

difunto/a dead; **Día** (*m.*) **de los Difuntos** Day of the Dead

digestión *f.* digestion

digital digital; **brecha digital** digital gap

dígito digit

dignidad *f.* dignity

dilema *m.* dilemma

diligente diligent

dimensión *f.* dimension

diminutivo *gram. n.* diminutive

Dinamarca Denmark

dinero money (2); **sacar (qu) dinero** to withdraw money

dinoflagelado *type of marine plankton*

dios *m. s.* god; **Dios** God; **por Dios** for heaven's sake (14)

diosa goddess

diptongo *gram.* diphthong

dirección *f.* address (7)

directo direct; **complemento directo** *gram.* direct object

director(a) director; conductor (13)

directorio directory

dirigir (dirijo) to direct (13) (pido) (i)

discapacidad *f.* disability

discapacitado/a disabled

disco disc; **disco duro** hard drive (12)

discoteca discotheque; **ir a una discoteca** to go to a disco (10)

discriminación *f.* discrimination (18)

disculpa apology, excuse; **pedir (pido) (i) disculpas** to apologize (14)

disculpar to excuse, pardon; **disculpa, discúlpame** pardon me (*fam. s.*) (14); I'm sorry (*fam. s.*) (14); **disculpe, discúlpeme** pardon me (*form. s.*) (14); I'm sorry (*form. s.*) (14)

discurso speech

discusión *f.* argument; discussion

discutir (con/sobre) to argue (with/about) (9)

diseñador(a) designer

diseñar to design (13)

diseño design

disfraz *m.* (*pl.* **disfraces**) costume, disguise

disfrutar (de) to enjoy

disminuir (*like* **construir**) to diminish

disparar to shoot

dispensario clinic

disponible available

disposición *f.* disposition

dispositivo device

dispuesto/a ready; prepared (*to do something*)

disputarse to compete for

distancia distance

distante distant

distinción *f.* distinction

distintivo/a distinctive

distinto/a different

distracción *f.* distraction

distraer (*like* **traer**) to distract

distraído/a absentminded; distracted (14); **ir distraído/a** to be distracted (14)

distribuido/a distributed

distrito district

disuadir to dissuade

diversidad *f.* diversity

diversión *f.* fun activity (10)

diverso/a diverse

divertido/a fun; **ser divertido/a** to be fun (10)

divertirse (me divierto) (i) to have a good time; to enjoy oneself (5)

dividirse to be divided

divorciado/a (de) divorced (from) (16)

divorciarse (de) to get divorced (from) (16)

divorcio divorce (16)

divulgar (gu) to divulge

doblar to turn (15)

doble *m.* double

doce twelve (1)

dócil docile

doctor(a) doctor

doctorado doctorate

documento document

dólar *m.* dollar

doler (duele) (*like* **gustar**) to hurt; to ache (11)

dolor (*m.*) **(de)** pain, ache (in) (11); **dolor de cabeza** headache; **tener dolor de** to have a pain/ache in (11)

doméstico/a domestic, related to the home (10); domesticated, tame (15); **animal** (*m.*) **doméstico** pet; **aparato doméstico** home appliance (10); **tarea doméstica** household chore

domicilio home

dominación *f.* domination

dominar to control; to dominate

domingo Sunday (5)

dominicano/a *n., adj.* Dominican

dominio control

don *m. title of respect used with a man's first name*

donar to donate

donde where

¿dónde? where? (1); **¿de dónde eres (tú)?** where are you (*fam. s.*) from? (1); **¿de dónde es usted?** where are you (*form. s.*) from? (1)

doña *title of respect used with a woman's first name*

dormir (duermo) (u) to sleep (5); **dormir la siesta** to take a nap (5); **dormirse** to fall asleep (5)

dormitorio bedroom

dos two (1); **dos veces** twice (11)

doscientos/as two hundred (4)

drama *m.* drama (13)

dramático/a dramatic

dramatizar(c) to dramatize

dramaturgo/a playwright (13)

droga drug

dromedario dromedary

ducha *n.* shower
ducharse to take a shower (5)
duda *n.* doubt
dudar to doubt (12)
dudoso/a doubtful
duelo duel
dueño/a landlord, landlady (12); owner (7)
dulce *adj.* sweet
dulces *m. pl.* sweets; candy (7)
duración *f.* duration
duradero/a lasting
durante during (5)
durar to last (18)
duro/a hard; **disco duro** hard drive (12)
DVD *m.* DVD (12)

E

e and (*used instead of* **y** *before words beginning with stressed* **i** *or* **hi,** *except* **hie**-)
echar to throw out
ecocasa ecological house
ecología ecology
ecológico/a ecological
ecologista *m., f.* ecologist
economía economy; *s.* economics (2)
económico/a economical
economista *m., f.* economist
economizar (c) to economize (17)
ecoturismo ecotourism
ecoturista *m., f.* ecotourist
ecoturístico/a *adj.* ecotourist
ecuador *m.* equator
ecuatoguineano/a of or from Equatorial Guinea
ecuatoriano/a Ecuadoran
edad *f.* age
edificio building (2); **edificio de apartamentos** apartment building (12)
editar to edit
editorial *f.* publishing house
educación *f.* education
educador(a) educator
educarse (qu) to be educated
educativo/a educational
efectivo cash (17); **en efectivo** in cash (17)
efectivo/a effective
efecto effect
efectuar (efectúo) to carry out, execute
eficiencia efficiency
eficiente efficient
Egipto Egypt
egoísmo selfishness
egoísta *m., f.* selfish
ejecutivo/a *n., adj.* executive
ejemplar exemplary
ejemplificar (qu) to exemplify

ejemplo example; **por ejemplo** for example (14)
ejercer (ejerzo) to apply, exercise
ejercicio exercise (5); **hacer ejercicio** to exercise (5); **hacer ejercicios aeróbicos** to do aerobics (11)
ejército army (18)
el *def. art. m. s.* the; **el cual** which; **el lunes (martes...)** on Monday (Tuesday . . .) (5); **el primero de** the first of (*month*) (6); **el próximo (martes...)** next (Tuesday . . .) (5)
él *sub. pron.* he (2)
elaboración *f.* elaboration
elección *f.* choice; *pl.* election
electricidad *f.* electricity (12); electric bill (12)
electricista *m., f.* electrician (17)
eléctrico/a electrical; **energía eléctrica** electrical energy (15)
electrónica electronic equipment
electrónico/a electronic; **billete** (*m.*) (*Sp.*) / **boleto** (*L.A.*) **electrónico** e-ticket (8); **equipo electrónico** electronic equipment (12)
elefante *m.* elephant (15)
elegante elegant
elegir (elijo) (i) to select; to elect
elemento element
elevado/a high
elevador *m.* elevator
elevarse to rise
eliminar to eliminate
ella *sub. pron.* she (2)
ello: por ello therefore
ellos/as *sub. pron.* they (2); *obj. (of prep.)* them (2)
e-mail *m.* e-mail (12)
embarazada pregnant
embargo: sin embargo nevertheless
embarque: puerta de embarque boarding gate (8); **tarjeta de embarque** boarding pass (8)
emberá Embera person
emblema *m.* emblem
emblemático/a emblematic
embotellamiento traffic jam
embutido sausage
emergencia emergency
emigración *f.* emigration
emigrante *m., f.* emigrant
emigrar to emigrate
emisario/a emissary
emitir to emit
emoción *f.* emotion (9)
emocionado/a excited
emocional emotional
emocionante exciting
emocionarse to get excited
emoticono emoticon
empacar (qu) to pack

empanada *turnover pie or pastry*
emparedado sandwich
emparejar to match
empezar (empiezo) (c) to begin, start (5); **empezar a** + *inf.* to begin to (*do something*) (5) 1
empleado/a employee
empleador(a) employer
emplear to use to employ
empleo job, position (17); **empleo bien/ mal pagado** well-/poorly paid job/ position (17); **empleo de tiempo completo/parcial** full-/part-time job/ position (17)
empresa corporation (17); business (17); **administración** (*f.*) **de empresas** business administration (2)
empresario/a businessman/woman
en in (1); on (1); at (*a place*) (1); **en casa** at home (2); **en caso de** *prep.* in case (16); **en caso de que** *conj.* in case (16); **en cuanto** as soon as (17); **en efectivo** in cash (17); **en negrilla** boldface; **en onda** in style; **en punto** on the dot (*time*) (1); **en rebaja** on sale; **en resumen** in summary; **en seguida** immediately (5); **en vez de** instead of
enamorado/a (de) in love (with) (16)
enamorarse (de) to fall in love (with) (16)
enano/a dwarf
encantado/a pleased to meet you (1); enchanted
encantar (*like* **gustar**) to like very much; to love (8)
encanto charm
encapuchado/a hooded
encarcelado/a incarcerated
encargado/a in charge
encender (enciendo) to turn on (*appliance, machine*) (12); to light
encerado blackboard
encima de on top of (6)
encomendarse (me encomiendo) a to commend yourself to
encontrar (encuentro) to find (9); **encontrarse (con)** to meet (*someone somewhere*) (11)
encuentro encounter
encuesta survey
encuestar to survey
endeble unstable
endémico/a endemic
enemigo enemy
energía energy (15); **energía eléctrica** electrical energy (15); **energía eólica** wind energy (15); **energía nuclear** nuclear energy (15); **energía renovable** renewable energy (15); **energía solar** solar energy (15)
enérgico/a energetic

enero January (6)
enfado anger
énfasis *m. inv.* emphasis
enfático/a emphatic
enfatizar (c) to emphasize
enfermarse to get sick (11)
enfermedad *f.* illness, sickness (11)
enfermero/a nurse (11)
enfermo/a sick (6)
enfilado/a in a line
enfocar (qu) to focus
enfoque *m.* focus
enfrentar(se) (a) to face
enfrente de *prep.* in front of (*across from, facing*)
englobar to encompass
engordar to gain weight; to fatten
enhorabuena congratulations
enojado/a angry (9)
enojarse (con) to get angry (with) (9)
enorme enormous
enriquecer (enriquezco) to enrich
ensalada salad (7)
ensayista *m., f.* essayist
ensayar to test
ensayo essay
enseñanza teaching
enseñar to teach (2); **enseñar a + inf.** to teach to (*do something*)
ensuciarse to get dirty
entender (entiendo) to understand (5)
enterarse (de) to find out; to learn (about) (18)
entero/a entire
enterrado/a buried
entidad *f.* entity
entonces then (*in that case*)
entrada entrance; ticket (*for a show*)
entrante: año entrante next year
entrañable moving, touching
entrar to enter; **entrar en internet** to go on the internet (12); **entrar en Facebook** to go onto Facebook (12)
entre *prep.* between; among (6)
entregar (gu) to hand in (8)
entrenador(a) trainer, coach
entrenamiento training
entrenar to practice, train (10)
entresemana during the week
entrevista interview (17)
entrevistado/a interviewee (17)
entrevistador(a) interviewer (17)
entrevistar to interview
entusiasmar to enthuse
envase *m.* container
envenenar to poison
enviar (envío) to send
envidia envy
envuelto/a covered
eólico/a: energía eólica wind energy (15)

episodio chapter
epitafio epitaph
época era, time (*period*)
equilibrar to balance
equilibrio balance
equipaje *m.* baggage, luggage (8); **facturar el equipaje** to check baggage (8)
equipar to equip
equipo team (10); equipment (12); **equipo electrónico** electronic equipment (12)
equivalente *m.* equivalent
equivaler (*like* **salir**) to equal
equivocarse (qu) (de) to make a mistake (about) (14)
eructar to burp, belch
erupción *f.* eruption (18)
escala stop (8); **hacer escalas** to make stops (8)
escalador(a) climber
escalar to climb
escalera staircase; *pl.* stairs (14)
escándalo scandal
escanear to scan
escáner *m.* scanner (12)
escapar(se) (de) to escape (from)
escaparate *m.* store (display) window
escaso/a scarce
escena scene (13)
escenario stage (13); scenery (13)
esclavitud *f.* slavery
esclavo/a slave
esclusa lock (*of canal*)
escoba broom
escoger (escojo) to choose; to select
escolar *adj.* school
Escorpión *m.* Scorpio
escribir (*p.p.* **escrito**) to write (3)
escrito/a (*p.p. of* **escribir**) written (14); **informe** (*m.*) **escrito** written report (14)
escritor(a) writer (13)
escritorio desk (2)
escuálido/a scrawny
escuchar to listen (to) (2)
escuela school (10); **escuela primaria** elementary school; **escuela secundaria** high school; **maestro/a de escuela** schoolteacher (17)
esculpir to sculpt
escultor(a) sculptor (13)
escultura sculpture (13)
ese/a *adj.* that (4)
esencia essence
esencial essential
esfuerzo effort
eso (*neuter pron.*) that (4); **eso quiere decir...** that means . . . (11); **por eso** for that reason; that's why (3)
esos/as *adj.* those (4)

espacial *adj.* space; **nave** (*f.*) **espacial** spaceship; **transbordador** (*m.*) **espacial** space shuttle
espacio space; **espacio de almacenamiento** storage space (12)
espacioso/a spacious
espalda back
espantapájaros *m. inv.* scarecrow
espantar to scare
español *m.* Spanish (*language*) (2)
español(a) *n.* Spaniard; *adj.* Spanish (3)
espárragos *m. pl.* asparagus (7)
especial special
especialidad *f.* specialty
especialización *f.* major (*academic*); specialization
especializarse (c) (en) to major (in)
especie *f.* species (15); **especie en peligro de extinción** endangered species (15)
especificar (qu) to specify
específico/a specific
espectacular spectacular
espectáculo show (13)
espectador(a) spectator (13); *pl.* audience (13)
especulación *f.* speculation
espejo mirror
espera wait; **llamada de espera** call-waiting; **sala de espera** waiting room (8)
esperanza hope, wish (18)
esperar to wait (for) (7); to expect (7); to hope (12)
espeso/a thick
espinaca spinach
espíritu *m.* spirit
espiritual spiritual
esplendor *m.* splendor
esposado/a handcuffed
esposo/a husband/wife (3)
esqueleto skeleton
esquema *m.* outline
esquí *m.* skiing (10)
esquiador(a) skier
esquiar (esquío) to ski (10)
esquina (street) corner (15)
esta noche tonight (6)
estabilidad *f.* stability
estable stable
establecer (establezco) to establish
estación *f.* station (8); season (6); **estación de autobuses** bus station (8); **estación de radio** radio station (18); **estación de servicio** gas station (15); **estación de trenes** train station/(8)
estacionamiento parking place/lot (15)
estacionar to park (14)
estadio stadium
estadísticas *f. pl.* statistics
estadístico/a statistical**

estado state (3); **estado afectivo** emotional state (9); **estado de ánimo** state of mind; **estado libre asociado** commonwealth; **Estados** (*m. pl.*) **Unidos de América** United States of America

estadounidense *n., adj.* of the United States of America (3)

estancia stay (*in a hotel*)

estante *m.* bookshelf (5)

estar to be (2); **¿cómo está?** how are you (*form. s.*)? (1); **¿cómo estás?** how are you (*fam. s.*)? (1); **está bien** it's fine, OK (6); **está de moda** it's trendy (hot) (4); **está (muy) nublado** it's (very) cloudy, overcast (6); **estar a dieta** to be on a diet (7); **estar al corriente** to be up to date; **estar al día** to be up to date (18); **estar bajo muchas presiones** to be under a lot of pressure (14); **estar bien** to be comfortable (*temperature*) (6); **estar casado/a (con)** to be married (to) (16); **(no) estar de acuerdo** to (dis)agree (3); **estar de vacaciones** to be on vacation (8); **(no) estar seguro/a de** to (not) be sure of (13)

estatal *adj.* state, of the government

estatua statue

estatura height; **de estatura mediana** of medium height

este *m.* east (6)

este/a *adj.* this (3)

estéreo stereo

estereotípico/a stereotypical

estereotipo stereotype

estético/a aesthetic

estilizado/a slender

estilo style

estimar to estimate

estipendio stipend

estipular to stipulate

estirar to stretch

esto (*neuter pron.*) this (3)

estómago stomach (11)

estornudo sneeze

estos/as *adj.* these (3)

estrategia strategy

estrecho *n.* straight; **Estrecho de Magallanes** Strait of Magellan

estrella star

estrépito crashing

estrés *m. inv.* stress (14)

estresado/a stressed out, under stress (14)

estresante stressful

estresar to cause stress

estricto/a strict

estrofa verse (*poem*)

estructura structure

estructurar to structure

estuario estuary

estudiantado student body

estudiante *m., f.* student (2)

estudiantil *adj.* (of) student(s)

estudiar to study (2)

estudio office (*in a home*) (5); studio (*television*) *pl.* studies (*education*)

estudioso/a studious

estufa stove (5)

estupendo/a stupendous

etapa stage, phase (16)

etcétera etcetera

eterno/a eternal

ético/a ethical

etnia ethnicity

étnico/a ethnic

etnolingüístico/a ethnolinguistic

Europa Europe

europeo/a *n., adj.* European

euskera *m.* Basque (*language*)

evaluación *f.* evaluation

evangélico/a *n., adj.* evangelical

evangelismo evangelism

evento event

evidencia evidence

evidente evident

evitar to avoid (15)

evolución *f.* evolution

exacto/a exact

exagerado/a exaggerated

examen *m.* exam, test (4)

examinar to examine

exceder to exceed

excelencia excellence

excelente excellent

excepción *f.* exception

excepcional exceptional

excepto except

excesivo/a excessive

exceso excess

exclamar to exclaim

excluir (*like* **construir**) to exclude

exclusivo/a exclusive

excursión *f.* excursion

excusa excuse

exigente demanding

exigir (exijo) to demand

exiliarse to go into exile

existencia existence

existir to exist

éxito success; **tener éxito** to be successful

exitoso/a successful

exótico/a exotic

expandir to expand

expectativa expectation

expedición *f.* expedition

experiencia experience

experto/a expert

expiatorio/a expiatory

explicación *f.* explanation

explicar (qu) to explain (8)

exploración *f.* exploration

explorador(a) explorer

explotación *f.* exploitation

explotar to exploit

exponer (*like* **poner**) (*p.p.* **expuesto**) to display; to propose

exportador(a) exporter

exportar to export

exposición *f.* exposition; **de exposición** expository

expresar to express

expresión *f.* expression; **expresión artística** artistic expression (13); **expresión de cortesía** courteous expression (1)

expresionista expressionist

expresivo/a expressive

expulsar to expel

expulsión *f.* expulsion

exquisito/a exquisite

extender (extiendo) to extend

extensión *f.* extension

externo/a external

extinción *f.* extinction; **especie** (*f.*) **en peligro de extinción** endangered species (15)

extinguirse (me extingo) to become extinct

extracto extract

extranjero/a *n.* foreigner (2); *adj.* foreign; **ir al extranjero** to go abroad (8); **lengua extranjera** foreign language (2)

extrañar to miss

extraño/a strange; **es extraño que** it's strange that (13); **¡qué extraño que... !** how strange that . . . ! (13)

extraordinario/a extraordinary

extravagante extravagant

extremo/a extreme

extrovertido/a extrovert(ed)

F

fábrica factory (15)

fabricar (qu) to manufacture (15)

fábula fable

fabuloso/a fabulous

Facebook *m.* Facebook (12); **entrar en Facebook** to go into Facebook (12)

fácil easy (6)

facilidad *f.* ease

facilitar to facilitate

factor *m.* factor

factura bill (17)

facturar el equipaje to check baggage (8)

facultad *f.* (*university*) department

falda skirt (4)

fallar to crash (*computer*) (12)

falso/a false

falta lack (15); absence (15)

faltar (a) to be absent (from); to not attend (9)

fama fame
familia family (3)
familiar *adj.* (of the) family
famoso/a famous
fantasía fantasy
fantasma *m.* ghost
fantástico/a fantastic
farmacéutico/a pharmacist (11)
farmacia pharmacy
faro lighthouse
fascinante fascinating
fascinar (*like* **gustar**) to fascinate (13)
fastidioso/a tedious
fatal *sl.* bad, awful
fatalista *m., f.* fatalist
fauna animal species
fauno faun
favor *m.* favor; **a favor de** in favor of; **por favor** please (1)
favorito/a favorite
fax *m.* FAX (12)
fe *f.* faith
febrero February (6)
fecha date (*calendar*) (6); **¿cuál es la fecha de hoy?** what's today's date? (6); **fecha límite** deadline; **¿qué fecha es hoy?** what's today's date? (6)
federación *f.* federation
federativo/a federative
felicidades *f. pl.* congratulations
felicitaciones *f. pl.* congratulations
felicitar to congratulate
feliz (*pl.* **felices**) happy (9)
femenino/a feminine
fenicio/a Phoenician
fénix *m.* phoenix
fenomenal phenomenal
fenómeno phenomenon
feo/a ugly (3)
feria fair
feriado/a: día (*m.*) **feriado** holiday
fertilidad *f.* fertility
festejar to celebrate
festividad *f.* festival
festivo/a festive, celebratory (9); **día** (*m.*) **festivo** holiday (9)
ficción *f.* fiction; **ciencia ficción** science fiction
ficticio/a fictitious
fiebre *f.* fever (11); **tener fiebre** to have a fever
fiel faithful (3)
fiesta party (2); **dar/hacer una fiesta** to have/give/throw a party (9); **fiesta patronal** party dedicated to a patron saint
fiestero/a happy; fond of parties
figura figure
fijarse (en) to notice
fijo/a set, fixed; **precio fijo** fixed, set price (4); **teléfono fijo** landline (12)

fila line
Filadelfia Philadelphia
filantrópico/a philanthropic
Filipinas *f. pl.* Philippines
filipino/a *n., adj.* Philippine
filmar to film; to record
filosofía philosophy (2)
filosófico/a philosophical
fin *m.* end; **a fines de** at the end of; **fin de año** end of the year (9); **fin de semana** weekend (2); **por fin** finally (5); **sin fines de lucro** non-profit
final *m.* end
finalmente finally (5)
financiar to finance
financiero/a financial
finanzas *f. pl.* finances
finca farm (15)
Finlandia Finland
fino/a fine
firmar to sign
física physics (2)
físico/a physical
flaco/a skinny
flamenco *music and dance form of southern Spain*
flan *m.* (baked) custard (7)
flauta flute
flexibilidad *f.* flexibility
flor *f.* flower (8)
flora plant species
flota fleet
folclore folklore
folclórico/a traditional (13)
folclorista *m., f.* folklorist
folklórico/a traditional
fomentar to encourage; to promote
fondo background; fund; bottom
fontanero/a plumber (*Sp.*)
forma form, shape (4); way; **de forma presencial** in person
formación *f.* formation; education, training
formar to form
formato format
formidable tremendous
fórmula formula
formulario form (17)
fortalecer (fortalezco) to strengthen
fortaleza fort
fosforescente phosphorescent
foto(grafía) photo(graph) (8); **sacar (qu) fotos** to take photos (8)
fotocopia photocopy (12); **hacer fotocopia** to copy (12)
fotocopiadora copy machine (12)
fotocopiar to photocopy
fotografía photography (13)
fotógrafo/a photographer (17)
fotomontaje *m.* photo montage
fragmentado/a fragmented
fragmento fragment; excerpt
francés *m.* French (*language*) (2)

francés, francesa *n.* French person; *adj.* French
Francia France
franja stripe, band; border, fringe
frase *f.* phrase; sentence
fraternidad *f.* fraternity
frecuencia frequency; **con frecuencia** frequently (2); **¿con qué frecuencia... ?** how often . . . ? (3)
frecuente frequent
frecuentemente frequently (11)
frenos *m. pl.* brakes (15)
frente a facing; **hacer frente a** to face up to
fresa strawberry
fresco: hace fresco it's cool (weather) (6)
fresco/a fresh (7)
frigorífico refrigerator
frijoles *m. pl.* beans (7)
frío cold(ness); *adj.* cold; **hace (mucho) frío** it's (very) cold (*weather*); **tener (mucho) frío** to be (very) cold (6)
frito/a fried (7); **papa/patata frita** French fried potato (7)
frituras *f. pl.* fried food
frontera border
frotar to rub
frustración *f.* frustration
frustrado/a frustrated
fruta fruit (7); **jugo de fruta** fruit juice (7)
frutería fruit store, stand
frutilla strawberry
fruto fruit
fuego fire
fuente *f.* source; fountain; serving dish
fuera *adv.* outside
fuerza force; **fuerzas** (*f. pl.*) **armadas** armed forces
fumador(a) smoker; **sala de fumadores** smoking area (8)
fumar to smoke (8); **sala de fumar** smoking area (8)
funcionamiento *n.* functioning, working
funcionar to work; to function (12); to run (*machines*) (12)
fundación *f.* foundation
fundador(a) founder
fundar to found
furia rage; **furia al volante** road rage; **furia caminera** road rage
furioso/a furious, angry (6)
fútbol *m.* soccer (10); **fútbol americano** football (10)
futbolista *m., f.* soccer player
futuro *n.* future
futuro/a *adj.* future

G

gabinete *m.* cabinet
gafas *f. pl.* glasses (4); **gafas de sol** sunglasses (4)

gaita *Colombian indigenous flute*
galán *m.* handsome man
gallego Galician (*language*)
galleta cookie (7)
gallo/a rooster, hen; **Misa del Gallo** Midnight Mass
galope *m. traditional dance of Paraguay*
galopera *traditional dance of Paraguay*
gambas *f. pl.* shrimp (*Sp.*)
ganador(a) winner
ganancia earning
ganar to win (10); to earn (*income*) (13)
ganas: tener ganas de + *inf.* to feel like (*doing something*) (4)
gandules *m. pl.* pigeon peas
ganga bargain (4)
garaje *m.* garage (5)
garantizar (c) to guarantee
garbanzos *m. pl.* chickpeas (7)
garganta throat (11)
garifunas *m. pl.* Black Caribs (*descendents of Carib indigenous people and African slaves in Honduras*)
gas *m.* gas (*not for cars*) (12)
gaseosa soft drink
gasolina gasoline (15)
gasolinera gas station (15)
gastar to spend (*money*) (9); to use (*gas*) (15)
gasto expense (12)
gastronómico/a gastronomic
gato cat (3)
gaucho *Argentine cowboy*
gazpacho *cold tomato soup of southern Spain*
gemelo/a twin
genealógico/a: árbol (*m.*) **genealógico** family tree
generación *f.* generation
general general; **en general** in general; **por lo general** generally (5)
generar to generate; to create
genérico/a generic
género genre; gender
generosidad *f.* generosity
generoso/a generous
gente *f. s.* people (8)
genuinamente genuinely
geografía geography
geográfico/a geographic
geología geology
geométrico/a geometric
gerente *m., f.* manager (17)
gerundio *gram.* gerund
gigante *adj.* giant
gimnasio gym(nasium)
ginecólogo/a gynecologist
gira tour
gitano/a *n., adj.* gypsy
globalización *f.* globalization
gobernador(a) governor

gobierno government (15)
gol *m.* goal (*soccer*)
golf *m.* golf (10)
golfo gulf
golpe *m.* blow; **golpe de estado** coup d'état
gordo/a fat (3)
gorila *m.* gorilla (15)
gorra baseball cap (4)
gótico/a Gothic
GPS *m.* GPS (12)
grabadora (tape) recorder/player
grabar to record (12); to tape (12)
gracia grace
gracias thank you (1); **Día** (*m.*) **de Acción de Gracias** Thanksgiving; **gracias por** + *noun/inf.* thanks for (9); **muchas gracias** thank you very much (1)
grado grade, year (*in school*); degree (*temperature*)
graduarse (me gradúo) (en) to graduate (from) (17)
gráfico/a graphic
grafiti *m.* graffiti
gramática grammar
gramo gram
gran, grande large, big; great (3); **Gran Bretaña** Great Britain; **pantalla grande** big screen (monitor) (12)
granero barn
granizo hail
granja farm
grano grain
grasa fat
gratis *inv.* free (of charge)
gratuito/a free (of charge)
grave serious
Grecia Greece
griego/a *n., adj.* Greek
grifo faucet
gripa flu (*Mex.*)
gripe *f.* flu (11)
gris gray (4)
gritar to shout
grito shout; cry
grueso/a thick
grupo group; band
guagua bus (*Carib.*)
guaguanco *subgenre of rumba*
guampa *cup made from a hollowed bull's horn used to drink mate; cup used to drink* **tereré**
guanábana soursop (*tropical fruit*)
guancasco *traditional dance of the Lenca of Honduras*
guante *m.* glove
guapo/a handsome; good-looking (3)
guaraní *m. indigenous language of South America*
guardacostas *m. inv.* Coast Guard

guardar to keep (12); to save (*documents*) (12); **guardar cama** to stay in bed (11); **guardar un puesto** to save a place (*in line*) (8)
guatemalteco/a *n., adj.* Guatemalan
gubernamental governmental
guerra war (18); **guerra civil** civil war
guerrero/a warrior
guía *m., f.* guide (13)
guiado/a guided
guion *m.* script (13)
güiro *Latin American musical instrument*
guitarra guitar
guitarrista *m., f.* guitarist
gustar to be pleasing (8); **¿a usted le gusta... ?** do you (*form. s.*) like . . . ? (1); **me gustaría (mucho)...** I would (really) like . . . (8); **(no,) no me gusta** (no,) I don't like . . . (1); **(sí,) me gusta...** (yes,) I like . . . (1); **¿te gusta... ?** do you (*fam. s.*) like . . . ? (1)
gusto like preference; *pl.* likes (1); **mucho gusto** nice to meet you (1)

H

haber (*inf. of* **hay**) there is, there are; to have (*aux. verb*) (12)
habichuelas *f. pl.* beans
habilidad *f.* ability
habitación *f.* bedroom
habitante *m., f.* inhabitant
habitar to inhabit
hábito habit
hablante *m., f.* speaker
hablar to speak; to talk (2); **hablar con soltura** to speak fluently; **hablar por teléfono** to talk on the phone (2)
hacer to do; to make (5); **hace** + *time* + **que** + *present* to have been (*doing something*) for (*time*) (14); **hace** + *time* + **que** + *preterite* ago (14); *present* + **desde hace** + *time* to have been (*doing something*) for (*time*) (14); *preterite* + **hace** + *time* ago (14); **hace (muy) buen/mal tiempo** it's very good/bad weather (6); **hace (mucho) calor** it's (very) hot (weather) (6.); **hace fresco** it's cool (weather) (6.); **hace (mucho) frío** it's (very) cold (*weather*); **hacer autostop** to hitchhike; **hacer** *camping* to go camping (8); **hacer clic** to click (12) **hacer cola** to stand in line (8); **hacer (foto)copia** to copy (12); **hacer (el método) Pilates** to do Pilates (11); **hacer (el) yoga** to do yoga (10); **hacer ejercicio** to exercise (5); **hacer ejercicios aeróbicos** to do aerobics (11); **hacer escalas** to make stops (8); **hacer frente a** to face up to; **hacer la cama** to make the bed (10); **hacer la(s) maleta(s)** to pack

one's suitcase(s) (8); **hacer paradas** to make stops (8); **hacer planes** (*m.*) **para** + *inf.* to make plans to (*do something*) (10); **hacer reserva** to make a reservation; **hacer** *surfing* to surf (10); **hacer un** *picnic* to have a picnic (10); **hacer un viaje** to take a trip (5); **hacer una fiesta** to have/throw a party (9); **hacer una juerga** to throw a party; **hacer una pregunta** to ask a question (5); **hacerse daño** to hurt oneself (14); **hacerse daño en** to hurt one's (*body part*) (14); **¿qué tiempo hace?** what's the weather like? (6)

hacia *prep.* towards

hada (*but* **el hada**) fairy

hallaca *Venezuelan meat pastry*

hamaca hammock

hambre *f.* hunger; **pasar hambre** to go hungry; **tener (mucha) hambre** to be (very) hungry (7)

hamburguesa hamburger (7)

harina flour

hasta *adv.* until; even; *prep.* until; **hasta luego** see you later (1); **hasta mañana** see you tomorrow (1); **hasta pronto** see you soon; **hasta que** until (17)

hay there is/are (1); **hay que** + *inf.* it is necessary to (*do something*) (13); **no hay** there is/are not (1); **no hay de qué** you're welcome (1)

hebreo Hebrew (*language*)

hecho *n.* fact; event (9)

hecho/a (*p.p. of* **hacer**) made

hectárea *land measure equal to 2.5 acres*

helado ice cream (7)

heliconia *flowering tropical plant*

hemisferio hemisphere

herbolario/a herbalist

heredar to inherit

herencia inheritance

hermanastro/a stepbrother, stepsister

hermano/a brother/sister (3); *m. pl.* siblings (3)

hermoso/a beautiful

héroe *m.* hero

heroína heroine

hervir (hiervo) (i) to boil

híbrido/a hybrid (15)

hidalgo nobleman

hidroeléctrico/a hydroelectric

hielo ice

hierba grass

hígado liver

hijastro/a stepson, stepdaughter

hijo/a son/daughter (3); *m. pl.* children (3)

himno hymn; **himno nacional** national anthem

hipopótamo hippopotamus

hispánico/a Hispanic

hispano/a Hispanic (3)

Hispanoamérica Hispanic America

hispanoamericano/a *adj.* Hispanic American

hispanohablante *adj. m., f.* Spanish-speaking

historia history (2); story (8)

historiador (a) historian

histórico/a historical

hockey *m.* hockey (10)

hogar *m.* home

hoja leaf

¡hola! hi!; hello! (1)

Holanda Holland

hombre *m.* man (2); **hombre de negocios** businessman (17)

homeópata *m., f.* homeopath

homeopático/a homeopathic

homogeneidad *f.* homogeneity

homogéneo/a homogenous

hondureño/a *n., adj.* Honduran

honesto/a honest

hongo mushroom; toadstool; fungus; **sombrero hongo** bowler hat, derby

honor *m.* honor

honrado/a honest; honorable

hora hour; time; **¿a qué hora... ?** at what time . . . ? (1); **es hora de... ** it's time to . . . ; **hora punta** peak hour **¿qué hora es?** what time is it? (1)

horario schedule (14)

horchata *Mexican drink made from rice*

hormona hormone

horno oven; **horno de microondas** microwave oven (10)

horóscopo horoscope

horror *m.* horror

hospital *m.* hospital

hospitalario/a hospitable

hospitalidad *f.* hospitality

hospitalización *f.* hospitalization

hotel *m.* hotel

hoy today (1); **¿cuál es la fecha de hoy?** what's today's date? (6); **¿qué día es hoy?** what day is today? (5); **¿qué fecha es hoy?** what's today's date? (6)

huelga strike (*labor*) (18)

huella mark; (finger)print

huerto orchard

hueso bone

huésped *m., f.* guest

huevo egg (7)

huipil *m. traditional Mayan blouse*

huir (*like* **construir**) to flee

humanidad *f.* humanity; *pl.* humanities (2)

humanista *n., adj.* humanist

humanitario/a humanitarian

humanizar (c) to make more human

humano/a human (11); **cuerpo humano** human body (11); **ser** (*m.*) **humano** human being

humedad *f.* humidity

húmedo/a humid

humilde humble

humorístico/a humorous

huracán *m.* hurricane

I

ibérico/a *adj.* Iberian

íbero/a *n.* Iberian

icónico/a iconic

ícono icon

ida: billete (*m.*) (*Sp.*) / **boleto** (*L.A.*) **de ida** one-way ticket (8); **billete** (*m.*) (*Sp.*) / **boleto** (*L.A.*) **de ida y vuelta** round-trip ticket (8)

idealista *m., f.* idealistic

idear to think up: to conceive (*idea*)

idéntico/a identical

identidad *f.* identity; **carnet** (*m.*) **de identidad** identification card

identificación *f.* identification; **carnet** (*m.*) **de identificación** identification card; **tarjeta de identificación** identification card (14)

identificar (se) (qu) to identify (oneself)

idioma *m.* language

idiomático/a idiomatic

ídolo idol

iglesia church (16)

ignorante ignorant

ignorar to ignore

igual same; equal

igualdad *f.* equality (18)

igualitario/a egalitarian

igualmente likewise; same here (1)

ilimitado/a unlimited

ilógico/a illogical

ilusorio/a false

ilustrar to illustrate

ilustrativo/a illustrative

imagen *f.* image (13)

imaginación *f.* imagination

imaginar(se) to imagine

imaginativo/a imaginative

imitar to imitate

impaciente impatient

impacto impact

impedimento impediment

impedir (*like* **pedir**) to impede

imperfecto *gram.* imperfect

imperio empire

impermeable *m.* raincoat (4); *adj.* impermeable

impertinente impertinent
implementar to implement
implicar (qu) to imply
imponer (*like* **poner**) to impose
importancia importance
importante important
importar (*like* **gustar**) to matter; to be important
imposible impossible (13); **es imposible que** it's impossible that (13); **no es imposible que** it's not impossible (13)
impresión *f.* impression
impresionante impressive
impresionar to impress
impreso/a printed
impresora printer (12)
imprimir to print (12)
improbable unlikely (13); **es improbable que** it's unlikely, improbable that (13); **no es improbable que** it's not improbable (13)
improvisar to improvise
impuesto tax
impulsivo/a impulsive
inalámbrico/a wireless
inauguración *f.* inauguration
inca *n. m., f.* Inca; *adj. m., f.* Incan
incaico/a *adj.* Inca
incapacidad *f.* inability
incendio fire
incidente *m.* incident
incienso incense
inclinación *f.* inclination
inclinarse to lean
incluir (*like* **construir**) to include
incómodo/a uncomfortable
incompleto/a incomplete
inconcebible inconceivable
inconveniencia inconvenience
inconveniente *n. m; adj.* inconvenient
incorporar to incorporate; to include
incorrecto/a incorrect
incrédulo/a incredulous
increíble incredible (13); **es increíble que** it's incredible that (13)
incrementar to increase
incremento increment
indefinido/a indefinite; **artículo indefinido** *gram.* indefinite article; **palabra indefinida y negativa** *gram.* indefinite and negative word (7)
indeleble indelible
independencia independence
independiente independent
independizarse (c) to become independent
indescriptible indescribable
indicación *f.* instruction; direction
indicar (qu) to indicate
indicativo *gram.* indicative

índice *m.* index
Índico Indian (Ocean)
indiferente indifferent
indígena *n. m., f.* indigenous person; *adj. m., f.* indigenous
indigenista *m., f.* pertaining to indigenous topics and themes
indio/a *n., adj.* Indian
indirecto/a indirect; **complemento indirecto** *gram.* indirect object
indiscreto/a indiscreet
indispensable indispensible, essential
indistinto/a indistinct
individualidad *f.* individuality
individuo *n.* individual
individuo/a *adj.* individual
industria industry
inesperado/a unexpected
inexistente nonexistent
infancia infancy; childhood (16)
infantil *adj.* child, children's
infatigable tireless
infección *f.* infection
inferir (infiero) (i) to infer
infiltrarse to infiltrate
infinitivo *gram.* infinitive
inflexibilidad *f.* inflexibility
influencia influence
influir (*like* **construir**) to influence
influyente influential
infografía computer graphic
información *f.* information
informar to inform (18)
informática computer science
informativo/a informative
informe *m.* **(oral/escrito)** (oral/written) report (14)
infraestructura infrastructure
infrecuente infrequent
infusión *f.* infusion
ingeniería engineering
ingeniero/a engineer (17)
ingenioso/a ingenious
Inglaterra England
inglés *m.* English (*language*) (2)
inglés, inglesa *n., adj.* English (3)
ingrediente *m.* ingredient
ingresar to deposit (*in an account*)
ingreso income
inicial *f.* initial (*letter*)
iniciar to start
iniciativa initiative
inicio beginning
injusticia injustice
injusto/a unfair
inmediato/a immediate
inmenso/a immense
inmerso/a immersed
inmigración *f.* immigration
inmigrante *n., m., f.* immigrant
inmobiliario/a *adj.* real estate; property

inmóvil unmoving
innecesario/a unnecessary
innumerable countless
inocente innocent
inolvidable unforgettable
inquilino/a tenant (12); renter (12)
inscribir(se) (*p.p.* **inscrito**) **(en)** to sign up; to register (for)
inscripción *f.* inscription
inscrito/a (*p.p. of* **inscribir**) registered
insecto insect
insistir (en) to insist (on) (12)
insoportable unbearable
inspiración *f.* inspiration
instalación *f.* facility
instalar to install (12)
instantáneo/a instantaneous
instante: al instante right away
institución *f.* institution
instituto institute
instrucciones *f, pl.* instructions
instructor(a) instructor
instrumento instrument
insulina insulin
insulto insult
integración *f.* integration
integrarse to integrate oneself
intelectivo/a cognitive
intelectual intellectual
inteligencia intelligence
inteligente intelligent (3)
intención *f.* intention
intencionadamente intentionally
intensidad *f.* intensity
intensificar (qu) to intensify
intenso/a intense
intentar to attempt to
interacción *f.* interaction
interactivo/a interactive
intercambiar to exchange
intercambio exchange
interés *m.* interest (17)
interesante interesting
interesar (*like* **gustar**) to interest (*someone*) (8)
intergaláctico/a intergalactic
interior interior; inner; **ropa interior** underwear (4)
intermedio/a intermediate
interminable endless
internacional international; **Día** (*m.*) **Internacional de la No Violencia Contra la Mujer** International No Violence Against Women Day
internauta *m., f.* internet user
internet *m.* internet (12); **buscar (qu) en internet** to look for on the internet (12); **entrar en internet** to go on the internet (12)
interno/a internal
interplanetario/a interplanetary

interpretación *f.* interpretation
interpretar to interpret
interrogación: signo de interrogación question mark
interrogativo/a *gram.* interrogative (1)
interrumpir to interrupt
interrupción *f.* interruption
intervención *f.* intervention
intimidad *f.* intimacy
íntimo/a intimate; close
intolerancia intolerance
intranquilidad *f.* restlessness
introducción *f.* introduction
introducir (*like* **conducir**) to introduce
inundación *f.* flood
inútil useless
invadido/a invaded
inválido/a disabled
invasión *f.* invasion
invasor(a) *adj.* invading
inventar to invent
inversión *f.* investment
invertir (invierto) (i) to invest
investigación *f.* investigation; research
investigador(a) researcher
investigar (gu) to investigate; to research
invierno winter (6)
invitación *f.* invitation
invitado/a guest (9)
invitar to invite (7)
invocar (qu) to invoke
inyección *f.* injection (11); **ponerle una inyección** to give (*someone*) a shot (11)
iPhone *m.* iPhone (12)
iPod *m.* iPod (12)
ir to go (4); **ir a** + *inf.* to be going to (*do something*) (4); **ir a un bar** to go to a bar (10); **ir a un concierto** to go to a concert (10); **ir a una discoteca** to go to a disco (10); **ir al extranjero** to go abroad (8); **ir de compras** to go shopping (4); **ir de safari** to go on a safari; **ir de vacaciones a...** to go on vacation in/to . . . (8); **ir distraído/a** to be distracted (14); **ir en...** to go/travel by . . . (8); **ir en autobús** to go/travel by bus (8); **ir en avión** to go/travel by plane (8); **ir en barco** to go/travel by boat, ship (8); **ir en tren** to go/travel by train (8); **irse** to leave; **vamos** let's go (4)
ira al manejar road rage
iraní (*pl.* **iraníes**) *n., adj.* Iranian
iraquí (*pl.* **iraquíes**) *n., adj.* Iraqi
iridiscencia iridescence
Irlanda Ireland
irlandés, irlandesa *n., adj.* Irish
ironía irony
irónico/a ironic
irresponsable irresponsible
isla island (6)

Islandia Iceland
islote *m.* islet
israelí (*pl.* **israelíes**) *n., adj.* Israeli
Italia Italy
italiano Italian (*language*) (2)
italiano/a *n., adj.* Italian
itinerario itinerary
-ito/a *diminuitive suffix* (10)
izquierda *n.* left-hand side; **a la izquierda de** to the left of (6)
izquierdo/a *adj.* left; **levantarse con el pie izquierdo** to get up on the wrong side of the bed (14)

J

jaguar *m.* jaguar
jamaica hibiscus
jamás never (7)
jamón *m.* ham (7)
Japón *m.* Japan
japonés *m.* Japanese (*language*)
japonés, japonesa *n., adj.* Japanese
jarabe *m.* (cough) syrup (11)
jardín *m.* garden (5)
jarra jar
jazz *m.* jazz
jeans *m. pl.* blue jeans (4)
jefe/a boss
jerarquía hierarchy
jersey *m.* sweater; pullover
jirafa giraffe
jornada de tiempo parcial part-time job
joropo *folkloric music of Venezuela*
joven *n. m., f.* (*pl.* **jóvenes**) youth; *adj.* young (3); **de joven** as a youth (10)
joyería jewelry
jubilarse to retire (17)
judaísmo Judaism
juego game; **Juegos Olímpicos** Olympic Games
juerga party; **hacer una juerga** to have/throw a party
jueves *m. inv.* Thursday (5)
jugador(a) player (10)
jugar (juego) (gu) (a, al) to play (*a game, sport*) (5); **jugar a las cartas / al ajedrez / a los videojuegos** to play cards/chess/videogames (10)
jugo (de fruta) (fruit) juice (7)
juguete *m.* toy
julio July (6)
junio June (6)
junto a *prep.* near
juntos/as together (8)
jurar to swear (*oath*)
justicia justice
justificación *f.* justification
justificar (qu) to justify
justo/a fair
juvenil *adj.* youth; youthful; **diabetes** (*f.*) **juvenil** childhood diabetes
juventud *f.* youth (16)

juzgar (gu) to judge

K

kaki: color (*m.*) **kaki** khaki
kilo(gramo) kilo(gram)
kilómetro kilometer

L

la *def. art. f. s.* the; *d.o. f. s.* you (*form.*); her, it; **a la(s)...** at . . . (*time of day*) (1); **la cual** which
labor *f.* work, job
laboral *adj.* work, work-related (17)
laboratorio laboratory
lácteo/a *adj.* dairy
lado side; **al lado de** alongside of (6); **por el otro lado** on the other hand; **por un lado** on one hand
ladrar to bark
ladrón, ladrona thief
lagarto lizard
lago lake (15)
lágrima tear
lamentar to regret; to feel sorry (13)
laminado/a laminated
lámpara lamp (5)
lana wool (4); **de lana** wool (4)
langosta lobster (7)
lapicero pen
lápiz *m.* (*pl.* **lápices**) pencil (2)
largo/a long (3)
las *def. art. s. pl.* the; *d.o. f. pl.* you (*form. pl.*); **a la(s)...** at . . . (*time of day*) (1); **las cuales** which
lasaña lasagne
lástima shame; **es una lástima que** it's a shame that (13); **¡qué lástima que... !** what a shame that . . . ! (13)
lastimarse to hurt (*a body part*) (14)
lata can
latín *m.* Latin (*language*)
latino/a *adj.* Latin; **América Latina** Latin America
Latinoamérica Latin America
latinoamericano/a *n., adj.* Latin American
lavabo (bathroom) sink (5)
lavadora washing machine (10)
lavandería laundry
lavaplatos *m. inv.* dishwasher (10)
lavar to wash (10); **lavarse** to wash (oneself)
lealtad *f.* loyalty
lección *f.* lesson
leche *f.* milk (7)
lechón *m.* suckling pig; **lechón asado** roast suckling pig
lechuga lettuce (7)
lector(a) reader
lectura reading
leer (*like* **creer**) to read (3)
legislación *f.* legislation
legumbre *f.* legume

lejos *adv.* far; **lejos de** *prep.* far from (6)

lema *m.* motto

lempira *currency of Honduras*

lengua language (2); tongue (11); **lenguas extranjeras** foreign languages (2); **sacar (qu) la lengua** to stick out one's tongue (11)

lentes *m. pl.* glasses (11); **lentes de contacto** contact lenses (11)

lentillas *f. pl.* contact lenses (*Sp.*)

lento/a slow

león *m.* lion; **león marino** sea lion

leopardo leopard

letra letter (*of the alphabet*); lyrics (*song*) (7)

levantar to raise; to lift; **levantar pesas** to lift weights (11); **levantarse** to get up (out of bed) (5); to stand up (5); **levantarse con el pie izquierdo** to get up on the wrong side of the bed (14)

leve *adj.* light

ley *f.* law (18)

leyenda legend

libanés, libanesa lebanese

liberar(se) to free (oneself)

libertad *f.* freedom, liberty

libertador(a) liberator

libra pound (*measurement*)

libre free, unoccupied (10); **al aire** (*m.*) **libre** outdoors (10); **estado libre asociado** commonwealth; **libre comercio** free trade; **ratos** (*m. pl.*) **libres** spare (free) time (10); **tiempo libre** free time (10)

librería bookstore (2)

libro book (2); **libro de texto** textbook (2)

licencia license (15); **licencia de manejar/conducir** driver's license (15)

licor *m.* liqueur

licuar (licúo) to liquefy

líder *m., f.* leader

liga league

ligero/a light, not heavy (7)

lima lime

limeño/a *adj.* from Lima, Peru

limitación *f.* limitation

limitar to limit

límite *m.* limit; **fecha límite** deadline; **límite de velocidad** speed limit (15)

limón *m.* lemon

limonada lemonade

limonero lemon tree

limosina limousine

limpiar (la casa) to clean (the) house (10)

limpieza cleanliness

limpio/a clean (6)

lindo/a pretty

línea line

lingüístico/a linguistic

linterna flashlight

lío problem; trouble; **meterse en líos** to get into trouble

liquidación *f.* liquidation

líquido liquid

Lisboa Lisbon

lista list

listo/a smart; clever (3); **estar listo/a** to be ready

literario/a literary

literatura literature (2)

litoral *m.* coast

llamada call; **bloqueo de llamadas** call blocker

llamar to call (7); **¿cómo se llama usted?** what is your (*form. s.*) name? (1); **¿cómo te llamas?** what is your (*fam. s.*) name? (1); **llamarse** to be called (5); **me llamo...** my name is . . . (1) **llamarse** to be called (5)

llanero Venezuelan cowboy

llanero/a of or pertaining to the plains

llano *n.* plain

llanta (desinflada) (flat) tire (15)

llanura *n.* plain

llave *f.* key (5)

llegada arrival (8)

llegar (gu) to arrive (3); **¿cómo se llega a... ?** how do you get to . . . ? (15); **llegar a ser** to become

llenar to fill (up) (15); to fill out (*a form*) (17)

lleno/a full

llevar to wear (4); to carry (4); to take (4); **llevar una vida sana/tranquila** to lead a healthy/calm life (11); **llevarse bien/mal (con)** to get along well/poorly (with) (16)

llorar to cry (9)

llover (llueve) to rain (6); **llueve** (it's raining) (6)

lluvia rain

lluvioso/a *adj.* rainy; of rain; **bosque** (*m.*) **tropical lluvioso** tropical rain forest

lo *d.o. m. s.* you (*form.*); him; it; **lo bueno** the good news/thing (11); **lo cual** which; **lo malo** the bad news/thing (11); **lo que** what, that which (5); **lo siento (mucho)** I'm (very) sorry (14); **lo suficiente** enough (11); **por lo general** generally (5); **por lo menos** at least (9); **por lo regular** in general

lobo/a wolf

localidad *f.* ticket (*to movie, play*)

localización *f.* location

loco/a crazy (6)

locutor(a) commentator

lógico/a logical

logotipo logo

lograr to achieve

logro achievement

Londres London

longitud *f.* longitude

los *def. art. m. pl.* the; *d.o. m. pl.* you (*form. pl.*) them; **los cuales** which; **los lunes (los martes...)** on Mondays (Tuesdays . . .) (5)

lotería lottery

lubricar (qu) to lubricate

lucha fight, struggle (18)

luchar to fight (18)

lucro: sin fines de lucro non-profit

luego then, afterward, next (5); **hasta luego** see you later (1)

lugar *m.* place (2)

lujo luxury

lujoso/a luxurious

luminiscente luminescent

luminoso/a lit up

luna moon; **luna de miel** honeymoon (16)

lunares: de lunares polka-dot (4)

lunes *m. inv.* Monday (5); **el lunes** on Monday (5); **los lunes** on Mondays (5); **el lunes que viene** next Monday (5)

Luxemburgo Luxembourg

luz *f.* (*pl.* **luces**) light (14)

M

madera wood

madrastra stepmother

madre *f.* mother (3); **Día** (*m.*) **de la Madre** Mother's Day

madrileño/a of or pertaining to Madrid

madrina godmother

madrugada dawn

madurez *f.* middle age (16)

maduro/a mature

maestría master's degree

maestro/a (de escuela) schoolteacher (17); *adj.* master; **obra maestra** masterpiece (13)

Magallanes: Estrecho de Magallanes Strait of Magellan

mágico/a *adj.* magic

magnífico/a magnificent

mago wizard

mahones *m. pl.* jeans

maíz *m.* (*pl.* **maíces**) corn

mal *adv.* poorly (2); **caerle mal a alguien** to make a bad impression on someone; **empleo mal pagado** poorly paid job/position (17); **llevarse mal (con)** to get along poorly (with) (16); **pasarlo mal** to have a bad time (9); **portarse mal** to misbehave (9); **salir mal** to come/turn out badly; to do poorly (5)

mal, malo/a *adj.* bad (3); **lo malo** the bad news/thing (11); **tener mala**

suerte to have bad luck; to be unlucky (14)

maleducado/a spoiled

malestar *m.* discomfort

maleta suitcase (8); **hacer la(s) maleta(s)** to pack one's suitcase(s) (8)

maletero porter (8)

malvado/a evil

mamá mother, mom (3)

mami mom, mommy

mamífero mammal

mancha stain

mandar to send (2); to order (*someone to do something*) (12); **mandar un mensaje** to (send a) text (2)

mandarín *m.* Mandarin (*language*)

mandato command (7)

manejar to drive (12); to operate (a *machine*) (12); **ira al manejar** road rage; **licencia de manejar** driver's license (15)

manera way, manner; **de manera que** so that, in such a way that

manga sleeve

manifestación *f.* demonstration, march (18)

maniquí *m.* mannequin

mano *f.* hand (11); **darse la mano** to shake hands (11)

mansión *f.* mansion

mantener (*like* tener) to maintain; to keep (18); **mantenerse en contacto** to stay in touch

mantequilla butter (7)

manzana apple (7); (city) block

mañana tomorrow (1); **de la mañana** in the morning, A.M. (1); **hasta mañana** see you tomorrow (1); **pasado mañana** the day after tomorrow (5); **por la mañana** in the morning (2)

mapa *m.* map

mapudungun *m. language of the Mapuche people*

máquina machine

mar *m.* sea (8); **mar Caribe** Caribbean Sea

maracuyá *m.* passion fruit

maratón *m.* marathon

maravilla wonder, marvel

maravillar to delight

maravilloso/a marvelous

marca brand; label

marcar (qu) to mark

marcial martial

mareado/a dizzy (11); nauseated (11)

marido husband (3)

marihuana marijuana

marinera *folkloric dance of coastal Peru*

marino/a marine; **león** (*m.*) **marino** sea lion

mariscos *m. pl.* shellfish (7)

marítimo/a maritime; sea, marine

marketing m. marketing

marrón *adj., m., f.* brown

martes *m. inv.* Tuesday (5); **los martes** on Tuesdays (5)

Maruecos Morocco

marzo March (6)

más more (2); **cada vez más** increasingly; **más de** + *number* more than + *number* (6); **más... que** more (-er) . . . than (6)

masa mass; dough

máscara mask

mascota pet (3)

masculino/a masculine

masivo/a massive

masticar (qu) to chew

matar to kill (18)

mate *m. traditional drink of Argentina*

matemáticas *f. pl.* math (2)

materia subject area (2); material (4)

materialidad *f.* material aspect; outward appearance

materialista *m., f.* materialistic

maternidad *f.* maternity

materno/a maternal

matinal *adj.* morning

matriarcado matriarchy

matriarcal matriarchal

matrícula tuition (2)

matricularse to enroll; to register

matrimonio marriage; married couple (16)

máximo/a maximum

maya *n., adj. m., f.* Mayan

mayo May (6)

mayor older (6); oldest; greater; greatest; **Antillas** (*f. pl.*) **Mayores** Greater Antilles; **cada vez mayor** greater and greater

mayoría majority

mayoritariamente primarily

mayoritario/a *adj.* majority

mayúscula capital (letter), uppercase

me *d.o.* me; *i.o.* to/for me; *refl. pron.* myself; **me gustaría (mucho)...** I would (really) like . . . (8); **me llamo...** my name is . . . (1); **(no,) no me gusta** (no,) I don't like . . . (1); **(sí,) me gusta...** (yes,) I like . . . (1)

mecánico/a mechanic (15)

mecanización *f.* mechanization

mecanografía typing

medalla medal

mediano/a: de estatura mediana of medium height

medianoche *f.* midnight (6)

mediante *prep.* by, with

medias *f. pl.* stockings (4)

medicamento medicine

medicina medicine (11)

médico/a (medical) doctor (3)

medio *n.* medium; means; *pl.* mass media (18); **medio ambiente** environment (15); **medio de comunicación** medium of communication (18); **medio de transporte** means of transportation (8)

medio/a *adj.* half; middle; average; **media naranja** better half; **y media** half past (*the hour*) (1)

medioambiental environmental

medioambiente *m.* environment

mediodía *m.* noon (6)

medir (mido) (i) to measure

meditar to meditate

megadiverso/a megadiverse

megalópolis *f.* super-city

mejor better; best (6)

mejora improvement

mejorar(se) to improve; to get better

mellizo/a fraternal twin

melódico/a melodious

memoria memory (12)

mencionar to mention

menonito/a *adj.* Mennonite

menor younger (6); youngest; less; least

menorá menorah

menos less; least; minus; **a menos que** *conj.* unless (16); **al menos** at least; **menos cuarto** a quarter to (*hour*) (1); **menos de** + *number* fewer than + *number* (6); **menos quince** fifteen minutes till (*hour*) (1); **por lo menos** at least (9)

mensaje *m.* message; **mandar un mensaje** to (send a) text (2)

mensual monthly

mente *f.* mind

mentir (miento) (i) to lie

mentira lie (12)

menú *m.* menu (7)

menudo: a menudo *adv.* often

mercadeo marketing

mercader *m., f.* merchant

mercado market(place) (4)

mercadotecnia marketing

merecer (merezco) to deserve

merendar (meriendo) to have a snack (7)

merengue *m. dance from the Dominican Republic*

merienda snack (7)

mes *m.* month (6)

mesa table (2); **poner la mesa** to set the table (10); **quitar la mesa** to clear the table (10)

meseta plateau

mesita end table (5)

mesoamericano/a *n., adj.* Meso-American

mestizaje *m.* mixing of races

meta goal

metáfora metaphor

metal *m.* metal

metálico/a metallic

metalúrgico/a metallurgical

meteorológico/a meteorological

meter to put (*into*); to place; **meterse en líos** to get into trouble

método method; **hacer (el método) Pilates** to do Pilates (11)

metro subway; **parada del metro** subway stop (12)

metrópoli *f.* metropolis

metropolitano/a urban

mexicano/a Mexican (3)

mexicoamericano/a Mexican American

mezcla mix

mezclar to mix

mezclilla denim

mezquita mosque

mí *obj. of prep.* me (6)

mi(s) *poss. adj.* my (3)

microbio microbe

microcuento very short story

microondas: horno de microondas microwave oven (10)

microorganismo microorganism

miedo fear; **tener miedo (de)** to be afraid (of) (4)

miel *f.* honey; **luna de miel** honeymoon (16)

miembro/a member

mientras while (10)

miércoles *m. inv.* Wednesday (5); **ayer fue miércoles...** yesterday was Wednesday . . . (5)

mierda shit

mil (one) thousand (4)

milagro miracle

milenario/a thousand-year

mililitro milliliter

militar *n. m., f.* soldier; (17) *adj.* military; **servicio militar** military service (18)

milla mile

millón: un millón (de) one million (4)

millonario/a millionaire

mimar to spoil; to pamper

mineral: agua *f.* (*but* **el agua**) **(mineral)** (mineral) water (7)

minidiálogo minidialogue

mínimo minimum

ministerio ministry

ministro/a minister

minoría minority

minuto minute

mío/a(s) *poss. adj.* my; *poss. pron.* (of) mine (17)

mirada look

mirar to look at; to watch (3); **mirar la tele(visión)** to watch television (3)

misa mass; **misa del gallo** midnight mass

miseria misery

misil *n.* missile

misión *f.* mission

mismo/a same (6); **ahora mismo** right now (6)

misterio mystery

misterioso/a mysterious

mitad *f.* half

mixto/a mixed

moái *m. statue on Easter Island, Chile*

mochila backpack (2)

moda fashion; style; **a la moda** in fashion, in a stylish way; **es de última moda** it's trendy (hot) (4); **está de moda** it's trendy (hot) (4)

modales *m. pl.* manners

modelar to model

modelo model, example

módem *m.* modem (12)

moderación *f.* moderation

modernidad *f.* modernity

modernismo modernism

modernista *m., f.* modernist

moderno/a modern (13)

modificar (qu) to modify

modismo idiom

modista dressmaker

modo way, matter; mode; *gram.* mood; **de modo que** in such a way that

mole *m. Mexican sauce*

molestar (*like* **gustar**) to bother (11)

molestia *n.* bother

molesto/a annoyed (6)

molino: rueda de molino treadmill

momento moment

momia mummy

monarquía monarchy

monasterio monastery

moneda coin (17); currency

monedero coin purse

monitor *m.* monitor

monitoreo monitoring

monitorizar (c) to monitor

mono monkey

monolingüe *adj.* monolingual

monoparental *adj.* single-parent

monopatín *m.* skateboard

monotonía monotony

monótono/a monotonous

monovolumen *m.* minivan

monstruo monster

montaje *m.* montage

montaña mountain (8)

montañoso/a mountainous

montar to ride; **montar a caballo** to ride a horse (10); **montar en bicicleta** to ride a bicycle (10)

montón: un montón a lot

montuno *traditional hat of Panama*

monumento monument

morado/a purple (4)

morales *f. pl.* morals

morderse (me muerdo) to bite

moreno/a brunet(te) (3)

morir(se) ([me] muero) (u) (*p.p.* **muerto**) to die (9)

moro/a *n.* Moor; *adj.* Moorish

mosaico mosaic

mosca fly

mostrador *m.* counter (8)

mostrar (muestro) to show (8)

motivación *f.* motivation

motivo motive

moto(cicleta) motorcycle (15)

motor *m.* motor

mover (muevo) to move

móvil mobile

movimiento movement

muchacho/a young boy/girl

mucho *adv.* much (2); a lot (2); **lo siento mucho** I'm very sorry (14); **me gustaría mucho...** I would really like . . . (8); **muchísimo** an awful lot (8)

mucho/a a lot (of) (3); *pl.* many (3); **estar bajo muchas presiones** to be under a lot of pressure (14); **muchas gracias** thank you very much (1); **mucho gusto** nice to meet you (1); **tener (mucha) hambre** to be (very) hungry (7); **tener (mucha) sed** to be (very) thirsty (7); **tener muchas presiones** to be under a lot of stress (14); **tener (mucho) calor** to be (very) warm, hot (6); **tener (mucho) frío** to be (very) cold (6)

mudanza *n.* move

mudarse to move (*residence*) (12)

mueble *m.* piece of furniture (5)

muela molar, back tooth (11); **sacarle (qu) una muela** to extract (*someone's*) molar (11)

muerte *f.* death (16)

muerto/a (*p.p. of* **morir**) dead; **Día (m.) de los Muertos** Day of the Dead

mujer *f.* woman (2); wife (3); **Día (m.) Internacional de la No Violencia Contra la Mujer** International No Violence Against Women Day; **mujer de negocios** businesswoman (17); **mujer soldado** female soldier (17)

mula mule

mulato/a mulatto

multa fine

multilingüe multilingual

multinacional multinational

múltiple multiple

multiplicarse (qu) to multiply; to grow in number

multirracial multiracial

mundial *adj.* world; **Copa Mundial** World Cup

mundo world (3); **Copa del Mundo** World Cup (soccer)

municipio municipality

muñeca doll

mural *m.* mural (13)

muralismo muralism

muralista *m., f.* muralist

muralla city wall

murciélago bat

muro wall

músculo muscle

museo museum; **visitar un museo** to visit a museum (10)

música music (13)

musical musical (13)

músico *m., f.* musician (13)

musulmán, musulmana Muslim

mutuo/a mutual

muy very (1); **muy bien** fine, very well (1); **muy buenas** good morning/afternoon/evening (1)

N

nacer (nazco) to be born (16)

nacimiento birth

nación *f.* nation; **Organización (f.) de Naciones Unidas (ONU)** United Nations (U.N.)

nacional national; **himno nacional** national anthem; **producto nacional bruto** gross national product

nacionalidad *f.* nationality; **adjetivo de nacionalidad** adjective of nationality (3)

nada nothing, not anything (7); **de nada** you're welcome (1); **para nada** at all (8)

nadar to swim (8)

nadie no one, nobody, not anybody (7)

náhuatl *m.* Nahuatl (*language of the Aztecs*)

nana *fam.* grandma

naranja orange (7); **media naranja** better half

nariz *f.* (*pl.* **narices**) nose (11)

narración *f.* narration

narrador(a) narrator

narrar to narrate

natación *f.* swimming (10)

natal: casa natal house where someone was born

nativo/a native

natural natural; **ciencias (f. pl.) naturales** natural sciences (2); **recurso natural** natural resource (15)

naturaleza nature (15)

naturópata *m., f.* naturopath

náufrago shipwreck

nave (*f.*) **espacial** spaceship

navegable navigable

navegación *f.* navigation

navegar (gu) to navigate (12); **navegar la Red** to surf the internet

Navidad *f.* Christmas (9)

navideño/a *adj.* Christmas

neblina mist; fog

necesario/a necessary (3)

necesidad *f.* need, necessity

necesitar to need (2)

negación *f.* negation

negar (niego) (gu) to deny (13)

negativo/a negative; **palabra indefinida y negativa** *gram.* indefinite and negative word (7)

negociar to negotiate

negocio business; **hombre** (*m.*) **de negocios** businessman (17); **mujer** (*f.*) **de negocios** businesswoman (17)

negrilla: en negrilla boldface

negro/a black (4)

neoyorquino/a *adj.* pertaining to New York

nerviosismo nervousness

nervioso/a nervous (6)

neumático tire (*automobile*)

neutralizar (c) to neutralize

neutro/a neutral

nevar (nieva) to snow (6); **nieva** it's snowing (6)

nevera refrigerator

ni neither; nor; **ni... ni** neither . . . nor

nicaragüense *n., adj. m., f.* Nicaraguan

niebla fog

nieto/a grandson/granddaughter (3)

ningún (ninguna) no, not any (7)

niñero/a baby-sitter (10)

niñez *f.* (*pl.* **niñeces**) childhood (16)

niño/a small child; boy/girl (3); **de niño/a** as a child (10)

nivel *m.* level

no no (1); **no creer** to not think/believe (13); **no es seguro/(im)posible, (im)probable** it's not sure/(im)possible, (im)probable (13); **no estar de acuerdo** to disagree (3); **no estar seguro/a de** to not be sure of (13); **no hay** there is/are not (1); **no hay de qué** you're welcome (1); **no obstante** however; **no tener razón** to be wrong (4); **ya no** no longer

¿no? right, don't they (you...)? (4)

noche *f.* night; **buenas noches** goodnight (1); **de la noche** in the evening, P.M. (1); **esta noche** tonight (6); **por la noche** at night, in the evening (2)

Nochebuena Christmas Eve (9)

Nochevieja New Year's Eve (9)

nombrar to name

nombre *m.* name (7)

nopal *m.* cactus

noreste *m.* northeast

norma rule; norm

normal normal; **es normal que** it's normal that (13)

normalidad *f.* normality

noroeste *m.* northwest

norte *m.* north (6)

Norteamérica North America

norteamericano/a North American

nos *d. o. pron.* us; *i. o. pron.* to/for us; *refl. pron.* ourselves; **nos vemos** see you around (1)

nosotros/as *subj. pron.* we (2); *obj.* (*of prep.*) us (2)

nota grade (*academic*) (5); note

notar to note, to notice

noticias *f. pl.* news (5)

noticiero newscast (18)

notificación *f.* notification

novecientos/as nine hundred (4)

novela novel (13)

novelista *m., f.* novelist (13)

noveno/a ninth (13)

noventa ninety (3)

noviazgo engagement (16)

noviembre *m.* November (6)

novio/a boyfriend/girlfriend (6); fiancé(e) (16); groom/bride (16)

nube *f.* cloud

nublado/a cloudy; **está (muy) nublado** it's (very) cloudy, overcast (6)

nuclear: energía nuclear nuclear energy (15)

nuestro/a(s) *poss. adj.* our (3); *poss. pron.* ours, of ours (17)

nueve nine (1)

nuevo/a new (3); **Año Nuevo** New Year; **Nueva York** New York

numérico/a numerical

número number (1); **número ordinal** ordinal number (13)

numeroso/a numerous

nunca never (3); **casi nunca** almost never (3)

nupcial nuptial; **votos** (*m. pl.*) **nupciales** wedding vows

nutritivo/a nutritious

O

o or (1)

obedecer (obedezco) to obey (15)

obispo bishop

objetivo *n.* objective

objeto object (2)

obligación *f.* obligation

obligado/a customary

obligatorio/a obligatory

obra work; **obra de arte** work of art (13); **obra de teatro** play (13); **obra maestra** masterpiece (13); **obra teatral** play

obrero/a worker, laborer (17)

observación *f.* observation

observar to observe

obstáculo obstacle

obstante: no obstante however

obtener (*like* **tener**) to get; to obtain (12)

obvio/a obvious

ocasión *f.* occasion

ocasionar to cause

océano ocean (8); **océano Pacífico** Pacific Ocean

ochenta eighty (3)

ocho eight (1)

ochocientos/as eight hundred (4)

octavo/a eighth (13)

octillizo/a octuplet

octubre *m.* October (6)

oculista *m., f.* ophthalmologist

oculto/a hidden

ocupación *f.* occupation

ocupado/a busy (6)

ocupar to hold; to occupy

ocurrir to occur (14)

odiar to hate (8)

oeste *m.* west (6)

ofensivo/a offensive

off: voz en off voice over

oficial official

oficina office (2)

oficio trade (*profession*) (17)

ofrecer (ofrezco) to offer (8)

ofrenda *n.* offering

oído inner ear (11)

oír to hear (5); to listen to (*music, the radio*) (5)

ojalá (que) I hope (that) (13)

ojo eye (11); **ojo alerta** eagle eye; **¡ojo!** *interj.* watch out!

olímpico/a: Juegos (*m. pl.*) **Olímpicos** Olympic Games

oliva: aceite (*m.*) **(de oliva)** (olive) oil (7)

olor *m.* odor

olvidar to forget (9)

omnipresente omnipresent

once eleven (1)

onda wave; **¿cuál es tu onda?** what's your style?; **en onda** in style; **¿qué onda?** what's new/happening?

onomatopeya onomatopoeia

onomatopéyico/a onomatopoeic

ONU *f.* **(Organización** [*f.*] **de Naciones Unidas)** U.N. (United Nations)

opción *f.* option

opcional optional

ópera opera (13)

operación *f.* operation

opinar to think; to have/express an opinion

opinión *f.* opinion

oponerse (a) (*like* **poner**) to oppose

oportunidad *f.* opportunity

optar (por) to opt (for)

optimista *m., f.* optimist; *adj.* optimistic

opuesto/a opposite

oración *f.* sentence

oral oral (14); **informe** (*m.*) **oral** oral report (14)

órale *interj. sl.* wow!

orangután *m.* orangutan

órbita orbit

orden *m.* order

ordenado/a neat (6)

ordenador *m. Sp.* computer

ordenar to put in order

ordinal: número ordinal ordinal number (13)

ordinario/a ordinary

oreja (outer) ear (11)

orgánico/a organic

organismo organism

organización *f.* organization

organizar (c) to organize

órgano organ

orgullo pride

orgulloso/a proud

orientación *f.* orientation

oriental eastern

origen *m.* origin

originario/a native

originarse to come from

oriundo/a native

oro gold (4); **de oro** gold (4)

orquesta orchestra (13)

orquídea orchid

ortogar (gu) to give

ortografía spelling

ortográfico/a: acento ortográfico accent mark

oscuridad *f.* darkness

oso/a bear

ostra oyster

otavaleno/a resident of Otavalo (*Ecuador*)

otoño fall, autumn (6)

otorgar (gu) to grant

otro/a other, another (3); **otra vez** again; **por el otro lado** on the other hand

oveja sheep

ozono: capa de ozono ozone layer (15)

P

paciencia patience

paciente *n. m., f.* patient (11); *adj.* patient

pacífico/a Pacific; **océano Pacífico** Pacific Ocean

padrastro stepfather

padre *m.* father (3); *m. pl.* parents (3); **Día** (*m.*) **del Padre** Father's Day

padrino godfather

paella *Spanish dish made with rice, shellfish, and often chicken, and flavored with saffron*

pagado/a: empleo bien/mal pagado well-/poorly paid job/ position (17)

pagar (gu) to pay (for) (2)

página page; **página web** webpage (12)

país *m.* country (3)

pájaro bird (3)

Pakistán Pakistan

pakistaní *m., f.* Pakistani

palabra word (1); **palabra indefinida y negativa** *gram.* indefinite and negative word (7)

palacio palace

palestino/a Palestinian

palma palm tree

palmera palm tree

palo stick

palomitas *f. pl.* popcorn

pampa plain (*geography, Arg.*)

pan *m.* bread (7); **pan tostado** toast (7)

panadería bakery

panameño/a *n., adj.* Panamanian

páncreas *m. inv.* pancreas

pandemia pandemic

pandilla gang

pánel (*m.*) **solar** solar panel

panhispano/a Pan-Hispanic

pánico panic

panorama *m.* panorama

pantalla (grande/plana) (big/flat) screen (monitor) (12)

pantalones *m. pl.* pants (4); **pantalones cortos** shorts (4)

pañuelo handkerchief

papa (frita) (French fried) potato (7)

papá *m.* father, dad (3); *m. pl.* parents

papel *m.* paper (2); role (13)

papi *m.* dad, daddy

par *m.* pair

para (intended) for; in order to (3); **para +** *inf.* (do something) (10); **para nada...** at all (8); **para que** so that (16)

parabrisas *m. inv.* windshield (15)

paracaídas *m. inv.* parachute

paracaidismo skydiving

parada stop (8); **hacer paradas** to make stops (8); **parada del autobús** bus stop (12); **parada del metro** subway stop (12)

paraguayo/a *n., adj.* Paraguayan

parar to stop (15)

parcial partial; **empleo de tiempo parcial** part-time job/position (17); **trabajo de tiempo parcial** part-time job (14)

pardo/a brown

parecer (parezco) (*like* gustar) to seem; **parecerse (a)** to resemble

pared *f.* wall (5)

pareja (married) couple; partner (16)

paréntesis *m. inv.* parentheses

pariente *m.* relative (3)

parlamentario/a parliamentary

parque *m.* park

parqueadero parking lot

parquear to park

párrafo paragraph

parranda Christmas party (*Cuba*)

parrilla grill

parte *f.* part (5); **por todas partes** everywhere (14)

participación *f.* participation

participante *m., f.* participant

participar to participate

particular particular; unique; **en particular** particularly

partida: punto de partida starting point

partido game, match (10); political party (18)

partir: a partir de beyond (4)

pasado/a past, last (11); **el año pasado** last year; **pasado mañana** the day after tomorrow (5)

pasaje *m.* fare, price (*of a transportation ticket*) (8)

pasajero/a passenger (8)

pasaporte *m.* passport (8)

pasar to spend (*time*) (6); to happen (6); **pasar hambre** to go hungry; **pasar la aspiradora** to vacuum (10); **pasar las vacaciones en...** to spend one's vacation in . . . (8); **pasar por el control de seguridad** to go/pass through security (check) (8); **pasar por la aduana** to go/pass through customs (8); **pasarlo bien/mal** to have a good/bad time (9)

pasatiempo pastime (10)

Pascua Easter (9)

pasear to take a walk, stroll; to go for a ride; **pasear en bicicleta** to ride a bicycle (10)

paseo walk, stroll; **dar un paseo** to take a walk (10)

pasillo aisle (8)

pasión *f.* passion

paso step

pastel *m.* cake (7); pie (7); **pastel de cumpleaños** birthday cake (9)

pastilla pill (11)

pastor(a) minister

pata leg (*of an animal*)

patata (frita) (French fried) potato (7)

paternidad *f.* paternity

paterno/a paternal

patinaje *m.* skating (10)

patinar to skate (10)

patio patio (5); yard (5)

patojo/a *sl.* young man/woman (*Guat.*)

patriarcal patriarchal

Patricio: Día (*m.*) **de San Patricio** St. Patrick's Day

patrimonio patrimony

patriota *m., f.* patriot

patriótico/a patriotic

patronal: fiesta patronal *party dedicated to patron saint*

pavo turkey (7)

paz *f.* (*pl.* **paces**) peace (18)

peca freckle

pecho chest

pedazo piece

pedir (pido) (i) to ask for (5); to order (5); **pedir disculpas** to apologize (14); **pedir prestado/a** to borrow (17)

pegar (gu) to hit (14); **pegarse con/contra** to run, bump into/against (14)

peinarse to comb/brush one's hair (5)

Pekín Peking

pelado/a *sl.* young man/woman (*Col.*)

pelear to fight (10)

pelícano pelican

película movie (5)

peligro danger; **especie** (*f.*) **en peligro de extinción** endangered species (15)

peligroso/a dangerous

pelo hair; **teñirse (me tiño) (i) el pelo** to dye one's hair; **tomarle el pelo** to pull someone's leg

pelota ball (10)

pelotero/a baseball player

peluche: animal (*m.*) **de peluche** stuffed animal

peluquero/a hairstylist (17)

pen drive *m.* memory stick (12)

pena pity

pendiente *m.* earring (*Sp.*)

península peninsula

pensar (pienso) (de/en) to think (about) (5); **pensar** + *inf.* to intend, plan to (*do something*) (5); **pensar que** to think that (5)

penúltimo/a next to last

peor worse (6)

pepino cucumber (7)

pequeño/a small (3)

percatarse to realize

percepción *f.* perception

percibir to perceive

percusión *f.* percussion

perder (pierdo) to lose; to miss (*an event*) (5)

perdón excuse me (1)

perdonar to forgive

perdurable lasting

peregrinación *f.* pilgrimage

perezoso/a lazy (3)

perfección *f.* perfection

perfecto/a perfect

pérfido/a treacherous

perfil *m.* profile

perforación *f.* drilling (*well*)

perfume *m.* perfume

periódico newspaper (3)

periodismo journalism

periodista *m., f.* journalist (17)

período period (*of time*)

permanecer (permanezco) to remain, stay

permanente permanent

permiso permission; permit; **(con) permiso** excuse me (1); **permiso de manejar** driving permit

permitir to permit, allow (12)

pero but (1)

perro dog (3)

persecución *f.* persecution

perseguir (*like* seguir) to chase; to pursue

persona person (2)

personaje *m.* character (*book, movie*)

personal (*m.*) **médico** medical personnel (11)

personal *adj.* personal; **pronombre** (*m.*) **personal** *gram.* personal pronoun (2)

personalidad *f.* personality

perspectiva perspective

persuasivo/a persuasive

pertenecer (pertenezco) a to belong to

perturbar to perturb, bother

peruano/a *n., adj.* Peruvian

pesado/a boring; difficult (10); heavy

pesar to weigh; **a pesar de** in spite of

pesas: levantar pesas to lift weights (11)

pescadería fish market

pescado fish (7)

pescar (qu) to fish

pesimista *m., f.* pessimistic

peso weight

pestaña eyelash

petición *f.* request

petróleo petroleum, oil (15)

petrolero/a *adj.* oil; petroleum

pez *m.* (*pl.* **peces**) fish (15)

picante hot, spicy (7)

picar (qu) to bite; to sting

picnic: **hacer un** *picnic* to have a picnic (10)

pico peak

pie *m.* foot (11); **dedo del pie** toe; **levantarse con el pie izquierdo** to get up on the wrong side of the bed (14)

piedra stone

piel *f.* skin
pierna leg (11)
pieza piece
pila battery; **ponerse las pilas** to get one's act together; to energize oneself
pilar *m.* pillar
Pilates: hacer (el método) Pilates to do Pilates (11)
píldora pill
piloto *m., f.* pilot (8)
pimienta pepper (*condiment*) (7)
pingüino penguin
pino pine (tree)
pinola *m. typical Nicaragua drink*
pintar to paint (13)
pintor(a) painter (13)
pintura painting (*general*) (13)
piña pineapple
pirámide *f.* pyramid
piraña piranha
Pirineos *m. pl.* Pyrenees
piscina swimming pool (5)
Piscis *m.* Pisces
pisco *alcoholic beverage of Peru and Chile*
piso floor (*of a building*) (12); **barrer (el piso)** to sweep (the floor) (10); **primer piso** first floor (second story) (12); **segundo piso** second floor (third story) (12)
pizarra chalkboard
pizarrón *m.* (chalk)board (2); **pizarrón blanco** whiteboard (2)
placa license plate
placer *m.* pleasure
plan *m.* plan (10); **hacer planes para + inf.** to make plans to (*do something*) (10)
planchar to iron (10)
planeación *f.* planning
planear to plan
planeta *m.* planet (15)
planetario/a planetary
plano map (*of a city*); blueprint
plano/a flat; **pantalla plana** flat screen (monitor) (12)
planta plant
planta baja ground floor (12)
plantación *f.* plantation
plasma: televisión plasma *f.* plasma television (12)
plástico plastic
plata *n.* silver (4); **de plata** *adj.* silver (4)
plátano plantain
platino platinum
plato dish; course (7); plate (5); **plato principal** main course (7)
playa beach (6)
plaza plaza, square (4)
plazo deadline (14); **a plazos** in installments (17)

pleno/a complete; full
plomero/a plumber (17)
pluma pen
plurinacional multinational
población *f.* population (15)
pobre poor (3)
pobreza poverty
poco (a) little (2); few (4); **un poco (de)** a little bit (of) (2)
poder *v.* to be able, can (4)
poder *n. m.* power; **poder adquisitivo** purchasing power
poderoso/a powerful
poema *m.* poem (13)
poesía poetry
poeta *m., f.* poeta (13)
poético/a poetic
polaco/a Polish
policía *m., f.* police officer (15); *f.* police (*force*); **mujer (*f.*) policía** policewoman
polinésico/a Polynesian
política politics; policy (18)
político/a *n.* politician (18); *adj.* political; **ciencias (*f. pl.*) políticas** political science (2)
pollera *indigenous skirt of the Andes*
pollo chicken (7); **pollo asado** roast chicken (7); **pollo frito** fried chicken
polvo dust
poner to put (5); to place (5); to turn on (*an appliance*) (12); **poner atención** to pay attention; **poner la mesa** to set the table (10); **ponerle una inyección** to give (*someone*) a shot (11); **ponerse** to put on (*an article of clothing*) (5); **ponerse + adj.** to become, get + *adj.* (9); **ponerse las pilas** to get one's act together; to energize oneself; **ponerse rojo/a** to blush (9)
popularidad *f.* popularity
por about (6); because of (6); through (8); for (8); by (14); **gracias por + noun/ inf.** thanks for (9); **por consiguiente** as a result; **por Dios** for heaven's sake (14); **por ejemplo** for example (14); **por el otro lado** on the other hand; **por ello** therefore; **por eso** for that reason (3); **por favor** please (1); **por fin** finally (5); **por la mañana** in the morning (2); **por la noche** at night, in the evening (2); **por la tarde** in the afternoon (2); **por lo general** generally (5); **por lo menos** at least (9); **por lo regular** in general; **por primera/última vez** for the first/ last time (14); **por si acaso** just in case (14); **por todas partes** everywhere (14); **por un lado** on one hand
porcentaje *m.* percentage
porción *f.* portion, part
pormenorizado/a detailed
poro pore
porotos *m. pl.* beans

porque because (3)
portafolio portfolio
portarse bien/mal to (mis)behave (9)
portátil portable; **computadora portátil** laptop (computer) (2); **ordenador (*m.*) portátil** (*Sp.*) laptop computer (12)
portero/a building manager; doorman (12)
portón *m.* front door; gate
portugués *m.* Portuguese (*language*)
portugués, portuguesa *n., adj.* Portuguese
posar to pose
posesión *f.* possession
posesivo/a possessive (17); **adjetivo posesivo** *gram.* possessive adjective (3)
posibilidad *f.* possibility
posible possible (3); **es posible que** it's possible that (13) **no es posible** it's not possible (13)
posición *f.* position
positivo/a positive
posponer (*like* poner) to postpone
postal: tarjeta postal postcard (8)
posterior later, subsequent
postre *m.* dessert (7)
postularse to run (18); **postularse como candidato/a** to run as a candidate (18); **postularse para un cargo como candidato/a** to run for a position as a candidate (18)
postura posture
potencia power
potencial *m.* potential; *adj.* potential
práctica practice
practicar (qu) to practice (2); **practicar el alpinismo** to mountain climb; **practicar un deporte** to play a sport
práctico/a practical
pradera meadow
preadolescencia preadolescence
precedente *m.* precedent
preceder to precede
precio (fijo) (fixed, set) price (4)
precioso/a precious
precipicio precipice
precipitado/a hasty
precisamente precisely
precolombino/a pre-Columbian
predicción *f.* prediction
predominante predominant
predominar to predominate
preescolar *adj.* preschool
preferencia preference (1)
preferir (prefiero) (i) to prefer (4)
¿por qué? why? (3)
pregunta question (5); **hacer una pregunta** to ask a question (5)
preguntar to ask (*a question*) (8)
prehistórico/a prehistoric
premio prize

prenda article of clothing
prender to fasten
prensa (print) press (18); news media (18); **quiosco de prensa** newsstand (18)
prensado/a pressed
preocupación *f.* worry
preocupado/a worried (6)
preocupar(se) to worry
preparación *f.* preparation
preparar to prepare (7); **prepararse** to prepare oneself; to get ready
preparatoria (prepa) pre-university study
preposición *f. gram.* preposition (5)
prescribir to prescribe
preseleccionado/a pre-selected
presencia presence
presencial: de forma presencial in person
presentación *f.* presentation
presentador(a) presenter; (television) anchor
presentar to introduce; to present
presente *m.* present (*time*); *gram.* present tense; *adj.* present
preservar to preserve
presidencia presidency
presidencial presidential
presidente/a president
presión *f.* pressure (14); **estar bajo muchas presiones** to be under a lot of pressure (14); **tener muchas presiones** to be under a lot of stress (14)
preso/a prisoner
prestado/a: pedir prestado/a to borrow (17)
préstamo loan (17)
prestar to lend (8)
prestigioso/a prestigious
presupuestario/a budgetary
presupuesto budget (17)
pretérito *gram.* preterite
preuniversitario/a pre-university
prevenir (*like* **venir**) to warn
primario/a primary; first; elementary; **escuela primaria** elementary school
primavera spring (6)
primer(o/a) first (5); **el primero de** the first of (*month*) (6); **primer piso** first floor (second story) (12); **por primera vez** for the first time (14)
primo/a cousin (3); *m. pl.* cousins (3)
princesa princess
principal main; **plato principal** main course (7)
príncipe *m.* prince
principiante *m., f.* beginner; novice
principio beginning; **al principio de** at the beginning of (17)

priorizar (c) to prioritize
prisa: tener prisa to be in a hurry (4)
privacidad *f.* privacy
privado/a private
privilegio privilege
probabilidad *f.* probability
probable probable (13); **es probable que** it's likely, probable that (13); **no es probable que** it's not probable (13)
probar (pruebo) to try, taste
problema *m.* problem
problemático/a problematic
procedimiento procedure
procesión *f.* procession
proceso process
proclamar to proclaim
procurar to procure
producción *f.* production
producir (*like* **conducir**) to produce
productivo/a productive
producto product; **producto nacional bruto** gross national product
productor(a) producer
profesión *f.* profession (17)
profesional *n. m., f.* professional, person with a profession; *adj.* professional
profesionista *n. m., f.* professional, person with a profession
profesor(a) professor (1)
profesorado faculty
profundidad *f.* depth
profundo/a deep
programa *m.* program; **programa (del curso)** (course) syllabus (14)
programación *f.* programming
programador(a) programmer (17)
progresivo/a progressive
progreso progress
prohibir (prohíbo) to prohibit, forbid (12)
proliferación *f.* proliferation
promedio average
promesa promise
prometer to promise (8)
prominente prominent
promover (promuevo) to promote
pronombre *m. gram.* pronoun; **pronombre personal** *gram.* personal pronoun (2); **pronombre relativo** *gram.* relative pronoun
pronosticar (qu) to forecast
pronóstico forecast
pronto soon; **hasta pronto** see you soon; **tan pronto como** as soon as (17)
prontuario guide
pronunciación *f.* pronunciation
pronunciar to pronounce
propiedad *f.* property; characteristic
propio/a own, one's own (17)
proponer (*like* **poner**) to propose
proporción *f.* proportion

proporcionar to provide
propósito purpose
prórroga extension
protagonista *m., f.* protagonist
protección *f.* protection
protector(a) protective
proteger (protejo) to protect (15)
proteína protein
protestante *n., adj. m., f.* Protestant
protestantismo Protestantism
protestar to protest
provecho: ¡buen provecho! enjoy your meal!
proveedor(a) provider
proveer (*like* **creer**) to provide
proverbio proverb
providencia providence
provincia province
provocar (qu) to cause
próximo/a next; **el próximo (martes...)** next (Tuesday . . .) (5); **la próxima semana** next week (5)
proyección *f.* projection
proyecto project
prudente prudent
prueba quiz; test (14); proof
psicología psychology
psicólogo/a psychologist
publicación *f.* publication
publicar (qu) to publish (12)
publicidad *f.* publicity
publicitario/a *adj.* advertising
público *n.* audience (13)
público/a *adj.* public (15); **transporte** (*m.*) **público** public transportation
pueblo town
puente *m.* bridge
puerco pig
puerta door (2); **puerta de embarque** boarding gate (8)
puerto port (8)
puertorriqueño/a *n., adj.* Puerto Rican
pues *conj.* well
puesto job; position; place (*in line*) (8)
pulgada inch
pulido/a polished
pulmones *m. pl.* lungs (11)
pulpería grocery store (*C.A.*)
pulpo octopus
punto point; **a punto de** + *inf.* about to + *inf.*; **en punto** on the dot (*time*) (1); **hora punta** peak hour; **punto cardinal** cardinal point (6); **punto de partida** starting point; **punto de vista** point of view
puntuación *f.* punctuation
pupusa *thick stuffed corn tortilla*
puro cigar
puro/a pure (15)
púrpura *n.* purple
purpúreo/a *adj.* purple

Q

que that, which (3); who (3); **así que** therefore, consequently, so; **hasta que** *conj.* until; **que Dios te bendiga** God bless you; **ya que** since

¿qué? what? which?; **¿a qué hora... ?** at what time . . . ? (1); **¿con qué frecuencia... ?** how often . . . ? (3); **¿por qué?** why? (3)

¡qué... ! what . . . !; **¡qué bacán!** fantastic! **¡qué yuca!** how difficult!

quebrarse (me quiebro) to break

quedar to remain; to be left (14); to stay; to remain (*in a place*) (6)

quehacer (*m.*) **doméstico** household chore (10)

quejarse (de) to complain (about) (8)

quemada *n.* burn

quemar to burn

querer to want (4); to love (16); **eso quiere decir...** that means . . . (11); **fue sin querer** I didn't mean to do it (14); **quererse** to love each other; to be fond of each other (11); **querido/a** dear (6)

querido/a dear (6)

queso cheese (7)

quetzal currency of Guatemala

quien who; whom

¿quién(es)? who? whom?; **¿de quién?** whose? (3)

química chemistry (2)

quince fifteen (1); **menos quince** fifteen minutes till (*hour*) (1); **y quince** fifteen minutes after (*the hour*) (1)

quinceañera young woman's fifteenth birthday party; young woman who is turning fifteen (9)

quinientos/as five hundred (4)

quintillizo/a quintuplet

quinto/a fifth (13)

quiosco de prensa newsstand (18)

quiropráctico/a chiropractor

quitar to remove; **quitar la mesa** to clear the table (10); **quitarse** to take off (*an article of clothing*) (5)

quizás *adv.* perhaps

R

rabia rutera road rage

ración *f.* portion

radiante bright, shining, radiant

radical *m. gram.* root

radio *m.* radio (*apparatus*) (12); *f.* radio (*medium*); **estación** (*f.*) **de radio** radio station (18)

radioyente *m., f.* radio listener; *m. pl.* radio audience

raíz *f.* (*pl.* **raíces**) root

rama branch

rana frog

ranchera *traditional music of Mexico sung by mariachis*

rancho ranch

rap *m.* rap music

rapanui *n. m., f. indigenous person of Easter Island*

rápido *adv.* quickly

rápido/a fast; **comida rápida** fast food

rápidos *m. pl.* rapids

raqueta racket

raro/a rare; strange

rascacielos *m. inv.* skyscraper (15)

rata rat

rato while, short time; **ratos libres** spare (free) time (10)

ratón *m.* mouse (12)

raya: de rayas striped (4)

rayar to scratch

raza race (*ethnic*)

razón *f.* reason; **no tener razón** to be wrong (4); **tener razón** to be right (4)

reacción *f.* reaction

reaccionar to react

real royal; real

realidad *f.* reality

realismo realism

realista *m., f.* realistic

realizar (c) to achieve; to attain

rebaja sale, reduction; *pl.* sales, reductions (4); **en rebaja** on sale

rebanada slice

rebasar to pass (*vehicle*)

rebelde *n. m., f.* rebel; *adj.* rebellious

rebelión *f.* rebellion

recado message

recámara bedroom

recepción *f.* reception

recepcionista *m., f.* receptionist

receptor *m.* receiver; recipient

receta recipe (7); prescription (11)

recetar to prescribe

recibir to receive (3)

recibo receipt (17)

reciclaje *m.* recycling (15)

reciclar to recycle (15)

recién recently; **recién casado/a (con)** newlywed (to) (16)

reciente recent

recipiente *m.* container

recíproco/a reciprocal

recitar to recite

recoger (recojo) to collect (14); to pick up (14)

recomendable recommendable

recomendación *f.* recommendation

recomendar (recomiendo) to recommend (8)

reconocer (like **conocer**) to recognize

reconocimiento recognition

reconquista reconquest

reconstituido/a remarried; hybrid (*of a family*)

reconstituir (*like* **construir**) to reconstitute; to reconstruct

recordar (recuerdo) to remember (9)

recrear to recreate

recreo recess

recto/a straight; **(todo) recto** straight ahead (15)

rector(a) university president

recuerdo memory

recuperación *f.* recuperation

recuperador(a) recuperative

recuperar to recuperate

recurso resource; **recurso natural** natural resource (15)

red *f.* network; internet; **navegar (gu) la Red** to surf the internet; **red social** social network (12)

redacción *f.* editing

redactar to write; to edit

reducción *f.* reduction

reducir (*like* **conducir**) to reduce

reemplazar (c) to replace

referencia reference

referirse (me refiero) (i) (a) to refer (to)

refinado/a refined

reflejar to reflect

reflexivo/a reflexive; **verbo reflexivo** *gram.* reflexive verb (5)

reforma change

refrán *m.* saying, proverb

refresco soft drink (7)

refrigerador *m.* refrigerator (10)

refrigeradora refrigerator

refugio refuge

regalar to give (*as a gift*) (8)

regalo present, gift (3)

regatear to haggle; to bargain (4)

regateo bartering

reggae *m.* reggae

régimen *m.* regime

región *f.* region

regir (rijo) (i) to govern

registración *f.* registration

registrar to register

registro register; record

regla rule

regresar to return (*to a place*) (2); **regresar a casa** to go home (2)

regulador(a) regulator

regular *adj.* so-so (1); **por lo regular** in general; *v.* to regulate

regularidad *f.* regularity

reina queen (18)

reinar to reign

reino kingdom

reírse (río) (i) (de) to laugh (about) (9)

reiterar to reiterate

reivindicación *f.* vindication

reivindicar (qu) to reclaim

reja bar (*of prison*)

relación *f.* relation; relationship; **relación sentimental** emotional relationship (16)

relacionar to relate

relajado/a relaxed

relajante relaxing

relajarse to relax

relámpago lightning

relativo/a: pronombre (*m.*) **relativo** *gram.* relative pronoun

relevante relevant

religión *f.* religion

religioso/a religious

relleno/a filled

reloj *m.* watch (4)

remarcar (qu) to remark

remate: de remate hopeless(ly)

remedio remedy

remodelado/a remodeled

remoto/a: control (*m.*) **remoto** remote control (12)

remuneración *f.* remuneration

renovable renewable (15); **energía renovable** renewable energy (15)

renovar (renuevo) to renew

rentar to rent (*Mex.*)

renunciar (a) to resign (from) (17)

reparar to repair (15)

repasar to review

repaso review

repeler to repel

repente: de repente suddenly (11)

repetición *f.* repetition

repetir (repito) (i) to repeat

repetitivo/a repetitive

reportaje *m.* report (*on a news show*)

reportar to report

reportero/a reporter (18)

represa dam

representación *f.* representation

representante *n. m., f.* representative; **representante al congreso** Congressional representative (18)

representar to represent

representativo/a *adj.* representative

reprobar (repruebo) to fail

república republic

republicano/a republican

requerir (requiero) (i) to require

requisito requirement

rescatar to rescue

reseña review (*book, movie*)

reserva reserve; reservation (*Sp.*); **hacer reserva** to make a reservation

resfriado *n.* cold (11)

resfriado/a *adj.* congested, stuffed up (11)

resfriarse (me resfrío) to catch/get a cold (11)

residencia dormitory (2); **residencia de ancianos** nursing home (12)

residencial *m.* building (*housing*)

residente *m., f.* resident

residuos *m. pl.* waste

resistente resistant; strong

resistir to resist

resolver (resuelvo) (*p.p.* **resuelto**) to solve; to resolve (15)

respectivo/a respective

respecto: a este respecto in this regard; (**con**) **respecto a** regarding

respetar to respect

respeto respect

respiración *f.* breathing

respirar to breathe (11)

responder to respond

responsabilidad *f.* responsibility (18); **responsabilidad cívica** civic duty (18)

responsable responsible

respuesta answer (6)

restablecimiento re-establishment; restoration

restaurante *m.* restaurant (7)

resto rest, remainder

restricción *f.* restriction

resuelto/a (*p.p. of* **resolver**) resolved

resultado result

resumen *m.* summary; **en resumen** in summary

resumir to summarize

resurrección *f.* resurrection

retribuir (*like* **contribuir**) to reward

retrospectivo/a retrospective

retumbar to resound

reunión *f.* meeting

reunirse (me reúno) (con) to get together (with) (9)

revelar to reveal

revés: al revés backwards

revisar to check (15)

revista magazine (3)

revolucionario/a revolutionary

revolver (*like* **volver**) to stir

rey *m.* king (18)

rezar (c) to pray

Ricitos de Oro Goldilocks

rico/a rich (3); tasty, savory; rich (7)

ridículo/a ridiculous

riesgo risk; **de alto riesgo** high risk

rígido/a rigid

rima rhyme

rimar to rhyme

rincón *m.* corner

rinoceronte *m.* rhinoceros

riñón *m.* kidney

río river (15)

rioplatense *adj., m., f.* from the **Río de la Plata** area

riqueza richness

risa laughter

ritmo rhythm; **ritmo de la vida** pace of life (15)

rito rite; ritual

robar to rob; to steal

robo theft; robbery

rodante: cinta rodante treadmill

rodeado/a (de) surrounded (by)

rodear to go around

rojo/a red (4)

Roma Rome

romano/a Roman

romántico/a romantic

romper(se) (*p.p.* **roto**) to break (14); **romper (con)** to break up (with) (16)

ron *m.* rum

ropa clothing (4); **ropa interior** underwear (4)

ropero wardrobe

rosa rose; **rosa té** tea rose

rosado/a pink (4)

rosario rosary

rostro face

roto/a (*p.p. of* **romper**) broken

rotulador *m.* felt-tipped pen

rubio/a blond(e) (3)

rueda wheel, tire; **rueda de molino** treadmill

ruido noise (5)

ruidoso/a noisy

ruina ruin (13)

ruso Russian (*language*)

ruso/a *n., adj.* Russian

ruta route

rutero/a: rabia rutera road rage

rutina routine (5)

rutinario/a *adj.* routine

S

sábado Saturday (5)

saber to know (7); **saber + *inf.*** to know how to (*do something*) (7)

sabiduría wisdom

sabio/a wise

sabor *m.* flavor

sabroso/a tasty

sacar (qu) to extract (11); get (*grades*) (14); to withdraw, take out (17); **sacar dinero** to withdraw money; **sacar fotos** to take photos (8); **sacar la basura** to take out the trash (10); **sacar la lengua** to stick out one's tongue (11); **sacarle un diente / una muela** to extract (*someone's*) tooth/molar (11)

sacerdote *m.* priest

safari: ir de safari to go on a safari

Sagitario Sagittarius

sagrado/a sacred

sal *f.* salt (7)

sala living room (5); **sala de espera** waiting room (8); **sala de fumadores/ de fumar** smoking area (8); **sala de urgencias** emergency room

salarial: brecha salarial wage gap

salario pay, wages (*often per hour*) (17)

salchicha sausage; hot dog (7)

salida departure (8)

salir (de) to leave (*a place*) (5); **salir bien/mal** to come/turn out well/ badly; to do poorly/well (5); **salir (con)** to go out (with) (5); **salir de vacaciones** to leave on vacation (8); **salir (para)** to leave (for) (*a place*) (5)

salmón *m.* salmon (7)

salón (*m.*) **de clase** classroom (2)

salsa sauce (7); salsa (*music*)

salsero/a *adj.* salsa (*music*)

saltar to jump

salud *f.* health (11)

saludable healthy

saludarse to greet each other (11)

saludo greeting (1)

salvadoreño/a *n., adj.* Salvadoran

salvaje wild (15)

salvar to save

san, santo/a *n.* saint; **Día** (*m.*) **de San Patricio** St. Patrick's Day; **Día** (*m.*) **de San Valentín** St. Valentine's Day

sanador(a) healer

sancocho *stew made with meat, cassava, and plantains*

sandalias *f. pl.* sandals (4)

sandía watermelon

sándwich *m.* sandwich (7)

sangre *f.* blood (11)

sangriento/a bloody

sanitario/a health; **asistencia sanitaria** health care

sano/a healthy (11); **llevar una vida sana** to lead a healthy life (11)

santo saint

santo/a holy

santuario sanctuary

sarcástico/a sarcastic

sartén *f.* skillet

satélite *m.* satellite

satírico/a satirical

satisfacción *f.* satisfaction

satisfactorio/a satisfactory

satisfecho/a satisfied

Saudito/a: Arabia Saudita Saudi Arabia

sazonar to season

secadora clothes dryer (10)

secar(se) (qu) to dry (oneself)

sección *f.* section

seco/a dry

secretario/a secretary (2)

secreto *n.* secret

secreto/a *adj.* secret

secuencia sequence

secundario/a secondary; **escuela secundaria** high school

sed *f.* thirst; **tener (mucha) sed** to be (very) thirsty (7)

seda silk (4); **de seda** *adj.* silk (4)

sedentario/a sedentary

seducir (*like* **conducir**) to seduce

segmento segment

seguida: en seguida immediately (5)

seguidor(a) follower

seguimiento following

seguir (sigo) (i) to follow (6); to keep on going (15)

según according to (3)

segundo/a second (13); **segundo piso** second floor (third story) (12)

seguridad *f.* security; safety; **control** (*m.*) **de seguridad** security (check) (8); **pasar por el control de seguridad** to go/pass through security (check) (8)

seguro *n.* insurance

seguro/a *adj.* sure, certain (6); **es seguro que** it's a sure thing that (13) **no es seguro** it's not sure (13); **no estar seguro/a de** to not be sure of (13)

seis six (1)

seiscientos/as six hundred (4)

selección *f.* selection; choice

seleccionador(a) *adj.* selection

seleccionar to select; to choose

selva jungle; **Selva Amazónica** Amazon Jungle

selvático/a *adj.* jungle

semáforo traffic signal (15)

semana week; **días** (*m. pl.*) **de la semana** days of the week (5); **fin** (*m.*) **de semana** weekend (2); **la próxima semana** next week (5); **la semana que viene** next week (5); **una vez a la semana** once a week (3)

semanal *m., f.* weekly

sembrar (siembro) to sow, plant

semejante similar

semejanza similarity

semestre *m.* semester

semi-cerrado/a semiclosed

semilla seed

senado senate

senador(a) senator (18)

sencillo/a simple

senda path

senderismo *n.* hiking

sendero path

sensación *f.* sensation

sensibilidad *f.* sensitivity

sensible sensitive

sentarse (me siento) to sit down (5)

sentido sense

sentimental: relación (*f.*) **sentimental** emotional relationship (16)

sentimiento feeling, emotion

sentir (siento) (i) to regret; to feel sorry (13), **lo siento (mucho)** I'm (very) sorry (14); **sentirse** to feel (*an emotion*) (9)

señalar to note; to point out

señor (Sr.) *m.* man; Mr.; sir (1)

señora (Sra.) woman; Mrs.; ma'am (1)

señorita (Srta.) young woman; Miss; Ms. (1)

separación *f.* separation (16)

separar(se) (de) to separate (from) (16)

septiembre *m.* September (6)

séptimo/a seventh (13)

ser to be (1); **ayer fue (miércoles...)** yesterday was (Wednesday . . .) (5); **¿cómo es usted?** what are you (*form. s.*) like? (1); **¿de dónde eres (tú)?** where are you (*fam. s.*) from? (1); **¿de dónde es usted?** where are you (*form. s.*) from? (1); **de última moda** it's trendy (hot) (4); **eres** you are (1); **es** he/she is, you (*form. s.*) are (1); **es absurdo que** it's absurd that (13); **es cierto que** it's certain that (13); **es de...** it is made of . . . (4); **es extraño que** it's strange that (13); **es (im)posible que** it's (im)possible that (13); **es (im)probable que** it's (un) likely, (im)-probable that (13); **es increíble que** it's incredible that (13); **es la una** it's one o'clock (1); **es normal que** it's normal that (13); **es seguro que** it's a sure thing that (13); **es terrible que** it's terrible that (13); **es una lástima que** it's a shame that (13); *es urgente que* + *subj.* it's urgent that *(12);* **fue sin querer** I didn't mean to do it (14); **llegar (gu) a ser** to become; **no es seguro/(im)posible, (im)probable que** + *subj.* it is not sure/(im)possible, (im)probable that (13); **pasar de ser** to go from being; **¿qué hora es?** what time is it? (1); **ser aburrido/a** to be boring (10); **ser aficionado/a (a)** to be a fan (of) (10); **ser casado/a** to be a married person (16); **ser divertido/a** to be fun (10); **ser en** + *place* to take place in/at (*a place*) (9); **son las...** it's . . . o'clock (1); **(yo) soy de...** I am from . . . (1)

ser (*m.*) **humano** human being

serie *f.* series

serio/a serious

serpiente *f.* snake

servicio service (15); **estación** (*f.*) **de servicio** gas station (15); **servicio militar** military service (18)

servilleta napkin

servir (sirvo) (i) to serve (5); **servir para** to be used for (5)

sesenta sixty (3)

sesión *f.* session

setecientos/as seven hundred (4)

setenta seventy (3)

sevillano/a of or pertaining to Seville

sexismo sexism

sexo sex

sextillo/a sextuplet

sexto/a sixth (13)

si if (4); **por si acaso** just in case (14)

sí yes (1); **sí, me gusta...** yes, I like . . . (1)

sicología psychology (2)

sicólogo/a psychologist (17)

siempre always (3)

sierra mountain

siesta nap; **dormir la siesta** to take a nap

siete seven (1)

siglo century

significado meaning

significar (qu) to mean

significativo/a significant

signo sign

siguiente following (5)

sílaba syllable

silencio silence

silla chair (2)

sillón *m.* armchair (5)

simbólico/a symbolic

simbolizar (c) to symbolize

símbolo symbol

similaridad *f.* similarity

similitud *f.* similarity

simpático/a nice, likeable (3)

sin without (5); **fue sin querer** I didn't mean to do it (14); **sin duda** without a doubt; **sin embargo** nevertheless (6); **sin que** *conj.* without; unless (16)

sinagoga synagogue

sinceridad *f.* sincerity

sincero/a sincere

sino but (rather); **sino que** *conj.* but (rather)

sinónimo synonym

sintético/a synthetic

síntoma *m.* symptom (11)

siquiatra *m., f.* psychiatrist (17)

sísmico/a seismic

sismorresistente earthquake resistant

sistema *m.* system; **analista** (*m., f.*) **de sistemas** systems analyst (17)

sistemático/a systematic

sitio place, location; **sitio web** website (12)

situación *f.* situation

situado/a situated

situarse (me sitúo) to situate oneself; to be placed (*in time*)

snowboard *m.* snowboarding

soberano/a sovereign

sobre *prep.* about (4); on; on top of; over

sobremesa after-dinner conversation

sobrenatural *adj.* supernatural

sobresaliente outstanding

sobresalir (like **salir**) to stand out

sobreviviente *adj., m., f.* surviving

sobrevivir to survive

sobrino/a nephew/niece (3)

social social; **ciencias** (*f. pl.*) **sociales** social sciences (2); **red** (*f.*) **social** social network (12); **trabajador(a) social** social worker (17)

socialismo socialism

socialista *n., adj. m., f.* socialist

socializar (c) to socialize

sociedad *f.* society

socioeconómico/a socioeconomic

sociología sociology (2)

sodio sodium

sofá *m.* couch (5)

soja soybean

sol *m.* sun; **gafas** (*f. pl.*) **de sol** sunglasses (4) **hace (mucho) sol** it's (very) sunny (6.); **tomar el sol** to sunbathe (8)

solar solar; **bloqueador** (*m.*) **solar** sunscreen (8); **energía solar** solar energy (15); **pánel** (*m.*) **solar** solar panel

solas: a solas alone

soldado soldier (17); **mujer** (*f.*) **soldado** female soldier (17)

soleado/a sunny

soledad *f.* solitud

soler (suelo) to tend to

solicitante *m., f.* applicant

solicitar to apply for (*a job*) (17)

solicitud *f.* application (*form*) (17)

sólido/a solid

solitario/a solitary, lonely

solo *adv.* only (2)

solo/a *adj.* alone (5)

soltero/a single (*not married*) (16)

soltura: hablar con soltura to speak fluently

solución *f.* solution

sombra shadow; shade

sombrero hat (4); **sombrero hongo** bowler hat, derby

sonar (sueno) to ring; to sound (10)

sonido sound

sonreír (*like* **reír**) to smile (9)

sopa soup (7)

soportar to bear

sor *f.* sister (*religious*)

sorber to absorb

sorprendente surprising

sorprender (*like* **gustar**) to surprise (13)

sorpresa surprise

sospechoso/a suspicious

sostenible sustainable

sostenido/a held

su(s) *poss. adj.* his, her, its, your (*form. s.*); their, your (*form. pl.*) (3)

suave pleasant

subir (a) to go up; to get on (*a vehicle*) (8)

subjuntivo *gram.* subjunctive

subordinado/a: cláusula subordinada *gram.* subordinate clause

subregión *f.* subregion

substituir (*like* **construir**) to substitute

subtítulo subtitle

suburbio suburb

suceder to occur; to happen

suceso happening

sucesor(a) successor

sucio/a dirty (6)

sudadera sweatshirt (4)

Sudamérica South America

sudamericano/a South American

Suecia Sweden

sueco/a Swedish

suegro/a father-in-law, mother-in-law

sueldo salary (17)

suelo floor

sueño dream; **tener sueño** to be sleepy (4)

suerte *f.* luck (14); **tener buena/mala suerte** to have good/bad luck; to be (un)lucky (14)

suéter *m.* sweater (4)

suficiente enough (11); **lo suficiente** enough (11)

sufijo *gram.* suffix

sufrimiento suffering

sufrir (de) to suffer (from, with) (14)

sugerencia suggestion

sugerir (sugiero) (i) to suggest (9)

suicidio suicide

suizo/a Swiss

sujeto *gram.* subject

sumo/a supreme

superar to overtake

superhombre *m.* superman

superlativo *gram.* superlative

supermercado supermarket (12)

superstición *f.* superstition

supersticioso/a superstitious

supervisor(a) supervisor

suplemento supplement

suponer (*like* **poner**) to suppose

supremo/a supreme

supuesto: ¡por supuesto! of course! (14)

sur *m.* south (6)

sureste *m.* southeast

surfear to surf

surfing: **hacer** *surfing* to surf (10)

suroeste *m.* southwest

surrealismo Surrealism

surrealista *adj. m., f.* surrealist

suscripción *f.* subscription

suspender to suspend

suspenso suspense

sustantivo *gram.* noun (2)
sustrato essence
sutil subtle
SUV *m.* SUV (15)
suyo/a(s) *poss. adj.* your (*form. s., pl.*); his, her, its, their; *poss. pron.* (of) your, yours (*form. s., pl.*); (of) his, her, its, their; (of) theirs (17)

T

tabaco tobacco
tabla table; chart
tableta tablet
tabú *f.* taboo
tacón *m.* heel
taconeo heel tap
tailandés, tailandesa Thai
Tailandia Thailand
taíno/a *pre-Columbian culture of the Caribbean*
tal such, such a; **con tal de** provided (16); **con tal (de) que** *conj.* provided (that) (16); **¿qué tal?** how are you? (1); **tal como** just as; **tal vez** perhaps
taladro drill
talento talent
talla size
taller *m.* (repair) shop (15)
tamal *m.* tamale
tamalada *get-together to make and eat tamales*
tamaño size
también also (1)
tambor *m.* drum
tambora African drum
tampoco neither, not either (7)
tan *adv.* so; as; **tan... como** as . . . as (6); **tan pronto como** as soon as (17)
tanque *m.* tank (15)
tanto/a *adj.* as much, so much; such (a); *pl.* so many; as many; **tanto como** as much as (6); **tanto/a(s)... como** as much/many . . . as (6)
tapa lid
tapar to cover
tapas *f. pl.* appetizers (9)
tapir *m.* tapir
taquigrafía shorthand
tardar to be long / take (a long) time
tarde *adv.* late (2)
tarde *f.* afternoon; **buenas tardes** good afternoon (1); **de la tarde** in the afternoon, P.M. (1); **por la tarde** in the afternoon (2)
tarea homework (5); **tarea doméstica** household chore
tarjeta card (8); **tarjeta bancaria** debit card (17); **tarjeta de crédito** credit card (7); **tarjeta de embarque** boarding pass (8); **tarjeta de identidad** identification card; **tarjeta de identificación**

identification card (14); **tarjeta postal** postcard (8)
tarta cake
tartamudo/a stutterer
tata *fam.* grandpa
tatuaje *m.* tattoo
taza cup (14)
té *m.* tea (7); **rosa té** tea rose
teatral theatrical; **obra teatral** play
teatro theater; **ir al teatro** to go to the theater (10); **obra de teatro** play (13)
techo roof
teclado keyboard
técnico/a technician (17)
tecnología technology
tecnológico/a technological
teja tile
tejedor(a) weaver
tejer to weave (13)
tejido weaving; *pl.* woven goods (13); textiles
tela cloth
tele *f.* T.V.
telediario news program
telefonear to phone
telefonía telephone systems
telefónico/a *adj.* telephone
teléfono phone (2); **hablar por teléfono** to talk on the phone (2); **teléfono celular** cell phone (2); **teléfono fijo** landline (12)
telegrama *m.* telegram
telenovela soap opera
telespectador(a) television viewer
televidente *m., f.* television viewer
televisión (*f.*) (**plasma**) (plasma) television (12); **mirar la tele(visión)** to watch television (3)
televisor *m.* television set
tema *m.* theme, topic
temblar (tiemblo) to tremble
temblor *m.* trembling
temer to fear; to be afraid (13)
temperatura temperature (11); **tomarle la temperatura** to take (*someone's*) temperature (11)
templo temple
temporada season (*hunting, fashion, etc.*)
temporal temporary
temprano *adv.* early (2)
tendencia tendency
tender (tiendo): tender la cama to make the bed
tenedor *m.* fork
tener to have (4); **no tener razón** to be wrong (4); **tener... años** to be . . . years old (3); **tener buena/mala suerte** to have good/bad luck; to be (un)lucky (14); **tener cuidado** to be careful; **tener dolor de** to have a pain/ache in (11); **tener éxito** to be successful; **tener fiebre** to have a

fever; **tener ganas de** + *inf.* to feel like (*doing something*) (4); **tener la culpa** to be at fault; **tener miedo (de)** to be afraid (of) (4); **tener (mucha) hambre** to be (very) hungry (7); **tener (mucha) sed** to be (very) thirsty (7); **tener muchas presiones** to be under a lot of stress (14); **tener (mucho) calor** to be (very) warm, hot (6); **tener (mucho) frío** to be (very) cold (6); **tener prisa** to be in a hurry (4); **tener que** + *inf.* to have to (*do something*) (4); **tener razón** to be right (4); **tener sueño** to be sleepy (4)
tenis *m. inv.* tennis (10); *pl.* tennis shoes (4)
tensión *f.* tension; **tensión arterial** blood pressure
tentación *f.* temptation
tentempié *m.* snack
teñirse (me tiño) (i) el pelo to dye one's hair
teoría theory
terapeuta *m., f.* therapist
terapia therapy
tercer(o/a) third (13)
tereré *m. traditional Paraguayan drink*
terminación *f. gram.* ending
terminal *m.* station, terminal
terminar to finish
término term
termómetro thermometer
ternura tenderness
terraza terrace
terremoto earthquake
terreno piece of land
terrestre *adj.* earth
terrible terrible (13); **es terrible que** it's terrible that (13)
territorio territory
terrorismo terrorism (18)
terrorista *m., f.* terrorist (18); **ataque** (*m.*) **terrorista** (terrorist) attack (18)
tertulia get-together
tesis *f. inv.* thesis
testigo *m., f.* witness (18)
testimonio testimony
texteo text (message)
textil *adj.* textile
texto text; **libro de texto** textbook (2)
ti (*obj. of prep.*) you (*fam.*) (6)
tibetano/a Tibetan
tiempo weather; time (6); *gram.* tense; **a tiempo** on time (8); **conjunción** (*f.*) **de tiempo** conjunction of time (17); **empleo de tiempo completo/parcial** full-/part-time job/position (17); **hace (muy) buen/mal tiempo** it's (very) good/bad weather (6); **jornada de tiempo parcial** part-time job; **¿qué tiempo hace?** what's the weather like? (6); **tiempo libre** free time (10); **trabajo**

de tiempo completo/parcial full/part-time job (14)

tienda shop, store (4); **tienda de acampar** tent; **tienda (de campaña)** tent (8)

tierra land

Tierra Earth (15)

tigre *m.* tiger

tihuanaco/a Tiwanakan (*of or pertaining to the pre-Columbian Tiwanaku civilization of Bolivia*)

tilma poncho; shawl

timbre *m.* doorbell

tímido/a shy

tina bathtub

tinieblas *f. pl.* darkness

tinto/a: vino tinto red wine (7)

tío/a uncle/aunt (3); *m. pl.* aunts and uncles (3)

típico/a typical

tipo type, kind; **de todo tipo** of all kinds

tira cómica comic strip

tirar to throw

tiritar to shiver

títere *m.* puppet

título title

toalla towel (5)

toallero towel rack

tocar (qu) to touch; to play (*a musical instrument*) (2); to honk (15); **tocarle a uno** to be someone's turn (10)

tocineta bacon

todavía still (6)

todo *n.* everything; **de todo** everything (4); **de todo tipo** of all kinds

todo/a *adj.* all (3); every (3); **por todas partes** everywhere (14); **todo derecho/recto** straight ahead (15); **todos los días** every day (2)

todoterreno *inv.* all-terrain (15)

tolerante tolerant

tomar to take (2); to drink (2); **tomar el sol** to sunbathe (8); **tomar unas vacaciones** to take a vacation (8); **tomarle la temperatura** to take (*someone's*) temperature (11); **tomarle el pelo** to pull (*someone's*) leg

tomate *m.* tomato (7)

tono tone

toque *f.* touch

tonto/a silly, foolish (3)

torno: en torno a around

toro bull (15)

torpe clumsy (14)

torre *f.* tower

torta sandwich (*Mex.*)

tortilla potato omelet (*Sp.*); *thin unleavened cornmeal or flour pancake* (*Mex.*)

tortuga turtle

tos *f.* cough (11)

tosco/a rustic; crude

toser to cough (11)

tostado/a toasted (7); **pan** (*m.*) **tostado** toast (7)

tostadora toaster (10)

tostones *m. pl. crispy fried plantain slices*

totalidad *f.* totality

trabajador(a) *adj.* hardworking (3)

trabajador(a) *n.* worker; **trabajador(a) social** social worker (17)

trabajar to work (2)

trabajo work; job (12); report, (piece of) work (14); **carga de trabajo** workload; **trabajo de tiempo completo/parcial** full-/part-time job (14)

trabajólico/a workaholic

trabalenguas *m. inv.* tongue twister

tractor *m.* tractor

tradición *f.* tradition; **tradición cultural** cultural tradition (13)

tradicional traditional

traducción *f.* translation

traducir (*like* **conducir**) to translate

traductor(a) translator (17)

traer to bring (5)

tráfico traffic (15)

tragedia tragedy

trágico/a tragic

traje *m.* suit (4); **traje de baño** swimsuit (4)

trámite *m.* step; procedure

tranquilo/a calm (9); **llevar una vida tranquila** to lead a calm life (11)

transatlántico *n.* ocean liner

transbordador (*m.*) **espacial** space shuttle

transformar to transform

transición *f.* transition

tránsito traffic (15)

transmitir to pass on; to transmit

transnacional international

transporte *m.* transportation; **medio de transporte** means of transportation (8); **transporte público** public transportation

tras *prep.* after

trasero/a back, rear

trasladarse to move

trastienda back room (*of a store*)

tratable treatable

tratado treaty

tratamiento treatment (11)

tratar de + *inf.* to try to (*do something*) (13); **tratar de** + *noun* to deal with + *noun*

través: a través de across; through; throughout

travieso/a mischievous

trayectoria trajectory; path

trébol *m.* clover

trece thirteen (1)

treinta thirty (1); **y treinta** thirty minutes past (*the hour*) (1)

tren *m.* train (8); **estación** (*f.*) **de trenes** train station (8); **ir en tren** to go/travel by train (8)

tres three (1)

trescientos/as three hundred (4)

triángulo triangle

tribu *f.* tribe

tributo tribute

trigo wheat

trillizo/a triplet

trilogía trilogy

trimestre *m.* trimester

triste sad (6)

tristeza sadness

triunfar to triumph

trofeo trophy

trompeta trumpet

tropical tropical; **bosque** (*m.*) **tropical lluvioso** tropical rain forest

trópico *n.* tropics

tropiezo mistake

trotadora treadmill

trozo piece

trucha trout

trueno thunder

tú *subj. pron.* you (*fam. s.*) (2); **¿de dónde eres (tú)?** where are you (*fam. s.*) from? (1); **¿y tú?** and you (*fam. s.*)? (1)

tu(s) your (*fam. s.*) (3)

tuit *m.* tweet (12)

tuitear to tweet

tumba tomb

tuna cactus fruit

turismo tourism

turista *n. m., f.* tourist

turístico/a *adj.* tourist

turnarse to take turns

turno shift (*on a job*)

turrón *m. type of candy traditionally eaten at Christmas*

tutor(a) tutor

tuyo/a(s) *poss. adj.* your (*fam. s.*); *poss. pron.* yours; of yours (*fam. s.*) (17)

Twitter *m.* Twitter (12)

U

u or (*used instead of* **o** *before words beginning with* **o** *or* **ho**)

ubicación *f.* placement, location

ubicar (qu) to locate

ucraniano/a Ukranian

¡uf! *interj.* oof!; whew!

último/a last, final (14); **es de última moda** it's trendy (hot) (4); **por última vez** for the last time (14)

ultramoderno/a ultramodern

un, uno/a one (1); *ind. art.* a, an; **un millón (de)** one million (4); **un poco (de)** a little bit (of) (2); **una vez a la semana** once a week (3)

unánime unanimous

único/a *adj.* only; unique

unidad *f.* unity

unido/a united; **Estados** (*m. pl.*) **Unidos de América** United States of America; **Naciones** (*f. pl.*) **Unidas** United Nations; **Organización** (*f.*) **de Naciones Unidas (ONU)** United Nations (U.N.)

unificar (qu) to unify

unión *f.* union

unir to join (together); to unite; **unirse a** to join (*a cause, organization*)

universidad *f.* university (2)

universitario/a *adj.* (of the) university (14)

universo universe

urbanístico/a *adj.* of urban development

urbano/a urban

urgencias: sala de urgencias emergency room

urgente urgent (12); **es urgente (que)** + *subj.* it's urgent (that) (12)

uruguayo/a *n., adj.* Uruguayan

usar to wear; to use (4)

uso use

usted (Ud., Vd.) *sub. pron.* you (*form. s.*) (2); *obj.* (*of prep.*) you (*form. s.*) (2); **¿a usted le gusta... ?** do you (*form. s.*) like . . . ? (1); **¿cómo es usted?** what are you (*form. s.*) like? (1); **¿cómo se llama usted?** what is your (*form. s.*) name? (1); **¿de dónde es usted?** where are you (*form. s.*) from? (1); **¿y usted?** and you (*form. s.*)? (1)

ustedes (Uds., Vds.) *sub. pron.* you (*form. pl.*); *obj.* (*of prep.*) you (*form pl.*) (2)

usuario/a user (12)

útil useful

utilidad *f.* utility

utilizar (c) to use; to utilize

uva grape

¡uy! *interj.* oh!; ah!

V

vaca cow (15)

vacaciones *f. pl.* vacation; **de vacaciones** on vacation (8); **estar de vacaciones** to be on vacation (8); **ir de vacaciones a...** to go on vacation in/to . . . (8); **pasar las vacaciones en...** to spend one's vacation in . . . (8); **salir de vacaciones** to leave on vacation (8); **tomar unas vacaciones** to take a vacation (8)

vacuna vaccine (11)

vacunación *f.* vaccination

vacunarse to get a shot

vainilla vanilla

valenciano/a Valencian

Valentín: Día (*m.*) **de San Valentín** St. Valentine's Day

valiente courageous

valioso/a valuable

valle *m.* valley

vallenato *Colombian folk music*

valor *m.* value

valorar to value

valorización *f.* appreciation

vals *m. inv.* waltz

vampiro vampire

vanagloriarse to brag

vandalismo vandalism

vapor *m.* mist

vaquero/a cowboy/cowgirl

variación *f.* variation

variante variant

variar (varío) to vary

variedad *f.* variety

varios/as several

vasco/a *n., adj.* Basque

vasija earthenware pot; vessel

vaso (drinking) glass

vasto/a vast

vecindario neighborhood

vecino/a neighbor (12)

vegano/a *n., adj.* vegan

vegetariano/a *n., adj.* vegetarian

vehículo vehicle (15)

veinte twenty (1)

veinticinco twenty-five

veinticuatro twenty-four

veintidós twenty-two

veintinueve twenty-nine

veintiocho twenty-eight

veintiséis twenty-six

veintisiete twenty-seven

veintitrés twenty-three

veintiún, veintiuno/a twenty-one

vejez *f.* (*pl.* **vejeces**) old age (16)

vela candle (9)

velocidad *f.* speed; **límite** (*m.*) **de velocidad** speed limit (15)

vena vein

vendedor(a) salesperson (17)

vender to sell (3)

Venecia Venice

venerar to revere; to venerate

venezolano/a *n., adj.* Venezuelan

venir to come (4); **el año que viene** next year; **el lunes** (*m.*) **que viene** next Monday (5); **la semana que viene** next week (5)

venta sale

ventaja advantage

ventana window (2)

ventanilla small window (*on a plane*) (8)

ver (*p.p.* **visto**) to see (5); **a ver** let's see; **nos vemos** see you around (1)

verano summer (6)

veras: ¿de veras? really

verbo *gram.* verb (2); **verbo reflexivo** *gram.* reflexive verb (5)

verdad *f.* truth; **es verdad que** it's true that (13)

¿verdad? right, don't they (you...)? (4)

verdadero/a true; real

verde green (4)

verdura vegetable (7)

vergonzoso/a shameful

vergüenza embarrassment

verificar (qu) to verify

versión *f.* version

verso verse; line of a poem

verter (vierto) (i) to spill; to shed (*a tear*)

vestido dress (4)

vestir (visto) (i) to dress; **vestirse** to get dressed (5)

veterano/a *n.* veteran

veterinario/a veterinarian (17)

vez *f.* (*pl.* **veces**) time; **a veces** sometimes, at times (3); **alguna vez** once; ever; **cada vez más** increasingly; **cada vez mayor** greater and greater; **dos veces** twice; **en vez de** instead of; **otra vez** again; **por primera/última vez** for the first/last time (14); **tal vez** perhaps; **una vez** once; **una vez a la semana** once a week (3)

viajar to travel (8)

viaje *m.* trip (5); **agencia de viajes** travel agency; **agente de viajes** travel agent; **de viaje** on a trip, traveling (8); **hacer un viaje** to take a trip (5)

viajero/a traveler

vial *adj.* road

vicepresidente/a vice president

víctima victim (18)

victoria victory

vicuña vicuna (llama)

vida life (11); **vida académica** academic life (14); **llevar una vida sana/tranquila** to lead a healthy/calm life (11); **ritmo de la vida** pace of life (15)

video video (12)

videocasetera video cassette recorder

videojuego videogame; **jugar (juego) (gu) a los videojuegos** to play videogames (10)

videollamada video call

videoturismo videotourism

vidrio glass

viejo/a old (3)

viento wind (6); **hace (mucho) viento** it's (very) windy (6)

viernes *m. inv.* Friday (5)

vietnamita *n., adj. m., f.* Vietnamese

vikingo/a Viking

vinagre *m.* vinegar

vino (blanco, tinto) (white, red) wine (7)

violación *f.* violation

violencia violence; **Día** (*m.*) **Internacional de la No Violencia Contra la Mujer** International No Violence Against Women Day

violento/a violent

violín *m.* violin

Virgen *f.* Virgin (Mary)

virreinato viceroyalty

virus *m. inv.* virus

visión *f.* vision

visita visit

visitante *m., f.* visitor

visitar to visit (10); **visitar un museo** to visit a museum (10)

víspera eve

vista view (12); **punto de vista** point of view

viudo/a widower/widow (16)

vivienda housing (12)

vivir to live (3)

vivo/a lively; bright (*of colors*)

vocabulario vocabulary

vocal *f.* vowel

voga: en voga in vogue

volante *m.* steering wheel; **furia al volante** road rage

volar (vuelo) to fly; **volar en avión** to fly; to go by plane (8)

volcán *m.* volcano

volcánico/a volcanic

voleibol *m.* volleyball (10)

voltear to turn (over)

volumen *m.* volume

voluntario/a volunteer

volver (vuelvo) (*p.p.* **vuelto**) to return (*to a place*) (5); **volver a** + *inf.* to (*do something*) again (5)

vos *subj. pron.* you (*fam. s. C.A., S.A.*)

vosotros/as *sub. pron.* you (*fam. pl. Sp.*); *obj.* (*of prep.*) you (*fam. pl. Sp.*) (2)

votación *f.* vote; voting

votante *m., f.* voter

votar to vote (18)

votos (*m. pl.*) **nupciales** wedding vows

voz *f.* (*pl.* **voces**) voice; **voz en off** voice over

vudú *m.* voodoo

vuelo flight (8); **asistente** (*m., f.*) **de vuelo** flight attendant (8)

vuelta: billete *m.* (*Sp.*) / **boleto** (*L.A.*) **de ida y vuelta** round-trip ticket (8)

vuelto/a (*p.p. of* **volver**) returned

vuestro/a(s) your (*fam. pl. Sp.*) (3); *poss. pron.* your (*fam. pl. Sp.*) (17)

vulnerar to violate; to hurt

W

web: página web webpage (12); **sitio web** website (12)

Y

y and (1); **y cuarto** a quarter (fifteen minutes) after (*the hour*) (1); **y media** half past (*the hour*) (1); **y quince** fifteen minutes after (*the hour*) (1); **y treinta** thirty minutes past (*the hour*) (1)

ya already (9); **ya no** no longer; **ya que** since

yacimiento deposit (*mineral*)

yerba herb

yerno son-in-law

yo *sub. pron.* I (2); **yo soy de...** I am from . . . (1)

yoga *m.* yoga; **hacer (el) yoga** to do yoga (10)

yogur *m.* yogurt (7)

yuca cassava, manioc; **¡qué yuca!** how difficult!

Z

zalamería flattery

zampoña *South American panpipe*

zanahoria carrot (7)

zancudo mosquito

zapatería shoe store

zapato shoe; *pl.* shoes (4)

zarzuela *traditional Spanish operetta*

zócalo central plaza (*Mex.*)

Zodíaco Zodiac

zona zone, area (12)

zoología zoology

zumo juice (*Sp.*)

VOCABULARIES

English-Spanish Vocabulary

A

@ **arroba** (12)
A.M. **de la mañana** (1)
able: to be able **poder** (4)
about **por** (6); **sobre** (4)
abroad: to go abroad **ir al extranjero** (8)
absence **falta** (15)
absent: to be absent (from) **faltar (a)** (9)
absentminded **distraído/a** (14)
absurd: it's absurd that **es absurdo que** (13)
academic **académico/a** (14); academic life **vida académica** (14)
accelerated **acelerado/a** (15)
accident **accidente** m. (14)
according to **según** (3)
account **cuenta** (17); to charge to an account **cargar (gu) a una cuenta** (17)
accountant **contador(a)** (17)
ache n. (in) **dolor (de)** (11); v. **doler (duele)** (like **gustar**) (11); to have an ache in **tener dolor de** (11)
acquainted: to be acquainted with **conocer (conozco)** (7)
act v. **actuar (actúo)** (13)
activity: fun activity **diversión** f. (10)
actor **actor** m. (13)
actress **actriz** f. (pl. **actrices**) (13)
additional **adicional** (1)
address **dirección** f. (7)
adjective gram. **adjetivo** (3); adjective of nationality **adjetivo de nacionalidad** (3); possessive adjective **adjetivo posesivo** (3)
administration: business administration **administración** (f.) **de empresas** (2)
adolescence **adolescencia** (16)
adolescent: as an adolescent **de adolescente** (10)
advice (piece of) **consejo** (7)
advisor **consejero/a** (2)
aerobics: to do aerobics **hacer ejercicios aeróbicos** (11)
affection **cariño** (16)
affectionate **cariñoso/a** (6)
afraid: to be afraid (of) **tener miedo (de)** (4), **temer** (13)
after prep. **después de** (5), conj. **después (de) que** (17)
afternoon: good afternoon **buenas tardes** (1); **muy buenas** (1); in the afternoon **de la tarde** (1), **por la tarde** (2)
afterward **luego** (5); afterwards **después** (5)
agent **agente** m., f. (8)
ago **hace** + time + **que** + preterite (14); preterite + **hace** + time (14)
agree **estar de acuerdo** (3)
agriculture **agricultura** (15)
ahead: straight ahead **(todo) derecho** (15), **todo recto** (15)
air **aire** m. (15)
airplane **avión** m. (8)
airport **aeropuerto** (8)
aisle **pasillo** (8)
alarm clock **despertador** m. (14)
all **todo/a** (3)
all-terrain **todoterreno** inv. (15)
allow **permitir** (12)
almost **casi** inv. (3); almost never **casi nunca** (3)
alone **solo/a** (5)
alongside of **al lado de** (6)
already **ya** (9)
also **también** (1)
always **siempre** (3)
am: I am **soy** (1); I am from **soy de** (1)
America: of the United States of America n., adj. **estadounidense** (3)
among prep. **entre** (6)
analyst: systems analyst **analista** (m., f.) **de sistemas** (17)
and **y** (1); and you? **¿y tú?** fam. s. (1), **¿y usted?** form. s. (1)
android **android** m. (12)
angry **enojado/a** (9); **furioso/a** (6); to get angry (with) **enojarse (con)** (9)
animal **animal** m. (15)
announce **anunciar** (8)
annoyed **molesto/a** (6)
another **otro/a** (3)
answer n. **respuesta** (6); v. to answer **contestar** (7)
antibiotic **antibiótico** (11)
anxiety **ansiedad** f. (14)
any **algún (alguna/os/as)** (7)
anybody: not anybody **nadie** (7)
anyone **alguien** (7)
anything **algo** (7); not anything **nada** (7)
apartment **apartamento** (2); apartment building **edificio de apartamentos** (12)
apologize **pedir disculpas** (14)
app(lication) **app** f. (12)
appetizers **botanas** f. pl. (Mex.) (9); **tapas** f. pl. (9)
apple **manzana** (7)
appliance: home appliance **aparato doméstico** (10)
applicant **aspirante** m., f. (17)
application (form) **solicitud** f. (17)
apply for (a job) **solicitar** (17)
appointment **cita** (11)
April **abril** m. (6)
architect **arquitecto/a** (13)
architecture **arquitectura** (13)
am: you (fam. s.) are **eres** (1); you (form. s.) are **es** (1)
area **zona** (12); smoking area **sala de fumadores/de fumar** (8)
argue (with/about) **discutir (con/por/sobre)** (9)
arm **brazo** (11)
armchair **sillón** m. (5)
armoire **armario** (5)
army **ejército** (18)
arrival **llegada** (8)
arrive **llegar (gu)** (3)
art **arte** m. (2); arts and crafts **artesanía** (13); the arts **artes** f. pl. (13); work of art **obra de arte** (13)
artist **artista** m., f. (13)
artistic **artístico/a** (13); artistic expression **expresión** (f.) **artística** (13)
as: as . . . as **tan... como** (6); as a child **de niño/a** (10); as a youth **de adolescente** (10); as much as **tanto como** (6); as much/many . . . as **tanto/a(s)... como** (6); as soon as **en cuanto** (17), **tan pronto como** (17)
ask (a question) **hacer una pregunta** (5), **preguntar** (8); to ask for **pedir** (5)
asleep: to fall asleep **dormirse** (5)
asparagus **espárragos** m. pl. (7)
assassinate **asesinar** (18)
assassination **asesinato** (18)
astronaut **astronauta** m., f. (17)
at **en** (1); at . . . (time of day) **a la(s)...** (1); at all **(para) nada** (8); at home **en casa** (2); at least **por lo menos** (9); at the beginning of **al principio de** (17);

at times **a veces** (3); at what time . . . ? **¿a qué hora...?** (1)

attack: terrorist attack **ataque** (*m.*) **terrorista** (18)

attend (*class, function*) **asistir (a)** (3); to not attend **faltar (a)** (9)

attendant: flight attendant **asistente** (*m., f.*) **de vuelo** (8)

attract **atraer** (*like* **traer**) (*like* **gustar**) (13)

audience **espectadores** *m. pl.* (13); **público** (13)

August **agosto** (6)

aunt **tía** (3); aunts and uncles **tíos** *m. pl.* (3)

author **autor(a)** (13)

auto **auto** (15)

automatic teller machine (ATM) **cajero automático** (17)

automobile **auto(móvil)** *m.* (15)

autumn **otoño** (6)

avenue **avenida** (12)

avocado **aguacate** *m.* (7)

avoid **evitar** (15)

awful: an awful lot **muchísimo** (8)

B

baby-sitter **niñero/a** (10)

back tooth **muela** (11)

backpack **mochila** (2)

bad **mal, malo/a** (3); (very) bad (weather) out **(muy) mal tiempo** (6); the bad news/thing **lo malo** (11); to have a bad time **pasarlo mal** (9); to have bad luck **tener mala suerte** (14)

badly: to come/turn out badly **salir mal** (5)

baggage **equipaje** *m.* (8); to check baggage **facturar el equipaje** (8)

baked custard **flan** *m.* (7)

ball **pelota** (10)

ballet **ballet** *m.* (13)

banana **banana** (7)

bank **banco** (17)

bar: to go to a bar **ir a un bar** (10)

barbecue **barbacoa** (7)

bargain *n.* **ganga** (4); *v.* **regatear** (4)

baseball **béisbol** *m.* (10); baseball cap **gorra** (4)

basketball **basquetbol** *m.* (10)

bath: to take a bath **bañarse** (5)

bathroom **baño** (5); bathroom sink **lavabo** (5)

bathtub **bañera** (5)

battery **batería** (15)

be **estar** (2); **ser** (1), (3); to be . . . years old **tener... años** (3); to be a fan (of) **ser aficionado/a (a)** (10); to be a married person **ser casado/a** (16); to be able **poder** (4); to be absent (from) **faltar (a)** (9); to be afraid **temer** (13); to be afraid (of) **tener miedo (de)** (4); to be born **nacer (nazco)** (16); to be (very) cold **tener (mucho) frío** (6); to

be comfortable (*temperature*) **estar bien** (6); to be distracted **ir distraído/a** (14); to be fond of each other **quererse** (11); to be fun **ser divertido/a** (10); to be happy (about) **alegrarse (de)** (12); to be (very) hungry **tener (mucha) hambre** (7); to be in a hurry **tener prisa** (4); to be left **quedar** (14); to be lucky **tener buena suerte** (14); to be married (to) **estar casado/a (con)** (16); to be on a diet **estar a dieta** (7); to be on vacation **estar de vacaciones** (8); to be right **tener razón** (4); to be sleepy **tener sueño** (4); to be (very) thirsty **tener (mucha) sed** (7); to be under a lot of pressure **estar bajo muchas presiones** (14); to be unlucky **tener mala suerte** (14); to be up to date **estar al día** (18); to be used for **servir (sirvo) (i) para** (5); to be (very) warm, hot **tener (mucho) calor** (6); to be wrong **no tener razón** (4)

beach **playa** (6)

beans **frijoles** *m. pl.* (7)

beautiful **bello/a** (15)

because **porque** (3); because of **por** (6)

become + *adj.* **ponerse** + *adj.* (9)

bed **cama** (5); to get out of bed **levantarse** (5); to get up on the wrong side of the bed **levantarse con el pie izquierdo** (14); to go to bed **acostarse (me acuesto)** (5); to make the bed **hacer la cama** (10); to stay in bed **guardar cama** (11)

bedroom **alcoba** (5)

beer **cerveza** (7)

before *prep.* **antes de** (16); *conj.* **antes (de) que** (16)

begin **empezar (empiezo) (c)** (5); to begin to (*do something*) **empezar a + *inf.*** (5)

beginning: at the beginning of **al principio de** (17)

behave **portarse bien** (9)

behind *prep.* **detrás de** (6)

believe (in) **creer (en)** (3); to not believe **no creer** (13)

below *prep.* **debajo de** (6)

belt **cinturón** *m.* (4)

beside **al lado de** (6)

best **mejor** (6)

better **mejor** (6)

between *prep.* **entre** (6)

beyond **a partir de** (4)

bicycle **bicicleta** (10); to ride a bicycle **montar en bicicleta** (10); **pasear en bicicleta** (10)

bicycling **ciclismo** (10)

big **gran, grande** (3); big screen (monitor) **pantalla grande** (12)

bill **cuenta** (7); **factura** (17); electric bill **electricidad** *f.* (12); (*money*) **billete** *m.* (17)

bird **pájaro** (3)

birthday **cumpleaños** *m. inv.* (6); birthday cake **pastel** (*m.*) **de cumpleaños** (9); to have a birthday **cumplir años** (9)

black **negro/a** (4)

blog **blog** *m.* (12)

blond(e) **rubio/a** (3)

blood **sangre** *f.* (11)

blouse **blusa** (4)

blue **azul** (4)

blue jeans *jeans* *m. pl.* (4)

blush *v.* **ponerse rojo/a** (9)

board **pizarrón** *m.* (2)

boarding: boarding gate **puerta de embarque** (8); boarding pass **tarjeta de embarque** (8)

boat **barco** (8); to go/travel by boat **ir en barco** (8)

body: human body **cuerpo humano** (11)

bomb **bomba** (18)

book **libro** (2); textbook **libro de texto** (2)

bookshelf **estante** *m.* (5)

bookstore **librería** (2)

boots **botas** *f. pl.* (4)

bore **aburrir** (*like* **gustar**) (13)

bored **aburrido/a** (6); to get bored **aburrirse** (10)

boring **pesado/a** (10); to be boring **ser aburrido/a** (10)

born: to be born **nacer (nazco)** (16)

borrow **pedir prestado/a** (17)

bother **molestar** (*like* **gustar**) (11)

boy **niño** (3); **chico** (4)

boyfriend **novio** (6)

brain **cerebro** (11)

brakes **frenos** *m. pl.* (15)

bread **pan** *m.* (7)

break **romper(se)** (14); to break up (with) **romper (con)** (16)

breakfast **desayuno** (7); to have (eat) breakfast **desayunar** (7)

breathe **respirar** (11)

bride **novia** (16)

bring **traer** (5)

brother **hermano** (3)

brown **(de) color café** (4)

brunet(te) **moreno/a** (3)

brush one's hair **peinarse** (5); to brush one's teeth **cepillarse los dientes** (5)

budget **presupuesto** (17)

build **construir** (15)

building **edificio** (2); apartment building **edificio de apartamentos** (12); building manager **portero/a** (12)

bull **toro** (15)

bump against/into **chocar (qu) con/contra** (14); **pegarse (gu) con/contra** (14) bureau **cómoda** (5)

bus **autobús** *m.* (8); bus station **estación** (*f.*) **de autobuses** (8); bus stop **parada del autobús** (12); to go; to travel by bus **ir en autobús** (8)

business **empresa** (17); business administration **administración** (*f.*) **de empresas** (2)

businessman **hombre** (*m.*) **de negocios** (17)

businesswoman **mujer** (*f.*) **de negocios** (17)

busy **ocupado/a** (6)

but **pero** (1)

butter **mantequilla** (7)

buy **comprar** (2)

by **por** (14); by check **con cheque** (17)

C

cabin (*on a ship*) **cabina** (8)

cafeteria **cafetería** (2)

cake **pastel** *m.* (7); birthday cake **pastel de cumpleaños** (9)

calculator **calculadora** (2)

calendar **calendario** (14)

call **llamar** (7); to be called **llamarse** (5)

calm **tranquilo/a** (9); to lead a calm life **llevar una vida tranquila** (11)

camera **cámara** (12)

campground **camping** *m.* (8)

camping: to go camping **hacer camping** (8)

candidate (*for a job*) **aspirante** *m., f.* (17); (*political*) **candidato/a** (18); to run as a candidate **postularse como candidato/a** (18); to run for a position as a candidate **postularse para un cargo como candidato/a** (18)

candle **vela** (9)

candy **dulces** *m. pl.* (7)

cap (baseball) **gorra** (4)

car **coche** *m.* (3); **carro** (15); convertible car **carro descapotable** (15)

card: (post)card **tarjeta (postal)** (8); credit card **tarjeta de crédito** (7); debit card **tarjeta bancaria** (17); identification card **tarjeta de identificación** (14); to play cards **jugar (juego) (gu) a las cartas** (10)

cardinal point **punto cardinal** (6)

care: to take care of oneself **cuidarse** (11)

carrot **zanahoria** (7)

carry **llevar** (4)

case: in case *prep.* **en caso de** (16); conj. **en caso de que** (6); just in case **por si acaso** (14)

cash (*a check*) **cobrar** (17); *n.* **efectivo** (17); in cash **en efectivo** (17)

cashier **cajero/a** (17)

cat **gato** (3)

catch a cold **resfriarse (me resfrío)** (11)

CD **CD** *m.* (12)

CD-ROM **CD-ROM** *m.* (12)

celebrate **celebrar** (6)

celebratory **festivo/a** (9)

cell phone **teléfono celular** (2)

center (*political*) **centro** (18)

ceramics **cerámica** *s.* (13)

cereal **cereal** *m.* (7)

certain **seguro/a** (6); it's certain that **es cierto que** (13)

chair **silla** (2)

champagne **champán** *m.* (9)

change **cambiar (de)** (12)

channel **canal** *m.* (12)

charge (*someone for an item or service*) **cobrar** (17); to charge to an account **cargar (gu) a una cuenta** (17)

chat *n.* **chateo** (12)

check (*bank*) **cheque** *m.* (17); (*restaurant*) **cuenta** (7); by check **con cheque** (17); *v.* **revisar** (15); to check baggage **facturar el equipaje** (8)

check-up **chequeo** (11)

cheese **queso** (7)

chef **cocinero/a** (17)

chemistry **química** (2)

chess: to play chess **jugar (juego) (gu) al ajedrez** (10)

chicken **pollo** (7); roast chicken **pollo asado** (7)

chickpeas **garbanzos** *m. pl.* (7)

child: as a child **de niño/a** (10)

childhood **infancia** (16); **niñez** *f.* (16)

children **hijos** *m. pl.* (3)

chop: (pork) chop **chuleta (de cerdo)** (7)

chore: household chore **quehacer** (*m.*) **doméstico** (10)

Christmas **Navidad** *f.* (9)

Christmas Eve **Nochebuena** *f.* (9)

church **iglesia** (16)

citizen **ciudadano/a** (18)

city **ciudad** *f.* (3)

civic duty **responsabilidad** (*f.*) **cívica** (18)

class (*of students*) **clase** *f.* (2); (*academic*) **clase** *f.* (2)

classic(al) **clásico/a** (13)

classmate **compañero/a (de clase)** (2)

classroom **salón** (*m.*) **de clase** (2)

clean *adj.* **limpio/a** (6); to clean (the) house **limpiar (la casa)** (10)

clear the table **quitar la mesa** (10)

clerk **dependiente/a** (2)

clever **listo/a** (3)

click *v.* **hacer clic** (*m.*) (12)

client **cliente/a** (2)

climate **clima** *m.* (6)

clock: alarm clock **despertador** *m.* (14)

close **cerrar (cierro)** (5)

close to *prep.* **cerca de** (6)

closed **cerrado/a** (6)

closet (*free-standing*) **armario** (5)

clothes dryer **secadora** (10)

clothing **ropa** (4)

cloudy: it's (very) cloudy **está (muy) nublado** (6)

clumsy **torpe** (14)

coat **abrigo** (4)

coffee **café** *m.* (2)

coffeemaker **cafetera** (10)

cognate **cognado** (2)

coin **moneda** (17)

cold (*illness*) **resfriado** *n.* (11); it's (very) cold (*weather*) **hace (mucho) frío** (6); to be (very) cold **tener (mucho) frío** (6); to catch/get a cold **resfriarse (me resfrío)** (11)

collect **recoger (recojo)** (14)

collision **choque** *m.* (18)

color **color** *m.* (4)

comb one's hair **peinarse** (5)

come **venir** (4); to come out badly **salir mal** (5); to come out well **salir bien** (5)

comedy **comedia** (13)

comfortable **cómodo/a** (4); to be comfortable (*temperature*) **estar bien** (6)

coming (*time*) **que viene** (5)

command **mandato** (7)

communicate (with) **comunicarse (qu) (con)** (18)

communication (*subject*) **comunicaciones** *f. pl.* (2); medium of communication **medio de comunicación** (18)

comparison **comparación** *f.* (6)

complain (about) **quejarse (de)** (8)

compose **componer** (*like* **poner**) (13)

composer **compositor(a)** (13)

computer **computadora** (2); computer file **archivo** (12); computer science **computación** *f.* (2); laptop (computer) **computadora portátil** (2)

concert **concierto** (10); to go to a concert **ir a un concierto** (10)

conductor **director(a)** (13)

congested (*with a cold*) *adj.* **resfriado/a** (11)

congratulations! **¡felicitaciones!** (9)

Congressional representative **representante** (*m., f.*) **al congreso** (18)

conjunction *gram.* **conjunción** *f.* (17); conjunction of time **conjunción** (*f.*) **de tiempo** (17)

connect **conectarse** (12)

conserve **conservar** (15)

contact lenses **lentes** (*m. pl.*) **de contacto** (11)

contaminated **contaminado/a** (15)

content *adj.* **contento/a** (6)

continue **continuar (continúo)** (6); **seguir (sigo) (i)** (6) control: remote control **control** (*m.*) **remoto** (12)

convertible car **carro descapotable** (12)

cook *v.* **cocinar** (7); *n.* **cocinero/a** (17)

cookie **galleta** (7)

cool: it's cool (weather) **hace fresco** (6)

copy *n.*: copy machine **fotocopiadora** (12); *v.* **copiar** (12); **hacer (foto)copia** (12)

corner (*street*) **esquina** (15)

corporation **empresa** (17)

cost: how much does it (do they) cost? **¿cuánto cuesta(n)?** (4)

cotton **de algodón** *adj.* (4)

couch **sofá** *m.* (5)

cough *n.* **tos** *f.* (11); cough syrup **jarabe** *m.* (11); *v.* **toser** (11)

counter **mostrador** *m.* (8)

country **país** *m.* (3)

countryside **campo** (15)

couple (*married*) **pareja** (16); **matrimonio** (16)

course (*academic*) **clase** *f.* (2); (*of a meal*) **plato** (7); course syllabus **programa** (*m.*) **del curso** (14); main course **plato principal** (7); of course! **¡por supuesto!** (14)

courteous expression **expresión** (f.) **de cortesía** (1)

courtesy **cortesía** (1)

cousin **primo/a** (3); *pl.* **primos** (3)

cover **cubrir** (*p.p.* **cubierto**) (15)

cow **vaca** (15)

craft: arts and crafts **artesanía** (13)

crash *n.* **choque** *m.* (18); *v.* (*computer*) **fallar** (12)

crazy **loco/a** (6)

create **crear** (13)

credit card **tarjeta de crédito** (7)

crime **delito** (15)

cruise (ship) **crucero** (8)

cry **llorar** (9)

cucumber **pepino** (7)

cuisine **cocina** (7)

cultural **cultural** (13); cultural tradition **tradición** (f.) **cultural** (13)

cup **taza** (14)

current *adj.* **actual** (12)

currently **en la actualidad** (10)

custard: baked custard **flan** *m.* (7)

customs (*at a border*) **aduana** (8); to go/ pass through customs **pasar por la aduana** (8)

D

dad **papá** *m.* (3)

daily **diario/a** (5)

dance *n.* **baile** *m.* (13); **danza** (13); *v.* **bailar** (2)

dancer **bailarín, bailarina** (13)

date **cita** (11); (*calendar*) **fecha** (6); to be up to date **estar al día** (18); what's

today's date? **¿cuál es la fecha de hoy?** (6), **¿qué fecha es hoy?** (6)

daughter **hija** (3)

day **día** *m.* (2); day after tomorrow **pasado mañana** (5); days of the week **días** (*m. pl.*) **de la semana** (5); every day **todos los días** (2); the day before yesterday **anteayer** (5); what day is today? **¿qué día es hoy?** (5)

deadline **plazo** (14)

dear **querido/a** (6)

death **muerte** *f.* (16)

debit card **tarjeta bancaria** (17)

December **diciembre** *m.* (6)

delay **demora** (8)

demonstration **manifestación** *f.* (18)

demonstrative *gram.* **demostrativo/a** (4)

dense **denso/a** (15)

dentist **dentista** *m., f.* (11)

deny **negar (niego) (gu)** (13)

department store **almacén** *m.* (4)

departure **salida** (8)

deposit **depositar** (17)

design **diseñar** (13)

designer: graphic designer **diseñador(a) gráfico/a** (17)

desk **escritorio** (2)

dessert **postre** *m.* (7)

destination **destino** (8)

destroy **destruir** (*like* **construir**) (15)

detail **detalle** *m.* (9)

develop **desarrollar** (15)

development **desarrollo** (15)

dictator **dictador(a)** (18)

dictatorship **dictadura** (18)

dictionary **diccionario** (2)

die **morir(se) ([me] muero) (u)** (9)

diet: to be on a diet **estar a dieta** (7)

difficult **difícil** (6); **pesado/a** (10)

dining room **comedor** *m.* (5)

dinner **cena** (7); to have (eat) dinner **cenar** (7)

direct **dirigir (dirijo)** (13)

director **director(a)** (13)

dirty **sucio/a** (6)

disagree **no estar de acuerdo** (3)

disaster **desastre** *m.* (14)

disc: compact disc (CD) **disco compacto (CD** *m.*) (12)

disco: to go to a disco **ir a una discoteca** (10)

discover **descubrir** (*p.p.* **descubierto**) (15)

discrimination **discriminación** *f.* (18)

dish **plato** (7)

dishwasher **lavaplatos** *m. inv.* (10)

distracted **distraído/a** (14); to be distracted **ir distraído/a** (14)

divorce *n.* **divorcio** (16); *v.* **divorciarse (de)** (16)

divorced (from) **divorciado/a (de)** (16)

dizzy **mareado/a** (11)

do **hacer** (5); do you like . . . ? **¿a usted le gusta... ?** *form. s.* (1); to (*do something*) again **volver a** + *inf.* (5); to do aerobics **hacer ejercicios** (*m. pl.*) **aeróbicos** (11); to do Pilates **hacer (el método) Pilates** (11); to do poorly **salir mal** (5); to do well **salir bien** (5); to do yoga **hacer (el) yoga** (10)

doctor (*medical*) **médico/a** (3)

dog **perro** (3)

domestic (*related to the home*) **doméstico/a** (10)

domesticated **doméstico/a** (15)

don't they (you...)? **¿no?** (4), **¿verdad?** (4)

door **puerta** (2)

doorman **portero/a** (12)

dormitory **residencia** (2)

dot: on the dot (*time*) **en punto** (1)

doubt **dudar** (12)

download **bajar** (12); **descargar (gu)** (12)

downtown **centro** (4)

drama **drama** *m.* (13)

draw **dibujar** (13); (*attract*) **atraer** (*like* **traer**) (*like* **gustar**) (13)

drawer **dibujante** *m., f.* (13)

drawing **dibujo** (13)

dress **vestido** (4)

dressed: to get dressed **vestirse (me visto) (i)** (5)

dresser **cómoda** (5)

drink *n.* **bebida** (5); soft drink **refresco** (7); *v.* **beber** (3); **tomar** (2)

drive *n.*: hard drive **discoduro** (12); *v.* **manejar** (12); **conducir (conduzco)** (15)

driver **conductor(a)** (15); driver's license **licencia de conducir/ manejar** (15)

drop **caer** (14)

drum set **batería** (15)

dryer: clothes dryer **secadora** (10)

during **durante** (5)

duty: civic duty **responsabilidad** (*f.*) **cívica** (18)

DVD **DVD** *m.* (12)

E

e-mail **e-mail** *m.* (12); **correo electrónico** (12)

e-ticket **billete** (*m.*) (*Sp.*) / **boleto** (*L.A.*) **electrónico** (8)

each **cada** *inv.* (5)

ear **oreja** (11); inner ear **oído** (11)

early *adv.* **temprano** (2)

earn (*income*) **ganar** (13)

earrings **aretes** *m. pl.* (4)

Earth **Tierra** (15)

east **este** *m.* (6)

Easter **Pascua** (9)

easy **fácil** (6)

eat **comer** (3); to eat breakfast **desayunar** (7); to eat dinner, supper cenar (7); to eat lunch **almorzar (ue) (c)** (5)

economics **economía** (2)

economize **economizar (c)** (17)

economy **economía** (2)

egg **huevo** (7)

eight **ocho** (1)

eight hundred **ochocientos/as** (4)

eighteen **dieciocho** (1)

eighth **octavo/a** (13)

eighty **ochenta** (3)

either: not either **tampoco** (7)

electric bill **electricidad** *f.* (12)

electrical **eléctrico/a** (15); electrical energy **energía eléctrica** (15)

electrician **electricista** *m., f.* (17)

electricity **electricidad** *f.* (12)

elephant **elefante** *m.* (15)

elevator **ascensor** *m.* (12)

eleven **once** (1)

embarrassed **avergonzado/a** (9)

embrace **abrazarse (c)** (11)

emotion **emoción** *f.* (9)

emotional **afectivo/a** (9); emotional relationship **relación** *(f.)* **sentimental** (16); emotional state **estado afectivo** (9)

end of the year **fin** *(m.)* **de año** (9)

end table **mesita** (5)

endangered species **especie** *(f.)* **en peligro de extinción** (15)

energy **energía** (15); electrical energy **energía eléctrica** (15); nuclear energy **energía nuclear** (15); renewable energy **energía renovable** (15); solar energy **energía solar** (15); wind energy **energía eólica** (15)

engagement **noviazgo** (16)

engineer **ingeniero/a** (17)

English *(language)* **inglés** *n. m.* (2); *n., adj.* **inglés, inglesa** (3)

enjoy oneself **divertirse (me divierto) (i)** (5)

enough **bastante** (16), **suficiente** (11); **lo suficiente** (11)

environment **medio ambiente** (15)

equality **igualdad** *f.* (18)

equipment **equipo** (12); electronic equipment **equipo electrónico** (12)

eruption **erupción** *f.* (18)

evening: good evening **buenas noches** (1); **muy buenas** (1); in the evening **de la noche** (1); **por la noche** (2)

event **acontecimiento** (18); **hecho** (9)

every **cada** *inv.* (5); **todo/a** (3); every day **todos los días** (2)

everything **de todo** (4)

everywhere **por todas partes** (14)

exam **examen** *m.* (4)

example: for example **por ejemplo** (14)

excuse me **(con) permiso** (1), **perdón** (1)

exercise *n.* **ejercicio** (5); *v.* **hacer ejercicio** (5)

expect **esperar** (7)

expense **gasto** (12)

expensive **caro/a** (4)

explain **explicar (qu)** (8)

expression (phrase) **expresión** *f.* (1); artistic expression **expresión artística** (13)

extinction **extinción** *f.* (15)

extract **sacar (qu)** (11); to extract *(someone's)* tooth/molar **sacarle (qu) un diente / una muela** (11)

eye **ojo** (11)

F

Facebook **Facebook** *m.* (12); to go into Facebook **entrar en Facebook** (12)

fact **hecho** (9)

factory **fábrica** (15)

faithful **fiel** (3)

fall *(season)* *n.* **otoño** (6); *v.* **caer** (14); to fall asleep **dormirse** (5); to fall down **caerse** (14); to fall in love (with) **enamorarse (de)** (16)

familiar: to be familiar with **conocer (conozco)** (7)

family **familia** (3)

fan: to be a fan (of) **ser aficionado/a (a)** (10)

far from **lejos de** (6)

fare **pasaje** *m.* (8)

farm **finca** (15)

farmer **agricultor(a)** (15)

farming **agricultura** (15)

fascinate **fascinar** (like **gustar**) (13)

fast **acelerado/a** (15)

fat **gordo/a** (3)

father **padre** *m.* (3), **papá** *m.* (3)

FAX **fax** *m.* (12)

fear *n.* **miedo** (4); *v.* **temer** (13)

February **febrero** (6)

feel **sentir** (13); *(an emotion)* **sentirse** (9); to feel like *(doing something)* **tener ganas de** + *inf.* (4); to feel sorry **lamentar** (13)

female housekeeper **ama** *(f.)* *(but* **el ama) de casa** (17)

female soldier **mujer** *(f.)* **soldado** (17)

festive **festivo/a** (9)

fever **fiebre** *f.* (11)

few **poco/a** (4)

fiancé **novio** (16)

fiancée **novia** (16)

field **campo** (15)

fifteen **quince** (1); fifteen minutes till *(hour)* **menos cuarto/quince** (1); young woman's fifteenth birthday party **quinceañera** (9)

fifth **quinto/a** (13)

fifty **cincuenta** (3)

fight *n.* **lucha** (18); *v.* **luchar** (18), **pelear** (10)

file *(computer)* **archivo** (12)

fill (up) **llenar** (15); to fill out *(a form)* **llenar** (17)

final **último/a** (14)

finally **por fin** (5), **finalmente** (5)

find **encontrar (encuentro)** (9); to find out (about) **enterarse (de)** (18)

fine **muy bien** (1); it's fine **está bien** (6)

finger **dedo (de la mano)** (11)

finish **acabar** (14)

fire *(someone)* *(from a job)* **despedir** *(like* **pedir)** (17)

first *adv.* **primero** (5); *adj.* **primer(o/a)** (13); first floor (second story) **primer piso** (12); for the first time **por primera vez** (14); the first of *(month)* **el primero de** (6)

fish *(cooked)* **pescado** (7); *(live)* **pez** *m.* *(pl.* **peces)** (15)

five **cinco** (1)

five hundred **quinientos/as** (4)

fix **arreglar** (15)

fixed price **precio fijo** (4)

flat: flat screen *(monitor)* **pantalla plana** (12); flat tire **llanta desinflada** (15)

flexible **flexible** (14)

flight **vuelo** (8); flight attendant **asistente** *(m., f.)* **de vuelo** (8)

flip-flops **chanclas** *f. pl.* (4)

floor *(of a building)* **piso** (12); first/second floor (second/third story) **primer/segundo piso** (12); ground floor **planta baja** (12); to sweep the floor **barrer el piso** (10)

flower **flor** *f.* (8)

flu **gripe** *f.* (11)

fly by plane **volar (vuelo) en avión** (8)

folder *(computer)* **carpeta** (12)

follow **seguir (sigo) (i)** (6)

following *adj.* **siguiente** (5)

fond: to be fond of each other **quererse** (11)

food **comida** (7)

foodstuff **comestibles** *m. pl.* (7)

foolish **tonto/a** (3)

foot **pie** *m.* (11)

football **fútbol** *(m.)* **americano** (10)

for **para** (3); **por** (8); for example **por ejemplo** (14); for heaven's sake **por Dios** (14); for that reason **por eso** (3); for what purpose? **¿para qué... ?** (16); what for? **¿para qué... ?** (16)

forbid **prohibir (prohíbo)** (12)

foreign **extranjero/a** (2); foreign language **lengua extranjera** (2)

foreigner **extranjero/a** (2)

forest **bosque** *m.* (15)

forget **olvidar** (9)

form **forma** (4); *(to fill out)* **formulario** (17)

forty **cuarenta** (3)

four **cuatro** (1)

four hundred **cuatrocientos/as** (4)

fourteen **catorce** (1)

fourth *adj.* **cuarto/a** (13)

free (*unoccupied*) **libre** (10); free time **ratos** (*m. pl.*) **libres** (10), **tiempo libre** (10)

freeway **autopista** (15)

freezer **congelador** *m.* (10)

French (*language*) **francés** *m.* (2); French fried potato **papa/patata frita** (7)

frequently **con frecuencia** (2), **frecuentemente** (11)

fresh **fresco/a** (7)

Friday **viernes** *m. inv.* (5)

fried **frito/a** (7); French fried potato **papa/patata frita** (7)

friend **amigo/a** (2)

friendly **amistoso/a** (16)

friendship **amistad** *f.* (16)

from **de** (1); from the **del** (3); I am from . . . **(yo) soy de...** (1); where are you from? **¿de dónde eres (tú)?** *fam. s.* (1); **¿de dónde es usted?** *form. s.* (1)

front: in front of **delante de** (6)

frozen **congelado/a** (6)

fruit **fruta** (7); fruit juice **jugo de fruta** (7)

full-time job **empleo de tiempo completo** (17)

fun activity **diversión** *f.* (10); to be fun **ser divertido/a** (10)

function **funcionar** (12)

furious **furioso/a** (6)

furniture (*piece*) **mueble** *m.* (5)

G

game **partido** (10)

garage **garaje** *m.* (5)

garden **jardín** *m.* (5)

gas (*not for cars*) **gas** *m.* (12)

gas station **estación** (*f.*) **de servicio** (15), **gasolinera** (15)

gasoline **gasolina** (15)

gate: boarding gate **puerta de embarque** (8)

generally **por lo general** (5)

German (*language*) **alemán** *m.* (2); *n., adj.* **alemán, alemana** (3)

get **obtener** (*like* **tener**) (12); how do you get to . . . ? **¿cómo se llega a... ?** (15); to get **conseguir** (*like* **seguir**) (9); to get (*grades*) **sacar** (**qu**) (14); to get a cold **resfriarse** (**me resfrío**) (11); to get along poorly (with) **llevarse mal (con)** (16); to get along well (with) **llevarse bien (con)** (16); to get angry (with) **enojarse (con)** (9); to get down (from) **bajarse (de)** (8); to get dressed **vestirse (me visto) (i)** (5); to get off (of) (*a vehicle*) **bajarse (de)** (8); to get on (*a vehicle*) **subir (a)** (8); to get sick

enfermarse (11); to get tired **cansarse** (11); to get together (with) **reunirse (me reúno) (con)** (9); to get up (out of bed) **levantarse** (5); to get up on the wrong side of the bed **levantarse con el pie izquierdo** (14)

gift **regalo** (3)

girl **chica** (4), **niña** (3)

girlfriend **novia** (6)

give **dar** (8); to give (*as a gift*) **regalar** (8); to give someone a party **dar**le/**hacer**le una fiesta a alguien (9); to give (*someone*) a shot/vaccination **poner**le una inyección/una vacuna (11)

glasses **anteojos** *m. pl.* (11), **lentes** *m. pl.* (11)

go **ir** (4); let's go **vamos** (4); to be going to (*do something*) **ir a** + *inf.* (4); to go abroad **ir al extranjero** (8); to go by boat/ship **ir en barco** (8); to go by bus **ir en autobús** (8); to go by plane **ir/ volar (vuelo) en avión** (8); to go by train **ir en tren** (8); to go camping **hacer** *camping* (8); to go for a hike **dar** una caminata (10); to go home **regresar a casa** (2); to go onto Facebook **entrar en Facebook** (12); to go on the internet **entrar en internet** (12); to go on vacation in/to . . . **ir de vacaciones a...** (8); to go out (with) **salir (con)** (5); to go shopping **ir de compras** (4); to go through customs **pasar por la aduana** (8); to go through security (check) **pasar por el control de seguridad** (8); to go to (*a class, function*) **asistir (a)** (3); to go to a bar **ir a un bar** (10); to go to a concert **ir a un concierto** (10); to go to a disco **ir a una discoteca** (10); to go to bed **acostarse (me acuesto)** (5); to go to the theater **ir al teatro** (10); to go to a museum **ir a un museo** (10); to go up **subir (a)** (8); to go/travel by train **ir en tren** (8)

gold **oro** (4); **de oro** (4)

golf **golf** *m.* (10)

good **buen, bueno/a** (3); good afternoon **buenas tardes** (1); good afternoon/evening **muy buenas** (1); good morning **buenos días** (1); good night **buenas noches** (1); the good news/thing **lo bueno** (11); it's (very) good weather out **hace (muy) buen tiempo** (6); to have a good time **pasarlo bien** (9), **divertirse (me divierto) (i)** (5); to have good luck **tener buena suerte** (14)

good-bye **adiós** (1); to say good-bye (to) **despedir(se)** (*like* **pedir**) **(de)** (9)

good-looking **guapo/a** (3)

goods: woven goods **tejidos** *m. pl.* (13)

gorilla **gorila** *m.* (15)

government **gobierno** (15)

GPS **GPS** *m. inv.* (12)

grade (*academic*) **nota** (5)

graduate (*from*) **graduarse (me gradúo) (en)**

granddaughter **nieta** (3)

grandfather **abuelo** (3)

grandmother **abuela** (3)

grandparents **abuelos** *m. pl.* (3)

grandson **nieto** (3)

graphic designer **diseñador(a) gráfico/a** (17)

gray **gris** (4)

great **gran, grande** (3)

green **verde** (4)

green peas **arvejas** *f. pl.* (7)

greet each other **saludarse** (11)

greeting **saludo** (1)

groceries **comestibles** *m. pl.* (7)

groom **novio** (16)

ground floor **planta baja** (12)

grow **crecer (crezco)** (16)

guess **adivinar** (9)

guest **invitado/a** (9)

guide **guía** *m., f.* (13)

H

haggle **regatear** (4)

hairstylist **peluquero/a** (17)

half past (*the hour*) **y media** (1)

ham **jamón** *m.* (7)

hamburger **hamburguesa** (7)

hand **mano** *f.* (11); to shake hands **darse la mano** (11)

hand in **entregar (gu)** (8)

handbag **cartera** (4)

handsome **guapo/a** (3)

happen **pasar** (6); **ocurrir** (14)

happening **acontecimiento** (18)

happy **alegre** (6), **contento/a** (6); **feliz** (*pl.* **felices**) (9); to be happy (about) **alegrarse (de)** (12)

hard **difícil** (6)

hard drive **disco duro** (12)

hardworking **trabajador(a)** (3)

hat **sombrero** (4)

hate **odiar** (8)

have **tener** (4); (*auxilliary verb*) **haber** (12); to have a bad time **pasarlo mal** (9); to have a birthday **cumplir años** (9); to have a good time **divertirse (me divierto) (i)** (5), **pasarlo bien** (9); to have (a lot of) stress **tener muchas presiones** (14); to have a pain/ache in **tener dolor de** (11); to have a **picnic hacer un** *picnic* (10); to have a snack **merendar (meriendo)** (7); to have bad luck **tener mala suerte** (14); to have been (*doing something*) for (*time*) **hace** + *time* + **que** + *present* (14); *present* + **desde hace** + *time* (14);

to have breakfast **desayunar** (7); to have dinner, supper **cenar** (7); to have good luck **tener buena suerte** (14); to have just (*done something*) **acabar de** + *inf.* (7); to have lunch **almorzar (almuerzo) (c)** (5); to have to (*do something*) **tener que** + *inf.* (4)

he *sub. pron.* **él** (2); he is **es** (1)

head **cabeza** (11)

health **salud** *f.* (11)

healthy **sano/a** (11); to lead a healthy life **llevar una vida sana** (11)

hear **oír** (5)

heart **corazón** *m.* (11)

heating **calefacción** *f.* (12)

heaven: for heaven's sake **por Dios** (14)

hello! **¡hola!** (1)

help *n.* **ayuda** (7); *v.* **ayudar** (7); to help to (*do something*) *v.* **ayudar a** + *inf.* (7)

her *poss. adj.* **su(s)** (3); her, (of) hers *poss. adj., poss. pron.* **suyo/a(s)** (17)

here **aquí** (2)

hi! **¡hola!** (1)

highway **carretera** (15)

hike: to go for a hike **dar una caminata** (10)

his *poss. adj.* **su(s)** (3); his, of his *poss. adj., poss. pron.* **suyo/a(s)** (17)

Hispanic **hispano/a** (3)

history **historia** (2)

hit **pegar (gu)** (14)

hobby **afición** *f.* (10)

hockey **hockey** *m.* (10)

holiday **día** (*m.*) **festivo** (9)

home *n.* **casa** (3); at home **en casa** (2); nursing home **residencia de ancianos** (12); to go home **regresar a casa** (2); *adj.* (*related to the home*) **doméstico/a** (10)

home appliance **aparato doméstico** (10)

homework **tarea** (5)

honeymoon **luna de miel** (16)

honk **tocar (qu)** (15)

hope **esperanza** (18); I hope (that) **ojalá (que)** (13); to hope **esperar** (12)

horn (*car*) **bocina** (15)

horse: to ride a horse **montar a caballo** (10)

host (*of an event*) **anfitrión, anfitriona** (9)

hot (*spicy*) **picante** (7); (*temperature*) **caliente** (7); it's (very) hot (weather) **hace (mucho) calor** (6); it's hot (trendy) **está de moda** (4), **es de última moda** (4); to be (very) hot **tener (mucho) calor** (6)

hot dog **salchicha** (7)

house **casa** (3)

household chore **quehacer** (*m.*) **doméstico** (10)

housekeeper: female housekeeper **ama** (*f.*) (*but* **el ama**) **de casa** (17); male housekeeper **amo de casa** (17)

housing **vivienda** (12)

how + *adj.*! **¡qué** + *adj.*!** (14); how strange that . . . ! **¡qué extraño que... !** (13)

how? **¿cómo?** (1); how are you ? **¿cómo está(s)?** (1); **¿qué tal?** (1); how do you get to . . . ? **¿cómo se llega a... ?** (15); how many? **¿cuántos/as?** (2); how much? **¿cuánto?** (2); how much does it (do they) cost? **¿cuánto cuesta(n)?** (4); how often . . . ? **¿con qué frecuencia... ?** (3)

human **humano/a** (11); human body **cuerpo humano** (11)

humanities **humanidades** *f. pl.* (2)

hungry: to be (very) hungry **tener (mucha) hambre** (7)

hurry: to be in a hurry **tener prisa** (4)

hurt **doler (duele)** (*like* **gustar**) (11); to hurt oneself **hacerse daño** (14); to hurt (*a body part*) **lastimarse** (14); to hurt one's (*body part*) **hacerse daño en** (14)

husband **esposo** (3), **marido** (3)

hybrid **híbrido/a** (15)

I

I *sub. pron.* **yo** (2); I am **soy** (1); I am from . . . (**yo) soy de...** (1); I didn't mean to do it **fue sin querer** (14); I hope (that) **ojalá (que)** (13); I would (really) like . . . **me gustaría (mucho)...** (8); I'm sorry/ pardon me **disculpa, discúlpame** *fam. s.* (14); **disculpe, discúlpeme** *form. s.* (14); I'm (very) sorry **lo siento (mucho)** (14)

ice cream **helado** (7)

identification card **tarjeta de identificación** (14)

if **si** (4)

illness **enfermedad** *f.* (11)

image **imagen** *f.* (13)

immediately **en seguida** (5)

impossible **imposible** (13); it's impossible that **es imposible que** (13) it's not impossible **no es imposible** (13)

improbable **improbable** (13); it's improbable that **es improbable que** (13); it's not improbable **no es improbable** (13)

in **en** (1); in case **en caso de (que)** (16); in cash **en efectivo** (17); in front of **delante de** (6); in love (with) **enamorado/a (de)** (16); in order to (*do something*) **para** + *inf.* (10); in the afternoon **de la tarde** (1); in the evening **de la noche** (1); in the morning **de la mañana** (1); in the morning/afternoon/evening **por la mañana/tarde/noche** (2)

incredible **increíble** (13); it's incredible that **es increíble que** (13)

indefinite and negative word *gram.* **palabra indefinida y negativa** (7)

inequality **desigualdad** *f.* (18)

inexpensive **barato/a** (4)

infancy **infancia** (16), **niñez** *f.* (16)

inflexible **inflexible** (14)

inform **informar** (18)

injection **inyección** *f.* (11)

inner ear **oído** (11)

insist (on) **insistir (en)** (12)

install **instalar** (12)

installments: in installments **a plazos** (17)

intelligent **inteligente** (3)

intended for **para** (3)

interest *n.* **interés** *m.* (17); *v.* to interest (*someone*) **interesar** (*like* **gustar**) (8)

internet **internet** *m.* (12); to go on the internet **entrar en internet** (12); to look for on the internet **buscar (qu) en internet** (12)

interrogative *gram.* **interrogativo/a** (2); interrogative word **palabra interrogativa** (2)

interstate **autopista** (15)

interview **entrevista** (17)

interviewee **entrevistado/a** (17)

interviewer **entrevistador(a)** (17)

invite **invitar** (7)

iPhone **iPhone** *m.* (12)

iPod **iPod** *m.* (12)

iron *v.* **planchar** (10)

island **isla** (6)

issue **cuestión** *f.* (17)

it is... (*time*) **es la...** (1), **son las...** (1)

Italian (*language*) **italiano** (2)

its *poss. adj.* **su(s)** (3); (of) its *poss. adj., poss. pron.* **suyo/a(s)** (17)

J

jacket **chaqueta** (4)

January **enero** (6)

jeans **jeans** *m. pl.* (4)

job **empleo** (17), **trabajo** (12); full-time job **empleo de tiempo completo** (17), **trabajo de tiempo completo** (14); part-time job **empleo de tiempo parcial** (17), **trabajo de tiempo parcial** (14); poorly paid job **empleo mal pagado** (17); well-paid job **empleo bien pagado** (17)

joke **chiste** *m.* (8)

journalist **periodista** *m., f.* (17)

juice **jugo** (7); fruit juice **jugo de fruta** (7)

July **julio** (6)

June **junio** (6)

just in case **por si acaso** (14)

K

keep **guardar** (12); **mantener** (*like* **tener**) (18); to keep on going **seguir (sigo) (i)** (15)
key **llave** *f.* (5)
kill **matar** (18)
kind **amable** (3)
king **rey** *m.* (18)
kiss: to kiss each other **besarse** (11)
kitchen **cocina** (5)
know **conocer (conozco)** (7); **saber** (7); to know how to (*do something*) **saber** + *inf.* (7)

L

laborer **obrero/a** (17)
lack **falta** (15)
lake **lago** (15)
lamp **lámpara** (5)
landlady **dueña** (12)
landline **teléfono fijo** (12)
landlord **dueño** (12)
language **lengua** (2); foreign language **lengua extranjera** (2)
laptop (computer) **computadora portátil** (2)
large **gran, grande** (3)
last **pasado/a** (11); **último/a** (14); for the last time **por última vez** (14); last night *adv.* **anoche** (11); to last **durar** (18)
late *adj.* **atrasado/a** (8); *adv.* **tarde** (2)
later: see you later **hasta luego** (1)
laugh **reírse (de)** (9)
law **ley** *f.* (18)
lawyer **abogado/a** (17)
layer: ozone layer **capa de ozono** (15)
lazy **perezoso/a** (3)
lead a calm/healthy life **llevar una vida tranquila/sana** (11)
learn **aprender** (3); to learn (about) **enterarse (de)** (18); to learn how to (*do something*) **aprender a** + *inf.* (3)
least: at least **por lo menos** (9)
leather *adj.* **de cuero** (4)
leave (*a place*) **salir (de)** (5); to leave for (*a place*) **salir para** (5); to leave on vacation **salir de vacaciones** (8)
left: to the left of **a la izquierda de** (6); to be left **quedar** (*like* **gustar**) (14)
leg **pierna** (11)
lend **prestar** (8)
lenses: contact lenses **lentes** (*m. pl.*) **de contacto** (11)
less than **menos que** (6); less. . . than **menos... que** (6); less than + *number* **menos de** + *number* (6)
let (*someone*) go **despedir** (*like* **pedir**) (17)
let's go **vamos** (4)
letter **carta** (3)
lettuce **lechuga** (7)

librarian **bibliotecario/a** (2)
library **biblioteca** (2)
license: driver's license **licencia de conducir/manejar** (15)
lie **mentira** (12)
life **vida** (11); academic life **vida académica** (14); pace of life **ritmo de la vida** (15)
lift weights **levantar pesas** (11)
light *n.* **luz** *f.* (*pl.* **luces**) (14); *adj.* light (*not heavy*) **ligero/a** (7)
like *n.* **gusto** (1); do you like . . . ? **¿te gusta... ?** *fam. s.* (1); **¿a usted le gusta... ?** *form. s.* (1); I would (really) like . . . **me gustaría (mucho)...** (8); (no,) I don't like . . . **(no,) no me gusta** (1); to like **gustar** (8); to like very much **encantar** (*like* **gustar**) (8); what are you like? **¿cómo es usted?** *form. s.* (1); yes, I like . . . **sí, me gusta...** (1)
likeable **simpático/a** (3)
likely: it's likely that **es probable que** (13)
likewise **igualmente** (1)
limit: speed limit **límite** (*m.*) **de velocidad** (15)
line (*of people*) **cola** (8); to stand in line **hacer cola** (8)
listen to (*music, the radio*) **oír** (5); to listen (to) **escuchar** (2)
literature **literatura** (2)
little *adv.* (a) little **poco** (2); (adjective suffix) **-ito/a** (10); a little bit (of) **un poco (de)** (2); *adj.* **poco/a** (4)
live **vivir** (3)
living room **sala** (5)
loan **préstamo** (17)
lobster **langosta** (7)
long **largo/a** (3)
look at **mirar** (3); to look for **buscar (qu)** (2); to look for on the internet **buscar (qu) en internet** (12)
lose **perder (pierdo)** (5)
lot: a lot *adv.* **mucho** (2); a lot (of) **mucho/a** (3); an awful lot **muchísimo** (8); there's lots of **hay mucho/a** (6)
love *n.* **amor** *m.* (16); *adj.* in love (with) **enamorado/a (de)** (16); *v.* **amar** (16); **querer** (16); **encantar** (*like* **gustar**) (8); to fall in love (with) **enamorarse (de)** (16); to love each other **quererse** (11)
luck: to have bad/good luck **tener mala/buena suerte** (14)
lucky: to be lucky **tener buena suerte** (14)
luggage **equipaje** *m.* (8)
lunch *n.* **almuerzo** (7); to have lunch **almorzar (almuerzo) (c)** (5)
lungs **pulmones** *m. pl.* (11)
-ly (*adverbial suffix*) **-mente** (14)
lyrics **letra** (7)

M

ma'am **señora (Sra.)** (1)
machine: automatic teller machine (ATM) **cajero automático** (17)
made: it is made of . . . **es de...** (4)
magazine **revista** (3)
mailbox: voice mailbox **buzón** (*m.*) **de voz** (12)
main course **plato principal** (7)
maintain **mantener** (*like* **tener**) (18)
make **hacer** (5); to make a mistake (about) **equivocarse (qu) (de)** (14); to make plans to (*do something*) **hacer planes** (*m.*) **para** + *inf.* (10); to make stops **hacer escalas/paradas** (8); to make the bed **hacer la cama** (10)
male housekeeper **amo de casa** (17)
mall: shopping mall **centro comercial** (4)
man **hombre** *m.* (2); business man **hombre de negocios** (17)
manager **gerente** *m., f.* (17); building manager **portero/a** (12)
manufacture **fabricar (qu)** (15)
many **muchos/as** (3); as many . . . as **tanto/a(s) ... como** (6); how many? **¿cuántos/as?** (2)
march **manifestación** *f.* (18)
March **marzo** (6)
market(place) **mercado** (4)
marriage **matrimonio** (16)
married: to be a married person **ser casado/a** (16); to be married (to) **estar casado/a (con)** (16)
marry **casarse (con)** (16)
mass media **medios** *m. pl.* (18)
masterpiece **obra maestra** (13)
match (*game*) **partido** (10)
material **materia** (4)
math **matemáticas** *f. pl.* (2)
matter **cuestión** *f.* (17)
May **mayo** (6)
me *obj. of prep.* **mí** (6); with me **conmigo** (6)
meal **comida** (7)
mean: I didn't mean to do it **fue sin querer** (14); that means . . . **eso quiere decir...** (11)
means of transportation **medio de transporte** (8)
meat **carne** *f.* (7)
mechanic **mecánico/a** (15)
medical **médico/a** (11); medical office **consultorio** (11); medical personnel **personal** (*m.*) **médico** (11)
medicine **medicina** (11)
medium of communication **medio de comunicación** (18)
meet **conocerse (conozco)** (16); nice to meet you **mucho gusto** (1); to meet (*someone somewhere*) **encontrarse (me encuentro) (con)** (11)

memory **memoria** (12)

memory stick **pen drive** *m.* (12)

menu **menú** *m.* (7)

messy **desordenado/a** (6)

Mexican **mexicano/a** (3)

microwave oven **horno de microondas** (10)

middle age **madurez** *f.* (16)

midnight **medianoche** *f.* (6)

military *adj.* **militar** (18); military service **servicio militar** (18)

milk **leche** *f.* (7)

million: one million **un millón (de)** (4)

mine, (of) mine *poss. adj., poss. pron.* **mío/a(s)** (17)

mineral water **agua** (*f.;* but **el agua**) **mineral** (7)

minute: fifteen minutes till (*hour*) **menos quince** (1); thirty minutes past (*the hour*) **y treinta** (1)

misbehave **portarse mal** (9)

miss (*an event*) **perder (pierdo)** (5)

Miss **señorita (Srta.)** (1)

mistake: to make a mistake (about) **equivocarse (qu) (de)** (14)

modem **módem** *m.* (12)

modern **moderno/a** (13)

molar **muela** (11)

mom **mamá** (3)

Monday **lunes** *m. inv.* (5); next Monday **el lunes que viene** (5); on Monday **el lunes** (5); on Mondays **los lunes** (5)

money **dinero** (2)

monitor **pantalla** (12); big screen monitor **pantalla grande** (12); flat screen monitor **pantalla plana** (12)

month **mes** *m.* (6)

moped **moto(cicleta)** (15)

more **más** (2); more than **más que** (6); more . . . than **más... que** (6); more than + *number* **más de** + *number* (6)

morning: good morning **buenos días** (1); in the morning **por la mañana** (2); **de la mañana** (1)

mother **madre** *f.* (3); **mamá** (3)

motorcycle **moto(cicleta)** (15)

mountain **montaña** (8)

mouse **ratón** *m.* (12)

mouth **boca** (11)

move (*residence*) **mudarse** (12)

movie **película** (5); movie theater **cine** *m. s.* (5); movies **cine** *m. s.* (5)

Mr. **señor (Sr.)** *m.* (1)

Mrs. **señora (Sra.)** (1)

Ms. **señorita (Srta.)** (1)

much **mucho** (2); as much . . . as **tanto/a(s)... como** (6); as much as **tanto como** (6); how much? **¿cuánto?** (2); how much does it (do they) cost? **¿cuánto cuesta(n)?** (4)

mural **mural** *m.* (13)

museum **museo** (10); to visit a museum **visitar un museo** (10)

mushrooms **champiñones** *m. pl.* (7)

music **música** (13)

musical *n. m.* **musical** (13)

musician **músico/a** (13)

must (*do something*) **deber** + *inf.* (3)

my *poss. adj.* **mi(s)** (3); *poss. adj., poss. pron.* **mío/a(s)** (17)

N

name **nombre** *m.* (7); my name is . . . **me llamo...** (1); what is your name? **¿cómo se llama usted?** *form. s.* (1); **¿cómo te llamas?** *fam. s.* (1)

nap: to take a nap **dormir duermo (u) la siesta** (5)

narrate **contar (cuento)** (8)

nationality **nacionalidad** *f.* (3); adjective of nationality **adjetivo de nacionalidad** (3)

natural **natural** (15); natural resource **recurso natural** (15); natural sciences **ciencias** (*f. pl.*) **naturales** (2)

nature **naturaleza** (15)

nauseated **mareado/a** (11)

navigate **navegar (gu)** (12)

neat **ordenado/a** (6)

necessary **necesario/a** (3); it is necessary to (*do something*) **hay que** + *inf.* (13)

need **necesitar** (2)

negative: indefinite and negative word *gram.* **palabra indefinida y negativa** (7)

neighbor **vecino/a** (12)

neighborhood **barrio** (12)

neither **tampoco** (7)

nephew **sobrino** (3)

nervous **nervioso/a** (6)

network: social network **red** (*f.*) **social** (12)

never **jamás** (7), **nunca** (3); almost never **casi nunca** (3)

nevertheless **sin embargo** (6)

new **nuevo/a** (3)

New Year's Eve **Nochevieja** *f.* (9)

newlywed **recién casado/a** (16)

news **noticias** *f. pl.* (5); news media **prensa** (18); the bad news **lo malo** (11); the good news **lo bueno** (11)

newscast **noticiero** (18)

newsstand **quiosco de prensa** (18)

newspaper **periódico** (3)

next *adv.* **luego** (5); *adj.* **próximo/a** (5); next (Tuesday . . .) **el próximo (martes...)** (5); next Monday **el lunes** (*m.*) **que viene** (5); next week **la próxima semana** (5), **la semana que viene** (5)

nice **amable** (3), **simpático/a** (3); nice to meet you **mucho gusto** (1); (very) nice out **(muy) buen tiempo** (6)

niece **sobrina** (3)

night: at night **de la noche** (1), **por la noche** (2); last night *adv.* **anoche** (11)

nine **nueve** (1)

nine hundred **novecientos/as** (4)

nineteen **diecinueve** (1)

ninety **noventa** (3)

ninth **noveno/a** (13)

no **no** (1); **ningún (ninguna)** (7); no, I don't like . . . **(no,) no me gusta** (1)

no one **nadie** (7)

nobody **nadie** (7)

noise **ruido** (5)

noon **mediodía** *m.* (6)

normal **normal** (13); it's normal that **es normal que** (13)

north **norte** *m.* (6)

nose **nariz** *f.* (*pl.* **narices**) (11)

not any **ningún (ninguna)** (7)

notebook **cuaderno** (2)

notes (*academic*) **apuntes** *m., pl.* (14)

nothing **nada** (7)

noun *gram.* **sustantivo** (2)

novel **novela** (13)

novelist **novelista** *m., f.* (13)

November **noviembre** *m.* (6)

now **ahora** (2); right now **ahora mismo** (6)

nuclear energy **energía nuclear** (15)

number **número** (1); ordinal number *gram.* **número ordinal** (13)

nurse **enfermero/a** (11)

nursing home **residencia de ancianos** (12)

O

o'clock: it's . . . o'clock **son las...** (1)

obey **obedecer (obedezco)** (15)

object **objeto** (2)

obligation **deber** *m.* (18)

obtain **obtener** (*like* **tener**) (12); **conseguir** (*like* **seguir**) (9)

ocean **océano** (8)

October **octubre** *m.* (6)

of **de** (1); of course! **¡por supuesto!** (14); of the **del** (3)

off: to turn off **apagar (gu)** (12)

offer **ofrecer (ofrezco)** (8)

office **oficina** (2); (*in a home*) **estudio** (5); (*medical*) **consultorio** (11); (*political*) **cargo** (18)

often: how often . . . ? **¿con qué frecuencia... ?** (3)

oil (*cooking*) **aceite** *m.* (7); (*fuel*) **petróleo** (15)

OK: it's OK **está bien** (6)

old **viejo/a** (3); old age **vejez** *f.* (16)

older (than) **mayor (que)** (6)

olive oil **aceite** (*m.*) **de oliva** (7)

on **en** (1); on a trip **de viaje** (8); on Monday **el lunes** (5); on the dot (*time*) **en punto** (1); on top of **encima de** (6);

on Tuesdays **los martes** (5); on vacation **de vacaciones** (8)

once a week **una vez a la semana** (3)

one **uno** (1); it's one o'clock **es la una** (1)

one hundred **cien** (3); (*used with* 101–199) **ciento** (4)

one hundred ninety-nine **ciento noventa y nueve** (4)

one hundred one **ciento uno** (4)

one hundred two **ciento dos** (4)

one million **un millón (de** + *noun*) (4)

one thousand **mil** (4)

onion **cebolla** (7)

only *adv.* **solo** (2)

open *v.* **abrir** (*p.p.* **abierto**) (3); *adj.* **abierto/a** (6)

opera **ópera** (13)

operate (*a machine*) **manejar** (12)

or **o** (1)

oral **oral** (14); oral report **informe** (*m.*) **oral** (14)

orange *n.* **naranja** (7); *adj.* **anaranjado/a** (4)

orchestra **orquesta** (13)

order **mandar** (12); (*in a restaurant*) **pedir** (**pido**) **(i)** (5); in order to (*do something*) **para** + *inf.* (3)

ordinal number *gram.* **número ordinal** (13)

other **otro/a** (3); others **los/las demás** (12)

ought to (*do something*) **deber** + *inf.* (3)

our *poss. adj.* **nuestro/a(s)** (3); our, of ours *poss. adj., poss. pron.* **nuestro/a(s)** (17)

outdoors *adv.* **afuera** (6); **al aire libre** (10)

outer ear **oreja** (11)

outskirts **afueras** *f. pl.* (12)

overcast: it's (very) overcast **está (muy) nublado** (6)

own, one's own **propio/a** (17)

owner **dueño/a** (7)

ozone layer **capa de ozono** (15)

P

P.M. **de la noche** (1); **de la tarde** (1)

pace of life **ritmo de la vida** (15)

pack one's suitcase(s) **hacer la(s) maleta(s)** (8)

page: webpage **página web** (12)

paid: well/poorly paid job/position **empleo bien/mal pagado** (17)

pain (in) **dolor** *m.* **(de)** (11); to have a pain in **tener dolor de** (11)

paint **pintar** (13)

painter **pintor(a)** (13)

painting (*general*) **pintura** (13); (*specific piece*) **cuadro** (13)

pants **pantalones** *m. pl.* (4)

paper **papel** *m.* (2)

pardon me **con permiso** (1), **disculpa, discúlpame** *fam. s.* (14); **disculpe, discúlpeme** *form. s.* (14)

parents **padres** *m. pl.* (3)

park **estacionar** (14)

parking lot/place **estacionamiento** (15)

part **parte** *f.* (5)

part-time job/position **empleo de tiempo parcial** (17), **trabajo de tiempo parcial** (14)

partner **pareja** (16)

party **fiesta** (2); (political) party **partido (político)** (18); to throw a party **dar/hacer una fiesta** (9)

pass: boarding pass **tarjeta de embarque** (8)

pass through customs **pasar por la aduana** (8); to pass through security (check) **pasar por el control de seguridad** (8)

passenger **pasajero/a** (8)

passport **pasaporte** *m.* (8)

password **contraseña** (12)

past **pasado/a** (11)

pastime **pasatiempo** (10)

patient **paciente** *n. m., f.* (11)

patio **patio** (5)

pay *n.* (*often per hour*) **salario** (17); *v.* to pay (for) **pagar (gu)** (2)

pea: green peas **arvejas** *f. pl.* (7)

peace **paz** *f.* (*pl.* **paces**) (18)

peasant **campesino/a** (15)

pen **bolígrafo** (2); pen drive **pen drive** *m.* (12)

pencil **lápiz** *m.* (*pl.* **lápices**) (2)

people **gente** *f. s.* (8)

pepper (*condiment*) **pimienta** (7)

permit **permitir** (12)

person **persona** (2)

personal pronoun *gram.* **pronombre** (*m.*) **personal** (2)

personnel: medical personnel **personal** (*m.*) **médico** (11)

pet **mascota** (3)

petroleum **petróleo** (15)

pharmacist **farmacéutico/a** (11)

phase **etapa** (16)

philosophy **filosofía** (2)

phone **teléfono** (2); cell phone **teléfono celular** (2); to talk on the phone **hablar por teléfono** (2)

photo(graph) **foto(grafía)** (8); to take photos **sacar (qu) fotos** (8)

photocopier **fotocopiadora** (12)

photocopy **fotocopia** (12)

photographer **fotógrafo/a** (17)

photography **fotografía** (13)

pick up **recoger (recojo)** (14)

picnic: to have a picnic **hacer un** *picnic* (10)

pie **pastel** *m.* (7)

piece: piece of advice **consejo** (7); piece of furniture **mueble** *m.* (5)

Pilates: to do Pilates **hacer (el método) Pilates** (11)

pill **pastilla** (11)

pilot **piloto** *m., f.* (8)

pink **rosado/a** (4)

place *n.* **lugar** *m.* (2); (*in line*) **puesto** (8); parking place **estacionamiento** (15); *v.* **poner** (5)

plaid **de cuadros** (4)

plan **plan** *m.* (10); to make plans to **hacer planes para** (10)

plane **avión** *m.* (8); to fly; to go/travel by plane **volar (vuelo) en avión** (8); **ir en avión** (8)

planet **planeta** *m.* (15)

plasma television **televisión** (*f.*) **plasma** (12)

plate **plato** (5)

play (*dramatic*) *n.* **drama** *m.* (13), **obra de teatro** (13); (*a game, sport*) *v.* **jugar (juego) (gu) (a, al)** (5); (*a musical instrument*) **tocar (qu)** (2); to play cards **jugar (juego) (gu) a las cartas** (10); to play chess **jugar (juego) (gu) al ajedrez** (10); to play videgames **jugar (juego) (gu) a los videojuegos** (10)

player **jugador(a)** (10)

playwright **dramaturgo/a** (13)

plaza **plaza** (4)

pleasantry **expresión** (*f.*) **de cortesía** (1)

please **por favor** (1)

pleased to meet you **encantado/a** (1), **mucho gusto** (1)

pleasing: to be pleasing **gustar** (8)

plumber **plomero/a** (17)

poem **poema** *m.* (13)

poet **poeta** *m., f.* (13)

point: cardinal point **punto cardinal** (6)

police officer **policía** *m., f.* (15)

policy **política** (18)

political: political office **cargo** (18); political party **partido** (18); political science **ciencias** (*f. pl.*) **políticas** (2)

politician **político/a** (18)

politics **política** *s.* (18)

polka-dot **de lunares** (4)

pollute **contaminar** (15)

polluted **contaminado/a** (15)

pollution: there's (lots of) pollution **hay (mucha) contaminación** *f.* (6)

pool **piscina** (5)

poor **pobre** (3); poorly paid job/position **empleo mal pagado** (17); to do poorly **salir mal** (5); to get along poorly (with) **llevarse mal (con)** (16)

poorly **mal** (2)

population **población** *f.* (15)

pork chop **chuleta (de cerdo)** (7)

port **puerto** (8)

porter **maletero** (8)

position **empleo** (17); full-time / part-time position **empleo de tiempo completo / parcial** (17), **trabajo de tiempo parcial** (14); poorly paid position **empleo mal pagado** (17); to run for a position (as a candidate) **postularse para un cargo (como candidato/a)** (18); well-paid position **empleo bien pagado** (17)

possessive **posesivo/a** (17); possessive adjective *gram.* **adjetivo posesivo** (3)

possible **posible** (3); it's not possible **no es posible que** (13); it's possible that **es posible que** (13)

post (*as on Facebook*) **publicar (qu)** (12)

postcard **tarjeta postal** (8)

potato **papa/patata** (7); French fried potato **papa/patata frita** (7)

pottery **cerámica** (13)

practice (*play*) **practicar (qu)** (2); (*train*) **entrenar** (10)

prefer **preferir (prefiero) (i)** (4)

preference **preferencia** (1)

prepare **preparar** (7)

preposition *gram.* **preposición** *f.* (5)

prescription **receta** (11)

present **regalo** (3)

press **prensa** (18)

pressure **presión** (14); to be under a lot of pressure **estar bajo muchas presiones** (14)

pretty **bonito/a** (3)

price (*of a transportation ticket*) **pasaje** *m.* (8); fixed, set price **precio fijo** (4)

print **imprimir** (12)

printer **impresora** (12)

probable **probable** (13); it's not probable **no es probable que** (13); it's probable that **es probable que** (13)

profession **profesión** *f.* (17)

professor **profesor(a)** (1)

programmer **programador(a)** (17)

prohibit **prohibir (prohibo)** (12)

promise **prometer** (8)

pronoun: personal pronoun *gram.* **pronombre (m.) personal** (2)

protect **proteger (protejo)** (15)

provided **con tal de** (16); provided (that) **con tal (de) que** (16)

psychiatrist **siquiatra** *m., f.* (17)

psychologist **sicólogo/a** (17)

psychology **sicología** (2)

public *n.* **público** (13); *adj.* **público/a** (15)

publish **publicar (qu)** (12)

pure **puro/a** (15)

purple **morado/a** (4)

purpose: for what purpose? **¿para qué?** (16)

purse **bolso** (4)

put **poner** (5); to put on (*an article of clothing*) **ponerse** (5)

Q

quarter: a quarter (fifteen minutes) after (*the hour*) **y cuarto/quince** (1); a quarter to (*hour*) **menos cuarto/ quince** (1)

queen **reina** (18)

question **pregunta** (5); to ask a question **hacer una pregunta** (5), **preguntar** (8)

quit **dejar** (17)

quiz **prueba** (14)

R

radio (apparatus) **radio** *m.* (12); radio station **estación** (*f.*) **de radio** (18)

rain **llover (llueve)** (6); it's raining **llueve** (6)

raincoat **impermeable** *m.* (4)

rather **bastante** (16)

read **leer** (*like* **creer**) (3)

reason: for that reason **por eso** (3)

receipt **recibo** (17)

receive **recibir** (3)

recipe **receta** (7)

recommend **recomendar (recomiendo)** (8)

record **grabar** (12)

recycle **reciclar** (15)

recycling **reciclaje** *m.* (15)

red **rojo/a** (4); red wine **vino tinto** (7)

reflexive verb *gram.* **verbo reflexivo** (5)

refrigerator **refrigerador** *m.* (10)

regret **lamentar** (13), **sentir (siento) (i)** (13)

relationship: emotional relationship **relación** (*f.*) **sentimental** (16)

relative **pariente** *m.* (3)

remain (*in a place*) **quedarse** (6); to remain; to be left **quedar** (14)

remember **acordarse (me acuerdo) (de)** (13); **recordar (recuerdo)** (9)

remote control **control** (*m.*) **remoto** (12)

renewable **renovable** (15); renewable energy **energía renovable** (15)

rent *n.* **alquiler** *m.* (12); *v.* to rent **alquilar** (12)

renter **inquilino/a** (12)

repair **arreglar** (15), **reparar** (15); repair shop **taller** *m.* (15)

report **informe** (14), **trabajo** (14); oral report **informe** (*m.*) **oral** (14); written report **informe** (*m.*) **escrito** (14)

reporter **reportero/a** (18)

representative: Congressional representative **representante** (*m., f.*) **al congreso** (18)

resign (from) **renunciar (a)** (17)

resolve **resolver (resuelvo)** (15)

resource: natural resource **recurso natural** (15)

responsibility **deber** *m.* (18), **responsabilidad** *f.* (18)

rest **descansar** (5)

restaurant **restaurante** *m.* (7)

résumé **currículum** *m.* (17)

retire (*from a job*) **jubilarse** (17)

return (*something to someone*) **devolver** (*like* **volver**) (14);

(*to a place*) **regresar** (2), **volver (vuelvo)** (5); to return home **regresar a casa** (2)

review **repaso** (2)

rice **arroz** *m.* (7)

rich (*wealthy*) **rico/a** (3); (*tasty*) **rico/a** (7)

ride: to ride a bicycle **montar en bicicleta** (10); **pasear en bicicleta** (10); to ride a horse **montar a caballo** (10)

right (*legal*) **derecho** (18); **¿no?** (4), **¿verdad?** (4); right now **ahora mismo** (6); right now (*currently*) **en la actualidad** (10); to be right **tener razón** (4); to the right of **a la derecha de** (6)

ring **sonar (suena)** (10)

river **río** (15)

roast(ed) **asado/a** (7); roast chicken **pollo asado** (7)

role (*in a play, an event*) **papel** *m.* (13)

room **cuarto** (2); waiting room **sala de espera** (8)

roommate **compañero/a de cuarto** (2)

round-trip ticket **billete** *m.* (*Sp.*) / **boleto** (*L.A.*) **de ida y vuelta** (8)

routine **rutina** (5)

rug **alfombra** (5)

ruin **ruina** (13)

run **correr** (10); to run against/into **chocar (qu) contra/con** (14); **pegarse (gu) con/contra** (14); to run as a candidate **postularse como candidato/a** (18); to run for a position **postularse para un cargo** (18); (*machines*) **funcionar** (12); to run out of **acabar** (14)

S

sad **triste** (6)

sake: for heaven's sake **por Dios** (14)

salad **ensalada** (7)

salary **sueldo** (17)

sales **rebajas** *f. pl.* (4)

salesperson **vendedor(a)** (17)

salmon **salmón** *m.* (7)

salt **sal** *f.* (7)

same **mismo/a** (6); same here (likewise) **igualmente** (1)

sandals **sandalias** *f. pl.* (4)

sandwich **sándwich** *m.* (7)

Saturday **sábado** (5)

sauce **salsa** (7)

sausage **salchicha** (7)

save **conservar** (15); (*a place in line*) **guardar un puesto** (8); (*documents*) **almacenar** (12), **guardar** (12); (*money*) **ahorrar** (17)

savory **rico/a** (7)

say **decir** (8); to say good-bye (to) **despedirse** (*like* **pedir**) **(de)** (9) scanner **escáner** *m.* (12)

scene **escena** (13)

scenery **escenario** (13)

schedule **horario** (14)

school **escuela** (10)

schoolteacher **maestro/a de escuela** (17)

science **ciencia** (2); computer science **computación** *f.* (2); natural sciences **ciencias** (*f. pl.*) **naturales** (2); political science **ciencias** (*f. pl.*) **políticas** (2); social sciences **ciencias** (*f. pl.*) **sociales** (2)

screen **pantalla** (12); big screen (monitor) **pantalla grande** (12); flat screen (monitor) **pantalla plana** (12)

script **guion** *m.* (13)

sculpt **esculpir** (13)

sculptor **escultor(a)** (13)

sculpture **escultura** (13)

sea **mar** *m.* (8)

season (of the year) **estación** *f.* (6)

seat **asiento** (8)

second **segundo/a** (13); second floor (third story) **segundo piso** (12)

secretary **secretario/a** (2)

security (check) **control** (*m.*) **de seguridad** (8); to go/pass through security (check) **pasar por el control de seguridad** (8)

see **ver** (5); see you around **nos vemos** (1); see you later **hasta luego** (1); see you tomorrow **hasta mañana** (1)

sell **vender** (3)

senator **senador(a)** (18)

send a text **mandar un mensaje** (2)

separate (from) **separarse (de)** (16)

separated from **separado/a (de)** (16)

separation **separación** *f.* (16)

September **septiembre** *m.* (6)

serve **servir (sirvo) (i)** (5)

service **servicio** (15); military service **servicio militar** (18)

set price **precio fijo** (4)

set the table **poner la mesa** (10)

seven **siete** (1)

seven hundred **setecientos/as** (4)

seventeen **diecisiete** (1)

seventh **séptimo/a** (13)

seventy **setenta** (3)

shake hands **darse la mano** (11)

shame **lástima** (13); it's a shame that **es una lástima que** (13); what a shame that . . . ! **¡qué lástima que... !** (13)

shape **forma** (4)

share **compartir** (17)

shave **afeitarse** (5)

she *sub. pron.* **ella** (2); she is **es** (1)

shellfish **mariscos** *m. pl.* (7)

ship **barco** (8); cruise ship **crucero** (8); to go/travel by ship **ir en barco** (8)

shirt **camisa** (4)

shoes **zapatos** *m. pl.* (4)

shop **tienda** (4); repair shop **taller** *m.* (15)

shopping **de compras** (4); shopping mall **centro comercial** (4); to go shopping **ir de compras** (4)

short (*in height*) **bajo/a** (3); (*in length*) **corto/a** (3)

shorts **pantalones** (*m. pl.*) **cortos** (4)

shot: to give (*someone*) a shot **ponerle una inyección** (11)

should (*do something*) **deber** + *inf.* (3)

show *n.* **espectáculo** (13); *v.* **mostrar (muestro)** (8)

shower: to take a shower **ducharse** (5)

shrimp **camarones** *m., pl.* (7)

siblings **hermanos** *m. pl.* (3)

sick **enfermo/a** (6); to get/become sick **enfermarse** (11)

sickness **enfermedad** *f.* (11)

sidewalk **acera** (15)

silk *adj.* **de seda** (4)

silly **tonto/a** (3)

silver *adj.* **de plata** (4)

sing **cantar** (2)

singer **cantante** *m., f.* (13)

single (*not married*) **soltero/a** (16)

sink: bathroom sink **lavabo** (5)

sir **señor (Sr.)** *m.* (1)

sister **hermana** (3)

sit down **sentarse (me siento)** (5)

six **seis** (1)

six hundred **seiscientos/as** (4)

sixteen **dieciséis** (1)

sixth **sexto/a** (13)

sixty **sesenta** (3)

skate *v.* **patinar** (10)

skating **patinaje** *m.* (10)

ski **esquiar (esquío)** (10)

skiing **esquí** *m.* (10)

skirt **falda** (4)

skyscraper **rascacielos** *m. inv.* (15)

sleep **dormir (duermo) (u) (u)** (5)

sleepy: to be sleepy **tener sueño** (4)

slender **delgado/a** (3)

small **pequeño/a** (3); (*adjective suffix*) **-ito/a** (10); small child **niño/a** (3)

smart **listo/a** (3)

smile **sonreír** (*like* **reír**) (9)

smoke **fumar** (8)

smoking area **sala de fumadores/ de fumar** (8)

snack **merienda** (7); to have a snack **merendar (meriendo)** (7)

snow **nevar (nieva)** (6); it's snowing **nieva** (6)

so that **para que** (16)

so-so **regular** (1)

soccer **fútbol** *m.* (10)

social: social network **red** (*f.*) **social** (12); social sciences **ciencias** (*f. pl.*)

sociales (2); social worker **trabajador(a) social** (17)

sociology **sociología** (2)

socks **calcetines** *m. pl.* (4)

soft drink **refresco** (7)

solar energy **energía solar** (15)

soldier **militar** *m., f.* (17); **soldado** (17); female soldier **mujer** (*f.*) **soldado** (17)

solve **resolver (resuelvo)** (15)

some **algún (alguna/os/as)** (7)

someone **alguien** (7)

something **algo** (7)

sometimes **a veces** (3)

son **hijo** (3)

song **canción** *f.* (7)

soon: as soon as **en cuanto** (17), **tan pronto como** (17)

sorry: to feel sorry **lamentar** (13), *sentir* **(siento) (i)** (13); I'm (very) sorry **lo siento (mucho)** (14)

sound **sonar (suena)** (10)

soup **sopa** (7)

south **sur** *m.* (6)

space: storage space **espacio de almacenamiento** (12)

Spanish (*language*) **español** *m.* (2); *n., adj.* **español, española** (3)

spare (free) time **ratos** (*m. pl.*) **libres** (10)

speak **hablar** (2)

species **especie** *f.* (15); endangered species **especie en peligro de extinción** (15)

spectator **espectador(a)** (13)

speed **velocidad** *f.* (15); speed limit **límite** (*m.*) **de velocidad** (15)

spend (*money*) **gastar** (9); (*time*) **pasar** (6); to spend one's vacation in . . . **pasar las vacaciones en...** (8)

spicy **picante** (7)

sport **deporte** *m.* (10)

sporting **deportivo/a** (10)

sports, sports-loving *adj.* **deportivo/a** (10)

spring (*season*) **primavera** (6)

square **plaza** (4)

stage **escenario** (13); (*phase*) **etapa** (16)

stairs **escaleras** *f. pl.* (14)

stand up **levantarse** (5); to stand in line **hacer cola** (8)

start **empezar (empiezo) (c)** (5); to start up (*a car*) **arrancar (qu)** (15)

state **estado** (3); emotional state **estado afectivo** (9)

station **estación** *f.* (8); bus station **estación de autobuses** (8); gas station **estación de servicio** (15); radio station **estación de radio** (18); station wagon **camioneta** (8); train station **estación de trenes** (8)

stay **quedarse** (6); to stay in bed **guardar cama** (11)

steak **bistec** *m.* (7)

stick out one's tongue **sacar (qu) la lengua** (11)

still **todavía** (6)

stockings **medias** *f. pl.* (4)

stomach **estómago** (11)

stop *n.* **escala** (*in a trip*) (8), **parada** (*to board transportation*) (8); bus stop **parada del autobús** (12); subway stop **parada del metro** (12); to make stops **hacer escalas** (8), **hacer paradas** (8); to stop **parar** (15); to stop (*doing something*) **dejar de** + *inf.* (11)

storage (space) **(espacio de) almacenamiento** (12)

store *n.* **tienda** (4); *v.* (*computer*) **almacenar** (12)

story **historia** (8)

stove **estufa** (5)

straight ahead **(todo) derecho** (15), **todo recto** (15)

strange: how strange that . . . ! **¡qué extraño que... !** (13); it's strange that **es extraño que** (13)

street **calle** *f.* (12)

street corner **esquina** (15)

stress **estrés** *m.* (14); to have a lot of stress **tener muchas presiones** (14); under stress, stressed out **estresado/a** (14)

strike (*labor*) **huelga** (18)

striped **de rayas** (4)

struggle **lucha** (18)

student **estudiante** *m., f.* (2)

study **estudiar** (2)

stuffed up (*with a cold*) **resfriado/a** *adj.* (11)

subject area **materia** (2)

suburbs **afueras** *f. pl.* (12)

subway stop **parada del metro** (12)

succeed in (*doing something*) **conseguir** (*like* **seguir**) + *inf.* (9)

suddenly **de repente** (11)

suffer **sufrir (de)** (14)

sufficiently **bastante** (16)

sugar **azúcar** *m.* (7)

suggest **sugerir (sugiero) (i)** (9)

suit **traje** *m.* (4)

suitcase **maleta** (8); to pack one's suitcase(s) **hacer la(s) maleta(s)** (8)

summer **verano** (6)

sunbathe **tomar el sol** (8)

Sunday **domingo** (5)

sunglasses **gafas** (*f. pl.*) **de sol** (4)

sunny: it's (very) sunny **hace (mucho) sol** (6)

sunscreen **bloqueador** (*m.*) **solar** (8)

supermarket **supermercado** (12)

supper **cena** (7); to have (eat) supper **cenar** (7)

sure **seguro/a** (6); it's a sure thing that **es seguro que** (13); it's not sure **no es seguro que** (13); to not be sure of **no estar seguro/a de** (13)

surf **hacer** *surfing* (10)

surprise **sorprender** (*like* **gustar**) (13)

SUV **SUV** *m.* (15)

sweater **suéter** *m.* (4)

sweatshirt **sudadera** (4)

sweep (the floor) **barrer (el piso)** (10)

sweets **dulces** *m. pl.* (7)

swim **nadar** (8)

swimming **natación** *f.* (10); swimming pool **piscina** (5)

swimsuit **traje** (*m.*) **de baño** (4)

syllabus **programa** (*m.*) **del curso** (14)

symptom **síntoma** *m.* (11)

systems analyst **analista** (*m., f.*) **de sistemas** (17)

T

T-shirt **camiseta** (4)

table **mesa** (2); to clear the table **quitar la mesa** (10); to set the table **poner la mesa** (10)

take **tomar** (2); **llevar** (4); to take a bath **bañarse** (5); to take a nap **dormir (duermo) (u) la siesta** (5); to take a shower **ducharse** (5); to take a trip **hacer un viaje** (5); to take a vacation **tomar unas vacaciones** (8); to take a walk **dar un paseo** (10); to take care of oneself **cuidarse** (11); to take off (*an article of clothing*) **quitarse** (5); to take out **sacar (qu)** (17); to take out the trash **sacar (qu) la basura** (10); to take photos **sacar (qu) fotos** (8); to take place at/in (*a place*) **ser en** + *place* (9); to take someone's temperature **tomarle la temperatura** (11)

talk **hablar** (2); to talk on the phone **hablar por teléfono** (2)

tall **alto/a** (3)

tame **domesticado/a** (15)

tank **tanque** *m.* (15)

tape **grabar** (12)

tasty **rico/a** (7)

tea **té** *m.* (7)

teach **enseñar** (2)

teacher: school teacher **maestro/a de escuela** (17)

team **equipo** (10)

technician **técnico/a** (17)

teeth: to brush one's teeth **cepillarse los dientes** (5)

television: (plasma) television **televisión** (*f.*) **(plasma)** (12); to watch television **mirar la tele(visión)** (3)

tell **contar (cuento)** (8); **decir** (8)

teller **cajero/a** (17); automatic teller machine (ATM) **cajero automático** (17)

temperature **temperatura** (11); to take someone's temperature **tomarle la temperatura** (11)

ten **diez** (1)

tenant **inquilino/a** (12)

tennis **tenis** *m.* (10)

tennis shoes **tenis** *m. pl.* (4)

tent **tienda (de campaña)** (8)

tenth **décimo/a** (13)

terrible **terrible** (13); it's terrible that **es terrible que** (13)

terrorism **terrorismo** (18)

terrorist **terrorista** *m., f.* (18); terrorist attack **ataque** (*m.*) **terrorista** (18)

test **examen** *m.* (4); **prueba** (14)

text (*electronic*) **mensaje** *m.* (2); to (send a) text **mandar un mensaje** (2)

textbook **libro de texto** (2)

than: less . . . than **menos... que** (6); less than + *number* **menos de** + *number* (6); more . . . than **más... que** (6); more than + *number* **más de** + *number* (6); older than **mayor que** (6); younger than **menos que** (6)

thank you (very much) **(muchas) gracias** (1); thanks for **gracias por** + *inf./ noun* (9)

that *conj.* **que** (3); that *adj., pron.* **ese/a** (4); *neuter pron.* **eso** (4); that ([way] over there) *adj., pron.* **aquel, aquella** (4); that ([way] over there) *neuter pron.* **aquello** (4); that means . . . **eso quiere decir...** (11); that which **lo que** (5)

theater **teatro** (10); to go to the theater **ir al teatro** (10)

their *poss. adj.* **su(s)** (3); (of) theirs *poss. adj., poss pron.* **suyo/a(s)** (17)

them *obj.* (*of prep.*) **ellos/as** (2)

then **luego** (5)

there **allí** (4)

there: (way) over there **allá** (4)

there is/are **hay** (1); is there / are there? **¿hay?** (1); there is/are not **no hay** (1); there's (lots of) **hay (mucho/a[s])** (6); infinitive form of **hay haber** (12)

these *adj., pron.* **estos/as** (3)

they *sub. pron.* **ellos/as** (2)

thin **delgado/a** (3)

thing **cosa** (5); the bad thing **lo malo** (11); the good thing **lo bueno** (11)

think **creer (en)** (3); to not think **no creer** (13); to think (about) **pensar (pienso) (de/en)** (5); **pensar que** to think that (5)

third **tercer(o/a)** (13)

thirsty: to be (very) thirsty **tener (mucha) sed** (7)

thirteen **trece** (1)

thirty **treinta** (1); thirty minutes past (*the hour*) **y treinta** (1)

this *adj., pron.* **este/a** (3); *neuter pron.* **esto** (3) those *adj., pron.* **esos/as** (4); those ([way] over there) *adj., pron.* **aquellos/as** (4)

three **tres** (1)

three hundred **trescientos/as** (4)

throat **garganta** (11)

through **por** (8)

throw: to throw a party **dar/hacer una fiesta** (9)

Thursday **jueves** *m. inv.* (5)

ticket **billete** *m. (Sp.)* / **boleto** *(L.A.)* (8); one-way ticket **billete/bolleto de ida** (8); round-trip ticket **billete/boleto de ida y vuelta** (8)

tie **corbata** (4)

time **tiempo** (6); at what time . . . ? **¿a qué hora... ?** (1); at times **a veces** (3); conjunction of time **conjunción** *(f.)* **de tiempo** (17); for the first/last time **por primera/última vez** (14); free time **tiempo libre** (10); on time **a tiempo** (8); free time **ratos** *(m. pl.)* **libres** (10); to have a bad time **pasarlo mal** (9); to have a good time **divertirse (me divierto) (i)** (5); **pasarlo bien** (9); what time is it? **¿qué hora es?** (1)

tire **llanta** (15); flat tire **llanta desinflada** (15)

tired **cansado/a** (6); to get tired **cansarse** (11)

to **a** (1); to the **al** (4); to the left of **a la izquiera de** (6); to the right of **a la derecha de** (6)

toast **pan tostado** (7)

toasted **tostado/a** (7)

toaster **tostadora** (10)

today **hoy** (1); what day is today? **¿qué día es hoy?** (5); what's today's date? **¿cuál es la fecha de hoy?** (6), **¿qué fecha es hoy?** (6)

toe **dedo del pie** (11)

together **juntos/as** (8)

tomato **tomate** *m.* (7)

tomorrow **mañana** (1); see you tomorrow **hasta mañana** (1); the day after tomorrow **pasado mañana** (5)

tongue **lengua** (11); to stick out one's tongue **sacar (qu) la lengua** (11)

tonight **esta noche** (6)

too much **demasiado** *adv.* (9)

tooth **diente** *m.* (5); back tooth **muela** (11); to brush one's teeth **cepillarse los dientes** (5)

top: on top of **encima de** (6)

towel **toalla** (5)

trade *(profession)* **oficio** (17)

tradition: cultural tradition **tradición** *(f.)* **cultural** (13)

traditional **folclórico/a** (13)

traffic **circulación** *f.* (15), **tráfico** (15), **tránsito** (15); traffic signal **semáforo** (15)

train **tren** *m.* (8); to go/travel by train **ir en tren** (8); to train **entrenar** (10); train station **estación** *(f.)* **de trenes** (8)

translator **traductor(a)** (17)

transportation: means of transportation **medio de transporte** (8)

trash **basura** (10); to take out the trash **sacar (qu) la basura** (10)

travel **viajar** (8); to travel by bus **ir en autobús** (8); to travel by boat/ship **ir en barco** (8); to travel by plane **ir en avión** (8)

traveling **de viaje** (8)

treadmill **caminadora** (11)

treatment **tratamiento** (11)

tree **árbol** *m.* (9)

trendy: it's trendy **está de moda** (4), **es de última moda** (4)

trip **viaje** *m.* (5); on a trip **de viaje** (8); to take a trip **hacer un viaje** (5)

true: it's true that **es verdad que** (13)

try to *(do something)* **tratar de + *inf.*** (13)

Tuesday **martes** *m. inv.* (5); on Tuesdays **los martes** (5)

tuition **matrícula** (2)

tuna **atún** *m.* (7)

turkey **pavo** (7)

turn **doblar** (15); to be someone's turn **tocarle (qu) a uno** (10); to turn on *(appliance, machine)* **encender (enciendo)** (12); to turn on *(appliance, machine)* **poner** (12); to turn off *(appliance, machine)* **apagar (gu)** (14); to turn out badly **salir mal** (5); to turn out well **salir bien** (5)

tweet *n.* **tuit** *m.* (12); *v.* **Twitear** (12)

twelve **doce** (1)

twenty **veinte** (1)

twice **dos veces** (11)

Twitter **Twitter** *m.* (12)

two **dos** (1)

two hundred **doscientos/as** (4)

U

ugly **feo/a** (3)

uncle **tío** (3); aunts and uncles **tíos** *m. pl.* (3)

under stress **estresado/a** (14); to be under a lot of stress **tener muchas presiones** (14)

understand **comprender** (3); **entender (entiendo)** (5)

underwear **ropa interior** (4)

unfortunately **desgraciadamente** (11)

United States: of the United States of America *n., adj.* **estadounidense** (3)

university *n.* **universidad** *f.* (2); *adj.* **universitario/a** (14)

unless **a menos que** (16); **sin que** (16)

unlikely: it's unlikely that **es improbable que** (13)

unlucky: to be unlucky **tener mala suerte** (14)

unoccupied **libre** (10)

unpleasant **antipático/a** (3)

until *prep.* **hasta** (1); *conj.* **hasta que** (17)

up: to be up to date **estar al día** (18)

urgent **urgente** (12); it's urgent (that) **es urgente que** (12)

us *obj. (of prep.)* **nosotros/as** (2)

use **usar** (4); *(gas)* **gastar** (15); to be used for **servir (sirvo) (i) para** (5)

user **usuario/a** (12)

V

vacation: on vacation **de vacaciones** (8); to be on vacation **estar de vacaciones** (8); to go on vacation in/to . . . **ir de vacaciones a...** (8); to leave on vacation **salir de vacaciones** (8); to spend one's vacation at/on/in . . . **pasar las vacaciones en...** (8); to take a vacation **tomar unas vacaciones** (8)

vaccination **vacuna** (11)

vacuum cleaner **aspiradora** (10); to vacuum **pasar la aspiradora** (10)

van **camioneta** (8)

vegetables **verduras** *f. pl.* (7)

vehicle **vehículo** (15)

verb *gram.* **verbo** (2); reflexive verb *gram.* **verbo reflexivo** (5)

very *adv.* **muy** (1); very much **muchísimo** (8); very very **-ísimo** (9); very well **muy bien** (1)

veterinarian **veterinario/a** (17)

victim **víctima** (18)

video **video** (12); videogame **videojuego** (10); to play videogames **jugar (juego) (gu) a los videojuegos** (10)

view **vista** (12)

visit a museum **visitar un museo** (10)

voice mailbox **buzón** *(m.)* **de voz** (12)

volleyball **voleibol** *m.* (10)

vote **votar** (18)

W

wages *(often per hour)* **salario** (17)

wait (for) **esperar** (7)

waiter/waitress **camarero/a** (7)

waiting room **sala de espera** (8)

wake up **despertarse (me despierto)** (5)

walk **caminar** (10); to take a walk **dar un paseo** (10)

wall **pared** *f.* (5)

wallet **cartera** (4)

want **desear** (2); **querer** (4)

war **guerra** (18)

was **fue** (5)

wash **lavar** (10)

washing machine **lavadora** (10)

watch *n.* **reloj** *m.* (4); *v.* **mirar** (3); to watch television **mirar la tele(visión)** (3) water **agua** *f.* (*but* **el agua**) (7); mineral water **agua mineral** (7)

way over there **allá** (4)

we *sub. pron.* **nosotros/as** (2)

wear **llevar** (4), **usar** (4)

weather **tiempo** (6); what's the weather like? **¿qué tiempo hace?** (6); it's (very) good/bad weather **hace (muy) buen/ mal tiempo** (6)

weave **tejer** (13)

webpage **página web** (12)

website **sitio web** (12)

wed: newly wed **recién casado/a** (16)

wedding (*ceremony*) **boda** (16)

Wednesday **miércoles** *m. inv.* (5)

week **semana** (5); days of the week **días** (*m. pl.*) **de la semana** (5); next week **la próxima semana** (5), **la semana que viene** (5); once a week **una vez a la semana** (3)

weekend **fin** (*m.*) **de semana** (2)

weight: to lift weights **levantar pesas** (11)

welcome: you're welcome **de nada** (1), **no hay de qué** (1)

well **bien** (1); very well **muy bien** (1); to come/turn out well **salir bien** (5); to do well **salir bien** (5)

well-being **bienestar** *m.* (11)

well-paid job/position **empleo bien pagado** (17)

west **oeste** *m.* (6)

whale **ballena** (15)

what (that which) **lo que** (5)

what? **¿cómo?** (1); **¿cuál?** (2); **¿qué?** (1); at what time? **¿a qué hora... ?** (1); for what purpose? **¿para qué... ?** (16); what (a) + *noun*! **¡qué** + *noun*! (14); what a shame that . . . ! **¡qué lástima que... !** (13); what are you like? **¿cómo es usted?** *form. s.* (1); what day is today? **¿qué día es hoy?** (5); what for? **¿para qué... ?** (16); what is your name? **¿cómo se llama usted?** *form. s.* (1); **¿cómo te llamas?** *fam. s.* (1); what time is it? **¿qué hora es?** (1); what's the weather like? **¿qué tiempo hace?** (6); what's today's date? **¿cuál es la fecha de hoy?** (6), **¿qué fecha es hoy?** (6)

when? **¿cuándo?** (2)

where? **¿dónde?** (1); where (to)? **¿adónde?** (4); where are you from? **¿de dónde eres (tú)?** *fam. s.* (1); **¿de dónde es usted?** *form. s.* (1)

which *conj.* **que** (3)

which? **¿cuál?** (2)

while **mientras** (10)

white **blanco/a** (4); white wine **vino blanco** (7)

whiteboard **pizarrón** (*m.*) **blanco** (2)

who *rel. pron.* **que** (3)

who? **¿quién?** (1)

whose? **¿de quién?** (3)

why? **¿por qué?** (3)

widow **viuda** (16)

widower **viudo** (16)

wife **esposa** (3), **mujer** *f.* (3)

wifi **wifi** *m.* (12)

wild **salvaje** (15)

win **ganar** (10)

wind **viento** (6); wind energy **energía eólica** (15)

window **ventana** (2); small window (*on a plane*) **ventanilla** (8)

windshield **parabrisas** *m. inv.* (15)

windy: it's (very) windy **hace (mucho) viento** (6)

wine (white, red) **vino (blanco, tinto)** (7)

winter **invierno** (6)

wish **esperanza** (18)

with **con** (2); with me **conmigo** (6); with you *fam. s.* **contigo** (6)

withdraw (*from an account*) **sacar (qu)** (17)

without **sin** (5); **sin que** (16)

witness **testigo** *m., f.* (18)

woman **mujer** *f.* (2); business woman **mujer de negocios** (17)

wool **de lana** (4)

word **palabra** (1); indefinite and negative word *gram.* **palabra indefinida y negativa** (7); interrogative word **palabra interrogativa** (2)

work (labor) **trabajo** (12); (piece of) **trabajo** (14); to work (function) **funcionar** (12); to work (at a job) **trabajar** (2); work of art **obra de arte** (13); *adj.* **laboral** (17)

worker **obrero/a** (17); social worker **trabajador(a) social** (17)

world **mundo** (3)

worried **preocupado/a** (6)

worse **peor** (6)

woven goods **tejidos** *m. pl.* (13)

write **escribir** (*p.p.* **escrito**) (3)

writer **escritor(a)** (13)

written **escrito/a** (*p.p. of* escribir) (14); written report **informe** (*m.*) **escrito** (14)

wrong: to be wrong **no tener razón** (4); to get up on the wrong side of the bed **levantarse con el pie izquierdo** (14)

Y

yard **patio** (5)

year **año** (6); (*in school*) **grado** (10); end of the year **fin** (*m.*) **de año** (9); to be . . . years old **tener... años** (3)

yellow **amarillo/a** (4)

yes **sí** (1)

yesterday **ayer** (5); yesterday was . . . **ayer fue...** (5); the day before yesterday *adv.* **anteayer** (5)

yoga: to do yoga **hacer (el) yoga** (10)

yogurt **yogur** *m.* (7)

you *sub. pron.* **tú** *fam. s.* (2); **usted (Ud.)** *form. s.* (2); **vosotros/as** *fam. pl.* (*Sp.*) (2); **ustedes (Uds.)** *form. pl.* (2); *obj. of prep.* **ti** *fam. s.* (6); **usted** *form. s.;* **ustedes (Uds.)** *form. pl.* (6); and you? **¿y tú?** *fam. s.* (1); **¿y usted?** *form. s.* (1); how are you? **¿cómo está(s)?** (1), **¿qué tal?** (1); with you *fam. s.* **contigo** (6); you are *fam. s.* **eres** (1), *form. s.* **es** (1)

young **joven** (3); young woman **señorita (Srta.)** (1)

younger (than) **menor (que)** (6)

your *poss. adj.* **tu(s)** *fam. s.* (3); **su(s)** *form. s., pl.* (3); **vuestro/a(s)** *fam. pl.* (*Sp.*) (3); your, (of) yours *poss. adj., poss. pron.* **tuyo/a(s)** *fam. s.* (17); **suyo/a(s)** *form. s., pl.* (17); **vuestro/a(s)** *fam. pl.* (*Sp.*) (17)

you're welcome **de nada** (1), **no hay de qué** (1)

youth **juventud** *f.* (16); as a youth **de adolescente** (10)

Z

zero **cero** (1)

zone **zona** (12)

CREDITS

Photo Credits

Front Matter
Page iii: © Hero/Corbis/Glow Images

Chapter 1
Opener: (road) © Rodrigo Torres/Glow Images RF; p. 2 (Barcelona): © John Kellerman/Alamy; p. 2 (Mexico City): © Mark Lewis/Getty Images RF; p. 3: © Onoky Photography/SuperStock RF; p. 4 (teacher and student): © Tom Fowlks/Getty Images; p. 4 (greeting): © GoGo Images Corporation/Alamy RF; p. 5: © Hola Images/age fotostock RF; p. 8: © dynamicgraphics/ Jupiterimages RF; p. 9 (woman): © Kevin Peterson/Getty Images RF; p. 9 (man): © Andersen Ross/Getty Images RF; p. 11: © America/Alamy RF; p. 13 (class): © KidStock/Blend Images LLC RF; p. 13 (signs): © Julio López Saguar/Getty Images RF; p. 15: © Bob Thomas/Popperfoto/ Getty Images; p. 20-21 (all): © McGraw-Hill Education/Klic Video Productions; p. 22 (mountain): © Guy Edwardes/Getty Images; p. 22 (beach): © Pixtal/age fotostock RF; p. 22 (forest): © Adalberto Rios Szalay/Sexto Sol/Getty Images RF; p. 22 (desert): © ESO, CC BY 3.0 RF; p. 23 (glacier): © Image Source RF; p. 23 (Madrid): © Pixtal/age fotostock RF; p. 25: © Rodrigo Torres/ Glow Images RF.

Chapter 2
Opener: © Simon Jarratt/Corbis/Photolibrary RF; p. 27: © Onoky Photography/SuperStock RF; p. 30: © David R. Frazier Photolibrary, Inc./Alamy; p. 32: © Lifesize/Getty Images RF; p. 33: © McGraw-Hill Education/Klic Video Productions; p. 45: © BananaStock/PunchStock RF; p. 47 (woman): © Tetra images RF/Getty Images RF; p. 47 (students): © Digital Vision/Getty Images RF; p. 48: © Digital Vision RF; p. 51: © David A. Tietz/Editorial Image, LLC; p. 53: © McGraw-Hill Education/Klic Video Productions; p. 54: © David Peevers/Lonely Planet Images/Getty Images; p. 56: © Onoky Photography/SuperStock RF; p. 57: © McGraw-Hill Education.

Chapter 3
Opener: © UpperCut Images/Alamy RF; p. 61: © Onoky Photography/SuperStock RF; p. 62 (abuelo): © Jack Hollingsworth/Getty Images RF; p. 62 (abuela): © Blend Images; p. 62 (padre): © Seth Joel/Getty Images; p. 62 (madre): © Getty Images; p. 62 (tio): © Getty Images; p. 62 (tia): © John Henley/Blend Images/Getty Images RF; p. 62 (Patricia): © Glow Images/SuperStock RF; p. 62 (hermana): © Getty Images/Digital Vision RF; p. 62 (hermano): © Blend Images/ PunchStock RF; p. 62 (dog): © G.K. & Vikki Hart/Getty Images RF; p. 62 (primo): © Ryan McVay/Getty Images RF; p. 62 (prima): © Michael Matisse/Getty Images RF; p. 64 (abuela): © Blend Images; p. 64 (padre): © Seth Joel/Getty Images; p. 64 (madre): © Getty Images; p. 64 (tio): © Getty Images; p. 64 (tia): © John Henley/Blend Images/Getty Images RF; p. 64 (abuelo): © Jack Hollingsworth/Getty Images RF; p. 64 (Patricia): © Glow Images/SuperStock RF; p. 65: © AGE Fotostock; p. 67: © McGraw-Hill Education/Klic Video Productions; p. 69: © SuperStock/ Purestock RF; p. 72: © Van Vechten Collection, Library of Congress, LC-USZ62-42516; p. 73: © McGraw-Hill Education/Klic Video Productions; p. 74: © DEA/G Dagli Orti/age fotostock; p. 75 (man): © Corbis/SuperStock RF; p. 75 (woman): © Lifesize/Getty Images RF; p. 82 (1): © moodboard/SuperStock RF; p. 82 (2): © Terry Vine/Blend Images LLC RF; p. 82 (3): © Monashee Frantz/age fotostock RF; p. 82 (4): © Jose Luis Pelaez Inc/Blend RF; p. 82 (a): © McGraw-Hill Education; p. 82 (b): © Blend Images/Alamy RF; p. 82 (c): © Hero/Corbis/Glow Images RF; p. 82 (d): © Image Source RF; p. 83: © McGraw-Hill Education/Klic Video Productions; p. 84 (leer): © Glow Images; p. 84 (escribir): © Alamy Images; p. 84 (beber): © Blend Images; p. 84 (comer): © Getty Images; p. 85: © Sergio Salvador/Getty Images RF; p. 87: © Charlie Neuman/U-T San Diego/ZUMA Wire/Alamy; p. 88: © Pixtal/age fotostock RF; p. 89: © Ann Summa/Corbis; p. 91: © McGraw-Hill Education/Klic Video Productions; p. 92: © Anuska Sampedro/Getty Images RF; p. 93: © AP Photo/Ramon Espinosa; p. 94: © Onoky Photography/ SuperStock RF; p. 95: © McGraw-Hill Education.

Chapter 4

Opener: © Danny Lehman/Corbis; p. 99: © Onoky Photography/SuperStock RF; p. 100 (young woman): © drbimages/Getty Images RF; p. 100 (woman): © Glowimages RM/Alamy; p. 100 (man): © Peopleimages/Getty Images RF; p. 101 (man): © Andresr/Getty Images RF; p. 101 (woman): © drbimages/Getty Images RF; p. 101 (couple): © 4x6/Getty Images RF; p. 103 (crayons): © Nicemonkey/Alamy RF; p. 103 (art): Artwork courtesy of La Antigua Galería de Arte Antigua Guatemala, www.artintheamericas.com; p. 104: © Barry Barker/McGraw-Hill Education; p. 105: © brianlatino/Alamy RF; p. 107: © McGraw-Hill Education/Klic Video Productions; p. 114: © Onoky Photography/SuperStock RF; p. 117: © Lissa Harrison RF; p. 119: © Diego Lezama/Lonely Planet Images/Getty Images; p. 121: © Miami In Focus, Inc.; p. 122: © Apriori, LLC/Getty Images; p. 123: © McGraw-Hill Education/Klic Video Productions; p. 124: © Dorling Kindersley/Getty Images RF; p. 126: © Onoky Photography/SuperStock RF; p. 127 (woman in library): © Fancy Collection/Fancy Collection/SuperStock RF; p. 127 (man with skateboard): © Blue Jean Images/Corbis RF; p. 127 (woman in dress): © Ed Suter/Africa Media Online/The Image Works; p. 127 (woman in coat): © pbnj productions/SuperStock RF; p. 127 (man in suit): © Kelly Redinger/Design Pics RF; p. 127: © McGraw-Hill Education.

Chapter 5

Opener: © Jon Arnold Images Ltd/Alamy; p. 131: © Purestock/Getty Images RF; p. 134: © John Mitchell/Alamy; p. 138: © McGraw-Hill Education/Klic Video Productions; p. 142: © Jan Stromme/Alamy; p. 143: © Paul Taylor/Getty Images; p. 144: © BrazilPhotos.com/Alamy; p. 152: © Nicholas Gill/Alamy; p. 155: © EPA/Roberto Escobar/Corbis; p. 157: © McGraw-Hill Education/Klic Video Productions; p. 158: © Image Source RF; p. 160: © Purestock/Getty Images RF; p. 161 (library): © Andersen Ross/Blend Images LLC RF; p. 161 (gym): © Erik Isakson/Blend Images LLC RF; p. 161 (class): © Purestock/Alamy RF; p. 161 (café): © UpperCut Images/Glow Images RF; p. 161 (steps): © Caia Image/Glow Images RF; p. 161 (video): © McGraw-Hill Education.

Chapter 6

Opener: © Paul Souders/The Image Bank/Getty Images; p. 165: © Purestock/Getty Images RF; p. 168 (all): © Bill Brooks/Alamy RF; p. 169: © DEA/S. Buonamici/Getty Images; p. 172: © McGraw-Hill Education/Klic Video Productions; p. 173: © Janis Christie/Getty Images RF; p. 175: © imagebroker/Alamy RF; p. 178 (man): © Stockbyte/Getty Images RF; p. 178 (woman): © XiXinXing/Getty Images RF; p. 180: © Rodrigo Guerrero/LatinContent/Getty Images; p. 181: © BananaStock/PictureQuest RF; p. 182: © Jenni Kirk/McGraw-Hill Education; p. 185 (Buenos Aires): © Image Source/PunchStock RF; p. 185 (San Jose): © mtcurado/Getty Images RF; p. 189 (man): © John Lund/Sam Diephuis/Blend Images LLC RF; p. 189 (woman): © Pixtal/age fotostock RF; p. 190: © Jack Hollingsworth/Getty Images RF; p. 191: © Alamy; p. 192 (boy left): © Paul Bradbury/age fotostock RF; p. 192 (boy middle): © KidStock/Blend Images LLC RF; p. 192 (girl): © JGI/Jamie Grill/Blend Images LLC RF; p. 193: © McGraw-Hill Education/Klic Video Productions; p. 194: © Jenni Kirk/McGraw-Hill Education; p. 196: © Purestock/Getty Images RF; p. 197: © McGraw-Hill Education.

Chapter 7

Opener: © Elmer Martinez/AFP/Getty Images; p. 201: © Purestock/Getty Images RF; p. 204: © Nicholas Gill/Alamy; p. 206: © John Parra/Getty Images; p. 208: © McGraw-Hill Education/Klic Video Productions; p. 213: © Image Source RF; p. 218: © Lissa Harrison RF; p. 219: © Purestock/Getty Images RF; p. 223: © JJM Stock Photography/Alamy RF; p. 225: © McGraw-Hill Education/Klic Video Productions; p. 226: © Gonzalo Azumendi/The Image Bank/Getty Images; p. 227: © Nathan King/Alamy; p. 228: © Purestock/Getty Images RF; p. 229: © McGraw-Hill Education.

Chapter 8

Opener: © Christian Kober/Robert Harding World Imagery/Alamy; p. 233: © Rafael Guerrero/Photolibrary/Getty Images; p. 237: © Michael J. Doolittle/The Image Works; p. 238 (se habla...): © Elena Rooraid/PhotoEdit; p. 238 (colmado): © Jane Sweeney/AWL Images/Getty Images; p. 240 (all): © McGraw-Hill Education/Klic Video Productions; p. 245: © Alea Image/iStock/Getty Images RF; p. 251: © Reinhard Dirscherl/WaterFrame/Getty Images; p. 255 (bill): © Studio Works/Alamy; p. 255 (woman): © Tetra Images/Getty Images RF; p. 257: © MedioImages RF; p. 259: © McGraw-Hill Education/Klic Video Productions; p. 260: © Jon McLean/Alamy; p. 261 (camel): © Ingram Publishing/SuperStock RF; p. 261 (lake): © Lissa Harrison RF; p. 261 (falls): © Exactostock/SuperStock RF; p. 262: © Rafael Guerrero/Photolibrary/Getty Images; p. 263 (hikers): © Aurora Open/SuperStock RF; p. 263 (café): © Image Source RF; p. 263 (beach): © Purestock/Superstock RF; p. 263 (library): © Fancy/Veer/Corbis/Glow Images RF; p. 263 (camping): © Brand X Pictures/age fotostock RF; p. 263 (video): © McGraw-Hill Education.

Chapter 9

Opener: © Evelyn Paley/Alamy; p. 267: © Rafael Guerrero/Photolibrary/Getty Images; p. 269: © Adalberto Roque/AFP/Getty Images; p. 270: © AP Photo/Dado Galdieri; p. 273: © McGraw-Hill Education/Klic Video Productions; p. 276: © Boston Globe/Getty Images; p. 278: © C Bockermann/CHROMOR/agefotostock; p. 280: © Carl DeAbreu/Alamy; p. 285: © Frans Schellekens/Redferns/Getty Images; p. 286: © Beren Patterson/Alamy; p. 287: © McGraw-Hill Education/Klic Video Productions; p. 288: © Purestock/Superstock RF; p. 290: © Rafael Guerrero/Photolibrary/Getty Images; p. 291 (formal): © moodboard/Alamy RF; p. 291 (wedding): © Purestock/Superstock RF; p. 291 (dinner): © Cultura Creative/Alamy RF; p. 291 (pinata): © Ariel Skelley/Blend Images LLC RF; p. 291 (video): © McGraw-Hill Education.

Chapter 10

Opener: © Sylvain Grandadam/Robert Harding Picture Library/age fotostock; p. 295: © Rafael Guerrero/Photolibrary/Getty Images; p. 296 (riding): © Comstock Images/Alamy RF; p. 296 (walking): © David Planchet RF; p. 296 (yoga): © Ingram Publishing/SuperStock RF; p. 296 (skiing): © Ben Blankenburg/Corbis RF; p. 296 (family playing): © Chris Ryan/age fotostock RF; p. 296 (running): © Mark Anderson/Getty Images RF; p. 296 (hiking): © Brand X Pictures RF; p. 296 (clubbing): © Chris Ryan/age fotostock RF; p. 297: © Beck Diefenbach/Reuters/Corbis; p. 299: © Geordie Torr/Alamy; p. 301: © McGraw-Hill Education/Klic Video Productions; p. 307: United States Coast Guard; p. 310 (Lopez): © Stephane Cardinale/Sygma/Corbis; p. 310 (del Torres): © Stefanie Keenan/WireImage/Getty Images; p. 310 (Walker): © Focus on Sport/Getty Images; p. 313: © Helen H. Richardson/Denver Post/Getty Images; p. 313: © Glyn Genin/Alamy; p. 315: © McGraw-Hill Education/Klic Video Productions; p. 316: © Medioimages/Photodisc/Getty Images RF; p. 318: © Rafael Guerrero/Photolibrary/Getty Images; p. 319 (waterfall): © Hola Images/Getty Images RF; p. 319 (video): © McGraw-Hill Education.

Chapter 11

Opener: © ZUMA Press, Inc/Alamy; p. 323: © Rafael Guerrero/Photolibrary/Getty Images; p. 325: © Nicole Braun/Retna Ltd./Corbis; p. 327 (runner): © Royalty Free/Corbis RF; p. 327 (doctor): © Mike Watson/moodboard/Corbis RF; p. 327 (farmacia): © David R. Frazier Photolibrary, Inc./Alamy; p. 329: © McGraw-Hill Education/Klic Video Productions; p. 330: © Marty Granger/McGraw-Hill Education; p. 333: © DEA/M. Seemuller/De Agostini/Getty Images; p. 334: © Imagesource/Photolibrary RF; p. 335 (food): © Boston Globe/Getty Images; p. 335 (party): © Image Source/age fotostock RF; p. 337: © Jacques Jangoux/Alamy; p. 341: © Tommy Kay/Corbis; p. 343: © Keith Dannemiller/Corbis; p. 345: © McGraw-Hill Education/Klic Video Productions; p. 346: © Paula Bronstein/Getty Images; p. 348: © Rafael Guerrero/Photolibrary/Getty Images; p. 349: © McGraw-Hill Education.

Chapter 12

Opener: © Radius/SuperStock RF; p. 353: © Daniel Ernst/iStock/Getty Images RF; p. 357: © Jose Miguel Gomez/Reuters/Corbis; p. 359: © McGraw-Hill Education/Klic Video Productions; p. 363: © Mark Dierker/McGraw-Hill Education; p. 365: © Glow Images/Superstock RF; p. 373: © Ulf Andersen/Getty Images; p. 374: © Brand X Pictures/PunchStock RF; p. 374: © Brand X Pictures/PunchStock RF; p. 375: © Dave G. Houser/Corbis; p. 377: © McGraw-Hill Education/Klic Video Productions; p. 378: © Jane Sweeney/The Image Bank/Getty Images; p. 380 (insulin): © James R Clarke/Alamy; p. 380 (man): © Daniel Ernst/iStock/Getty Images RF; p. 381: © McGraw-Hill Education.

Chapter 13

Opener: © Bernai Velarde; p. 385: © Daniel Ernst/iStock/Getty Images RF; p. 388: © mediacolor's/Alamy; p. 389: © age fotostock/Alamy; p. 391: © McGraw-Hill Education/Klic Video Productions; p. 392: © Joe Sohm/The Image Works; p. 394: Blanton Museum of Art, The University of Texas at Austin, Barbara Duncan Fund, 1975. Photo by Rick Hall; p. 397: © Melanie Stetson Freeman/The Christian Science Monitor via Getty Images; p. 399: Aryballos-shaped vessel (ceramic), Incan/Museo Regional de Cuzco, Peru/Bildarchiv Steffens Henri Stierlin/The Bridgeman Art Library; p. 400 (market): © Nigel Pavitt/AWL Images/Getty Images; p. 400 (lake): © Christophe Boisvieux/Hemis/Alamy; p. 401 (tortoise): © Cleveland Metroparks Zoo/McGraw-Hill Education; p. 401 (iquana): © FAN Travelstock/Alamy RF; p. 404: © DEA/G Dagli Orti/Getty Images; p. 405: © Iberfoto/Iberfoto/Superstock; p. 407: © McGraw-Hill Education/Klic Video Productions; p. 408: © Aizar Raldes/AFP/Getty Images; p. 410: © Daniel Ernst/iStock/Getty Images RF; p. 411 (children): © SuperStock/age fotostock; p. 411 (video): © McGraw-Hill Education.

Text Credits

Chapter 1
Page 7 (table): From *Fox News Latino*; p. 11 (bottom): Source: 2010 U.S. Census; p. 12 (left – table): Source: 2006 U.S. Census.

Chapter 2
Page 55 (bottom right): From Cincilingua International Language Center, Cincinnati, Ohio.

Chapter 3
Page 64 (top left): From Instituto Nacional Electoral, Mexico; p. 65 (bottom): From Mexican Government.

Chapter 4
Page 106 (top): From Quo, HF Revistas; p. 125 (middle): Gregori Dolz, "Algo mas que ropa" in *Nexos Magazine* - © Ink-Global.

Chapter 5
Page 159 (middle): From Bienes Raíces Avisos de Ocasión.

Chapter 6
Page 195 (middle): From La U El Diario de Kampussia.

Chapter 7
Page 209 (top): From www.cnpp.usda.gov; p. 224 (middle): From CONABIP.

Chapter 8
Page 239 (middle): From En Lan; p. 246 (right): www.godominicanrepublic.com; p. 258 (cartoon): From David Sebastian Ojeda, Pasaje Blanco, 1662 Moron, prov. De Buenos Aires, artepiero@hotmail.com; p. 261 (middle): © I Love Viajes - www.iloveviajes.com.

Chapter 10
Page 308 (top): From Restaurant El Boricua.

Chapter 11
Page 340 (cartoon): © Joaquín Salvador Lavado (QUINO) Toda Mafalda - Ediciones de La Flor, 1993; p. 347 (middle): Nicanor Parra, "Epitafio", POEMAS Y ANTIPOEMAS © 1954, Nicanor Parra. Used by permission.

Chapter 12
Page 358 (top): From Vodafone; p. 364 (right): From Colombia Government - Industria y turismo; p. 379 (middle): "Cuadrados y angulos" by Alfonsina Storni, 1904.

Chapter 13
Page 409 (middle): Tito Matamala, "La opportunidad de Salomón Bobadilla" in *Con pocas palabras. Muestra de microcuentos*. Used with permission.

Chapter 14
Page 433 (bottom): From Asociacion todo ellos por; p. 439 (middle): Mario Benedetti, Poem **Oh** in *Poemas de la oficina* © Fundacion Mario Benedetti, c/o Schavelzon Graham Agencia Literaria, www.schavelzongraham.com.

Chapter 15
Page 449 (top right): © UTE; 464 (cartoon - left): © Joaquín Salvador Lavado (QUINO) iCuánta bondad! - Ediciones de La Flor, 1999; p. 464 (cartoon - right): Cartoon by MENA, ALI Brussels; p. 467 (middle): "Apocalipsis, I" by Marco Denevi from *Falsificaiones*.

Chapter 16
Page 491 (middle): Diego Muñoz Valenzuela, *Amor cibernauta*. Used with permission.

Chapter 17
Page 519 (middle): © Fundación Gloria Fuertes.

Chapter 18
Page 537 (cartoon): From Antonio Mingote; p. 549 (middle): Eduardo Galeano, Celebración de la voz humana/2 in *El libro de los abrazos* © Siglo XXI DE ESPAÑA EDITORES. Used by permission; p. 555 (bottom): www.hispanicfiesta.com.

INDEX

Note: The notation "n" after a page number indicates that it is a footnote.

origins, expressing with **ser**, 76
o to ue, 145–147
otro/a, 71

P

pagar, 43
Panama, 201, 206, 218, 223
para
    + *infinitive*, 78, 102
        por versus, 431–432, 442
        ser with, 76, 179
Paraguay, 473, 477, 482, 485, 490
Parra, Nicanor, 347
Parra, Violeta, 509
parts of the body, 324
partying (*vocabulary*), 52
pastimes, 316, 320
past participle, 454–455
    with **había** (past perfect), 462, 470
    used as an adjective, 455, 470
    See also Appendix 1; Appendix 5
past perfect tense, 462, 470
past progressive (**-ndo**), 305
past subjunctive, 532–534
    of irregular verbs, 533
    with **ojalá (que)**, 538
    uses, 534
    See also Appendix 5
pedir (*irregular*), 145, 279
    See also Appendix 5
pensar, 145, 147
    See also Appendix 5
peor, 188, 311
perfect tenses, 458–459
    See also Appendix 1; Appendix 4;
        Appendix 5
performing arts, 386–387
personal **a**, 210
    with **alguien** and **nadie**, 480
    specific persons or animals, 480
personal endings, 43
personal pronouns, 41–42, 85
Peru, 169, 273, 415, 423, 425, 429, 435
plural
    accent mark use, 109
    of adjectives, 70
    of adverbs, 117
    of nouns, 39
pluscuamperfecto de subjuntivo. *See*
        Appendix 4
poco, 117
poder (*irregular*), 114–115
    See also Appendix 5
poner (*irregular*), 139–140
    verbs derived from, 363
    See also Appendix 5
por, 46, 431
    adjectives with, 181
    in fixed expressions, 431
    para versus, 431–432, 442
porque, 78
position, of adjectives, 71
possession
    with **ser** and **de**, 76
    unstressed possessive adjectives,
        80–81
possessive adjectives, 80–81

definition, 80
    unstressed, 80
    See also Appendix 3
possessive pronouns, 503
    stressed, 503
preferir (*irregular*), 114–115
prepositions, + infinitive, 512
prepositions, 136–137
    defined, 136
    of location, 170
    with time of day, 46
    verbs requiring, 400
    See also Appendix 1
present indicative, 43, 84
    of **-ar** verbs, 42–44
    English equivalents, 85
    of **-er** and **-ir** verbs, 84–85
    present progressive and simple present
        compared, 183
    stem-changing verbs, 139–140, 145–147,
        162
    See also Appendix 5
present participle, 174, 454
    direct object pronouns with, 211
    with verbs other than **estar**, 177
present perfect subjunctive, 459, 470
present perfect tense, 458–459, 470
    See also Appendix 4
present progressive, 173–174, 198
    reflexive pronouns with, 174, 177
present subjunctive, 365–368
    after conjunctions of purpose and
        contingency, 483–484
    after nonexisting and indefinite
        antecedents, 479–480
    feelings and emotion, 393
    forms, 367, 367–368
    future or pending actions, 511–512
    indicative compared, 365–366, 479–480
    influence, emotion, doubt, and denial,
        402
    subjective actions or states, 365–368
    uncertainty, 397–399
    uses, 367, 371–372
    with verbs of influence, 371–372
preterite
    imperfect versus, 303, 304, 330–332
    irregular endings, 292
    of irregular verbs, 253, 274–275
    of regular verbs, 251–252
    of stem-changing verbs, 252, 278–279
    verbs that change meaning, 275, 332
    words and expressions associated with,
        333
    See also Appendix 1; Appendix 5
primer(o), 168
professions and trades (*vocabulary*),
        498–499
progressive, defined, 173
progressive forms, 173–174
    past, 305
    present, 174
    present progressive, 174, 198
    verbs other than **estar**, 177
pronouns
    definition, 41
    demonstrative. *See* Appendix 2
    direct object, 211

    double object, 282–283
    indirect object, 241–243
    as objects of prepositions, 170
    order of, 283
    possessive, 503
    reflexive, 150–152, 151, 162, 341
    relative, 338–339
    subject, 41–42, 85
    See also Appendix 1
pronunciation, 7
    diphthongs, 34, 108
    linking, 34
    rising or falling intonation, 48–49
    schwa, 7
    stress and written accent marks, 68,
        108–109
    vowels, 7
    y, 7n
Puerto Rico, 295, 299, 301, 307, 313, 316
punctuation
    comma and period uses, 105
    inverted question mark in tag questions,
        102

Q

¿qué?, 308–309
    ¿cuál? versus, 32
que, 339
    with subjunctive, 366
    in subjunctive, 371
querer (*irregular*), 114–115
    past subjunctive to express requests,
        534
    preterite changes in meaning, 275
    See also Appendix 5
questions
    information, 48
    inversion in, 49
    rising or falling intonation, 48–49
    yes/no, 48–49
    See also interrogative words
¿quien(es)?, 308, 339

R

radical changing verbs. *See* stem-changing
        verbs
reciprocal actions, 341
reflexive pronouns, 150–152, 151, 162
    placement, 152
    with present progressive, 174, 177
    reciprocal actions, 341
relative pronouns, 338–339
    definition, 338
República Dominicana. *See* Dominican
        Republic
romantic relationships (*vocabulary*),
        474–475

S

saber (*irregular*)
    conocer versus, 205, 275
    preterite changes in meaning, 275
    See also Appendix 5
salir, 139–140
    See also Appendix 5
schwa, 7

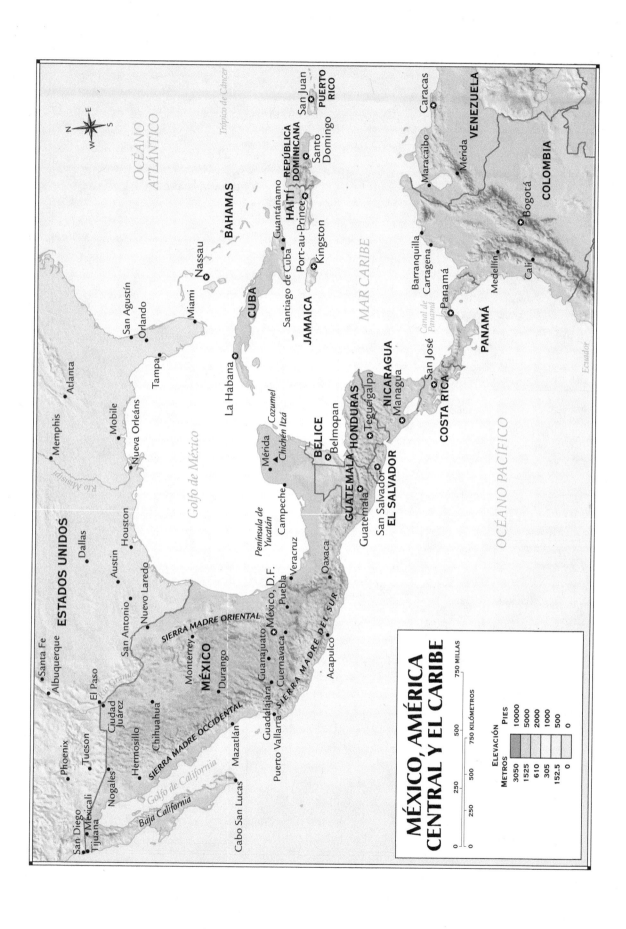

MÉXICO, AMÉRICA
CENTRAL Y EL CARIBE

N

OCÉANO ATLÁNTICO

Trópico de Cáncer

ESTADOS UNIDOS

Santa Fe
Albuquerque
Phoenix
Tucson
El Paso
Ciudad Juárez
Nogales
Mexicali
Tijuana
San Diego
Hermosillo
Chihuahua
Baja California
Cabo San Lucas
Mazatlán
Golfo de California

Río Grande

SIERRA MADRE OCCIDENTAL

Durango
Guadalajara
Puerto Vallarta
Guanajuato
Cuernavaca
México, D.F.
Puebla
Monterrey
Nuevo Laredo
San Antonio
Austin
Dallas
Houston

MÉXICO

SIERRA MADRE ORIENTAL

SIERRA MADRE DEL SUR

Acapulco
Oaxaca
Veracruz
Campeche

Memphis
Atlanta
Mobile
Nueva Orleáns
Tampa
Orlando
San Agustín
Miami

Río Misisipi

Golfo de México

Península de Yucatán

Mérida
Cozumel
Chichén Itzá

BAHAMAS
Nassau

CUBA

La Habana
Santiago de Cuba
Guantánamo

HAITÍ
Port-au-Prince

REPÚBLICA DOMINICANA
Santo Domingo

PUERTO RICO
San Juan

JAMAICA
Kingston

MAR CARIBE

BELICE
Belmopan

GUATEMALA
Guatemala

HONDURAS
Tegucigalpa

EL SALVADOR
San Salvador

NICARAGUA
Managua

COSTA RICA
San José

Canal de Panamá

PANAMÁ
Panamá

VENEZUELA
Caracas
Maracaibo
Mérida

COLOMBIA
Barranquilla
Cartagena
Medellín
Bogotá
Cali

Ecuador

OCÉANO PACÍFICO

ELEVACIÓN

METROS	PIES
3050	10000
1525	5000
610	2000
305	1000
152.5	500
0	0

0   250   500   750 KILÓMETROS

0   250   500   750 MILLAS

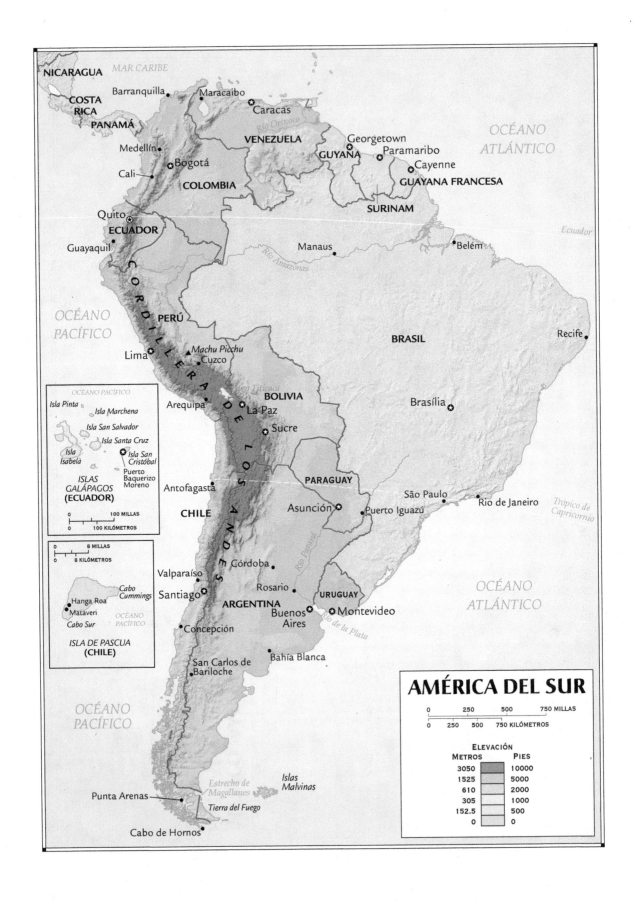

NICARAGUA

MAR CARIBE

COSTA
RICA

PANAMÁ

Barranquilla

Maracaibo

⊛ Caracas

Río Orinoco

VENEZUELA

Georgetown

Medellín

GUYANA ⊛

Paramaribo

⊛ Cayenne

⊛ Bogotá

Cali

COLOMBIA

GUAYANA FRANCESA

SURINAM

*OCÉANO
ATLÁNTICO*

Quito

⊛

ECUADOR

Ecuador

Guayaquil

Manaus

⊛ Belém

Río Amazonas

*OCÉANO
PACÍFICO*

PERÚ

BRASIL

Recife

C
O
R
D
I
L
L
E
R
A

Lima

▲ *Machu Picchu*
Cuzco

Lago Titicaca

D
E

OCÉANO PACÍFICO

Isla Pinta

Isla Marchena

BOLIVIA

⊛ La Paz

Arequipa

Brasília ⊛

Isla San Salvador

L
O
S

⊛ Sucre

Isla Santa Cruz

Isla
Isabela

⊛ *Isla San
Cristóbal*

Puerto
Baquerizo
Moreno

*ISLAS
GALÁPAGOS
(ECUADOR)*

A
N
D
E
S

PARAGUAY

São Paulo

0   100 MILLAS

Antofagasta

⊛ Asunción

0   100 KILÓMETROS

CHILE

Puerto Iguazú

Rio de Janeiro

*Trópico de
Capricornio*

Río Paraná

0   8 MILLAS

0   8 KILÓMETROS

Córdoba

Cabo
Cummings

Hanga Roa

Valparaíso

Santiago ⊛

Mataveri

Cabo Sur

*OCÉANO
PACÍFICO*

ARGENTINA

Rosario

URUGUAY

⊛ Montevideo

*OCÉANO
ATLÁNTICO*

*ISLA DE PASCUA
(CHILE)*

Buenos
Aires

Río de la Plata

Concepción

Bahía Blanca

San Carlos de
Bariloche

*OCÉANO
PACÍFICO*

*Islas
Malvinas*

*Estrecho de
Magallanes*

Punta Arenas

Tierra del Fuego

Cabo de Hornos

AMÉRICA DEL SUR

| 0 | 250 | 500 | 750 MILLAS |

| 0 | 250 | 500 | 750 KILÓMETROS |

ELEVACIÓN

METROS	PIES
3050	10000
1525	5000
610	2000
305	1000
152.5	500
0	0

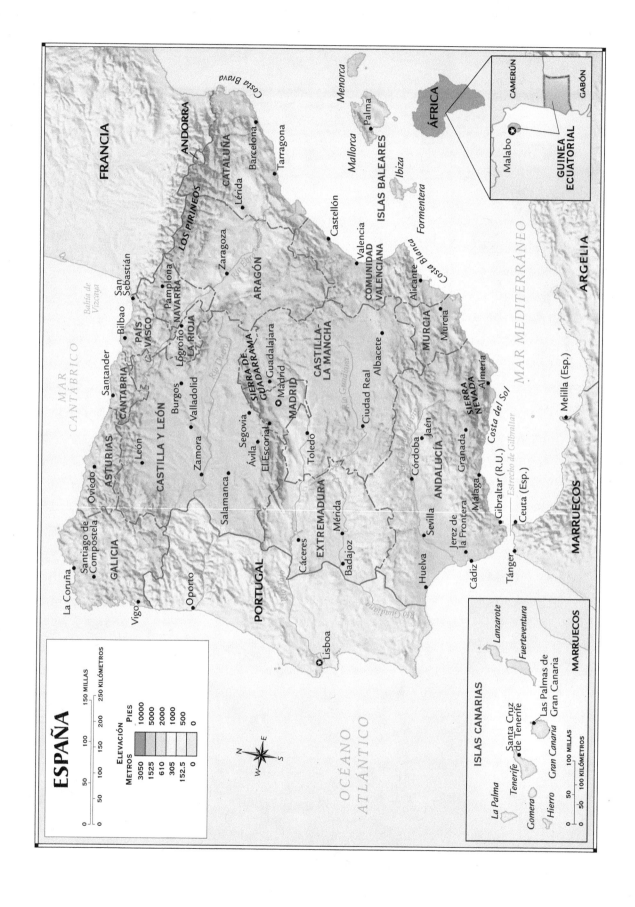

ESPAÑA

ELEVACIÓN

METROS	PIES
3050	10000
1525	5000
610	2000
305	1000
152.5	500
0	0

0 50 100 150 200 250 KILÓMETROS
0 50 100 150 MILLAS

N
W · E
S

OCÉANO
ATLÁNTICO

MAR
CANTÁBRICO

Bahía de
Vizcaya

FRANCIA

ANDORRA

Costa Brava

Menorca

Mallorca

Palma

ISLAS BALEARES

Ibiza

Formentera

MAR MEDITERRÁNEO

ARGELIA

MARRUECOS

Melilla (Esp.)

GALICIA

La Coruña

Santiago de
Compostela

Vigo

Oporto

PORTUGAL

Lisboa

ASTURIAS

Oviedo

Santander

CANTABRIA

Bilbao

San
Sebastián

PAÍS
VASCO

Pamplona

NAVARRA

Logroño

LA RIOJA

LOS PIRINEOS

CATALUÑA

Lérida

Barcelona

Tarragona

Zaragoza

Río Ebro

ARAGÓN

Castellón

Valencia

COMUNIDAD
VALENCIANA

Alicante

Costa Blanca

CASTILLA Y LEÓN

León

Burgos

Valladolid

Zamora

Salamanca

Río Duero

SIERRA DE
GUADARRAMA

Segovia

Ávila

El Escorial

Guadalajara

Madrid

MADRID

Toledo

CASTILLA-
LA MANCHA

Ciudad Real

Albacete

Río Guadiana

MURCIA

Murcia

Almería

SIERRA
NEVADA

EXTREMADURA

Cáceres

Mérida

Badajoz

Río Tajo

ANDALUCÍA

Huelva

Sevilla

Córdoba

Jaén

Granada

Málaga

Jerez de
la Frontera

Cádiz

Tánger

Costa del Sol

Gibraltar (R.U.)

Ceuta (Esp.)

Estrecho de Gibraltar

MARRUECOS

Río Guadalquivir

ÁFRICA

CAMERÚN

GABÓN

Malabo

GUINEA
ECUATORIAL

ISLAS CANARIAS

La Palma

Tenerife

Gomera

Hierro

Santa Cruz
de Tenerife

Gran Canaria

Las Palmas de
Gran Canaria

Lanzarote

Fuerteventura

MARRUECOS

0 50 100 KILÓMETROS
0 50 100 MILLAS